Fodor's 2011

CARIBBEAN PORTS OF CALL

Where to Stay and Eat for All Budgets

Must-See Sights and Local Secrets

Ratings You Can Trust

Fodor's Travel Publications   New York, Toronto, London, Sydney, Auckland
www.fodors.com

FODOR'S CARIBBEAN PORTS OF CALL 2011

Editor: Douglas Stallings

Editorial Contributors: Carol M. Bareuther, John Bigley, Linda Coffman, Michael de Zayas, Jennifer Edwards, Rena Havner-Philips, Lynne Helm, Michele Joyce, Marlise Kast, Lynda Lohr, Maribeth Mellin, Elise Meyer, Paris Permenter, Alice Powers, Vernon O'Reilly Ramesar, Jessica Robertson, Heather Rodino, Sam Sessa, Ramona Settle, Jordan Simon, Eilen Robinson Smith, Roberta Sotonoff, Cynthia Tourigny, Jeffrey Van Fleet, Chelle Koster Walton, Melanie Wetzel, Jane E. Zarem

Production Editor: Carolyn Roth

Maps & Illustrations: David Lindroth, Mark Stroud, *cartographers;* Bob Blake, Rebecca Baer, *map editors;* William Wu, *information graphics*

Design: Fabrizio La Rocca, *creative director;* Guido Caroti, Siobhan O'Hare, *art directors;* Tina Malaney, Chie Ushio, Ann McBride, Jessica Walsh, *designers;* Melanie Marin, *senior picture editor*

Cover Photo: (Deadman's Bay, Peter Islands, British Virgin Islands): Karl Weatherly/ Photographer's Choice RF/Getty Images

Production Manager: Angela L. McLean

ISBN 978-1-4000-0469-0

ISSN 1090–7343

SPECIAL SALES

This book is available at special discounts for bulk purchases for sales promotions or premiums. Special editions, including personalized covers, excerpts of existing books, and corporate imprints, can be created in large quantities for special needs. For more information, write to Special Markets/Premium Sales, 1745 Broadway, MD 6-2, New York, New York 10019, or e-mail specialmarkets@randomhouse.com.

AN IMPORTANT TIP & AN INVITATION

Although all prices, opening times, and other details in this book are based on information supplied to us at press time, changes occur all the time in the travel world, and Fodor's cannot accept responsibility for facts that become outdated or for inadvertent errors or omissions. So **always confirm information when it matters,** especially if you're making a detour to visit a specific place. Your experiences—positive and negative— matter to us. If we have missed or misstated something, **please write to us.** We follow up on all suggestions. Contact the Caribbean Ports of Call editor at editors@fodors.com or c/o Fodor's at 1745 Broadway, New York, NY 10019.

PRINTED IN THE UNITED STATES OF AMERICA

10 9 8 7 6 5 4 3 2 1

Be a Fodor's Correspondent

Your opinion matters. It matters to us. It matters to your fellow Fodor's travelers, too. And we'd like to hear it. In fact, we need to hear it.

When you share your experiences and opinions, you become an active member of the Fodor's community. That means we'll not only use your feedback to make our books better, but we'll publish your names and comments whenever possible. Throughout our guides, look for "Word of Mouth," excerpts of your unvarnished feedback.

Here's how you can help improve Fodor's for all of us.

Tell us when we're right. We rely on local writers to give you an insider's perspective. But our writers and staff editors—who are the best in the business—depend on you. Your positive feedback is a vote to renew our recommendations for the next edition.

Tell us when we're wrong. We're proud that we update most of our guides every year. But we're not perfect. Things change. Hotels cut services. Museums change hours. Charming cafés lose charm. If our writer didn't quite capture the essence of a place, tell us how you'd do it differently. If any of our descriptions are inaccurate or inadequate, we'll incorporate your changes in the next edition and will correct factual errors at fodors.com immediately.

Tell us what to include. You probably have had fantastic travel experiences that aren't yet in Fodor's. Why not share them with a community of like-minded travelers? Maybe you chanced upon a beach or bistro or B&B that you don't want to keep to yourself. Tell us why we should include it. And share your discoveries and experiences with everyone directly at fodors.com. Your input may lead us to add a new listing or highlight a place we cover with a "Highly Recommended" star or with our highest rating, "Fodor's Choice."

Give us your opinion instantly at our feedback center at www.fodors.com/feedback. You may also e-mail editors@fodors.com with the subject line "Caribbean Ports of Call Editor." Or send your nominations, comments, and complaints by mail to Caribbean Ports of Call Editor, Fodor's, 1745 Broadway, New York, NY 10019.

You and travelers like you are the heart of the Fodor's community. Make our community richer by sharing your experiences. Be a Fodor's correspondent.

Bon voyage!

Tim Jarrell, Publisher

CONTENTS

MAPS

ABOUT THIS BOOK

Our Ratings

Sometimes you find terrific travel experiences and sometimes they just find you. But usually the burden is on you to select the right combination of experiences. That's where our ratings come in.

As travelers we've all discovered a place so wonderful that its worthiness is obvious. And sometimes that place is so experiential that superlatives don't do it justice: you just have to be there to know. These sights, properties, and experiences get our highest rating, **Fodor's Choice** indicated by orange stars throughout this book.

Black stars highlight sights and properties we deem **Highly Recommended** places that our writers, editors, and readers praise again and again for consistency and excellence.

By default, there's another category: any place we include in this book is by definition worth your time, unless we say otherwise. And we will.

Disagree with any of our choices? Care to nominate a place or suggest that we rate one more highly? Visit our feedback center at www.fodors.com/feedback.

Budget Well

Hotel and restaurant price categories from ¢ to $$$$ are defined in the opening pages of each chapter. For attractions, we always give standard adult admission fees; reductions are usually available for children, students, and senior citizens. Want to pay with plastic? **AE, D, DC, MC, V** following restaurant and hotel listings indicate if American Express, Discover, Diners Club, MasterCard, and Visa are accepted.

Restaurants

Unless we state otherwise, restaurants are open for lunch and dinner daily. We mention dress only when there's a specific requirement and reservations only when they're essential or not accepted—it's always best to book ahead.

Hotels

Hotels have private bath, phone, TV, and air-conditioning and operate on the European Plan (aka EP, meaning without meals), unless we specify that they use the Breakfast Plan (BP, with a full breakfast), Continental Breakfast Plan (CP), or Modified American Plan (MAP, with breakfast and dinner daily), or Full American Plan (FAP, with three meals a day). We always list facilities but not whether you'll be charged an extra fee to use them, so when pricing accommodations, find out what's included.

Many Listings
- ★ Fodor's Choice
- ★ Highly recommended
- ⊠ Physical address
- ✦ Directions or Map coordinates
- ⬧ Mailing address
- ☎ Telephone
- 🖷 Fax
- ⊕ On the Web
- ✉ E-mail
- 🏷 Admission fee
- ☉ Open/closed times
- Ⓜ Metro stations
- ▭ Credit cards

Hotels & Restaurants
- 🏨 Hotel
- ⭹ Number of rooms
- ☕ Facilities
- ⑩ Meal plans
- ✗ Restaurant
- ⌨ Reservations
- 🏛 Dress code
- ⤬ Smoking
- ᵠ BYOB

Outdoors
- 🏌 Golf
- ⛺ Camping

Other
- ♻ Family-friendly
- ⇨ See also
- ⊠ Branch address
- ☞ Take note

Cruise Primer

WORD OF MOUTH

"[K]eeping in mind that I would like to keep the cruise on a lower budget, I have a few questions being a first-time cruiser: 1) Is a room with a window important, or would it be better to pick a room on a middle to higher floor with no window? 2) Is there an advantage to booking on the phone vs online? 3) Is there an advantage to booking airfare through the cruise line . . . ? Anything else I should consider before booking?"

—mmd1

By Linda
Coffman

If you're considering a cruise but can't decide whether it's really for you, it's tempting to ask, "What's so special about a cruise vacation?" It's a good question. Until the age of the airplane, ocean travel was simply a means to get to your far-flung destination—often the only way. But even in the early decades of the 20th century, venerable ocean liners such as the *Normandie* offered the occasional round-trip cruise to an exotic locale.

Passengers on those earliest cruises didn't have a fun-in-the-sun mindset as they sailed to faraway ports. They sailed to broaden their horizons and learn about ports of call that couldn't be reached by overland travel. Perhaps they booked a cruise to Panama to observe the construction of the canal or, like the *Normandie*'s passengers, were bound for Brazil and the daring excitement of Carnival.

Regardless of *why* they were cruising, early cruisers steamed toward the unfamiliar with many fewer comforts than contemporary passengers enjoy. On the *Normandie*, air-conditioned comfort was available only in the ship's first-class dining room, though at least passengers could find relief from Rio's heat by taking a dip in one of the era's few outdoor swimming pools at sea. In those days, if an ocean liner had a permanent swimming pool, it was often indoors and deep in the hull.

Carnival Cruise Lines executives like to reminisce about the tiny "gyms" on their early ships, which were converted ocean liners, and then point to how far ship designs have evolved. I remember the old ships well. It was even difficult to find the casino on Carnival's first "Fun Ship," *Mardi Gras,* let alone locate the indoor swimming pool. That's hardly the case today. Designed for contemporary travelers and tastes, modern cruise ships carry passengers amid conveniences unheard of in the heyday of the North Atlantic ocean liner or even in the earliest vessels permanently dedicated to cruises. As more than 14 million passengers discovered when they went to sea in 2010, there's a lot to like on ships these days.

The allure of a modern sea cruise is its ability to appeal to a wide range of vacationers as a safe and convenient way to travel. Today's cruise ships are lively and luxurious floating resorts that offer something to satisfy the expectations of almost everyone. The first thing you'll find is that although cruise ships differ dramatically in the details and how they craft and deliver the cruise experience, most ships have the same basic features. And although the decisions and considerations in booking one cruise over another can be complex, the more you know about cruise travel in general, the better prepared you will be when it comes to making your choices.

BEFORE YOU GO

To expedite your preboarding paperwork, most cruise lines have convenient forms on their Web sites. As long as you have your reservation number, you can provide the required immigration information, pre-reserve shore excursions, and even indicate any special requests from the comfort of your home. Less "wired" cruise lines might mail preboarding paperwork to you or your travel agent for completion after you make your final payment, and request that you return the forms by mail or fax. No matter how you submit them, be sure to make hard copies of any forms you fill out and bring them with you to the pier to smooth the embarkation process.

DOCUMENTS

It is every passenger's responsibility to have proper identification. If you arrive at the port without it, you may not be allowed to board, and the line will issue no fare refund. Most travel agents know the requirements and can guide you to the proper agency to obtain what you need if you don't have it.

Everyone must have proof of citizenship and identity to travel abroad. Effective June 1, 2009, travelers were required to present a passport or other approved document denoting citizenship and identity for all land *and* sea travel into the United States. Like most rules, there is a confusing exception—U.S. citizens traveling within the Caribbean on closed-loop cruises (cruises that begin and end in the same port) are still permitted to depart from or enter the U.S. with proof of identity, which includes a government-issued photo ID, such as a driver's license, along with proof of citizenship, such as a birth certificate. However, you may still be required to present a passport when you dock at a foreign port, depending on the islands or countries that your cruise ship is visiting. And if your cruise begins in one U.S. port and ends in a different port, you will be required to have a passport. Check with your cruise line to ensure you have the appropriate documents for the stops you'll be making on your cruise.

Even for cruises that begin and end in the same port, cruise lines strongly recommend that all passengers travel with a valid passport. That will enable you to fly from the U.S. to meet your ship at the first port should you miss the scheduled embarkation, as well as allow you to leave the ship without significant delays and complications before the cruise ends if you must fly back to the U.S. due to an emergency.

Children under the age of 18, when they are not traveling with both parents, almost always require a letter of permission from the absent parent(s). Airlines, cruise lines, and immigration agents can deny minor children initial boarding or entry to foreign countries without proper proof of identification and citizenship *and* a notarized permission letter from absent or noncustodial parents. Your travel agent or cruise line can help with the wording of such a letter.

WHAT TO PACK

In terms of your wardrobe, cruise wear falls into three categories: casual, informal, and formal. Cruise documents should include information indicating how many evenings fall into each category. You will know when to wear what by reading your ship's daily newsletter—each evening's dress code will be prominently announced.

For the day, you'll need casual wear. For warm-weather cruises, you'll typically need swimwear, a cover-up, and sandals for pool and beach. Time spent ashore touring and shopping calls for shorts topped with T-shirts or polo shirts and comfy walking shoes. Conservative is a rule to live by in the Caribbean (most Caribbean islands are very socially conservative), and mix-and-match will save room in your suitcase. Forget denim, which is too hot, and concentrate on lighter fabrics that will breathe in the Caribbean heat. Although jeans are allowed in the dining rooms of most mainstream ships, at night casual generally means khaki-type slacks and nice polo or sport shirts for men. Ladies' outfits are sundresses, skirts and tops, or pants outfits. By sticking to two or three complementary colors and a few accessories, you can mix up tops and bottoms for a different look every night.

Informal dress—sometimes called "resort" or "smart" casual—is a little trickier. It applies only to evening wear, and can mean different things depending on the cruise line. Informal for women is a dressier dress or pants outfit; for men it almost always includes a sport coat and sometimes a tie. Check your documents carefully.

Formal night means dressing up, but these days even that is a relative notion. You will see women in everything from simple cocktail dresses to elaborate glittering gowns. A tuxedo (either all black or with white dinner jacket) or dark suit is required for gentlemen. If you have been a "Mother-of-the-Bride" lately, chances are your outfit for the wedding is just perfect for formal night. For children, Sunday best is entirely appropriate.

Men can usually rent their formal attire from the cruise line, and if they do so, it will be waiting when they board. Be sure to make these arrangements in advance; your travel agent can get the details from the cruise line. But if you are renting a tux, buy your own studs: a surefire way to spot a rented tuxedo is by the inexpensive studs that come with it. Also, many men with a little "girth" consider a vest more comfortable than a cummerbund.

An absolute essential for women is a shawl or light sweater. Aggressive air-conditioning can make public rooms uncomfortable, particularly if you are sunburned from a day at the beach.

Put things you can't do without—such as prescription medication, spare eyeglasses, toiletries, a swimsuit, and change of clothes for the first day—in your carry-on. Most cruise ships provide soap, shampoo, and conditioner, so you probably won't need those.

And plan carefully. In fact, we'd strongly advise you to make a list so you don't forget anything.

ACCESSIBILITY ISSUES

As recently as the early 1990s, "accessibility" on a cruise ship meant little more than a few inside staterooms set aside for passengers with mobility issues. Most public restrooms and nearly all en suite bathrooms had a "step-over" threshold. Newer ships are more sensitive to the needs of passengers with disabilities, but many older ships still have physical barriers in both cabins and public rooms. And once you get off the ship—particularly in some Caribbean ports—your problems will be compounded.

All cruise lines offer a limited number of staterooms designed to be wheelchair- and scooter-accessible. Booking a newer vessel will generally assure more choices. On newer ships, public rooms are generally more accessible, and more facilities have been planned with wheelchair users in mind. Auxiliary aids, such as flashers for the hearing impaired and buzzers for visually impaired passengers, as well as lifts for swimming pools and hot tubs, are available upon request. However, more than the usual amount of preplanning is necessary for smooth sailing if you have special needs.

For example, when a ship is unable to dock—as is the case in Grand Cayman, for instance—passengers are taken ashore on tenders that are sometimes problematic even for the able-bodied to negotiate under adverse conditions. Some people with limited mobility may find it difficult to embark or disembark when docked due to the steep angle of gangways during high or low tide at certain times of day. In some situations, crew members may offer assistance that involves carrying guests, but if the sea is choppy when tendering is a necessity, that might not be an option.

Passengers who require continuous oxygen or have service animals have further hurdles to overcome. You can bring both aboard a cruise ship, but your service animal may not be allowed to go ashore with you if the port has strict laws regarding animal quarantines.

INSURANCE

We believe that comprehensive trip insurance is especially valuable if you're booking a very expensive or complicated trip (particularly to an isolated region) or if you're booking far in advance. Who knows what could happen six months down the road? But whether or not you get insurance has more to do with how comfortable you are assuming all that risk yourself.

Comprehensive travel policies typically cover trip-cancellation and interruption, letting you cancel or cut your trip short because of a personal emergency, illness, or, in some cases, acts of terrorism in your destination. Such policies also cover emergency evacuation and medical care. Some also cover you for trip delays because of bad weather or mechanical problems, as well as for lost or delayed baggage. Another type of coverage to look for is financial default—that is, when your trip is disrupted because a tour operator, airline, or cruise line goes out of business. Generally you must buy this when you book your trip or shortly thereafter, and it's only available to you if your operator isn't on a list of excluded companies.

If you're going abroad, consider buying medical-only coverage at the very least. Neither Medicare nor some private insurers cover medical expenses anywhere outside of the United States (including time aboard a cruise ship, even if it leaves from a U.S. port). Medical-only policies typically reimburse you for medical care (excluding that related to preexisting conditions) and hospitalization abroad, and provide for evacuation. You still have to pay the bills and await reimbursement from the insurer, though.

Expect comprehensive travel insurance policies to cost about 4% to 7% or 8% of the total price of your trip (it's more like 8%–12% if you're over age 70). A medical-only policy may or may not be cheaper than a comprehensive policy. Always read the fine print of your policy to make sure that you are covered for the risks that are of most concern to you. Compare several policies to make sure you're getting the best price and range of coverage available.

U.S. Travel Insurers Access America (☎ *800/284–8300* ⊕ *www. accessamerica.com*). **CSA Travel Protection** (☎ *800/711–1197* ⊕ *www. csatravelprotection.com*). **HTH Worldwide** (☎ *610/254–8700* or *888/243–2358* ⊕ *www.hthworldwide.com*). **Travelex Insurance** (☎ *800/228–9792* ⊕ *www. travelex-insurance.com*). **Travel Guard International** (☎ *715/345–0505* or *800/826–4919* ⊕ *www.travelguard.com*). **Travel Insured International** (☎ *800/243–3174* ⊕ *www.travelinsured.com*).

ARRIVING AND EMBARKING

Most cruise-ship passengers fly to the port of embarkation. If you book your cruise far enough in advance, you'll be given the opportunity to purchase an air-and-sea package, which may, or may not, save you money on your flight. You might get a lower fare by booking your flight independently, so it's a good idea to check for the best fare available.

If you buy an air-and-sea package from your cruise line, a uniformed cruise-line agent will meet you (usually in the baggage claim area) to smooth your way from airport to pier. You will need to claim your own bags and give them to the transfer driver so they can be loaded on the bus. Upon arrival at the pier, luggage is automatically transferred to the ship for delivery to your cabin. The cruise line ground transfer system can also be available to independent fliers. However, be sure to ask your travel agent how much it costs; you may find that a taxi or shuttle service is less expensive and more convenient.

In addition to the busiest embarkation ports such as Miami, Fort Lauderdale, and New York City, cruises now leave from less-familiar port cities all around the East and Gulf coasts. Galveston, Texas, and Port Canaveral, Florida, have become major home ports in recent years, and are considered now to be among the nation's top 10 cruise ports. Many people prefer to drive to these ports if they are close enough to home; happily, secure parking is always available, either within the port itself or nearby.

BOARDING

1

Once the planning, packing, and anticipation are behind them, veteran cruise passengers sometimes view embarkation day as anticlimactic. However, for first-time cruise travelers, embarking on their first ship can be more than exhilarating—it can be downright intimidating. What exactly can you expect?

CHECK-IN

Once inside the cruise terminal, you'll see a check-in line. Actual boarding time is often scheduled for noon, but some cruise lines will begin processing early arrivals and then direct them to a "holding" area. During check-in you will be asked to produce your documents and any forms you were sent to complete ahead of time, plus proof of citizenship and a credit card (to cover onboard charges). You are issued a boarding card that functions as your shipboard charge card and often also doubles as your stateroom "key." At some point—usually before you enter the check-in area—you and your hand luggage will pass through a security procedure similar to those at airports.

Check-in lines can be long, particularly at peak times. If check-in starts at noon but continues to 4 PM, you can expect lines to trail off as the boarding deadline approaches. All passengers are anxious to get on board and begin their vacation, so if you arrive at one of the busy periods, keep in mind that this is not the time to get cranky if you have to wait.

Although the gangway is generally not removed until 30 minutes before sailing, U.S. government security regulations require cruise lines to submit certain passenger information to law enforcement authorities at least 60 minutes prior to departure. To meet that requirement, they must have the necessary information in their records at least 90 minutes before departure. If you arrive too late and your information is not in the system before the deadline, you run the risk of being denied boarding even if the ship hasn't sailed.

BOARDING THE SHIP

Once boarding begins, you will inevitably have your first experience with the ship's photographer and be asked to pose for an embarkation picture. It only takes a second, so smile. Later, you'll find those photos for purchase in the ship's photo center.

Procedures vary somewhat once you are greeted by staff members lined up just inside the ship's hull; however, you'll have to produce your boarding card for the security officer. At some point—either at the check-in desk or when boarding the ship for the first time—you will be photographed for security purposes; your image will display when your boarding card is "swiped" into a computer as you leave and reboard the ship in ports of call. Depending on the cruise line, you will be directed to your cabin, or a steward will relieve you of your carry-on luggage and accompany you. Stewards on high-end cruise lines not only show you the way, but hand you a glass of champagne as a welcome-aboard gesture. However, if you board early, don't be surprised if you are told cabins are not "ready" for occupancy—passageways to accommodations may even be roped off. In that case you can explore the ship, have lunch, or simply relax until an announcement is made that you can go to your cabin.

ON BOARD

Check out your cabin to make sure that everything is in order. Try the plumbing and set the air-conditioning to the temperature you prefer. Your cabin may feel warm while docked but will cool off when the ship is underway. You should find a copy of the ship's daily schedule in the cabin. Take a few moments to look it over—you will want to know what time the muster drill takes place (a placard on the back of your cabin door will indicate directions to your emergency station; the drill will happen within the first 24 hours of your cruise), as well as meal hours and the schedule for various activities and entertainments.

Rented tuxedoes are either hanging in the closet or will be delivered sometime during the afternoon; bon voyage gifts sent by your friends or travel agent usually appear as well. Be patient if you are expecting deliveries, particularly on mega-ships. Cabin stewards participate in the ship's turnaround and are extremely busy, although yours will no doubt introduce himself at the first available opportunity. It will also be a while before your checked luggage arrives, so your initial order of business is usually the buffet, if you haven't already had lunch. Bring along the daily schedule to check over while you eat.

While making your way to the Lido buffet, you may see bar waiters offering trays of colorful and exotic drinks, often in souvenir glasses that you can keep. Beware—on most lines they are not complimentary! If you choose one, you will be asked to sign for it.

Do your plans for the cruise include booking shore excursions and indulging in spa treatments? The most popular tours sometimes sell out, and spas can be very busy during sea days, so your next stops should be the Shore Excursion Desk to book tours and the spa to make appointments.

Dining-room seating arrangements are another matter for consideration. Some people like to check the main dining room to determine where their table is located. If it is not to your liking, or if you requested a large table and find yourself assigned to a small one, you will want to see the head waiter. He or she will be stationed in a lounge with the seating charts handy to make changes. The daily schedule will indicate where and when to meet with him or her. If you plan to dine in the ship's specialty restaurant, make those reservations as soon as possible to avoid disappointment.

PAYING FOR THINGS ON BOARD

Let's step back a moment and take a look at what happened when you checked in at the pier. Because a cashless society prevails on cruise ships, an imprint was made of your credit card, or you had to place a cash deposit for use against your onboard charges. Then you were issued a charge card that usually doubles as your boarding card and stateroom "key." Most onboard expenditures are charged to your shipboard account with your signature as verification, with the possible exception of casino gaming—even so, you can often get "cash advances" against your account from the casino cashier.

An itemized bill is provided at the end of the voyage listing your purchases. In order to avoid surprises, it is a good idea to set aside your charge slips and request an interim printout of your bill from the purser to ensure accuracy. Should you change your mind about charging onboard purchases, you can always inform the purser and pay in cash or traveler's checks instead. If your cash deposit was more than you spent, you will receive a refund.

TIPPING

One of the most delicate—yet frequently debated—topics of conversation among cruise passengers involves the matter of tipping. Who do you tip? How much? What's "customary" and "recommended?" Should parents tip the full amount for children or is just half adequate? Why do you have to tip at all?

When transfers to and from your ship are a part of your air-and-sea program, gratuities are generally included for luggage handling. In that case, do not worry about the interim tipping. However, if you take a taxi to the pier and hand over your bags to a stevedore, be sure to tip him. Treat him with respect and pass along at least $5.

During your cruise, room-service waiters generally receive a cash tip of $1 to $3 per delivery. A 15% to 18% gratuity will automatically be added to each bar bill during the cruise. If you use salon and spa services, a similar percentage might be added to the bills there as well. If you dine in a specialty restaurant, you may be asked to provide a one-time gratuity for the service staff.

There will be a "Disembarkation Talk" on the last day of the cruise that explains tipping procedures. If you are expected to tip in cash, small white "tip" envelopes will appear in your stateroom that day. If you tip in cash, you usually give the tip envelope directly to each person on the last night of the cruise, but this practice is becoming increasingly rare. Most cruise lines now either automatically add gratuities to passengers' onboard charge accounts or offer the option. If that suits you, then do nothing further. However, you are certainly free to adjust the amounts up or down to more appropriate levels or ask that the charge be removed altogether if you prefer distributing cash gratuities.

Tips generally add up to about $10 to $15 per person per day. You tip the same amount for each person who shares the cabin, including children, unless otherwise indicated.

DINING

All food, all the time? Not quite, but it is possible to literally eat away the day and most of the night on a cruise. A popular cruise directors' joke is, "You came on as passengers, and you will be leaving as cargo." Although it is meant in fun, it does contain a ring of truth. Food—tasty and plentiful—is available 24 hours a day on most cruise ships, and the dining experience at sea has reached almost mythical proportions. Perhaps it has something to do with legendary midnight buffets, the absence of menu prices, or maybe it's the vast selection and availability.

RESTAURANTS

Every ship has at least one main restaurant and a Lido, or casual, buffet alternative. Increasingly important are specialty restaurants. Meals in the primary and buffet restaurants are included in the cruise fare, as are midday tea and snacks, late-night buffets, and most round-the-clock room service. Most mainstream cruise lines levy a surcharge for dining in alternative restaurants that may, or may not, also include a gratuity. With the exception of some connoisseur-wine-and-gourmet-food dining experiences, generally there is no additional charge on luxury cruise lines.

You may also find a pizzeria or a specialty coffee bar on your ship— increasingly popular favorites cropping up on ships old and new. Although pizza is complimentary, expect an additional charge for specialty coffees at the coffee bar and, quite likely, in the dining room as well. You will also likely be charged for sodas and drinks during meals other than iced tea, regular coffee, tap water, and fruit juice.

There is often a direct relationship between the cost of a cruise and the quality of its cuisine. The food is very sophisticated on some (mostly expensive) lines, among them Crystal, Cunard, Seabourn, SeaDream, Regent Seven Seas, and Silversea. In the more moderate price range, Oceania Cruises and Azamara Club Cruises have gained renown for their culinary stylings. The trend toward featuring specialty dishes and even entire menus designed by acclaimed chefs has spread throughout the cruise industry; however, on most mainstream cruise lines the food is the quality that you would find in any good hotel banquet—perfectly acceptable but certainly not great.

DINNER SEATINGS

If your cruise ship has traditional seatings for dinner, the one decision that may set the tone for your entire cruise is your dinner seating. Which is best? Early dinner seating is generally scheduled between 6 and 6:30 PM, while late seating can begin from 8:15 to 8:45 PM. So the "best" seating depends on you, your lifestyle, and your personal preference.

Families with young children and older passengers often choose an early seating. Early-seating diners are encouraged not to linger too long over dessert and coffee because the dining room has to be readied for late seating. Late seating is viewed by some passengers as more romantic and less rushed.

Cruise lines understand that strict schedules no longer satisfy the desires of all modern cruise passengers. Many cruise lines now include alternatives to the set schedules in the dining room, including casual dinner menus in their buffet facilities where more flexibility is allowed in dress and mealtimes. À la carte restaurants are showing up on more ships and offer yet another choice, though usually for an additional charge.

Open seating is primarily associated with more upscale lines; it allows passengers the flexibility to dine any time during restaurant hours and be seated with whomever they please.

Led by Norwegian Cruise Line and Princess Cruises, more contemporary and premium cruise lines, including Holland America Line, Celebrity Cruises, Royal Caribbean, and Carnival Cruise Lines, have introduced adaptations of open seating to offer variety and a more personalized experience for their passengers. Most cruise lines also offer casual evening meals in the Lido buffet, some featuring entrées similar to those served in the main dining room and with limited table service.

CHANGING TABLES

Cruise lines will never guarantee that you receive your preferred dinner seating, and table assignments are generally not confirmed until embarkation; however, every effort is made to satisfy all guests. Should there be a problem, see the maître d' for assistance. Changes after the first evening are generally discouraged, so if you want to change your seating or table, meet with dining-room staff and iron out problems on embarkation day. Check the daily program for time and location.

SPECIAL DIETS

Cruise lines make every possible attempt to ensure dining satisfaction. If you have special dietary considerations—such as low-salt, kosher, or food allergies—be sure to indicate them well ahead of time and check to be certain your needs are known by your waiter once on board. In addition to the usual menu items, "spa," vegetarian, low-calorie, low-carbohydrate, or low-fat selections, as well as children's menus are usually available. Requests for dishes not featured on the menu can often be granted if you ask in advance.

WINE

Wine typically costs about what you would expect to pay at a nice lounge or restaurant in a resort or a large U.S. city. Wine by the bottle is sometimes a more economical choice at dinner than ordering it by the glass. Any wine you don't finish will be kept for you and served the next night. Gifts of wine or champagne ordered from the cruise line (either by you, a friend, or your travel agent) can be taken to the dining room. Wine from any other source will incur a "corkage" fee of approximately $10 to $15 per bottle.

THE CAPTAIN'S TABLE

Legend has it that a nouveau-riche passenger's response to an invitation to dine with the captain during a round-the-world cruise was, "I didn't shell out all those bucks to eat with the help!" Although there are some cruise passengers who decline invitations to dine at the captain's table, there are far more who covet such an experience. You will know you have been included in that exclusive coterie when an embossed invitation arrives in your stateroom on the day of a formal dinner. RSVP as soon as possible—if you are unable to attend, someone else will be invited in your place.

Who is invited? If you are a frequent repeat cruiser, the occupants of an owner's suite, or if you hail from the captain's hometown or speak his native language, you may be considered. Honeymoon couples are

Drinking on Board

It's hard to avoid the ship's bars, since they are social centers, but alcoholic drinks are not usually included in your cruise fare, and bar bills can add up quickly. Drinks at the captain's welcome-aboard cocktail party and at cocktail parties held specifically for past cruisers are usually free. But if you pick up that boldly colored welcome-aboard cocktail as your ship pulls away from the dock, you may very well be asked to sign for it, and the cost will then be added to your shipboard account.

You should expect to pay about the same for a drink on board a cruise ship that you would pay in a bar at home: $5 to $6 for a domestic beer, $5 to $9 for a cocktail, $6 to $9 for a glass of wine, $1.25 to $2 for a soft drink. On virtually all ships, an automatic 15% gratuity will be added to your tab. What most people don't consider is that specialty coffees are also added to your bar tab, so if you order a cappuccino—and on some ships that applies even if it's in the dining room after dinner—you'll see a charge of $4 to $6 on your bar bill.

To save money on your bar bill, you can follow a few simple strategies. In lounges, request the less expensive bar brands or the reduced-price drink-of-the-day. On some ships, discounted "beverage cards" for unlimited fountain soft drinks and/or a set number of mixed drinks are available.

In international waters there are, technically, no laws against teenage drinking, but almost all ships now require passengers to be over 21 to purchase alcoholic beverages.

sometimes selected at random, as are couples celebrating a golden wedding anniversary. Attractive, unattached female passengers often round out an uneven number of guests. Requests made by travel agents on behalf of their clients sometimes do the trick.

ENTERTAINMENT

It's hard to imagine, but in the early years of cruise travel shipboard entertainment consisted of little more than poetry readings and recitals that exhibited the talents of fellow passengers. Those bygone days of sedate amusements in an intimate setting have been replaced by lavish showrooms where sequined and feathered showgirls strut their stuff on stage amid special effects not imagined in the past.

Seven-night Caribbean cruises usually include two original production shows. One of these might be a Las Vegas–style extravaganza and the other a best-of-Broadway show featuring old and new favorites from the Great White Way. Other shows highlight the talents of individual singers, dancers, magicians, comedians, and even acrobats. Don't be surprised if you are plucked from the audience to take the brunt of a comedian's jokes or act as the magician's temporary assistant. Sit in the front row if appearing onstage appeals to you.

Whether it is relegated to a late-afternoon interlude between bingo and dinner or a featured evening highlight, the passenger talent show is often a "don't miss" production. From pure camp to stylishly slick, what passes for talent is sometimes surprising but seldom boring. Stand-up comedy is generally discouraged; however, passengers who want their performance skills to be considered should answer the call for auditions and plan to rehearse the show at least once.

Enrichment programs have become a popular pastime at sea. It may come as a surprise that port lecturers on many large contemporary cruise ships offer more information on shore tours and shopping than insight into the ports of call. If more cerebral presentations are important to you, consider a cruise on a line that features stimulating enrichment programs and seminars at sea. Speakers can include destination-oriented historians, popular authors, business leaders, radio or television personalities, and even movie stars.

LOUNGES AND NIGHTCLUBS

If you find the show-lounge stage a bit intimidating and want to perform in a more intimate venue, look for karaoke. Singing along in a lively piano bar is another shipboard favorite for would-be crooners. Some passengers even take the place of the ship's pianist during breaks to demonstrate their skill.

Other lounges might feature easy-listening music, jazz, or combos for pre- and postdinner social dancing. Later in the evening, lounges pick up the pace with music from the 1950s and '60s; clubs aimed at a younger crowd usually have more contemporary dance music during the late-night hours.

CASINOS

A sure sign that your ship is in international waters is the opening of the casino. On most ships, lavish casinos pulsate with activity. The most notable exceptions are the family-oriented ships of Disney Cruise Line, which shun gaming in favor of more wholesome pastimes.

On ships that feature them, the rationale for locating casinos where most passengers must pass either through or alongside them is obvious—the unspoken allure of winning. In addition to slot machines in a variety of denominations, cruise-ship casinos might feature roulette, craps, and a variety of poker games—Caribbean Stud Poker, Let It Ride, Texas Hold 'Em, and blackjack, to name a few. Cruise lines strive to provide fair and professional gambling entertainment and supply gaming guides that set out the rules of play and betting limits for each game.

Casino hours vary based on the itinerary or location of the ship; most are required to close while in port, while others may be able to offer 24-hour slot machines and simply close table games. Every casino has a cashier, and you may be able to charge a cash advance to your onboard account, for a fee.

OTHER ENTERTAINMENT

Most vessels have a room for screening movies. On older ships and some newer ones, this is often a genuine cinema-style movie theater, while on other ships it may be just a multipurpose room. Over the course of a weeklong voyage a dozen films may be screened, each repeated several times. Theaters are also used for lectures, culinary demonstrations, religious services, and private meetings. The latest twist in video programming can be found on some Princess, Disney, and Carnival ships—huge outdoor LED screens where movies, music video concerts, news channels, and even the ship's activities are broadcast for passengers lounging poolside.

With a few exceptions, cruise ships equip their cabins with closed-circuit TVs showing movies (continuously on some newer ships), shipboard lectures, news channels, and regular programs (thanks to satellite reception). Pay-per-view movies (for a charge) are available on some ships. Ships with in-cabin VCRs or DVDs usually provide a selection of movies at no charge (a deposit is sometimes required).

Most medium and large ships have video arcades, and nearly all ships now have computer centers.

SPORTS AND FITNESS

Onboard sports facilities might include a court for basketball, volleyball, tennis—or all three—a jogging track, or even an in-line skating track. Some ships are even offering innovative and unexpected features, such as rock-climbing walls, bungee trampolines, and surfing pools on some Royal Caribbean ships. You'll even be able to bowl on certain NCL ships. For the less adventurous, there's always table tennis and shuffleboard.

Naturally, you will find at least one swimming pool and, possibly, several. Cruise-ship pools are generally on the small side—more appropriate for cooling off than doing laps—and the majority contain filtered saltwater. But some are elaborate affairs with waterslides. Princess Grand-class ships have challenging, freshwater "swim against the current" pools for swimming enthusiasts who want to get their low-impact exercise while on board.

Golf is a perennial seagoing favorite of players who want to take their games to the next level and include the Caribbean's most beautiful and challenging courses on their scorecards. Shipboard programs can include clinics, use of full-motion golf cages, and even individual instruction from resident pros using state-of-the-art computer analysis. Once ashore, escorted excursions include everything needed for a satisfying round of play, including equipment and tips from the pro, and the ability to schedule tee times at exclusive courses.

FITNESS CENTERS

Cruise vacations can be hazardous to your waistline if you are not careful. Eating "out" for all meals and sampling different cuisines tend to pile on unaccustomed calories. But shipboard fitness centers have become ever more elaborate, offering state-of-the-art exercise machines, treadmills, and stair steppers, not to mention weights and weight machines. As a bonus, many fitness centers with floor-to-ceiling windows have the world's most inspiring sea views.

For guests who prefer a more social atmosphere as they burn off sinful chocolate desserts, there are specialized fitness classes for all levels of ability. High-impact, energetic aerobics are not for everyone, but any

CLOSE UP

Health and Safety at Sea

Safety begins with you, the passenger. Once settled into your cabin, locate life vests and review posted emergency instructions. Make sure vests are in good condition and learn to secure them properly. If you have a physical infirmity that may hamper a speedy exit from your cabin, make certain the ship's purser knows, so that in an emergency he or she can quickly dispatch a crew member to assist you. If you're traveling with children, be sure that child-size life jackets are placed in your cabin.

Within 24 hours of embarkation, you'll be asked to attend a mandatory lifeboat drill. Do so and listen carefully. If you're unsure about how to use your vest, now is the time to ask. Only in the most extreme circumstances will you need to abandon ship—but it has happened. The time you spend learning the procedure may serve you well in a mishap.

In actuality, the greatest danger facing cruise-ship passengers is fire. All cruise lines must meet international standards for fire safety, which require sprinkler systems, smoke detectors, and other safety features. Fires on cruise ships are not common, but they do happen, and these rules have made ships much safer. You can do your part by *not* using an iron in your cabin and taking care to properly extinguish smoking materials. Never throw a lit cigarette overboard—it could be blown back into an opening in the ship and start a fire.

All large ships have an infirmary to deal with minor medical emergencies, but these infirmaries are not suitable for dealing with major procedures. The ship's doctor should be able to treat you as well as any general practitioner or clinic ashore for minor problems. For really complicated medical conditions, such as a heart attack or appendicitis, the ship's medical team evacuates passengers to the nearest hospital ashore. While at sea, evacuation expenses can rise as fast as the helicopter that whisks the patient away. You'll need supplementary insurance to cover evacuation costs.

Two of the most prevalent diseases that spread through cruise-ship populations are influenza and noroviruses that cause intestinal and stomach upsets. Annual influenza vaccination is the primary method for preventing influenza and its complications. But to prevent all kinds of infections—including noroviruses—frequent hand-washing is also essential; take advantage of the dispensers of hand-sanitizer, and use it when entering any dining room. Or slip into the restroom to wash your hands with soap and hot water.

---

class that raises the heart rate can be toned down and tailored to individual capabilities. Stretching classes help you warm up for a light jog or brisk walk on deck, and there are even sit-for-fitness classes for mature passengers or those with delicate joints. Fees are usually charged for specialty classes, such as Pilates, spinning, and yoga. Personal trainers are usually on board to get you off on the right foot, also for a fee.

SPAS

With all the usual pampering and service in luxurious surroundings, simply being on a cruise can be a stress-reducing experience. Add to that the menu of spa and salon services at your fingertips and you have a recipe for total sensory pleasure. Spas have also become among the most popular of shipboard areas.

Some spa offerings sound good enough to eat. A Milk-and-Honey Hydrotherapy Bath, Coconut Rub and Milk Ritual Wrap or Float, and a Javanese Steam Wrap incorporating cinnamon, ginger, coffee, sea salt, and honey are just a few of the tempting items found on spa menus. Not quite as exotic sounding, other treatments and services are nonetheless therapeutic for the body and soul. Steiner Leisure is the largest spa and salon operator at sea (the company also operates the Mandara- and the Greenhouse-brand spas), with facilities on more than 100 cruise ships worldwide.

In addition to facials, manicures, pedicures, massages, and sensual body treatments, other hallmarks of Steiner Leisure are salon services and products for hair and skin. Founded in 1901 by Henry Steiner of London, a single salon prospered when Steiner's son joined the business in 1926 and was granted a Royal Warrant as hairdresser to Her Majesty Queen Mary in 1937. In 1956 Steiner won its first cruise-ship contract to operate the salon on board the ships of the Cunard Line. By the mid-1990s, Steiner Leisure began taking an active role in creating shipboard spas offering a wide variety of wellness therapies and beauty programs for both women and men.

SHIPBOARD SERVICES

COMMUNICATIONS

Just because you are out to sea does not mean you have to be out of touch. Ship-to-shore telephone calls can cost $5 to $15 a minute, so it makes more economic sense to use e-mail to remain in contact with your home or office. Most ships have basic computer systems, while some newer vessels offer more high-tech connectivity—even in-cabin hookups or wireless connections for either your own laptop computer or one you can rent on board. Expect charges in the 50¢- to $1-per-minute range for the use of these Internet services. Ships usually offer some kind of package so that you get a reduced per-minute price if you pay a fee up front.

The ability to use your own mobile phone from the high seas is a relatively new alternative that is gaining popularity. It's usually cheaper than using a cabin phone if your ship offers the service, but it can still cost up to $4 or $5 a minute. It's a rather ingenious concept, with the ship acting as a cell "tower" in international waters—you use your own cell phone and your own number when roaming at sea. If using your cell phone is essential, contact your mobile service carrier before leaving home to enable international roaming and dialing, and be sure to understand their roaming agreements to be certain that your carrier has one with your cruise line. When in port, depending on the

CLOSE UP

Crime on Ships

1

Crime aboard cruise ships has occasionally become headline news, thanks in large part to a few well-publicized cases. Most people never have any type of problem, but you should exercise the same precautions aboard ship that you would at home. Keep your valuables out of sight—on big ships virtually every cabin has a small safe. Don't carry too much cash ashore, use your credit card whenever possible, and keep your money in a secure place, such as a front pocket that's harder to pick. Single women traveling with friends should stick together, especially when returning to their cabins late at night. When assaults occur, it often comes to light

that excessive drinking of alcohol is a factor. Be careful about befriending anyone, as you would anywhere, whether it's a fellow passenger or a member of the crew. Don't be paranoid, but do be prudent.

Your cruise is a wonderful opportunity to leave everyday responsibilities behind, but don't neglect to pack your common sense. After a few drinks it might seem like a good idea to sit on a railing or lean over the rail to get a better view of the ship's wake. Passengers have been known to fall. "Man overboard" is more likely to be the result of carelessness than criminal intent.

agreements your mobile service provider has established, you may be able to connect to local networks. Rates for using the maritime service, as well as any roaming charges from Caribbean islands, are established by your mobile service carrier and are worth checking into before you leave home. They can be substantial (i.e., up to $2 or $4 per minute); text messages are cheaper but are usually charged at the higher international roaming rate of 25¢ to 50¢ per message and will be charged separately, even if you have a text-message plan. Most GSM tri-band phones from the U.S. will work in the Caribbean if your carrier has a roaming agreement.

LAUNDRY AND DRY CLEANING

Most cruise ships offer valet laundry and pressing (and some also offer dry-cleaning) service. Expenses can add up fast, especially for laundry, since charges are per item and the rates are similar to those charged in hotels. If doing laundry is important to you and you do not want to send it out to be done, many cruise ships have a self-service laundry room (which usually features an iron and ironing board in addition to washer and dryer). If you book one of the top-dollar suites, laundry service may be included for no additional cost. Upscale ships, such as those in the Regent Seven Seas Cruises, Silversea Cruises, and Seabourn fleets, have complimentary self-service launderettes. On other cruise lines, such as Princess Cruises, Oceania Cruises, Carnival Cruise Lines, Disney Cruise Line, and Holland America Line (except Vista- and Signature-class ships), you can do your own laundry for about $3 or less per load; Norwegian Cruise Lines' laundry facilities are free, but you have to purchase your own laundry products. None of the vessels in the Royal Caribbean or Celebrity Cruises fleets has self-service laundry facilities.

SHORE EXCURSION DESK

Manned by a knowledgeable staff, the Shore Excursion Desk can not only book ship-sponsored tours, but may also be the place to learn more about ports of call and garner information to tour independently. Although staff members and the focus of their positions vary widely, the least you can expect is basic information and port maps. Happily, some shore-excursion staff members possess a wealth of information and share it without reservation. On some ships the port lecturer may emphasize shopping and "recommended" merchants, with little to impart regarding sightseeing or the history and culture of ports.

DISEMBARKATION

All cruises come to an end eventually, and it hardly seems fair that you have to leave when it feels like your vacation has just begun, but leave you must. The disembarkation process actually begins the day before you arrive at your ship's home port. During that day your cabin steward delivers special luggage tags to your stateroom, along with customs forms and instructions. Some lines allow you to carry your luggage off the ship, and if you choose to do that, then you will not have to worry about placing your bags outside your cabin door the night before disembarkation; verify with your cruise line whether it's possible for you to do this, assuming you want to.

The night before you disembark, you'll need to set aside clothing to wear the next morning when you leave the ship. Many people dress in whatever casual outfits they wear for the final dinner on board, or change into travel clothes after dinner. Also, do not forget to put your passport or other proof of citizenship, airline tickets, and medications in your hand luggage.

If you are not carrying your luggage off-ship, then after you finish packing, attach your new luggage tags (they are color- or number-coded according to post-cruise transportation plans and flight schedules). Follow the instructions provided and place the locked luggage outside your stateroom door for pickup during the hours indicated.

A statement itemizing your onboard charges is delivered before you arise on disembarkation morning. Plan to get up early enough to check it over for accuracy, finish packing your personal belongings, and vacate your stateroom by the appointed hour. Any discrepancies in your onboard account should be taken care of before leaving the ship, usually at the purser's desk.

Room service is not available on most ships on the last day; however, breakfast is served in the main restaurant as well as the buffet. After breakfast there is not much to do but wait comfortably in a lounge or on deck for your tag color or number to be called; some lines now allow you to wait in your cabin. Disembarkation procedures can sometimes be drawn out by passengers who are unprepared. This is no time to abandon your patience or sense of humor. An announcement will be made when it is your turn to disembark. Have your cruise card in hand for security to scan you off the vessel. Also have your passport or other identification and completed customs form handy.

Remember that all passengers must meet with customs and immigration officials during disembarkation, usually in the terminal. Procedures vary and are outlined in your instructions. In some ports passengers must meet with the officials at a specified hour (usually very early) in an onboard lounge; in other ports, customs forms are collected in the terminal and passports/identification papers are examined there as well.

Once in the terminal, locate your luggage and proceed to your bus or taxi, or retrieve your vehicle from the parking lot.

CUSTOMS AND DUTIES

U.S. CUSTOMS

Before a ship docks, each individual or family must fill out a customs declaration. If your purchases total less than the limit for your destination, you will not need to itemize them. Be prepared to pay whatever duties are owed directly to the customs inspector, with cash or check. Be sure to keep receipts for all purchases; and you may be asked to show officials what you've bought.

U.S. Customs preclears ships sailing into and out of some ports—it's done on the ship before you disembark. In other ports you must collect your luggage from the dock, then stand in line to pass through the inspection point. This can take up to an hour.

ALLOWANCES

You're always allowed to bring goods of a certain value back home without having to pay any duty or import tax. There's also a limit on the amount of tobacco and liquor you can bring back duty-free, and some countries have separate limits for perfumes; for exact figures, check with your customs department. The values of so-called "duty-free" goods are included in these amounts. When you shop abroad—and in the Caribbean, this means all islands except for Puerto Rico, which is considered a part of the U.S. for customs purposes—save all your receipts, as customs inspectors may ask to see them as well as the items you purchased. If the total value of your goods is more than the duty-free limit, then you'll have to pay a tax (most often a flat percentage) on the value of everything beyond that limit.

Individuals entering the United States from the Caribbean are allowed to bring in $800 worth of duty-free goods for personal use ($1,600 from the U.S. Virgin Islands), including 1 liter of alcohol (2 liters if one was produced in the Caribbean and 5 liters from the USVI), one carton of cigarettes (or five if four were purchased in the U.S. Virgin Islands), and 100 non-Cuban cigars. Antiques and original artwork are also duty-free.

SENDING PACKAGES HOME

Although you probably won't want to spend your time looking for a post office, you can send packages home duty-free, with a limit of one parcel per addressee per day (except alcohol or tobacco products or perfume worth more than $5). You can mail up to $200 worth of goods for personal use; label the package "personal use" and attach a list of the contents and their retail value. If the package contains your used personal belongings, mark it "personal goods returned" to avoid paying duty on your laundry. You may also send up to $100 worth of goods as gifts, with the same limit of one parcel per addressee per day ($200 from the U.S. Virgin Islands); mark the package "unsolicited gift." Items you mailed do not affect your duty-free allowance on your return.

NONCITIZENS

Non–U.S. citizens who are returning home within hours of docking may be exempt from all U.S. Customs duties. Everything you bring into the United States must leave with you when you return home, though. When you reach your own country, you will have to pay duties there.

Cruising the Caribbean

WORD OF MOUTH

"To just select a cruise line without doing some research or talking to a knowledgeable cruise [travel agent] is just asking for trouble. Cruise lines are different. They are not all the same. They offer different passenger demographics, different activities, different service, etc."

—golfette

By Linda
Coffman

More cruise ships ply the waters of the Caribbean than any other spot on Earth. Some are huge ships carrying more than 3,000 passengers; some are "midsize" ships welcoming about 1,500 cruisers; and others are comparatively small ships on which you'll find yourself with 300 or fewer other passengers. There are fancy ships and party ships, ships with sails, ships that pride themselves on the numbers of ports they visit, and ships that provide so much activity right on board that you hardly have time or inclination to go ashore. In peak season it's not uncommon for thousands of passengers to disembark from several ships into a small island port on the same day—a phenomenon not always enjoyed by locals. With such an abundance of cruise ships in this area, however, you can choose the ship and the itinerary that suit you best.

CHOOSING YOUR CRUISE

Some of the best "islands" in the Caribbean are the ones that float and move—they are called cruise ships. Just as Caribbean islands have distinct histories and cultures, cruise ships also have individual personalities. Determined by their size, the year they were built, and their style, on one hand, they can be bold, brassy, and exciting—totally unlike home, but a great place to visit. Big ships offer stability and a huge variety of activities and facilities. On the other hand, small ships feel intimate, like private clubs or, more appropriately, personal yachts. For every big-ship fan there is someone who would never set foot aboard a "floating resort." Examine your lifestyle—there's sure to be a cruise ship to match your expectations.

After giving some thought to your itinerary and where in the Caribbean you might wish to go, the ship you select is the most vital factor in your Caribbean cruise vacation, since it will not only determine which islands you will visit, but also how you will see them. Big ships visit major ports of call such as St. Thomas, St. Maarten/St. Martin, Nassau, and San Juan; when they call at smaller islands with shallower ports, passengers must disembark aboard shore tenders (small boats that ferry dozens of passengers to shore at a time). Or they may skip these smaller ports entirely. Small and midsize ships can visit smaller islands, such as St. Barths, St. Kitts, or Tortola, more easily; passengers are often able to disembark directly onto the pier without having to wait for tenders to bring them ashore.

ITINERARIES

You'll want to give some consideration to your ship's Caribbean itinerary when you are choosing your cruise. The length of the cruise will determine the variety and number of ports you visit, but so will the type of itinerary and the point of departure. **Round-trip cruises** start and end at the same point and usually explore ports close to one another; **one-way cruises** start at one point and end at another and range farther afield.

Almost all cruises in the Caribbean are round-trip cruises. On Caribbean itineraries you often have a choice of U.S. mainland departure points. Ships sailing out of San Juan can visit up to five ports in seven days, while cruises out of Florida can reach up to four ports in the same length of time. The Panama Canal can also be combined with a Caribbean cruise: the 50-mi (83-km) canal is a series of locks, which make up for the height difference between the Caribbean and the Pacific. Increasingly popular are partial transit cruises that enter the Panama Canal, anchor in Gatún Lake for a short time, and depart through the same set of locks.

EASTERN CARIBBEAN ITINERARIES

Eastern Caribbean itineraries consist of two or three days at sea as well as stops at some of the Caribbean's busiest cruise ports. A typical cruise will usually take in three or four ports of call, such as St. Thomas in the U.S. Virgin Islands, San Juan, or St. Maarten/St. Martin, along with a visit to the cruise line's "private" island for beach time. Every major cruise line has at least two of those popular islands on its itineraries. Some itineraries might also include others, such as Tortola, Dominica, Barbados, St. Kitts, or Martinique.

WESTERN CARIBBEAN ITINERARIES

Western Caribbean itineraries embarking from Galveston, Ft. Lauderdale, Miami, Port Canaveral, New Orleans, Mobile, or Tampa might include Belize, Cozumel or the Costa Maya Cruise Port in Mexico, Key West, Grand Cayman, or Jamaica—all perfect choices for passengers who enjoy scuba diving and snorkeling and look forward to exploring Mayan ruins. Ships often alternate itineraries in the Western Caribbean with itineraries in the Eastern Caribbean on a weekly basis, offering the ability to schedule a 14-night back-to-back cruise without repeating ports.

SOUTHERN CARIBBEAN ITINERARIES

Southern Caribbean cruises tend to be longer in duration, with more distant ports of call. They often originate in a port that is not on the U.S. mainland. Embarking in San Juan, for example, allows you to reach the lower Caribbean on a seven-day cruise with as many as four or five ports of call. Southern Caribbean itineraries might leave Puerto Rico for the Virgin Islands, Guadeloupe, Grenada, Curaçao, Barbados, Antigua, St. Lucia, Martinique, or Aruba. Smaller ships leave from embarkation ports as far south as Bridgetown, Barbados, and cruise through the Grenadines. Every major cruise line offers some Southern Caribbean itineraries, but these cruises aren't as popular as Western and Eastern Caribbean cruises.

OTHER ITINERARIES

In recent years shorter itineraries have grown in appeal to time-crunched and budget-constrained travelers. If you are planning your first cruise in the tropics, a short sailing to the Bahamas allows you to test your appetite for cruising before you take a chance on a longer and more expensive cruise. Embarking at Fort Lauderdale, Miami, Jacksonville, or Port Canaveral, you will cruise for three to five days, taking in at least one port of call (usually Nassau or Freeport in the Bahamas) and possibly a visit to a "private" island or Key West. Four- and five-night cruises may also include a day at sea. Cruises also depart from ports farther north on the east coast; you might depart from Charleston, Baltimore, or New York City and cruise to Bermuda or the Bahamas.

WHEN TO GO

Average year-round temperatures throughout the Caribbean are 78°F–85°F, with a low of 65°F and a high of 95°F; downtown shopping areas always seem to be unbearably hot. Low season runs from approximately mid-September through mid-April. Many travelers, especially families with school-age children, make reservations months in advance for the most expensive and most crowded summer months and holiday periods; however, with the many new cruise ships that have entered the market, you can often book fairly close to your departure date and still find room, although you may not get exactly the kind of cabin you would prefer. A summer cruise offers certain advantages: temperatures are virtually the same as in winter (cooler on average than in parts of the U.S. mainland), island flora is at its most dramatic, the water is smoother and clearer, and although there is always a breeze, winds are rarely strong enough to rock a ship. Some Caribbean tourist facilities close down in summer, however, and many ships move to Europe, Alaska, or the northeastern United States.

Hurricane season runs a full six months of the year—from June 1 through November 30. Although cruise ships stay well out of the way of these storms, hurricanes and tropical storms—their less-powerful relatives—can affect the weather throughout the Caribbean for days, and damage to ports can force last-minute itinerary changes.

CRUISE COSTS

The average daily price for Caribbean itineraries varies dramatically depending on several circumstances. The cost of a cruise on a luxury line such as Silversea or Seabourn may be three to four times the cost of a cruise on a mainstream line such as Carnival or even premium lines like Princess. When you sail will also affect your costs: published brochure rates are usually highest during the peak summer season and holidays. When snow blankets the ground and temperatures are in single digits, a

CLOSE UP

Saving Money on Your Cruise Fare

You can save on your cruise fare in several ways. Obviously, you should shop around. Some travel agents will discount cruise prices, though this is becoming a thing of the past. One thing never changes—do not ever, under any circumstances, pay brochure rate. You can do better, often as much as half off published fares. These are a few simple strategies you can follow:

■ Book early: Cruise lines discount their cruises if you book early, particularly during the annual "Wave" season between January and March.

■ Cruise during the off-season: If you take a cruise during the later months of hurricane season (especially October and November) or the period between Thanksgiving and Christmas, you'll often find specials.

■ Book late: Sometimes you can book a last-minute cruise at substantial savings if the ship hasn't filled all its cabins.

■ Choose accommodations with care: Cabins are usually standardized, and location determines the fare. Selecting a lower category can result in savings while giving up nothing in terms of cabin size and features.

■ Book a "guarantee": You won't be able to select your own cabin because the cruise line will assign you one in the category you book, but a "guarantee" fare can be substantially lower than a regular fare.

■ Cruise with friends and family: Book a minimum number of cabins, and your group can generally receive a special discounted fare.

■ Reveal your age and affiliations: Fare savings may be available for seniors and members of certain organizations, as well as cruise-line stockholders.

■ Cruise often: Frequent cruisers usually get discounts from their preferred cruise lines.

Caribbean cruise can be a welcome respite and less expensive than land resorts, which often command top dollar in winter months.

Solo travelers should be aware that single cabins have virtually disappeared from cruise ships. Taking a double cabin can cost twice the advertised per-person rates (which are based on double occupancy). Some cruise lines will find same-sex roommates for singles; each then pays the per-person, double-occupancy rate.

EXTRAS

In addition to the cost of your cruise, there are further expenses to consider, such as airfare to the port city. These days, virtually all cruise lines offer air add-ons, which are sometimes, but not always, less expensive than the lowest available airline fare. Shore excursions can also be a substantial expense; the best shore excursions are not cheap. But if you skimp too much on your excursion budget you'll deprive yourself of an important part of the Caribbean cruising experience. Finally, there will be many extras added to your shipboard account during the cruise, including drinks (both alcoholic and nonalcoholic), activity fees (you pay to use that golf simulator), dining in specialty restaurants, spa services, and even cappuccino and espresso on most ships. These add-ons are no longer nominal fees, either; you pay top-dollar for most extras onboard mainstream ships, and the average post-cruise bill may be as much as 50% of the base cost of your cruise.

TIPPING

Tipping is another add-on. At the end of the cruise, it's customary to tip your room steward, dining-room waiter, and the person who buses your table. You should expect to pay an average of $10 to $15 per person per day in tips. Most major cruise lines are moving away from the traditional method of tipping the service staff in cash at the end of the cruise, instead adding the recommended amount per day to your onboard account to cover tips, which you may adjust upward or downward according to the level of service you receive. Bar bills generally include an automatic 15%–18% gratuity, so the one person you don't need to tip is your bartender. Some cruise lines have gratuities-included policies, though some passengers tip for any extra services received anyway. Each cruise line offers guidelines.

CRUISE LINES

Seated in an airplane after a week of enjoying an exceptionally nice cruise, I overheard the couple behind me discussing their "dreadful" cruise vacation. What a surprise when they mentioned the ship's name. It was the one I'd just spent a glorious week on. I never missed a meal; they hated the food. My cabin was comfortable and cheery, if not large; their identical accommodations resembled a "cave." One size definitely does not fit all in cruising. What's appealing to one passenger may be unacceptable to another. Ultimately, most cruise complaints arise from passengers whose expectations were not met. The couple I eavesdropped on were on the wrong cruise line and ship for them.

I enjoy cruises. Some have suited me more than others, but I've never sailed on a cruise that was completely without merit. Make no mistake about it: cruise lines have distinct personalities, but not all luxury or mainstream cruise lines are alike, although they will share many basic similarities. The cruise industry is a fluid one—that means that when new features are introduced, they may not be found on all ships, even those within the same cruise line. For instance, you won't find an ice-skating rink on any but the biggest Royal Caribbean ships. However, most cruise lines attempt to standardize the overall experience throughout their fleets, which is why you'll find a waterslide on every Carnival ship.

Just as trends and fashion evolve over time, cruise lines embrace the ebb and flow of change. To keep pace with today's lifestyles, some cruise lines strive to include something that will appeal to everyone on their ships. Others focus on narrower elements and are more traditional. Today's passengers have higher expectations, and they sail on ships that are far superior to their predecessors. And they often do so at a much lower comparable fare than in the past.

So which cruise line is best? Only you can determine which is best for you. You won't find ratings by Fodor's—either quality stars or value scores. Why? Think of those people seated behind me on the airplane. Ratings are personal and heavily weighted to the reviewer's opinion. Your responsibility is to select the right cruise for you—no one knows your expectations better than you do yourself. It's your time, money, and vacation that are at stake. No matter how knowledgeable your travel agent it, how sincere your friends are, or what any expert can tell you, you are the only one who really knows what you like. The short wait for a table might not bother you because you would prefer a casual atmosphere with open seating; however, some people want the security of a set time at an assigned table served by a waiter who gets to know their preferences. You know what you are willing to trade off in order to get what you want.

The following cruise-line profiles offer a general idea of what you can expect in terms of overall experience, quality, and service from each major cruise line that operates in the Caribbean and the Bahamas. You will want to compare the features of several cruise lines to determine which ones come closest to matching your needs. Then narrow them down further to a few that appeal most to you. Keep in mind that not all ships belonging to the cruise lines described in the following profiles are deployed in the Caribbean year-round; some head for Alaska and Europe during summer months; others call port cities on the Pacific coast their home for part of the year.

LUXURY CRUISE LINES

Comprising only 5% of the market, the exclusive luxury cruise lines, which include Crystal, Cunard, Regent Seven Seas, Seabourn, SeaDream, Silversea, and Windstar, offer high staff-to-guest ratios for personal service, superior cuisine in a single seating (except Crystal, with two assigned seatings and an open-seating option, and Cunard, with dual-class dining assignments), and a highly inclusive product with few onboard charges. These small and midsize ships offer much more space per passenger than you will find on the mainstream lines' vessels. Lines differ in what they emphasize, with some touting luxurious accommodations and entertainment and others focusing on exotic destinations and onboard enrichment.

If you consider travel a necessity rather than a luxury and frequent posh resorts, then you will appreciate the extra attention and the higher level of comfort that luxury cruise lines offer.

Itineraries on these ships often include the big casino and most popular island beach resorts, but luxury ships also visit some of the more uncommon Caribbean destinations. With a shallow draft and intimate size, the smaller luxury ships can visit such ports as Anguilla, St. Barths, Tobago, and Jost Van Dyke and Virgin Gorda in the British Virgin Islands.

MAINSTREAM CRUISE LINES

More than 85% of the Caribbean is covered by nearly a dozen mainstream cruise lines. They offer the advantage of something for everyone and nearly every available sports facility imaginable. Some ships even have ice-skating rinks, 18-hole miniature golf courses, bowling alleys, and rock-climbing walls.

Generally speaking, the mainstream lines have two basic ship sizes—large cruise ships and mega-ships—in their fleets. These cruise ships have plentiful outdoor deck space, and many have a wraparound outdoor promenade deck that allows you to stroll or jog the ship's perimeter. In the newest vessels, traditional meets trendy. You'll find atrium lobbies and expansive sun and sports decks, picture windows instead of portholes, and cabins that open onto private verandas. For all their resort-style innovations, they still feature cruise-ship classics—afternoon tea, complimentary room service, and lavish pampering. The smallest ships carry 1,000 passengers or fewer, while the largest accommodate more than 3,000 passengers and are filled with diversions.

If you're into big, bold, brassy, and nonstop activity, these huge ships offer it all. The centerpiece of most mega-ships is a 3-, 5-, or even 11-story central atrium. However, these giant vessels are most readily distinguished by their profile: the boxy hull and superstructure rise as many as 14 stories out of the water and are capped by a huge sun- or sports deck with a jogging track and one or more swimming pools. Some mega-ships have a traditional wraparound promenade deck. Picture windows are standard equipment, and cabins in the top categories have private verandas. From their casinos and discos to their fitness centers, everything is bigger and more extravagant than on other ships. You may want to rethink a cruise aboard one of these ships if you want a little downtime, since you'll be joined by 1,500 to 5,400 fellow passengers.

OTHER CRUISE LINES

A few small cruise lines sail through the Caribbean and offer boutique to nearly bed-and-breakfast experiences. Notably, Windstar Cruises and Star Clippers appeal to passengers who eschew mainstream cruises. Most of these niche vessels accommodate 200 or fewer passengers, and their focus is on soft adventure. Cruising between nearby ports and anchoring out so passengers can swim and snorkel directly from the ship, their itineraries usually leave plenty of time for exploring and other activities on- or offshore. Many of these cruises schedule casual enrichment talks that often continue on decks, at meals, and during trips ashore.

AZAMARA CLUB CRUISES

"The adventuresome (yet pampered) soul has met its match" is the catchy new slogan for this ultra-premium cruise line newly launched by parent company Royal Caribbean in 2007. The line is comprised of two ships, both built for now-defunct Renaissance Cruises and refitted for the deluxe-cruise crowd. Designed to offer exotic, destination-driven itineraries, Azamara offers a more intimate onboard experience, while allowing access to the more unusual ports of call experienced travelers want to visit.

Enrichment programs, from culinary demonstrations to seminars by guest speakers and experts on a wide variety of topics, are some of the best on offer. The ships are designated resort casual, so there is no necessity to weigh down your luggage with formal attire—even though your butler is on hand to unpack for you. Evening entertainment leans toward sophisticated cabaret and jazz. Azamara ships are some of the most smoke-free at sea. Only two small sections are designated for smokers—one in a section of the observation lounge and the other in a forward area of the pool deck. No other areas on the ships allow smoking, including cabins and balconies.

Your Shipmates. Azamara is designed to appeal to discerning travelers, primarily American couples of any age who appreciate a high level of service in an unstructured atmosphere. The ships are not family-oriented and do not have facilities or programs for children.

Food. Expect all the classic dinner favorites but with an upscale twist, such as gulf shrimp with cognac and garlic, or a filet mignon with black-truffle sauce. In addition to the open-seating main dining room, each Azamara ship offers two specialty restaurants: the Mediterranean-influenced Aqualina and the stylish steak-and-seafood restaurant Prime C. Suite guests may dine in the specialty restaurants every night of their cruise at no charge. Passengers booked in Veranda, Oceanview, and Interior staterooms are guaranteed seating for two nights and may make additional reservations based on availability. A $15 cover charge applies to all stateroom guests. Daily in-cabin afternoon tea service and delivery of canapés are available to all passengers.

Fitness and Recreation. In addition to a well-equipped gym and an outdoor jogging track, Azamara's fitness program includes yoga at sunset, Pilates, and access to an onboard wellness consultant. Both ships offer a full menu of spa treatments, an outdoor spa relaxation lounge, and an aesthetics suite featuring acupuncture, laser hair removal, and micro-dermabrasion.

Service and Tipping. Gracious and polished service throughout the ships affords everyone an exclusive experience. Azamara offers butler service in every stateroom and suite. Gratuities are automatically charged to onboard accounts at the daily rate of $12.25 per person per day. Guests in suites experience superior Head Butler service in addition to Butler & Stateroom Attendant service and are charged an additional gratuity of $4 per person, per day. Amounts may be adjusted according to the level of service received. A standard 18% gratuity is added to beverage charges. It is recommended that a $5 per person gratuity be extended when dining in the specialty restaurants.

Contact Azamara Club Cruises (☏ 877/999–9553 ⊕ *www.azamaraclubcruises. com*).

CARNIVAL CRUISE LINES

☾ The world's largest cruise line originated the "Fun Ship" concept in 1972 with the relaunch of an aging ocean liner that got stuck on a sandbar during its maiden voyage. Sporting red-white-and-blue flared funnels, which are easily recognized from afar, new ships are continuously added to the fleet and rarely deviate from a successful pattern. Decor tends to be over the top; each ship features theme public rooms and huge casinos, spas, and lavish entertainment in massive show lounges.

Cabins are spacious and comfortable, often larger than on other ships in this price category, and feature the "Carnival Comfort Bed" sleep system consisting of plush mattresses, luxury duvets, high-quality linens, and cushy pillows.

Your Shipmates. Carnival's passengers are mostly American couples in their mid-30s to mid-50s. During holidays and school vacation periods you'll see many families with kids on board. "Camp Carnival" offers year-round programs for children and teens from age 2 to 17. Daytime group babysitting is offered for infants 2 and under until noon on all port days, as well as from 10 PM to 3 AM, when slumber party–style group babysitting is available for ages 4 months to 11 years. As long as diapers and supplies are provided, toddlers do not have to be toilet trained to participate.

Food. Carnival ships have both flexible dining options and casual alternative restaurants. Although the tradition of two set meal times for dinner prevails on Carnival ships, the line's open-seating concept has been implemented fleet-wide. Upscale supper clubs on the newest ships serve cuisine comparable to high-end steak houses and seafood restaurants ashore. "Georges Blanc Signature Selections" expand main-dining-room, Lido-restaurant, and Supper Club menus with a variety of gourmet-quality choices. In addition to the regular menu, vegetarian, low-calorie, low-carbohydrate, low-salt, no-sugar, and children's selections are available. If you don't feel like dressing up for dinner, the Lido buffet serves full meals and excellent pizza.

Fitness and Recreation. Carnival's trademark spas and fitness centers are some of the largest and best equipped at sea. State-of-the-art cardiovascular and strength-training equipment, a jogging track, and basic exercise classes are available at no charge in the fitness centers. There's a fee for personal training and specialized classes such as yoga and Pilates.

Service and Tipping. Service on Carnival ships is friendly but not polished. Stateroom attendants are not only recognized for their attention to cleanliness, but also for their expertise in creating towel animals that appear most nights during turn-down service. Gratuities of $10 per passenger, per day, are automatically added to onboard accounts. A 15% gratuity is automatically added to bar and beverage tabs.

Contact Carnival Cruise Lines (☎ *305/599–2600 or 800/227–6482* ⊕ *www. carnival.com*).

CELEBRITY CRUISES

Founded in 1989, Celebrity has gained a reputation for fine food and professional service. The cruise line has built premium, sophisticated ships and developed signature amenities, including a specialty coffee shop, martini bar, large standard staterooms with generous storage, spas, and butler service for passengers booking the top suites. ConciergeClass makes certain premium ocean-view and balcony staterooms almost the equivalent of suites in terms of amenities and service.

2

Entertainment choices range from Broadway-style productions, captivating lounge shows, and lively discos to Monte Carlo–style casinos and specialty lounges. Multimillion-dollar art collections grace the entire fleet, which merged with Royal Caribbean International in 1997.

Your Shipmates. Celebrity caters to Americans, primarily couples from their mid-30s to mid-50s. During summer months and holiday periods you'll see many families with kids aboard. Each vessel has a dedicated playroom and offers planned activities for children and teens ages 3 to 17, plus Toddler Time for parents and their children under age 3. Some activities have additional fees; evening in-cabin babysitting can also be arranged for a fee.

Food. In early 2007 Celebrity announced plans to advance its already distinguished fleetwide culinary program to the next level. Each ship in the fleet has highly experienced teams headed by executive chefs and food and beverage managers, who have developed their skills in some of the world's finest restaurants and hotels. Although the tradition of two set meal times for dinner is still popular on Celebrity ships, the line has introduced an open-seating concept fleet-wide. Alternative restaurants on all but *Celebrity Mercury* offer fine dining in classic ocean-liner splendor.

Fitness and Recreation. Celebrity's fitness centers and AquaSpa by Elemis are some of the most tranquil and nicely equipped at sea. State-of-the-art exercise equipment, a jogging track, and some fitness classes are available at no charge. Spa treatments include a variety of massages, body wraps, and facials. Each ship has an Acupuncture at Sea program administered by a specialist in Oriental medicine. Hair and nail services are offered in the salons.

Service and Tipping. Service on Celebrity ships is unobtrusive and polished. ConciergeClass adds an unexpected level of service and amenities that are usually reserved for passengers in top-category suites on other premium cruise lines. Gratuities, which may be adjusted, are automatically added to your onboard account on a daily basis in the following amounts: $11.50 per person per day for passengers in staterooms; $12 per person per day for passengers in ConciergeClass and AquaClass staterooms; and $15 per person per day for passengers in suites). An automatic gratuity of 15% is added to all beverage tabs.

Contact **Celebrity Cruises** (☎ *800/647–2251* ⊕ *www.celebritycruises.com*).

COSTA CRUISES

The Genoa-based Costa Crociere, parent company of Costa Cruises, had been in the shipping business for more than 100 years and in the passenger business for almost 50 years when Carnival Corporation gained sole ownership of the line in 2000, but the ships retain their original flavor. Costa's Italian-inspired vessels bring the Mediterranean vitality of *La Dolce Vita* to far-flung regions of the Caribbean. The ships are a combination of classic and modern design. A new vessel-building program has brought Costa ships into the 21st century with innovative, large-ship designs that reflect their Italian heritage and style without overlooking the amenities expected by modern cruisers.

Festive shipboard activities include games of boccie and a wacky toga party, yet there is also a nod to the traditional cruise-ship entertainment expected by North Americans. Supercharged social staffs work overtime to get everyone in the mood and encourage everyone to be a part of the action.

Your Shipmates. Passengers tend to be a little older than average—the average age is 54—and have an interest in all things Italian. Up to 80% of passengers are North Americans, and many of them are of Italian descent. You don't find a lot of first-time cruisers on Costa ships. Youth programs provide daily age-appropriate activities for children age 3 to 17. Group evening babysitting for youngsters ages 3 and up (children must be toilet trained) is available on request for a fee.

Food. Dining features regional Italian cuisines, a variety of pastas, chicken, beef, and seafood dishes, as well as authentic pizza. Costa dining is notable for its delicious, properly prepared pasta courses. Vegetarian and healthy diet choices are also offered. Alternative dining is by reservation only in the upscale supper clubs, which serve choice steaks and seafood from a Tuscan Steakhouse menu as well as traditional Italian specialties. Costa chefs continue to celebrate the tradition of lavish late-night buffets during Caribbean cruises.

Fitness and Recreation. Costa places continuing emphasis on wellness and sybaritic pleasures. Spa treatments include a variety of massages, body wraps, and facials. Hair and nail services are available in the salons. State-of-the-art exercise equipment in the terraced gym, a jogging track, and basic fitness classes for all levels of ability are available.

Service and Tipping. Service in dining areas can be spotty and rushed, but is adequate—if not always overly friendly. Gratuities are added to onboard accounts in the following amounts: $10 per adult per day for cruises up to eight nights; $7.50 per adult per day on longer cruises; 50% of that amount for teens between the ages of 14 and 17; and no charge for children under the age of 14. A 15% gratuity is automatically added to all beverage tabs.

Contact Costa Cruises (☎ *954/266–5600 or 800/462–6782* ⊕ *www.costacruises.com*).

CRYSTAL CRUISES

Crystal's midsize ships stand out for their modern design, amenities, and spaciousness. Built to deliver the first-rate service and amenities expected from a luxury line, these vessels nevertheless carry upward of 900 passengers—and have many big-ship facilities. Beginning with ship designs based on the principles of feng shui, no detail is too small to overlook to provide passengers with the best imaginable experience.

Crystal ships have long set standards for pampering—one reason these vessels often spend several days at sea rather than in port. To the typical litany of cruise-ship diversions, Crystal adds enrichment opportunities that include destination-oriented lectures and talks by scholars, political figures, and diplomats; hands-on classes in music and art; and deluxe theme cruises that emphasize such topics as food and wine or the fine arts.

Your Shipmates. Affluent, well-traveled couples, from their late-30s to retirees, are typical. Although the cruises are adult-oriented, there are dedicated facilities for children from 3 to 17 that are staffed for some sailings, especially during holiday periods and the summer season; however, Crystal limits the number of children under 3 and does not allow infants less than 6 months of age without a signed waiver of parental consent.

Food. The food is a good enough reason to book a Crystal cruise. Dining in the main restaurants is an event starring Continental-inspired cuisine served by European-trained waiters. Off-menu requests are honored when possible, and special dietary considerations are handled with ease. Unlike most luxury lines, Crystal still offers two assigned dinner seatings in the main restaurant. Happily, a flexible option is now offered—with Open Dining by Reservation you may reserve a table in dining room at the time of your choice each night of your cruise, Casual poolside dining from the grills is offered on some evenings in a relaxed, no-reservations-required option. A variety of hot and cold hors d'oeuvres are served in bars and lounges every evening before dinner and again during the wee hours. Where service and the dishes really shine are in the specialty restaurants; each ship has Asian-inspired and Italian specialty restaurants.

Fitness and Recreation. Large spas offer innovative treatments. Fitness centers feature a range of exercise and weight-training equipment and workout areas for aerobics classes, plus complimentary yoga and Pilates. Utilizing Le Monde Life Fitness bikes, Crystal ships offer "Tour de Spin," a complimentary indoor cycling program. In addition, golfers enjoy extensive shipboard facilities, including a driving-range practice cage and putting green.

Service and Tipping. Crystal's European-trained staff members provide gracious service in an unobtrusive manner. Tips are either personally distributed by passengers on the last night of the cruise or charged to onboard accounts. Suggested guidelines for stateroom and dining service gratuities (per person, per day) are: stewardess $5 (single travelers, $6 per day); senior waiter $5; waiter $3; butler (Penthouse Decks) $4. For specialty restaurants, the suggested gratuity is $7 per person per dinner. A 15% gratuity is automatically added to bar checks; the same is suggested for spa and beauty treatments.

Contact Crystal Cruises (☎ *310/785–9300 or 888/799–4625* ⊕ *www. crystalcruises.com*).

CUNARD LINE

One of the world's most distinguished names in ocean travel since 1840, Cunard Line has a history of deluxe transatlantic crossings and worldwide cruising that is legendary for comfortable accommodations, excellent cuisine, and personal service. Though the line is now owned by Carnival Corporation, its high-end ships retain a distinctly British sensibility. Cunard offers a short season of Caribbean cruises, which are highly prized by fans of the line.

Entertainment includes nightly production shows or cabaret-style performances and even plays. An authentic pub adds to the British ambience, while a wide variety of musical styles can be found for dancing and listening in other bars and lounges. Cunard's fine enrichment programs are presented by expert guest lecturers. You can preplan your activities prior to departure by consulting the syllabus of courses available online at Cunard Line's Web site.

Your Shipmates. Discerning, well-traveled British and American couples from their late-30s to retirees are drawn to Cunard's traditional style. The availability of spacious accommodations and complimentary self-service laundry facilities make Cunard liners a good option for families, but the number of kids on board is usually fairly limited. Kid-friendly features include a dedicated play area for children 1 to 6. Separate programs are reserved for older children ages 7 to 12 and teens up to 17. Toddlers are supervised by English nannies, and complimentary group babysitting is available in the evenings.

Food. In the tradition of multiclass ocean liners, dining-room assignments are made according to the accommodation category booked, so you get the luxury you pay for. Passengers in Junior Suites are assigned to single-seating Princess Grill, while the posh Queen's Grill serves passengers booked in the most lavish suites. All other passengers are assigned to one of two seatings in the dramatic Britannia Restaurant. Menus also include vegetarian and low-calorie selections. Specialty restaurants require reservations, and there is an additional charge.

Fitness and Recreation. Swimming pools, golf driving ranges, table tennis, paddle tennis, shuffleboard, and jogging tracks barely scratch the surface of onboard facilities dedicated to recreation. Fitness centers offer high-tech workout equipment, a separate weight room, and classes ranging from aerobics to healthy living workshops. The spas are top-notch, with a long menu of treatments and salon services for women and men.

Service and Tipping. Service is formal and sophisticated. Suggested gratuities of $13 per person per day (for Grill Restaurant accommodations) or $11 per person per day (all other accommodations) are automatically charged to shipboard accounts. A 15% gratuity is added to bar tabs. Direct gratuities for special service are allowed.

Contact Cunard Line (☎ 661/753–1000 or 800/728–6273 ⊕ www.cunard.com).

DISNEY CRUISE LINE

Disney Cruise Line launched its ships in 1998 and 1999, and is poised to introduce a third ship in 2011. Dozens of the best ship designers, industry veterans, and Disney creative minds planned intensely for multiple years to produce these vessels, which make a positive impression on adults and children alike. Exteriors are reminiscent of the great ocean liners of the early 20th century, resplendent with two funnels and black hulls, but interiors are technologically up-to-the-minute and full of novel developments in dining, cabin, and entertainment facilities. Accommodations are especially family-friendly, and most have a split-bathroom configuration with a sink and bathtub in one section and a sink and toilet in the other.

Entertainment leans heavily on popular Disney themes and characters. Parents are actively involved in the audience with their children at production shows, movies, "live" character meetings, deck parties, and dancing in the family nightclub. Teens have a supervised, no-adults-allowed club space. For adults, there are traditional no-kids-allowed bars and lounges with live music, dancing, theme parties, and late-night comedy as well as daytime wine-tasting sessions, game shows, culinary-arts and home-entertaining demonstrations, and behind-the-scenes lectures.

Your Shipmates. The young and not so young all find Disney Cruises appealing. Multigenerational family groups are the core clientele for these ships. As expected, Disney ships have extensive, age-appropriate programs for children and teens. A nursery for infants as young as 3 months is available for an hourly fee, and the diapers you supply will be changed by attendants—a service not available on most cruise lines. You might be surprised at the number of honeymooners on board.

Food. Don't expect top chefs and gourmet food; the fare is all-American for the most part. Naturally, all restaurants have children's menus. In a novel twist on dining, passengers "rotate" between theme dining rooms, accompanied each night by their waitstaff. Palo, the adults-only Italian restaurant on Disney Magic and Disney Wonder, requires reservations and has a cover charge. Similarly, adults on Disney Dream can opt for specialty dining in Remy, Disney's first-ever premier dining restaurant serving French-inspired cuisine. Fountain drinks at beverage stations are complimentary.

Fitness and Recreation. Three swimming pools are designated for different groups: children, families, and adults. The salon and spa rival any afloat. Unique to Disney ships are Spa Villas, indoor/outdoor treatment suites, each with a veranda with a hot tub and open-air shower. In addition to a nicely equipped fitness center and aerobics studio are a jogging track and basketball court.

Service and Tipping. Service is friendly, and particular importance is placed on treating children with the same courtesy extended to adults. Suggested gratuities are calculated on a per-person/per-cruise basis, and can be added to onboard accounts or offered in cash on the last night. For the dining-room server, assistant server, head server, and stateroom host/hostess, guidelines are $36 for three-night cruises, $48 for four-night cruises, and $84 for seven-night cruises. A 15% gratuity is added to bar service tabs.

Contact Disney Cruise Line (☎ *407/566–3500 or 888/325–2500.* ⊕ *www.disneycruise.com).*

HOLLAND AMERICA LINE

Founded in 1873, Holland America Line (HAL) is one of the oldest names in cruising. Its cruises are classic, conservative affairs renowned for their grace and gentility. As its ships attract a more youthful clientele, Holland America has taken steps to shed its "old folks" image, now offering stops at a private island in the Bahamas, trendier cuisine, a culinary arts center, and an expanded children's program. Still, these are not party cruises, and Holland America has managed to preserve the refined and relaxing qualities that have always been its hallmark, even on sailings that cater more to younger passengers and families.

Luxury bedding, magnifying makeup mirrors, robes, fresh-fruit baskets, flat-screen TVs, and DVD players are found in all cabins. In addition, suites have duvets, fully stocked minibars, personalized stationery, and access to the exclusive Neptune Lounge. Explorations Café, powered by the *New York Times,* combines a coffee bar, computer center with Wi-Fi, and cozy library-reading room complete with tabletop versions of the *Times'* crossword puzzles.

Your Shipmates. No longer your grandparents' cruise line, today's Holland America also attracts families and discerning couples, mostly from their late 30s and up. Retirees are often still in the majority; however, during holidays and summer months you'll find more families with kids. Group activities are planned for children ages 3 to 7 and 8 to 12 in Club HAL. After Hours offers late-night activities from 10 PM until midnight for an hourly fee. Teens ages 13 to 17 have their own lounge with activities.

Food. You have your choice of two assigned seatings or open seating for evening meals in the formal dining room. In the reservations-required Pinnacle Grill alternative restaurant ($20 dinner; $10 lunch), fresh seafood and premium cuts of beef are used to prepare creative specialty dishes. Delicious onboard traditions are afternoon tea, a Dutch Chocolate Extravaganza, and Holland America Line's signature bread pudding. Casual evening dining in the Lido restaurants offers a combination of buffet and waiter service. A portion of the Lido restaurant is transformed nightly into Canaletto, a complimentary casual Italian restaurant that requires reservations.

Fitness and Recreation. Well-equipped and fully staffed fitness facilities contain state-of-the-art exercise equipment; basic fitness classes are available at no charge, though you pay for personal training, yoga, and Pilates. You'll also find a jogging track, multiple swimming pools, and sports courts. Promenade decks encircle each ship and are popular for walking. The Greenhouse Spa offers a variety of treatments and salon services.

Service and Tipping. Professional, unobtrusive service by the Indonesian and Filipino staff is a fleetwide standard on Holland America Line. A standard gratuity of $11 per passenger per day is automatically added to shipboard accounts and is distributed to stewards and waitstaff. Room-service tips are offered in cash. An automatic 15% gratuity is added to bar-service tabs.

Contact **Holland America Line** (☎ *206/281–3535 or 800/577–1728.* ⊕ *www. hollandamerica.com*).

MSC CRUISES

With several seasons of Caribbean sailing behind them, MSC Cruises has outgrown its newcomer status. More widely known as one of the world's largest cargo shipping companies, parent company Mediterranean Shipping Company has operated cruises with an eclectic fleet since the late 1980s, but expanded its cruising reach by introducing graceful, modern ships in the Caribbean.

While sailing Caribbean itineraries, MSC Cruises adopts activities that appeal to American passengers without abandoning those preferred by Europeans—prepare for announcements in several languages in addition to English. In addition to trivia games, bingo, and cooking demonstrations, a popular option is Italian language classes. Nightly shows accentuate MSC Cruises' Mediterranean heritage—there might be an opera presentation in the main showroom and live music in the smaller lounges.

Your Shipmates. On Caribbean itineraries you will find about half of your fellow passengers are American couples in the 35- to 55-year-old range and families. Children ages 3 to 17 are welcome to participate in age-appropriate youth programs; the Teenage Club is for youths 13 years and older.

Food. Dinner on MSC ships is centered around authentic Italian fare. Menus list Mediterranean regional specialties and classic favorites prepared from scratch. "Healthy Choice" and vegetarian items are offered as well as sugar-free desserts. In a nod to American tastes, chicken, sirloin steak, grilled salmon, and Caesar salad are always available in addition to the regular dinner menu. A daily highlight is the bread and pasta, freshly made on board. Midnight buffets are a retro food feature missing from most of today's cruises. Alternative restaurants are featured throughout the fleet, but vary by ship class. Coffee bars and ice-cream bars charge for specialty coffee drinks and frozen treats.

Fitness and Recreation. Up-to-date exercise equipment, a jogging track, and basic fitness classes for all levels are available. Spa treatments include a variety of massages, body wraps, and facials that can be scheduled à la carte or combined in packages to encompass an afternoon or the entire cruise.

Service and Tipping. Service can be inconsistent, but is more than acceptable—if not overly gracious. The mainly Italian staff are sometimes still befuddled by American habits and expectations. Customary gratuities are automatically charged to onboard accounts in the amount of $12 per person per day for adults and $6 for children. Gratuities are included in all bar purchases.

Contact **MSC Cruises** (☎ *800/666–9333* ⊕ *www.msccruisesusa.com*).

NORWEGIAN CRUISE LINE

Norwegian Cruise Line (NCL) was established in 1966, when one of Norway's oldest and most respected shipping companies, Oslo-based Klosters Rederi A/S, acquired the *Sunward* and repositioned the ship from Europe to the then-obscure Port of Miami. With the formation of a company called Norwegian Caribbean Lines, the cruise industry as we know it today was born. NCL launched an entirely new concept with its regularly scheduled cruises to the Caribbean on a single-class ship. No longer simply a means of transportation, the ship became a destination unto itself, offering guests an affordable alternative to land-based resorts.

Always a cruise-industry innovator, Norwegian Cruise Line's "Freestyle" cruising introduced a wider variety of dining options in a casual, free-flowing atmosphere. Noted for top-quality, high-energy entertainment and emphasis on fitness facilities and programs, NCL combines action, activities, and a resort-casual atmosphere.

Your Shipmates. NCL's mostly American cruise passengers are active couples ranging from their mid-30s to mid-50s; some passengers may be in the over-55 age group. Many families enjoy cruising on NCL ships during summer months. Each NCL vessel offers the "Kid's Crew" program of supervised entertainment for young cruisers ages 2 to 17. For 13- to 17-year-olds there are clubs where they can hang out in adult-free zones.

Food. Main dining rooms serve what is traditionally deemed Continental fare, although it's about what you would expect at a really good hotel banquet. Where NCL stands above the ordinary is in their specialty restaurants, especially the French-Mediterranean Le Bistro (on all ships), the Pan-Asian restaurants, and steak houses (on the newer ships). In addition, you may find a Spanish tapas bar and an Italian trattoria. Most, but not all, specialty restaurants carry a cover charge and require reservations. An NCL staple, the late-night Chocoholic Buffet continues to be a favorite event.

Fitness and Recreation. Mandara Spa offers a long list of unusual and exotic spa treatments fleet-wide on NCL. State-of-the-art exercise equipment, jogging tracks, and basic fitness classes are available at no charge. There's a fee for personal training and specialized classes such as yoga and Pilates.

Service and Tipping. Although somewhat inconsistent, service is nonetheless congenial. A fixed service charge of $12 per person, per day, is added to shipboard accounts for passengers age 3 and up. An automatic 15% gratuity is added to bar tabs and 18% for spa services. Staff members are permitted to accept cash gratuities. Passengers in suites are asked to offer a cash gratuity to their concierge and butlers.

Contact Norwegian Cruise Line (☎ *305/436–4000 or 800/327–7030* ⊕ *www. ncl.com*).

OCEANIA CRUISES

This distinctive cruise line, founded by cruise-industry veterans with the know-how to satisfy inquisitive passengers with interesting ports of call and upscale touches for fares much lower than you would expect, is now owned by Prestige Cruise Holdings. Oceania uses midsize "R-class" ships from the now-defunct Renaissance Cruises fleet, and launched a new ship class in fall 2010. Varied, destination-rich itineraries are an important characteristic of Oceania Cruises, and most Caribbean sailings are in the 10- to 12-night range. Before arrival in ports of call, lectures are presented on the historical background, culture, and traditions of the islands.

Intimate and cozy public spaces reflect the importance of socializing on Oceania ships. Evening entertainment leans toward light cabaret, solo artists, music for dancing, and conversation with fellow passengers; however, you'll find lively karaoke sessions as well. On sea days jazz or easy-listening melodies are played poolside.

Your Shipmates. Oceania Cruises appeal to singles and couples from their late-30s to well-traveled retirees who have the time for and prefer longer cruises. Most are attracted to the casually refined atmosphere, creative cuisine, and European service. Oceania Cruises are adult-oriented and not a good choice for most families; there are no dedicated children's facilities.

Food. Master chef Jacques Pépin designed the menus for Oceania, and the results are sure to please the most discriminating palate. Oceania simply serves some of the best food at sea, particularly impressive for a cruise line that charges far less than luxury rates. The main open-seating restaurant offers trendy French-Continental cuisine with an always-on-the-menu steak, seafood, or poultry choice and vegetarian option. Intimate specialty restaurants require reservations, but there is no additional charge.

Fitness and Recreation. Although small, the spa, salon, and well-equipped fitness center on Regatta-class ships are adequate for the number of passengers on board. There is a walking/jogging track circling the top of the ship. The Canyon Ranch SpaClub treatment menus list massages, body wraps, and facials. Forward of the locker rooms you will find a large therapy pool and quiet deck for relaxation and sunning on padded wooden steamer chaises.

Service and Tipping. Highly personalized service by a mostly European staff is crisp and efficient without being intrusive. Butlers are on hand to satisfy the needs of suite guests and will even assist with packing and unpacking upon request. A charge of $12.50 per person, per day is added to onboard accounts, and an additional $4 per person, per day is added for suite occupants. An 18% gratuity is automatically added to all beverage purchases and spa and salon services.

Contact **Oceania Cruises** (☎ *305/514–2300 or 800/531–5658* ⊕ *www. oceaniacruises.com*).

Drinking and Gambling Ages

Many underage passengers have learned to their chagrin that the rules that apply on land are also adhered to at sea. On most mainstream cruise ships you must be 21 in order to imbibe alcoholic beverages. There are exceptions—for instance, on cruises departing from countries where the legal drinking age is typically lower than 21. By and large, if you haven't achieved the magic age of 21, your shipboard charge card will be coded as booze-free, and bartenders won't risk their jobs to sell you alcohol.

Gambling is a bit looser, and 18 year olds can try their luck on cruise lines such as Carnival, Celebrity, Azamara, Silversea, Norwegian, and Royal Caribbean; most other cruise lines adhere to the age-21 minimum. Casinos are trickier to patrol than bars, though, and minors who look "old enough" may get away with dropping a few coins in an out-of-the-way slot machine before being spotted on a hidden security camera. If you hit a big jackpot, you may have a lot of explaining to do to your parents.

PRINCESS CRUISES

Rising from modest beginnings in 1965, when it began offering cruises to Mexico with a single ship, Princess has become one of the world's best-known cruise lines. Catapulted to stardom in 1977, when its flagship became the setting for *The Love Boat* television series, Princess introduced millions of viewers to the still-new concept of a seagoing vacation. Altough the line does have some medium-size vessels, Princess more often follows the "big is better" trend. Its fleet sails to more destinations each year than any other major line, though many cruises depart from the West Coast.

All Princess ships feature the line's innovative "Personal Choice Cruising" program that gives passengers choice and flexibility in customizing their cruise experience—multiple dining locations, flexible entertainment, and affordable private balconies are all highlights. Enrichment programs feature guest lecturers and opportunities to learn new skills or crafts, but you'll still find staples such as bingo and art auctions. You can even earn PADI scuba-diving certification in just one week during select sailings.

Your Shipmates. Princess Cruises attract mostly American passengers ranging from their mid-30s to mid-50s. Longer cruises appeal to well-traveled retirees. Families can be found cruising together on the Princess fleet, particularly during summer months, when many children are on board. For young passengers ages 3 to 17, each Princess vessel (except Ocean and Pacific Princess) allows parents independent time ashore, youth centers operate as usual during port days.

Food. Personal choices regarding where and what to eat abound, but unless you opt for traditional assigned seating, you might have a short wait for a table in one of the open-seating dining rooms. Menus are varied and extensive, and the results are good to excellent. A special menu is designed especially for children. Alternative restaurants are

2

a staple throughout the fleet, but vary by ship class. Lido buffets on all ships are almost always open, and a pizzeria and grill offer casual daytime snack choices. The fleet's patisseries and ice-cream bars charge for specialty coffee, pastries, and ice-cream treats. With balcony accommodations, you can enjoy a private Champagne Breakfast or Ultimate Balcony Dinner.

Fitness and Recreation. Spa and salon rituals include massages, body wraps, facials, and numerous hair and nail services, including treatments designed specifically for men, teens, and couples. Modern exercise equipment, a jogging track, and basic fitness classes are available at no charge. Grand-class ships have a resistance pool for lap swimming.

Service and Tipping. Professional service by an international staff is efficient and friendly. Princess suggests tipping $11 per person per day for passengers in suites and minisuites and $10.50 per person, per day for all other passengers (including children). Gratuities are automatically added to onboard accounts; spa personnel are tipped at your discretion; 15% is added to bar bills.

Contact Princess Cruises (☎ 661/753–0000 or 800/774–6237 ⊕ www. princess.com).

REGENT SEVEN SEAS CRUISES

Regent Seven Seas Cruises sails an elegant fleet of vessels that offer a nearly all-inclusive cruise experience in sumptuous, contemporary surroundings. The line's spacious ocean-view staterooms have the industry's highest percentage of private balconies, and almost all drinks (except some premium brands) are now included.

Subtle improvements throughout the fleet are ongoing, such as computer service with Wi-Fi capability for your own laptop and cell phone access. New luxury bedding, Regent-branded bath amenities, flat-screen TVs, DVD players, and new clocks have been added to all cabins. Top suites also feature iPods and Bose speakers. Delightful ships feature exquisite service, generous staterooms with abundant amenities, a variety of dining options, and superior enrichment programs. Cruises are destination-focused, and most sailings host guest lecturers—historians, anthropologists, naturalists, and diplomats.

Your Shipmates. Regent Seven Seas Cruises are inviting to active, affluent, well-traveled couples ranging from their late 30s to retirees who enjoy the ships' elegance and destination-rich itineraries. Longer cruises attract passengers in the over-60 age group. Regent vessels are adult-oriented and do not have dedicated children's facilities; however, youth programs are offered on some sailings.

Food. Menus may appear to include the usual cruise-ship staples, but the results are some of the most outstanding meals at sea. Specialty dining varies within the fleet; when available, the sophisticated Signatures features the cuisine of Le Cordon Bleu of Paris; Prime 7 offers menus that rival the finest shoreside steak and seafood restaurants. In addition, Mediterranean-inspired bistro dinners are served in the daytime casual

Lido buffet restaurants. Wines chosen to complement dinner menus are freely poured each evening.

Fitness and Recreation. Although gyms and exercise areas are well equipped, these are not large ships, so the facilities tend to be on the small side. Each ship has a jogging track, and the larger ones feature a variety of sports courts. The spas and salons are operated by the legendary Canyon Ranch SpaClub.

Service and Tipping. The efforts of a polished European staff go almost unnoticed, yet special requests are handled with ease. Butlers provide an additional layer of personal service to guests in the top-category suites. Gratuities are included in the fare, and none are expected. Passengers are allowed to donate to a crew welfare fund that benefits the ship's staff.

Contact **Regent Seven Seas Cruises** (☎ *954/776–6123 or 877/505–5370* ⊕ *www.rssc.com*).

ROYAL CARIBBEAN INTERNATIONAL

Big, bigger, biggest! More than a decade ago, Royal Caribbean launched the first of the modern mega-cruise ships for passengers who enjoy traditional cruising with a touch of daring and whimsy tossed in. These large-to-giant vessels are indoor-outdoor wonders, with every conceivable activity in a resortlike atmosphere, including atrium lobbies, shopping arcades, large spas, expansive sundecks, and rock-climbing walls. Several ships have such elaborate facilities as 18-hole miniature-golf courses, ice-skating rinks, and in-line skating tracks. Oasis-class ships, RCI's latest additions, and presently the world's largest cruise ships, even have surf parks and a zip-line at sea. Plush new bedding has been installed fleetwide.

The centerpiece of Royal Caribbean mega-ships is the multideck atrium, a hallmark that has been duplicated by many other cruise lines. The brilliance of this design is that all the major public rooms radiate from this central point, so you can learn your way around these huge ships within minutes of boarding. Ships in the Vision class are especially bright and airy, with sea views almost anywhere you happen to be. The main problem with RCI's otherwise well-conceived vessels is that there are often too many people on board, making embarkation, tendering, and disembarkation exasperating. However, Royal Caribbean is still one of the best-run and most popular cruise lines.

Your Shipmates. Royal Caribbean cruises have a broad appeal for active couples and singles, mostly in their 30s to 50s. Families are partial to the newer vessels that have larger staterooms, excellent kids' facilities, and seemingly endless choices of activities and dining options. Supervised age-appropriate activities are designed for children ages 3 through 17. For infants and toddlers 6 to 36 months of age, interactive playgroup sessions are planned, while a teen center with a disco is an adult-free gathering spot. "Family-size" staterooms are available on most newer ships, but there are no self-service laundry facilities.

Food. Royal Caribbean offers the choice of an early or late dinner seating and an open-seating option that is available across the fleet. Windjammer Café and, on certain ships, the sunny Seaview Café are casual dining options. Each ship has a pizzeria, coffee bar, and ice-cream parlor, and Johnny Rockets 1950s-style diners (extra fee) can be found on most ships. Royal Caribbean doesn't place emphasis on celebrity chefs or specialty alternative restaurants, although the line has introduced a more intimate dinner experience in the form of an Italian-specialty restaurant and a steak house on some ships. The Oasis-class ships feature two-dozen dining spots, ranging from a seafood café and a cupcake bakery to more upscale specialty restaurants, many carrying extra charges.

Fitness and Recreation. Fabled for its range of top-of-the-line recreations, Royal Caribbean also delivers on the basics: most exercise classes, aimed at sweating off those extra calories, are included in the fare (although there's a fee for spinning, yoga, and Pilates classes, as well as personal training). Each ship has multiple swimming pools and a rock-climbing wall. Spas feature extensive treatment menus and full services for pampering adults and teens.

Service and Tipping. Service on Royal Caribbean ships is friendly but not consistent. Assigned meal seatings assure that most passengers get to know the waiters and their assistants, who in turn get to know the passengers' likes and dislikes; however, that can lead to a level of familiarity that some find uncomfortable. Tips can be prepaid when the cruise is booked, added onto shipboard accounts, or given in cash on the last night of the cruise. Suggested gratuities per passenger, per day, are: $3.50 for the cabin steward (or $5.75 for suite attendant); $3.50 for the waiter; $2 for the assistant waiter; and $0.75 for the head waiter. A 15% gratuity is automatically added to all bar tabs.

Contact **Royal Caribbean International** (✉ 305/539–6000 or 800/327–6700 ⊕ www.royalcaribbean.com).

SEABOURN CRUISE LINE

Ultraluxury pioneer Seabourn was founded on the principle that dedication to personal service in elegant surroundings would appeal to sophisticated, independent-minded passengers whose lifestyles demand the best. Its three nearly identical, all-suites ships received extensive makeovers in 2008, and were joined by newly launched larger vessels in 2009 and 2010. The "yachts" remain favorites with people who can take care of themselves but would rather do so aboard a luxury ship. Dining and evening socializing are generally more stimulating to Seabourn passengers than splashy song-and-dance reviews; however, proportionately scaled production and cabaret shows are presented in the main showroom and smaller lounge. The library stocks not only books but also movies.

You can expect complimentary wines and spirits, elegant amenities, and even the pleasure of minimassages while lounging poolside. Guest appearances by luminaries in the arts and world affairs highlight the enrichment program. Wine tasting, trivia contests, and other quiet pursuits might be scheduled, but most passengers prefer to simply do what pleases them.

Your Shipmates. Seabourn attracts mostly affluent, 50-plus and retired couples who are accustomed to evening formality. The ships are adult-oriented, with no children's programs or facilities, and are unable to accommodate children under 6 months (1 year for voyages of 15 days or longer).

Food. Exceptional cuisine created by celebrity chef-restaurateur Charlie Palmer is prepared to order and served in open-seating dining rooms. Creative menu offerings include foie gras, quail, and fresh seafood. Vegetarian dishes and offerings low in cholesterol, salt, and fat are prepared with the same care. Wines are chosen to complement each day's lunch and dinner menus, and caviar is always available. Evening dining alternatives include "Restaurant 2," which serves dinner nightly, and a second—even more laid-back—"Sky Grill," offering sizzling steaks and seafood, is sometimes offered in the open-air Sky Bar. Both require reservations but do not charge extra.

Fitness and Recreation. Complimentary "massage moments" offered poolside are mini-previews of the soothing treatments available in the spa. A full array of cardio, strength, and weight-training equipment and basic fitness classes are available in the small gym, while some specialized fitness sessions are offered for a fee. The water-sports marina is popular with active passengers who want to jet-ski, windsurf, kayak, or swim in the integrated saltwater "pool" while anchored in calm waters.

Service and Tipping. Personal service and attention by the professional staff are the order of the day. Your preferences are noted and fulfilled without the necessity of reminders. Tipping is neither required nor expected.

Contact Seabourn Cruise Line (☎ *305/463–3000 or 800/929–9391* 🖷 *305/463–3010* ⊕ *www.seabourn.com*).

SEADREAM YACHT CLUB

Launched in 1984 as Sea Goddess mega-yachts, these boutique ships have changed hands through the years, becoming SeaDream Yacht Club in 2002. Passengers enjoy an unstructured holiday at sea doing whatever pleases them, giving the diminutive vessels the feel of true private yachts with a select guest list. Other than a pianist in the tiny piano bar, a small casino, and movies in the main lounge, there is no roster of activities. The rocking late-night place to be is the Top of the Yacht Bar, where passengers gather to share the day's experiences and kick their shoes off to dance on the teak deck. The Captain hosts welcome-aboard and farewell cocktail receptions in the Main Salon each week. Otherwise, you are on your own to do as you please. A well-stocked library has books and movies for those who prefer quiet pursuits in the privacy of their staterooms.

Ports of call almost seem an intrusion on socializing amid the chic surroundings, although a picnic on a secluded beach adds the element of a private island paradise to each Caribbean cruise. While the ambience is sophisticated, all cruises are "yacht" casual, and you can leave your formal clothing at home. You can also leave your charge card in your pocket, as all beverages, including select wines and spirits are complimentary.

Your Shipmates. SeaDream yachts appeal to energetic, affluent travelers of all ages, as well as groups. Passengers tend to be couples from 45-year-olds and up to retirees. No children's facilities or organized activities are available, and these ships are not really suitable for passengers confined to wheelchairs. Although one stateroom on each vessel is designated "accessible," public facilities have thresholds, and the elevator doesn't reach the uppermost deck.

Food. Every meal is prepared to order using the freshest seafood and prime cuts of beef. Menus include vegetarian alternatives and Asian wellness cuisine for the health-conscious. Cheeses, petits fours, and chocolate truffles are offered with after-dinner coffee, and desserts are to die for. All meals are open seating, either in the main restaurant or, weather permitting, alfresco in the canopied Topsider Restaurant daily for breakfast, lunch, and special dinners. Wines are chosen to complement each luncheon and dinner menu.

Fitness and Recreation. Small gyms on each ship are equipped with treadmills, elliptical machines, recumbent bikes, and free weights. A personal trainer is available. SeaDream's unique Asian Spa facilities are also on the small side, yet offer a full menu of individualized gentle pampering treatments including massages, facials, and body wraps utilizing Eastern techniques. Mountain bikes are available for use ashore.

Service and Tipping. Personal service and attention to detail are amazing—you will be greeted by name within hours of boarding. Passenger preferences are shared among staff members who all work hard to assist one another. You seldom, if ever, have to repeat a request. Tipping is neither required nor expected.

Contact SeaDream Yacht Club (☎ *305/856–5622 or 800/707–4911* ⊕ *www. seadreamyachtclub.com*).

SILVERSEA CRUISES

Intimate ships, paired with exclusive amenities and unparalleled hospitality, are the hallmarks of Silversea luxury cruises. Personalization is a Silversea maxim. Ships offer more activities than other comparably sized luxury vessels, with guest lecturers on nearly every cruise. A multitiered show lounge is the setting for classical concerts, big-screen movies, and folkloric entertainers from ashore. All accommodations are spacious outside suites, most with private verandas. Silversea ships have large swimming pools in expansive Lidos. Silversea's third generation of ships introduced even more luxurious features when the 36,000-ton Silver Spirit launched late in 2009.

Although these ships schedule more activities than other comparably sized luxury vessels, you can either take part or opt instead for a good book and any number of quiet spots to read or snooze in the shade.

Silversea is so all-inclusive that you'll find your room key/charge card is seldom used for anything but opening your suite door.

Your Shipmates. Silversea Cruises appeal to sophisticated, affluent couples who enjoy the country club–like atmosphere, exquisite cuisine, and polished service. You might see the occasional child, but children less than 6 months old are not permitted, and the cruise line limits the number of children under the age of 3 on board.

Food. Dishes from the galleys of Silversea's master chefs are complemented by those of La Collection du Monde, created by Silversea's culinary partner, the world-class chefs of Relais & Châteaux. Perhaps more compelling is the line's flair for originality. The pasta chef's daily special is a passenger favorite, as is the galley brunch, held just once each cruise, when the galley is transformed into a buffet restaurant. Special off-menu orders are prepared whenever possible. Nightly alternative-theme dinners in La Terrazza (by day, the buffet restaurant) feature regional specialties from the Mediterranean; an intimate dining experience aboard each vessel is Le Champagne—the Wine Restaurant, which is run by Relais & Châteaux. Silver Spirit adds two additional dining options— Stars Supper Club, at no additional charge, and Asian-inspired Seishin Restaurant, for which there is a per-guest reservation fee.

Fitness and Recreation. The rather small gyms are well equipped with cardiovascular and weight-training equipment, and fitness classes are held in the mirror-lined, but somewhat confining, exercise room. South Pacific–inspired Mandara Spa offers numerous treatments, including exotic-sounding massages, facials, and body wraps.

Service and Tipping. Personalized service is exacting and hospitable, yet discreet; staff members strive for perfection and often achieve it. Personal preferences are remembered and satisfied. Tipping is neither required nor expected.

Contact **Silversea Cruises** (☎ 954/522–4477 or 800/722–9955 ⊕ www. silversea.com).

STAR CLIPPERS

In 1991 Star Clippers presented a new tall-ship alternative to sophisticated travelers whose wants included adventure at sea, but not on board a conventional cruise ship. Star Clippers vessels are the world's largest barkentine and full-rigged sailing ships—four- and five-masted sailing beauties filled with modern, high-tech equipment as well as amenities more often found on private yachts. The ships rely on sail power while at sea unless conditions require the assistance of the engines. Minimum heeling, usually less than 6%, is achieved through judicious control of the sails.

Star Clippers are not cruise ships in the ordinary sense, with strict agendas and pages of activities. You can lounge on deck and simply soak in the nautical ambience or learn about navigational techniques from the captain. Cabins, which are very compact, do include such amenities as hair dryers, TVs, and telephones. Star Clippers ships also have swimming pools. Other features fall somewhere between those of a true sailing yacht and the high-tech Windstar ships. The differences are more than just in the level of luxury—Star Clippers are true sailing vessels. Prices, however, are a bit more affordable and often less than you would pay on a high-end cruise ship.

Your Shipmates. Star Clippers cruises appeal to active, upscale American and European couples from their 30s on up who enjoy sailing, but in a casually sophisticated atmosphere with modern conveniences. Many sailings are split nearly equally between North American and European passengers. This is not a cruise line for the physically challenged; there are no elevators or ramps, nor are any staterooms or bathrooms wheelchair-accessible. Star Clippers ships are adult-oriented, and while children are allowed, there are no dedicated youth facilities.

Food. Not noted for gourmet fare, the international cuisine is what you would expect from a trendy shoreside bistro, albeit an elegant one. Fresh fruits and fish are among the best choices from Star Clippers' galleys. In a nod to American tastes, dinner menus include an alternative steak selection. Lunch buffets are quite a spread of seafood, salads, and grilled items. Casual fare is offered for lunch or late-afternoon snacking on deck. Room service is only available to occupants of suites aboard *Royal Clipper.*

Fitness and Recreation. Formal exercise sessions take a backseat to water sports, although aerobics classes and swimming are featured on all ships. Only *Royal Clipper* has a marina platform that can be lowered in calm waters to access water sports and diving, however, the smaller ships replicate the experience by using launches. A gym/spa with an array of exercise equipment, free weights, spa treatments, and unisex hair services are found only on *Royal Clipper.*

Service and Tipping. Service is friendly and gracious, similar to what you would find in a boutique hotel or restaurant. Star Clippers recommends the following gratuities (always in euros): room steward, €3 per day; dining-room staff, €5 per day. Tips are pooled and shared; individual tipping is discouraged. A 15% gratuity is added to bar bills. Gratuities may be charged to your shipboard account.

Contact Star Clippers (☎ *305/442–0550 or 800/442–0551* ⊕ *www. starclippers.com*).

WINDSTAR CRUISES

Are they cruise ships with sails or sailing ships designed for cruises? In actuality they are masted sailing yachts, pioneers in the upscale sailing niche. Although the sails add speed, Windstar ships seldom depend on wind alone to sail. However, if you are fortunate and conditions are perfect, the total silence of pure sailing is a thrill. Although the ships' designs may be reminiscent of sailing vessels of yore, the amenities and shipboard service are among the best at sea.

In keeping with the line's exacting standards, all ocean-view staterooms and suites provide the comforts of home with sitting area, luxury linens and mattresses, DVD/CD player, Apple iPod Nano and Bose Sound-Dock speakers, wireless Internet, safe, minibar/refrigerator, international direct-dial phones, L'Occitane bath toiletries, hair dryer, plenty of closet space, and plush robes and slippers. An array of international newspapers, books, and games can be found in the library, and a wide selection of DVD titles and CDs is available for complimentary use. Life on board is unabashedly sybaritic, attracting a sophisticated, relatively young crowd who are happy to sacrifice bingo and pool games for the attractions of remote islands and water sports; even motorized water sports are included, and passengers pay extra only for scuba diving. Unfortunately, only basic beverages are included in the fare.

Your Shipmates. Windstar cruises appeal to upscale professional couples in their late 30s to 60s. These ships are especially popular with honeymooners. The ships were not designed for accessibility, and are not a good choice for the physically challenged. *Wind Surf,* for example, has only two elevators, and the smaller ships have none. There are no staterooms or bathrooms deemed "accessible," and gangways can be difficult to navigate, depending on the tide and angle of ascent. The unregimented atmosphere is adult-oriented; children are not encouraged, and there are no dedicated children's facilities.

Food. Windstar menus feature dishes with tropical accents, using fresh local ingredients whenever possible. In a nod to healthful dining, low-calorie and low-fat spa cuisine and vegetarian dishes are always available in the open-seating restaurants. A mid-cruise deck barbecue featuring grilled seafood and other favorites is offered on all cruises. Aboard Wind Surf the specialty restaurant Degrees features themed dinners such as Italian, Indonesian, and Steak House at no additional charge, but reservations are required.

Fitness and Recreation. Windstar's massage and exercise facilities are quite small on *Wind Star* and *Wind Spirit,* as would be expected on ships that carry fewer than 150 passengers. However, on the larger *Wind Surf* the WindSpa and fitness areas are surprisingly large. An array of exercise equipment, free weights, and basic fitness classes are available in the gym and Nautilus room. A wide variety of massages, body wraps, and facial treatments are offered in the spa, while hair and nail services are available for women and men in the salon. Stern-mounted watersports marinas are popular with active passengers who want to kayak, windsurf, and water-ski.

Service and Tipping. Personal service is comprehensive, competent, and designed to create an elite and privileged atmosphere. Expect to be addressed by name within a short time of embarking. A service charge of $12 per person, per day is automatically added onto shipboard accounts. An automatic 15% gratuity is automatically added to all bar tabs.

Contact Windstar Cruises (☎ *206/281–3535 or 800/258–7245* ⊕ *www. windstarcruises.com*).

Ports of Embarkation

WORD OF MOUTH

"[The Fort Lauderdale airport] is only 45 minutes from the Port [of Miami], and you can grab a shared shuttle outside FLL baggage claim. . . . (Then to return to FLL, we just booked a private ride and the driver was waiting when we left the ship.)"

—cruisin_tigger

Miami is the world's cruise capital, and more cruise ships are based here year-round than anywhere else. Caribbean cruises depart for their itineraries from several ports on either of Florida's coasts, as well as from cities on the Gulf Coast and East Coast of the United States.

Generally, if your cruise is on an Eastern Caribbean itinerary, you'll likely depart from Miami, Fort Lauderdale, Jacksonville, or Port Canaveral; short three- and four-day cruises to the Bahamas also depart from these ports. Most cruises on Western Caribbean itineraries depart from Tampa, Mobile, New Orleans, Galveston, or Houston, though some depart from Miami as well. Cruises from farther up the East Coast of the United States, including such ports as Baltimore, Maryland; Charleston, South Carolina; and even New York City, usually go to the Bahamas or sometimes Key West and often include a private-island stop or a stop elsewhere in Florida. Cruises to the Southern Caribbean might depart from Miami if they are 10 days or longer, but more likely they will depart from San Juan, Puerto Rico, or some other port deeper in the Caribbean.

Regardless of which port you depart from, air connections may prevent you from leaving home on the morning of your cruise or going home the day you return to port. Or you may wish to arrive early simply to give yourself a bit more peace of mind, or you may just want to spend more time in one of these interesting port cities. Many people choose to depart from New Orleans or Mobile just to have an excuse to spend a couple of days in the city before or after their cruise.

PORT ESSENTIALS

CAR RENTAL

Major Agencies Alamo (☎ 800/462–5266 ⊕ www.alamo.com). **Avis** (☎ 800/230–4898 ⊕ www.avis.com). **Budget** (☎ 800/527–0700 ⊕ www. budget.com). **Hertz** (☎ 800/654–3131 ⊕ www.hertz.com). **National Car Rental** (☎ 800/227–7368 ⊕ www.nationalcar.com).

SURCHARGES

To avoid a hefty refueling fee, fill the tank just before you turn in the car, but be aware that gas stations near the rental outlet may charge more than those farther away. If you plan to do a lot of driving, it can be a better deal to buy a full tank of gas when you rent so you can return the car with an empty tank. However, it's never a good deal to pay the huge surcharge for not returning a tank full unless you simply have no other choice. Other surcharges may apply if you are under 25 or over 75, if you want to add an additional driver to the contract, or if you want to drive over state borders or out of a specific radius from your point of rental. You'll also pay extra for child seats, which are compulsory for children under 5, and for a GPS navigation system or electronic toll pass. You can sometimes avoid the charge for insurance if you have your own, either from your own policy or from a credit card, but know what you are covered for, and read the fine print before making this decision.

DINING

Unless otherwise noted, all prices are given in U.S. dollars. The following price categories are used in this book.

WHAT IT COSTS IN U.S. DOLLARS					
	¢	$	$$	$$$	$$$$
AT DINNER	under $8	$8–$12	$13–$20	$21–$30	over $30

Prices are per person for a main course at dinner and do not include any service charges or taxes.

LODGING

Whether you are driving or flying into your port of embarkation, it is often more convenient to arrive the day before or to stay for a day after your cruise. For this reason we offer lodging suggestions for each port of embarkation.

The lodgings we list are convenient to the cruise port and the cream of the crop in each price category. We always list the facilities that are available, but we don't specify whether they cost extra; when pricing accommodations, always ask what's included. Properties are assigned price categories based on the range between their least expensive standard double room in high season (excluding holidays) and the most expensive. But if you find everything sold out or wish to find a more predictable place to stay, there are chain hotels at almost all ports of embarkation.

Assume that hotels operate on the **European Plan** (EP, with no meals) unless we specify that they use either the **Continental Plan** (CP, with a Continental breakfast), **Breakfast Plan** (BP, with a full breakfast), or the **Modified American Plan** (MAP, with breakfast and dinner). The following price categories are used in this book.

WHAT IT COSTS IN U.S. DOLLARS					
	¢	$	$$	$$$	$$$$
FOR 2 PEOPLE	under $70	$70–$120	$120–$175	$175–$250	over $250

Prices are for a double room in high season, excluding service and taxes.

BALTIMORE, MARYLAND

Sam Sessa

Baltimore's charm lies in its neighborhoods. Although stellar downtown attractions such as the National Aquarium and Camden Yards draw torrents of tourists each year, much of the city's character can be found outside the Inner Harbor. Scores of Baltimore's trademark narrow red-brick row houses with white marble steps line the city's east and west

Security

All cruise lines have instituted stricter security procedures in recent years; however, you may not even be aware of all the changes.

Some of the changes will be more obvious to you. For example, only visitors who have been authorized well in advance are allowed onboard. Proper identification (a government-issued photo ID) is required in all instances to board the ship, whether you are a visitor or passenger. Ship security personnel are stationed at all points of entry to the ship. All hand-carried items are searched by hand in every port (this applies to both crew and passengers).

Some of the changes are more behind the scenes. All luggage is scanned, whether you carry it aboard with you or not, and all packages and provisions brought onboard are scanned.

In addition, every ship has added professionally trained security officers and taken many other measures to ensure the safety of all passengers. Many cruise-line security personnel are former navy or marine officers with extensive maritime experience. Some cruise lines recruit shipboard security personnel from the ranks of former British Gurkha regiments. From Nepal, the Gurkhas are renowned as soldiers of the highest caliber.

sides. Some neighborhood streets are still made of cobblestone, and grand churches and museums and towering, glassy high-rises fill out the growing skyline. Now the city's blue-collar past mixes with present urban-professional revitalization. Industrial waterfront properties are giving way to high-end condos, and corner bars formerly dominated by National Bohemian beer—once made in the city—are adding micro-brews to their beverage lists. And with more and more retail stores replacing old, run-down buildings and parking lots, Baltimore is one of the nation's up-and-coming cities.

ESSENTIALS

HOURS During the summer tourist season, most of Baltimore's stores and attractions usually open around 9 AM and close around 9 PM.

INTERNET **Enoch Pratt Free Library** (⊠ *400 Cathedral St., Mount Vernon* ☎ *410/396–5500* ⊕ *www.pratt.lib.md.us* ⊗ *Oct.–May, Mon.–Wed. 10–7, Thurs.–Sat. 10–5, Sun. 1–5; June–Sept., closed Sun.*)

VISITOR INFORMATION **Baltimore Visitor Center** (⊠ *401 Light St., Inner Harbor* ☎ *877/225–8466* ⊕ *www.baltimore.org*).

THE CRUISE PORT

Well marked and easily accessible by major highways, the South Locust Point Cruise Terminal is about a mile from center city. Several cruise lines offer seasonal cruises from the port, and *Carnival Pride* is based here permanently. Ships dock near the main cruise building, which itself is little more than a hub for arrivals and departures. There are few facilities for passengers in the immediate port area, which is out of walking distance to Baltimore's attractions.

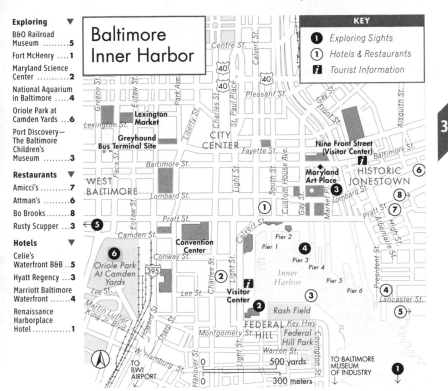

During cruise season, taxis are the best transportation to the downtown area. They cost about $5 one-way and frequent the port. Taxis to Baltimore–Washington International Airport charge a flat rate of $35. Rental cars are generally not necessary; if you fly into Baltimore, you can see the majority of Baltimore by taxi. Guided tours of the city range from $20 to $60.

Information Port of Baltimore (✉ 2001 E. McComas St. ☎ 410/962–8701 ⊕ www.cruisemaryland.com).

AIRPORTS

Baltimore-Washington International Airport (BWI; ✉ 10 mi south of Baltimore off Rte. 295/Baltimore–Washington Pkwy. ☎ 410/859–7111 for information and paging ⊕ www.bwiairport.com).

Airport Transfers Airport Taxis (☎ 410/859–1100 ⊕ www.bwiairporttaxi.com). **Arrow Taxicab** (☎ 410/358–9696). **BWI Airport rail station** (☎ 410/672–6167 ⊕ www.mtamaryland.com). **BWI SuperShuttle** (☎ 800/258–3826 ⊕ www. supershuttle.com). **Carey Limousines** (☎ 888/880–0999 ⊕ www.carey.com). **Maryland Area Rail Commuter** (MARC; ☎ 800/325–7245 or 410/539–5000 ⊕ www.mtamaryland.com). **Penn Station** (✉ Charles St. at Mt. Royal Ave., Mount Vernon ☎ 800/523–8720). **Private Car/RMA Worldwide Chauffeured Transportation** (☎ 410/519–0000 or 800/878–7743 ⊕ www.rmalimo.com).

PARKING

There's a secure parking lot next to the cruise terminal, where parking costs $15 per day. Drop off your luggage before parking.

EXPLORING BALTIMORE

Numbers in the margin correspond to points of interest on the Baltimore map.

⑤ B&O Railroad Museum. The famous Baltimore & Ohio Railroad was founded on the site that now houses this museum, which contains more than 120 full-size locomotives and a great collection of railroad memorabilia, from dining-car china and artwork to lanterns and signals. The 1884 roundhouse (240 feet in diameter and 120 feet high) adjoins one of the nation's first railroad stations. Train rides are available every day but Monday. The Iron Horse Café serves food and drinks. ⊠ *901 W. Pratt St., West Baltimore* ☎ *410/752–2490* ⊕ *www.borail.org* ⊠ *$14* ☉ *Mon.–Sat. 10–4, Sun. 11–4.*

① Fort McHenry. This star-shaped brick fort is forever associated with Francis Scott Key and "The Star-Spangled Banner," which Key penned while watching the British bombardment of Baltimore during the War of 1812. A visit to the fort includes a 15-minute history film, guided tour, and frequent living-history displays on summer weekends. To see how the formidable fortifications might have appeared to the bombarding British, catch a water taxi from the Inner Harbor to the fort instead of driving. ⊠ *E. Fort Ave., from Light St., take Key Hwy. for 1½ mi and follow signs, Locust Point* ☎ *410/962–4290* ⊕ *www.nps.gov/fomc* ⊠ *$7* ☉ *Memorial Day–Labor Day, daily 8–8; Labor Day–Memorial Day, daily 8–5.*

FodorsChoice ★

② Maryland Science Center. Originally known as the Maryland Academy of Sciences, this 200-year-old scientific institution is one of the oldest in the United States. Now housed in a contemporary building, the three floors of exhibits on the Chesapeake Bay, Earth science, physics, the body, dinosaurs, and outer space are an invitation to engage, experiment, and explore. The center has a planetarium, a simulated dinosaur dig, an IMAX movie theater with a screen five stories high, and a playroom especially designed for young children. ⊠ *601 Light St., Inner Harbor* ☎ *410/685–5225* ⊕ *www.mdsci.org* ⊠ *$14.95, IMAX $8* ☉ *Memorial Day–Labor Day, Thurs.–Sat. 10–8, Sun.–Wed. 10–6; Labor Day–Memorial Day, Tues.–Fri. 10–5, Sat. 10–6, Sun. 11–5.*

④ National Aquarium. The most-visited attraction in Maryland has more than 10,000 fish, sharks, dolphins, and amphibians dwelling in 2 million gallons of water. Animal Planet Australia: Wild Extremes, a new exhibit built to mimic a river running through a gorge (with all its native wildlife), opened in 2006. The aquarium also features reptiles, birds, plants, and mammals in its rain-forest environment inside a glass pyramid 64 feet high. The aquarium's famed shark tank and Atlantic coral-reef exhibits are spectacular; you can wind through an enormous glass enclosure on a spiral ramp while hammerheads and brightly hued tropical fish glide by. ■TIP➔ Arrive early to ensure admission, which is by timed intervals; by noon the wait is often two or three hours. ⊠ *Pier 3, Inner*

FodorsChoice ★

Harbor ☎ *410/576–3800* ⊕ *www.
aqua.org* ✉ *$29.95* ⊙ *Nov.–Feb.,
Mon.–Thurs. 10–4, Fri. 10–8,
Sat.–Sun. 10–5; Mar.–June, Sept.,
Sat.–Thurs. 9–5, Fri. 9–8; Oct.,
Mon.–Thurs. 9–5, Fri. 9–8, Sat.–
Sun. 9–5; July–Aug., Mon.–Thurs.
9–5; Fri.–Sat. 9–8, Sun. 9–6; visitors
may tour for up to 1½ hrs after closing. Timed tickets may be required
on weekends and holidays; purchase
these early in the day or in advance
on the aquarium's Web site.*

❻ **Oriole Park at Camden Yards.** Home
☾ of the Baltimore Orioles, Camden
★ Yards and the nearby area bustle

> **BALTIMORE BEST BETS**
>
> ■ **Camden Yards.** Tour the sta-
> dium or, better yet, see an Orioles
> game if the team is playing while
> you're in town.
>
> ■ **Fort McHenry.** This historic fort
> is where Francis Scott Key saw the
> Stars and Stripes flying during the
> War of 1812.
>
> ■ **The National Aquarium.** This
> excellent museum is a great desti-
> nation for families or adults.

3

on game days. Since it opened in 1992, this nostalgically designed
baseball stadium has inspired other cities to emulate its neotraditional
architecture and amenities. The Eutaw Street promenade, between
the warehouse and the field, has a view of the stadium; look for the
brass baseballs embedded in the sidewalk that mark where home runs
have cleared the fence, or visit the Orioles Hall of Fame display and
the monuments to retired Orioles. Daily 90-minute tours take you
to nearly every section of the ballpark, from the massive JumboTron
scoreboard to the dugout to the state-of-the-art beer-delivery system.
⊠ *333 W. Camden St., Downtown* ☎ *410/685–9800 general information, 410/547–6234 tour times, 888/848–2473 tickets to Orioles home
games* ⊕ *www.theorioles.com* ✉ *Eutaw St. Promenade free; tour $9*
⊙ *Eutaw St. promenade daily 10–3, otherwise during games and tours;
tours Mar.–Sept., Mon.–Sat. at 11, noon, 1, and 2; Oct., weekdays at
11:30 and 1:30, Sat. at 11, noon, 1, and 2, Sun. at 12:30, 1, 2, and 3;
Nov., Mon.–Sat. at 11:30 and 1:30, Sun. at 12:30 and 2:30.*

❸ **Port Discovery—The Baltimore Children's Museum.** At this interactive
☾ museum adults are encouraged to play every bit as much as children.
A favorite attraction is the three-story KidWorks, a futuristic jungle
gym on which the adventurous can climb, crawl, slide, and swing their
way through stairs, slides, ropes, zip-lines, and tunnels, and even cross a
narrow footbridge three stories up. Changing interactive exhibits allow
for even more play. ⊠ *35 Market Pl., Inner Harbor* ☎ *410/727–8120*
⊕ *www.portdiscovery.com* ✉ *$12.95* ⊙ *Memorial Day–Labor Day,
Mon.–Sat. 10–5, Sun. noon–5; Sept., Fri. 9:30–4:30, Sat. 10–5, Sun.
noon–5; Oct.–Memorial Day, Tues.–Fri. 9:30–4:30, Sat. 10–5, Sun.
noon–5.*

SHOPPING

Baltimore isn't the biggest shopping town, but it does have some malls
and good stores here and there. Hampden (the "p" is silent), a neighborhood west of Johns Hopkins University, has funky shops selling
everything from housewares to housedresses along its main drag, 36th

Street (better known as "The Avenue"). Some interesting shops can be found along Charles Street in Mount Vernon and along Thames Street in Fells Point. Federal Hill has a few fun shops, particularly for furnishings and vintage items. At the Inner Harbor, the Pratt Street and Light Street pavilions of **Harborplace and the Gallery** (☎ *410/332–4191*) contain almost 200 specialty shops that sell everything from business attire to children's toys. The Gallery has J. Crew, Banana Republic, and the Gap, among others.

NIGHTLIFE

Both Fells Point, just east of the Inner Harbor, and Federal Hill, due south, have hosts of bars, restaurants, and clubs that draw a rowdy, largely collegiate, crowd. If you're seeking quieter surroundings, head for the upscale comforts of downtown or Mount Vernon clubs and watering holes.

BARS AND LOUNGES

Upstairs at **The Brewer's Art** (✉ *1106 N. Charles St., Mount Vernon* ☎ *410/547–6925* ⊕ *www.belgianbeer.com*) is an elegant bar and lounge with armchairs, marble pillars, and chandeliers, plus a dining room with terrific food; downstairs, the dark basement bar specializes in Belgian-style beers. With its stylized art deco surroundings, the funky **Club Charles** (✉ *1724 N. Charles St., StationNorth Arts District* ☎ *410/727–8815*) is a favorite hangout for an artsy crowd, moviegoers coming from the Charles Theater across the street, and, reputation has it, John Waters. **Club Hippo** (✉ *1 W. Eager St., Mount Vernon* ☎ *410/547–0069* ⊕ *www.clubhippo.com*) is Baltimore's longest-reigning gay bar. A dance club, martini bar, and pub have all helped make **Grand Central** (✉ *1003 N. Charles St., Mount Vernon* ☎ *410/752–7133*) into a hip gay hot spot. Beer lovers should visit **Max's Taphouse** (✉ *737 S. Broadway, Fells Point* ☎ *410/675–6297* ⊕ *www.maxs.com*), which has more than 70 brews on tap and about 300 more in bottles. **Red Maple** (✉ *930 N. Charles St., Mount Vernon* ☎ *410/547–0149* ⊕ *www.930redmaple. com*) is one of the city's most stylish spots for drinks and tapas. At the top of the Belvedere Hotel, the **13th Floor** (✉ *1 E. Chase St., Mount Vernon* ☎ *410/347–0888*) offers a great view, a long martini list, and live dance music.

COMEDY CLUBS

The Comedy Factory (✉ *36 Light St., Inner Harbor* ☎ *410/752–4189*) is the best local spot to see live standup.

WHERE TO EAT

Baltimore loves crabs. Soft- or hardshell crabs, crab cakes, crab dip—the city's passion for clawed crustaceans seems to have no end. Flag down a Baltimore native and ask them where the best crab joint is, and you'll get a list of options. In addition to crabs and seafood, Baltimore's restaurant landscape also includes Italian, Afghan, Greek, American, tapas, and other cuisines. The city's dining choices may not compare with those of

New York, or even Washington, but it does have some real standouts. Note that places generally stop serving by 10 PM, if not earlier.

For price categories, see ⇨ Dining at the beginning of this chapter.

$-$$ ✕ **Amicci's.** At this self-proclaimed "very casual eatery," you don't have
ITALIAN   to spend a fortune to get a satisfying taste of Little Italy. Blue jean–clad
☺   diners and walls hung with movie posters make for a fun atmosphere. Service is friendly and usually speedy, and the food comes in large portions. Try the chicken Lorenzo: breaded chicken breast covered in a Marsala wine sauce, red peppers, prosciutto, and provolone. ⊠ *231 S. High St., Little Italy* ☎ *410/528–1096* ⊕ *www.amiccis.com* ▭ *AE, D, DC, MC, V.*

¢–$ ✕ **Attman's.** Open since 1915, this authentic New York–style deli near
ISRAELI   the Jewish Museum is the king of Baltimore's "Corned Beef Row." Of
★   the three delis on the row, Attman's has the longest waits and steepest prices, but delivers the highest-quality dishes. Don't be put off by the long lines—they move fairly quickly, and the outstanding corned-beef sandwiches are worth the wait, as are the pastrami, homemade chopped liver, and other oversize creations. Attman's closes at 6:30 PM daily. ⊠ *1019 Lombard St., Historic Jonestown* ☎ *410/563–2666* ⊕ *www. attmansdeli.com* ▭ *AE, DC, MC, V* ☉ *Closed Sat.*

$$-$$$ ✕ **Bo Brooks.** Picking steamed crabs on Bo Brooks's waterfront deck
SEAFOOD   with a pitcher of cold beer at hand as sailboats and tugs ply the harbor
★   is a quintessential Baltimore pleasure. Locals spend hot summer days cracking into warm, spicy crabs while a cool breeze blows in from the harbor. Brooks serves its famous crustaceans year-round, along with a menu of Chesapeake seafood classics. Locals know to stick to the Maryland crab soup, crab dip, jumbo lump crab cakes, and fried oysters. ⊠ *2701 Boston St., Canton* ☎ *410/558–0202* ⊕ *www.bobrooks. com* ▭ *AE, D, MC, V.*

$$-$$$ ✕ **Rusty Scupper.** A tourist favorite, the Rusty Scupper undoubtedly has
SEAFOOD   the best view along the waterfront; sunset here is magical, with the sun sinking slowly into the harbor as lights twinkle on the city's skyscrapers. The interior is decorated with light wood and windows from floor to ceiling; the house specialty is seafood, particularly the jumbo lump crab cake, but the menu also includes beef, chicken, and pasta. Reservations are essential on Friday and Saturday, and service can be spotty. ⊠ *402 Key Hwy., Inner Harbor* ☎ *410/727–3678* ▭ *AE, D, DC, MC, V.*

WHERE TO STAY

When booking a hotel or bed-and-breakfast in Baltimore, focus on the Inner Harbor, where you're likely to spend a good deal of time. The downside to staying in hotels near downtown is the noise level, which can rise early in the morning and stay up late into the night—especially if there's a baseball or football game. For quieter options, head to neighborhoods like Fells Point and Canton.

$$-$$$ 🏨 **Celie's Waterfront Bed & Breakfast.** Proprietors Nancy and Kevin Kupec
B&B   oversee every detail of this small inn in the heart of Fells Point. Guest rooms, all with private bath, are furnished in Early American style; two suites accommodate large groups. Upscale amenities include down

comforters, terry robes, fireplaces, and whirlpool baths. Continental breakfast is served in the cozy dining room. The rooftop deck provides a wonderful view of Baltimore's skyline and harbor. **Pros:** intimate accommodations; situated next to an entertainment district. **Cons:** prices high for what you get; it can get noisy late at night. ✉ *1714 Thames St., Fells Point* ☎ *410/522–2323 or 800/432–0184* ⊕ *www.celieswaterfront.com* ↩ *7 rooms, 2 suites* ♿ *In-room: Wi-Fi* ▭ *AE, D, MC, V* ⧆ *CP.*

$$$$ ⊞ **Hyatt Regency.** This stretch of Light Street is practically a highway,
HOTEL   but the unenclosed skyways allow ready pedestrian access to both Inner Harbor attractions and the convention center. Rooms have rich gold and black-purple prints and cherrywood furniture; most rooms have views of the harbor or the city. The lobby has glass elevators and the chain's trademark atrium. The 12th floor is the Club level, with evening hors d'oeuvres and a private concierge available. Atop the hotel, the Pisces restaurant and lounge provides stunning city views, especially at night. **Pros:** the Inner Harbor is just a skywalk away. **Cons:** service can be slow and unhelpful. ✉ *300 Light St., Inner Harbor* ☎ *410/528–1234 or 800/233–1234* ⊕ *baltimore.hyatt.com* ↩ *488 rooms, 26 suites* ♿ *In-room: Wi-Fi. In-hotel: restaurant, bars, tennis courts, pool, gym, parking (paid), no-smoking rooms* ▭ *AE, D, DC, MC, V.*

$$$–$$$$ ⊞ **Marriott Baltimore Waterfront.** The city's tallest hotel and the only one
HOTEL   directly on the Inner Harbor itself, this upscale 31-story Marriott has a neoclassical interior that uses multihue marbles, rich jewel-tone walls, and photographs of Baltimore architectural landmarks. Although it's at the eastern end of the Inner Harbor, all downtown attractions are within walking distance; there's also a water-taxi stop right by the front door. Most rooms offer unobstructed views of the city and harbor; ask for one that faces west toward downtown for a splendid panorama of the waterfront and skyscrapers. **Pros:** nice amenities; great location and view. **Cons:** pricey, compared to nearby hotels. ✉ *700 Aliceanna St., Inner Harbor East* ☎ *410/385–3000* ⊕ *www.marriotthotels.com/ bwiwf* ↩ *751 rooms* ♿ *In-room: safe, refrigerator, Internet. In-hotel: restaurant, bar, pool, gym, parking (paid), no-smoking rooms* ▭ *AE, D, DC, MC, V.*

$$$–$$$$ ⊞ **Renaissance Harborplace Hotel.** The most conveniently located of the
HOTEL   Inner Harbor hotels—across the street from the shopping pavilions— the Renaissance Harborplace meets the needs of tourists, business travelers, and conventioneers. Guest rooms are light and cheerful, with amenities that include coffeemakers, terry robes, hair dryers, and ironing boards. Some rooms have a view of the harbor, the downtown landscape, or the indoor courtyard. The hotel adjoins the Gallery, a four-story shopping mall. **Pros:** snappy service. **Cons:** some rooms can be a bit threadbare. ✉ *202 E. Pratt St., Inner Harbor* ☎ *410/547–1200 or 800/468–3571* ⊕ *www.renaissancehotels.com/bwish* ↩ *562 rooms, 60 suites* ♿ *In-room: Wi-Fi, refrigerator. In-hotel: restaurant, bar, pool, gym, parking (paid), no-smoking rooms* ▭ *AE, D, DC, MC, V.*

CHARLESTON, SOUTH CAROLINA

Eileen Robinson Smith

Charleston looks like a movie set, an 18th-century etching brought to life. The spires and steeples of more than 180 churches punctuate her low skyline, and tourists ride in horse-drawn carriages that pass grandiose, centuries-old mansions and gardens brimming with heirloom plants. Preserved through the poverty following the Civil War and natural disasters like fires, earthquakes, and hurricanes, much of Charleston's earliest public and private architecture still stands. And thanks to a rigorous preservation movement and strict Board of Architectural Review, the city's new structures blend with the old ones. If you're boarding your cruise ship here, it's worth coming a few days early to explore the historic downtown and to eat in one of the many superb restaurants. In late spring, plan in advance for the Spoleto U.S.A. Festival. For more than 30 memorable years, arts patrons have gathered to enjoy the international dance, opera, theater, and other performances at venues citywide. Piccolo Spoleto showcases local and regional concerts, dance, theater, and comedy shows.

ESSENTIALS

HOURS Most shops are open from 9 or 10 AM to at least 6 PM, but some are open later. A new city ordinance requires bars to close by 2 AM.

INTERNET While almost all hotels (and even B&Bs) offer some kind of Internet service, Internet cafés are rare in the Charleston historic district; however, many coffee shops, including all the local Starbucks, offer Wi-Fi.

VISITOR INFORMATION **Charleston Visitor Center** (⌖ *375 Meeting St., Upper King* ☞ *423 King St., 29403* ☎ *843/853–8000 or 800/868–8118* ⊕ *www.charlestoncvb.com*).

THE CRUISE PORT

Cruise ships sailing from Charleston depart from the Union Pier Terminal, which is in Charleston's historic district. If you are driving, however, and need to leave your car for the duration of your cruise, take the East Bay Street exit off the new, majestic Arthur Ravenel, Jr. Bridge on I–17 and follow the CRUISE SHIP signs. On ship embarkation days police officers will direct you to the ship terminal from the intersection of East Bay and Chapel streets. Cruise parking is located adjacent to Union Pier.

INFORMATION

Port of Charleston (⌖ *196 Concord St., Market area, at foot of Market St.* ☎ *843/958–8298 for cruise information* ⊕ *www.port-of-charleston.com*).

AIRPORT TRANSFERS

Several cab companies service the airport, including the new Charleston Black Cab Company, which operates a fleet of genuine London cabs with uniformed drivers and costs about $10 more than calling a regular cab—about $50 to downtown. Airport Ground Transportation arranges shuttles, which cost $15 per person to the downtown area, $40 to $45 for a return trip to the airport. CARTA's bus No. 11, a public bus, now goes to the airport for a mere $1.25; it leaves downtown from

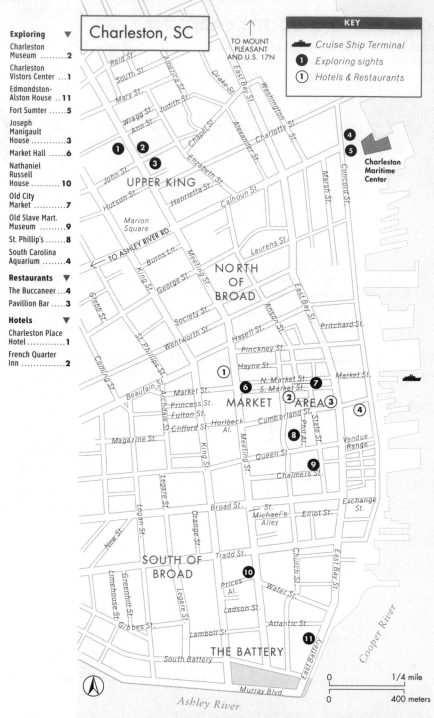

Charleston, SC

TO MOUNT PLEASANT AND U.S. 17N

KEY

🚢 Cruise Ship Terminal

❶ Exploring sights

① Hotels & Restaurants

Charleston Maritime Center

UPPER KING

Marion Square

NORTH OF BROAD

MARKET AREA

SOUTH OF BROAD

THE BATTERY

Cooper River

Ashley River

0   1/4 mile

0   400 meters

the Meeting/Mary St. parking garage every 50 minutes, from 5:45 AM until 11:09 PM.

PARKING

Parking costs $15 per day ($105 per week) for regular vehicles, $35 per day ($245 per week) for RVs or other vehicles more than 20 feet in length. You pay in advance by cash, check or credit card. A free shuttle bus takes you to the cruise-passenger terminal. Be sure to drop your large luggage off at Union Pier before you park your car; only carry-on size luggage is allowed on the shuttle bus, so if you have any bags larger than 22 inches by 14 inches, they will have to be checked before you park. Also, you'll need your cruise tickets to board the shuttle bus

EXPLORING CHARLESTON

Numbers in the margin correspond to points of interest on the Charleston map.

The heart of the city is on a peninsula, sometimes just called "downtown" by the nearly 60,000 residents who populate the area. Walking Charleston's peninsula is the best way to get to know the city. The main downtown historic district is roughly bounded by Lockwood Boulevard to the west, Calhoun Street to the north, the Cooper River to the east, and the Battery to the south. Nearly 2,000 historic homes and buildings occupy this fairly compact area divided into South of Broad (Street) and North of Broad. King Street, the main shopping street in town, cuts through Broad Street, and the most trafficked tourist area ends a few blocks south of the Crosstown, where U.S. 17 cuts across Upper King. If you don't wish to walk, there are bikes, pedicabs, and trolleys. Street parking is irksome, as meter readers are among the city's most efficient public servants. Parking garages, both privately and publicly owned, charge around $1.50 an hour.

❷ Charleston Museum. Founded in 1773, the country's oldest museum is housed in a contemporary complex. The museum's decorative-arts holdings and its permanent Civil War exhibit are extraordinary. There are more than 500,000 items in the collection, including silver, toys, and snuffboxes. There are also fascinating exhibits on natural history, archaeology, and ornithology. Temporary exhibitions are even more scintillating, like the recent "Charleston During the Civil War." ■TIP→ **Combination tickets that give you admission to the Joseph Manigault House and the Heyward-Washington House are a bargain at $22. Visit: www.charlestonmuseummile.com for an incredible combo ticket.** ✉ *360 Meeting St., Upper King* ☎ *843/722–2996* ⊕ *www.charlestonmuseum.org* ✇ *$10* ⊙ *Mon.–Sat. 9–5, Sun. 1–5.*

❶ Charleston Visitors Center. The center's 20-minute film *Forever Charleston* is a fine introduction to the city. **The first 30 minutes are free at the parking lot, making it a real bargain.** ✉ *375 Meeting St., Upper King* ☎ *843/853–8000 or 800/868–8118* ⊕ *www.charlestoncvb.com* ✇ *Free* ⊙ *Apr.–Oct., daily 8:30–5:30; Nov.–Mar. 31, daily 8:30–5.*

⓫ Edmondston-Alston House. First built in 1825 in late-Federal style, the Edmondston-Alston House was transformed into the imposing Greek

Revival structure you see today during the 1840s. Tours of the home—furnished with antiques, portraits, silver, and fine china—are informative. ✉ *21 E. Battery, South of Broad* ☎ *843/722–7171* ⊕ *www.middletonplace.org* ✉ *$10; $41 with combination ticket for Middleton Place* ⊙ *Tues.–Sat. 10–4:30, Sun. 1:30–4:30, Mon. 1–4:30*

❺ Fort Sumter National Monument. The first shot of the Civil War was fired ☾ at Fort Sumter on April 12, 1861. After a 34-hour battle, Union forces ★ surrendered the fort, which became a symbol of Southern resistance. The Confederacy held it, despite almost continual bombardment, from August of 1863 to February of 1865. When it was finally evacuated, the fort was a heap of rubble. Today the National Park Service oversees it. The **Fort Sumter Liberty Square Visitor Center** (✉ *340 Concord St., Upper King* ☎ *843/577–0242* ✉ *Free* ⊙ *Daily 8:30–5*), next to the South Carolina Aquarium, contains exhibits on the Civil War. This is a departure point for ferries headed to the island where you can find Fort Sumter itself. Rangers conduct guided tours of the restored **Fort Sumter.** To reach the fort, you have to take a ferry; boats depart from Liberty Square Visitor Center and from Patriot's Point in Mount Pleasant. There are six crossings daily between mid-March and mid-August. The schedule is abbreviated the rest of the year, so call ahead for details. ✉ *Charleston Harbor* ☎ *843/577–0242* ⊕ *www.nps.gov/fosu* ✉ *Fort free; ferry $15, kids 9 and under $5* ⊙ *Daily 8:30–5.*

❸ Joseph Manigault House. An outstanding example of Federal architecture, this home was designed by Charleston architect Gabriel Manigault in 1803. It's noted for its carved-wood mantels, elaborate plasterwork, and garden "folly." The pieces of rare tricolor Wedgwood are noteworthy. ✉ *350 Meeting St., Upper King* ☎ *843/722–2996* ⊕ *www.charlestonmuseum.org* ✉ *$10* ⊙ *Mon.–Sat. 10–5, Sun. 1–5.*

❻ Market Hall. Built in 1841, this imposing landmark was modeled after the Temple of Nike in Athens. The hall contains the **Confederate Museum,** in which the United Daughters of the Confederacy display flags, uniforms, swords, and other Civil War memorabilia. ✉ *188 Meeting St., Market area* ☎ *843/723–1541* ✉ *$5* ⊙ *Tues.–Sat. 11–3:30.*

❿ Nathaniel Russell House. One of the nation's finest examples of Adam-**Fodor's Choice** style architecture, the Nathaniel Russell House was built in 1808. The ★ interior is distinguished by its ornate detailing, its lavish period furnishings, and the "free-flying" staircase that spirals three stories with no visible support. The garden is well worth a stroll. ✉ *51 Meeting St., South of Broad* ☎ *843/724–8481* ⊕ *www.historiccharleston.org* ✉ *$10; $16 with admission to Aiken-Rhett House* ⊙ *Mon.–Sat. 10–5, Sun. 2–5.*

❼ Old City Market. This area is often called the Slave Market, because it's ☾ where house slaves once shopped for produce and fish. Today stalls are lined with restaurants and shops selling children's toys, leather goods, and regional souvenirs. Local "basket ladies" weave and sell sweetgrass, pine-straw, and palmetto-leaf baskets—a craft passed down through generations from their West African ancestors; unfortunately, these baskets are now pretty expensive; the majority of stands have budget prices and flea-market merchandise. ✉ *N. and S. Market Sts.,* *between Meeting and E. Bay Sts., Market area* ☎ *No phone* ◷ *Daily 9–dusk.*

❾ Old Slave Mart Museum. This is likely the only building still in existence that was used for slave auctioning, which ended in 1863. It is part of a complex called Ryan's Mart, which contains the slave jail, the kitchen, and the morgue. The history of Charleston's role in the slave trade is recounted here. As unpleasant as slavery must have been, its history is vital, but not proud. Charleston once served as the center of commercial activity for the South's plantation economy, and slaves were the primary source of labor both within the city and on the surrounding plantations. The museum is on one of the few remaining cobblestone streets in town. Closed for years, it finally reopened in 2008 with updated exhibits. ✉ *6 Chalmers St., Market area* ☎ *843/958–6467* ⊕ *www.charlestoncity.info* ☐ *$10* ◷ *Mon.–Sat. 9–5.*

Fodor's Choice
★

CHARLESTON BEST BETS

■ **Viewing Art.** The city is home to some 120 galleries, exhibiting art from Charleston, the South, and around the world. The Gibbes Museum of Art and a half-dozen other museums add to the cultural mix.

■ **The Battery.** The views from the point—both natural and man-made—are the loveliest in the city. Look west to see the harbor; to the east you'll find elegant Charleston mansions.

■ **Historic Homes.** Charleston's preserved, centuries-old, stately homes, including the Nathaniel Russell House, are highlights.

3

---

❽ St. Philip's (Episcopal) Church. The namesake of Church Street, this graceful late-Georgian building is the second on its site: the congregation's first building burned down in 1835 and was replaced in 1838. During the Civil War the steeple was a target for shelling; one Sunday a shell exploded in the churchyard. The minister bravely continued his sermon. Afterward, the congregation gathered elsewhere for the duration of the war. Notable Charlestonians like John C. Calhoun are buried in the twin graveyards. ✉ *146 Church St., Market area* ☎ *843/722–7734* ⊕ *www.stphilipschurchsc.org* ◷ *Church weekdays 9–11 and 1–4; cemetery daily 9–4.*

❹ South Carolina Aquarium. The 380,000-gallon Great Ocean Tank has the tallest aquarium window in North America. Exhibits display more than 10,000 creatures, representing more than 500 species. You travel through the five major regions of the Southeast Appalachian Watershed: the Blue Ridge Mountains, the Piedmont, the coastal plain, the coast, and the ocean. Little ones can pet stingrays at one touch tank and horseshoe crabs and conchs at another. Surprising developments are common, including such new offerings as turtle hospital tours or a rare albino alligator in the newly renovated Blackwater Swamp Exhibit. Magellanic penguins may not be indigenous to South Carolina, but watching them dive, swim, and play will tickle you. ✉ *100 Aquarium Wharf, Upper King* ☎ *843/720–1990 or 800/722–6455* ⊕ *www.scaquarium.org* ☐ *$18* ◷ *Mar.–Aug., daily 9–5; Sept.–Feb., daily 9–4.*

SHOPPING

The Market area is a cluster of shops and restaurants centered around the **Old City Market** (✉ *E. Bay and Market Sts., Market area*). Sweetgrass basket weavers work here, and you can buy the resulting wares. **King Street** is the major shopping street in town. Lower King (from Broad to Market streets) is lined with high-end antiques dealers. Middle King (from Market to Calhoun streets) is a mix of national chains, including Saks Fifth Ave. and Banana Republic. Upper King (from Calhoun to Cannon streets) is the up-and-coming area where fashionistas like the alternative shops. If you're lucky, you'll be present for one of the celebratory King Street Walk nights, with include wine service.

NIGHTLIFE

The elegant **Charleston Grill** (✉ *Charleston Place Hotel, 224 King St., Market area* ☎ 843/577–4522) has live jazz nightly, and draws a mature, upscale clientele, hotel guests, and more recently an urbane thirtysomething crowd. Those who want to stare into each others eyes choose either a high cocktail table or a comfy chair in the lounge in front of the musicians. Make a reservation for dinner, or you can have something at the classy, sophisticated bar. **Mercato** (✉ *102 N. Market St., Market area* ☎ 843/722–6393) is a popular restaurant that has become almost as well known for its roster of live entertainment, which can be heard nightly Monday through Saturday from 6 to 10 PM. Although musicians and sounds change, they may include Charleston's well-respected pianist Frank Duvall with his jazz instrumentalists, a gypsy trio, or the legendary Ann Caldwell accompanied by a jazz and blues trio. Come early to get a seat at the long, elegant bar, or reserve one of the 12 downstairs tables for dinner. **Southend Brewery** (✉ *161 E. Bay St., Market area* ☎ 843/853–4677) has a lively bar serving beer brewed on the premises. Try the wood-oven pizzas and the smokehouse barbecue. Thursday is salsa night; on weekends entertainment varies, but may include a bluegrass band, a guitarist, or a jazz trio. You can dance if the music moves you; in fact, it is encouraged. At **Tommy Condon's** (✉ *15 Beaufain St., Market area* ☎ 843/577–3818), a rollicking Irish pub, you can listen to authentic Irish musicfrom Wednesday through Sunday; on Friday and Saturday the music starts later and ends later.

WHERE TO EAT

$–$$

SOUTHERN

✕ **The Buccaneer.** Housed in a historic warehouse, this family-friendly restaurant is pirate-themed, as the name might suggest, but also has a talented chef, who has improved the quality of the food offerings. Soak in some colorful Charleston history and sip a Painkiller, while supping on the bounty of the sea and produce from the local farmer's market. The fresh catch of the day might be a delicate Vidalia onion–encrusted snapper with an emerald sauce of basil oil, snap peas, and tomatoes. Sandwich favorites include the crab cake and a fried green tomato BLT. The classic she-crab soup bows only to the pastry-encrusted wild-mushroom soup. Do order dessert: the bread pudding has a soufflé texture coupled with a bananas Foster sauce. Lunch is served late (until 4 PM), when the dinner menu goes into effect, but has many of the same entrées at lower prices. ⊠ *5 Faber St., Market area* ☎ *843/805–5065* ⊕ *www.thebuccaneerrestaurant.com* ⊟ *AE, D, MC, V.*

$$ ✕ **Pavilion Bar.** Known among the
ECLECTIC high-end, cocktail-hour crowd for its lively nighttime scene, this rooftop terrace restaurant of the classy Market Pavilion hotel also serves a

CHARLESTON CRUISE PACKAGES

For a listing of all hotel package discounts you can book along with your cruise, not to mention discounted tours (including the popular plantation tours), attractions, and shopping and dining coupons, visit ⊕ *www.charlestoncruisepackages.com.*

great upscale lunch. You can view the boating action in the harbor as you groove to the new lounge music and sip something creative like a mango mojito or a pomegranate "Paviliontini." Although the restaurant is generally considered pricey, you can order a delicious gourmet pizza suitable for two for $16. Charleston crab-cake salad is an intelligent choice, as is a Greek salad with a feta vinaigrette. The baked Carolina trifle with its raspberry sorbet and ice cream, candied peanuts, and capped by a toasted meringue is a refreshing dessert. And if you're a hotel guest (a wise suggestion), you can also jump into the pool or take a siesta on one of the chaise longues. ⊠ *225 East Bay St., Market area* ☎ *843/723–0500* ⊕ *www.marketpavilion.com* ⊟ *AE, D, MC, V.*

WHERE TO STAY

While the city's best hotels and B&Bs are in the historic district, most of them do not have free parking. If you stay outside of downtown in a chain hotel, you will give up much in charm and convenience but pay significantly less, not to mention park for free. High-season rates are traditionally in effect from March through May and September through November.

$$$$ ⬜ **Charleston Place.** Even casual passersby enjoy gazing up at the hand-
★ blown Murano glass chandelier in the hotel's open lobby, clicking across the Italian marble floors, and admiring the antiques from Sotheby's. A gallery of upscale shops completes the ground-floor offerings. Rooms are furnished with period reproductions. The impeccable service is what you would expect from an Orient-Express property, particularly on the Club Level, where rooms carry a $100 surcharge that gets you a breakfast spread, afternoon tea, and cocktails and pastries in the evening. A truly deluxe day spa, with an adjacent fitness room, has an inviting indoor salt- and mineral-water pool with a retractable roof and illuminated skylight for night swimming. Cruise passengers get a small discount (10%) as well as 15% off most food and spa bills. **Pros:** two great restaurants; in the historic district on the best shopping street; pet-friendly. **Cons:** no Wi-Fi; rooms aren't as big as one would expect for the price; much of the business is conference groups in shoulder seasons. ⊠ *130 Market St., Market area* ☎ *843/722–4900 or 800/611–5545* ⊕ *www.charlestonplacehotel.com* ↝ *400 rooms, 42 suites* ♿ *In-room:*

3

safe, refrigerator, Internet. In-hotel: 2 restaurants, bars, pool, gym, spa, Internet terminal, parking (paid), some pets allowed, no-smoking rooms ⊟ AE, D, DC, MC, V ⍑⍜⍑ EP.

$$$$ 　⊞ **French Quarter Inn.** The first architectural detail you'll notice in this
★　boutique hotel known for its chic French style is a circular staircase with a wrought-iron bannister embellished with iron leaves. Guests appreciate the lavish breakfasts, the afternoon wine and cheese reception, and evening cookies and milk. The pillow menu is a luxury; you can order whatever kind you desire, including big body pillows. Some rooms have fireplaces, others balconies. Among the best are No. 220, a business suite with a corner office niche overlooking the courtyard, and No. 104, with a spacious L-shaped design. You'll get champagne at check-in, too. **Pros:** in the heart of the market area yet a quiet haven; excellent restaurant (Tristan) on premises; within 5 minutes of the cruise pier. **Cons:** no pool or fitness area; being smack in the busy Market has its downside. ⊠ *166 Church St., Market area* ☎ *843/722–1900 or 866/812–1900* ⊕ *www.fqicharleston.com* ↯ *46 rooms, 4 suites* ⚒ *In-room: safe (some), refrigerator (some), Internet, Wi-Fi. In-hotel: restaurant, bar, parking (paid), no-smoking rooms* ⊟ *AE, MC, V* ⍑⍜⍑ *CP.*

FORT LAUDERDALE, FLORIDA

Lynne Helm　　In the 1960s Fort Lauderdale's beachfront was lined with T-shirt shops interspersed with quickie-food outlets, and downtown consisted of a lone office tower, some dilapidated government buildings, and motley other structures waiting to be razed. Today the beach is home to upscale shops and restaurants, while downtown has exploded with new office and luxury residential development. The entertainment and shopping areas—Las Olas Boulevard, Las Olas Riverfront, and Himmarshee Village—are thriving. And Port Everglades is giving Miami a run for its money in passenger cruising, with a dozen cruise-ship terminals, including the world's largest, hosting more than 20 cruise ships with some 3,000 departures annually. A captivating shoreline with wide ribbons of sand for beachcombing and sunbathing makes Fort Lauderdale and Broward County a major draw for visitors, and often tempts cruise-ship passengers to spend an extra day or two in the sun. Fort Lauderdale's 2-mi (3-km) stretch of unobstructed beachfront has been further enhanced with a sparkling promenade designed more for the pleasure of pedestrians than vehicles.

ESSENTIALS

HOURS　Many museums close on Monday.

INTERNET　If you have your own laptop, Broward County has created a fairly extensive Wi-Fi network with numerous hotspots in downtown Fort Lauderdale, providing free Internet access to anyone using suitably equipped laptops. There's also free Wi-Fi in the airport.

BOAT TOURS　**Water Bus** (☎ 954/467–6677 ⊕ www.watertaxi.com) provides service along the intracoastal waterway in Fort Lauderdale between the 17th Street Causeway and Oakland Park Boulevard, and west into downtown along New River daily from 10 AM until midnight. A day-pass costs $15.

Fort Lauderdale

N. W. 13th St.

Sunrise Blvd.

W. Sunrise Blvd.

Sistrunk Blvd.

N. W. 4th St.

Broward Blvd.

S. W. 2nd St.

Performing
Art Center

S. W. 6th St.

Las Olas Blvd.

S. W. 10th St.

Davie Blvd.

17th St. Causeway

S. W. 24th St.

New River

ATLANTIC OCEAN

Port
Everglades

N. W. 7th Ave.

Andrews Ave.

N. E. 3rd Ave.

N. E. 14th Ave.

S. Ocean Blvd.

S. W. 9th Ave.

S. W. 4th Ave.

A1A

842

95

84

595

Federal Hwy.

0   1 mile
0   1 km

KEY

● Exploring sights

① Hotels & Restaurants

VISITOR
INFORMATION
Greater Fort Lauderdale Convention and Visitors Bureau (☎ 954/765–4466 ⊕ *www.broward.org*).

THE CRUISE PORT

Port Everglades, Fort Lauderdale's cruise port (nowhere near the Everglades, but happily near the beach and less than 2 mi [3 km] from the airport), is among the world's largest, busiest ports. It's also the straightest, deepest port in the southeastern United States, meaning you'll be out to sea in no time flat once your ship sets sail. At a cost of $75 million, Cruise Terminal 18 has been tripled in size to accommodate Royal Caribbean's Oasis-class ships, including the 5,400-passenger Oasis of the Seas and sister Allure of the Seas (which debuted in late 2010). The terminal's mega-size (240,000 square feet) accommodates both arriving and departing passengers and their luggage, simultaneously going through processing procedures. The port is south of downtown Fort Lauderdale, spread out over a huge area extending into Dania Beach, Hollywood, and a patch of unincorporated Broward County. A few words of caution: Schedule plenty of time to navigate the short distance from the airport, your hotel, or wherever else you might be staying, especially if you like to be among the first to embark for your sailing. Increased security (sometimes you'll be asked for a driver's license and/or other identification, and on occasion for boarding documentation upon entering the port, other times not) combined with increased traffic, larger parking facilities, construction projects, roadway improvements, and other obstacles mean the old days of popping over to Port Everglades and running up a gangplank in the blink of an eye are history.

If you are driving, there are two entrances to the port. One is from 17th Street, west of the 17th Street Causeway Bridge, turning south at the traffic light onto Eisenhower Boulevard. Or to get to the main entrance, take either State Road 84, running east–west, to the intersection of Federal Highway and cross into the port, or take I–595 east straight into the Port (I–595 becomes Eller Drive once inside the Port). I–595 runs east–west with connections to the Fort Lauderdale–Hollywood International Airport, U.S. 1 (Federal Highway), I–95, State Road 7 (U.S. 441), Florida's Turnpike, Sawgrass Expressway, and I–75.

FORT LAUDERDALE BEST BETS

The Beach. With more than 20 mi of ocean shoreline, the scene at Greater Fort Lauderdale's best beaches, including those along Lauderdale-by-the-Sea Fort Lauderdale, and Hollywood, is not to be missed.

The Everglades. Take in the wild reaches in or near the Everglades with an airboat ride. Mosquitoes are friendly, so arm yourself accordingly.

The Riverwalk. This is a great place to stroll before and after performances, dinner, libations, and other entertainment.

Contact Port Everglades (✉ 1850 Eller Dr., Fort Lauderdale, FL ☎ 954/523–3404 ⊕ www.porteverglades.org).

AIRPORT TRANSFERS

Fort Lauderdale–Hollywood International Airport is 4 mi (6 km) south of downtown and 2 mi (3 km) (about 5 to 10 minutes) from the docks. If you haven't arranged an airport transfer with your cruise line, you can take a taxi to the cruise-ship terminals. The ride in a metered taxi costs about $15 to $18, depending on your departure terminal. Taxi fares for up to five passengers, regulated by the county, are $4.50 for the first mile and $2.40 for each additional mile, 40¢ per minute for waiting time, plus a $2 surcharge for cabs departing from the airport. Yellow Cab is a major presence, and Go Airport Shuttle provides limousine or shared-ride service to and from Port Everglades to all parts of Broward County; fares to most Fort Lauderdale beach hotels are in the $25 to $30 range.

Contacts Yellow Cab (☎ 954/777–7777). **Go Airport Shuttle** (☎ 954/561–8888 ⊕ goairportshuttle.com).

PARKING

Two covered parking facilities close to the terminals are Northport (expanded to 4,250 spaces) and Midport (for 2,000 vehicles). Use the Northport garage if your cruise leaves from Pier 1, 2, or 4; use Midport if your cruise leaves from Pier 18, 19, 21, 22/24, 25, 26, 27, or 29. The Midport Surface Lot, between piers 18 and 19, has 400 spaces. The cost is $15 per day for either garage or surface lot ($19 for oversized vehicles up to 40 feet). To save a few bucks on your parking tab, two separate companies, Park 'N Fly ($12.95 per day) and Park 'N Go ($12 per day) provide remote parking just outside Port Everglades, at the exit off I–595, with shuttles to all cruise terminals.

Contacts Park 'N Fly (✉ 2200 N.E. 7th Ave., Dania Beach ✛ at the Port Everglades exit off I–595 ☎ 954/779–1776 ⊕ www.pnf.com).**Park 'N Go** (✉ 1101 Eller Dr., Fort Lauderdale ✛ at the Port Everglades exit off I–595 ☎ 954/760–4525 ⊕ www.parkngo.net).

3

EXPLORING FORT LAUDERDALE

Like its southeast Florida neighbors, Fort Lauderdale has been busily revitalizing for several years. In a state where gaudy tourist zones often stand aloof from workaday downtowns, Fort Lauderdale is unusual in that the city exhibits consistency at both ends of the 2-mi (3-km) Las Olas corridor. The sparkling look results from efforts to thoroughly improve both beachfront and downtown. Matching the downtown's innovative arts district, cafés, and boutiques is an equally inventive beach area with its own share of cafés and shops facing an undeveloped shoreline.

Numbers in the margin refer to points of interest on the Fort Lauderdale map.

❻ A stretch from Fort Lauderdale's beaches, but worth the hour-plus
↻ drive, is the **Big Cypress Seminole Reservation** with its two very different attractions. At the **Billie Swamp Safari,** experience the majesty of the Everglades firsthand. Daily tours of wildlife-filled wetlands and hammocks yield sightings of deer, water buffalo, bison, wild hogs, hawks, eagles, alligators, and, if you're really lucky, the rare Florida panther. Animal and reptile shows ($8) are entertaining. Ecotours ($25) are conducted aboard motorized swamp buggies, and airboat rides ($15) are available, too. The on-site Swamp Water Café serves gator nuggets, frogs' legs, catfish, and Indian fry bread with honey. Overnight in a chickee ($35 for 2) or a dorm ($65 for up to 8). ✉ *19 mi north of I–75 Exit 49* ☎ *863/983–6101 or 800/949–6101* ⊕ *www.seminoletribe. com* ⊠ *Free; combined ecotour, reptile or critter show, and airboat ride, $43.20* ☉ *Daily 8–5.*

A couple of miles or so from Billie Swamp Safari is **Ah-Tah-Thi-Ki Museum,** whose name means "a place to learn, a place to remember." This museum documents the traditions and culture of the Seminole Tribe of Florida through artifacts, exhibits, and reenactments of rituals and ceremonies. The 60-acre site includes a living-history Seminole village, nature trails, and a wheelchair-accessible boardwalk through a cypress swamp. ✉ *17 mi north of I–75 Exit 49* ☎ *863/902–1113* ⊕ *www.seminoletribe.com* ⊠ *$9* ☉ *Tues.–Sun. 9–5.*

❷ **Bonnet House.** A 35-acre oasis in the heart of the beach area, this sub-
★ tropical estate on the National Register of Historic Places stands as a tribute to the history of Old South Florida. The charming home was the winter residence of the late Frederic and Evelyn Bartlett, artists

whose personal touches and small surprises are evident throughout. For architecture, artwork, or the natural environment, this place is special. Be on the lookout for playful monkeys swinging from trees, a source of amusement at even some of the most solemn weddings on the grounds. Hours can vary, so call first. ⊠ *900 N. Birch Rd.* ☎ *954/563–5393* ⊕ *www. bonnethouse.org* ⊑ *$20 for house tours, $10 for grounds only* ⊙ *Tues.–Sat. 10–4, Sun. noon–4.*

> **IT'S A GIRL**
>
> Even as far back as ancient times, mariners have traditionally referred to their ships as "she." To a seaman, a ship is as beautiful and comforting as his mother or sweetheart. You could say a good ship holds a special place in his heart.

❶ Butterfly World. As many as 80 butterfly species from South and Central America, the Philippines, Malaysia, Taiwan, and other Asian nations are typically found within the serenity of this 3-acre site inside Tradewinds Park. A screened aviary called North American Butterflies is reserved for native species. The Tropical Rain Forest Aviary is a 30-foot-high construction, with observation decks, waterfalls, ponds, and tunnels filled with thousands of colorful butterflies. Kids bug out at the bug zoo with Asian cockroaches as big as your hand. ⊠ *3600 W. Sample Rd., Coconut Creek* ☎ *954/977–4400* ⊕ *www.butterflyworld.com* ⊑ *$24.95* ⊙ *Mon.–Sat. 9–5, Sun. 11–5.*

❺ Museum of Art Fort Lauderdale. Currently in an Edward Larrabee Barnes–designed building that's considered an architectural masterpiece, this museum was started in a nearby storefront about 50 years ago. MOAFL now coordinates with Nova Southeastern University to host world-class touring exhibits and has an impressive permanent collection of 20th-century European and American art, including works by Picasso, Calder, Dalí, Mapplethorpe, Warhol, and Stella, as well as works by celebrated Ashcan School artist William Glackens. ⊠ *1 E. Las Olas Blvd.* ☎ *954/763–6464* ⊕ *www.moafl.org* ⊑ *$10* ⊙ *Feb.–mid-Dec., Wed.–Mon. 11–5, Thurs. 11–8; mid-Dec.–Jan., Fri.–Wed. 11–5, Thurs. 11–8.*

❸ Museum of Discovery & Science/AutoNation IMAX Theater. Open 365 days barring weather-related events, this museum aims to entertain children—*and* adults—with wonders of science. The courtyard's 52-foot-tall Great Gravity Clock lets arrivals know cool experiences await. Exhibits include Kidscience, encouraging youngsters to explore the world; and Gizmo City, a look at how gadgets work. Florida Ecoscapes has a living coral reef, plus sharks, rays, and eels. The AutoNation IMAX theater, part of the complex, shows films, some in 3-D. A Subway sandwich shop is on the premises. ⊠ *401 S.W. 2nd St.* ☎ *954/467–6637 museum, 954/463–4629 IMAX* ⊕ *www.mods.org* ⊑ *Museum $11, $16 with one IMAX show* ⊙ *Mon.–Sat. 10–5, Sun. noon–6.*

❹ Riverwalk. Lovely views and entertainment prevail on this paved promenade on the New River's north bank. On the first Sunday of every month a free jazz brunch attracts visitors. The walk has been extended 2 mi on both sides of the urban stream, connecting the facilities of the Arts and Science District.

BEACHES

Fort Lauderdale's **beachfront** offers the best of all possible worlds, with easy access not only to a wide band of beige sand but also to restaurants and shops. For 2 mi (3 km) heading north, beginning at the Bahia Mar yacht basin, along Route A1A you'll have clear views, typically across rows of colorful beach umbrellas, of the sea, and of ships passing into and out of nearby Port Everglades. If you're on the beach, gaze back on an exceptionally graceful promenade.

Pedestrians rank above vehicles in Fort Lauderdale. Broad walkways line both sides of the beach road, and traffic has been trimmed to two gently curving northbound lanes, where in-line skaters skim past slow-moving cars. On the beach side, a low masonry wall doubles as an extended bench, separating sand from the promenade. At night the wall is accented with ribbons of fiber-optic color, quite pretty when working, although outages are frequent. The most crowded portion of beach is between Las Olas and Sunrise boulevards. Tackier aspects of this onetime strip—famous for the springtime madness spawned by the film *Where the Boys Are*—are now but a fading memory, with the possible exception of the icon Elbo Room, an ever-popular bar at the corner of Las Olas and A1A.

North of the redesigned beachfront are another 2 mi (3 km) of open and natural coastal landscape. Much of the way parallels the **Hugh Taylor Birch State Recreation Area,** preserving a patch of primeval Florida.

SHOPPING

When you're downtown, check out **Las Olas Riverfront** (⊠ *1 block west of Andrews Ave. along New River*), a shopping, dining, and entertainment complex with constantly evolving shops for everything from meals and threads to cigars and tattoos. If only for a stroll and some high-end window-shopping, don't miss **Las Olas Boulevard** (⊠ *1 block off New River east of Andrews Ave.*). The city's best boutiques plus top restaurants and art galleries line a beautifully landscaped street.

Just north of Las Olas Boulevard on Route A1A is **The Gallery at Beach Place** (⊠ *17 S. Fort Lauderdale Beach Blvd.*). Browse shops, enjoy lunch or dinner, or carouse at assorted nightspots. Lower-level eateries tend toward the more upscale, whereas upper-level prices are lower (go figure), with superior ocean views. ■ TIP→ **Beach Place has covered parking, but you can pinch pennies by using a nearby municipal lot that's metered.** Just west of the Intracoastal Waterway, the split-level **Galleria Mall** (⊠ *2414 E. Sunrise Blvd.*) entices with Neiman Marcus, Dillard's, and Macy's, plus 150 specialty shops for anything from cookware to exquisite jewelry. Chow down at Capital Grille, Blue Martini, Mama Sbarro's, and Seasons 52, or head for the food court, a decided cut above at this upscale mall open 10 AM–9 PM Monday through Saturday, noon–5:30 Sunday. The **Swap Shop** (⊠ *3291 W. Sunrise Blvd.*) is the South's largest flea market, with 2,000 vendors open daily. While exploring this indoor–outdoor entertainment and shopping complex, hop on the carousel or stick around for movies at the 14-screen Swap Shop drive-in.

NIGHTLIFE

Coyote Ugly (✉ 214 S.W. 2nd St. ☎ 954/764–8459) continues a tradition of being one of the hottest spots in Broward. **Hooters of Beach Place** (✉ The Gallery at Beach Place, 17 S. Fort Lauderdale Beach Blvd. ☎ 954/767–0014) extends its reputation for tacky and unrefined fun to this seaside setting with a fabulous view. Around since 1948, **Kim's Alley Bar** (✉ 1920 E. Sunrise Blvd. ☎ 954/763–2143) has two bar areas, a jukebox, and pool tables that provide endless entertainment. **Maguire's Hill 16** (✉ 535 N. Andrews Ave. ☎ 954/764–4453) hosts live music in classic Irish-pub surroundings. **Parrot Lounge** (✉ 911 Sunrise La. ☎ 954/563–1493) favored by Philadelphia Eagles fans, backs up libations and revelry with wings, fingers, poppers, and skins.

WHERE TO EAT

$$$$
SEAFOOD
★
✗ Blue Moon (EAST) Fish Company. Most tables have stellar views of the Intracoastal Waterway, but Blue Moon East's true magic comes from the kitchen, where chefs Baron Skorish and Bryce Statham create moon-and-stars-worthy seafood dishes. Start with the raw bar, a sushi sampler, or pan-seared fresh-shucked oysters. Salads include hydroponic lettuce with candied walnuts, and among the entrée favorites are lump crab and corn-roasted grouper with asparagus risotto and peppercorn-crusted big-eye tuna with sticky rice. Carnivores might opt for prosciutto-stuffed veal tenderloin. Wrap up an evening with the tartelette of bananas Foster. For Sunday champagne brunches book early, even in the off-season. For the record, a Blue Moon West has risen in Coral Springs. ✉ 4405 W. Tradewinds Ave. ☎ 954/267–9888 ▤ AE, D, DC, MC, V.

$$
AMERICAN
✗ Floridian. This Las Olas landmark is plastered with photos of Monroe, Nixon, and local notables past and present in a succession of brightly painted rooms with funky chandeliers. The kitchen dishes up some of the best breakfasts around (no matter the hour), with oversize omelets that come with biscuits, toast, or English muffins, plus a choice of grits or tomato. With sausage or bacon on the side, you'll forget about eating again soon. Count on savory sandwiches and hot platters for lunch, tempting meat-loaf plates for dinner, and friendly, efficient service. It's open 24 hours—even during hurricanes, as long as the power holds out. Feeling flush? Try the Fat Cat Breakfast (New York strip steak, hash browns or grits, toast, and worthy champagne) or the Not-So-Fat-Cat, with the same grub and a lesser-quality vintage. ✉ 1410 E. Las Olas Blvd. ☎ 954/463–4041 ▤ No credit cards.

$
SEAFOOD
✗ Southport Raw Bar. You can't go wrong at this unpretentious spot where the motto, on bumper stickers for miles around, proclaims EAT FISH, LIVE LONGER, EAT OYSTERS, LOVE LONGER, EAT CLAMS, LAST LONGER. Raw or steamed clams, raw oysters, and peel-and-eat shrimp are market priced. Sides range from Bimini bread to key lime pie, with conch fritters, beer-battered onion rings, and corn on the cob in between. Order

wine by the bottle or glass, and beer by the pitcher, bottle, or can. Eat outside overlooking a canal, or inside at booths, tables, or in the front or back bars. Limited parking is free, and a grocery-store parking lot is across the street. ⊠ *1536 Cordova Rd.* ☎ *954/525–2526* ⊕ *www. southportrawbar.com* ▭ *MC, V.*

WHERE TO STAY

Fort Lauderdale has a growing and varied roster of lodging options, from beachfront luxury suites to intimate B&Bs to chain hotels along the Intracoastal Waterway. If you want to be on the beach, be sure to mention this when booking your room, since many hotels advertise "waterfront" accommodations that are actually on inland waterways, not the beach.

For price categories, see ⇨ *Lodging at the beginning of this chapter.*

$$$–$$$$
Fodor's Choice
★

🏨 **Hyatt Regency Pier Sixty-Six Resort & Spa.** Unfortunately, the trademark of this high-rise resort—the rooftop Pier Top Lounge—has closed. Happily, that space with the most eye-popping views around is open to the public for a pricey Sunday brunch with unlimited champagne ($65 per head). The iconic 17-story tower dominates a lovely 22-acre spread that includes the full-service Spa 66. Each room has a balcony with views of the 142-slip marina, pool, ocean, or the Intracoastal Waterway. Some guests prefer the ground-level lanai rooms. Lush landscaping and convenience to beach and causeway, shopping, and restaurants add to overall allure, plus each room has complimentary Wi-Fi. Hail the Water Taxi at the resort's dock for access to downtown or the beach. **Pros:** great views; plenty of activities; ideal location. **Cons:** not on the beach; spa's location seems like an afterthought. ⊠ *2301 S.E. 17th St. Causeway* ☎ *954/525–6666 or 800/327–3796* ⊕ *www.pier66.com* ⇱ *380 rooms, 8 suites* ⚐ *In-room: safe, refrigerator, Wi-Fi. In-hotel: 6 restaurants, bars, tennis courts, pools, gym, spa, water sports, Wi-Fi hotspot* ▭ *AE, D, DC, MC, V.*

$$$–$$$$
☼
★

🏨 **Pelican Grand Beach Resort.** Smack on the beach, this already lovely property has been transformed with a new tower, restaurant and lounge, an old-fashioned ice-cream parlor, and a circulating lazy-river pool that allows guests to float round and round. Most rooms and one-bedroom suites have ocean views. (Pelican fans of old may care to know that the original Sun Tower has gotten a makeover, but now operates separately from the resort.) Free Wi-Fi is available in public spaces and by the pool. **Pros:** you can't get any closer to the beach in Fort Lauderdale. **Cons:** you'll need wheels to access Las Olas beach-area action. ⊠ *2000 N. Atlantic Blvd.* ☎ *954/568–9431 or 800/525–6232* ⊕ *www. pelicanbeach.com* ⇱ *121 rooms (remainder of 155 total are condominiums)* ⚐ *In-room: safe, refrigerator, Internet. In-hotel: restaurant, bar, pool, Wi-Fi hotspot* ▭ *AE, DC, MC, V.*

GALVESTON, TEXAS

Updated by
Rena Havner-
Philips

A thin strip of an island in the Gulf of Mexico, Galveston is big sister Houston's beach playground—a year-round coastal destination just 50 mi away. Many of the first public buildings in Texas, including a post office, bank, and hotel, were built here, but most were destroyed in the Great Storm of 1900. Those that endured have been well preserved, and the Victorian character of the Strand shopping district and the neighborhood surrounding Broadway is still evident. On the Galveston Bay side of the island (northeast), quaint shops and cafés in old buildings are near the Seaport Museum, harbor-front eateries, and the cruise-ship terminal. On the Gulf of Mexico side (southwest), resorts and restaurants line coastal Seawall Boulevard. The 17-foot-high seawall abuts a long ribbon of sand and provides a place for rollerblading, bicycling, and going on the occasional surrey ride. The city was badly damaged from flooding during Hurricane Ike in 2008; at this writing, most of the businesses that had been closed were reopening.

Galveston is a port of embarkation for cruises on Western Caribbean itineraries. It's an especially popular port of embarkation for people living in the southeastern states who don't wish to fly to their cruise. At this writing, both Carnival and Royal Caribbean have ships based in Galveston, offering four-, five-, and seven-day cruises along the Mexican coast and to Jamaica, Grand Cayman, and Honduras.

ESSENTIALS

HOURS   Shops in the historic district are usually open until at least 7, but some stay open later. This is also the city's nightlife district, and is hopping until late.

INTERNET   The best place to check your e-mail is at your hotel. Most of the hotels in Galveston offer some kind of Internet service, though usually for a fee. If you have a laptop, the city has a relatively extensive network of free Wi-Fi zones, including several spots on the Strand.

VISITOR
INFORMATION
Strand Visitors Center (✉ 2215 Strand ⊕ www.galveston.com).

THE CRUISE PORT

The relatively sheltered waters of Galveston Bay are home to the Texas Cruise Ship Terminal. It's only 30 minutes to open water from here. Driving south from Houston on I–45, you cross a long causeway before reaching the island. Take the first exit, Harborside Drive, left after you've crossed the causeway onto Galveston Island. Follow that for a few miles to the port. Turn left on 22nd Street (also called Kempner Street); there is a security checkpoint before you continue down a driveway. The drop-off point is set up much like an airport terminal, with pull-through lanes and curbside check-in.

Port Contacts **Port of Galveston** (✉ Harborside Dr. and 22nd St. ☎ 409/765–9321 ⊕ www.portofgalveston.com).

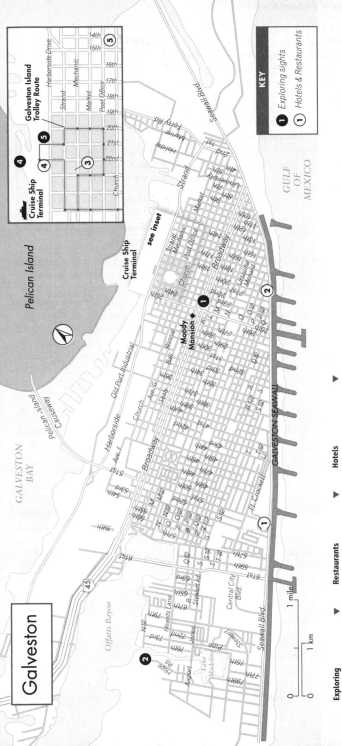

Galveston

Pelican Island

GALVESTON BAY

GULF OF MEXICO

Galveston Island Trolley Route

Cruise Ship Terminal

see inset

KEY

- **1** Exploring sights
- **1** Hotels & Restaurants

Moody Mansion

GALVESTON SEAWALL

Exploring ▶

Broadway	**1**
Moody Gardens	**2**
Pier 21 Theater	**5**
The Strand	**3**
Texas Seaport Museum	**4**

Restaurants ▶

Fisherman's Wharf	**4**
Mosquito Café	**5**

Hotels ▶

Hotel Galvez	**2**
San Luis Resort	**1**
Tremont House	**3**

AIRPORT TRANSFERS

The closest airports are in Houston, 50 mi from Galveston. Houston has two major airports: Hobby Airport, 9 mi (15 km) southeast of downtown, and George Bush Intercontinental, 15 mi (24 km) northeast of the city. Traffic into Galveston can be delayed because of ongoing construction.

Unless you have arranged airport transfers through your cruise line, you'll have to make arrangements to navigate the miles between the Houston airport at which you land and the cruise-ship terminal in Galveston. Galveston Limousine Service provides scheduled transportation (return reservations required) between either airport and Galveston hotels or the cruise-ship terminal. Hobby is a shorter ride (1 hour, $45 one-way, $80 round-trip), but Intercontinental (2 hours, $55 one-way, $100 round-trip) is served by more airlines, including international carriers. Taking a taxi allows you to set your own schedule, but can cost twice as much (it's also important to note that there aren't always enough taxis to handle the demands of disembarking passengers, so you might have to wait after you leave your ship). Negotiate the price before you get in.

Contacts Galveston Limousine Service (☎ 800/640–4826 ⊕ *www. galvestonlimousineservice.com*).

> **GALVESTON BEST BETS**
>
> ■ **Historic Homes.** The island has some lovely historic homes to explore, particularly during early May, when the Historic Homes Tour lets you into many that aren't usually open to the public.
>
> ■ **Moody Gardens.** There are enough activities at this park to keep any kid happy.
>
> ■ **The Strand.** Galveston's historic district is a great place to stroll, shop, and eat.

PARKING

Parking is coordinated by the Port Authority. After you drop off your checked luggage and passengers at the terminal, you receive a color-coded parking pass from the attendant, with directions to a parking lot for your cruise departure. The lots are approximately ½ mi (1 km) from the terminal. Check-in, parking, and boarding are generally allowed four hours prior to departure. A shuttle bus (carry-on luggage only) runs back and forth between the lots and the terminal every 7 to 12 minutes on cruise arrival and departure days (be sure to drop off your luggage *before* you park the car). The lot is closed other days. Port Authority security checks the well-lighted, fenced-in lots every two hours; there is also a limited amount of covered parking. Parking for a 5-day cruise is $50, 7-day is $70 ($80 covered). Cash, traveler's checks, and credit cards (Visa and MasterCard only) are accepted for payment.

EXPLORING GALVESTON

❶ **Broadway.** The late 1800s were the heyday of Galveston's port (before Houston's was dug out). Victorian splendor is evident in the meticulously restored homes of this historic district, some of which are now museums. If you're in town the first two weekends of May, don't miss the **Galveston Historic Homes Tour.** In addition to visiting the neighborhood's museums, you can walk through privately owned homes dating from the 1800s. For more information about area house museums or the tour, contact the Heritage Visitors Center. **Moody Mansion** (✉ *2618 Broadway* ☎ *409/762–7668* ⊕ *www.moodymansion.org*), the residence of generations of one of Texas's most powerful families, was completed in 1895. Tour its interiors of exotic woods and gilded trim filled with family heirlooms and personal effects. It's open from 11 to 3 daily, charging $7 admission.

② **Moody Gardens** is a multifaceted entertainment and educational complex inside pastel-color glass pyramids. Attractions include the 13-story **Aquarium Pyramid,** showcasing marine life from four oceans in tanks and touch pools; **Rainforest Pyramid,** a 40,000-square-foot tropical habitat for exotic flora and fauna; **Discovery Museum,** which has changing exhibits; and two **IMAX theaters,** one of which has a space adventure ride. Outside, **Palm Beach** has a white-sand beach, landscaped grounds, man-made lagoons, a kid-size waterslide and games, and beach chairs. ✉ *1 Hope Blvd.* ☎ *409/741–8484 or 800/582–4673* ⊕ *www.moodygardens.com* ☜ *$8.95–$18.95 per venue, $39.95 day pass or $49.95 2-day pass* ☉ *Daily 10–6.*

⑤ Pier 21 Theater. At this theater on the Strand, watch the Great Storm of 1900 come back to life in a multimedia presentation that includes video clips of archival drawings, still photos, and narrated accounts from survivors' diaries. Also playing is a film about the exploits of pirate Jean Lafitte, who used the island as a base. ✉ *Pier 21, Harborside Dr. and 21st St.* ☎ *409/763–8808* ⊕ *www.galveston.com/pier21theatre* ☜ *Great Storm $5, Pirate Island $4* ☉ *Memorial Day–Labor Day, Wed.–Mon. 11–6; Labor Day–Memorial Day, Wed.–Mon. 11–5.*

③ The Strand. This shopping area is defined by the architecture of its 19th- and early-20th-century buildings, many of which survived the storm of 1900 and are on the National Register of Historic Places. When Galveston was still a powerful port city—before the Houston Ship Channel was dug, diverting most boat traffic inland—this stretch, formerly the site of stores, offices, and warehouses, was known as the Wall Street of the South. As you stroll up the Strand, you'll pass dozens of shops and cafés. ✉ *Between Strand and Postoffice St., 25th and 19th Sts.*

④ Texas Seaport Museum. Aboard the restored 1877 tall ship *Elissa*, detailed interpretive signs provide information about the shipping trade in the 1800s, including the routes and cargoes this ship carried into Galveston. Inside the museum building is a replica of the historic wharf and information about the ethnic groups that immigrated through this U.S. point of entry after 1837. ✉ *Pier 21* ☎ *409/763–1877* ⊕ *www.tsm-elissa.org* ☜ *$8* ☉ *Daily 10–5.*

BEACHES

The **Seawall** (✉ *Seawall Blvd. from 61st St. to 25th St.*) on the Gulf-side waterfront attracts runners, cyclists, and rollerbladers. Just below it is a long, free beach near many big hotels and resorts. **Stewart Beach Park** (✉ *6th St. and Seawall Blvd.* ☎ *409/765–5023* ☜ *$8 per vehicle*) has a bathhouse, amusement park, bumper boats, miniature-golf course, and a water coaster in addition to saltwater and sand. It's open weekdays 9 to 5, weekends 8 to 6 from March through May; weekdays 8 to 6 and weekends 8 to 7 from June through September; and weekends 9 to 6 during the first two weekends of October. **Galveston Island State Park** (✉ *3 Mile Rd., 10 mi (16 km) southwest on Seawall Blvd.* ☎ *409/737-1222* ✉ *$5* ⊙ *Daily dawn–dusk*), on the western, unpopulated end of the island, is a 2,000-acre natural beach habitat ideal for birding, walking, and renewing your spirit.

> **BOARDING PASSES**
>
> Modern ID cards and scanning equipment record passenger comings and goings on the majority of cruise ships these days. With a swipe through a machine (it looks much like a credit-card swipe at the supermarket), security personnel know who is on board the vessel at all times. On most large ships passengers' pictures are recorded digitally at check-in.

SHOPPING

The **Strand** (✉ *Bounded by Strand and Postoffice St. [running east–west] and 25th and 19th Sts. [running north–south]*) is the best place to shop in Galveston. Old storefronts are filled with gift shops, antiques stores, and one-of-a-kind boutiques. More than 50 antiques dealers are represented at the **Emporium at Eibands** (✉ *2201 Postoffice St.* ☎ *409/750–9536*), an upscale showroom filled with custom upholstery, bedding and draperies, antique furniture, and interesting architectural finds. The **Firm** (✉ *2220 Postoffice St.* ☎ *409/762–8300*) was the first retail business along quaint Postoffice Street. Today it is a favorite place to shop for trendy, unique women's fashions from Los Angeles, while reveling in the boutique's shabby-chic decor. **Old Strand Emporium** (✉ *2112 Strand* ☎ *409/515–0715*) is a charming deli and grocery reminiscent of an old-fashioned ice-cream parlor and sandwich shop, with candy bins, packaged nuts, and more.

NIGHTLIFE

For a relaxing evening, choose any of the harborside restaurant-bars on piers 21 and 22 to sip a glass of wine or a frozen Hurricane as you watch the boats go by. The **Grand 1894 Opera House** (✉ *2020 Postoffice St.* ☎ *409/765–1894 or 800/821–1894* ⊕ *www.thegrand.com*) stages musicals and hosts concerts year-round. It's worth visiting for the ornate architecture alone. Sarah Bernhardt and Anna Pavlova both performed on this storied stage.

WHERE TO EAT

For price categories, see ⇨ *Dining at the beginning of this chapter.*

$$$–$$$$
SEAFOOD
✗ **Fisherman's Wharf.** Even though Landry's has taken over this harborside institution, locals keep coming here for the reliably fresh seafood and reasonable prices. Dine indoors or watch the boat traffic (and waiting cruise ships) from the patio. Start with a cold combo, like

boiled shrimp and grilled rare tuna. For entrées, the fried fish, shrimp, and oysters are hard to beat. ✉ *Pier 22, Harborside Dr. and 22nd St.* ☎ *409/765–5708* ⊟ *AE, D, DC, MC, V.*

$$–$$$ ✕**Mosquito Café.** This chichi eatery in Galveston's historic East End
AMERICAN serves fresh, contemporary food—including some vegetarian dishes—in a hip, high-ceilinged dining room and on an outdoor patio. Wake up to a fluffy egg frittata or a homemade scone topped with whipped cream, or try a large gourmet salad for lunch. The fish of the day is always a hit. ✉ *628 14th St.* ☎ *409/763–1010* ⊟ *AE, D, MC, V* ⊗ *Closed Mon. No dinner Sun.*

WHERE TO STAY

For price categories, see ⇨ Lodging at the beginning of this chapter.

$$$–$$$$ ⊡ **Hotel Galvez: A Wyndham Historic Hotel.** This renovated six-story Spanish-colonial hotel, built in 1911, was once called "Queen of the Gulf." Teddy Roosevelt and Howard Hughes are just two of the many well-known guests who have stayed here. Traditional dark wood and plush upholstery pieces furnish both the public and private areas. A pool, swim-up bar, and outdoor grill have been added to the tropical garden facing the sea. **Pros:** directly on beach; incredible pool area; beautiful grounds. **Cons:** rooms can be small (especially the bathrooms). ✉ *2024 Seawall Blvd.* ☎ *409/765–7721* ⊕ *www.wyndham.com* ⤶ *231 rooms* ⚬ *In-hotel: Wi-Fi. In-hotel: restaurant, pool, gym, laundry service, Internet terminal, no-smoking rooms* ⊟ *AE, DC, MC, V.*

$$–$$$ ⊡ **San Luis Resort, Spa and Conference Center.** A long marble staircase alongside a slender fountain with sculpted dolphins welcomes you to the beachfront elegance of this resort. The upper-floor facade isn't much to look at, but don't let that fool you; inside, the colors of cool, cream marble and taupe stone in the lobby are echoed in the guest rooms. The sculptural lines of pink granite on the headboards and armchairs say "Italian villa." All rooms have balconies facing the Gulf, and prices rise with the floor height. New Club Ten guest rooms on the 10th floor offer upgraded linens, down comforters, iPod docking stations, and huge plasma TVs. Back on ground level, step into the meandering (and heated) grotto pool with a rock waterfall set amid coconut palms and bougainvillea; then have a Balinese massage (or a wildflower compress) at the Spa San Luis. The resort offers free parking for the duration of a cruise as well as transportation to the cruise terminal. **Pros:** great Gulf views; nice pool area. **Cons:** public parking (nonvalet) is not convenient. ✉ *5222 Seawall Blvd.* ☎ *409/744–1500 or 800/445–0090* ⊕ *www.sanluisresort.com* ⤶ *244 rooms* ⚬ *In-room: Internet. In-hotel: restaurant, room service, bars, tennis courts, pools, gym, spa, children's programs (ages 4–12), laundry service, Internet terminal, parking (free), no-smoking rooms* ⊟ *AE, D, DC, MC, V.*

$$–$$$ ⊡ **Tremont House: A Wyndham Historic Hotel.** A four-story atrium lobby, with ironwork balconies and full-size palm trees, showcases an 1872 hand-carved rosewood bar in what was once a busy dry-goods warehouse. This actually is a historic place: Republic of Texas president Sam Houston presented his last speech at this hotel, both Confederate

3

and Union soldiers bunked here, and Great Storm victims took refuge under this roof. Rooms have high ceilings and 11-foot windows. Period reproduction furniture and Victorian-pattern wallpapers add to the authenticity. It's the closest full-service lodging to the port, just a short walk from shopping on the Strand—and it's also a completely no-smoking environment. Damaged heavily during Hurricane Ike, the hotel was completely renovated in 2009. **Pros:** beautiful, historic environment; great location. **Cons:** not a fun scene for young single travelers. ⌧ *2300 Ship's Mechanic Row* ☎ *409/763–0300* ⊕ *www.wyndham. com* ↪ *119 rooms* ☼ *In-room: Internet. In-hotel: restaurant, room service, bar, laundry service, Internet terminal, parking (paid), no-smoking rooms* ⊟ *AE, D, DC, MC, V.*

JACKSONVILLE, FLORIDA

Jennifer
Edwards

One of Florida's oldest cities and at 730 square mi (1,891 square km) the largest city in the continental United States, Jacksonville is underrated, and makes a worthwhile vacation spot for an extra day or two before or after your cruise. It offers appealing downtown riverside areas, handsome residential neighborhoods, the region's only skyscrapers, a thriving arts scene, and, for football fans, the NFL Jaguars and the NCAA Gator Bowl. Remnants of the Old South flavor the city, especially in the Riverside/Avondale historic district, where moss-draped oak trees frame prairie-style bungalows and Tudor Revival mansions, and palm trees, Spanish bayonet, and azaleas populate Jacksonville's landscape.

ESSENTIALS

HOURS Many museums close on Monday.

INTERNET Most people access the Internet in their hotel, and most hotels offer some kind of Internet access, often Wi-Fi.

VISITOR
INFORMATION **Jacksonville and The Beaches Convention & Visitors Bureau** (⌧ *550 Water St., Suite 1000, Jacksonville* ☎ *904/798–9100 or 800/733–2668* ⊕ *www. visitjacksonville.com*).

THE CRUISE PORT

Limited in the sizes of ships it can berth, JAXPORT currently serves as home port to the *Carnival Fascination,* which departs weekly on four- and five-night cruises to Key West and the Bahamas during the fall and winter cruising seasons. The facility is fairly sparse, consisting basically of some vending machines and restrooms, but the embarkation staff receives high marks. The terminal itself is a temporary structure; a permanent cruise terminal has been under consideration for some time, but its fate is uncertain at this writing.

JAXPORT is about 15 minutes from Jacksonville International Airport. Take I–95 South to S.R. 9-A East. Follow 9-A to Heckscher Drive (S.R. 105) west until you reach August Drive. Head south on August Drive, and follow the signs to the cruise terminal.

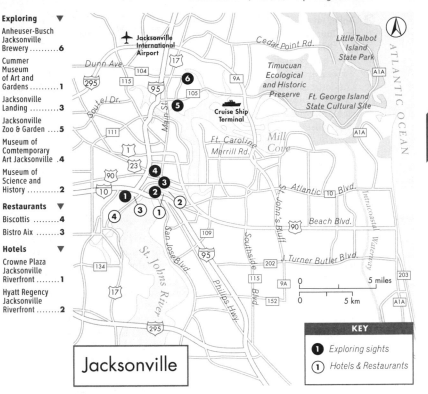

Jacksonville

KEY
1 Exploring sights
1 Hotels & Restaurants

Port Contacts Jacksonville Port Authority (✉ 9810 August Dr., Jacksonville ☎ 904/630-3006 ⊕ www.jaxport.com).

AIRPORT TRANSFERS

The transfer from Jacksonville airport takes about 15 minutes and costs $30 for up to three passengers by taxi, not including tip. **Yellow Cab–Jacksonville** (☎ *904/260–1111). Note that this number reaches dispatchers for several city cabs, including Yellow Cab and Gator City Taxi.*

PARKING

There is a fenced and guarded parking lot next to the cruise terminal, within walking distance. Parking costs $15 per day for regular vehicles, $25 for RVs. You must pay in advance by cash or major credit card.

EXPLORING JACKSONVILLE

Because Jacksonville was settled along both sides of the twisting St. Johns River, a number of attractions are on or near a riverbank. Both sides of the river, which is spanned by myriad bridges, have downtown areas and waterfront complexes of shops, restaurants, parks, and museums; some attractions can be reached by water taxi or the Skyway Express monorail system—scenic alternatives to driving back and forth across the bridges—but a car is generally necessary.

⑥ Anheuser-Busch Jacksonville Brewery Tour. Beer lovers will appreciate this behind-the-scenes look at how barley, malt, rice, hops, and water form the "King of Beers." Guided tours take guests through the entire brewing and bottling process. Or you can hightail it through the self-guided tour and head straight to the free beer tastings (for guests 21 years and older, that is). ⊠ *111 Busch Dr.* ☎ *904/696–8373* ⊕ *www.budweisertours.com* ⊠ *Free* ⊘ *Mon.–Sat. 10–4; guided tours Mon.–Sat. 10–3 on the ½ hr.*

❶ Cummer Museum of Art & Gardens. The world-famous Wark Collection of early-18th-century Meissen porcelain is just one reason to visit this former riverfront estate, which includes 13 permanent galleries with more than 5,000 items spanning more than 8,000 years, and 3 acres of riverfront gardens reflecting northeast Florida's blooming seasons and indigenous varieties. Art Connections allows kids to experience art through hands-on, interactive exhibits. One of the museum's newest additions, the Thomas H. Jacobsen Gallery of American Art, focuses on works by American artists, including Max Weber, N.C. Wyeth, and Paul Manship. ⊠ *829 Riverside Ave.* ☎ *904/356–6857* ⊕ *www.cummer.org* ⊠ *$10, free Tues. 4–9* ⊘ *Tues. 10–9, Wed.–Sat. 10–5, Sun. noon–5.*

❸ Jacksonville Landing. During the week, this riverfront festival marketplace caters to locals and tourists alike, with specialty shops, full-service restaurants—including a sushi bar, Italian bistro, and a steak house—and an internationally flavored food court. On weekends the Landing hosts more than 250 events each year, ranging from the good clean fun of the Lighted Boat Parade and Christmas Tree Lighting to the just plain obnoxious Florida/Georgia game after-party, as well as live music (usually of the local cover-band variety) in the courtyard. ⊠ *2 Independent Dr.* ☎ *904/353–1188* ⊕ *www.jacksonvillelanding.com* ⊠ *Free* ⊘ *Mon.–Thurs. 10–8, Fri. and Sat. 10–9, Sun. noon–5:30; restaurant hrs vary.*

❺ Jacksonville Zoo and Gardens. Encompassing more than 120 acres on Jacksonville's north side, this midsize zoo is home to 1,000 unique plant species and 1,500 rare and exotic animals, from barking tree frogs and Madagascar hissing cockroaches to dusky pygmy rattlesnakes and giant anteaters. Among the zoo's outstanding exhibits are its collection of rare waterfowl and the Serona Overlook, which showcases some of the world's most venomous snakes. The Florida Wetlands is a 2½-acre area with black bears, bald eagles, white-tailed deer, and other animals native to Florida. The African Veldt has alligators, elephants, and white rhinos, among other species of African birds and mammals; and the Range of the Jaguar, winner of the Association of Zoos and Aquarium's Exhibit of the Year, includes 4 acres of exotic big cats as well as 20 other species of animals. New additions include Play

Ⓒ
Fodor'sChoice
★

Park, complete with a splash park, forest play area, maze, and discovery building; and Stingray Bay, a 17,000-gallon pool where visitors can pet and feed the mysterious creatures. ⊠ *370 Zoo Pkwy., off Heckscher Dr. E* ☎ *904/757–4463* ⊕ *www.jaxzoo.org* ⊠ *$13* ⊙ *Daily 9–5; extended hours offered during summer weekends and holidays.*

> **BRING GEORGE**
>
> Whenever you leave for a cruise, bring a supply of one-dollar bills. They will come in handy for tipping both airport and port personnel.

3

❹ **Museum of Contemporary Art Jacksonville.** In this loftlike downtown building, the former headquarters of the Western Union Telegraph Company, a permanent collection of 20th-century art shares space with traveling exhibitions. The museum encompasses five galleries and ArtExplorium, a highly interactive educational exhibit for kids, as well as a funky gift shop and Café Nola, open for lunch on weekdays and for dinner on Thursday and Friday. MOCA Jacksonville (previously known as the Jacksonville Museum of Modern Art) also hosts film series, lectures, and workshops throughout the year, and packs a big art-wallop into a relatively small 14,000 square feet. Sunday is free for families. ⊠ *Hemming Plaza, 333 N. Laura St.* ☎ *904/366–6911* ⊕ *www.mocajacksonville.org* ⊠ *$8* ⊙ *Tues., Wed., Fri., and Sat. 10–4, Thurs. 10–8, Sun. noon–4; hrs subject to change.*

Fodor's Choice ★

❷ **Museum of Science & History.** You won't find any mad scientists here, but ⓒ you'll probably find lots of giggling ones. Targeted at the elementary- and middle-school set, MOSH aims to educate and entertain kids about science and history through a variety of interactive exhibits like the JEA Science Theatre, where they'll participate in live experiments related to electricity and electrical safety; the Florida Naturalist's Center, where they can explore northeast Florida wildlife (like American alligators, gopher turtles, and various native snakes and birds); and the Universe of Science, where they'll learn about properties of physical science through hands-on demonstrations. Other permanent exhibits include Atlantic Tails, an exploration of whales, dolphins, and manatees; Currents of Time, chronicling 12,000 years of northeast Florida history; and Prehistoric Park, featuring a life-size Allosaurus skeleton. The Alexander Brest Planetarium hosts daily shows on astronomy, and, on weekends, Cosmic Concerts, 3-D laser shows set to pop music. ⊠ *1025 Museum Circle* ☎ *904/396–6674* ⊕ *www.themosh.org* ⊠ *$9 adult, planetarium $1 and Extreme Science Show $1 (in addition to admission), Cosmic Concerts $7–$9* ⊙ *Weekdays 10–5, Sat. 10–6, Sun. 1–6.*

SHOPPING

At **Five Points** (⊠ *Intersection of Park, Margaret, and Lomax Sts., Riverside*) you'll find a small but funky shopping district of new and vintage-clothing boutiques, shoe stores, and antiques shops, as well as a handful of eateries and bars, not to mention some of the most colorful characters in the city. **The Shoppes of Avondale** (⊠ *St. Johns Ave., between Talbot Ave. and Dancy St.*) highlight upscale clothing and accessories boutiques, art galleries, home-furnishings shops, a choco-latier, and trendy restaurants. **San Marco Square** (⊠ *Intersection of San Marco and Atlantic Blvds.*) has dozens of interesting apparel, home, and jewelry stores and restaurants in 1920s Mediterranean-revival–style buildings. One of northeast Florida's newest shopping destinations, **St. Johns Town Center** (⊠ *4663 River City Dr., Southside* ☎ *904/642–8339*) is an outdoor "lifestyle center" with shops not found anywhere else in northeast Florida, including Anthropologie, Apple, Lucky Brand Jeans, and Sephora, as well as the Cheesecake Factory, P.F. Changs, and Maggiano's Little Italy.

NIGHTLIFE

Technically, **Eclipse** (⊠ *4219 St. Johns Ave.* ☎ *904/387–3582*) is a dance club that serves up a mix of moods and music styles for the twentysomething set. Wine snobs, rejoice! At **The Grotto** (⊠ *2012 San Marco Blvd.* ☎ *904/398–0726* ⊕ *www.grottowine.com*) you can enjoy more than 70 wines by the glass. **Harmonious Monks** (⊠ *10550 Old St. Augustine Rd.* ☎ *904/880–3040*) claims to have "the world's most talented waitstaff." They certainly might be the most energetic, performing throughout the night and encouraging customers to dance on the bar. **Jack Rabbits** (⊠ *1528 Hendricks Ave.* ☎ *904/398–7496* ⊕ *www.jackrabbitsonline.com*) welcomes the latest and greatest indie bands and budding rock stars. The self-proclaimed "neighborhood lounge with a dash of dance club style," **Mark's** (⊠ *315 E. Bay St.* ☎ *904/355–5099* ⊕ *www.marksjax.com*) attracts the beautiful people for theme nights like Indie Lounge Tuesdays. **Metro** (⊠ *2929 Plum St.* ☎ *904/388–8719* ⊕ *www.metrojax.com*) is more than just a gay bar: it's like seven gay bars rolled into one, including a piano bar, dance club, lounge, and drag-show cabaret. Fans of Christian music flock to the **Murray Hill Theatre** (⊠ *932 Edgewood Ave. S* ☎ *904/388–7807* ⊕ *www.murrayhilltheatre.com*), a no-smoking, no-alcohol club. At 12,000 square feet, **Plush** (⊠ *845 University Blvd. N* ☎ *904/743–1845* ⊕ *plushjax.com*) is certainly Jacksonville's largest nightclub; it's also the loudest. **Square One** (⊠ *1974 San Marco Blvd.* ☎ *904/306–9004*) has an upscale singles' scene, with live music on weekends.

WHERE TO EAT

JAXPORT's location on Jacksonville's Westside means there aren't too many nearby restaurants. But by taking a 10- to 15-minute drive south, you'll find a wealth of restaurants for all tastes and price categories.

For price categories, see ⇨ Dining at the beginning of this chapter.

¢   × **Biscottis.** The local artwork on the redbrick walls is a mild distraction
AMERICAN from the jovial crowds (from yuppies to soccer moms to metrosexuals) jockeying for tables in this midsize restaurant. Elbows almost touch, but no one seems to mind. The menu offers the unexpected: wild mushroom ravioli with a broth of corn, leek, and dried apricot; or curry-grilled swordfish with cucumber-fig bordelaise sauce. Be sure to sample from Biscottis' decadent dessert case (we hear the peanut-butter ganache

is illegal in three states). Brunch, a local favorite, is served until 3 on weekends. ⊠ *3556 St. Johns Ave., Avondale* ☎ *904/387–2060* ⊕ *www. biscottis.net* ⚲ *Reservations not accepted* ⊟ *AE, MC, V.*

$$$

ECLECTIC

✗ **Bistro Aix.** When a Jacksonville restaurant can make Angelinos feel like they haven't left home, that's saying a lot. With its slick black-leather booths, 1940s brickwork, velvet drapes, and intricate marbled globes, Bistro Aix (pronounced "X") is just that place. Regulars can't get enough of the creamy onion soup, crispy calamari, and house-made potato chips with warm blue-cheese appetizers or entrées like oak-fired fish Aixoise, grilled salmon, and filet mignon. Adventurous diners can sample diverse dishes on a prix-fixe menu for $29. Aix's resident pastry chef ensures no sweet tooth leaves unsatisfied. For the most part, wait-staff are knowledgeable and pleasant, though some patrons find their demeanor snooty, except, of course, the ones from L.A. Call for preferred seating. ⊠ *1440 San Marco Blvd., San Marco* ☎ *904/398–1949* ⊕ *www.bistrox.com* ⚲ *Reservations not accepted* ⊟ *AE, D, DC, MC, V* ☉ *No lunch weekends.*

WHERE TO STAY

Hotels near the cruise terminals are few and far between, so most cruisers needing a room make the drive to Downtown (15 minutes) or to the Southbank or Riverside (20 minutes).

For price categories, see ⇨ *Lodging at the beginning of this chapter.*

$$$

⛫ **Crowne Plaza Jacksonville Riverfront.** A staple on Jacksonville's south bank for decades, the former Hilton Jacksonville Riverfront maintains its commanding presence but now as a Crowne Plaza property. Its location on the south side of the St. Johns River puts it within walking distance of restaurants, the Automated Skyway Express, and the water taxi; the swanky Ruth's Chris Steak House is one of the on-site restaurants. Guests wanting to live like a king can book the San Marco (aka the Elvis Room), a premier suite with Jacuzzi tub and two balconies that Presley called home during numerous trips to Jacksonville. **Pros:** newly renovated rooms; riverfront balconies; friendly staff. **Cons:** small bathrooms; loud air-conditioning units; no free parking. ⊠ *1201 Riverplace Blvd.* ☎ *904/398–8800* ⊕ *www.cpjacksonville.com* ⬚ *292 rooms, 30 suites* ⚴ *In-room: refrigerator (some), Wi-Fi. In-hotel: 2 restaurants, room service, bars, pool, gym, laundry service, Wi-Fi hotspot, parking (paid)* ⊟ *AE, D, MC, V.*

$$$

⛫ **Hyatt Regency Jacksonville Riverfront.** In Jacksonville it doesn't get much more convenient than this downtown waterfront hotel. Perched on the north bank of the St. Johns River, the 19-story property is within walking distance of the Jacksonville Landing, Florida Theatre and Times-Union Center, corporate office towers, and the county courthouse. The former Adam's Mark Hotel now includes the Plaza III Steakhouse and rooms updated with Florida-style decor, triple-sheeted beds, pillow-top mattresses, and sliding-glass doors. Since northeast Florida's largest hotel encompasses 110,000 square feet of meeting space, chances are pretty good you'll share an elevator with someone wearing a name tag (if you're not wearing one yourself). **Pros:** riverfront location; newly renovated; rooftop pool and gym. **Cons:** not all rooms are riverfront; slow valet service; no minibars. ⊠ *225 E. Coastline Dr.* ☎ *904/588–1234* ⊕ *www.jacksonville.hyatt.com* ⇌ *966 rooms, 21 suites* ⑁ *In-room: refrigerator (some), DVD (some), Internet. In-hotel: 3 restaurants, room service, bar, pool, gym, laundry facilities, laundry service, parking (paid), some pets allowed, Wi-Fi hotspot* ⊟ *AE, D, DC, MC, V.*

MIAMI, FLORIDA

Lynne Helm

Miami is the busiest of Florida's very busy cruise ports. Because there's so much going on here, you might want to schedule an extra day or two before and/or after your cruise to explore North America's most Latin city. Downtown is a convenient place to stay if you are meeting up with a cruise ship, but at night, except for Bayside Marketplace, the American Airlines Arena, and a few ever-changing clubs in warehouses, the area is deserted. Travelers spend little time here, since most tourist attractions are in other neighborhoods. Miami Beach, particularly the Art Deco District in South Beach—the square-mile section between 6th and 23rd streets—is the heart of Miami's vibrant nightlife and restaurant scene. But you may also want to explore beyond the beach, including the Little Havana, Coral Gables, and Coconut Grove sections of the city.

THE CRUISE PORT

The Port of Miami, in downtown Miami near Bayside Marketplace and the MacArthur Causeway, justifiably bills itself as the Cruise Capital of the World. Home to eight cruise lines and the largest year-round cruise fleet in the world, the port accommodates more than 3 million passengers a year for sailings from three to 14 days and sometimes longer duration. Air-conditioned terminals include the newer terminals D and E, with dramatic public art installations reflecting sun-drenched waters off the Florida coastline and the Everglades ecosystems. There's duty-free shopping and limousine service. You can get taxis at all the terminals, and car-rental agencies offer shuttles to off-site lots.

If you are driving, take I–95 north or south to I–395. Follow the directional signs to the Biscayne Boulevard exit. When you get to Biscayne Boulevard, make a right. Go to 5th Street, which becomes Port Boulevard (look for the American Airlines Arena); then make a left and go over the Port Bridge. Follow the directional signs to your terminal.

Contacts Port of Miami (⊠ *1015 North American Way, Miami* ☎ *305/371–7678* ⊕ *www.co.miami-dade.fl.us/portofmiami).*

AIRPORT TRANSFERS

If you have not arranged an airport transfer through your cruise line, you have a couple of options for getting to the cruise port. The first is a taxi, and fares are regulated by the county, with a flat fare of $24 from Miami International Airport (MIA). This fare is per trip, not per passenger, and includes tolls and $1 airport surcharge but not a tip. Super-Shuttle vans transport passengers between MIA and local hotels, as

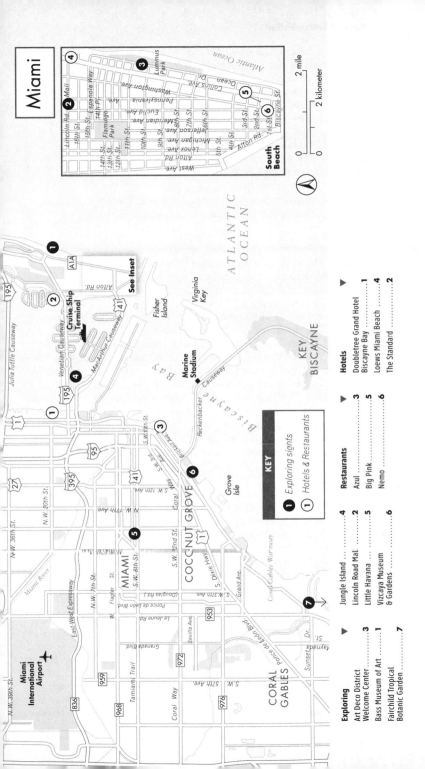

Miami

Lincoln Rd. ② Mall
③ Lummus Park
④

16th St.
16th St. Espanola Way
14th St.
14th Pl.
Flamingo Park
Espanola Way
Washington Ave.
Pennsylvania Ave.
Euclid Ave.
Meridian Ave.
Jefferson Ave.
Michigan Ave.
Lenox Ave.
West Ave.
Alton Rd.
Lincoln Rd.
14th St.
13th St.
12th St.
11th St.
10th St.
9th St.
8th St.
7th St.
6th St.
5th St.
4th St.
3rd St.
2nd St.
1st St.
Collins Ave.
Ocean Dr.
Biscayne St.
Atlantic Ocean

South Beach

⑤
⑥

0 ———— 2 mile
0 ———— 2 kilometer

ATLANTIC OCEAN

Miami International Airport ✈

N.W. 36th St.
N.W. 20th St.
East-West Expressway
Miami River
N.W. 7th St.
W. Flagler St.
Ponce de León Blvd.
Le Jeune Rd. (Douglas Rd.)
Granada Blvd
Sevilla Ave.
Coral Way
S.W. 57th Ave.
Tamiami Trail
Sunset Dr.
Maynada St.
Coral Gables Waterway
Ponce de León Blvd.
S. Dixie Hwy.
Grand Ave.
S.W. 37th Ave.
S.W. 32nd St.
S.W. 22nd St.
Coral Way
S.W. 12th Ave.
N.W. 17th Ave.
S.W. 8th St.
S.W. 12th St.
S.W. 13th St.
Brickell Ave.
S.W. 2nd Ave.

CORAL GABLES
COCONUT GROVE
MIAMI

Grove Isle

Julia Tuttle Causeway
Venetian Causeway
MacArthur Causeway
Alton Rd.
Cruise Ship Terminal
See Inset

Fisher Island
Virginia Key

Biscayne Bay

Marine Stadium
Rickenbacker Causeway
KEY BISCAYNE

195
195
95
395
27
836
959
972
968
976
953
A1A
41
41
1

① ❶
② ❶
④ ❶
③ ❶
⑤ ❶
⑥ ❶
⑦ ❶

KEY

① Exploring sights
① Hotels & Restaurants

Exploring ▶

Art Deco District **3**
Welcome Center **1**
Bass Museum of Art **1**
Fairchild Tropical
Botanic Garden **7**
Jungle Island **4**
Lincoln Road Mall **2**
Little Havana **5**
Vizcaya Museum
& Gardens **6**

Restaurants ▶

Azul **3**
Big Pink **5**
Nemo **6**

Hotels ▶

Doubletree Grand Hotel
Biscayne Bay **1**
Loews Miami Beach **4**
The Standard **2**

well as the Port of Miami. At MIA the vans pick up at the ground level of each concourse (look for clerks with yellow shirts, who will flag one down). SuperShuttle service from MIA is available on demand; for the return it's best to make reservations 24 hours in advance. The cost from MIA to the cruise port is $16 per person, or $55 if you want the entire van to yourselves.

CAUTION
Airline carry-on restrictions are being updated continuously. Check with your airline before packing, and be aware that large purses will sometimes be counted as a carry-on item!

Information SuperShuttle (☎ *305/871–2000 from MIA, 954/764–1700 from Fort Lauderdale, 800/258–3826 elsewhere ⊕ www.supershuttle.com*).

PARKING
Street-level lots are right in front of each of the cruise terminals. In 2010 the $15-million Parking Garage D (with 873 spaces on four levels) opened near two recently constructed terminals serving Carnival Cruise Lines. Altogether the port's three parking garages (each with an open-air top floor) accommodate 5,871 vehicles, with 56 spaces designated for handicapped guests and another half-dozen or so for passengers with infants. The cost for all, payable in advance, is $20 per day ($40 for RVs) and $7 for short-term parking of less than 4 hours for drop-off/pick-up. You can pay with cash or a credit card, although only with American Express, Master Card, or Visa. There is no valet parking, but a shuttle for cruise passengers (one is wheelchair accessible) can pick you up at the parking garage/lot, take you to the appropriate terminal, and return you to your vehicle after your cruise.

VISITOR INFORMATION
Greater Miami Convention & Visitors Bureau (✉ *701 Brickell Ave., Suite 2700, Miami* ☎ *305/539–3000, 800/933–8448 in U.S.* ⊕ *www.gmcvb.com*).

EXPLORING MIAMI

In the 1950s Miami was best known for alligator wrestlers and you-pick strawberry fields or citrus groves. Well, things have changed. Miami on the mainland is South Florida's commercial hub, while its sultry sister Miami Beach (America's Riviera) encompasses 17 islands in Biscayne Bay. Seducing winter refugees with its sunshine, beaches, palms, and nightlife, this is what most people envision when planning a trip to what they think of as Miami. If you want to do any exploring, you'll have to drive.

❸ Art Deco district Welcome Center. Run by the Miami Design Preservation League, the center provides information about the buildings in the district. A gift shop sells 1930s–50s art deco memorabilia, posters, and books on Miami's history. Several tours—covering Lincoln Road, Española Way, North Beach, and the entire Art Deco district, among others—start here. You can rent audiotapes for a self-guided tour, join one of the regular morning (Friday through Wednesday) or Thursday-evening walking tours. All of the options provide detailed histories of the art deco hotels. Don't miss the special boat tours during Art Deco Weekend, in early January. ✉ *1001 Ocean Dr., at Barbara Capitman Way (10th St.)* ☎ *305/531–3484* ☒ *Tours $20* ☾ *Sun.–Thurs. 10–7, Fri. and Sat. 10–6.*

❶ Bass Museum of Art. The Bass, in historic Collins Park, is part of the Miami Beach Cultural Park, which includes the Miami City Ballet's Arquitectonica-designed facility and the Miami Beach Regional Library. The original building, constructed of keystone, has unique Maya-inspired carvings. The expansion designed by Japanese architect Arata Isozaki houses another wing and an outdoor sculpture garden. Special exhibitions join a diverse collection of European art. Works on permanent display include *The Holy Family,* a painting by Peter Paul Rubens; *The Tournament,* one of several 16th-century Flemish tapestries; and works by Albrecht Dürer and Henri de Toulouse-Lautrec. Special exhibits often cost a little extra. ✉ *2121 Park Ave., at 21st St.* ☎ *305/673–7530* ⊕ *www.bassmuseum.org* ☒ *$8* ☾ *Wed.–Sun. noon–5.*

❼ Fairchild Tropical Botanic Garden. With 83 acres of lakes, sunken gardens, a 560-foot vine pergola, orchids, bellflowers, coral trees, bougainvillea, rare palms, and flowering trees, Fairchild is the largest tropical botanical garden in the continental United States. The tram tour highlights the best of South Florida's flora; then set off exploring on your own. A 2-acre rain-forest exhibit showcases tropical plants from around the world, complete with a waterfall and stream. The conservatory, Windows to the Tropics, is home to rare tropical plants, including the Titan Arum (*Amorphophallus titanum*), a fast-growing variety that attracted thousands of visitors when it bloomed in 1998. (It was only the sixth documented bloom in this country in the 20th century.) The Keys Coastal Habitat, created in a marsh and mangrove area in 1995 with assistance from the Tropical Audubon Society, provides food and shelter to resident and migratory birds. Check out the Montgomery Botanical Center, a research facility devoted to palms and cycads. Spicing up Fairchild's calendar are plant sales, afternoon teas, and genuinely special events year-round, such as the International Mango Festival the second weekend in July. The excellent bookstore–gift shop carries books on gardening and horticulture, and the Garden Café serves sandwiches and, seasonally, smoothies made from the garden's own crop of tropical fruits. ✉ *10901 Old Cutler Rd., Coral Gables* ☎ *305/667–1651* ⊕ *www.fairchildgarden.org* ☒ *$20* ☾ *Daily 9:30–5.*

❹ Jungle Island. South Florida's original tourist attraction, the park is home to just about every unusual and endangered species you would want to see, including a rare albino alligator, a liger (lion and tiger mix), a 28-foot-long "crocosaur," and a myriad of exotic birds. The most intriguing offerings are the interactive animal tours, including the Lemur Experience ($45 for 45 minutes), in which the highly social primates make themselves at home on your lap or shoulders, and the Penguin Encounter ($30 for 30 minutes), where you can pet and feed warm-weather South African penguins. ✉ *1111 Parrot Jungle Trail, off MacArthur Causeway (I–395)* ☎ *305/400–7000* ⊕ *www.jungleisland. com* ☒ *$29.95, $23.95 for kids, plus $7 parking* ☾ *Daily 10–6.*

② **Lincoln Road Mall.** Renovated in the '60s by architect Morris Lapidus, known for his Miami Modern (MiMo) design, Lincoln Road, a pedestrian mall just a few blocks from the beach and convention center, is fun, lively, and friendly for people old, young, gay, and straight—and their dogs. Folks skate, scoot, bike, or jog here past the electronics stores at the Collins Avenue end toward the chichi boutiques and outdoor cafés heading west. An 18-screen movie theater anchors the west end. The best times to hit the road are during Sunday-morning farmers' markets and on weekend evenings when cafés are bustling; galleries, like pop artist Romero Britto's Britto Central, schedule openings; street performers take the stage; and bookstores, import shops, and clothing stores are open late. ⊠ *Lincoln Rd., between Collins Ave. and Alton Rd.*

⑤ **Little Havana.** More than 40 years ago the tidal wave of Cubans fleeing the Castro regime flooded into an older neighborhood west of downtown Miami. Don't expect a sparkling and lively reflection of 1950s Havana, however. What you will find are ramshackle motels and cluttered storefronts. With a million Cubans and other Latinos—who make up more than half the metropolitan population—dispersed throughout Greater Miami, Little Havana and neighboring East Little Havana remain magnets for Hispanics and Anglos alike, who come to experience the flavor of traditional Cuban culture. That culture, of course, functions in Spanish. Many Little Havana residents and shopkeepers speak little or no English.

Two blocks in the heart of Little Havana, which are known as **Cuban Memorial Boulevard,** are filled with monuments to Cuba's freedom fighters. Among the memorials are the *Eternal Torch of the Brigade 2506,* commemorating those killed in the failed Bay of Pigs invasion of 1961; a bust of 19th-century hero Antonio Maceo; and a bas-relief map of Cuba depicting each of its *municipios.* There's also a bronze statue honoring Bay of Pigs invasion participant Tony Izquierdo. ⊠ *S.W. 13th Ave., south of S.W. 8th St., Little Havana.*

Through the giant storefront windows of **El Credito Cigar Factory** you can see cigars being rolled. One worker, at this family business dating back three generations, learned his trade in prerevolutionary Cuba. Today the tobacco leaf used comes primarily from the Dominican Republic, Honduras, Nicaragua, and Mexico, and wrappers are from Ecuador, making for a truly multinational product. Visitors are invited to check out the walk-in humidor, where the tobacco treasure is stored. ⊠ *1106 S.W. 8th St., near S.W. 11th Ave., Little Havana* ☎ *305/858–4162* ⊕ *www.elcreditocigars.com* ☉ *Weekdays 8–5, Sat. 9–4. Factory closed Sat., but store is open.*

⑥ **Vizcaya Museum and Gardens.** Of the 10,000 people living in Miami between 1912 and 1916, about 1,000 of them were gainfully employed by Chicago industrialist James Deering to build this European-inspired residence. Once comprising 180 acres, this national historic landmark now occupies a 30-acre tract that includes a native hammock and more than 10 acres of formal gardens with fountains overlooking Biscayne Bay. The house, open to the public, contains 70 rooms, 34 of which are filled with paintings, sculpture, antique furniture, and other fine and decorative arts. The collection spans 2,000 years and represents the Renaissance, baroque, rococo, and neoclassical periods. So unusual and impressive is Vizcaya that visitors have included many major heads of state. Guided tours are available. Moonlight tours, offered on evenings that are nearest the full moon, provide a magical look at the gardens; call for reservations. ✉ *3251 S. Miami Ave.* ☎ *305/250–9133* ⊕ *www. vizcayamuseum.org* 🖂 *$15* ⊙ *Daily 9:30–4:30.*

BEACHES

SOUTH BEACH
Fodor's Choice
★

The 10-block stretch of white sandy beach hugging the turquoise waters along **Ocean Drive**—from 5th to 15th streets—is one of the most popular in America, known for drawing unabashedly modelesque sunbathers and posers. The beaches crowd quickly on the weekends with a blend of European tourists, young hipsters, and sun-drenched locals offering Latin flavor. Separating the sand from the traffic of Ocean Drive is palm-fringed Lummus Park, with its volleyball nets and chickee huts (huts made of palmetto thatch over a cypress frame) for shade. The beach at 12th Street is popular with gays, a section often marked with rainbow flags. Locals hang out on 3rd Street beach, where they watch fit Brazilians play foot volley, a variation of volleyball that uses everything but the hands. Because much of South Beach leans toward skimpy sunning—women are often in G-strings and casually topless—many families prefer the tamer sections of Mid- and North Beach. Metered parking spots next to the ocean are a rare find. Instead, opt for a public garage a few blocks away and enjoy the people-watching as you walk to find your perfect spot on the sand. ✉ *Ocean Dr., between 1st and 22nd Sts., Miami Beach* ☎ *305/673–7714.*

SHOPPING

In Greater Miami you're never more than 15 minutes from a major commercial area that serves as both a shopping and entertainment venue for tourists and locals. The shopping is great on a two-block stretch of **Collins Avenue** between 6th and 8th streets. The busy **Lincoln Road Mall** is just a few blocks from the beach and convention center, making it popular with locals and tourists. There's an energy here, especially on weekends, when the pedestrian mall is filled with locals. Creative merchandise, galleries, and a Sunday-morning antiques market can be found among the art galleries and cool cafés. An 18-screen movie theater anchors the west end of the street.

NIGHTLIFE

Miami's pulse pounds with nonstop nightlife that reflects the area's potent cultural mix. On sultry, humid nights with the huge full moon rising out of the ocean and fragrant night-blooming jasmine intoxicating the senses, who can resist Cuban salsa, Jamaican reggae, and Dominican merengue, with some disco and hip-hop thrown in for good measure? When this place throws a party, hips shake, fingers snap, bodies touch. It's no wonder many clubs are still rocking at 5 AM.

WHERE TO EAT

At many of the hottest spots you'll need a reservation to avoid a long wait for a table. And when you get your check, note whether a gratuity is included; most restaurants add 15% (ostensibly for the convenience of—and protection from—Latin-American and European tourists who are used to this

---

PACK IT, POST IT

Pack a pad of Post-It notes when you take a cruise. They come in handy when you need to leave messages for your cabin steward, family, and shipboard friends.

---

practice in their homelands and would not normally tip), but you can reduce or supplement it depending on your opinion of the service. One of Greater Miami's most popular pursuits is bar-hopping. Bars range from intimate enclaves to showy see-and-be-seen lounges to loud, raucous frat parties. There's a New York–style flair to some of the newer lounges, which are increasingly catering to the Manhattan party crowd who escape to South Beach for long weekends. If you're looking for a relatively non-frenetic evening, your best bet is one of the chic hotel bars on Collins Avenue.

For price categories, see ⇨ Dining at the beginning of this chapter.

$$$$
ECLECTIC
Fodor's Choice
★

✕ **Azul.** From chef Clay Conley's exotically rendered Asian-Mediterranean cuisine to the thoughtful service staff who graciously anticipate your broader dining needs, Azul has sumptuously conquered the devil in the details. Does your sleeveless blouse leave you too cold to properly appreciate the Moroccan lamb and seared red snapper? Forgot your reading glasses and can't decipher the hanger steak with foie-gras sauce? Request a pair from the host. A risotto with Alba white truffles is typical of the way Azul will reach across the globe for the finest ingredients. The Moroccan-inspired Colorado lamb with eggplant and harissa is a perennial favorite. There is a lot of new competition for dining attention in town, but Azul is still at the pinnacle of its game. ⊠ *Mandarin Oriental Hotel, 500 Brickell Key Dr., Downtown Miami* ☎ *305/913–8358* ⚐ *Reservations essential* ▤ *AE, MC, V* ☉ *Closed Sun. No lunch weekends.*

$
AMERICAN
Fodor's Choice
★

✕ **Big Pink.** The decor in this innovative, super-popular diner may remind you of a roller-skating rink—everything is pink Lucite, stainless steel, and campy (think sports lockers as decorative touches)—and the menu is 3 feet tall, complete with a table of contents. Food is solidly all-American, with dozens of tasty sandwiches, pizzas, turkey or beef burgers, and side dishes, each and every one composed with gourmet flair. Big Pink also makes a great spot for brunch. ⊠ *157 Collins Ave., South Beach* ⊕ *www.mylesrestaurantgroup.com* ☎ *305/532–4700* ▤ *AE, MC, V.*

$$$$
SEAFOOD

✕ **Nemo.** The SoFi (South of 5th Street) neighborhood may have emerged as a South Beach hot spot, but Nemo's location is not why this casually comfortable restaurant receives rave reviews. It's the menu, which often changes but always delivers, blending Caribbean, Asian, Mediterranean, and Middle Eastern influences and providing an explosion of cultures in each bite. Popular appetizers include citrus-cured salmon rolls with tobiko caviar and wasabi mayo, and crispy duck-leg confit served with lentils in a tangy pineapple sauce. Main courses might include wok-charred salmon or grilled Indian-spice pork chop. Bright colors and copper fixtures highlight the tree-shaded courtyard. ⊠ *100 Collins Ave., South Beach* ☎ *305/532–4550* ⊕ *www.mylesrestaurantgroup.com* ⊟ *AE, DC, MC, V.*

WHERE TO STAY

Staying in downtown Miami will put you close to the cruise terminals, but there is little to do at night. South Beach is the center of the action in Miami Beach, but it's fairly distant from the port. Staying in Miami Beach, but north of South Beach's Art Deco District, will put you on the beach but nominally closer to the port.

For price categories, see ⇨ *Lodging at the beginning of this chapter.*

$$ ☷ **Doubletree Grand Hotel Biscayne Bay.** Like the Biscayne Bay Marriott, this elegant waterfront option is at the north end of downtown off a scenic marina, and near many of Miami's headline attractions: the Port of Miami, Bayside, the Arena, and the Carnival Center. Rooms are spacious, and most have a view of Biscayne Bay and the port. Some suites have full kitchens. You can rent Jet Skis or take deep-sea-fishing trips from the marina. **Pros:** great bay views; deli and market on-site. **Cons:** need a cab to get around. ⊠ *1717 N. Bayshore Dr., Downtown Miami* ☎ *305/372–0313 or 800/222–8733* ⊕ *www.doubletree.com* ⇝ *152 suites* ♿ *In-room: a/c, safe, kitchen (some), Wi-Fi. In-hotel: restaurant, room service, bar, pool, gym, spa, Wi-Fi hotspot, parking (paid)* ⊟ *AE, D, DC, MC, V.*

$$$$ ☷ **Loews Miami Beach Hotel.** The oldest of South Beach's "new hotels," Loews Miami Beach is marvelous for families, businesspeople, and groups. The 800-room mega-hotel combines top-tier amenities, a massive new spa, a great pool, and a direct beachfront setting in its pair of enormous 12- and 18-story towers. When it was built in 1998, Loews managed not only to snag 99 feet of beach, but also to take over the vacant St. Moritz next door and restore it to its original 1939 art deco beauty. The entire complex combines boutique charm with updated opulence. How big is it? The Loews has 85,000 square feet of meeting space and an enormous ocean-view grand ballroom. Emeril Lagasse opened a restaurant here, and a three-story spa has 15 treatment rooms and a state-of-the-art fitness center. In the grand lobby you'll find a dozen black-suited staffers behind the counter, and a half dozen other bellboys and valets. Rooms are great: contemporary and very comfortable, with flat-screen TVs and high-end amenities. If you like big hotels with all the services, this is your choice in South Beach. **Pros:** top-notch amenities include a beautiful oceanfront pool and immense spa. **Cons:** intimacy is lost due to its large size. ⊠ *1601 Collins Ave., South Beach* ☎ *305/604–1601 or 800/235–6397* ⊕ *www.loewshotels.com/ miamibeach* ⇝ *733 rooms, 57 suites* ♿ *In-room: a/c, Internet, Wi-Fi. In-hotel: 3 restaurants, room service, bars, pool, gym, spa, beachfront, laundry service, Internet terminal, parking (paid), Wi-Fi hotspot, some pets allowed* ⊟ *AE, D, DC, MC, V.*

$$ ⊡ **The Standard.** An extension of André Balazs's trendy budget hotel chain, the Standard is a Hollywood newcomer that set up shop a few minutes from South Beach on an island just over the Venetian Causeway. The message: we'll do what we please, and the cool kids will follow. The scene is trendy 30- and 40-year-olds interested in the hotel's many "do-it-yourself" spa activities, including mud bathing, scrubbing with sea salts, soaking in hot or arctic-cold waters, and yoga. An 8-foot, 103-degree cascade into a Roman hot tub is typical of the handful of adult pleasures spread around the pool deck. An informal restaurant overlooks the bay's Mediterranean-style mansions and the cigarette boats that float past. If you choose, you can go kayaking around the island. On the hotel facade you'll see the monumental signage of a bygone occupant, the Lido Spa Hotel, and the much smaller sign of its current occupant, hung, with a wink, upside down. The rooms are small and simple, though they have thoughtful touches like a picnic basket and embroidered fabric covers for the small flat-screen TVs. First-floor rooms have outdoor soaking tubs but very limited privacy, so few take that plunge. **Pros:** interesting island location; free bike and kayak rentals; swank pool scene; great spa; inexpensive. **Cons:** removed from South Beach nightlife; small rooms with no views; outdoor tubs are gimmicks; mediocre service. ⊠ *40 Island Ave., Belle Isle* ☎ *305/673–1717* ⊕ *www.standardhotel.com* ⤳ *104 rooms, 1 suite* ⚭ *In-room: a/c, safe, refrigerator, DVD, Internet, Wi-Fi. In-hotel: restaurant, room service, bars, pool, gym, spa, water sports, bicycles, laundry service, Wi-Fi hotspot, parking (paid), some pets allowed, no kids under 14* ▭ *AE, D, DC, MC, V.*

MOBILE, ALABAMA

Updated by
Rena Havner-
Philips

Fort Condé was the name given by the French in 1711 to the site known today as Mobile; around it blossomed the first white settlement in what is now Alabama. For eight years it was the capital of the French colonial empire, and it remained under French control until 1763, long after the capital had moved to New Orleans. Mobile, known as the "Port City"—not to mention the birthplace of Mardi Gras—is noted for its tree-lined boulevards fanning westward from the riverfront. In the heart of busy downtown is Bienville Square, a park with an ornate cast-iron fountain and shaded by centuries-old live oaks. One of the city's main thoroughfares, Dauphin Street, has many thriving restaurants, bars, and shops.

THE CRUISE PORT

Carnival Cruises bases one ship here year-round, doing shorter (four- and five-day) Mexico itineraries as well as several seven-day cruises to Jamaica and the Cayman Islands. The cruise terminal is near the downtown area. Free shuttles from Mobile's public transit system, Moda, are provided to the cruise terminal from throughout downtown Mobile on days when ships are in port. It's a good home port to consider if you want to drive, but it's less convenient by air, with just a few airlines

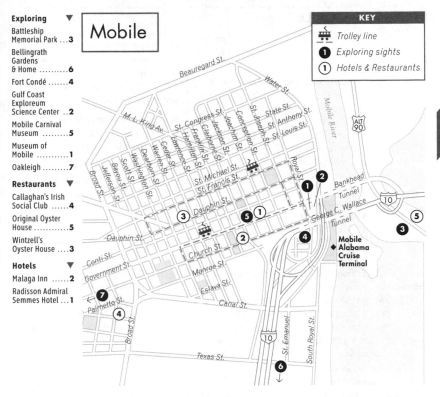

KEY

🚃 *Trolley line*

❶ *Exploring sights*

① *Hotels & Restaurants*

flying to the Mobile Regional Airport; however, the Biloxi and Pensacola airports are a relatively short drive away.

Contacts Mobile Alabama Cruise Terminal (✉ *201 S. Water St., Mobile* ☎ *251/338–7447* ⊕ *www.shipmobile.com*).

AIRPORT TRANSFERS

Taxis are available to the cruise terminal, or you can call the Mobile Regional Airport Shuttle, which will transport you for $13 per person ($25 round-trip). Mobile Bay Transportation Company also operates airport transfers. A taxi costs about $30 each way, but that is for the trip not per-passenger.

Contacts Mobile Bay Transportation Company (☎ *251/633–5693 or 800/272–6234* ⊕ *www.mobilebaytransportation.com*). **Mobile Regional Airport Shuttle** (☎ *251/633–0313 or 800/357–5373* ⊕ *www.mobairport.com*).

PARKING

Parking is available in a garage next to the cruise terminal. It costs $15 a day for cars, $30 for RVs. You can pay by cash or credit card.

VISITOR INFORMATION

Mobile Bay Convention & Visitor's Bureau (✉ *1 S. Water St., Mobile* ☎ *251/208–2000 or 800/566–2453* ⊕ *www.mobilebay.org*).

EXPLORING MOBILE

Numbers in the margin refer to points of interest on the Mobile map.

❸ Battleship Memorial Park. Mobile Bay, east of downtown, is the site of the 155-acre park where the battleship USS *Alabama* is anchored. A self-guided tour gives a fascinating glimpse into the World War II vessel, which had a crew of 2,500. Drydocked next to it is the USS *Drum*, a World War II submarine. Other exhibits include the B-52 bomber *Calamity Jane*. ✉ *2703 Battleship Pkwy., Mobile* ☎ *251/433–2703 or 800/426–4929* ⊕ *www.ussalabama.com* ✑ *$12* ☉ *Apr.–Sept., daily 8–6; Oct.–Mar., daily 8–4.*

> ### MOBILE BEST BETS
>
> ■ **Bellingrath Gardens.** One of the finest gardens in the South is just outside Mobile.
>
> ■ **Battleship Memorial Park.** Many people come to Mobile just to tour the USS *Alabama.*
>
> ■ **Oakleigh.** This well-preserved antebellum home is furnished with period antiques; it's a great experience if you like history.

❻ Bellingrath Gardens and Home. One of the most popular gardens in the South is Bellingrath, famous for its magnificent azaleas, which are part of 65 acres of gardens set amid a 905-acre semitropical landscape. Showtime for the azaleas is mid- to late-March, when some 250,000 plantings of 200 different species are ablaze with color. But Bellingrath is a year-round wonder, with more than 75 varieties of roses blooming in summer, 60,000 chrysanthemum plants cascading in fall, and red fields of poinsettias brightening winter. Countless species and flowering plants spring up along the Fowl River, surround streams, and a lake populated by ducks and swans. A free map lets you plan your own strolls along flagstone paths across charming bridges. In April and October large numbers of migratory birds drop by. You can also visit the home of Coca-Cola bottling pioneer Walter D. Bellingrath. Forty-five-minute boat cruises on the Fowl River aboard the *Southern Belle* leave from the dock next to the home several times daily from March through Thanksgiving. Take I–10 West to Exit 15, then follow CR 59 South to Theodore. ✉ *12401 Bellingrath Gardens Rd., Theodore* ☎ *251/973–2217, 800/247–8420, 800/247–8420 for boat cruises* ⊕ *www.bellingrath.org* ✑ *Gardens $11; gardens and home $19; gardens, home, and cruise $27* ☉ *Gardens daily 8–5, home daily 9–4.*

❹ Ft. Condé. In 1711 France built this fort that would one day expand and become Mobile. The city's French origins endure in its creole cuisine. Now, 150 years after the fort was destroyed, its remains were discovered during construction of the I–10 interchange. A reconstructed portion houses the city's **visitor center,** as well as a museum. Costumed guides conduct tours. ✉ *150 S. Royal St., Mobile* ☎ *251/208–7304* ⊕ *www. museumofmobile.com* ✑ *Free* ☉ *Daily 8–5.*

❷ Gulf Coast Exploreum Science Center. Near Ft. Condé, Mobile's science museum for children hosts traveling exhibits and an IMAX dome theater. ✉ *65 Government St., Mobile* ☎ *251/208–6883 or 877/625–4386* ⊕ *www.exploreum.com* ✑ *Museum $14, IMAX $8, both $18*

Fodor's Choice
★

admission charges are sometimes increased for special exhibitions ⊙ *Weekdays 9–5, Sat. 10–5, Sun. noon–6.*

❺ Mobile Carnival Museum. Mobile celebrates its heritage in this converted 1870 town house dedicated to all things Mardi Gras. The pre-Lenten festival was first celebrated in the

> **FRESH, WRINKLE-FREE**
>
> You can tuck fabric-softener sheets between garments as you pack to keep your clothing smelling fresh during travel. Dry-cleaning bags are good for keeping out wrinkles.

New World here in Mobile in 1703, and the museum allows the party to continue 365 days a year. Displays include regal costumes of past kings and queens, traditional Mardi Gras "throws" (items that are thrown from the floats during parades), and even full-sized floats. ⊠ *355 Government St.* *251/432–3324* ⊕ *www.mobilecarnivalmuseum.com* *$5* ⊙ *Mon., Wed., Fri., Sat. 9–4.*

❻ Museum of Mobile. The museum opened in 2001 in the renovated circa-1857 Southern Market/Old City Hall building next to the Exploreum. Interactive exhibits and special collections of antique silver, weapons, and more tell the 300-year history of Mobile. ⊠ *111 S. Royal St., Mobile* ☎ *251/208–7569* ⊕ *www.museumofmobile.com* ⌂ *$5* ⊙ *Mon.–Sat. 9–5, Sun. 1–5.*

❼ ★ Oakleigh. About 1½ mi (2 ½ km) from Ft. Condé, in the heart of the historic Oakleigh Garden District, is an antebellum Greek Revival–style mansion built between 1833 and 1838. Costumed guides give tours of the home, which has fine period furniture, portraits, silver, jewelry, kitchen implements, toys, and more. Tickets include a tour of neighboring **Cox-Deasy House,** an 1850s cottage furnished with simple 19th-century pieces. ⊠ *300 Oakleigh Pl., Mobile* ☎ *251/432–1281* ⊕ *www. historicmobile.org* ⌂ *$7* ⊙ *Thurs.–Sat. 10–4, Sun. 1–4; Mon.–Wed. by appointment.*

SHOPPING

Most shopping in Mobile is in malls and shopping centers in the suburbs. Stores are generally open Monday to Saturday 10–9, Sunday noon–6. Antiques buffs may be interested in Mobile's many antiques stores that are in the Loop area of midtown (where Government Street, Airport Boulevard, and Dauphin Island Parkway converge); several shops are within walking distance of each other.

Bel Air Mall (⊠ *3299 Bel Air Mall* ☎ *251/478–1893*) has more than 130 stores, including Belk's, Dillard's, Sears, JCPenney, and Target. **Eastern Shore Centre** (⊠ *30500 State Hwy. 181, at I–10, Spanish Fort* ☎ *251/625–0060*) is one of the newest shopping complex in the Mobile area, with 75 stores, including a Dillard's. It's about 10 minutes from downtown.

NIGHTLIFE

Most of Mobile's nightlife centers around the downtown's former commercial district, Dauphin Street, which today has a number of restaurants and nightspots spread out over several blocks. Mobilians have taken to calling the area LoDa, short for Lower Dauphin. In midtown Mobile the **Double Olive** (✉ 2033 Airport Blvd. ☎ 251/450–5001) is an artsy, urbane martini bar that draws hip crowds. **Soul Kitchen** (✉ 219 Dauphin St. ☎ 251/433–5958) is one of several almost indistinguishable bars that host local bands as well as a few national ones, drawing crowds of twentysomethings on Friday and Saturday nights.

> **CAUTION**
>
> Notify the cruise line of any special dietary restrictions when booking your cruise, and then follow up on the arrangements a couple of months before boarding.

WHERE TO EAT

For price categories, see ⇨ Dining at the beginning of this chapter.

$–$$ ✕ **Callaghan's Irish Social Club.** A neighborhood pub situated in the his-
AMERICAN toric Oakleigh neighborhood near downtown, Callaghan's is known for having one of the best burgers in town. But you also can't go wrong with a chicken club and a side of cucumber and tomato salad. Regulars enjoy the casual atmosphere, local music acts on the weekends, and brunch on Sundays. ✉ 916 Charleston St., Oakleigh ☎ 251/433–9374 ▭ AE, D, DC, MC, V.

$–$$ ✕ **Original Oyster House.** Destroyed during Hurricane Katrina, this
SEAFOOD Mobile Bay Causeway restaurant relocated a few months later about a mile from its original site, causing seafood lovers, who continue to pack the restaurant, to breathe a collective sigh of relief. Specialties include fried crab claws, Mike's grilled shrimp, shrimp and grits, and blackened mahimahi topped with fried crawfish tails and tasso ham cream sauce. ✉ 3733 Battleship Pkwy., Spanish Fort ☎ 251/626–2188 ▭ AE, D, MC, V ⊘ Closed Mon.

$–$$ ✕ **Wintzell's Oyster House.** "Oysters—fried, steamed, or nude" is the
SEAFOOD motto for this downtown Mobile institution. Founded in 1938 by Oliver Wintzell, the restaurant is in the same location and with few cosmetic changes since it was founded, the walls still covered by Oliver's homespun sayings. You can get your oysters by the dozen or half-dozen, but won't go wrong sampling any of the seafood on the menu or simply enjoying a cup of homemade gumbo. ✉ 605 Dauphin St. ☎ 251/432–4605 ▭ AE, D, DC, MC, V.

WHERE TO STAY

Several local hotels offer cruise packages that include lodging, parking for the duration of your cruise, and a shuttle to the cruise terminal.

For price categories, see ⇨ Lodging at the beginning of this chapter.

$–$$ ▥ **Malaga Inn.** A delightful, romantic getaway, this place comprises two town houses built by a wealthy landowner in 1862. The lobby is furnished with 19th-century antiques and opens onto a landscaped central courtyard with a fountain. The rooms are large, airy, and furnished with antiques. The Malaga is on a quiet street downtown, within walking distance of the Museum of Mobile and the Gulf Coast Exploreum, and offers a cruise package. ✉ *359 Church St.* ☎ *251/438–4701 or 800/235–1586* ⊕ *www.malagainn.com* ☛ *35 rooms, 3 suites* ♿ *In-room: Wi-Fi. In-hotel: pool, Wi-Fi* ▤ *AE, D, MC, V.*

$–$$ 🖼 **Radisson Admiral Semmes Hotel.** This restored 1940 hotel in the historic district is a favorite with local politicians. It's also popular with partygoers, particularly during Mardi Gras, because of its excellent location directly on the parade route. The spacious, high-ceiling rooms have a burgundy-and-green color scheme and are furnished in Queen Anne and Chippendale styles. ✉ *251 Government St.,* ☎ *251/432–8000 or 800/333–3333* ⊕ *www.radisson.com* ☛ *148 rooms, 22 suites* ♿ *In-room: refrigerator, Internet. In-hotel: restaurant, bar, pool, laundry service, Wi-Fi* ▤ *AE, D, DC, MC, V.*

3

NEW ORLEANS, LOUISIANA

The spiritual and cultural heart of New Orleans is the French Quarter, where the city was settled by the French in 1718. You could easily spend several days visiting museums, shops, and eateries in this area, but you can get a small sense of the place quickly. If you have time, the rest of the city's neighborhoods, radiating out from this focal point, also make for rewarding rambling. The mansion-lined streets of the Garden District and Uptown, the aboveground cemeteries that dot the city, and the open air along Lake Pontchartrain provide a nice balance to the commercialization of the Quarter. Despite its sprawling size, New Orleans has a small-town vibe, perhaps due to locals' shared cultural habits and history.

ESSENTIALS

HOURS Shops in the French Quarter tend to be open late, but stores in most of the malls close by 9. Restaurants tend to be open late as well.

INTERNET **French Quarter Postal Emporium** (✉ *1000 Bourbon St.* ☎ *504/525–6651* ⊕ *www.frenchquarterpostal.com*) offers Internet service and is also a mailing center.

VISITOR **New Orleans Convention & Visitors Bureau** (✉ *2020 St. Charles Ave., Garden* INFORMATION *District* ☎ *800/672–6124 or 504/566–5011* ⊕ *www.neworleanscvb.com*). **New Orleans Multicultural Tourism Network** (⊕ *www.soulofneworleans.com*).

THE CRUISE PORT

The Julia Street Cruise Terminal is at the end of Julia Street on the Mississippi River; the Erato Street Terminal is just to the north. Both terminals are behind the Ernest M. Morial Convention Center. You can walk to the French Quarter from here in about 10 minutes; it's a short taxi ride to the Quarter or nearby hotels. Carnival, Royal Caribbean, and Norwegian base ships here at least part of the year.

If you are driving, you'll probably approach New Orleans on I-10. Take the Business 90 West/Westbank exit, locally known as Pontchartrain Expressway, and proceed to the Tchoupitoulas Street/South Peters Street exit. Continue to Convention Center Boulevard, where you will take

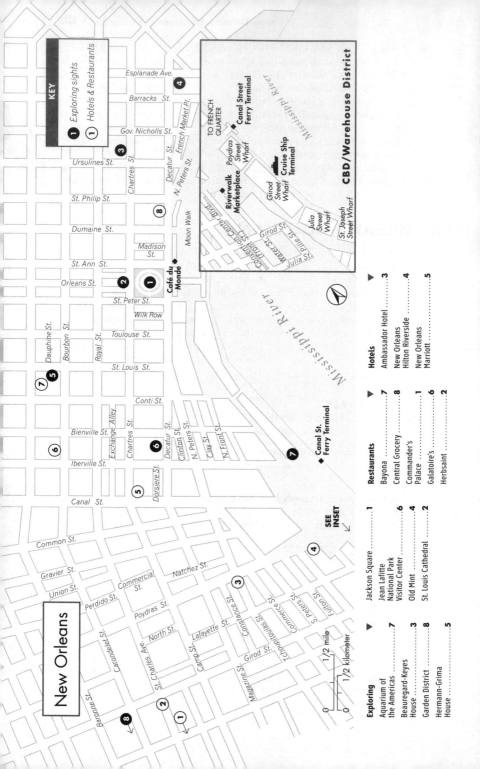

New Orleans

KEY
- 1 Exploring sights
- 1 Hotels & Restaurants

CBD/Warehouse District

Mississippi River

Esplanade Ave.
Barracks St.
Gov. Nicholls St.
Ursulines St.
St. Philip St.
Dumaine St.
St. Ann St.
Orleans St.
St. Peter St.
Wilk Row
Toulouse St.
St. Louis St.
Conti St.
Bienville St.
Iberville St.
Canal St.
Common St.
Gravier St.
Union St.
Perdido St.
Poydras St.
Commercial St.
Natchez St.
Lafayette St.

Café du Monde
Madison St.
Moon Walk

Chartres St.
Decatur St.
French Market Pl.
N. Peters St.

Dauphine St.
Bourbon St.
Royal St.
Exchange Alley
Chartres St.
Decatur St.
Clinton St.
N. Peters St.
Clay St.
N. Front St.
Dorsiere St.

To French Quarter
Canal Street Ferry Terminal
Poydras Street Wharf
Cruise Ship Terminal
Riverwalk Marketplace
Girod Street Wharf
Julia Street Wharf
St. Joseph Street Wharf

Girod St.
Pilie St.
Water St.
Convention Center Blvd.
Julia St.

Mississippi River

Canal St. Ferry Terminal

SEE INSET

0   1/2 mile
0   1/2 kilometer

St. Charles Ave.
Carondelet St.
Baronne St.
Camp St.
Magazine St.
Girod St.
Tchoupitoulas St.
Commerce St.
Constance St.
S. Peters St.
Fulton St.
North St.

Exploring
- Aquarium of the Americas 7
- Beauregard-Keyes House 3
- Garden District 8
- Hermann-Grima House 5
- Jackson Square 1
- Jean Lafitte National Park Visitor Center 6
- Old Mint 4
- St. Louis Cathedral 2

Restaurants
- Bayona 7
- Central Grocery 8
- Commander's Palace 1
- Galatoire's 6
- Herbsaint 2

Hotels
- Ambassador Hotel 3
- New Orleans Hilton Riverside 4
- New Orleans Marriott 5

a right turn. Continue to Henderson Street, where you will turn left, and then continue to Port of New Orleans Place. Take a left on Port of New Orleans Place to Julia Street Terminals 1 and 2, or take a right to get to the Robin Street Wharf.

Port Contacts Port of New Orleans
(✉ *Port of New Orleans Pl. at foot of Julia St.* ☎ *504/522–2551* ⊕ *www.portno.com*).

AIRPORT TRANSFERS
Shuttle-bus service to and from the airport and the cruise port is available through Airport Shuttle New Orleans. Buses leave regularly from the ground level near the baggage claim. Return trips to the airport need to be booked in advance. The cost one-way is $15 per person, and the trip takes about 45 minutes.

A cab ride to or from the airport from uptown or downtown New Orleans costs $28 for the first two passengers and $12 for each additional passenger; there's a fuel surcharge of $1 per trip (not per passenger). At the airport, pick-up is on the lower level, outside the baggage claim area. There may be an additional charge for extra baggage.

Contacts Airport Shuttle New Orleans (☎ *504/522–3500*).

PARKING
If you are spending some time in the city before or after your cruise, finding a parking space is fairly easy in most of the city, except for the French Quarter, where meter maids are plentiful and tow trucks eager. If in doubt about a space, pass it up and pay to use a parking lot. Avoid parking spaces at corners and curbs: less than 15 feet between your car and the corner will result in a ticket. Watch for temporary NO PARKING signs, which pop up along parade routes and film shoots. Long-term and overnight parking are extremely expensive at hotels and garages. Parking for the duration of your cruise is available for $16 per night and is on Erato Street; if you want, SeaCaps will take your bags directly to the ship so you just have to deal with your hand luggage. RVs can park in a lot on Poydras Street next to Terminal 2 at the Julia Street dock for $32 per night.

NEW ORLEANS BEST BETS

■ **Aquarium of the Americas.** Especially good for families is this fantastic aquarium near the city's convention center.

■ **Eating Well.** A highlight in New Orleans is dining. If you ever wanted to splurge on a great restaurant meal, this is the place to do it. At the very least, have a beignet at Café du Mond.

■ **Hermann-Grima House.** This is one of the best-preserved historic homes in the French Quarter.

EXPLORING NEW ORLEANS

Bullets in the margins refer to points of interest on the New Orleans map.

The **French Quarter,** the oldest part of the city, lives up to all you've heard: it's alive with the sights, sounds, odors, and experiences of a major entertainment hub. At some point, ignore your better judgment and take a stroll down **Bourbon Street,** past the bars, restaurants, music clubs, and novelty shops that have given this strip its reputation as the playground of the South. Be sure to find time to stop at Café du Monde for chicory-laced coffee and beignets. With its beautifully landscaped gardens surrounding elegant antebellum homes, the **Garden District** is mostly residential, but most home-owners do not mind your enjoying the sights from outside the cast-iron fences surrounding their magnificent properties.

⑦ **Aquarium of the Americas.** Power failures during Hurricane Katrina
ᶜᵇ resulted in the major loss of the Aquarium's collection of more than
Fodor'sChoice 7,000 aquatic creatures. In a dramatic gesture of solidarity, aquariums
★ around the country joined together to repopulate its stock. Each of the four major exhibit areas—the Amazon Rain Forest, the Caribbean Reef, the Mississippi River, and the Gulf Coast—has fish and animals native to that environment. A fun exhibit called Beyond Green houses more than 25 frog species and includes informative displays. The aquarium's spectacular design allows you to feel part of the watery worlds by providing close-up encounters with the inhabitants. A gift shop and café are on the premises. You can get a combined ticket for the aquarium and the Audubon Zoo, including a round-trip cruise down the river. ⊠ *1 Canal St., French Quarter* ☎ *504/581–4629 or 800/774–7394* ⊕ *www. auduboninstitute.org* ⊠ *Aquarium $13.50; combination ticket with IMAX $24; combination ticket for aquarium, zoo, and insectarium $30* ☉ *Aquarium Tues.–Sun. 10–5.*

③ **Beauregard-Keyes House.** This stately 19th-century mansion with period furnishings was the temporary home of Confederate general P. G. T. Beauregard. The house and grounds had severely deteriorated by the 1940s, when the well-known novelist Frances Parkinson Keyes moved in and helped restore it. Her studio at the back of the large courtyard remains intact, complete with family photos, original manuscripts, and her doll, fan, and teapot collections. Keyes wrote 40 novels in this studio, all in longhand, among them the local favorite, *Dinner at Antoine's*. The house suffered some roof damage during the storm, resulting in water stains along the dining-room ceiling. Undaunted, the staff has reopened the site and continues its normal tour schedule. If you do not have time to tour the house, take a peek through the gates at the beautiful walled garden at the corner of Chartres and Ursulines streets. Landscaped in the same sun pattern as Jackson Square, the garden is in bloom throughout the year. ⊠ *1113 Chartres St., French Quarter* ☎ *504/523–7257* ⊠ *$10* ☉ *Mon.–Sat. 10–3, tours on the hr.*

⑧ **Garden District.** The Garden District is divided into two sections by Jackson Avenue. Upriver from Jackson is the wealthy **Upper Garden District,** where the homes are meticulously kept. Below Jackson, the **Lower Garden District** is considerably rougher. Though the homes here are often just as structurally beautiful, most of them lack the recent restorations of those of the Upper Garden District. The streets are also less well patrolled; wander cautiously. **Magazine Street,** lined with antiques shops and coffeehouses (ritzier along the Upper Garden District, hipper along the Lower Garden District), serves as a southern border to the Garden District, and St. Charles Avenue forms the northern border.

⑤ **Hermann-Grima House.** One of the largest and best-preserved examples of American architecture in the Quarter, this Georgian-style house has the only restored private stable and the only working 1830s Creole kitchen in the Quarter. American architect William Brand built the house in 1831. The house fortunately sustained only minor damage during the storm and is open for visits and tours. Cooking demonstrations on the open hearth are held here all day Thursday from October through May. You'll want to check the gift shop, which has many local crafts and books. ⊠ *820 St. Louis St., French Quarter* ☎ *504/525–5661* ⊠ *$10, combination ticket with the Gallier House $18* ⊘ *Tours Mon., Tues., Thurs., Fri. 10, 11, noon, 1, 2, Sat. noon, 1, 2, 3.*

FodorsChoice ★

3

❶ **Jackson Square.** Surrounded by historic buildings and filled with plenty of the city's atmospheric street life, the heart of the French Quarter is today a beautifully landscaped park. Originally called the Place d'Armes, the square was founded in 1718 as a military parade ground. It was also the site of public executions carried out in various styles, including burning at the stake, beheading, breaking on the wheel, and hanging. A **statue of Andrew Jackson,** victorious leader of the Battle of New Orleans in the War of 1812, commands the center of the square; the park was renamed for him in the 1850s. President George W. Bush made a major address to the nation here after Katrina, in which he celebrated the importance of the city in the history of the country and the federal government's commitment to its recovery.

Among the notable buildings around the square are **St. Louis Cathedral** and **Faulkner House.** Two Spanish colonial–style buildings, the **Cabildo** and the **Presbytère,** flank the cathedral. The handsome rows of brick apartments on each side of the square are the **Pontalba Buildings.** The park is landscaped in a sun pattern, with walkways set like rays streaming out from the center, a popular garden design in the royal court of King Louis XIV, the Sun King. In the daytime, dozens of artists hang their paintings on the park fence and set up outdoor studios where they work on canvases or offer to draw portraits of passersby. These artists are easy to engage in conversation and are knowledgeable about many aspects of the Quarter and New Orleans. You can also be entertained by musicians, mimes, tarot-card readers, and magicians who perform on the flagstone pedestrian mall surrounding the square, many of them day and night. ⊠ *French Quarter* ⊘ *Park daily 8 AM–dusk; flagstone paths on park's periphery open 24 hrs.*

❻ **Jean Lafitte National Park Visitor Center.** This center has free visual and sound exhibits on the customs of various communities throughout the state, as well as information-rich daily history tours of the French Quarter. The one-hour daily tour leaves at 9:30 AM; tickets are handed out one per person (you must be present to get a ticket), beginning at 9 AM, for that day's tours only. Arrive at least 15 minutes before tour time to be sure of a spot. The office also supervises and provides information on Jean Lafitte National Park Barataria Unit, a nature preserve (complete with alligators) across the river from New Orleans, and the Chalmette Battlefield, where the Battle of New Orleans was fought in the War of 1812. Each year in January, near the anniversary of the battle, a reenactment is staged at the Chalmette site. ✉ *419 Decatur St., French Quarter* ☎ *504/589–2636* ⊙ *Daily 9–5.*

4 Old Mint. Minting began in 1838 in
★ this ambitious, Ionic structure, a project of President Andrew Jackson. The New Orleans mint was to provide currency for the South and the West, which it did until the Confederacy began minting its own currency here in 1861. When supplies ran out, the building served as a barracks, then a prison, for Confederate soldiers; the production of U.S. coins recommenced only in

1879. It stopped again, for good, in 1909. After years of neglect, the federal government handed the Old Mint over to Louisiana in 1966; the state now uses the quarters to exhibit collections of the Louisiana State Museum. At the Barracks Street entrance, notice the one remaining sample of the mint's old walls—it'll give you an idea of the building's deterioration before its restoration. Hurricane Katrina ripped away a large section of the copper roof, and for months the twisted metal remained on the ground here, one of the most dramatic reminders of the storm in the French Quarter. Repairs to the building have begun in earnest, but the museum's reopening date remains in question. At the foot of Esplanade Avenue, notice the memorial to the French rebels against early Spanish rule, the first instance of a New World rebellion against a European power. The rebel leaders were executed on this spot and give nearby Frenchmen Street its name. The principal exhibit here is the **New Orleans Jazz Collection,** a brief but evocative tour through the history of traditional New Orleans jazz. In addition to informative written explanations, a wealth of artifacts movingly tells the story of the emergent art form. Among the gems are the soprano saxophone owned by Sidney Bechet, the trumpets of Pops Celestin and Dizzy Gillespie, and the cornet given to Louis Armstrong at the juvenile home where he spent much of his youth. Across the hall from the jazz exhibit are a few rooms filled with the beautiful and locally treasured Newcomb pottery. ✉ *400 Esplanade Ave., French Quarter* ☎ *504/568–6968* ⌦ *Old US Mint $5.*

2 St. Louis Cathedral. The oldest active cathedral in the United States, this church at the heart of the Old City is named for the 13th-century French king who led two crusades. The current building, which replaced two structures destroyed by fire, dates from 1794 (although it was remodeled and enlarged in 1851). The austere interior is brightened by murals covering the ceiling and stained-glass windows along the first floor. Pope John Paul II held a prayer service for clergy here during his New Orleans visit in 1987; to honor the occasion, the pedestrian mall in front of the cathedral was renamed Place Jean Paul Deux. Nearly every evening in December brings a free concert held inside the cathedral. The statue of the Sacred Heart of Jesus dominates **St. Anthony's Garden,** which extends behind the rectory to Royal Street. This statue was damaged during the storm, losing the thumb and forefinger of one hand. The pieces have been recovered, but the statue's injuries have yet to be repaired. The garden is also the site of a monument to 30 members of a French ship who died in a yellow-fever epidemic in 1857. ✉ *615 Père Antoine Alley, French Quarter* ☎ *504/525–9585* 🎫 *Free.*

SHOPPING

The fun of shopping in New Orleans is in the regional items available throughout the city, in the smallest shops or the biggest department stores. You can take home some of the flavor of the city: its pralines (pecan candies), seafood (packaged to go), Louisiana red beans and rice, coffee (pure or with chicory), and creole and Cajun spices (cayenne pepper, chili, and garlic). There are even packaged mixes of such local favorites as jambalaya, gumbo, beignets, and the sweet red local cocktail called the Hurricane. Cookbooks also share the secrets of preparing distinctive New Orleans dishes. The French Quarter is well known for its fine antiques shops, located mainly on Royal and Chartres streets. The main shopping areas in the city are the French Quarter, with narrow, picturesque streets lined with specialty, gift, fashion, and antiques shops and art galleries; the Central Business District (CBD), populated mostly with jewelry, specialty, and department stores; the Warehouse District, best known for contemporary arts galleries and cultural museums; Magazine Street, home to antiques shops, art galleries, home-furnishing stores, dining venues, fashion boutiques, and specialty shops; and the Riverbend/Maple Street area, filled with clothing stores and some specialty shops.

Jax Brewery (✉ *600 Decatur St., French Quarter* ☎ *504/566–7245* ⊕ *www.jacksonbrewery.com*) was a factory for Jax beer, but now holds a Jax Beer museum and an upscale mall filled with both local shops and national chains. **Riverwalk Marketplace** (✉ *1 Poydras St., Warehouse* ☎ *504/522–1555* ⊕ *www.riverwalkmarketplace.com*), with 180-some stores, was built in what once was the International Pavilion of the 1984 World's Fair.

NIGHTLIFE

No American city places such a premium on pleasure as New Orleans. From swank hotel lounges to sweaty dance clubs, refined jazz clubs and raucous Bourbon Street bars, this city is serious about frivolity. And famous for it. Partying is more than an occasional indulgence in this city—it's a lifestyle. Bars tend to open in the early afternoon and stay open into the morning hours; live music, though, follows a more restrained schedule. Some jazz spots and clubs in the French Quarter stage evening sets around 6 PM or 9 PM; at a few clubs, such as the Palm Court, the bands actually finish by 11 PM. But this is the exception: for the most part, gigs begin between 10 and 11 PM, and locals rarely emerge for an evening out before 10. Keep in mind that the lack of legal closing time means that shows advertised for 11 may not start until after midnight.

Harrah's New Orleans. Commanding the foot of Canal Street, this Beaux Arts–style casino is the largest in the South. Its 100,000 square feet hold 2,900 slots and 120 gaming tables. There's an upscale steak restaurant run by local celebrity-chef John Besh. Valet parking is available. ⊠ *4 Canal St., CBD* ☎ *504/533–6000 or 800/427–7247* ⊕ *www.harrahs.com.*

Mulate's. Across the street from the Convention Center, this large restaurant seats 400, and the dance

GET MUGGED
Take along an insulated mug with a lid that you can fill at the beverage station in the buffet area. Your drinks will stay hot or cold, and you won't have to worry about spills. Most bartenders will fill the mug with ice and water or a soft drink. With a straw, your ice will not melt instantly while you lounge at the pool.

floor quickly fills with couples twirling and two-stepping to authentic Cajun bands from the countryside. Regulars love to drag first-timers to the floor for impromptu lessons. The home-style Cajun cuisine is quite good, and the bands play until 10:30 or 11 PM. ⊠ *201 Julia St., Warehouse* ☎ *504/522–1492.*

★ **Pat O'Brien's.** Sure, it's touristy, but there are reasons Pat O's has been a must-stop on the New Orleans cocktail trail for so long. For one thing, there's plenty of room to spread out, from the elegant side bar and piano bar that flank the carriageway entrance to the lush (and in winter, heated) patio. Friendly staff, an easy camaraderie among patrons, and a signature drink—the pink, cloying, and extremely potent Hurricane, which comes with a souvenir glass—make this French Quarter stalwart a pleasant afternoon diversion. ⊠ *718 St. Peter St., French Quarter* ☎ *504/525–4823.*

★ **Preservation Hall.** The jazz tradition that flowered in the 1920s is enshrined in this cultural landmark by a cadre of distinguished New Orleans musicians, most of whom were schooled by an ever-dwindling group of elder statesmen. There is limited seating on benches—many patrons end up squatting on the floor or standing in back—and no beverages are served or allowed. Nonetheless, the legions of satisfied customers regard an evening here as an essential New Orleans experience. Cover charge is $10, but can run a bit higher for special appearances. Call ahead for performance times; sometimes the show ends before you even begin pre-partying. ⊠ *726 St. Peter St., French Quarter* ☎ *504/522–2841 or 504/523–8939.*

Fodor's Choice **The Spotted Cat.** Jazz, funk, and blues bands perform nearly every night,
★ with early-afternoon sets weekends, at this rustic club right in the thick of the Frenchmen Street action. A rattan seat near the front window makes for good people-watching. ⊠ *623 Frenchmen St., Faubourg Marigny* ☎ *504/943–3887.*

★ **Tipitina's.** A bust of legendary New Orleans pianist Professor Longhair, or "Fess," greets visitors at the door of this Uptown landmark, which takes its name from one of his most popular songs. As the concert posters pinned to the walls attest, Tip's hosts a wide variety of touring bands and local acts. The long-running Sunday-afternoon Cajun dance still packs the floor. The Tipitina's Foundation has an office and workshop upstairs, where local musicians affected by Hurricane Katrina can network, gain access to resources, and search for gigs. ⊠ *501 Napoleon Ave., Uptown* ☎ *504/895–8477.*

SIGHTSEEING TOURS

Several local tour companies give two- to four-hour city tours by bus that include the French Quarter, the Garden District, uptown New Orleans, and the lakefront. Prices range from $25 to $125 per person, depending on the kind of experience. Both Gray Line and New Orleans Tours offer a longer tour that combines a two-hour city tour by bus with a two-hour steamboat ride on the Mississippi River. Gray Line and Tours by Isabelle both offer tours of Hurricane Katrina devastation as well.

Tour Contacts Gray Line (☎ *800/535–7786 or 504/569–1401* ⊕ *www. graylineneworleans.com*). **New Orleans Tours** (☎ *504/592–1991* ⊕ *www. notours.com*). **Tours by Isabelle** (☎ *877/665–8687 or 504/398–0365* ⊕ *www.toursbyisabelle.com*).

WHERE TO EAT

For price categories, see ⇨ *Dining at the beginning of this chapter.*

Don't miss beignets and rich, chicory-laced coffee at **Café du Monde** (⊠ *800 Decatur St., French Quarter* ☎ *504/525–4544* ▭ *No credit cards*) in the French Quarter, though there's also an outlet in the Riverwalk.

$$$
SOUTHERN ✕ **Bayona.** "New World" is the label Louisiana native Susan Spicer applies to her cooking style, which results in such special dishes as the Caribbean pumpkin soup with coconut, and Niman Ranch pork chop with a spicy adobo glaze. The lunch omelet of andouille, smoked cheddar, and fried oysters is about as authentic as Louisiana cooking can be. These and other imaginative dishes are served in an early-19th-century Creole cottage that glows with flower arrangements, elegant photographs, and trompe-l'oeil murals suggesting Mediterranean landscapes. Don't skip pastry chef Christy Phebus's sweets, such as a maple semolina cake with golden raisin compote and pomegranate sauce. ⊠ *430 Dauphine St., French Quarter* ☎ *504/525–4455* ⊕ *www.bayona.com* ⚞ *Reservations essential* ▭ *AE, DC, MC, V* ⊙ *Closed Sun. No lunch Mon. or Tues.*

$
CAFÉ ✕ **Central Grocery.** This old-fashioned Italian grocery store produces authentic muffulettas, one of the gastronomic gifts of the city's Italian immigrants. Good enough to challenge the po'boy as the local sandwich champ, it's made by filling round loaves of seeded bread with ham, salami, mozzarella, and a salad of marinated green olives. Sandwiches, about 10 inches in diameter, are sold in wholes and halves. ■**TIP➜ The muffulettas are huge! Unless you're starving, you'll do fine with a half.** You can eat your muffuletta at a counter, or get it to go and dine on a bench on Jackson Square or the Moon Walk along the Mississippi riverfront. The Grocery closes at 5:30 PM. ⊠ *923 Decatur St., French Quarter*

☎ *504/523–1620* ▭*D, MC, V* ☾ *No dinner.*

$$$ ✕ **Commander's Palace.** No restaurant captures New Orleans's gastronomic heritage and celebratory spirit as well as this one, long considered the grande dame of New Orleans's fine dining. The recent

CREOLE
Fodor's Choice
★

> **CAUTION**
>
> Items confiscated by airport security will not be returned to you. If you are uncertain whether something will pass the security test, pack it in your checked luggage.

renovation has added new life, especially upstairs, where the Garden Room's glass walls have marvelous views of the giant oak trees on the patio below; other rooms promote conviviality with their bright pastels. The menu's classics include sugarcane-grilled pork tenderloin; a spicy and meaty turtle soup; terrific bourbon-lacquered Mississippi quail; and a wonderful griddle-seared gulf fish. Among the addictive desserts is the bread-pudding soufflé. Weekend brunches are a New Orleans tradition. Jackets are preferred at dinner. ✉ *1403 Washington Ave., Garden District* ☎ *504/899–8221* ⊕ *www.commanderspalace.com* ✍ *Reservations essential* ▭ *AE, D, DC, MC, V.*

$$$ ✕ **Galatoire's.** Galatoire's has always epitomized the old-style French-
CREOLE Creole bistro. Many of the recipes date to 1905. Fried oysters and bacon
Fodor's Choice en brochette are worth every calorie, and the brick-red rémoulade sauce
★ sets a high standard. Other winners include veal chops in béarnaise sauce, and seafood-stuffed eggplant. The setting downstairs is a single, narrow dining room lighted with glistening brass chandeliers; bentwood chairs and white tablecloths add to its timelessness. You may reserve a table in the renovated upstairs rooms, though the action is on the first floor, where partying regulars inhibit conversation but add good people-watching entertainment value. Friday lunch starts early and continues well into early evening. A jacket is required. ✉ *209 Bourbon St., French Quarter* ☎ *504/525–2021* ⊕ *www.galatoires.com* ▭ *AE, D, DC, MC, V* ☾ *Closed Mon.*

$$ ✕ **Herbsaint.** Upscale food and moderate prices are among Herbsaint's
SOUTHERN assets. Chef Donald Link turns out food that sparkles with robust flavors and top-grade ingredients. Small plates and side dishes such as charcuterie, a knock-'em-dead shrimp bisque, house-made pasta, and cheese- or nut-studded salads are mainstays. Don't overlook the rich and flavorful Louisiana cochon with turnips, cabbage, and cracklins. Also irresistible: smoked beef brisket with horseradish potato salad. For dessert, the layered spice cake with figs and pecans will ensure future return trips. The plates provide most of the color in the light-hearted, often noisy, rooms. The wine list is expertly compiled and reasonably priced. ✉ *701 St. Charles Ave., CBD* ☎ *504/524–4114* ⊕ *www.herbsaint.com* ✍ *Reservations essential* ▭ *AE, D, DC, MC, V* ☾ *Closed Sun. No lunch Sat.*

WHERE TO STAY

You can stay in a large hotel near the cruise-ship terminal or in more intimate places in the French Quarter. Hotel rates in New Orleans tend to be on the high end, though deals abound.

For price categories, see ⇨ Lodging at the beginning of this chapter.

$$ ⚏ **Ambassador Hotel.** Guest rooms at this hotel bordering the CBD and Warehouse District have real character, with hardwood floors, oversize windows, and high ceilings. Four-poster iron beds, armoires, and local jazz prints are among the furnishings. Exposed-brick walls and ceiling fans add to the ambience of the pre–Civil War building. This is a good alternative to the huge convention hotels; you're just steps from the major downtown attractions and the Convention Center, and Harrah's New Orleans Casino is a five-minute walk. **Pros:** distinctive decor; urban-chic atmosphere. **Cons:** some first-floor rooms let in too much noise from street and lobby area. ⊠ *535 Tchoupitoulas St., CBD* ☏ *504/527–5271 or 800/455–3417* ⊕ *www.ambassadorneworleans. com* ☞ *165 rooms* ♿ *In-room: Wi-Fi. In-hotel: restaurant, bar, parking (paid)* ⊟ *AE, D, DC, MC, V.*

$$$ ⚏ **New Orleans Hilton Riverside.** The sprawling multilevel Hilton complex sits right on the Mississippi, with superb views. Guest rooms have French provincial furnishings, and the 180 rooms that share a concierge have fax machines. The lavish Sunday brunch is consistently outstanding. Adjacent to Riverwalk Shopping Center, the hotel is directly across the street from Harrah's New Orleans Casino; the Riverfront streetcar stops out front. The health club is among the best in town, and the hotel has a resident golf pro and a four-hole putting green. Designed for large convention groups, this hotel is also a great choice for independent travelers. **Pros:** well-maintained facilities; hotel runs like a well-oiled machine. **Cons:** the city's biggest hotel; typical chain service and surroundings; garage needs better lighting and security. ⊠ *Poydras St. at the Mississippi River, CBD* ☏ *504/561–0500 or 800/445–8667* ⊕ *www. hilton.com* ☞ *1,600 rooms, 67 suites* ♿ *In-room: Wi-Fi. In-hotel: 3 restaurants, tennis courts, pools, gym, parking (paid), no-smoking rooms* ⊟ *AE, D, DC, MC, V.*

$$$ ⚏ **New Orleans Marriott Hotel.** The Marriott has a fabulous view of the Quarter, the CBD, and the river. It's an easy walk from the Canal Place mall, the Riverwalk, and the Convention Center. Rooms are comfortable, service is friendly (if uneven), and nightly jazz enlivens the lobby—but the hotel lacks New Orleans charm. The Canal Street streetcar line provides convenient access to most parts of the city. Keep in mind that this high-rise convention hotel is located on Canal Street, the busiest street in the downtown area. **Pros:** good location; very clean; stunning city and river views. **Cons:** typical chain hotel; inconsistent service. ⊠ *555 Canal St., French Quarter* ☏ *504/581–1000 or 800/228–9290* ⊕ *www.neworleansmarriott.com* ☞ *1,290 rooms, 54 suites* ♿ *In-room: Internet. In-hotel: restaurant, bar, pool, gym, Wi-Fi hotspot, parking (paid)* ⊟ *AE, D, DC, MC, V.*

NEW YORK, NEW YORK

A few cruise lines now base Caribbean-bound ships in New York City year-round, though most of the market is made up of ships doing seasonal cruises to New England and Bermuda. If you're coming to the city from the immediate area, you can easily arrive the day before and do a bit of sightseeing and perhaps take in a Broadway show. The cruise port in Manhattan is fairly close to Times Square and Midtown hotels and theaters. But the New York City region now has three major cruise ports. You can also leave from Cape Liberty Terminal in Bayonne, New Jersey, on both Celebrity and Royal Caribbean ships. In 2006 a new cruise-ship terminal opened in Red Hook, Brooklyn, and this terminal serves Carnival and Princess ships as well as Cunard's *Queen Mary 2*.

ESSENTIALS

HOURS They say that New York never sleeps, and that's particularly true around Times Square, where some stores are open until 11 PM or later even during the week. But most stores outside of the immediate Times Square area are open from 9 or 10 until 6 or 7. Many museums close on Monday.

INTERNET Internet service is offered by most New York hotels, and there are independent Internet cafés all over town. You might even see cheap Internet service in pizzerias and delis. Starbucks offers wireless service for a fee, but if you have your own laptop you can use the free outdoor Wi-Fi network in Bryant Park (6th Avenue, between 42nd and 41st streets).

VISITOR INFORMATION **NYC & Company Convention & Visitors Bureau** (✉ *810 7th Ave., between W. 52nd and W. 53rd Sts., 3rd fl., Midtown West* ☎ *212/484–1222* ⊕ *www.nycgo. com*). **Times Square Information Center** (✉ *1560 Broadway, between 46th and 47th Sts., Midtown West* ☎ *212/768–1560* ⊕ *www.timessquarenyc.org*).

THE CRUISE PORT

The New York Passenger Ship Terminal is on the far west side of Manhattan, five very long blocks from the Times Square area, between 48th and 52nd streets; the vehicle entrance is at 55th Street. Traffic can be backed up in the area on days that cruise ships arrive and depart, so allow yourself enough time to check in and go through security. There are no nearby subway stops, though city buses do cross Midtown at 50th and 42nd streets. If you don't have too much luggage, it is usually faster and more convenient to have a taxi drop you off at the intersection of 50th Street and the West Side Highway, directly across the street from the entrance to the lower-level of the terminal; then you can walk right in and take the escalator or elevator up to the embarkation level.

Cape Liberty Terminal in Bayonne is off Route 440. From the New Jersey Turnpike, take Exit 14A, then follow the signs for 440 South, and make a left turn into the Cape Liberty Terminal area (on Port Terminal Boulevard). If you are coming from Long Island, you cross Staten Island, and after crossing the Bayonne Bridge take 440 North, making a right into the terminal area. If you are coming from Manhattan, you can also reach the terminal by public transit. Take the New Jersey Transit light-rail line that connects to the PATH trains in Hoboken; get off at the Bayonne stop, and from there you can take a taxi to the terminal (about 2 mi [3 km] away); there may be free shuttle bus on cruise sailing dates, but confirm that with your cruise line.

The Brooklyn cruise terminal at Pier 12 in Red Hook, which opened in April 2006, is not convenient to public transportation, so you

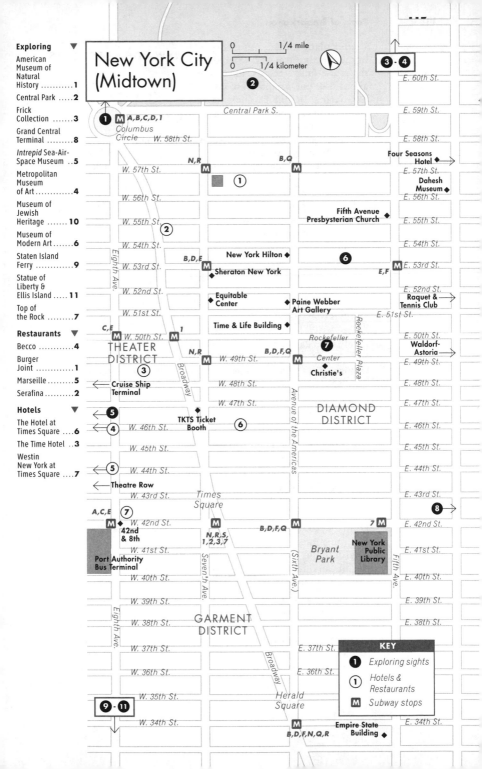

New York City (Midtown)

0 — 1/4 mile
0 — 1/4 kilometer

Central Park S.

Columbus Circle

W. 58th St.
W. 57th St.
W. 56th St.
W. 55th St.
W. 54th St.
W. 53rd St.
W. 52nd St.
W. 51st St.
W. 50th St.
W. 49th St.
W. 48th St.
W. 47th St.
W. 46th St.
W. 45th St.
W. 44th St.
W. 43rd St.
W. 42nd St.
W. 41st St.
W. 40th St.
W. 39th St.
W. 38th St.
W. 37th St.
W. 36th St.
W. 35th St.
W. 34th St.

E. 60th St.
E. 59th St.
E. 58th St.
E. 57th St.
E. 56th St.
E. 55th St.
E. 54th St.
E. 53rd St.
E. 52nd St.
E. 51st St.
E. 50th St.
E. 49th St.
E. 48th St.
E. 47th St.
E. 43rd St.
E. 42nd St.
E. 41st St.
E. 40th St.
E. 39th St.
E. 38th St.
E. 37th St.
E. 36th St.
E. 34th St.

Eighth Ave.

A,B,C,D,1
N,R
B,Q
B,D,E
C,E
N,R
B,D,F,Q
E,F
B,D,F,Q
A,C,E
N,R,S 1,2,3,7
7
B,D,F,N,Q,R

Four Seasons Hotel ◆

Dahesh Museum ◆

Fifth Avenue Presbysterian Church ◆

New York Hilton ◆

Sheraton New York

Equitable Center ◆

◆ Paine Webber Art Gallery

Time & Life Building ◆

THEATER DISTRICT

Broadway

Rockefeller Center

Rockefeller Plaza

Christie's ◆

Raquet & Tennis Club

Waldorf-Astoria

Cruise Ship Terminal

DIAMOND DISTRICT

Avenue of the Americas

TKTS Ticket Booth

Theatre Row

Times Square

Seventh Ave.

42nd & 8th

Port Authority Bus Terminal

Bryant Park

New York Public Library

(Sixth Ave.)

Fifth Ave.

GARMENT DISTRICT

Herald Square

Broadway

Empire State Building ◆

KEY

❶ *Exploring sights*

① *Hotels & Restaurants*

Ⓜ *Subway stops*

should plan to take a taxi, drive, or take the bus transfers offered by the cruise lines (the cost for this is about $40 per person from either LaGuardia or JFK). There is a secure, 500-car outdoor parking lot on-site. To reach the terminal from La Guardia Airport, take I–278 W (the Brooklyn-Queens Expressway), Exit 26, Hamilton Avenue; the terminal entrance is actually off Browne Street. From JFK, take I–278 E (again, the Brooklyn-Queens Expressway), and then the same exit. If you arrive early, there's not much in the neighborhood, but there are a few neighborhood delis and restaurants about 15 minutes away on foot; the area is a safe place to walk around during daylight hours, though it's very industrial and unattractive. Red Hook is the home of ships from the Carnival, Princess, and Cunard cruise lines.

> ## NEW YORK BEST BETS
>
> ■ **An Art Museum.** Take your pick: the Met, MOMA, or the Frick, but this is a true highlight of New York.
>
> ■ **A Broadway Show.** The theater experience in New York is better than almost anywhere else in the world.
>
> ■ **Statue of Liberty.** Just the sight of Lady Liberty will melt the coldest heart, though the highlight of the trip is actually the Ellis Island museum, not the statue itself.

Information Cape Liberty Terminal (✉ *14 Port Terminal Blvd., Bayonne, NJ* ☎ *201/823-3737* ⊕ *www.cruiseliberty.com*). **New York Passenger Ship Terminal** (✉ *711 12th Ave., Midtown West, New York, NY* ☎ *212/246-5450* ⊕ *www.nycruiseterminal.com* ✉ *Pier 12, Bldg. 112, Red Hook, Brooklyn, NY* ☎ *718/858-3450*).

AIRPORT TRANSFERS

A cab to or from JFK to the passenger-ship terminal in **Manhattan** will cost $45 (a flat fare) plus toll and tip; expect to pay at least $35 on the meter if you are coming from LaGuardia and at least $50 or $60 (not including tolls of about $10 and the tip) from Newark in a regular taxi (from Newark airport, it's usually more cost-effective to call for a car service to pick you up; these services have a flat fare of about $48, not including the tolls and tip).

From Newark Airport it's approximately $30 to **Cape Liberty,** $75 from JFK (plus tolls and tip, so count on at least $100), and $80 from La Guardia (plus tolls and tip; count on paying more than $100). Royal Caribbean offers bus service from several Mid-Atlantic and Northeast cities on sailing dates, but confirm that with the cruise line.

If your cruise is leaving from **Red Hook,** the taxi fare will be much cheaper if you fly into either La Guardia (about $30) or JFK (about $40); you'll pay at least $70 from Newark Airport. Cruise lines provide bus transfers from all three of the area's airports, but it may be cheaper to take a taxi if you are traveling with more than one other person. Note that all these taxi fares do not include tolls and tips. From Newark, the tolls to Brooklyn can be substantial, adding almost $20 to the fare.

PARKING

You can park at the New York Passenger Ship Terminal for a staggering $30 a day; the fee is payable in advance in cash or traveler's checks (no credit cards).

Parking at Cape Liberty Terminal in Bayonne is $19 per day, payable only in cash, traveler's checks, and major credit cards.

Parking at Red Hook, Brooklyn, costs $23 for the first 24 hours and then $20 per day.

TOP ATTRACTIONS

There's no way to do justice to even the most popular tourist stops in New York. Below is information about several top attractions. If you have only a day in the city, choose one or two attractions and buy a daily unlimited subway pass to get around. There's a moving series of panels about the World Trade Center at the so-called "Ground Zero" site across from the Millennium Hotel (take the 1 train to Cortlandt Street or the E to World Trade Center); there's another series of memorial panels underneath at the World Trade Center PATH station, which is accessible from the main, streetside memorial area.

Bullets in the margins refer to points of interest on the Midtown Manhattan map.

❶ American Museum of Natural History. With 45 exhibition halls and more than 32 million artifacts and specimens, the world's largest and most important museum of natural history can easily occupy you for half a day. The dioramas might seem dated, but are fun. The dinosaur exhibits are probably the highlight. Attached to the museum is the **Rose Center for Earth and Space,** with various exhibits and housing the **Hayden Planetarium** and an **IMAX Theater.** ⊠ *Central Park West at W. 79 St., Upper West Side* ☎ *212/769–5200* ⊕ *www.amnh.org* ☜ *$20 suggested donation, includes admission to Rose Center for Earth and Space* ☉ *Daily 10–5:45. Rose Center until 8:45 on Fri.*

❷ Central Park. Without Central Park's 843 acres of meandering paths, tranquil lakes, ponds, and open meadows, New Yorkers might be a lot less sane. You can drop by the zoo (near 64th Street, on the east side) or the famous Bethesda Fountain (mid-park, at around 72nd Street), but the main draw is just to wander the lanes. Central Park has one of the lowest crime rates in the city. Still, use common sense and stay within sight of other park visitors, and don't go into the park after dark. Directions, park maps, and events calendars can be obtained from volunteers at two 5th Avenue **information booths,** at East 60th Street and East 72nd Street. ☎ *212/310–6600 for schedule of park events, 212/360–2726 for schedule of walking tours* ⊕ *www.centralparknyc. org* Ⓜ *Subway: A, C, or 1 to Columbus Circle.*

❸ Frick Collection. Coke-and-steel baron Henry Clay Frick (1849–1919) ★ amassed this superb art collection far from the soot and smoke of Pittsburgh, where he made his fortune. The mansion was designed by Thomas Hastings and built in 1913–14. It opened in 1935, but still resembles a gracious private home, albeit one with bona fide masterpieces in almost every room. This is the best small museum in town by a mile. ✉ *1 E. 70th St., at 5th Ave., Upper East Side* ☎ *212/288–0700* ⊕ *www. frick.org* 🎫 *$18* ☉ *Tues.–Sat. 10–6, Sun. 11–5* Ⓜ *6 to 68th St./Hunter College.*

> **CAUTION**
>
> If you still use film, do not pack it in checked luggage, since the newest airport screening equipment will ruin it. Put it in your carry-on instead.

⑧ Grand Central Terminal. Grand Cen-

★ tral is not only the world's largest (76 acres) and the nation's busiest (500,000 commuters and subway riders use it daily) railway station, but also one of the world's greatest public spaces ("justly famous," as critic Tony Hiss noted, "as a crossroads, a noble building . . . and an ingenious piece of engineering"). A massive four-year renovation completed in October 1998 restored the 1913 landmark to its original splendor—and then some. *Main entrance* ✉ *E. 42nd St. at Park Ave., Midtown East* ☎ *212/935–3960* ⊕ *www. grandcentralterminal.com* Ⓜ *4, 5, 6, 7, S to 42nd St./Grand Central.*

⑤ *Intrepid* Sea-Air-Space Museum. Formerly the USS *Intrepid,* this 900-foot
⏳ aircraft carrier is serving out its retirement as the centerpiece of Manhattan's only floating museum. An A-12 Blackbird spy plane, lunar landing modules, helicopters, seaplanes, and two dozen other aircraft are on deck. Docked alongside, and also part of the museum, are the *Growler,* a strategic-missile submarine; the *Edson,* a Vietnam-era destroyer; and several other battle-scarred naval veterans. Children can explore the ships' skinny hallways and winding staircases, as well as manipulate countless knobs, buttons, and wheels. This museum is within easy walking distance of the main cruise piers in Manhattan. ✉ *Hudson River, Pier 86, 12th Ave. at W. 46th St., Midtown West* ☎ *212/245–0072 or 877/957–7447* ⊕ *www.intrepidmuseum.org* 🎫 *$22; free to active and retired U.S. military personnel and children under 3* ☉ *Apr.–Sept., weekdays 10–5, weekends 10–6; Oct.–Mar., Tues.–Sun. 10–5; last admission 1 hr before closing* Ⓜ *A, C, E to 42nd St.; M42 bus to pier.*

④ The Metropolitan Museum of Art. If the city held no other museum than the colossal Metropolitan Museum of Art, you could still occupy yourself
★ for days roaming its labyrinthine corridors. Because the Metropolitan Museum has something approaching 3 million works on display over its more than 7 square mi, you're going to have to make some hard choices. Looking at everything here could take a week. ✉ *5th Ave. at 82nd St., Upper East Side* ☎ *212/535–7710* ⊕ *www.metmuseum.org* 🎫 *$20 suggested donation* ☉ *Tues.–Thurs. and Sun. 9:30–5:30, Fri. and Sat. 9:30–9.*

⑩ Museum of Jewish Heritage—A Living Memorial to the Holocaust. In a granite hexagon rising 85 feet above Robert F. Wagner Jr. Park at the southern end of Battery Park City, this museum pays tribute to the 6 million Jews who perished in the Holocaust. It's one of the best such museums in the country. ✉ *36 Battery Pl., Battery Park City, Lower Manhattan* ☎ *646/437–4200* ⊕ *www.mjhnyc.org* 🎫 *$12, free on Wed. from 4–10* ☉ *Thurs. and Sun.–Tues. 10–5:45, Wed. 10–8, Fri. and eve of Jewish holidays 10–3* Ⓜ *4, 5 to Bowling Green.*

6 Museum of Modern Art (MoMA). The masterpieces—Monet's *Water Lilies,* Picasso's *Les Demoiselles d'Avignon,* Van Gogh's *Starry Night*—are still here, but for now the main draw at MoMA is, well, MoMA. A "modernist dream world" is how critics described the museum after its $425 million face-lift. Unfortunately, the museum was an instant success, which means lines are sometimes down the block. For the shortest wait, get here before the museum opens; you can avoid some of the crowding by entering through the 54th Street side. Be prepared for sticker shock when you buy your ticket. ✉ *11 W. 53rd St., between 5th and 6th Aves., Midtown East* ☎ *212/708–9400* ⊕ *www.moma.org* ✉ *$20* ☉ *Sat.–Mon., Wed., and Thurs. 10:30–5:30, Fri. 10:30–8* Ⓜ *Subway: E, V to 5th Ave./53rd St.; B, D, E to 7th Ave.; B, D, F, V to 47th–50th Sts./Rockefeller Center.*

9 Staten Island Ferry. The best transit deal in town is the Staten Island Ferry, a free 20- to 30-minute ride across New York Harbor providing great views of the Manhattan skyline, the Statue of Liberty, the Verrazano-Narrows Bridge, and the New Jersey coast. Ferries embark on various schedules: every 15 minutes during rush hours, every 20–30 minutes most other times, and every hour on weekend nights and mornings. If you can manage it, catch one of the older blue-and-orange ferries, which have outside decks. ✉ *State and South Sts., Lower Manhattan* ☎ *718/390–5253* ✉ *Free* Ⓜ *Subway: 4, 5 to Bowling Green; 1, 9 to South Ferry.*

⑪ Statue of Liberty and Ellis Island. Though you must endure a long wait and onerous security, it's worth the trouble to see one of the iconic images of New York. But the truth is that a trip to the statue is time-consuming and laborious; Ellis Island is a much better investment of your time, especially if you have only a day or two in New York. You're allowed access to the statue's museum only as part of one of the free tours of the promenade (which surrounds the base of the pedestal) or the observatory (at the pedestal's top). The tours are limited to 3,000 participants a day; to guarantee a place, particularly on the observatory tour, you must order tickets ahead of time—they can be reserved up to 180 days in advance, by phone or over the Internet. The narrow, double-helix stairs leading to the statue's crown closed after 9/11, but access reopened on July 4, 2009. Approximately 240 people are allowed to visit the crown each day; tickets are available online. If you can't get tickets to the crown, you get a good look at the statue's inner structure on the observatory tour. Much more interesting—and well worth exploring—is the Ellis Island museum, which traces the story of immigration in New York City with moving exhibits throughout the restored processing building. Go early if you want to see everything, and allow plenty of time for security and lines. The ferry stops first at the statue and then continues to Ellis Island. ✉ *Liberty Island* ☎ *212/363–3200; 877/523–9849 ticket reservations* ⊕ *www.statuecruises.com* ✉ *Free; ferry $12 round-trip; crown tickets $3* ☉ *Daily 9:30–5; extended hrs in summer (current hours available at* ⊕ *www.nps.gov/stli/planyourvisit/hours.htm).*

3

❼ **Top of the Rock.** Rockefeller Center's multifloor observation deck, first
Fodor's Choice opened in 1933, and closed in the early 1980s, reopened in 2005.
★ Though overpriced, the experience is infinitely better than that at
the Empire State Building, where interminable lines spoil most of the
fun. Arrive just before sunset for the best views (which include the
Empire State Building). ✉ *Entrance on 50th St., between 5th and 6th
Aves., Midtown West* ☎ *877/692–7625 or 212/698–2000* ⊕ *www.
topoftherocknyc.com* ⛝ *$20* ☉ *Daily 8–midnight; last elevator at 11
PM* Ⓜ *B, D, F, V to 47th–50th Sts./Rockefeller Center.*

SHOPPING

You can find almost any major store from virtually any designer or
chain in Manhattan. High-end designers tend to be along **Madison Avenue,** between 55th and 86th streets. Some are along **57th Street,** between
Madison and 7th avenues. **Fifth Avenue,** starting at Saks Fifth Avenue (at
50th Street) and going up to 59th Street, is a hodgepodge of high-end
stores and more accessible options, including the high-end department
store Bergdorf-Goodman, at 58th Street. More interesting and individual stores can be found in **SoHo** (between Houston and Canal, West
Broadway and Lafayette), and the **East Village** (between 14th Street and
Houston, Broadway and Avenue A). **Chinatown** is chock-full of designer
knockoffs, crowded streets, and dim sum palaces; though frenetic during the day, it's a fun stop. The newest group of stores in Manhattan is
at the **Time-Warner Center,** at Columbus Circle (at 8th Avenue and 59th
Street); the high-rise mall has upscale stores and some of the city's best-
reviewed and most expensive new restaurants.

BROADWAY SHOWS

Scoring tickets to Broadway shows is fairly easy except for the very top
draws. For the most part, the top ticket price for Broadway musicals is
now over $120; the best seats for Broadway plays can run as high as
$100. **Telecharge** (☎ *212/239–6200* ⊕ *www.telecharge.com*). **Ticketmaster**
(☎ *212/307–4100* ⊕ *www.ticketmaster.com*).

For seats at 25%–50% off the usual price, go to one of the **TKTS booths**
(✉ *Duffy Sq. at W. 47th St. and Broadway, Midtown West* Ⓜ *1, 2, 3,
7, N, Q, R, S, W to 42nd St./Times Sq.; N, R, W to 49th St.; 1 to 50th
St.* ✉ *South St. Seaport at Front and John Sts., Lower Manhattan* Ⓜ *2,
3, 4, 5, A, C, E, J, M, Z to Fulton St./Broadway-Nassau* ✉ *Downtown
Brooklyn, at the Myrtle St. Promenade and Jay St., Brooklyn* Ⓜ *A, C,
F to Jay St.-Borough Hall; M, R, 2, 3, 4, 5 to Court St.-Borough Hall*
⊕ *www.tdf.org*).

WHERE TO EAT

The restaurants we recommend below are all in Midtown West, near
Broadway theaters and hotels. Make reservations at all but the most
casual places or face a numbing wait.

For price categories, see ⇨ *Dining at the beginning of this chapter.*

$$$
ITALIAN

✕**Becco.** An ingenious concept makes Becco a prime Restaurant Row choice for time-constrained theatergoers. There are two pricing scenarios: one includes an all-you-can-eat selection of antipasti and three pastas served hot out of pans that waiters circulate around the dining room; the other adds a generous entrée to the mix. The pasta selection changes daily, but often includes gnocchi, fresh ravioli, and fettuccine in a cream sauce. The entrées include braised veal shank, grilled double-cut pork chop, and rack of lamb, among other selections. ✉ *355 W. 46th St., between 8th and 9th Aves., Midtown West* ☎ *212/397-7597* ⊕ *www.becco-nyc.com* ✍ *Reservations essential* ▭ *AE, D, DC, MC, V* Ⓜ *A, C, E to 42nd St.*

> **CAUTION**
>
> Store any irreplaceable valuables in the ship purser's safe rather than the one in your cabin. Some insurance policies will not cover the loss of items left in your cabin.

3

¢
BURGER
Fodor's Choice
★

✕**Burger Joint.** What's a college burger bar, done up in particleboard and rec-room decor straight out of a Happy Days episode, doing hidden inside of a five-star Midtown hotel? This tongue-in-cheek lunch spot, hidden behind a heavy red velvet curtain in the Parker Meridien hotel, does such boisterous midweek business that lines often snake through the lobby. Stepping behind the curtain, you can find baseball cap–wearing grease-spattered cooks dispensing paper-wrapped cheeseburgers and crisp thin fries. Forget Kobe beef or foie gras—these burgers are straightforward, cheap, and delicious. ✉ *118 W. 57th St., between 6th and 7th Aves., Midtown West* ☎ *212/245-5000* ⊕ *www.parkermeridien.com* ▭ *No credit cards* Ⓜ *F, N, Q, R, W to 57th St.*

$$
MEDITERRANEAN

✕**Marseille.** With great food and a convenient location near several Broadway theaters, Marseille is perpetually packed. Executive chef and partner Andy d'Amico's Mediterranean creations are continually impressive. His bouillabaisse, the signature dish of the region for which the restaurant is named, is a mélange of mussels, shrimp, rouget, and bass swimming in a fragrant fish broth, topped with a garlicky crouton and served with rouille on the side. Leave room for the spongy beignets with chocolate and raspberry dipping sauces. ✉ *630 9th Ave., at W. 44th St., Midtown West* ☎ *212/333-2323* ⊕ *www.marseillenyc.com* ✍ *Reservations essential* ▭ *AE, MC, V* Ⓜ *A, C, E to 42nd St./Port Authority Bus Terminal.*

$$
ITALIAN

✕**Sosa Borella.** This is one of the Theater District's top spots for reliable food at a reasonable cost. This bi-level, casual Italian eatery is an inviting and friendly space where diners choose from a wide range of options. The lunch menu features staples like warm sandwiches and entrée-size salads, while the dinner menu is slightly gussied up with meat, fish, and pasta dishes (the rich agnolotti with lamb Bolognese sauce, topped with a wedge of grilled pecorino cheese is a must-try). The freshly baked bread served at the beginning of the meal with pesto dipping sauce is a nice touch as you wait for your meal. The service, at times, can be slow, so leave yourself plenty of time before the show. ✉ *832 8th Ave., between 50th and 51st Sts., Midtown West* ☎ *212/262-8282* ⊕ *www.sosaborella.com* ▭ *AE, MC, V* Ⓜ *C, E, 1 to 50th St.*

WHERE TO STAY

There are no real bargains in the Manhattan hotel world, and you'll find it difficult to get a decent room for under $250. However, occasional weekend deals can be found. All the hotels we recommend for cruise passengers are on the West Side, in relatively easy proximity to the cruise ship terminal.

For price categories, see ⇨ Lodging at the beginning of this chapter.

¢ ☷ **The Hotel at Times Square.** Yes, there really is a Super 8 in Times Square—though it no longer goes by that name. The rooms are motel-plain with an unfortunate sea-foam color scheme, but most are well maintained. If you're an unfussy traveler who wants to be in the thick of the madness, it's not a bad option. This small prewar hotel shares its block with a plethora of Brazilian restaurants and is near many theaters and Rockefeller Center. The peculiar lobby has a narrow corridor that snakes off around a corner and is decorated with some rather handsome Art Deco Bakelite lamps. **Pros:** free breakfast; free Wi-Fi; free local calls. **Cons:** peremptory, low-frills service; noisy area. ⊠ *59 W. 46th St., between 5th and 6th Aves., Midtown West* ☎ *212/719–2300 or 800/848–0020* ⊕ *www.applecorehotels.com* ⇨ *209 rooms* ♿ *In-room: a/c, Wi-Fi. In-hotel: bar, gym, Internet terminal, parking (paid)* ▤ *AE, D, DC, MC, V* Ⓜ *B, D, F, V to 47th–50th Sts./Rockefeller Center.*

$$ ☷ **The Time Hotel.** One of the neighborhood's first boutique hotels, this spot half a block from the din of Times Square tempers trendiness with a touch of humor. A ridiculously futuristic glass elevator—eggshells line the bottom of the shaft—transports guests to the second-floor lobby. In the adjoining bar nature videos lighten up the low-slung, serious, gray-scale furnishings, while local DJs spin a fresh selection of music in the trendy Time Lounge. The smallish guest rooms, each themed to one of the primary colors—red, yellow, or blue—have mood lighting and even specific "color" aromas that create a unique, if contrived, hotel experience. Whatever your primary color, they boast iPod docks, large flat-screen TVs, and modern, if not especially comfortable, beds and couches. **Pros:** acclaimed and popular Serafina restaurant downstairs; surprisingly quiet for Times Square location; good turndown service. **Cons:** decor makes the rooms a little dated; service is inconsistent; water pressure is lacking. ⊠ *224 W. 49th St., between Broadway and 8th Ave., Midtown West* ☎ *212/320–2900 or 877/846–3692* ⊕ *www.thetimeny. com* ⇨ *164 rooms, 29 suites* ♿ *In-room: a/c, safe, Internet. In-hotel: restaurant, room service, bar, gym, laundry service, Internet terminal, parking (paid)* ▤ *AE, D, DC, MC, V* Ⓜ *1, C, E to 50th St.*

$ ☷ **Westin New York at Times Square.** Renovations are ongoing at this Westin in the heart of it all, so your experience can vary wildly depending on what type of room you get. Older rooms are a bit tired, though all come with the Heavenly Bed, flat-screen televisions, and Ethernet. For even more comfort, spa-floor rooms come with massage chairs, aromatherapy candles, and other pampering pleasures. Though it costs $10 for entry, the gym is impressive, and it even includes Wii Fit and running tours throughout the city. The huge lobby gets crowded during busy check-in and check-out times; Shula's Steakhouse is a pricey dining option. **Pros:** busy Times Square location; big rooms; great gym. **Cons:** busy Times Square location; small bathroom sinks; some rooms need to be refreshed. ✉ *270 W. 43rd St., at 8th Ave., Midtown West* ☎ *212/201–2700 or 866/837–4183* ⊕ *www.westinny.com* ⤷ *737 rooms, 126 suites* ⌂ *In-room: a/c, safe, refrigerator, Internet, Wi-Fi. In-hotel: restaurant, room service, bars, gym, spa, laundry service, Internet terminal, Wi-Fi hotspot, parking (paid), some pets allowed* ⊟ *AE, D, DC, MC, V* Ⓜ *A, C, E to 42nd St./Times Sq.*

NORFOLK, VIRGINIA

Alice Powers

Founded in 1680, Norfolk is no newcomer to the cruise business. One famous passenger, Thomas Jefferson, arrived here in November 1789 after a two-month crossing of the Atlantic. More than 200 years later, this historic seaport welcomes more than 300,000 cruise passengers annually. Situated at the heart of nautical Hampton Roads, Norfolk is home to the largest naval base in the world and is also a major commercial port.

ESSENTIALS

HOURS Most stores are open weekdays from 10 to 9. Some museums close on Monday and/or Tuesday.

INTERNET Most of the hotels offer free Wi-Fi service if you have your own laptop. If not, you may be able to find an Internet café, but the local Norfolk Public Library has free Internet access, so why pay? **Norfolk Public Library** (✉ *235 E. Plume St.* ☎ *757/664–7323* ⊕ *www.npl.lib.va.us*).

VISITOR INFORMATION **Norfolk Convention and Visitors Bureau** (✉ *232 E. Main St.* ☎ *757/664–6620* ⊕ *www.norfolktoday.com*).

THE CRUISE PORT

The new Half Moone Cruise and Celebration Center, as Norfolk calls its cruise terminal is in the center of the attractive, downtown waterfront. It's within walking distance of numerous attractions and amenities. From I–264, take the City Hall exit (Exit 10). At the light, turn right on St. Paul's Boulevard, and follow the signs to the Cedar Grove parking lot.

INFORMATION

Half Moone Cruise and Celebration Center (✉ *1 Waterside Dr.* ⊕ *www. cruisenorfolk.org*).

AIRPORT TRANSFERS

Norfolk International Airport (ORF) is 9 mi (15 km) and 20 minutes away from the cruise terminal. One-way, shared shuttle costs range from $7.50 to $22 per person, and a taxi costs about $18 to $25.

Contacts **Norfolk Airport Express** (☎ *877/455–7462* ⊕ *www. norfolkairportexpress.com*). **Norfolk International Airport** (*ORF;* ✉ *2200 Norview Ave., Norfolk* ☎ *757/857–3351* ⊕ *norfolkairport.com*).

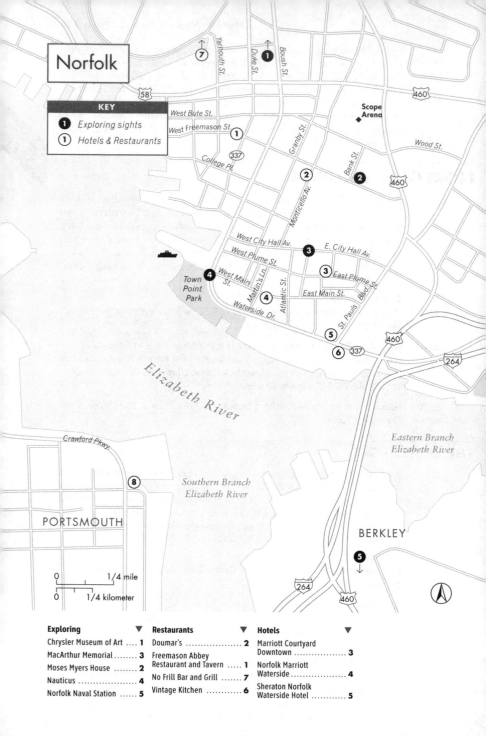

Norfolk

PARKING

Cedar Grove Parking is the designated facility for cruise passengers. The parking fee ($10 daily) is paid upon entering the lot; Visa, MasterCard, American Express, cash, and traveler's checks are accepted. Less than 1 mi (1½ km) from I–264, this lot is located on Monticello Avenue between Virginia Beach Boulevard and Princess Anne Road in Downtown Norfolk. Shuttles run regularly to the cruise terminal.

EXPLORING NORFOLK

History meets high-tech in this waterfront city. From 18th-century historic homes and a major art museum to 20th-century battleships and nuclear-powered aircraft carriers, Norfolk has many interesting sites to explore, several of them free and most within walking distance of the cruise terminal.

Bullets in the margins refer to points of interest on the Norfolk map.

❶ ★ Chrysler Museum of Art. By any standard, this downtown institution qualifies as one of America's major art museums. The permanent collection includes works by Rubens, Gainsborough, Renoir, Picasso, Cézanne, Matisse, Warhol, and Pollock, a list that suggests the breadth available here. Classical and pre-Columbian civilizations are also represented. The decorative-arts collection includes exquisite English porcelain and art nouveau furnishings. The Chrysler is home to one the most important glass collections in America, which includes glass objects from the 6th century BC to the present, with particularly strong holdings in Tiffany, French art glass, and English cameo, as well as artifacts from ancient Rome and the Near and Far East. ⊠ *245 W. Olney Rd.* ☎ *757/664–6200* ⊕ *www.chrysler.org* ▢ *Free* ◯ *Wed. 10–9, Thurs.– Sat. 10–5, Sun. 12–5.*

❸ MacArthur Memorial. This is the burial place of one of America's most distinguished military officers. General Douglas MacArthur (1880–1964) agreed to this navy town as the site for his monument because it was his mother's birthplace. In the rotunda of the old City Hall, converted according to MacArthur's design, is the mausoleum; 11 adjoining galleries house mementos of MacArthur's career, including his signature corncob pipe and the Japanese instruments of surrender that concluded World War II. However, this is a monument not only to General MacArthur but to all those who served in wars from the Civil to the Korean War. Its Historical Center holds 2½ million documents and more than 100,000 photographs, and assists scholars, students, and researchers from around the world. The general's staff car is on display in the gift shop, where a 24-minute biography is shown. ⊠ *198 Bank St., MacArthur Square* ☎ *757/441–2965* ⊕ *www.macarthurmemorial.org* ▢ *Free* ◯ *Mon.–Sat. 10–5, Sun. 11–5.*

❷ Moses Myers House. The Federal redbrick house built by its namesake between 1792 and 1796, is exceptional, and not just for its elegance. The furnishings, 70% of them original, include family portraits by Gilbert Stuart and Thomas Sully. A transplanted New Yorker as well as Norfolk's first Jewish resident, Myers made his fortune in Norfolk in shipping, then served as a diplomat and a customhouse officer. His grandson married James Madison's grandniece; his great-grandson served as mayor; and the family kept the house for five generations. ⊠ *323 E. Free Mason St.* ☎ *757/333–1086* ⊕ *www.chrysler. org/houses.asp* ⊠ *Free* ⊙ *Wed.–Sat. 10–4, Sun. noon–4.*

❹ **Nauticus,** a popular attraction on
☾ Norfolk's redeveloped downtown
★ waterfront, is a maritime science museum featuring hand-on exhibits, interactive theaters, and high-definition films that celebrate the local connection to the seaport. Visitors can touch a shark, learn about weather and underwater archaeology, and explore the mysteries of the Elizabeth River. A NOAA Environmental Resource Center is an invaluable stop for education materials. Temporary exhibits in both the Changing Gallery and Forecastle Gallery keep things fresh. The Hampton Roads Naval Museum, operated by the Navy on the second floor, and the Battleship *Wisconsin,* adjacent to the building (which has been taken over by the city of Norfolk) are also popular attractions, and are included in the Nauticus admission. ⊠ *1 Waterside Dr.* ☎ *757/664–1000* ⊕ *www.nauticus.org* ⊠ *$10.95* ⊙ *Memorial Day–Labor Day, daily 9–5; Labor Day–Memorial Day, Tues.–Sat. 10–5, Sun. noon–5.*

❺ **Norfolk Naval Station.** On the northern edge of the city, this U.S. Navy
☾ installation is an impressive sight, home to more than 100 ships of the
Fodor's Choice Atlantic Fleet. The base was built on the site of the Jamestown Expo-
★ sition of 1907; many of the original buildings survive and are still in use. Several large aircraft carriers, built at nearby Newport News, call Norfolk home port and can be seen from miles away, especially at the bridge-tunnel end of the base. You may see two, each with a crew of up to 6,300, beside slightly smaller amphibious carriers that discharge marines in both helicopters and amphibious assault craft. The submarine piers, floating dry docks, supply center, and air station are all worth seeing. The *Victory Rover* and *Carrie B.* provide boat tours from downtown Norfolk to the naval station, and Hampton Roads Transit operates tour trolleys most of the year, departing from the naval-base tour office. Visitor access is by tour only, and photo ID is required to enter the base. ⊠ *9079 Hampton Blvd.* ☎ *757/444–0948 for tour information* ⊕ *www.cnic.navy.mil/norfolksta/* ⊠ *Tour $10 (cash only)* ⊙ *The 45-minute tours are conducted between one and four times daily, depending on the month. Call ahead for detailed information.*

NORFOLK BEST BETS

■ **Chrysler Museum of Art.** Though far from New York, Chicago, or Los Angeles, this is one of the major art museums in the U.S.

■ **Nauticus.** The National Maritime Center is one of the region's most popular attractions, and especially good for families.

■ **Norfolk Naval Station.** This giant naval base, the home of the Atlantic Fleet, is an impressive site in itself.

SHOPPING

If you forget to pack something for your cruise, you'll find stores galore within walking distance of the cruise terminal at the handsome MacArthur Center Mall.

> **BEACH AND BUY**
>
> A nylon tote bag that folds compactly into its own pocket can be used as a beach bag during your cruise and as an extra carry-on for your return home.

3

You can meet painters, sculptors, glassworkers, jewelers, photographers, and other artists at work in their studios at **d'Art Center** (✉ *Selden Arcade, 208 E. Main St.* ☎ *757/625–4211*); the art is for sale. An eclectic mix of chic shops, including antiques stores, bars, and eateries, lines the streets of **Ghent,** a turn-of-the-20th-century neighborhood that runs from the Elizabeth River to York Street, to West Olney Road and Llewellyn Avenue. The intersection of Colley Avenue and 21st Street is the hub. A car is useful if you want to visit this area. The center of Norfolk's downtown, the **MacArthur Center** (✉ *300 Monticello Ave.* ☎ *757/627–6000*) has more than 100 stores, including anchors Nordstrom and Dillard's. There are restaurants downstairs and numerous fast-food outlets upstairs offering a variety of reasonably tolerable food. In Ghent the upscale clothing and shoe boutiques at the **Palace Shops** (✉ *21st St. at Llewellyn Ave.*) are a good place to search out some finery.

WHERE TO EAT

In addition to hotel restaurants, downtown Norfolk has many fine-dining restaurants as well as casual eateries in Waterside Festival Marketplace, where there's a versatile food court, and in the MacArthur Center Mall, including Johnny Rockets and Kincaid's—good food values for the price.

For price categories, see ⇨ *Dining at the beginning of this chapter.*

¢
BARBECUE
✕ **Doumar's.** After he introduced the world to its first ice-cream cone at the 1904 World's Fair in St. Louis, Abe Doumar founded this drive-in institution in 1934. It's still operated by his family. Waitresses carry to your car the specialties of the house: barbecue, limeade, and ice cream in waffle cones made according to an original recipe. For breakfast, try the Egg-O-Doumar, a bargain at $2.70. The Food Network's "Diners, Drive-Ins, and Dives" featured Doumars twice in 2008. ✉ *1919 Monticello Ave.* ☎ *757/627–4163* ⊕ *www.doumars.com* ▭ *MC, V* ⊗ *Closed Sun.*

$
AMERICAN
✕ **Freemason Abbey Restaurant and Tavern.** This former church near the historic business district has been drawing customers for a long time, and not without reason. It has 40-foot-high cathedral ceilings and large windows, making for an airy, and dramatic, dining experience. You can sit upstairs, in the large choir loft, or in the main part of the church downstairs. Beside the bar just inside the entrance is an informal sort of "diner" area, but with the whole menu to choose from. Regular appetizers include artichoke dip and Santa Fe shrimp. There's a dinner special every weeknight, such as lobster, prime rib, and wild game (wild boar

or alligator, for example). ✉ *209 W. Freemason St.* ☎ *757/622–3966* ⊕ *www.freemasonabbey.com* ▭ *AE, D, DC, MC, V.*

$ ✕ **No Frill Bar and Grill.** This expansive café is in an antique building in
CAFÉ the heart of Ghent. Beneath a tin ceiling and exposed ductwork, a cen-
★ tral bar is surrounded by several dining spaces with cream-and-mustard
walls and wooden tables. Signature items include its ribs; the Funky
Chicken Sandwich, a grilled chicken breast with bacon, tomato, melted
Swiss cheese, and Parmesan pepper dressing on rye; and the Spotswood
Salad of baby spinach, Granny Smith apples, and blue cheese. ✉ *806
Spotswood Ave., at Colley Ave.* ☎ *757/627–4262* ⊕ *www.nofrillgrill.
com* ▭ *AE, MC, V.*

$$–$$$ ✕ **Vintage Kitchen.** The Vintage Kitchen has racked up many accolades
AMERICAN for its focus on local foods, artisan cheeses, and microbrews. The chef is
Paris trained, but local, and knows the specialties of the area. It's a place
where you can order "Five Spice Duck Breast" and also a superb cheese-
burger. A special seven-course tasting meal is available by appointment
Monday through Wednesday. ✉ *Dominion Tower, 999 Waterside Dr.*
☎ *757/625–3370* ⊕ *www.vintage-kitchen.com* ⌂ *Reservations essential*
▭ *AE, D, MC, V* ☉ *No dinner Mon.–Wed. Closed Sun.*

WHERE TO STAY

There are hotels within walking distance of the cruise port, or if you
have a car, there are numerous chain motels on the outskirts of town
where you can save a little money.

For price categories, see ⇨ *Lodging at the beginning of this chapter.*

$$ 🏨 **Marriott Courtyard Downtown.** Built in 2005, this eight-story hotel is
near everything visitors want to see and where business travelers need to
be. It's next door to the MacArthur Memorial and near the MacArthur
Center and Nauticus. A handsome, inviting lobby has a tailored look;
the modern guest rooms have a large desk, comforters, hair dryers,
coffeemakers, irons, ironing boards, and a free daily newspaper. **Pros:**
convenient downtown location. **Cons:** Nearby light rail construction
may make access to hotel difficult. ✉ *520 Plume St.* ☎ *757/963–6000 or
888/236–2427* ⊕ *www.marriott.com* ⬱ *137 rooms, 3 suites* ⌂ *In-room:
refrigerator, Wi-Fi. In-hotel: restaurant, room service, pool, laundry
facilities, laundry service, parking (paid)* ▭ *AE, D, DC, MC, V.*

$$$ 🏨 **Norfolk Waterside Marriott.** This hotel in the redeveloped downtown
area is connected to the Waterside Festival Marketplace shopping area
by a ramp and is close to Town Point Park, site of many festivals. The
handsome lobby, with wood paneling, a central staircase, silk tapestries,
and Federal-style furniture, sets a high standard that continues throughout the hotel. Rooms are somewhat small, but each has most everything
the business traveler could ask for—including two telephones, voice
mail, and Internet access. **Pros:** great central location; two blocks from
the Waterside Festival Marketplace. **Cons:** parking is pricey; Internet
service is $10 a day. ✉ *235 E. Main St.* ☎ *757/627–4200 or 800/228–
9290* ⊕ *www.marriott.com* ⬱ *396 rooms, 8 suites* ⌂ *In-room: Wi-Fi.
In-hotel: 2 restaurants, bar, pool* ▭ *AE, D, DC, MC, V.*

$$$ ☷ **Sheraton Norfolk Waterside Hotel.** Modern is the word for this hotel's furnishings, from the bright, spacious lobby to the ample rooms and large suites. A ground-floor bar with dramatic 30-foot windows overlooks the Elizabeth—many rooms also have a beautiful view over the water. This property is convenient to the Waterside Festival Marketplace shopping area. **Pros:** the only hotel that is truly on the waterfront. **Cons:** again, parking—for Norfolk—is pricey. ⊠ *777 Waterside Dr.* ☎ *757/622–6664* ⊕ *www.starwood.com* ⌁ *426 rooms, 20 suites* ⚐ *Inhotel: restaurant, bar, pool* ⊟ *AE, D, DC, MC, V.*

3

PORT CANAVERAL, FLORIDA

Jennifer
Edwards

This once-bustling commercial fishing area is still home to a small shrimping fleet, charter boats, and party fishing boats, but its main business these days is as a cruise-ship port. Cocoa Beach itself isn't the spiffiest place around, but what *is* becoming quite clean and neat is the north end of the port, where the Carnival, Disney, and Royal Caribbean cruise lines set sail, as well as Sun Cruz and Sterling casino boats. Port Canaveral is now Florida's second-busiest cruise port. Because of Port Canaveral's proximity to Orlando theme parks (about an hour away), many cruisers combine a short cruise with a stay in the area. The port is also convenient to popular Space Coast attractions such as the Kennedy Space Center and United States Astronaut Hall of Fame in Titusville.

ESSENTIALS

HOURS Most of the area's attractions are open every day.

INTERNET Most people choose to go online at their hotel.

VISITOR
INFORMATION **Space Coast Office of Tourism** (⊠ *430 Brevard Ave., Suite 150, Cocoa Village* ☎ *321/433–4470* ⊕ *www.space-coast.com*).

THE CRUISE PORT

Port Canaveral is the second-busiest cruise port in the world, with more than 4.6 million passengers passing through its terminals annually. The port expects its business to grow, predicting for instance that it will soon host twice the number of one-day ship visits it did in 2009, for a total of 126.

The port has six cruise terminals and is home to ships from Carnival Cruise Lines, Disney Cruise Line, and Royal Caribbean International. Other cruise lines, such as Holland America and Norwegian Cruise Line, operate seasonally. The port serves as the embarkation point for three-, four-, and seven-day cruises to the Bahamas, Key West, Mexico, Jamaica, and the Virgin Islands.

In Brevard County, Port Canaveral is on State Road (S.R.) 528, also known as the Beeline Expressway, which runs straight to Orlando, which has the nearest airport. To drive to Port Canaveral from there, take the north exit out of the airport, staying to the right, to S.R. 528 (Beeline Expressway) East. Take S.R. 528 directly to Port Canaveral; it's about a 45-minute drive.

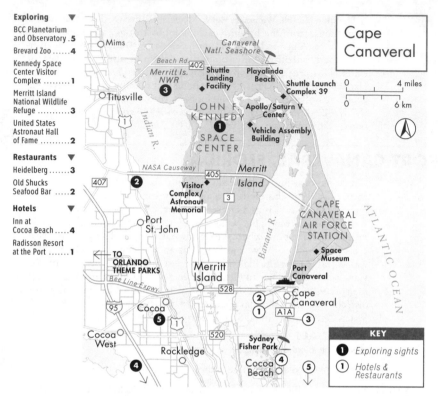

Port Contacts Canaveral Port Authority (✉ *9150 Christopher Columbus Dr., Cape Canaveral* ☎ *321/783–7831 or 888/767–8226* ⊕ *www.portcanaveral.org*).

AIRPORT TRANSFERS

If you are flying into the area, the Orlando airport is 45 minutes away from the docks. If you have not arranged airport transfers with your cruise line, you will need to make your own arrangements. Taxis are expensive, but many companies offer shared minivan and bus shuttles to Port Canaveral. They are all listed on the Canaveral Port Authority Web site. Some shuttles charge for the entire van, which is a good deal for groups but not for individuals or couples; some will charge a per-person rate. Expect to pay at least $38 per person round-trip, and check the Internet for coupons and special offers.

You will need to make a reservation in advance regardless of which service you use. Some cruisers who want to do some exploring before the cruise rent a car at the airport and drop it off at the port, which houses several major rental-car agencies.

Contacts AAA Cruise Line Connection (☎ *407/908–5566* ⊕ *www. aaasuperride.com*). **Busy Traveler Transport Service** (☎ *321/453–5278 or 800/496–7433* ⊕ *www.abusytraveler.com*).

PARKING

Outdoor, gated lots and a six-story parking garage are near the terminals and cost $15 per day for vehicles up to 20 feet in length and $26 per day for vehicles over 20 feet, which must be paid in advance, either in cash, traveler's checks, or by major credit card (MasterCard and Visa only).

EXPLORING THE CAPE CANAVERAL AREA

3

With the Kennedy Space Center just 20 minutes away, there is plenty to do in and around Cape Canaveral, though many folks opt to travel the extra hour into Orlando to visit the popular theme parks.

⑤ BCC Planetarium & Observatory. Based at Brevard Community College, this planetarium and observatory has one of Florida's largest public-access telescopes. The 24-inch telescope allows visitors to view objects in the solar system and deep space. The on-campus planetarium has two theaters, one showing a changing roster of nature documentaries, the other hosting laser-light shows as well as changing planetarium shows. Science Quest Exhibit Hall has hands-on exhibits, including scales calibrated to other planets (Vegas-era Elvis would have weighed just 62 pounds on the moon). The International Hall of Space Explorers displays exhibits on space travel. Show schedules and opening hours may vary, so it's best to call ahead. ⊠ *1519 Clearlake Rd., Bldg. 19* ☎ *321/433-7373* ⊕ *www.brevardcc.edu/planet* ⊠ *Observatory and exhibits free; film or planetarium show $7; both shows $11; laser show $7, triple combination $16* ⊙ *Call for schedule.*

④ Brevard Zoo. At the only American Zoo and Aquarium Association–accredited zoo built by a community, stroll along the shaded boardwalks and get a close-up look at alligators, crocodiles, giant anteaters, marmosets, jaguars, eagles, river otters, kangaroos, exotic birds, and kookaburras. Alligator, crocodile, and river-otter feedings are held on alternate afternoons—although the alligators do not dine on the otters. Stop by Paws-On, an interactive learning playground where kids and adults can crawl into human-size gopher burrows, beehives, and spider webs; get cozy with several domestic animals in Animal Encounters; hand-feed a giraffe in Expedition Africa or a lorikeet in the Australian Free Flight Aviary; and step up to the Wetlands Outpost, an elevated pavilion that's a gateway to 22 acres of wetlands through which you can paddle kayaks and keep an eye open for the 4,000 species of wildlife that live in these waters and woods. ⊠ *8225 N. Wickham Rd.* ☎ *321/254-9453* ⊕ *www.brevardzoo.org* ⊠ *$12.50 for general admission; $17 for admission, a train ride, and food for the lorikeets* ⊙ *Daily 9:30–5, last admission at 4:15.*

① Kennedy Space Center Visitor Complex. This must-see attraction, just southeast of Titusville, is one of Central Florida's most popular sights. Located on a 140,000-acre island 45 minutes outside Orlando, Kennedy Space Center is NASA's launch headquarters, where the space shuttle is prepared for flight, launched into space, and returns after its mission. The Visitor Complex gives guests a unique opportunity to

Fodor's Choice
★

Fodor's Choice
★

learn about—and experience—the past, present, and future of America's space program.

The Shuttle Launch Experience uses a sophisticated motion-based platform, special-effects seats, and high-fidelity visual and audio components to simulate the sensations experienced in an actual Space Shuttle launch. It's included in the basic admission price, which also includes whatever film is showing in the IMAX theater. The basic bus tour includes many different exhibits and activities, including a stop at the **Launch Complex 39 Observation Gantry,** which has an unparalleled view of the twin space-shuttle launchpads. An outdoor display includes examples of many different rockets. The most moving exhibit is the **Astronaut Memorial,** a tribute to those who have died while in pursuit of space exploration. You can pay for many different additional experiences, including a daily Q&A session, a lunch with an astronaut, or a NASA Up Close tour. ⊠ *Rte. 405, Kennedy Space Center* ☎ *321/449–4444* ⊕ *www.kennedyspacecenter.com* ⊠ *General admission includes bus tour, IMAX movies, Visitor Complex shows and exhibits, and the Astronaut Hall of Fame, $38* ⊙ *Space Center opens daily at 9, closing times vary according to season (call for details), last regular tour 3 hrs before closing; closed certain launch dates.*

❸
Fodor'sChoice
★
Merritt Island National Wildlife Refuge. Adjoining the Canaveral National Seashore, this refuge acts as a buffer around Kennedy Space Center, while protecting 500 species of wildlife, including 10 considered threatened or endangered. It's an immense area dotted by brackish estuaries and marshes and patches of land consisting of coastal dunes, scrub oaks, pine forests and flatwoods, and palm and oak hammocks. You can borrow field guides and binoculars at the visitor center to track down various types of falcons, ospreys, eagles, turkeys, doves, cuckoos, loons, geese, skimmers, terns, warblers, wrens, thrushes, sparrows, owls, and woodpeckers. A 20-minute video about refuge wildlife and accessibility—only 10,000 acres are developed—can help orient you. You might take a self-guided tour along the 7-mi **Black Point Wildlife Drive.** On the **Oak Hammock Foot Trail** you can see wintering migratory waterfowl and learn about the plants of a hammock community. If you exit the north end of the refuge, look for the **Manatee Observation Area** just north of the Haulover Canal (maps are at the visitor center). They usually show up in spring and fall. The refuge is closed four days before a shuttle launch. ⊠ *Rte. 402, across Titusville Causeway* ☎ *321/861–0667, 321/861–0668 visitor center* ⊕ *www.fws.gov/ merrittisland* ⊠ *Free* ⊙ *Daily sunrise–sundown; visitor center weekdays 8–4:30, weekends 9–5 (Nov.–Mar.).*

❷ **United States Astronaut Hall of Fame.** The original Mercury 7 team and the later Gemini, Apollo, Skylab, and shuttle astronauts contributed to make this the world's premium archive of astronauts' personal stories. Authentic memorabilia and equipment from their collections tell the story of human space exploration. You'll watch videotapes of historic moments in the space program and see one-of-a-kind items like Wally Schirra's relatively archaic Sigma 7 Mercury space capsule, Gus Grissom's spacesuit (colored silver only because NASA thought silver looked more "spacey"), and a flag that made it to the moon. The exhibit **First on the Moon** focuses on crew selection for *Apollo 11* and the Soviet Union's role in the space race. Definitely don't miss the **Astronaut Adventure,** a hands-on discovery center with interactive exhibits that help you learn about space travel. One of the more challenging activities is a space-shuttle simulator that lets you try your hand at landing the craft—and afterward replays a side view of your rolling and pitching descent. ✉ *Rte. 405, Kennedy Space Center* ☎ *321/449–4444, 321/449–4400 ATX* ⊕ *www.kennedyspacecenter. com* 🖾 *$17* ☉ *Hall of Fame opens daily at 9, closing times vary according to season (call for details).*

PORT CANAVERAL BEST BETS

■ **Kennedy Space Center.** Kennedy Space Center in Titusville is the region's biggest attraction.

■ **Merritt Island.** If you want to get out and commune with nature, this is the place, especially for bird-watchers.

■ **Orlando Theme Parks.** With Orlando just an hour away, many cruisers combine a theme-park visit with their cruise.

ORLANDO THEME PARKS

☺ **SeaWorld Orlando.** In the world's largest marine adventure park, every attraction is devoted to demonstrating the ways that humans can protect the mammals, birds, fish, and reptiles that live in the ocean and its tributaries. The presentations are gentle reminders of our responsibility to safeguard the environment, and you'll find that SeaWorld's use of humor plays a major role in this education. The park is small enough that, armed with a map that lists show times, you can plan a chronological approach that flows easily from one attraction to the next. Near the intersection of I–4 and the Beeline Expressway; take I–4 to Exit 71 or 72 and follow signs. ✉ *7007 Sea Harbor Dr., International Drive Area, Orlando* ☎ *888/800–5447* ⊕ *www.seaworld.com* 🖾 *$74.95 for a 1-day ticket* ☉ *Daily 9–6 or 7, until as late as 10 summer and holidays; educational programs daily, some beginning as early as 6:30* AM.

☺ **Universal Orlando.** The resort consists of **Universal Studios** (the original movie theme park), **Islands of Adventure** (the second theme park), and **CityWalk** (the dining-shopping-nightclub complex). Although it's bordered by residential neighborhoods and thickly trafficked International Drive, Universal Orlando is surprisingly expansive yet intimate and accessible, with two massive parking complexes, easy walks to all attractions, and a motor launch that cruises to the hotels. Universal Orlando emphasizes "two parks, two days, one great adventure," but you may find the presentation, creativity, and cutting-edge technology bring you back for more. ✉ *1000 Universal Studios Plaza, Orlando* ☎ *407/363–8000* ⊕ *www.universalorlando.com* 🖾 *1-day, 1-park ticket $79.99* ☉ *Usually daily 9–7, but hrs vary seasonally; CityWalk restaurants and bars have individual open hrs.*

☺ **Walt Disney World.** Walt Disney World is a huge complex of theme parks and attractions, each of which is worth a visit. Parks include the **Magic Kingdom,** a family favorite and the original here; **Epcot,** Disney's international, educational park; Disney–MGM Studios, a movie-oriented theme park; and Disney's Animal Kingdom, which is much more than a zoo. Beyond these, there are water parks, elaborate minigolf courses, a sports center, resorts, restaurants, and nightlife. If you have only one day, you'll have to concentrate on a single park;

> **WRITE EASY**
>
> Preaddress a page of stick-on labels before you leave home; use them for postcards to the folks back home and you will not have to carry along a bulky address book.

Disney–MGM Studios or Animal Kingdom are easiest to do in a day, but arrive early and expect to stay until park closing, which might be as early as 5 PM for Animal Kingdom or as late as 11 PM during busy seasons at the Magic Kingdom. The most direct route to the Disney Parks from Port Canaveral is S.R. 528 (the Beeline Expressway) to I–4; when you get through Orlando, follow the signs to Disney and expect traffic. ⊠ *Lake Buena Vista* ☎ *407/824–4321* ⊕ *disneyworld.disney. go.com* ✉ *1-day, 1-park pass $79* ⊙ *Most parks open by 9 AM; closing hrs vary, but usually 5 PM for Animal Kingdom and 6–11 PM for other parks, depending on season.*

BEACHES

Alan Shepard Park. Named for the former astronaut, this 5-acre ocean-front park, aptly enough, provides excellent views of shuttle launches. Facilities include 10 picnic pavilions, shower and restroom facilities, and more than 300 parking spaces. Those spaces are in high-demand on launch days, but the park's are a nice break any other day, too. Parking is $7 per day, $10 per day on weekends and holidays from early March through Labor Day. Shops and restaurants are within walking distance. ⊠ *East end of Rte. 250* ☎ *321/868–3274.*

Playalinda Beach. The southern access for the Canaveral National Sea-shore, remote Playalinda Beach has pristine sands and is the longest stretch of undeveloped coast on Florida's Atlantic seaboard. Its isolation explains why there are limited services (no phones, food service, drinking water, or lifeguards from May 30 to September 1) and why a remote strand of the beach is popular with nude sunbathers. Aside from them, hundreds of giant sea turtles come ashore here from May through August to lay their eggs. Eight parking lots anchor the beach at 1-mi intervals. To get here, take Interstate 95 Exit 220 east and follow the signs. Take bug repellent in case of horseflies. ⊠ *Rte. 402/Beach Rd.* ☎ *321/867–4077* ⊕ *www.nps.gov/cana* ✉ *$3 per person (admission to the National Seashore)* ⊙ *Nov.–Mar., daily 6–6; Apr.–Oct., daily 6–8.*

Sidney Fischer Park. The 10-acre oceanfront has showers, playgrounds, changing areas, picnic areas with grills, snack shops, and plenty of well-maintained, inexpensive surfside parking lots. Beach vendors carry necessities for sunning and swimming. The parking fee is $5 for cars and RVs. ⊠ *2100 block of Rte. A1A* ☎ *321/868–3252.*

SHOPPING

Cocoa Beach Surf Company (⊠ *4001 N. Atlantic Ave.* ☏ *321/799–9930*) is the world's largest surf complex, with three floors of boards, apparel, sunglasses, and anything else a surfer, wannabe-surfer, or souvenir-seeker could need. Also on-site are a 5,600-gallon fish and shark tank, the Shark Pit Bar & Grill, and the **East Coast Surfing Hall of Fame and Museum.**

Fodor's Choice
★ It's impossible to miss the **Ron Jon Surf Shop** (⊠ *4151 N. Atlantic Ave., Rte. A1A* ☏ *321/799–8888* ⊕ *www.ronjonsurfshop.com*). With a giant surfboard and an aqua, teal, and pink art-deco facade, Ron Jon takes up nearly two blocks along Route A1A. What started in 1963 as a small T-shirt and bathing-suit shop has evolved into a 52,000-square-foot superstore that's open every day 'round the clock. The shop has water-sports gear as well as chairs and umbrellas for rent and sells every kind of beachwear, surf wax, plus the requisite T-shirts and flip-flops.

■ **TIP**➔ For up-to-the-minute surfing conditions, call the store and press 3 and then 7 for the Ron Jon Surf and Weather Report.

WHERE TO EAT

The Cove at Port Canaveral has several restaurants if you are looking for a place to eat right at the port.

For price categories, see ⇨ *Dining at the beginning of this chapter.*

$$$
GERMAN
✕ **Heidelberg.** As the name suggests, the cuisine here is definitely German, from the sauerbraten served with potato dumplings and red cabbage to the beef Stroganoff and spaetzle to the classically prepared Wiener schnitzel. All the soups and desserts are homemade; try the Viennese-style apple strudel and the rum-zapped almond-cream tortes. Elegant interior touches include crisp linens and fresh flowers. There's live music Friday and Saturday evenings. You can also dine inside the jazz club, Heidi's, next door. ⊠ *7 N. Orlando Ave., opposite City Hall* ☏ *321/783–6806* ⊕ *www.heidisjazzclub.com* ▭ *AE, MC, V* ⊙ *Closed Mon. Closed Tues. in summer. No lunch Sun.*

$
SEAFOOD
✕ **Oh Shucks Seafood Bar.** At the only open-air seafood bar on the beach, at the entrance of the Cocoa Beach Pier, the main item is oysters, served on the half shell. You can also grab a burger here, crab legs by the pound, or Oh Shucks' most popular item, coconut beer shrimp. Some diners complain that the prices don't jibe with the ultracasual atmosphere (e.g., plastic chairs), but they're also paying for the "ex-Pier-ience." There's live entertainment on Friday and Saturday. ⊠ *401 Meade Ave., Cocoa Beach Pier* ☏ *321/783–7549* ▭ *AE, D, MC, V.*

WHERE TO STAY

Many local hotels offer cruise packages that include one night's lodging, parking for the duration of your cruise, and transportation to the cruise port.

For price categories, see ⇨ Lodging at the beginning of this chapter.

$$$ 🏨 **Inn at Cocoa Beach.** One of the area's best, this charming oceanfront ★ inn has spacious, individually decorated rooms with four-poster beds, upholstered chairs, and balconies or patios; most have ocean views. Deluxe rooms are much larger, with a king-size bed, sofa, and sitting area; most also have a dining table. Jacuzzi rooms are different sizes. Included in the rate are afternoon socials in the breezeway, evening wine and cheese, and a Continental breakfast. **Pros:** quiet; romantic; honor bar. **Cons:** no on-site restaurant; "forced" socializing. ✉ *4300 Ocean Beach Blvd.* ☎ *321/799–3460, 800/343–5307 outside Florida* ⊕ *www.theinnatcocoabeach.com* 🛏 *50 rooms* ♿ *In-room: safe, DVD (some). In-hotel: pool, beachfront, parking (free), Wi-Fi hotspot* ▭ *AE, D, MC, V* 🍽 *CP.*

$$$ 🏨 **Radisson Resort at the Port.** For cruise-ship passengers who can't wait to get under way, this splashy resort, done up in pink and turquoise, already feels like the Caribbean. Guest rooms have wicker furniture, hand-painted wallpaper, tropical-theme decor, and ceiling fans. The pool is lushly landscaped and features a cascading 95-foot mountain waterfall, tiki bar, and occasional appearances by the "Radisson parrots," about a dozen renegade birds who call the resort home (can you blame them?). This resort, directly across the bay from Port Canaveral, is not on the ocean, but it does provide complimentary transportation to the beach, Ron Jon Surf Shop, and the cruise-ship terminals at Port Canaveral. **Pros:** cruise-ship convenience; pool area; free shuttle. **Cons:** three-day cancellation policy; rooms around the pool can be noisy; loud air-conditioning in some rooms; no breakfast. ✉ *8701 Astronaut Blvd.* ☎ *321/784–0000 or 888/201–1718* ⊕ *www.radisson.com/ capecanaveralfl* 🛏 *284 rooms, 72 suites* ♿ *In-room: kitchen (some), refrigerator (some), Internet, Wi-Fi. In-hotel: restaurant, bar, tennis court, pool, gym, laundry facilities, laundry service, Wi-Fi hotspot* ▭ *AE, D, MC, V.*

SAN JUAN, PUERTO RICO

Heather Rodino

In addition to being a major port of call, San Juan is also a common port of embarkation for cruises on Southern Caribbean itineraries.

For information on dining, shopping, nightlife, and sightseeing see ⇨ San Juan, Puerto Rico in Chapter 4.

THE CRUISE PORT

Most cruise ships dock within a couple of blocks of Old San Juan. The Paseo de la Princesa, a tree-lined promenade beneath the city wall, is a nice place for a stroll—you can admire the local crafts and stop at the refreshment kiosks. A tourist information center is in the cruise terminal area. Major sights in Old San Juan are mere blocks from the piers, but be aware that the streets are narrow and steeply inclined in places. Even if you have only a few hours before your cruise, you'll have time to do a little sightseeing. A few ships dock across the bay, which will require you to take a taxi everywhere.

EXTRA BATTERIES
Even if you don't think you'll need them, bring along extra camera batteries and change them before you think the old ones are dead.

AIRPORT TRANSFERS

The ride from the Luis Muñoz Marín International Airport, east of downtown San Juan, to the docks in Old San Juan takes about 20 minutes. The white TAXI TURISTICO cabs, marked by a logo on the door, have a fixed rate of $19 to the cruise-ship piers; there is a $1 charge for each piece of luggage. Other taxi companies charge by the mile, which can cost a little more. Be sure the driver starts the meter, or agree on a fare beforehand.

VISITOR INFORMATION **Puerto Rico Tourism Company** (✉ *Edificio Ochoa, 500 Calle de la Tanca, across from Pier 1, Old San Juan* ☎ *787/721–2400 or 787/722–1709* ⊕ *www. gotopuertorico.com*).

WHERE TO STAY

If you are planning to spend one night in San Juan before your cruise departs, you'll probably find it easier to stay in Old San Juan, where the cruise-ship terminals are. But if you want to spend a few extra days in the city, there are other possibilities near good beaches a bit farther out. We make some nightlife suggestions in the San Juan port of call section (*see* ⇨ *San Juan in Chapter 4*).

For price categories, see ⇨ *Lodging at the beginning of this chapter.*

$$$$ **Hotel El Convento.** Carmelite nuns once inhabited this 350-year-old
HOTEL convent, but they never had high-tech gadgets such as in-room broad-
Fodor'sChoice band connections or plasma TVs. The accommodations here beautifully
★ combine the old and the new. All the guest rooms are lavish and inviting, and have a mix of wrought-iron and hand-hewn wood furniture,
shuttered windows, and mahogany-beamed ceilings, but some have
extra appeal—hence the hotel was featured in the May 2002 issue of
Architectural Digest. Room 508 has two views of the bay, while rooms
216, 217, and 218 have private walled patios. Guests gather on the
second floor for the complimentary wine and hors d'oeuvres that are
served before dinner, with a lovely view over the nearby cathedral. The
second-floor El Picoteo and the courtyard Café del Níspero are good
dining choices. **Pros:** lovely building; atmosphere to spare; plenty of
nearby dining options. **Cons:** near some noisy bars. ✉ *100 Calle Cristo,
Old San Juan* ⊕ *Box 1048, 00902* ☎ *787/723–9020 or 800/468–2779*
⊕ *www.elconvento.com* ✍ *63 rooms, 5 suites* ⚹ *In-room: safe, DVD,
Ethernet, Wi-Fi. In-hotel: 3 restaurants, bars, pool, gym, concierge,
laundry service, public Internet, public Wi-Fi, parking (fee), no-smoking
rooms* ▭ *AE, D, DC, MC, V* ⏐⊙⏐ *EP.*

$–$$
HOTEL

🖵 **Howard Johnson Plaza de Armas.** On Old San Juan's main square, this hotel couldn't be more convenient. All the most popular sights are within easy walking distance. Some of the building's best architectural details, such as the tile floors, have been preserved. The best rooms are in the front, where shuttered doorways lead to balconies overlooking the Plaza de Armas. Some of the inner rooms are a bit cramped, as is the lobby, which has a streetfront café with Internet. Decor is a tad frumpy, but all the essentials are in place, and the hotel is kept spic and span. The interior courtyard has a hip little bar area. **Pros:** great location; quiet courtyard; good value. **Cons:** some rooms have very small windows; some street noise. ⊠ *202 Calle San José, Old San Juan* ☎ *787/722–9191* ⊕ *www.hojo.com* ⥽ *51 rooms* ⚫ *In-room: refrigerator (some). In-hotel: bar* ▭ *AE, D, DC, MC, V* ⏺⏺ *CP.*

$$$$
HOTEL

🖵 **Sheraton Old San Juan Hotel.** This hotel's triangular shape subtly echoes the cruise ships docked nearby. Rooms facing the water have dazzling views of these behemoths as they sail in and out of the harbor. (Interior rooms, however, face black concrete walls.) The plushly furnished rooms have nice touches like custom-designed beds, but they feel institutional. On the top floor you'll find a sunny patio with a pool and whirlpool bath, as well as a spacious gym with the latest equipment. Facilities here include two restaurants—a steak house and a burger joint—and a casino, which dominates the lobby. **Pros:** harbor views; near many dining options; good array of room types. **Cons:** motel feel to guest rooms; noise from casino overwhelms lobby and restaurants; extra charges for everything from bottled water to Internet access. ⊠ *100 Calle Brumbaugh, Old San Juan* ☎ *787/721–5100 or 866/376–7577* ⊕ *www.sheratonoldsanjuan.com* ⥽ *200 rooms, 40 suites* ⚫ *In-room: safe, refrigerator, Ethernet. In-hotel: restaurant, room service, bar, pool, gym, laundry service, executive floor, public Internet, parking (fee), no-smoking rooms* ▭ *AE, D, DC, MC, V* ⏺⏺ *EP.*

TAMPA, FLORIDA

Christina
Tourigny

Although glitzy Miami seems to hold the trendiness trump card and Orlando is the place your kids want to visit annually until they hit middle school, the Tampa Bay area has that elusive quality that many attribute to the "real Florida." The state's second-largest metro area is less fast-lane than its biggest (Miami), or even Orlando, but its strengths are just as varied, from broad cultural diversity to a sun-worshiping beach culture. Florida's third-busiest airport, a vibrant business community, world-class beaches, and superior hotels and resorts—many of them historic—make this an excellent place to spend a week or a lifetime. Several ships are based here year-round and seasonally, most doing Western Caribbean itineraries.

ESSENTIALS

HOURS   Some museums are closed on Monday.

INTERNET   Most people choose to access the Internet through their hotels. Most Starbucks outlets offer Internet service for a fee if you have your own laptop.

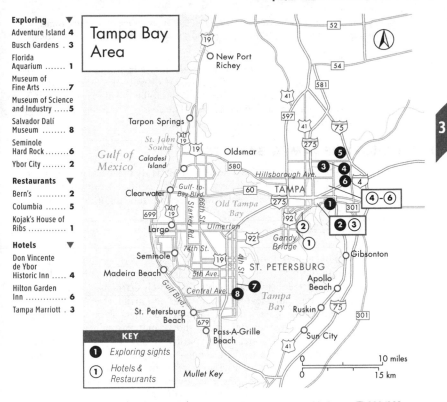

KEY

❶ *Exploring sights*

① *Hotels &
Restaurants*

VISITOR **Tampa Bay & Company** (✉ *401 E. Jackson St., Suite 2100, Tampa* ☎ *800/368–*
INFORMATION *2672 or 813/223–1111* ⊕ *www.visittampabay.com).* **Ybor City Chamber Visitor**
Bureau (✉ *1600 E. 8th Ave., Suite B104, Tampa* ☎ *813/241–8838* ⊕ *www.ybor.org*).

THE CRUISE PORT

Tampa is the largest shipping port in the state of Florida, and it's becoming ever more important to the cruise industry, now with three passenger
terminals. In Tampa's downtown area, the port is linked to nearby Ybor
City and the rest of the Tampa Bay Area by the TECO streetcar line.

To reach the port by car, take I–4 West to Exit 1 (Ybor City), and go
south on 21st Street. To get to terminals 2 and 6, turn right on Adamo
Drive (Highway 60), then left on Channelside Drive.

Contacts Tampa Port Authority (✉ *1101 Channelside Dr.* ☎ *813/905–7678,*
813/905–5045, or 800/741–2297 ⊕ *www.tampaport.com*).

AIRPORT TRANSFERS

Both Bay Shuttle and Super Shuttle provide shared van service to and
from the airport and the cruise terminal. Expect to pay about $14 per
person.

Information Bay Shuttle (☎ 813/259–9998 ⊕ www.tampabayshuttle.com).
Super Shuttle (☎ 727/572–1111 or 800/282–6817 ⊕ www.supershuttle.com).

PARKING

Parking is available at the port directly across from the terminals. For terminals 2 and 3 (Carnival and Royal Caribbean), parking is in a garage across the street. For Terminal 6 (Holland America), parking is outdoors in a guarded, enclosed lot. The cost is $14 a day, payable by credit card (MasterCard or Visa) or in cash.

EXPLORING THE TAMPA BAY AREA

Florida's west-coast crown jewel as well as its business and commercial hub, Tampa has high-rises and heavy traffic. Amid the bustle is the region's greatest concentration of restaurants, nightlife, stores, and cultural events.

Numbers in the margin refer to points of interest on the Tampa Bay Area map.

❹ **Adventure Island.** From spring until mid-fall, rides named Tampa Typhoon, Gulf Scream, and Key West Rapids promise heat relief at this corporate cousin and neighbor of Busch Gardens. Tampa's most popular "wet" park features waterslides and artificial wave pools in a 30-acre package. One of the attraction's headliners, Riptide, challenges you to race three other riders on a sliding mat through twisting tubes and hairpin turns. Planners of this park also took the younger kids into account, with offerings such as Fabian's Funport, which has a scaled-down wave pool and interactive water gym. Along with a volleyball complex and a surf pool, there are cafés, snack bars, picnic and sun-bathing areas, and changing rooms. ⊠ *1001 Malcolm McKinley Dr., less than 1 mi north of Busch Gardens, Central Tampa* ☎ *813/987–5660 or 888/800–5447* ⊕ *www.adventureisland.com* ⌐ *$44.95; parking $10* ⊙ *Mid-Mar.–late Oct., daily 10–5.*

❸ **Busch Gardens.** Nearly 4½ million vacationers and locals flock here each year. The hook: five roller coasters are an irresistible lure for thrill-ride jockeys. But this state-of-the-art attraction also is a world-class zoo, with more than 2,000 animals, and a live-entertainment venue that provides a full day (or more) of entertainment for the whole family. The 335-acre adventure park's habitats offer views of some of the world's most endangered and exotic animals. You can experience up-close animal encounters (for an extra charge), and there are many individual shows and special exhibit areas to bring you up close and personal with a wide variety of animals. Not to mention those rides. Allow six to eight hours to experience Busch Gardens. ⊠ *3000 E. Busch Blvd., 8 mi northeast of downtown Tampa and 2 mi east of I–275 Exit 50, Central Tampa* ☎ *813/987–5000 or 888/800–5447* ⊕ *www.buschgardens.com* ⌐ *$74.95; parking $12* ⊙ *Daily 10–6.*

FodorśChoice
★

❶ **Florida Aquarium.** Eels, sharks, and stingrays may be the headliners, but this is much more than a giant fishbowl. It is a dazzling architectural landmark with an 83-foot-high multitier glass dome and 200,000 square feet of air-conditioned exhibit space. It has more than 10,000 aquatic plants, and animals representing species native to Florida and the rest of the world. The major exhibit areas reflect the diversity of Florida's natural habitats—Wetlands, Bays and Beaches, and Coral Reef. Creature-specific exhibits are the No Bone Zone (lovable invertebrates) and Sea Hunt, with predators ranging from sharks to exotic lionfish. The aquarium's most impressive single exhibit is the Coral Reef Gallery, in a 500,000-gallon tank ringed with viewing windows, including an awesome 43-foot-wide panoramic opening. Part of the tank is a walkable tunnel, almost giving the illusion of venturing into underwater depths. There you see a thicket of elkhorn coral teeming with tropical fish. A dark cave reveals sea life you would normally see only on night dives. ✉ *701 Channelside Dr., Downtown, Tampa* ☎ *813/273–4000* ⊕ *www.flaquarium.org* ✉ *Aquarium $19.95, Ecotour $21.95; Aquarium/Ecotour combo $35.95; parking $6* ☾ *Daily 9:30–5.*

> ### TAMPA BEST BETS
>
> ■ **Busch Gardens.** The area's best theme park is a good family destination.
>
> ■ **Florida Aquarium.** The aquarium is next to the cruise port, so you can just walk, making it a good option even if you have a couple of hours to kill before boarding (they'll even store your luggage if you want to visit after disembarking).
>
> ■ **Ybor City.** For nightlife and restaurants, this historic district is Tampa's hot spot.

7 Museum of Fine Arts. Outstanding examples of European, American, pre-Columbian, and Far Eastern art are at St. Petersburg's major art museum. There are also photographic exhibits. Staff members give narrated gallery tours two to five times a day. ✉ *255 Beach Dr. NE* ☎ *727/896–2667* ⊕ *www.fine-arts.org* ✉ *$14* ☾ *Tues.–Sat. 10–5, Sun. 1–5.*

5 Museum of Science and Industry (MOSI). This is a fun and stimulating scientific playground, though at times some exhibits aren't working properly. When it's hitting on all cylinders, you learn about Florida weather, anatomy, flight, and space by seeing *and* by doing. At the Gulf Coast Hurricane Exhibit you can experience what a hurricane and its 74-MPH winds feel like, though crowds sometimes mean a long wait. The BioWorks Butterfly Garden is a 6,400-square-foot engineered ecosystem project that demonstrates how wetlands can clean water plus serve as a home for butterflies. The 100-seat Saunders Planetarium—Tampa's only planetarium—has afternoon and evening shows, one of them a trek through the universe. For adventurous spirits, there's a high-wire bicycle ride 30 feet above the floor. There's also an impressive IMAX theater, where films are projected on a hemispherical 82-foot dome. ✉ *4801 E. Fowler Ave., 1 mi north of Busch Gardens, Northeast Tampa* ☎ *813/987–6100 or 800/995–6674* ⊕ *www.mosi.org* ✉ *$23.95* ☾ *Weekdays 9–5, weekends 9–6.*

8 Salvador Dalí Museum. The collection includes 95 oils, more than 100 watercolors and drawings, and 1,300 graphics, sculptures, photographs, and objets d'art, including floor-to-ceiling murals. Frequent tours are led by well-informed docents. How did the collection end up here? A rich northern industrialist and friend of Dalí, Ohio magnate A. Reynolds

Fodor's Choice ★

Morse, was looking for a museum site after his huge personal Dalí collection began to overflow his mansion. The people of St. Petersburg vied admirably for the collection, and the museum was established here as a result. At this writing, a new museum—twice the size of this facility—was scheduled to open just south of the Mahaffey Theater and Baker in January 2011. ⊠ *1000 3rd St. S* ☎ *727/823–3767 or 800/442–3254* ⊕ *www.salvadordalimuseum.org* ⊡ *$15* ⊙ *Mon.–Wed. and Sat. 9:30–5:30, Thurs. 9:30–8, Fri. 9:30–6:30, Sun. noon–5:30.*

❻ **Seminole Hard Rock Hotel & Casino.** The latest buzz at the casino is about the much-anticipated upgrade that may add blackjack and baccarat to the gaming areas. Until the formalities are addressed (including legislative action and a possible legal challenge), gamers can still get their kicks at the casino's poker tables, slot machines, and video gaming machines. The casino lounge serves drinks 24 hours a day. Floyd's restaurant has dinner and nightlife. ⊠ *5223 N. Orient Rd., off I–4 at N. Orient Rd. Exit* ☎ *813/627–7625 or 866/502–7529* ⊕ *www.seminolehardrock. com* ⊡ *Free* ⊙ *Daily 24 hrs.*

❷ **Ybor City.** Tampa's lively Latin quarter is one of only four National

Fodor's Choice Historic Landmark districts in Florida. It has antique-brick streets and

★ wrought-iron balconies. Cubans brought their cigar-making industry to Ybor (pronounced *ee*-bore) City in 1886, and the smell of cigars—hand-rolled by Cuban immigrants—still wafts through the heart of this east Tampa area, along with the strong aroma of roasting coffee. These days the neighborhood is one of Tampa's hot spots, if at times a rowdy one, as empty cigar factories and historic social clubs have been transformed into trendy boutiques, art galleries, restaurants, and nightclubs.

Step back into the past at **Centennial Park** (⊠ *8th Ave. and 18th St.*), which re-creates a period streetscape and hosts the Fresh Market every Saturday. The **Ybor City Museum State Park** provides a look at the history of the cigar industry. Admission includes a tour of La Casita, one of the shotgun houses occupied by cigar workers and their families in the late 1890s. ⊠ *1818 E. 9th Ave., between Nuccio Pkwy. and 22nd St., from 7th to 9th Ave., Tampa* ☎ *813/247–6323* ⊕ *www.ybormuseum. org* ⊡ *$4, walking tours $6* ⊙ *Daily 9–5; walking tours Sat. 10:30.*

BEACHES

Spread over five small islands, or keys, 1,136-acre **Fort De Soto Park** (⊠ *3500 Pinellas Bayway S, Tierra Verde* ☎ *727/582–2267* ⊡ *Free*) lies at the mouth of Tampa Bay. It has 7 mi of beaches, two fishing piers, a 4-mi hiking-skating trail, picnic and camping grounds, and a historic fort that kids of any age can explore. The fort for which it's named was built on the southern end of Mullet Key to protect sea-lanes in the gulf during the Spanish-American War. Roam the fort or wander the beaches of any of the islands within the park. **Pass-A-Grille Beach** (⊠ *Off Gulf Blvd. [Rte. 699], St. Pete Beach*), at the southern end of St. Pete Beach, has parking meters, a snack bar, restrooms, and showers. It and Clearwater Beach are two of the area's most popular saltwater swimming holes.

SHOPPING

Ybor City's destination within a destination is the dining and entertainment palace **Centro Ybor** (✉ *1600 E. 8th Ave., Ybor City*). It has shops, trendy bars and restaurants, a 20-screen movie theater, and GameWorks, an interactive playground developed by Steven Spielberg. **Channelside** (✉ *615 Channelside Dr., Downtown*) offers movie theaters, shops, restaurants, and clubs. The official Tampa Bay visitor center is also here. If you want to grab something at Neiman Marcus or Nordstrom on your way to the airport, the upscale **International Plaza** (✉ *2223 N. West Shore Blvd., Airport Area*) has Betsey Johnson, J. Crew, L'Occitane, Louis Vuitton, Tiffany & Co., and many other shops. **Old Hyde Park Village** (✉ *Swan Ave. near Bayshore Blvd., Hyde Park*) is a typical shopping district, just like the ones you find in every major American city. Williams-Sonoma and Brooks Brothers are mixed in with bistros and sidewalk cafés.

NIGHTLIFE

Although there are more boarded storefronts than in the past, the biggest concentration of nightclubs, as well as the widest variety, is found along 7th Avenue in Ybor City. It becomes a little like Bourbon Street in New Orleans on weekend evenings. **Centro Cantina** (✉ *1600 E. 8th Ave., Ybor City* ☎ *813/241–8588*) has a balcony overlooking the crowds on 7th Avenue. There's live music Thursday through Sunday nights, a large selection of margaritas, and more than 30 brands of tequila. Food is served until 2 AM. International Plaza's **Bay Street** (✉ *2223 N. West Shore Blvd., Airport Area*) has become one of Tampa's dining and imbibing hot spots. Considered something of a dive—but a lovable one—by a loyal and young local following that ranges from esteemed jurists to nose-ring-wearing night owls, the **Hub** (✉ *719 N. Franklin St., Downtown* ☎ *813/229–1553*) is known for having one of Tampa's best martinis and one of its most eclectic jukeboxes.

WHERE TO EAT

For price categories, see ➪ *Dining at the beginning of this chapter.*

$$$$
STEAK
Fodor'sChoice
★

✕**Bern's Steak House.** With the air of an exclusive club, this is one of Florida's finest steak houses. Rich mahogany paneling and ornate chandeliers define the legendary Bern's, where the chef ages his own beef, grows his own organic vegetables, roasts his own coffee, and maintains his own saltwater fish tanks. There's also a Cave Du Fromage, housing a discriminating selection of artisanal cheeses from around the world. Cuts of topmost beef are sold by weight and thickness. There's a 60-ounce strip steak that's big enough to feed your pride (of lions), but for most appetites the veal loin chop or 8-ounce chateaubriand is more than enough. The wine list includes approximately 7,000 selections (with 1,000 dessert wines). After dinner, tour the kitchen and wine cellar before having dessert upstairs in a cozy booth. The dessert room is a hit. For a real jolt, try the Turkish coffee with an order of Mississippi mud pie. Casual business attire is recommended. ✉ *1208 S.*

Howard Ave., Hyde Park ☎ *813/251–2421* ⊕ *www.bernssteakhouse. com* ⌂ *Reservations essential* ⊟ *AE, D, MC, V.*

$$
SPANISH
Fodor'sChoice
★

✕ **Columbia**. Make a date for some of the best Latin cuisine in Tampa. A fixture since 1905, this magnificent structure with an Old World air, spacious dining rooms, and a sunny courtyard takes up an entire city block, and seems to feed the entire city—locals as well as travelers— throughout the week, but especially on weekends. The paella, bursting with seafood, chicken, and pork, is arguably the best in Florida, and the 1905 salad—with ham, olives, cheese, and garlic—is legendary. The menu has Cuban classics such as *boliche criollo* (tender eye of round stuffed with chorizo sausage), *ropa vieja* (shredded beef with onions, peppers, and tomatoes), and *arroz con pollo* (chicken with yellow rice). Don't miss the flamenco dancing show every night but Sunday. ✉ *2117 E. 7th Ave., Ybor City* ☎ *813/248–4961* ⊕ *www.columbiarestaurant. com* ⊟ *AE, D, DC, MC, V.*

$
SOUTHERN

✕ **Kojak's House of Ribs**. Few barbecue joints can boast the staying power of this family-owned and -operated pit stop, which had its debut in 1978. In the last three decades it has earned a following of sticky-fingered regulars who have turned it into one of the most popular barbecue stops in central Florida. It could pass for a century-old Cracker house complete with veranda, pillars supporting the overhanging roof, and brick steps. Day and night, three indoor dining rooms and an outdoor dining porch have a steady stream of hungry patrons digging into tender pork spareribs that are dry-rubbed and tanned overnight before visiting the smoker for a couple of hours. Then they're bathed in the sauce of your choice. Kojak's also has a nice selection of sandwiches, including sloppy chicken and country-style sausage. ✉ *2808 Gandy Blvd., South Tampa* ☎ *813/837–3774* ⊕ *www.kojaksbbq.com* ⊟ *AE, D, MC, V* ✷ *Closed Mon.*

WHERE TO STAY

If you want to be close to the cruise-ship terminal, then you'll have to stay in Tampa, but if you want to spend more time in the area and perhaps stay on the beach, St. Petersburg and the beaches are close by.

For price categories, see ⇨ *Lodging at the beginning of this chapter.*

$$$
★

▥ **Don Vicente de Ybor Historic Inn**. Built as a home in 1895 by town founder Don Vicente de Ybor, this inn shows that the working-class cigar city had an elegant side, too. From the beige-stucco exterior to the white marble staircase in the main lobby, this boutique hotel is an architectural tour de force. Rooms have parquet floors, canopy beds, and private baths; most have wrought-iron balconies. Common areas have crystal chandeliers, Tiffany lamps, and Persian carpets. **Pros:** elegant rooms; rich in history; walking distance to nightlife. **Cons:** rowdy neighborhood on weekend nights. ✉ *1915 Republica de Cuba, Ybor City* ☎ *813/241–4545 or 866/206–4545* ⊕ *donvicenteinn.com* ⇆ *13 rooms, 3 suites* ⌂ *In-room: Internet, Wi-Fi. In-hotel: restaurant, bar, laundry service, Wi-Fi hotspot* ⊟ *AE, D, DC, MC, V* ❙⃝❙ *BP.*

$$–$$$
★

▥ **Hilton Garden Inn Tampa Ybor Historic District**. Although its modern architecture makes it seem out of place in this historic district, this chain hotel's location across from Centro Ybor is a plus. There is an on-site restaurant that serves breakfast, but be sure to take at least one day off to visit one of the nearby eateries for a traditional breakfast of *café cubano* or *café con leche* with a wedge of Cuban bread slathered with butter. **Pros:** good location for business travelers; reasonable rates. **Cons:** chain-hotel feel; far from downtown. ⊠ *1700 E. 9th Ave., Ybor City* ☎ *813/769–9267* ⊕ *www.hiltongardeninn.com* ⇆ *93 rooms, 2 suites* ♿ *In-room: refrigerator, Internet, Wi-Fi. In-hotel: restaurant, pool, laundry facilities, laundry service, Wi-Fi hotspot* ☰ *AE, D, DC, MC, V.*

$$$–$$$$ 🔲 **Tampa Marriott Waterside Hotel & Marina.** Across from the Tampa Convention Center, this downtown hotel was built for conventioneers, but is also convenient to tourist spots such as the Florida Aquarium and the Channelside and Hyde Park shopping districts. At least half the rooms and most of the suites overlook the concrete-walled channel to Tampa Bay, which has sparse boat traffic except on weekends; the bay itself is visible from the higher floors of the 27-story tower. The pillared lobby has real palm trees growing out of the gleaming tile floors, and the coffee bar overlooks the water. Il Terrazzo is the hotel's formal dining room. **Pros:** great downtown location; near shopping. **Cons:** gridlock during rush hour; area sketchy after dark; chain-hotel feel. ⊠ *700 S. Florida Ave., Downtown* ☎ *888/268–1616* ⊕ *www.marriott. com* ⇆ *681 rooms, 36 suites* ♿ *In-room: safe, kitchen (some), Internet, Wi-Fi. In-hotel: 3 restaurants, room service, bars, pool, gym, spa, laundry facilities, laundry service, parking (paid), Wi-Fi hotspot* ☰ *AE, D, DC, MC, V.*

Ports of Call

WORD OF MOUTH

"I research the ports, select what we want to do, and engage a cab driver when we get off the ship to take us around. It's much cheaper than the ship's shore excursion and personalized to our interests. Other people book excursions through private companies, and seem quite happy with that."

—abram

NOWHERE IN THE WORLD are conditions better suited to cruising than in the Caribbean Sea. Tiny island nations, within easy sailing distance of one another, form a chain of tropical enchantment that curves from Cuba in the north all the way down to the coast of Venezuela. There's far more to life here than sand and coconuts, however. The islands are vastly different, with a variety of cultures, topographies, and languages represented. Colonialism has left its mark, and the presence of the Spanish, French, Dutch, Danish, and British is still felt. Slavery, too, has left its cultural legacy, blending African overtones into the colonial/Indian amalgam. The one constant, however, is the weather. Despite the islands' southerly latitude, the climate is surprisingly gentle, due in large part to the cooling influence of the trade winds.

The Caribbean is made up of the Greater Antilles and the Lesser Antilles. The former consist of those islands closest to the United States: Cuba, Jamaica, Hispaniola (Haiti and the Dominican Republic), and Puerto Rico. (The Cayman Islands lie south of Cuba.) The Lesser Antilles, including the Virgin, Windward, and Leeward islands and others, are greater in number but smaller in size, and constitute the southern half of the Caribbean chain.

GOING ASHORE

Traveling by cruise ship presents an opportunity to visit many places in a short time. The flip side is that your stay in each port of call will be brief. For this reason cruise lines offer shore excursions, which maximize passengers' time. There are a number of advantages to shore excursions arranged by your ship: in some destinations, transportation may be unreliable, and a ship-packaged tour is the best way to see distant sights. Also, you don't have to worry about missing the ship. The disadvantage of a shore excursion is the cost—you usually pay more for the convenience of having the ship do the legwork for you, but it's not always a lot more. Of course, you can always book a tour independently, hire a taxi, or use foot power to explore on your own. For each port of call included in this guide we've provided some suggestions for the best ship-sponsored excursions—in terms of both quality of experience and price—as well as some suggestions for what to do if you want to explore on your own.

ARRIVING IN PORT

When your ship arrives in a port, it will tie up alongside a dock or anchor out in a harbor. If the ship is docked, passengers walk down the gangway to go ashore. Docking makes it easy to move between the shore and the ship.

TENDERING

If your ship anchors in the harbor, you will have to take a small boat—called a launch or tender—to get ashore. Tendering is a nuisance; however, participants in shore excursions are given priority. Passengers wishing to disembark independently may be required to gather in a public room, get sequenced boarding passes, and wait until their numbers are called. The ride to shore may take as long as 20 minutes. If you don't like waiting, plan to go ashore an hour or so after the ship drops its anchor. On a very large ship, the wait for a tender can be quite long and frustrating.

Because tenders can be difficult to board, passengers with mobility problems may not be able to visit certain ports. The larger ships are more likely to use tenders. It is usually possible to learn before booking a cruise whether the ship will dock or anchor at its ports of call.

Before anyone is allowed to walk down the gangway or board a tender, the ship must be cleared for landing. Immigration and customs officials board the vessel to examine passports and sort through red tape. It may be more than an hour before you're allowed ashore. You will be issued a boarding pass, which you'll need to get back on board.

4

RETURNING TO THE SHIP

Cruise lines are strict about sailing times, which are posted at the gangway and elsewhere and announced in the daily schedule of activities. Be sure to be back on board (not on the dock waiting to get a tender back to the ship) at least an hour before the announced sailing time or you may be stranded. If you are on a shore excursion that was sold by the cruise line, however, the captain will wait for your group before casting off. That is one reason many passengers prefer ship-packaged tours.

If you're not on one of the ship's tours and the ship sails without you, immediately contact the cruise line's port representative, whose phone number is often listed on the daily schedule of activities. You may be able to hitch a ride on a pilot boat, although that is unlikely. Passengers who miss the boat must pay their own way to the next port.

CARIBBEAN ESSENTIALS

CURRENCY

The U.S. dollar is the official currency on Puerto Rico, the U.S. Virgin Islands, the Turks and Caicos, and the British Virgin Islands. On Grand Cayman you will usually have a choice of Cayman or U.S. dollars when you take money out of an ATM, and you may even be able to get change in U.S. dollars. In Cozumel, Calica, Costa Maya, and Progreso, the Mexican peso is the official currency. The euro is used in a handful of French island (St. Barth, St. Martin, Martinique, Guadeloupe). In most Caribbean ports U.S. paper currency (not coins) is accepted readily. When you pay in dollars you'll almost always get change in local currency, so it's best to carry bills in small denominations. If you need local currency (say, for a trip to one of the French islands that uses the euro), change money at a local bank or use an ATM for the best rate. Most major credit cards are accepted all over the Caribbean, except at local market stalls and small establishments.

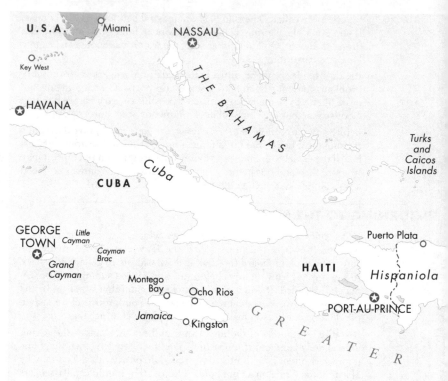

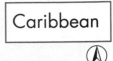

Caribbean

ATLANTIC OCEAN

4

LEEWARD ISLANDS

DOMINICAN REPUBLIC

St. John
St. Thomas
Tortola
Virgin Gorda
Anguilla
St. Barthélemy

⊕ SANTO DOMINGO

⊕ SAN JUAN
Puerto Rico

St. Croix

St. Maarten/
St. Martin
St. Eustatius
St. Kitts
Nevis

Saba

Barbuda

Antigua

A N T I L L E S

Montserrat
Guadeloupe

Marie Galante

Dominica

WINDWARD

Martinique
Fort-de-France ○

St. Lucia ○

Sea

Barbados
Bridgetown ○

St. Vincent
Bequia
The Grenadines
Carriacou
St. George's ○
Grenada

WILLEMSTAD

Aruba

Bonaire
⊕ Curaçao

Islas Los Roques

L E S S E R   A N T I L L E S

Tobago

Port of Spain ○ Trinidad

La Guaira
⊕
CARACAS

VENEZUELA

0		200 miles
0		300 km

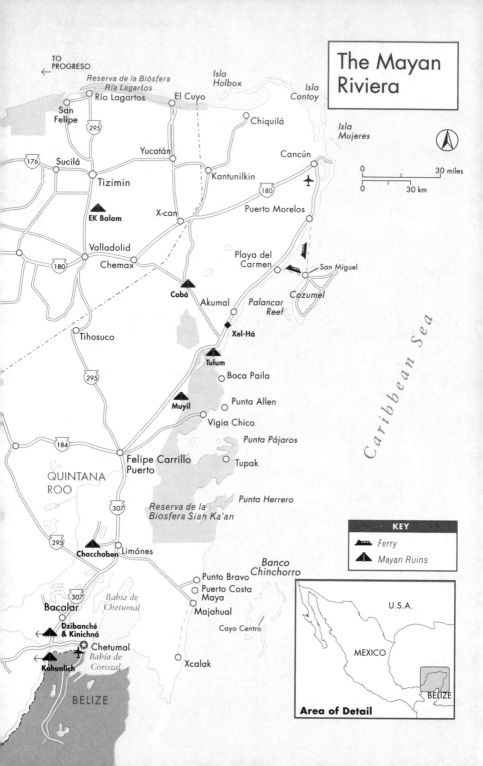

KEEPING IN TOUCH

Internet cafés are now fairly common on many islands, and you'll sometimes find Internet cafés in the cruise-ship terminal itself—or perhaps in an attached or nearby shopping center. If you want to call home, most cruise-ship facilities have phones that accept credit cards or local phone cards (local phone cards are almost always the cheapest option). And on most islands GSM multi-band mobile phones will work, though roaming charges may be steep (some plans include Puerto Rico and the U.S. Virgin Islands in their nationwide calling regions).

> ### BUYING LIQUOR AND PERFUME
>
> If you buy duty-free liquor or perfume while in a Caribbean port, don't forget that you may not bring it aboard your flight home. You will have to put it in your checked bags. Many liquor stores will pack your bottles in bubble wrap and pack them in a good cardboard box. Take advantage of this service.

WHERE TO EAT

Cuisine on the Caribbean's islands is as varied as the islands themselves. The region's history as a colonial battleground and ethnic melting pot creates plenty of variety and adds lots of unusual tropical fruit and spices. In fact, the one quality that defines most Caribbean cooking is its spiciness, acquired from nutmeg, mace, allspice, peppers, saffron, and many other seasonings grown in the islands. Dress is generally casual, although throughout the islands beachwear is inappropriate most anywhere except on the beach. Unless otherwise noted, prices are given in U.S. dollars. The following price categories are used in this book.

WHAT IT COSTS IN U.S. DOLLARS				
	¢	$	$$	$$$	$$$$
At Dinner	under $8	$8–$11	$12–$19	$20–$30	over $30

Prices are per person for a main course at dinner and do not include any service charges.

SHORE EXCURSIONS

Typical excursions include an island or town bus tour, a visit to a beach or rum factory, a boat trip, a snorkeling or diving trip, and charter fishing. In recent years, however, shore excursions have gotten more adventurous, with mild river-rafting, parasailing, jet-skiing, hiking, and biking added to the mix. It's often easier to take a ship-arranged excursion, but it's almost never the cheapest option.

If you prefer to break away from the pack, find a knowledgeable taxi driver or tour operator—they're usually within a stone's throw of the pier—or wander around on your own. A group of four to six people will usually find this option more economical and practical than will a single person or a couple.

Renting a car is also a good option on many islands—again, the more people, the better the deal. But get a good island map before you set off, and be sure to find out how long it will take you to get around.

Conditions are ideal for water sports of all kinds—scuba diving, snorkeling, windsurfing, sailing, waterskiing, and fishing excursions abound. Your shore-excursion director can usually arrange these activities for you if the ship offers no formal excursion.

PRIVATE ISLANDS

Linda Coffman   When evaluating the "best" Caribbean ports of call, many repeat cruise passengers often add the cruise lines' own private island to their lists of preferred destinations.

The cruise lines established "private" islands to provide a beach break on an island (or part of one) reserved for their exclusive use. While most passengers don't select an itinerary based solely upon calling at a private island, they usually consider them a highlight of their cruise vacation. The very least you can expect of your private island is lush foliage and a wide swath of beach surrounded by azure water. Facilities vary, but a beach barbecue, water-sports equipment rental, lounge chairs, hammocks, and restrooms are standard. Youth counselors come ashore to conduct sand-castle building competitions and lead junior pirates on swashbuckling island treasure hunts.

The use of strollers and wheelchairs equipped with all-terrain wheels may be offered on a complimentary first-come, first-served basis. However, with the exception of some participation sports on the beach, plan to pay for most water toys and activities. Costs associated with private-island fun and recreation can range from $8 for use of a snorkel vest (you may use your own snorkel equipment; however, in the event a floatation vest is required for safety, you must rent one) to $30 for rental of an entire snorkeling outfit for the day (mask, fins, snorkel vest, a mesh bag, fish identification card, and fish food). You can often take a banana-boat ride for $16 to $19 (15-minute ride), sail a small boat or catamaran for $30 to $50 (one hour), paddle a kayak for $18 to $38 (half-hour to hour-and-a-half), ride Jet Skis for $59 to $95 (45 minutes to one hour), parasail for a hefty $79 to $84 (10 minutes or less), or fly through the treetops on a zip line for $85. Floating mats are a relative bargain at $10 to $12 for all-day lounging in the water. You might also find open-air massage cabanas with pricing comparable to the spa charges onboard.

There is generally no charge for food or basic beverages such as those served onboard ship. While soft drinks and tropical cocktails can usually be charged to your shipboard account, you might want to bring a small amount of cash ashore for souvenir shopping, which is usually possible from vendors set up on or near the beach. You will also want to bring beach towels ashore and return them to the ship at the end of the day, because, as Princess Cruises reminds passengers, "Although the locals may offer to do this for you, unfortunately we seldom see the towels again!"

Even if you do nothing more than lie in a shaded hammock and sip fruity tropical concoctions, the day can be one of the most fun and relaxing of your entire cruise.

ISLANDS BY CRUISE LINE

Carnival Cruise Lines is currently the only major cruise line without an extensive private island experience available to the entire fleet. However, select Carnival itineraries include calls at Half Moon Cay, Holland America Line's private paradise, where "Fun Ship" passengers can use all the facilities and participate in organized activities. Similarly, certain Regent Seven Seas cruises include beach days at Princess Cays or Cayo Levantado, located off the Samaná Peninsula on the northeast coast of the Dominican Republic.

Although they do not stop at "private islands" in the strictest sense, the smaller ships of Seabourn and SeaDream offer passengers a day ashore on secluded private beaches where they can enjoy lavish barbecues and take a break from swimming and snorkeling to indulge in champagne and caviar served in the surf.

COSTA CRUISES

An unspoiled island paradise, Costa's **Catalina Island** is just off the coast of the Dominican Republic. Passengers can participate in Costa's "Beach Olympics," schedule a seaside massage, or just kick back on a chaise longue or a complimentary water float. Water-toy rentals, banana-boat rides, and sailing tours are available from independent concessionaires. Local vendors set up souvenir shops offering crafts and T-shirts. The ship provides the food for a lunch barbecue and tropical beverages at the beach bar.

Activities: Snorkeling, sailing, jet-skiing, waterskiing, hiking, volleyball, organized games, massages, shopping.

DISNEY CRUISE LINE

Disney's **Castaway Cay** has a dock, so passengers simply step ashore (rather than tendering, as is required to reach most cruise lines' private islands). Like everything associated with Disney, the line's private island is almost too good to be true. Located in the Abacos, a chain in the Bahamas, only 10% of Castaway Cay is developed, leaving plenty of unspoiled area to explore in Robinson Crusoe fashion. Trams are provided to reach separate beaches designated for children, teens, families, and adults, and Disney is the only line to offer age-specific activities and extensive, well-planned children's activities. Biking and hiking are so popular that a second nature trail, complete with an observation tower, has been added. Passengers can swim to a water platform complete with two slides or cool off in a 2,400-square-foot water-play area equipped with water jets and a splash pad. A 1,200-square-foot soft wet deck area provides freshwater fun for children with an array of pop jets, geysers, and bubblers. There is no charge for the water-play facilities. Excursions range from as passive as a glass-bottom boat tour to the soaring excitement of parasailing. An interactive experience with stingrays is educational and safe—the gentle creatures' barbs are blunted for safety. In addition to barbecue fare and several beverage stations, beach games, island-style music, and a shaded game pavilion, there are shops, massage cabanas by the sea, and even a post office. Popular with couples as well as families, 20 private rental cabanas provide the luxury of a deluxe beach retreat with an option to add the personalized service of a cabana host.

Activities: Snorkeling, kayaking, parasailing, sailing, jet-skiing, paddleboats, water cycles, fishing, bicycles, basketball, billiards, hiking, Ping-Pong, shuffleboard, soccer, volleyball, organized games, massages, shopping.

HOLLAND AMERICA LINE

Little San Salvador, one of the Bahamian out-islands, was renamed **Half Moon Cay** by Holland America Line to honor Henry Hudson's ship (depicted on the cruise line's logo) as well as to reflect the beach's crescent shape. Even after development, the island is still so unspoiled that it has been named a Wild Bird Preserve by the Bahamian National Trust. Passengers, who are welcomed ashore at a West Indies Village complete with shops and straw market, find Half Moon Cay easily accessible—all facilities are connected by hard-surfaced and packed-sand pathways and meet and exceed ADA requirements. An accessible tram also connects the welcome center with the food pavilion; wheelchairs with balloon tires are available. In addition to the beach area for lazing in the sun or shade, the island has a post office, Bahamian-style chapel, a lagoon where you can interact with stingrays, and, for family fun, you'll find a beachfront water park with waterslides and fanciful sea creatures tethered to the sandy bottom of the shallow water. Massage services are available, as are fitness activities. Air-conditioned cabanas can be rented for the day, with or without the services of your own butler.

Activities: Scuba diving, snorkeling, windsurfing, kayaking, parasailing, sailing, jet-skiing, Aqua Bikes, fishing, bicycles, basketball, hiking, horseback riding, shuffleboard, volleyball, massages, shopping.

NORWEGIAN CRUISE LINE

Only 120 mi east of Fort Lauderdale in the Berry Island chain of the Bahamas, much of **Great Stirrup Cay** looks as it did when it was acquired by Norwegian Cruise Line in 1977, with bougainvillea, sea grape, and coconut palms as abundant as the colorful tropical fish that inhabit the reef. The first uninhabited island purchased to offer cruise-ship passengers a private beach day, Great Stirrup Cay's white-sand beaches are fringed by coral and ideal for swimming and snorkeling, but become very crowded when a large number of passengers are ashore. Permanent facilities have been added to and improved in the intervening years and a seawall was erected to reduce beach erosion and preserve the environment. A straw market, water-sports centers, bars, volleyball courts, beachside massage stations, a food pavilion, and an inflatable waterslide round out the current facilities. Sand wheelchairs are available on the island, but the only paved pathway is along the seawall. However, extensive island improvements began in 2010 with the excavation of a new entrance channel for tenders and construction of tender docking facilities and a welcome pavilion that will be the site for future landings. When the tender dock is complete, the current beachfront will be expanded significantly to alleviate crowding. With a completion date in 2011, plans include the addition of private beachfront cabanas, a kid's play area, wave runners, a floating Aqua Park with a variety of water toys, kayak tours through man-made rivers within the island, an eco-cruise, and a stingray encounter experience.

Activities: Snorkeling, kayaking, parasailing, sailing, paddleboats, Ping-Pong, hiking, volleyball, organized games, massages, shopping.

PRINCESS CRUISES

Princess Cays is a 40-acre haven on the southern tip of Eleuthera Island in the Bahamas. Not quite an uninhabited island, it nevertheless offers a wide ribbon of beach, long enough for passengers to splash in the surf, relax in a hammock, or limbo to the beat of local music and never feel crowded. In a similar fashion to booking shore excursions, water-sports equipment can be reserved ahead of time, either onboard the ship or through the Princess Web site. Nestled in a picturesque palm grove, private bungalows with air-conditioning and ceiling fans and a deck for lounging can be rented for parties of up to six. A pirate-theme play area for children is supervised. In addition to three tropical bars and the area where a Bahamian barbecue is served, permanent facilities include small shops that sell island crafts and trinkets, but if you head around the back and through the fence, independent vendors sell similar goods for lower prices.

Activities: Snorkeling, kayaking, parasailing, sailing, paddleboats, Aqua Bikes, hiking, organized games, shopping.

ROYAL CARIBBEAN, CELEBRITY CRUISES, AND AZAMARA CLUB CRUISES

Royal Caribbean, Azamara Club Cruises, and Celebrity Cruises passengers have twice as many opportunities to visit a private island. The lines share two, and many Caribbean itineraries include one or the other.

Coco Cay is a 140-acre island in the Berry Island chain between Nassau and Freeport. Originally known as Little Stirrup Cay, it's within view of Great Stirrup Cay (NCL's private island) and the snorkeling is just as good, especially around a sunken airplane and a replica of Blackbeard's flagship, *Queen Anne's Revenge*. In addition to activities and games ashore, Coco Cay boasts the largest Aqua Park in the Caribbean, where children and adults alike can jump on an in-water trampoline or climb a floating sand castle before they dig into a beach barbecue or explore a nature trail. The newest attractions include an inflatable 40-foot waterslide (fun for adults and kids alike) and a Power Wheels track, where youngsters age 3 to 8 can take a miniature car for a spin at a sedate 3 MPH.

Activities: Scuba diving, snorkeling, jet-skiing, kayaking, parasailing, hiking, volleyball, organized games, shopping.

Labadee is a 260-acre peninsula approximately 6 mi (10 km) from Cap Haitien on the secluded north coast of Haiti (the port of call is sometimes called "Hispaniola"). Passengers can step ashore at a new dock, from which water taxis and five different walking paths, trails, and avenues lead to many areas throughout the peninsula, including the Labadee Town Square and Dragon's Plaza, where a welcome center and central tram station are located. In addition to swimming, water sports, an Aqua Park with floating trampolines and waterslides, and nature trails to explore, bonuses on Labadee are an authentic folkloric show presented by island performers and a market featuring work of local artists and crafters, where you might find an interesting painting or unique wood carving. More adventurous activities include an Alpine Coaster, a thrilling roller coaster experience, and one of the most exciting—and at 2,600 feet in length the longest—zip-line experiences in the Caribbean, which takes place 500 feet above the beaches of Labadee, where riders can reach speeds of 40 to 50 MPH over the water. Due to the proximity of Labadee to mainland Haiti, in the past it has occasionally been necessary to cancel calls there due to political unrest. In that event, an alternate port is usually scheduled.

Activities: Snorkeling, jet-skiing, kayaking, parasailing, hiking, volleyball, organized games, shopping.

ANTIGUA (ST. JOHN'S)

Jordan Simon

Some say Antigua has so many beaches that you could visit a different one every day for a year. Most have snow-white sand, and many are backed by lavish resorts that offer sailing, diving, windsurfing, and snorkeling. The largest of the British Leeward Islands, Antigua was the headquarters from which Lord Horatio Nelson (then a mere captain) made his forays against the French and pirates in the late 18th century. You may wish to explore English Harbour and its carefully restored Nelson's Dockyard, as well as tour old forts, historic churches, and tiny villages. Appealing aspects of the island's interior include a small tropical rain forest ideal for hiking and ziplining, ancient Native American archaeological digs, and restored sugar mills. Due to time constraints, it's best to make trips this far from port with an experienced tour operator, but you can easily take a taxi to any number of fine beaches on your own and escape from the hordes descending from the ship.

ESSENTIALS

CURRENCY   Eastern Caribbean (EC) dollar (EC$2.67 to US$1). U.S. dollars are generally accepted, but change is given in EC.

INTERNET   There are some small Internet cafés in St. John's and English Harbour; ask at the tourist information booth at the cruise-ship pier.

TELEPHONES   A GSM tri-band mobile phone will usually work in Antigua. You can use a LIME (formerly Cable & Wireless) Phone Card (available in $5, $10, and $20 denominations in most hotels and post offices) for local and long-distance calls. To call the United States and Canada, dial 1 + the area code + the seven-digit number, or use the phone card or one of the CALL USA phones, which are available at several locations, including the cruise terminal at St. John's and the English Harbour Marina.

COMING ASHORE

Though some ships dock at the deepwater harbor in downtown St. John's, most use Heritage Quay, a multimillion-dollar complex with shops, condominiums, a casino, and a food court. Most St. John's attractions are an easy walk from Heritage Quay; the older part of the

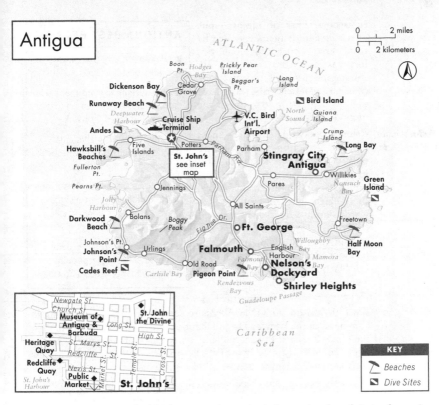

Antigua

ATLANTIC OCEAN

0 _____ 2 miles
0 _____ 2 kilometers

Boon Pt. Hodges Bay Prickly Pear Island
Beggar's Pt. Long Island
Dickenson Bay Cedar Grove
Runaway Beach Bird Island
Deepwater Harbour North Sound Guiana Island
Cruise Ship Terminal
Andes V.C. Bird Int'l. Airport
Five Islands Potters Crump Island
Hawksbill's Beaches Parham Rd. Parham Long Bay
Fullerton Pt. **St. John's see inset map** **Stingray City Antigua**
Pearns Pt. Jennings Willikies Green Island
Pares Nunsuch Bay
Jolly Harbour All Saints
Darkwood Beach Bolans Boggy Peak Fig Tree Dr. **Ft. George** Freetown
Johnson's Pt. Urlings English Harbour Willoughby Bay **Half Moon Bay**
Johnson's Point **Falmouth** Falmouth Bay Mamora Bay
Cades Reef Old Road Pigeon Point **Nelson's Dockyard**
Carlisle Bay **Shirley Heights**
Rendezvous Bay
Guadeloupe Passage

Caribbean Sea

KEY
⟋ Beaches
◰ Dive Sites

St. John's inset

Newgate St.
Church St.
Museum of Antigua & Barbuda Long St. **St. John the Divine**
Heritage Quay St. Marys St. High St.
Redcliffe St.
Redcliffe Quay Nevis St.
St. John's Harbour **Public Market** Market St. Temple St. Cross St. **St. John's**

city is eight blocks away. A tourist information booth is in the main docking building.

If you intend to explore beyond St. John's, consider hiring a taxi driver–guide. Taxis meet every cruise ship. They're unmetered; fares are fixed, and drivers are required to carry a rate card. Agree on the fare before setting off (make sure you know the price quoted is one-way or round-trip), and plan to tip drivers 10%. Some cabbies may take you from St. John's to English Harbour and wait for a "reasonable" amount of time (about a half-hour) while you look around, for about $50; you can usually arrange an island tour for around $25 per hour. Renting your own car isn't usually practical, since you must purchase a $20 temporary driving permit in addition to the car-rental fee, which is usually about $50 per day in the high season.

EXPLORING ANTIGUA

Falmouth. This town sits on a lovely bay backed by former sugar plantations and sugar mills. The most important historic site here is St. Paul's Church, which was rebuilt on the site of a church once used by troops during the Horatio Nelson period.

Ft. George. East of Liberta—one of the first settlements founded by freed slaves—on Monk's Hill, this fort was built from 1689 to 1720. Among the ruins are the sites for 32 cannons, water cisterns, the base of the old flagstaff, and some of the original buildings.

Fodor's Choice
★ **Nelson's Dockyard.** Antigua's most famous attraction is the world's only Georgian-era dockyard still in use, a treasure trove for history buffs and nautical nuts alike. In 1671 the governor of the Leeward Islands wrote to the Council for Foreign Plantations in London, pointing out the advantages of this landlocked harbor. By 1704 English Harbour was in regular use as a garrisoned station.

> **ANTIGUA BEST BETS**
>
> ■ **Dickenson Bay Beach.** One of Antigua's best beaches.
>
> ■ **Ecotourism.** Explore the island's forested interior on foot or surrounding coves by kayak.
>
> ■ **Jolly Harbour.** A cheap day pass at the Jolly Harbour Resort is a great day at the beach.
>
> ■ **Nelson's Dockyard.** This is one of the Caribbean's best historic sights, with many stores, restaurants, and bars.
>
> ■ **St. John's.** There's excellent duty-free shopping, especially in Heritage Quay and Redcliffe Quay.

In 1784, 26-year-old Horatio Nelson sailed in on the HMS *Boreas* to serve as captain and second-in-command of the Leeward Island Station. Under him was the captain of the HMS *Pegasus,* Prince William Henry, duke of Clarence, who was later crowned King William IV. The prince acted as best man when Nelson married Fannie Nisbet on Nevis in 1787.

When the Royal Navy abandoned the station at English Harbour in 1889, it fell into a state of decay, though adventuresome yachties still lived there in near-primitive conditions. The Society of the Friends of English Harbour began restoring it in 1951; it reopened with great fanfare as Nelson's Dockyard on November 14, 1961. Within the compound are crafts shops, restaurants, and two splendidly restored 18th-century hotels, the Admiral's Inn and the Copper & Lumber Store Hotel, worth peeking into. (The latter, occupying a supply store for Nelson's Caribbean fleet, is a particularly fine example of Georgian architecture and has an interior courtyard evoking Old England.) The Dockyard is a hub for oceangoing yachts and serves as headquarters for the annual Sailing Week Regatta in late April and early May. Water taxis will ferry you between points for EC$5. The Dockyard National Park also includes serene nature trails accessing beaches, rock pools, and crumbling plantation ruins and hilltop forts.

The **Dockyard Museum,** in the original Naval Officer's House, presents ship models, mock-ups of English Harbour, displays on the people who worked there and typical ships that docked, silver regatta trophies, maps, prints, antique navigational instruments, and Nelson's very own telescope and tea caddy. ⊠ *English Harbour* ☎ *268/481–5022; 268/463–1060; 268/460–1379 for National Parks Authority* ⊕ *www. antiguamuseums.org* ⊠ *$2 suggested donation* ☉ *Daily 8–5.*

St. John's. Antigua's capital, with some 45,000 inhabitants (approximately half the island's population), lies at sea level at the inland end of a sheltered northwestern bay. Although it has seen better days, a couple of notable historic sites and some good waterfront shopping areas make it worth a visit. At the far south end of town, where Market Street forks into Valley and All Saints roads, haggling goes on every Friday and Saturday, when locals jam the **Public Market** to buy and sell fruits, vegetables, fish, and spices. Ask before you aim a camera; your subject may expect a tip. This is old-time Caribbean shopping, a jambalaya of sights, sounds, and smells.

Signs at the **Museum of Antigua and Barbuda** say PLEASE TOUCH, encouraging you to explore Antigua's past. Try your hand at the educational video games or squeeze a cassava through a *matapi* (grass sieve). Exhibits interpret the nation's history, from its geological birth to its political independence in 1981. There are fossil and coral remains from some 34 million years ago; models of a sugar plantation and a wattle-and-daub house; an Arawak canoe; and a wildly eclectic assortment of objects from cannonballs to 1920s telephone exchanges. The museum occupies the former courthouse, which dates from 1750. The superlative museum gift shop carries such unusual items as calabash purses, seed earrings, warri boards (warri being an African game brought over to the Caribbean), and lignum vitae pipes, as well as historic maps and local books (including engrossing, detailed monographs on varied subjects by the late Desmond Nicholson, a longtime resident). ⊠ *Long and Market Sts.* ☎ *268/462–1469* ⊕ *www.antiguamuseums.org* ⌸ *$2 suggested donation* ☉ *Sun.–Thurs. 8:30–4, Fri. 8:30–3, Sat. 10–2.*

At the south gate of the **Anglican Cathedral of St. John the Divine** are figures of St. John the Baptist and St. John the Divine, said to have been taken from one of Napoléon's ships and brought to Antigua. The original church was built in 1681, replaced by a stone building in 1745, and destroyed by an earthquake in 1843. The present neo-baroque building dates from 1845; the parishioners had the interior completely encased in pitch pine, hoping to forestall future earthquake damage. Tombstones bear eerily eloquent testament to the colonial days. ⊠ *Between Long and Newgate Sts.* ☎ *268/461–0082.*

Fodor's Choice
★ Redcliffe Quay, at the water's edge just south of Heritage Quay, is the most appealing part of St. John's. Attractively restored (and superbly re-created) buildings in a riot of cotton-candy colors house shops, restaurants, and boutiques and are linked by courtyards and landscaped walkways.

Shirley Heights. This bluff affords a spectacular view of English Harbour. The heights are named for Sir Thomas Shirley, the governor who fortified the harbor in 1787. At the top is Shirley Heights Lookout, a restaurant built into the remnants of the 18th-century fortifications. Most notable for its boisterous Sunday barbecues that continue into the night with live music and dancing, it serves dependable burgers, pumpkin soup, grilled meats, and rum punches.

Not far from Shirley Heights is the **Dows Hill Interpretation Centre,** where observation platforms provide still more sensational vistas of the English Harbour area. A multimedia sound-and-light presentation on island history and culture, spotlighting lifelike figures and colorful tableaux accompanied by running commentary and music, results in a cheery, if bland, portrait of Antiguan life from Amerindian times to the present. ☎ *268/460–1379 for National Parks Authority* ✉ *EC$15* ☉ *Daily 9–5.*

☪ **Stingray City Antigua** (✉ *Seaton's Village* ☎ *268/562–7297* ⊕ *www. stingraycityantigua.com*) is a carefully reproduced "natural" environment nicknamed by staffers the "retirement home," though the 30-plus stingrays, ranging from infants to seniors, are frisky. You can stroke, feed, even hold the striking gliders, as well as snorkel in deeper, protected waters. The tour guides do a marvelous job of explaining the animals' habits, from feeding to breeding, and their predators (including man).

SHOPPING

Redcliffe Quay, on the waterfront at the south edge of St. John's, is by far the most appealing shopping area. Several restaurants and more than 30 boutiques, many with one-of-a-kind wares, are set around landscaped courtyards shaded by colorful trees. **Heritage Quay,** in St. John's, has 35 shops—including many that are duty-free—that cater to the cruise-ship crowd, which docks almost at its doorstep. Outlets here include Benetton, the Body Shop, Sunglass Hut, Dolce & Gabbana, and Oshkosh B'Gosh. There are also shops along **St. John's, St. Mary's, High,** and **Long streets.** The tangerine-and-lilac-hue four-story **Vendor's Mall** at the intersection of Redcliffe and Thames streets gathers the pushy, pesky vendors that once clogged the narrow streets. It's jammed with stalls; air-conditioned indoor shops sell some higher-price, if not higher-quality, merchandise. On the west coast the Mediterranean-style, arcaded **Jolly Harbour Marina** holds some interesting galleries and shops, as do the marinas and Main Road snaking around English and Falmouth Harbours.

ACTIVITIES

ADVENTURE TOURS

★ **Adventure Antigua** (☎ *268/727–3261 or 268/726–6355* ⊕ *www. adventureantigua.com*) is run by enthusiastic Eli Fuller, who is knowledgeable not only about the ecosystem and geography of Antigua but also about its history and politics (his grandfather was the American consul). His thorough seven-hour excursion (Eli dubs it "re-creating my childhood explorations") includes stops at Guiana Island (for lunch and guided snorkeling; turtles, barracuda, and stingrays are common sightings), Pelican Island (more snorkeling), Bird Island (hiking to vantage points to admire the soaring ospreys and frigate and red-billed tropic birds), and Hell's Gate (a striking limestone rock formation where the more intrepid may hike and swim through sunken caves and tide pools painted with pink and maroon algae). The company also offers a fun, shorter "Xtreme amusement park ride" variation on a racing boat catering to adrenaline junkies who "feel the need for speed" that also visits Stingray City, as well as a more sedate Antigua Classic Yacht sail-and-snorkel experience that explains the rich West Indian history of boatbuilding.

Play Tarzan and Jane at **Antigua Rainforest Canopy Tours** (✉ *Fig Dr., Wallings* ☎ *268/562–6363* ⊕ *www.antiguarainforest.com*). You should be in fairly good condition for the ropes challenges, which require upper-body strength and stamina, but anyone (vertigo or acrophobia sufferers, beware) can navigate the intentionally rickety "Indiana Jones–inspired" suspension bridges, then fly (in secure harnesses) over a rain-forest-filled valley from one towering turpentine tree to the next. There are 21 stations, as well as a snack bar and interpretive signage. First-timers, fear not: the "rangers" are affable, amusing, and accomplished. Admission varies slightly, but is usually $85. It's open Monday–Saturday from 8 to 6.

DIVING

Antigua is an unsung diving destination, with plentiful undersea sights to explore, from coral canyons to sea caves. Barbuda alone features roughly 200 wrecks on its treacherous reefs. The most accessible wreck is the 1890s bark *Andes,* not far out in Deep Bay, off Five Islands Peninsula. Among the favorite sites are **Green Island, Cades Reef,** and **Bird Island** (a national park). Memorable sightings include turtles, stingrays, and barracuda darting amid basalt walls, hulking boulders, and stray 17th-century anchors and cannon. One advantage is accessibility in many spots for shore divers and snorkelers. Double-tank dives run about $90.

Dive master Bryan Cunningham took over Wolf Krebs's Montserratian **Sea Wolf Diving School** (✉ *Falmouth Harbour* ☎ *268/783–3466 or 268/561–5258* ⊕ *www.seawolfdivingschool.com*) and eventually moved it to Antigua. It offers PADI and NAUI certification; shore, night, and boat dives, including Torpedo Diver propulsion vehicles; snorkeling trips; and underwater photography classes. It's the island's only dive retail shop, guaranteeing premium state-of-the-art equipment, and the only outfit diving Barbuda. Trips are open to four divers maximum, ensuring personalized attention. Rates are quite competitive, and Bryan and wife Tish are particularly good with kids. The shop stocks underwater Frisbees and torpedoes, as well as specialized children's gear, and Tish entertains little ones with art classes ashore.

KAYAKING

★ **"Paddles" Kayak Eco Adventure** (✉ *Seaton's Village* ☎ *268/463–1944* ⊕ *www.antiguapaddles.com*) takes you on a 3½-hour tour of serene mangroves and inlets with informative narrative about the fragile ecosystem of the swamp and reefs and the rich diversity of flora and fauna. The tour ends with a hike to sunken caves and snorkeling in the North Sound Marine Park, capped by a rum punch at the fun creole-style clubhouse. Experienced guides double as kayaking and snorkeling instructors, making this an excellent opportunity for novices. Conrad and Jennie's brainchild is one of Antigua's better bargains.

BEACHES

Dickenson Bay. Along a lengthy stretch of powder-soft white sand and exceptionally calm water you can find small and large hotels, water sports, concessions, and beachfront restaurants. There's decent snorkeling at either point.

Half Moon Bay. This ½-mi (1-km) ivory crescent is a prime snorkeling and windsurfing area. On the Atlantic side, the water can be rough at times, attracting intrepid hard-core surfers and wake-boarders. The northeastern end, where a protective reef offers spectacular snorkeling, is much calmer. A tiny bar has restrooms, snacks, and beach chairs. Half Moon is a real trek, but one of Antigua's showcase beaches. ⊠ *On southeast coast, 1½ mi (2½ km) from Freetown.*

Johnson's Point/Crabbe Hill. This series of connected, deserted beaches on the southwest coast looks out toward Montserrat, Guadeloupe, and St. Kitts. Notable beach bar–restaurants include OJ's, Gibson's, and Turner's. The water is generally placid, though not good for snorkeling. ⊠ *3 mi (5 km) south of Jolly Harbour complex on main west-coast road.*

Pigeon Point. Near Falmouth Harbour lie two fine white-sand beaches. The leeward side is calmer, the windward side is rockier, and there are sensational views and snorkeling around the point. Several restaurants and bars are nearby, though Bumpkin's satisfies most on-site needs. ⊠ *Off main south-coast road, southwest of Falmouth.*

WHERE TO EAT

$$$–$$$$
CONTINENTAL
★

✕**Coconut Grove.** Coconut palms grow through the roof of this open-air thatched restaurant, flickering candlelight illuminates colorful local murals, waves lap the white sand, and the warm waitstaff provides just the right level of service. Jean-François Bellanger's superbly presented dishes fuse French culinary preparations with island ingredients. Top choices include linguini with smoked salmon, sun-dried tomatoes, and tapenade; pan-seared snapper medallions served with roasted sweet potato in a saffron white-wine curry; Caribbean bouillabaisse with coconut milk and pumpkin aioli; and chicken stuffed with creole vegetables in mango-kiwi sauce. The kitchen can be uneven, the wine list is unimaginative and overpriced, and the buzzing happy-hour bar crowd lingering well into dinnertime can detract from the otherwise romantic atmosphere. Nonetheless, Coconut Grove straddles the line between casual beachfront boîte and elegant eatery with aplomb. ⊠ *Siboney Beach Club, Dickenson Bay* ☎ *268/462–1538* ⚐ *Reservations essential* ⊟ *AE, D, MC, V.*

$$–$$$
CARIBBEAN

✕**Commissioner Grill.** White-tile floors, powder-blue chairs, floral tablecloths, glass buoys, Antiguan pottery, conch shells, and historic maps give this converted, 19th-century tamarind warehouse a timeless island feel. Specials might include whelks in garlic butter, bacon-wrapped plantains in mustard sauce, snapper in lobster sauce, or mahimahi creole. Local seafood is the obvious choice, although beef and poultry are also reliable. Lunch is considerably cheaper and more authentic. ✉ *Commissioner Alley and Redcliffe St., St. John's* ☎ *268/462–1883* 🗏 *AE, D, MC, V.*

ARUBA (ORANJESTAD)

Vernon
O'Reilly
Ramesar

Few islands can boast the overt dedication to tourism and the quality of service that Aruba offers. The arid landscape is full of attractions to keep visitors occupied, and the island offers some of the most dazzling beaches in the Caribbean. Casinos and novelty nightclubs abound in Oranjestad, giving the capital an almost Las Vegas appeal. To keep tourists coming back year after year, the island boasts a tremendous variety of restaurants ranging from upscale French eateries to toes-in-the-sand casual dining. Aruba may not be an unexplored paradise, but hundreds of thousands of tourists make it a point to beat a path here every year. Because it's not a very large island, cruise-ship visitors can expect to see a large part of the island on their day ashore. Or they can simply see several of the beautiful beaches. Whether you're planning to be active or to simply relax, this is an ideal cruise port.

ESSENTIALS

CURRENCY   The Aruban florin (AFl 1.79 to US$1). The florin is pegged to the U.S. dollar, and Arubans accept U.S. dollars readily, so you need only acquire local currency for pocket change. Note that the Netherlands Antilles florin used on Bonaire and Curaçao is not accepted on Aruba.

INTERNET   **Café Internet** (✉ *8 Royal Plaza Mall, Oranjestad* ☎ *297/582–4609*).

TELEPHONE   When making calls to anywhere in Aruba, simply dial the seven-digit number. AT&T customers can dial 800–8000 from special phones at the cruise dock and in the airport's arrival and departure halls. Otherwise dial 121 to contact the international operator to place an international call.

COMING ASHORE

The Port of Oranjestad is a busy place and is generally full of eager tourists looking for souvenirs or a bite to eat. The port can accommodate up to five ships at a time (and frequently does). The Renaissance Mall is right on the port, as are a number of souvenir shops and some decent and inexpensive eating places. The main shopping areas of Oranjestad are all within 10 minutes' walk of the port.

Taxis can be flagged down on the street that runs alongside the port (look for license plates with a TX tag). Rates are fixed (i.e., there are no meters; the rates are set by the government and displayed on a chart), though you and the driver should agree on the fare before your ride begins. Rides to Eagle Beach run about $10; to Palm Beach, about $11. If you want to rent a car, you can do so for a reasonable price; driving is on the right, just as in the U.S., and it's pretty easy to get around, though a four-wheel drive vehicle does help in reaching some of the more out-of-the-way places.

4

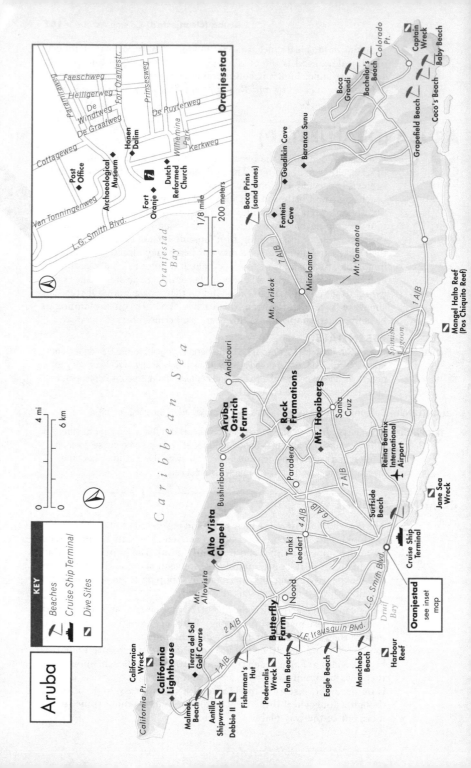

Aruba

KEY

Beaches
Cruise Ship Terminal
Dive Sites

Caribbean Sea

Californian Wreck
California Pt.
California Lighthouse
Tierra del Sol Golf Course
Mt. Altovista
Malmok Beach
Antilla Shipwreck
Debbie II
Fisherman's Hut
Pedernalis Wreck
Palm Beach
Butterfly Farm
Eagle Beach
Manchebo Beach
Harbour Reef
Noord
Tanki Leendert
Alto Vista Chapel
Bushiribana
Aruba Ostrich Farm
Rock Formations
Mt. Hooiberg
Paradera
Santa Cruz
Andicouri
Mt. Arikok
Miralamar
Mt. Yamanota
Boca Prins (sand dunes)
Guadikin Cave
Baranca Sunu
Fontein Cave
Boca Grandi
Bachelor's Beach
Captain Wreck
Baby Beach
Coco's Beach
Colorado Pt.
Grapefield Beach
Mangel Halto Reef (Pos Chiquito Reef)
Spanish Lagoon
Reina Beatrix International Airport
Jane Sea Wreck
Surfside Beach
Cruise Ship Terminal
Oranjestad see inset map
L.G. Smith Blvd.
Druif Bay
J.E. Irausquin Blvd.
1 A/B
2 A/B
4 A/B
6 A/B
7 A/B

Oranjestad

Faeschweg
Paramhaweg
Helligerweg
De Windtweg
De Graafweg
Cottageweg
Van Tonningenweg
L.G. Smith Blvd.
Fort Oranjestr.
Prinsesweg
De Ruyterweg
Wilhemina Park
Kerkweg
Honen Dalim
Archaeological Museum
Post Office
Fort Oranje
Dutch Reformed Church

1/8 mile
200 meters

Oranjestad Bay

4 mi
6 km

EXPLORING ARUBA

Alto Vista Chapel. Alone near the island's northwest corner sits the scenic little Alto Vista Chapel. The wind whistles through the simple mustard-color walls, eerie boulders, and looming cacti. Along the side of the road back to civilization are miniature crosses with depictions of the stations of the cross and hand-lettered signs exhorting PRAY FOR US SINNERS and the like—a simple yet powerful evocation of faith. ⊹ *To get here, follow the rough, winding dirt road that loops around the island's northern tip, or, from the hotel strip, take Palm Beach Road through three intersections and watch for the asphalt road to the left just past the Alto Vista Rum Shop.*

★ **Aruba Ostrich Farm.** Everything you ever wanted to know about the world's largest living birds can be found at this farm. A large *palapa* (palm-thatched roof) houses a gift shop and restaurant (popular with large bus tours), and tours of the farm are available every half hour. This operation is virtually identical to the facility in Curaçao; it's owned by the same company. ⊠ *Makividiri Rd., Paradera* ☎ *297/585–9630* ⊕ *www.arubaostrichfarm.com* ⊟ *$12* ☉ *Daily 9–5.*

Butterfly Farm. Hundreds of butterflies from around the world flutter about this spectacular garden. Guided 20- to 30-minute tours (included in the price of admission) provide an entertaining look into the life cycle of these insects, from egg to caterpillar to chrysalis to butterfly. There's a special deal offered here: after your initial visit, you can return as often as you like for free during your vacation. ⊠ *J. E. Irausquin Blvd., Palm Beach* ☎ *297/586–3656* ⊕ *www.thebutterflyfarm.com* ⊟ *$13* ☉ *Daily 9–4:30; last tour at 4.*

California Lighthouse. The lighthouse, built by a French architect in 1910, stands at the island's far northern end. Although you can't go inside, you can ascend the hill to the lighthouse base for some great views. In this stark landscape, you might feel as though you've just landed on the moon. The lighthouse is surrounded by huge boulders that look like extraterrestrial monsters and sand dunes embroidered with scrub that resembles undulating sea serpents.

Mt. Hooiberg. Named for its shape (*hooiberg* means "haystack" in Dutch), this 541-foot peak lies inland just past the airport. If you have the energy, climb the 562 steps to the top for an impressive view of Oranjestad (and Venezuela on clear days).

ARUBA BEST BETS

■ **Oranjestad.** Aruba's capital is pretty and easy to explore on foot, and it's impossible to get lost.

■ **Eagle Beach.** One of the most beautiful beaches in the Caribbean, with miles of white sand.

■ **Nightlife.** If your ship stays in port late, take advantage of the island's great bar scene and its many casinos.

■ **Snorkeling.** Though you can't dive here, you can snorkel to get a glimpse of what's under the sea.

■ **Windsurfing.** Constant wind allows this adrenaline sport to thrive in Aruba.

4

Oranjestad. Aruba's charming capital is best explored on foot. L. G. Smith Boulevard, the palm-lined thoroughfare in the center of town, runs between pastel-painted buildings, old and new, of typical Dutch design. You'll find many malls with boutiques and shops here.

The **Archaeological Museum of Aruba** has two rooms chock-full of fascinating artifacts from the indigenous Arawak people, including farm and domestic utensils dating back hundreds of years. ⊠ *J. E. Irausquin Blvd. 2A, Oranjestad* ☎ *297/582–8979* ☜ *Free* ☉ *Weekdays 8–noon and 1–4.*

★ Learn all about aloe—its cultivation, processing, and production—at **Aruba Aloe,** Aruba's own aloe farm and factory. Guided tours lasting about a half hour will show you how the gel—revered for its skin-soothing properties—is extracted from the aloe vera plant and used in a variety of products, including after-sun creams, soaps, and shampoos. Though not the most exciting tour on the island and unlikely to keep kids entertained, it might be a good option in the event of a rainy day. You can purchase the finished goods in the gift shop. ⊠ *Pitastraat 115, Oranjestad* ☎ *297/588–3222* ☜ *$8* ☉ *Weekdays 8:30–4:30, Sat. 9–1.*

☾ One of the island's oldest edifices, **Ft. Zoutman** was built in 1796 and played an important role in skirmishes between British and Curaçao troops in 1803. The Willem III Tower, named for the Dutch monarch of that time, was added in 1868 to serve as a lighthouse. Over time, the fort has been a government office building, a police station, and a prison; now its historical museum displays Aruban artifacts in an 18th-century house. ⊠ *Zoutmanstraat, Oranjestad* ☎ *297/582–6099* ☜ *Free* ☉ *Weekdays 8–noon and 1–4.*

★ The **Numismatic Museum** displays more than 40,000 historic coins and paper money from around the world. A few pieces were salvaged from shipwrecks in the region. Some of the coins circulated during the Roman Empire, the Byzantine Empire, and the ancient Chinese dynasties; the oldest date to the 3rd century BC. The museum had its start as the private collection of an Aruban who dug up some old coins in his garden. It's now run by his granddaughter. ⊠ *Weststraat, Oranjestad* ☎ *297/582–8831* ☜ *$5* ☉ *Mon.–Fri. 8–12 and 1–4 (also open on weekends depending on cruise ship traffic).*

Rock Formations. The massive boulders at Ayo and Casibari are a mystery, as they don't match the island's geological makeup. You can climb to the top for fine views of the arid countryside. On the way you'll doubtless pass Aruba whiptail lizards—the males are cobalt blue, and the females are blue-gray with light-blue dots. The main path to Casibari has steps and handrails, and you must move through tunnels and along narrow steps and ledges to reach the top. At Ayo you can find ancient pictographs in a small cave (the entrance has iron bars to protect the drawings from vandalism). You may also encounter boulder climbers, who are increasingly drawn to Ayo's smooth surfaces. Access to Casibari is via Tanki Highway 4A; you can reach Ayo via Route 6A. Watch carefully for the turnoff signs near the center of the island on the way to the windward side.

SHOPPING

Oranjestad's **Caya G. F. Betico Croes** is Aruba's chief shopping street, lined with several shops advertising "duty-free prices" (again, these are not truly duty-free), boutiques, and jewelry stores noted for the aggressiveness of their vendors on cruise-ship days.

Stores at the **Port of Call Marketplace** (✉ *L.G. Smith Blvd. 17, Oranjestad*) sell fine jewelry, perfumes, low-priced liquor, batiks, crystal, leather goods, and fashionable clothing. **Paseo Herencia** (✉ *L.G. Smith Blvd., Palm Beach* ☎ *297/586–6533*) is the newest mall in Aruba, just minutes away from the high-rise hotel area. It's all about style, and from the great bell tower to the nightly dancing-waters shows and the selection of restaurants, the aim here is to pull in shoppers. Offerings include Cuban cigars, the fine leather goods of Mario Hernandez, Italian denim goods at Moda & Stile, perfumes, cosmetics, and a variety of souvenir shops.

Five minutes from the cruise-ship terminal, the **Renaissance Mall** (✉ *L.G. Smith Blvd. 82, Oranjestad*), also known as Seaport Mall, has more than 120 stores selling merchandise to meet every taste and budget; the Crystal Casino is also here. The **Royal Plaza Mall** (✉ *L.G. Smith Blvd. 94, Oranjestad*), across from the cruise-ship terminal, has cafés, a post office (open weekdays 8 to 3:30), and such stores as Nautica, Benetton, Tommy Hilfiger, and Gandelman Jewelers. There's also a cybercafé for those who want to send e-mail and get their caffeine fix all in one stop.

DIVING AND SNORKELING

With visibility of up to 90 feet, the waters around Aruba are excellent for snorkeling and diving. Advanced and novice divers alike will find plenty to occupy their time, as many of the most popular sites—including some interesting shipwrecks—are found in shallow waters ranging from 30 to 60 feet.

★ **De Palm Watersports** (✉ *L. G. Smith Blvd. 142, Oranjestad* ☎ *297/582–4400 or 800/766–6016* ⊕ *www.depalm.com*) is one of the best choices for your undersea experience, and the options go beyond basic diving. You can don a helmet and walk along the ocean floor near De Palm Island, home of huge blue parrot fish. You can even do Snuba—which is like scuba diving but without the heavy air tanks—from either a boat or from an island; it costs $133 for 4 hours.

GOLF

★ **Tierra del Sol** (✉ *Malmokweg* ☎ *297/586–0978*), a stunning course, is on the northwest coast near the California Lighthouse. Designed by Robert Trent Jones Jr., this 18-hole championship course combines Aruba's native beauty—cacti and rock formations—with the lush greens of the world's best courses. The greens fees vary depending on the time of day (from December to March it is $159 in the morning, $124 for early afternoon, and $100 from 3 PM). The fee includes a golf cart equipped with a communications system that allows you to order drinks for your return to the clubhouse. Half-day golf clinics, a bargain at $45, include lunch in the clubhouse (available Monday, Tuesday, and Thursday). The pro shop is one of the Caribbean's most elegant, with an extremely attentive staff.

KAYAKING

Kayaking is a popular sport on Aruba, especially along the south coast, where the waters are calm. It's a great way to explore the coastline. **Aruba Kayak Adventure** (⊠ *Ponton 90, Oranjestad* ☎ *297/587–7722* ⊕ *www.arubakayak.com*) has excellent half-day kayak trips, which start with a quick lesson before you paddle through caves and mangroves and along the scenic coast. The tour makes a lunch stop at De Palm Island, where snorkeling is included as part of the $99 package.

BEACHES

The beaches on Aruba are beautiful, clean, and easily reached from the cruise-ship terminal in Oranjestad.

Fodor'sChoice **Eagle Beach** (⊠ *J. E. Irausquin Blvd., north of Manchebo Beach*), on
★ the southwestern coast, is one of the Caribbean's—if not the world's—best beaches. Not long ago it was a nearly deserted stretch of pristine sand dotted with the occasional thatched picnic hut. Now that the resorts have been completed, this mile-plus-long beach is always hopping. **Manchebo Beach** (⊠ *J. E. Irausquin Blvd., at the Manchebo Beach Resort*) is impressively wide; the shoreline in front of the Manchebo Beach Resort is where officials turn a blind eye to the occasional topless sunbather. This beach merges with Druif Beach, and most locals use the name Manchebo to refer to both. **Palm Beach** (⊠ *J. E. Irausquin Blvd. between the Westin Aruba Resort, Spa & Casino and the Marriott Aruba Ocean Club*) from the Westin Aruba to the Marriott Aruba Ocean Club is the center of Aruban tourism, offering good opportunities for swimming, sailing, and other water sports. In some spots you might find a variety of shells that are great to collect, but not as much fun to step on barefoot—bring sandals just in case.

WHERE TO EAT

$$–$$$ ✕ **Cuba's Cookin'.** This funky little establishment is tucked away on an
CUBAN unprepossing street downtown. Nightly entertainment, great authentic
★ Cuban food, and a lively crowd are the draws here. The empanadas are excellent, as is the chicken stuffed with plantains. Don't leave without trying the roast pork, which is pretty close to perfection. The signature dish is the *ropa vieja,* a sautéed flank steak served with a rich sauce (the name literally translates as "old clothes"). Service can be a bit spotty at times, depending on how busy it gets. There's always a crowd, as loyal fans and fun-seekers usually flock to the bar area. ⊠ *Wilhelminastraat 27, Oranjestad* ☎ *297/588–0627* ⊕ *www.cubascookin.com* ⊟ *AE, D, MC, V* ☺ *Closed Sun. mid-Apr.–mid-Dec.*

$$–$$$ ✕ **Rumba Bar & Grill.** In the heart of Oranjestad, this lively bistro has an
CARIBBEAN open kitchen where you can watch the chef prepare tasty international

fare (mostly grilled seafood and beef) over a charcoal grill. The presentations are fanciful, with entrées forming towering shapes over beds of colorful vegetables and sauces. You can dine on the terrace and soak up the local color, or inside amid wicker and warm pink hues; the crowd is always worth watching. ⊠ *Havenstraat 4, Oranjestad* ☎ *297/588–7900* ⊕ *www.rumba-aruba.com* ⊟ *AE, D, MC, V* ☺ *Closed Sun.*

BARBADOS (BRIDGETOWN)

Jane E. Zarem

Barbadians (Bajans) are a warm, friendly, and hospitable people, who are genuinely proud of their country and culture. Although tourism is the island's number one industry, the island has a sophisticated business community and stable government, so life here doesn't skip a beat after passengers return to the ship. Barbados is the most "British" island in the Caribbean. Afternoon tea is a ritual, and cricket is the national sport. The atmosphere, though, is hardly stuffy. This is still the Caribbean, after all. Beaches along the island's south and west coasts are picture-perfect, and all are available to cruise passengers. On the rugged east coast the Atlantic Ocean attracts world-class surfers. The northeast is dominated by rolling hills and valleys, while the interior of the island is covered by acres of sugarcane and dotted with small villages. Historic plantations, a stalactite-studded cave, a wildlife preserve, rum distilleries, and tropical gardens are among the island's attractions. Bridgetown is the capital city, and its downtown shops and historic sites are a short walk or taxi ride from the pier.

ESSENTIALS

CURRENCY The Barbados dollar (BDS$) is pegged to the U.S. dollar at the rate of BDS$1.99 to US$1. U.S. dollars (but not coins) are accepted universally across the island, but change is given in Barbados currency.

INTERNET You'll find Internet cafés in and around Bridgetown and at St. Lawrence Gap on the south coast. Rates range from $2 for 15 minutes to $8 or $9 per hour. **Bean-n-Bagel Internet Cafe** (⊠ *The Wharf, Bridgetown*). **Connect Internet Cafe** (⊠ *Shop #9, 27 Broad St., Bridgetown*).

TELEPHONE Your cell phone should work in Barbados, although roaming charges can be costly. Alternatively, you can purchase phone cards at the cruise-ship terminal. Direct-dialing to the United States, Canada, and other countries is efficient and reasonable. Some toll-free numbers cannot be accessed in Barbados. To charge your overseas call on a major credit card or U.S. calling card without incurring a surcharge, dial 800/225–5872 (1-800/CALL-USA) from any phone.

COMING ASHORE

Up to eight ships at a time can dock at Bridgetown's Deep Water Harbour, on the northwest side of Carlisle Bay near Bridgetown. The cruise-ship terminal has duty-free shops, handicraft vendors, a post office, a telephone station, a tourist information desk, and a taxi stand. To get downtown, follow the shoreline to the Careenage. It's a 15-minute walk or a $3 taxi ride.

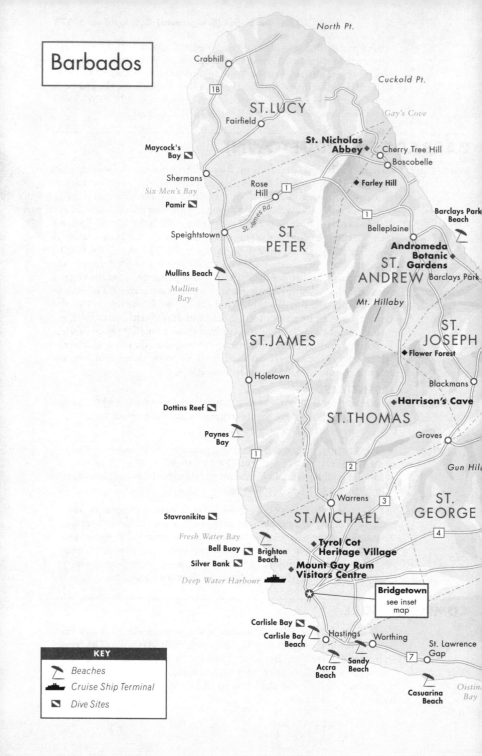

Barbados

North Pt.

Crabhill

Cuckold Pt.

1B

ST.LUCY

Fairfield

Gay's Cove

Maycock's
Bay

St. Nicholas
Abbey ◆   Cherry Tree Hill
Boscobelle

Shermans

Six Men's Bay

Rose
Hill   1   ◆ Farley Hill

Pamir

1

Barclays Park
Beach

ST
PETER

Belleplaine

Speightstown

Andromeda
Botanic
Gardens ◆
ST.
ANDREW   Barclays Park

Mullins Beach

Mullins
Bay

ST.JAMES

Mt. Hillaby

ST.
JOSEPH

◆ Flower Forest

Holetown

Blackmans

Dottins Reef

◆ Harrison's Cave

ST.THOMAS

Groves

Paynes
Bay

Gun Hil

1

2

Stavronikita

Warrens   3

ST.
GEORGE

ST.MICHAEL

4

Fresh Water Bay

Bell Buoy   Brighton
Beach

Silver Bank

◆ Tyrol Cot
Heritage Village

Mount Gay Rum
Visitors Centre

Deep Water Harbour

Bridgetown
see inset
map

Carlisle Bay

Carlisle Bay
Beach   Hastings   Worthing

St. Lawrence
Gap

7

Accra
Beach

Sandy
Beach

Casuarina
Beach

Oistin
Bay

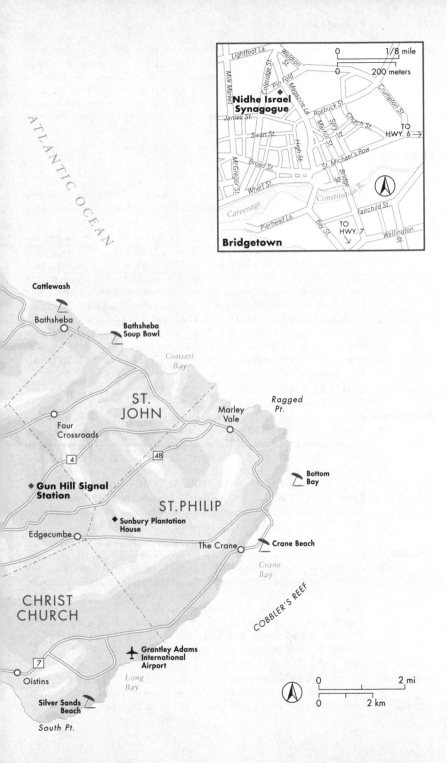

Bridgetown

Lightfoot La.
Waldron St.
Coleridge St.
Pin Fold
Magazine La.
Milk Market

Nidhe Israel Synagogue

James St.
Swan St.
Roebuck St.
Church St.
Crumpton St.
Spry St.
Marhill St.
High St.
Broad St.
St. Michael's Row
McGregor St.
Wharf St.
Bridge St.
Constitution R.
Careenage
Pierhead La.
Bay St.
Fairchild St.
Wellington St.

TO HWY. 6 →

TO HWY. 7 ↓

0   1/8 mile
0   200 meters

ATLANTIC OCEAN

Cattlewash

Bathsheba

Bathsheba Soup Bowl

Consett Bay

ST. JOHN

Marley Vale

Ragged Pt.

Four Crossroads

4   4B

◆ Gun Hill Signal Station

Bottom Bay

ST. PHILIP

◆ Sunbury Plantation House

Edgecumbe

The Crane

Crane Beach

Crane Bay

CHRIST CHURCH

COBBLER'S REEF

7

Oistins

✈ Grantley Adams International Airport

Long Bay

Silver Sands Beach

South Pt.

0   2 mi
0   2 km

Taxis await ships at the pier. Drivers accept U.S. dollars and appreciate a 10% tip. Taxis are unmetered and operate at a fixed hourly rate of $25 per carload (up to three passengers). Most drivers will cheerfully narrate an island tour. You can rent a car with a valid driver's license, but rates are steep—up to $85 per day during the high season—and some agencies require a two-day rental at that time. Note, too, that driving is on the left, British-style.

EXPLORING BARBADOS

BRIDGETOWN

This bustling capital city is a major duty-free port with a compact shopping area. The principal thoroughfare is Broad Street, which leads west from National Heroes Square.

Nidhe Israel Synagogue. Providing for the spiritual needs of one of the oldest Jewish congregations in the Western Hemisphere, this synagogue was formed by Jews who left Brazil in the 1620s and introduced sugarcane to Barbados. The adjoining cemetery has tombstones dating from the 1630s. The original house of worship, built in 1654, was destroyed in an 1831 hurricane, rebuilt in 1833, and restored with the assistance of the Barbados National Trust in 1987. Friday-night services are held during the winter months, but the building is open to the public year-round. Shorts are not acceptable during services but may be worn at other times. ⊠ *Synagogue La., St. Michael* ☎ *246/426–5792* ✉ *Donation requested* ☉ *Weekdays 9–4.*

CENTRAL AND WEST

☾ **Gun Hill Signal Station.** The 360-degree view from Gun Hill, 700 feet above sea level, gave this location strategic importance to the 18th-century British army. Using lanterns and semaphore, soldiers based here could communicate with their counterparts at the Garrison on the south coast and at Grenade Hill in the north. Time moved slowly in 1868, and Captain Henry Wilkinson whiled away his off-duty hours by carving a huge lion from a single rock—which is on the hillside just below the tower. Come for a short history lesson, but mainly for the view; it's so gorgeous, military invalids were once sent here to convalesce. ⊠ *Gun Hill, St. George* ☎ *246/429–1358* ✉ *$5* ☉ *Weekdays 9–5.*

Fodor's Choice
★

☾ **Harrison's Cave.** This limestone cavern, complete with stalactites, stalagmites, subterranean streams, and a 40-foot waterfall, is a rare find in the Caribbean—and one of Barbados's most popular attractions. The cave reopened in early 2010, after extensive renovations comprising a new visitor center with interpretive displays, life-size models and sculptures, a souvenir shop, improved restaurant facilities, and access for people with disabilities. The one-hour tours are conducted via electric trams, which fill up fast; reserve ahead of time. ⊠ *Hwy. 2, Welchman Hall, St. Thomas* ☎ *246/438–6640* ⊕ *www.harrisonscave.com* ✉ *$20* ☉ *Wed.–Sun. 9–3:45 (last tour).*

Fodor's Choice
★

Fodor's Choice
★ **Mount Gay Rum Visitors Centre.** On this popular tour you learn the colorful story behind the world's oldest rum—made in Barbados since 1703. Although the distillery is in the far north, in St. Lucy Parish, tour guides

explain the rum-making procedure. Both historic and modern equipment is on display, and rows and rows of barrels are stored in this location. The 45-minute tour runs hourly (last tour begins at 3:30) and concludes with a tasting and an opportunity to buy bottles of rum and gift items—and even have lunch or cocktails, depending on the time of day. ⊠ *Spring Garden Hwy., Brandons, St. Michael* ☎ *246/425–8757* ⊕ *www.mountgay.com* ⊠ *$7, $40 with lunch; $30 with cocktails* ⊘ *Weekdays 9–5.*

NORTH AND EAST

Fodor's Choice **Andromeda Botanic Gardens.** Beautiful and unusual plant specimens from around the world are cultivated in 6 acres of gardens nestled among streams, ponds, and rocky outcroppings overlooking the sea above the Bathsheba coastline. The gardens were created in 1954 with flowering plants collected by the late horticulturist Iris Bannochie. They're now administered by the Barbados National Trust. The Hibiscus Café serves snacks and drinks. ⊠ *Bathsheba, St. Joseph* ☎ *246/433–9384* ⊠ *$10* ⊘ *Daily 9–5.*

Fodor's Choice **St. Nicholas Abbey.** There's no religious connection here at all. The island's oldest greathouse (circa 1650) was named after the original British owner's hometown, St. Nicholas Parish near Bristol, and Bath Abbey nearby. Its stone-and-wood architecture makes it one of only three original Jacobean-style houses still standing in the western hemisphere. It has Dutch gables, finials of coral stone, and beautiful grounds that include an old sugar mill. The first floor, fully furnished with period furniture and portraits of family members, is open to the public. Fascinating home movies, shot by a previous owner's father, record Bajan life in the 1930s. ⊠ *Cherry Tree Hill, St. Peter* ☎ *246/422–5357* ⊕ *www.stnicholasabbey.com* ⊠ *$15* ⊘ *Sun.–Fri., 10–3:30.*

SOUTH

Fodor's Choice **Sunbury Plantation House and Museum.** Lovingly rebuilt after a 1995 fire destroyed everything but the thick flint-and-stone walls, Sunbury offers an elegant glimpse of the 18th and 19th centuries on a Barbadian sugar estate. Period furniture, old prints, and a collection of horse-drawn carriages lend an air of authenticity. A buffet luncheon is served daily in the courtyard for $30 per person. A five-course candlelight dinner is served ($100 per person, reservations required) two nights a week at the 200-year-old mahogany dining table in the Sunbury dining room. ⊠ *Off Hwy. 5, Six Cross Roads, St. Philip* ☎ *246/423–6270* ⊕ *www.barbadosgreathouse.com* ⊠ *$7.50* ⊘ *Daily 9:30–4:30.*

BARBADOS BEST BETS

■ **The East Coast.** The island's windward coast, with its crashing surf, is striking.

■ **Harrison's Cave.** This extensive cave system is in the limestone deep beneath Barbados.

■ **Mount Gay Rum Visitors Centre.** Take a tour and a tasting.

■ **Flower Gardens.** Andromeda Botanic Gardens and the Flower Forest are both scenic and fragrant.

■ **St. Nicholas Abbey.** Not an abbey at all, this is one of the oldest Jacobean-era houses still standing in the western hemisphere.

4

☺ **Tyrol Cot Heritage Village.** This coral-stone cottage just south of Bridgetown was constructed in 1854 and is preserved as an example of period architecture. In 1929 it became the home of Sir Grantley Adams, the first premier of Barbados and the namesake of its international airport. Part of the Barbados

> **TIP**
>
> If you don't want to rely on shipboard wake-up calls, be sure to bring your own travel alarm clock; most staterooms do not have clocks.

National Trust, the cottage is filled with antiques and memorabilia that belonged to the late Sir Grantley and Lady Adams. It's also the centerpiece of an outdoor "living museum," where artisans and craftsmen have their workshops in a cluster of traditional chattel houses. Workshops are open, crafts are for sale, and refreshments are available at the "rum shop" primarily during the winter season and when cruise ships are in port. ⊠ *Rte. 2, Codrington Hill, St. Michael* ☎ *246/424–2074 or 246/436–9033* ▣ *$6* ☉ *Weekdays 8–4.*

SHOPPING

Duty-free shopping is found in Bridgetown's Broad Street stores and their branches in Holetown and at the cruise-ship terminal. Stores are generally open weekdays 8:30–4:30, Saturday 8:30–1. ■**TIP→ To purchase items duty-free, you must show your passport and cabin key card.**

Best of Barbados (⊠ *Worthing, Christ Church* ☎ *246/421–6900* ⊕ *www.best-of-barbados.com*) was the brainchild of architect Jimmy Walker as a place to showcase the works of his artist wife. Now with seven locations, the shops offer products that range from Jill Walker's frameable prints, housewares, and textiles to arts and crafts in both "native" style and modern designs. Everything is made or designed on Barbados.

Fodor's Choice **Earthworks Pottery** (⊠ *No. 2, Edgehill Heights, St. Thomas* ☎ *246/425–*
★ *0223* ⊕ *www.earthworks-pottery.com*) is a family-owned and -operated pottery shop where you can purchase anything from a dish or knickknack to a complete dinner service or one-of-a-kind art piece. You can find the characteristically blue or green pottery for sale in gift shops throughout the island, but the biggest selection (including some "seconds") is at Earthworks, where you also can watch the potters work.

★ **Pelican Craft Centre** (⊠ *Princess Alice Hwy., Bridgetown, St. Michael* ☎ *246/427–5350*) is a cluster of workshops halfway between the cruise-ship terminal and downtown Bridgetown where craftspeople create and sell locally made leather goods, batik, basketry, carvings, jewelry, glass art, paintings, pottery, and other items. It's open weekdays 9 to 5 and Saturday 9 to 2, with extended hours during holidays or cruise-ship arrivals.

ACTIVITIES

FISHING

Billfisher II (☎ 246/431–0741), a 40-foot Pacemaker, accommodates up to six passengers with three fishing chairs and five rods. Captain Winston ("The Colonel") White has been fishing these waters since 1975. His full-day charters include a full lunch and guaranteed fish (or a 25% refund); all trips include drinks and transportation to and from the boat. *Blue Jay* (☎ 246/429–2326 ⊕ *www.bluemarlinbarbados.com*) is a spacious, fully equipped, 45-foot Sport Fisherman with a crew that knows the water's denizens—blue marlin, sailfish, barracuda, and kingfish. Four to six people can be accommodated—it's the only charter boat on the island with four chairs. Most fishing is done by trolling. Drinks, snacks, bait, tackle, and transfers are provided.

GOLF

Barbados Golf Club (✉ *Hwy. 7, Durants, Christ Church* ☎ 246/428–8463 ⊕ *www.barbadosgolfclub.com*), the first public golf course on Barbados, is an 18-hole championship course (6,805 yards, par 72) redesigned in 2000 by golf course architect Ron Kirby. Greens fees are $135 for 18 holes, plus a $20 per-person cart fee. Unlimited three-day and seven-day golf passes are available. Several hotels offer preferential tee-time reservations and reduced rates. Club and shoe rentals are available.

Fodor's Choice At the prestigious **Country Club at Sandy Lane** (✉ *Hwy. 1, Paynes Bay, St.*
★ *James* ☎ 246/444–2500 ⊕ *www.sandylane.com/golf*) golfers can play on the Old Nine or on either of two 18-hole championship courses: the Tom Fazio–designed Country Club Course or the spectacular Green Monkey Course, reserved for hotel guests and club members only. Golfers have complimentary use of the club's driving range. The Country Club Restaurant and Bar, which overlooks the 18th hole, is open to the public. Greens fees in high season are $150 for 9 holes ($130 for hotel guests) or $235 for 18 holes ($200 for hotel guests). Golf carts, caddies, or trolleys are available for hire, as are clubs and shoes. Carts are equipped with GPS, which alerts you to upcoming traps and hazards, provides tips on how to play the hole, and allows you to order refreshments!

BEACHES

All beaches on Barbados are open to cruise-ship passengers. The west coast has the stunning coves and white-sand beaches dear to the hearts of postcard publishers, plus calm, clear water for snorkeling and swimming. Waterskiing and parasailing are also available on most beaches along the south and west coasts. Windsurfing is best on the south coast.

Accra Beach, also known as Rockley Beach, is next to the Accra Beach Hotel. Look forward to gentle surf and a lifeguard, plenty of nearby restaurants for refreshments, a children's playground, and beach stalls for renting chairs and equipment for snorkeling and other water sports. Parking is available at an on-site lot. **Brighton Beach.** Calm as a lake, this is where you can find locals taking a quick dip on hot days. Just north of Bridgetown, Brighton Beach is also home to the Malibu Beach

Club. **Carlisle Bay,** adjacent to the Hilton Barbados and Grand Barbados hotels just south of Bridgetown, is a broad half-circle of white sand and one of the island's best beaches—but it can become crowded on weekends and holidays. Park at Harbour Lights or the Boatyard, both on Bay Street, where you can also rent umbrellas and beach chairs and buy refreshments. **Mullins Beach,** just south of Speightstown, is a perfect place to spend the day. The water is safe for swimming and snorkeling, there's easy parking on the main road, and Mannie's Suga Suga restaurant serves snacks, meals, and drinks—and rents chairs and umbrellas. **Paynes Bay** is lined with luxury hotels. It's a pretty area, with plenty of beach to go around and good snorkeling. Public access is available at several locations along Highway 1; parking is limited. Grab a bite to eat and liquid refreshments at Bomba's Beach Bar.

WHERE TO EAT

$$–$$$ ✕ **Cliffside at New Edgewater.** The outdoor deck of this restaurant in
CARIBBEAN   the New Edgewater hotel provides one of the prettiest, breeziest ocean views in all Barbados and, therefore, is a good stop for lunch when touring the east coast. From noon to 3 PM, choose the Bajan buffet or select from the menu. Either way, you might enjoy fried flying fish, roast or stewed chicken, local lamb chops, rice and peas, steamed root vegetables, sautéed plantains, and salad. Afternoon tea with scones, pastries, and sandwiches is served from 3:30 to 6 PM. Dinner is also served, but mostly to hotel guests and local residents, who are able to find their way home in the dark on the neighborhood's winding, often unmarked roads. ⊠ *New Edgewater Hotel, Bathsheba, St. Joseph* ☎ *246/433–9900* ⊕ *www.newedgewater.com* ⚲ *Reservations essential* ▭ *AE, MC, V.*

$$$–$$$$ ✕ **Waterfront Café.** This friendly bistro alongside the Careenage is the
CARIBBEAN   perfect place to enjoy a drink, snack, or meal—and to people-watch. Locals and tourists alike gather for all-day alfresco dining on sandwiches, salads, fish, pasta, pepper-pot stew, and tasty Bajan snacks such as buljol, fish cakes, or plantation pork (plantains stuffed with spicy minced pork). The panfried flying-fish sandwich is especially popular. In the evening you can gaze through the arched windows while savoring nouvelle Caribbean cuisine, enjoying cool trade winds, and listening to live jazz. There's a special Caribbean buffet and steel-pan music on Tuesday night from 7 to 9. ⊠ *The Careenage, Bridgetown, St. Michael* ☎ *246/427–0093* ⊕ *www.waterfrontcafe.com.bb* ▭ *AE, DC, MC, V* ☉ *Closed Sun.*

BELIZE CITY, BELIZE

Jeffrey Van
Fleet

Belize probably has the greatest variety of flora and fauna of any country of its size in the world. Here you'll often find more iguanas or howler monkeys than humans. A few miles off the mainland is the Belize Barrier Reef, a great wall of coral stretching the entire 200-mi (333-km) length of the coast. Over 200 cayes (pronounced keys) dot the reef like punctuation marks, and three coral atolls lie farther out

to sea. All are superb for diving and snorkeling. Many, like Ambergris Caye (pronounced *Am*-bur-griss Key) and Caye Caulker, are jolly resort islands with ample supplies of bars and restaurants, easily reachable on day trips from Belize City. The main choice you'll have to make is whether to stay in Belize City for a little shopping, a little walking, and perhaps lunch or a dram at one of the Fort George hotels or restaurants, or alternatively to head out by boat, rental car, taxi, or tour on a more active adventure.

ESSENTIALS

CURRENCY The Belize dollar (BZ$2 to US$1). Since the U.S. dollar is universally accepted, there's no need to acquire Belize currency.

FLIGHTS Especially if you are going to Ambergris Caye, you may prefer to fly, or you can water-taxi over and fly back to maximize your time. There are hourly flights on two airlines. The flight to Caulker takes about 10 minutes and that to San Pedro about 25 minutes. The cost is about BZ$240 round-trip to either island. Be sure you fly out of Belize City's Municipal, not out of the international airport north of the city. **Maya Island Airways** (✉ *Box 458, Municipal Airport, Belize City* ☎ *223–1140, 800/225–6732 in U.S.* ⊕ *www.mayaregional.com*). **Tropic Air** (✉ *Box 20, San Pedro* ☎ *226–2012, 800/422–3435 in U.S.* ⊕ *www.tropicair.com*).

INTERNET   **Click and Sip Internet Café** (✉ *Fort St., in Fort Street Tourism Village* ☎ *223–1305*). **Mail Boxes Etc.** (✉ *166 N. Front St., Belize City* ☎ *227–6046*).

TELEPHONE   Calling locally or internationally is easy, but rates are high; around BZ$1.50 a minute for calls to the U.S. To call the United States, dial 001 or 10–10–199 plus the area code and number. Pay phones, which are located in the Fort Street Tourism Village where you are tendered, and elsewhere downtown, accept only prepaid Belize Telecommunications Ltd. phone cards, available in shops in denominations from $5 to $50. Special "USA Connect" prepaid cards, for sale at some stores in Belize City, in denominations of $5 to $20, claim discounts of as much as 57% for calls to the U.S. only. Your U.S.-based GSM phone will probably work on Belize's GSM 1900 system. Foreign calling cards are generally blocked in Belize. Call 113 for local directory assistance, and 115 for an operator.

> ### BELIZE CITY BEST BETS
>
> ■ **Belize Zoo.** Though small, this collection of native Belize wildlife is excellent.
>
> ■ **Cave Tubing.** If you are not claustrophobic, this is an unforgettable excursion.
>
> ■ **Diving.** Belize is becoming known as one of the world's best dive destinations. For the certified, this is a must.
>
> ■ **Snorkeling in Hol Chan.** The water is teeming with fish, and you don't need to be certified to enjoy the underwater world here.

COMING ASHORE

Because Belize City's harbor is shallow, passengers are tendered in. If you're going the independent route, try to get in line early for the tenders, as it sometimes takes 90 minutes or more for all the passengers to be brought ashore. You arrive at the Fort Street Tourism Village complex. It has an antiseptic collection of gift shops, restaurants, and tour operators nicely situated along the harbor. Bathrooms are spick-and-span, too. At this writing, construction is sputtering on a much-delayed $50-million cruise terminal south of the city center; when it will finally open is anyone's guess.

Taxis, tour guides, and car-rental desks are readily available. Taxi trips—official taxis have green license plates—within Belize City are supposed to be set at BZ$6 to BZ$10 for one person between any two points in the city, plus BZ$1 for each additional person. Outside the city, and from downtown to the suburbs, you're charged by the distance you travel. Hourly rates are negotiable, but expect to pay around $30, or $150 for the day. There's no need to tip cab drivers. You can also rent a car at the Tourism Village, but rates can be high (at least $75 per day), and gas is also expensive. Green directional signs point you to nearby destinations such as the Belize Zoo. The Wet Lizard, next to the Tourism Village, also organizes tours for cruise-ship passengers.

EXPLORING BELIZE

Numbers in the margin correspond to points of interest on the Belize City map.

Belize City. Many Belize hands will tell you that the best way to see Belize City is through a rearview window. But, with an open mind to its peculiarities, and with a little caution (the city has a crime problem, but the tourist police keep a close watch on cruise-ship passengers), you may decide Belize City has a raffish, atmospheric charm rarely found in other Caribbean ports of call. You might even see the ghost of Graham Greene at a hotel bar. A 5- to 10-minute stroll from the perky Fort Street Tourism Village brings you into the other worlds of Belize City. On the north side of Haulover Creek is the colonial-style world of the Fort George section, where large old homes, stately but sometimes down at the heels, take the breezes off the sea and share their space with hotels and restaurants. On the south side is the bustling world of Albert Street, the main commercial thoroughfare. But don't stroll too far. Parts of Belize City are unsafe by night or day. During the daylight hours, as long as you stay within the main commercial district and the Fort George area—and ignore the street hustlers—you should have no problem.

House of Culture, the city's finest colonial structure, is said to have been designed by the illustrious British architect Sir Christopher Wren. Built in 1814, it was once the residence of the governor-general, the queen's representative in Belize. ⊠ *Regent St. at Southern Foreshore* ☎ *227–3050* ⌲ *BZ$10* ⊗ *Weekdays 9–4.*

Towering over the entrance to Belize Harbor, the **Fort George Lighthouse and Bliss Memorial** stands guard on the tip of Fort George Point. It was designed and funded by the country's greatest benefactor, Baron Bliss. The English nobleman never actually set foot on the Belizean mainland, but in his will he bequeathed most of his fortune to the people of Belize, and the date of his death, March 9, is celebrated as a national holiday. He is buried here, in a small, low mausoleum perched on the seawall, up a short run of limestone stairs. The lighthouse is for photo ops only—you can't enter it. ⊠ *Marine Parade.*

This small but interesting **Museum of Belize** was a Belize City jail from the 1850s to 1993. Displays on Belize history and culture include ancient Mayan artifacts, eclectic memorabilia, colorful Belize postage stamps, and an actual jail cell. Exhibitions change frequently. ⊠ *Gabourel La.* ☎ *223–4524* ⌲ *BZ$10* ⊗ *Weekdays 9–5.*

St. John's Cathedral, at the south end of Albert Street, is the oldest Anglican church in Central America, and the only one outside England where kings were crowned. From 1815 to 1845 four kings of the Mosquito Coast (a British protectorate along the coast of Honduras and Nicaragua) were crowned here. ⊠ *Albert St.* ☎ *227–2137* ⊗ *Weekdays 6–6.*

Altun Ha. If you've never visited an ancient Maya site, make a trip to Altun Ha, 28 mi (45 km) north of Belize City. ✧ *From Belize City, take the Northern Hwy. north to Mile 18.9. Turn right (east) on the Old Northern Hwy., which is only partly paved, and go 10½ mi (17 km) to* *the signed entrance road to Altun Ha on the left. Follow this paved road 2 mi (3 km) to the visitor center ☎ 609–3540 ☒ BZ$10 ☉ Daily 9–5.*

☺ **Belize Zoo.** One of the smallest, but arguably one of the best, zoos in the
Fodor'sChoice world, this park houses only animals native to Belize. Highlights include
★ spotted and rare black jaguars, pumas, margays, ocelots, jaguarondi, and the Baird's tapir, the national animal of Belize. ☒ *Western Hwy., 30 mi (49 km) west of Belize City* ☎ *220–8004* ⊕ *www.belizezoo.org* ☒ *BZ$16 adults, BZ$8 children* ☉ *Daily 8–5.*

☺ **Community Baboon Sanctuary.** This interesting wildlife conservation project is actually a haven for nearly 1,000 black howler monkeys and numerous other species of birds and mammals. ☒ *Community Baboon Sanctuary, 31 mi (50 km) northwest of Belize City* ☎ *220–2181* ⊕ *www. howlermonkeys.org* ☒ *BZ$14* ☉ *Daily 8–5.*

Crooked Tree Wildlife Sanctuary. A paradise for birders and animal lovers, this wildlife sanctuary encompasses a chain of inland waterways around the Northern Lagoon covering about 3,000 acres. Traveling through by canoe, you're likely to see iguanas, crocodiles, coatis, and turtles. The sanctuary's most prestigious visitors, however, are the jabiru storks, several of which usually visit between November and May. ☒ *Turn west off Northern Hwy. at Mile 30.8, then drive 2 mi (3 km)* ☎ *223–4987 for Belize Audubon Society* ⊕ *www.belizeaudubon.org/parks/ctws.htm* ☒ *BZ$8* ☉ *Daily 8–4:30.*

Hummingbird Highway. At Belmopan, the paved Hummingbird Highway is Belize's most scenic road, cutting 54 mi (90 km) southeast through the Maya Mountains to Dangriga, passing Five Blues Lake and Blue Hole national parks. Mile markers on the Hummingbird start in Dangriga.

☺ Less than a half-hour south of Belmopan, the 575-acre **St. Herman's Blue Hole Natural Park** has a natural turquoise pool surrounded by mosses and lush vegetation, excellent for a cool dip. ☒ *Mile 42.5, Hummingbird Hwy.* ⊕ *www.belizeaudubon.org* ☒ *BZ$8* ☉ *Daily 8–4:30*

THE CAYES

Ambergris Caye. Ambergris is the queen of the cayes. With a population of around 5,000, the island's only town, San Pedro, remains a small, friendly, and prosperous village. It has one of the highest literacy rates in the country and an admirable level of awareness about the fragility of the reef. The large number of substantial private houses being built on the edges of town is proof of how much tourism has enriched San Pedro. A water taxi from the Marine Terminal takes about 75 minutes and costs BZ$20 each way. You can also fly.

Fodor'sChoice **Hol Chan Marine Reserve** (Maya for "little channel") is 4 mi (6 km)
★ from San Pedro at the southern tip of Ambergris. Because fishing is forbidden here, snorkelers and divers can see teeming marine life. You can also snorkel with nurse sharks and rays (which gather here to be fed) at Shark-Ray Alley, a sandbar that is part of the reserve. You need above-average swimming skills, as the current is often strong. ☒ *Southern tip of Ambergris Caye* ⊕ *www.holchanbelize.org* ☒ *BZ$25 marine reserve fee.*

Caye Caulker. On Caye Caulker, where the one village is home to around 800 people, brightly painted houses on stilts line the coral-sand streets. Although the island is being developed more each year, flowers still outnumber cars 10 to 1 (golf carts, bicycles, and bare feet are the preferred means of transportation). The living is easy, as you might guess from all the NO SHIRT, NO SHOES, NO PROBLEM signs at the bars. This is the kind of place where most of the listings in the telephone directory give addresses like "near football field." A water taxi from the Marine Terminal costs about BZ$20 each way and takes about 45 minutes.

SHOPPING

Belize does not have the crafts tradition of its neighbors, Guatemala and Mexico, and imported goods are expensive due to high duties, but hand-carved items of ziricote or other local woods make good souvenirs. Near the Swing Bridge at Market Square is the **Commercial Center,** which has some food and craft vendors on the first floor and a restaurant and shops on the second. The **Fort Street Tourism Village,** where the ship tenders come in, is a collection of bright and clean gift shops selling T-shirts and Belizean and Guatemalan crafts. Beside the Tourism Village is an informal **Street Vendor Market,** with funkier goods and performances by a "Brukdown" band or a group of Garifuna drummers.

National Handicraft Center (⊠ *2 South Park St., in Fort George section* ☎ *223–3636*) has Belizean souvenir items, including hand-carved figurines, handmade furniture, pottery, and woven baskets. The prices are about as good as you'll find anywhere in Belize, and the sales clerks are friendly. It faces the small Memorial Park, which commemorates the Battle of St. George's Caye and is just a short stroll from the harbor front, the Tourism Village, and many of the hotels in the Fort George area, including the Radisson, Chateau Caribbean, and Great House.

ACTIVITIES

CANOPY TOURS

You may feel a little like Tarzan as you dangle 80 feet above the jungle floor, suspended by a harness, moving from one suspended platform to another. **Jaguar Paw Lodge** (☎ *820–2023, 877/624–3770 in the U.S.* ⊕ *www.jaguarpaw.com*), off Mile 37 of the Western Highway, has seven platforms set 100 to 250 feet apart. At the last platform you have to rappel to the ground. The cost is BZ$150 to BZ$200, depending on whether lunch and transportation are included. There's a 240-pound weight limit.

CAVE TUBING

Very popular with cruise passengers are river-tubing trips that go through a cave, where you'll turn off your headlamp for a minute of absolute darkness, but these are not for the claustrophobic or those afraid of the dark. **Cave-Tubing in Belize** (☎ *605–1575* ⊕ *www.cavetubing.com*) specializes in cave-tubing trips. The cost is BZ$90 (not including transportation from the cruise pier); for BZ$150, you can do both the cave-tubing and an ATV trip in the jungle.

DIVING AND SNORKELING

Most companies on Ambergris Caye offer morning and afternoon single-tank dives; snorkel trips begin mid-morning or early afternoon. Dive and snorkeling trips that originate in Caye Caulker are a bit cheaper. **Amigos del Mar** (⊠ *Off Barrier Reef Dr., near Mayan Princess Hotel, Ambergris Caye* ☎ *226–2706* ⊕ *amigosdive.com*) is perhaps the island's most consistently recommended dive operation. It offers a range of local dives as well as trips to Turneffe Atoll and Lighthouse Reef in a fast 48-foot dive boat.

Go out for a snorkel on a sailboat with **Raggamuffin Tours** (⊠ *Front St., Caye Caulker* ☎ *226–0348* ⊕ *www.raggamuffintours.com*), which goes to Hol Chan for BZ$90, including the park entrance fee.

INDEPENDENT TOURS

Several Belize City–based tour guides and operators offer custom trips for ship passengers; companies will usually meet you at the Fort Street Tourism Village. Katie Valk, who owns **Belize Trips** (⌂ *Box 1108, Belize City* ☎ *223–0376 in Belize, 561/210–7015 in U.S.* ⊕ *www.belize-trips. com*), is a transplanted New Yorker. Her company can organize a custom trip to just about anywhere in the country. **Ecological Tours & Services.** (⊠ *Fort Street Tourism Village, Belize City* ☎ *223–4874* ⊕ *www. ecotoursbelize.com*), based in Belize City, specializes in organizing independent tours for cruise-ship passengers.

BEACHES

Although the barrier reef just offshore limits the wave action, which, over eons, builds classic wide sandy beaches, and there is a good deal of seagrass on the shore bottom, Ambergris Caye's beaches are among the best in Belize. All beaches in Belize are public. **Mar de Tumbo,** 1½ mi (3 km) south of town near the Tropica Hotel, is the best beach on the south end of the island. **North Ambergris,** accessible by water taxi from San Pedro or by golf cart over the new bridge to the north, has miles of narrow beaches and fewer people. **Ramon's Village's beach,** right across from the airstrip, is the best in the town area. The beaches on Caulker are not as good as those on Ambergris. Along the front side of the island is a narrow strip of sand, but the water is shallow and swimming conditions are poor. The **Split,** on the north end of the village (turn to your right from the main public pier), is the best place on Caye Caulker for swimming.

WHERE TO EAT

$$$–$$$$ ✗ **Harbour View.** For the most romantic setting in the city, ask for a
SEAFOOD table on the wraparound balcony overlooking the harbor. The friendly
★ staff and consistently excellent food also make the Harbour View a favorite of Belize's power brokers. The seafood is especially good; try the snapper with mango chutney, cooked in a banana leaf. Pork dishes, especially Pork Picasso with a hot pepper relish, also are delicious. ⊠ *Fort St., near Tourism Village* ☎ *223–6420* ▭ *AE, D, MC, V* ☉ *No lunch weekends.*

$-$$
SEAFOOD

✗ **Wet Lizard.** Right next to the Tourism Village, overlooking the board-walk where cruise-ship tenders drop off passengers, there's no question of the target market of the Wet Lizard. Even so, it's become a popular bar and a place to grab a sandwich or hamburger, even for those not on a cruise ship. An expansion added a gift shop, snack bar, and tour operation. ⊠ *1 Fort St.* ☎ *223/2664* ⊟ *MC, V* ☽ *Closed Sun. and Mon.*

BERMUDA

Basking in the Atlantic, 508 mi (817 km) due east of Cape Hatteras, North Carolina, restrained, polite Bermuda is a departure from other sunny, beach-strewn isles. You won't find laid-back locals wandering around barefoot proffering piña coladas. Bermuda is somewhat formal, and despite the gorgeous weather, residents wearing stockings and heels or jackets, ties, Bermuda shorts, and knee socks are a common sight, whether on the street by day or in restaurants at night. On Bermuda's 22 square mi (57 square km) you will discover that pastel cottages, quaint shops, and manicured gardens betray a more staid, suburban way of life. A self-governing British colony since 1968, Bermuda has maintained some of its English character even as it is increasingly influenced by American culture. Most cruise ships make seven-night loops from U.S. embarkation ports, with four nights at sea and three tied up in port. Increasingly popular are round-trip itineraries originating in northeastern embarkation ports that include a single day or overnight port call in Bermuda before continuing south to the Bahamas or the Caribbean.

4

ESSENTIALS

CURRENCY The Bermuda dollar (B$) is on par with the U.S. dollar. You can use American money anywhere, but change is often given in Bermudian currency. ATMs are common.

INTERNET Expect to pay as much as $12 per hour to check your e-mail on Bermuda. **Logic Communications** (⊠ *The Walkway, 10–12 Burnaby St., Hamilton* ☎ *441/296–9600*).

TELEPHONE To make a local call, simply dial the seven-digit number. You can find specially marked AT&T USADirect phones at the airport, the cruise-ship dock in Hamilton, and King's Square and Ordnance Island in St. George's. You can also make international calls with a calling card from the main post office. You can make prepaid international calls from the Cable & Wireless Office, which also has international telex, cable, and fax services Monday through Saturday from 9 to 5.

COMING ASHORE

Three Bermuda harbors serve cruise ships: Hamilton (the capital), St. George's, and King's Wharf at the Royal Naval Dockyard.

In Hamilton, cruise ships tie up right on the city's main street, Front Street. A Visitors Service Bureau is next to the ferry terminal, also on Front Street and nearby; maps and brochures are displayed in the cruise terminal itself.

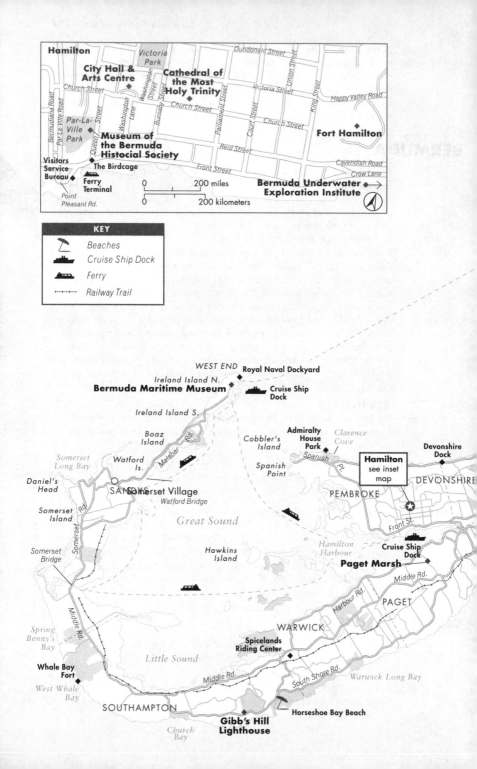

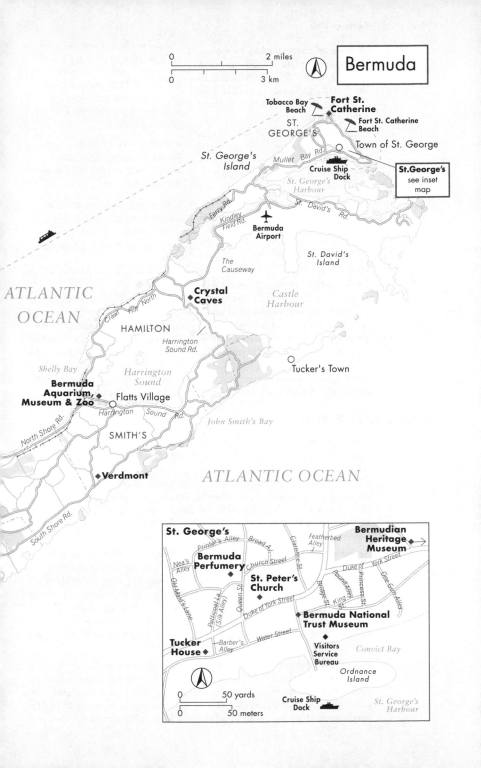

St. George's actually has two piers that accommodate cruise ships. One is on Ordnance Island, which is in the heart of the city; another pier is nearby. Visitors Service Bureau offices are at each pier.

King's Wharf, in the Royal Naval Dockyard at the westernmost end of the island, is the most isolated of the three cruise-ship berthing areas, and it is where the largest vessels dock. But it is well connected to the rest of the island by taxi, bus, and ferry. The nearby Cooperage has a Visitors Service Bureau office, and bus stops and the ferry pier are clearly marked.

> **BERMUDA BEST BETS**
>
> ■ **Gibbs Hill Lighthouse.** Make the climb to the top, where the reward is an expansive view of the inlets and harbors.
>
> ■ **Bermuda Maritime Museum.** Absorb Bermuda's nautical and military history in this Royal Navy Dockyard museum.
>
> ■ **St. George's.** Attend the pier-side show hosted by the town crier, where gossips and nagging wives are drenched in a dunking stool.

Taxis are the fastest and easiest way to get around the island, but they are also quite expensive. Four-seaters charge $6.40 for the first mile and $2 for each subsequent mile. You can hire taxis for around $40 per hour (three-hour minimum for up to four passengers) if you want to do some exploring, and if you can round up a group of people, this is often cheaper than an island tour offered by your ship. Tip drivers 15%. Rental cars are prohibited, but the island has a good bus and ferry system. You can also rent scooters, but this can be dangerous for the unitiated and is not recommended.

EXPLORING BERMUDA

HAMILTON

Bermuda's capital since 1815, the city of Hamilton is a small, bustling harbor town. It's the economic and social center of Bermuda, with busy streets lined with shops and offices. International influences, from both business and tourism, have brought a degree of sophistication unusual in so small a city. There are several museums and galleries to explore, but the favorite pastimes are shopping in Hamilton's numerous boutiques and dining in its many upscale restaurants.

♺ **Bermuda Underwater Exploration Institute (BUEI).** The 40,000-square-foot
★ Ocean Discovery Centre has numerous multimedia and interactive displays designed to acquaint you with the deep sea and its inhabitants. Never heard of a bathysphere? See a replica of this deep-sea diving vehicle, which allowed oceanographer William Beebe and Otis Barton to venture ½ mi down into the deep in 1934. ⊠ *40 Crow La., off E. Broadway* ☎ *441/292-7219* ⊕ *www.buei.org* ⊠ *$12.50* ☉ *Weekdays 9–5, weekends 10–5; last admission at 4.*

★ **Cathedral of the Most Holy Trinity.** Designed with early Greek Revival flourishes, the cathedral was constructed out of Bermuda limestone and materials imported from France, Nova Scotia, and Scotland. The cathedral was completed in 1911. It has a copper roof, unusual in Bermuda's sea of white-topped buildings. After exploring the interior, you can purchase tickets to climb the 150-odd steps (143 feet) of the tower ⊠ *29 Church St.* ☎ *441/292–4033* ⊕ *www.anglican.bm* ⊡ *Cathedral free; tower $3* ☉ *Cathedral daily 7:30–5 and for Sun. services; tower weekdays 10–4.*

↻ **City Hall and Arts Centre.** Set back from the street behind a fountain and
★ lily pond, City Hall contains Hamilton's administrative offices as well as two art galleries and a performance hall. Instead of a clock, its tower is topped with a bronze wind vane—a prudent choice in a land where the weather is as important as the time. Massive cedar doors open into a large lobby with beautiful chandeliers and high ceilings. On the first landing, in the East Exhibition Room, is the **Bermuda National Gallery,** the home of Bermuda's national art collection. Farther up the stairs, in the West Wing, the **Bermuda Society of Arts Gallery** displays work by its members. ⊠ *17 Church St.* ☎ *441/292–1234* ☉ *City Hall weekdays 9–5; National Gallery weekdays 10–4, Sat. 10–2; Society of the Arts weekdays 10–4, Sat. 10–2.*

↻ **Fort Hamilton.** This imposing moat-ringed fortress has underground pas-
★ sageways that were cut through solid rock by Royal Engineers in the 1860s. Built to defend the West End's Royal Naval Dockyard from land attacks, it was outdated even before its completion, but remains a fine example of a polygonal Victorian fort. Even if you're not a big fan of military history, the hilltop site's stellar views and stunning gardens make the trip worthwhile. ⊠ *Happy Valley Rd.* ☎ *441/292–1234* ⊡ *Free* ☉ *Daily 8–sunset.*

★ **Museum of the Bermuda Historical Society/Bermuda Public Library.** This building was once the home of Hamilton's first postmaster, William Bennet Perot, and his family. Mark Twain once lamented that the rubber tree in the front yard didn't bear fruit in the form of hot-water bottles and rubber overshoes. The library was founded in 1839, and its reference section has virtually every book ever written about Bermuda. The museum depicts Bermuda history with household goods and other artifacts, including an 18th-century sedan chair. ⊠ *13 Queen St.* ☎ *441/295–2905 library; 441/295–2487 museum* ⊕ *www.bnl.bm* ⊡ *Library free; museum donations accepted* ☉ *Library Mon.–Thurs. 8:30–7 Fri. 10–5, Sat. 9–5, Sun. 1–5; closed Sun and at 6 Mon.–Thur. in July and Aug.; museum weekdays 10–2* ☞ *Tours by appointment.*

ST. GEORGE'S

The settlement of Bermuda began in what is now the town of St. George nearly 400 years ago, when the *Sea Venture* was shipwrecked on Bermuda's treacherous reefs on its way to the colony of Jamestown, Virginia. No trip to Bermuda is complete without a visit to this historic town and UNESCO World Heritage Site.

★ **Bermuda National Trust Museum at the Globe Hotel.** This building was erected in 1700. During the American Civil War, Confederate Major Norman Walker was stationed in the building, where he coordinated the flow of guns, ammunition, and war supplies through Union blockades in American ports. The house saw service as the Globe Hotel during the mid-19th century and became a National Trust property in 1951. ⊠ *32 Duke of York St.* ☎ *441/297–1423* ⊕ *www.bnt.bm* ⊡ *$5;*

$10 combination ticket includes admission to Tucker House and Verdmont ⊙ Apr.–Sept., Tues., Wed., Fri., and Sat. 10–4; limited hours in winter.

★ **Bermuda Perfumery & Gardens.** In 2005 the perfumery moved from Bailey's Bay in Smith's Parish, where it had been based since 1928, to historic Stewart Hall. Although the location changed, the techniques it uses did not: the perfumery still manufactures and bottles all its island-inspired scents on-site using essential oils extracted from frangipani, jasmine, oleander, and passionflower. Guides are available to explain the entire process, and there's a small museum that outlines the company's history. You can also wander around the gardens and stock up on your favorite fragrances in the showroom. ⊠ *Stewart Hall, 5 Queen St.* ☎ *441/293–0627* ⊕ *www.lilibermuda.com* ☐ *Free* ⊙ *Mon.–Sat. 9–5.*

Ⓒ ★ **Ordnance Island.** A splendid bronze statue of Sir George Somers dominates the island. The dunking stool is a replica of the one used to dunk gossips, nagging wives, and suspected witches. Demonstrations are sometimes given, although volunteers report that getting dunked is no picnic. Also on the island is the *Deliverance II*, a replica of one of two ships—the other was the *Patience*—built by the survivors of the 1609 wreck of the *Sea Venture* to carry them to Jamestown, Virginia, their original destination. ⊠ *Across from King's Sq.*

Fodor's Choice ★ **St. Peter's Church.** Because parts of this church date back to 1620, it holds the distinction of being the oldest continuously operating Anglican church in the western hemisphere. It was not the first church to stand on this site, however. It replaced a 1612 structure of posts and palmetto leaves that was destroyed in a storm. The present church was extended in 1713, and the galleries on either side were added in 1833. ⊠ *33 Duke of York St.* ☎ *441/297–2459* ⊕ *www.anglican.bm* ☐ *Donations accepted* ⊙ *Mon.–Sat. 10–4, Sun. service at 11:15.*

★ **Tucker House.** Constructed out of native limestone, Tucker House is typical of many early Bermudian houses. It was built in 1711 for a merchant who used the basement as storage space for his wares, and it was originally close to the shore—landfill has since moved the water back. The house is at the corner of Barber's Alley, named for Joseph Haine Rainey, a freed slave from South Carolina who fled to Bermuda at the outbreak of the American Civil War and made his living here as a barber. After the war, Rainey returned home and, in 1870, became the first black man to be elected to the U.S. House of Representatives. ⊠ *5 Water St.* ☎ *441/297–0545* ⊕ *www.bnt.bm* ☐ *$5; $10 combination ticket includes admission to National Trust Museum in Globe Hotel and Verdmont* ⊙ *Tues.–Thurs. 10–2.*

ELSEWHERE ON THE ISLAND

Ⓒ Fodor's Choice ★ **Bermuda Aquarium, Museum and Zoo.** The aquarium has always been a pleasant diversion, but thanks to an ambitious expansion project it has become truly great. The 145,000-gallon tank holding the North Rock Exhibit, in the main gallery, gives you a diver's view of Bermuda's famed living coral reefs and colorful marine life. ⊠ *40 N. Shore Rd., Flatts Village, Hamilton Parish* ☎ *441/293–2727* ⊕ *www.bamz.org* ☐ *$10*

⊙ *Daily 9–5, last admission at 4; North Rock dive talk at 1:10 daily and seal feeding at 1:30 and 4 daily.*

☾ **Bermuda Maritime Museum and Dolphin Quest.** Inside Bermuda's largest
Fodor'sChoice fort, built between 1837 and 1852, the Maritime Museum exhibits its
★ collections in six old stone munitions warehouses, which surround the
parade grounds and the Keep Pond. On top of the hill is the Commis-
sioner's House, an unusual cast-iron building constructed from 1823
to 1828 in England and shipped to Bermuda for the chief administra-
tor of the Dockyard.

The Maritime Museum's most popular attraction is **Dolphin Quest**
(☎ 441/234–4464 ⊕ *www.dolphinquest.org*) within the fortress's historic keep. Several programs designed for adults and/or children age
five and older let you get into the water and touch, play with, and
swim alongside dolphins. ⊠ *National Museum of Bermuda, Dockyard*
☎ *441/234–1418* ⊕ *www.bmm.bm* ⊠ *$10 for museum, $175–$299 for
Dolphin Quest* ⊙ *Daily 9:30–4.*

☾ **Crystal Caves.** This fantastic cavern 120 feet underground, which was
Fodor'sChoice discovered in 1907, has spectacular stalactite formations. ⊠ *8 Crys-
★ tal Caves Rd., off Wilkinson Ave., Bailey's Bay, Hamilton Parish*
☎ *441/293–0640* ⊕ *www.bermudacaves.com* ⊠ *One cave $20; com-
bination ticket $27* ⊙ *Daily 9:30–4:30; last combination tour at 4.*

☾ **Fort St. Catherine.** This restored fortress is one of the most impressive
★ on the island. The original fort was built around 1613, but it was
remodeled and enlarged at least five times. As you travel through the
tunnels, you'll come across some startlingly lifelike figures tucked into
niches. ⊠ *15 Coot Pond Rd., St. George's Parish* ☎ *441/297–1920* ⊠ *$7*
⊙ *Weekdays 10–4.*

☾ **Gibb's Hill Lighthouse.** The second cast-iron lighthouse ever built soars
★ above Southampton Parish. Designed in London and opened in 1846,
the tower stands 117 feet high and 362 feet above the sea. It's a long
haul up the 185 spiral stairs, but you can stop to catch your breath at
platforms along the way, where photographs and drawings of the lighthouse divert your attention. ⊠ *68 St. Anne's Rd., Southampton Parish*
☎ *441/238–8069* ⊕ *www.bermudalighthouse.com* ⊠ *$2.50* ⊙ *Daily
9–4.30. Closed mid-Jan.–mid-Feb.*

Fodor'sChoice **Paget Marsh.** This small, easily walkable slice of unspoiled native Ber-
★ muda is just minutes from bustling Hamilton. Listen for the cries of
the native and migratory birds that visit this natural wetland, jointly
owned and preserved by the Bermuda National Trust and the Bermuda
Audubon Society. ⊠ *Lovers La., Paget Parish* ☎ *441/236–6483* ⊕ *www.
bnt.bm* ⊠ *Free* ⊙ *Daily sunrise–sunset.*

☾ **Verdmont.** Though it was used as a home until the mid-20th century, the
★ house has had virtually no structural changes since it was built in about
1710. Verdmont holds a notable collection of historic furnishings. Some
are imported from England—such as the early-19th-century piano—
but most of the furniture is 18th-century cedar, crafted by Bermudian
cabinetmakers. ⊠ *6 Verdmont La., off Collector's Hill, Smith's Parish*
☎ *441/236–7369* ⊕ *www.bnt.bm* ⊠ *$5; $10 combination ticket with
Bermuda National Trust Museum in Globe Hotel and Tucker House*

◔ *Nov.–Apr., Tues., Wed., Fri., and Sat. 10–4; May–Oct., Tues., Wed., Thurs., and Sat. 10–4.*

SHOPPING

Hamilton has the greatest concentration of shops in Bermuda, and Front Street is its pièce de résistance. Lined with small, pastel-color buildings, this most fashionable of Bermuda's streets houses sedate department stores and snazzy boutiques, with several small arcades and shopping alleys leading off it. A smart canopy shades the entrance to the 55 Front Street Group, which houses Crisson Jewelers. Modern Butterfield Place has galleries and boutiques selling, among other things, Louis Vuitton leather goods. The Emporium, a renovated building with an atrium, has a range of shops, from antiques to souvenirs.

St. George's Water Street, Duke of York Street, Hunters Wharf, Penno's Wharf, and Somers Wharf are the sites of numerous renovated buildings that house branches of Front Street stores, as well as artisans' studios. Historic King's Square offers little more than a couple of T-shirt and souvenir shops.

In the West End, **Somerset Village** has a few shops, but they hardly merit a special shopping trip. However, the **Clocktower Mall**, in a historic building at the Royal Naval Dockyard, has a few more shopping opportunities, including branches of Front Street shops and specialty boutiques. The Dockyard is also home to the Craft Market, the Bermuda Arts Centre, and Bermuda Clayworks.

ACTIVITIES

BICYCLING

The best and sometimes only way to explore Bermuda's nooks and crannies—its little hidden coves and 18th-century tribe roads—is by bicycle or motor scooter. A popular option for biking in Bermuda is the **Railway Trail,** a dedicated cycle path blissfully free of cars. Running intermittently the length of the old Bermuda Railway (old "Rattle 'n' Shake"), this trail is scenic, paved, and restricted to pedestrian and bicycle traffic. You can ask the staff at any bike-rental shop for advice on where to access the trail.

Eve's Cycle Livery. In three convenient locations around the island, Eve's rents standard-size mountain bikes, as well as motor scooters, including your mandatory helmet. The staff readily supplies advice on where to ride, and there's no charge for a repair waiver. Eve's Cycles on Water Street is convenient if you arrive in Bermuda on a cruise docking in St. George's—the shop is literally a few yards away from the cruise terminal. ✉ *114 Middle Rd., near S. Shore Rd., Paget Parish* ☎ *441/236–6247* ✉ *1 Water St., St. George's* ☎ *441/236–0839* ✉ *Maritime La., Dockyard* ☎ *441/236–6748.*

GOLF

Golf courses make up nearly 17% of the island's 21.6 square mi. The scenery on the courses is usually spectacular, with flowering trees and shrubs decked out in multicolor blossoms against a backdrop of brilliant blue sea and sky. The layouts are remarkably challenging, thanks to capricious ocean breezes, daunting natural terrain, and the clever work of world-class golf architects.

Fairmont Southampton Golf Club is known for its steep terrain. ⊠ *Fairmont Southampton Resort, 101 South Rd., Southampton Parish* ☎ *441/239–6952* ⊕ *www.fairmont.com/Southampton* ☜ *Greens fees $84 before 2:30 PM with cart mandatory, $65 after 2:30 PM with cart or $45 walking.*

★ **Mid Ocean Club,** a classic 1921 Charles Blair Macdonald design revamped by Robert Trent Jones Sr. in 1953, is ranked as one of the top 50 courses outside the U.S. by *Golf Digest.* ⊠ *1 Mid Ocean Dr., off S. Shore Rd., Tucker's Town* ☎ *441/293–1215* ⊕ *www.themidoceanclubbermuda. com* ☜ *Greens fees $250 ($100 when playing with a member). Nonmembers must be sponsored by a club member (your hotelier can arrange this); nonmember starting times available Mon., Wed., and Fri. except holidays. Caddies $55 for double or $65 for single per bag (tip not included). Cart rental $30 per person. Shoe rentals $6. Club rentals $45. Lessons $55 a half hour, $100 per hour.*

SNORKELING

Snorkeling cruises are generally offered from April through November. Smaller boats, which limit capacity to 10 to 16 passengers, offer more personal attention and focus more on the beautiful snorkeling areas themselves. Guides on such tours often relate interesting historical and ecological information about the island. Some larger boats take up to 40 passengers.

Jessie James Cruises. Half-day trips aboard the 31-foot glass-bottomed boat *Pisces*, which holds up to 17 people, cost $65, $45 for children (ages 8–10). The boat takes you to three different sites, including at least two shipwrecks. ⊠ *6 Glen Ct., Warwick* ☎ *441/236–4804* ⊕ *www. jessiejames.bm.*

BEACHES

☾ **Elbow Beach.** Swimming and bodysurfing are great at this beach, which
★ is bordered by the prime strand of sand reserved for guests of the Elbow Beach Hotel on the left, and the ultraexclusive Coral Beach Club beach area on the right. Protective coral reefs make the waters the safest on the island, and a good choice for families. A lunch wagon sells fast food and cold drinks during the day, and Mickey's beach bar (part of the Elbow Beach Hotel) is open for lunch and dinner, though it may be difficult to get a table. ⊠ *Off South Rd., Paget Parish* Ⓜ *Bus 2 or 7 from Hamilton.*

☾ **Horseshoe Bay Beach.** When locals say they're going to "the beach," they're
Fodor's Choice generally referring to Horseshoe Bay Beach, the island's most popular.
★ With clear water, a ⅓-meter crescent of pink sand, a vibrant social scene, and the uncluttered backdrop of South Shore Park, Horseshoe Bay has everything you could ask of a Bermudian beach. A snack bar, changing rooms, beach-rental facilities, and lifeguards add to its appeal. The undertow can be strong, especially on the main beach. ⊠ *Off South Rd., Southampton Parish* ☎ *441/238–2651* Ⓜ *Bus 7 from Hamilton.*

Tobacco Bay Beach. The most popular beach near St. George's—about 15 minutes northwest of the town on foot—this small north-shore strand is huddled in a coral cove. Its beach house has a snack bar, equipment rentals, toilets, showers, changing rooms, and ample parking. It's a 10-minute hike from the bus stop in the town of St. George's, or you can flag down a St. George's Minibus Service van and ask for a lift ($2 per person). In high season the beach is busy, especially midweek, when cruise ships are docked. ⊠ *Coot Pond Rd., St. George's Parish* ☎ *441/297–2756* Ⓜ *Bus 1, 3, 10, or 11 from Hamilton.*

WHERE TO EAT

$ ✕ **Docksider.** Locals come to mingle at this sprawling Front Street sports
BRITISH   bar. It's generally more popular as a drinking venue, as it can get quite overcrowded and rowdy. But if you want to catch the game on the big screen with everyone else, an all-day menu of standard pub fare is available, as well as local fish. Go for the English beef pie, fish-and-chips, or a fish sandwich and sip your dessert—a Dark 'n Stormy—out on the porch as you watch Bermuda stroll by. Or if you can't make up your mind, you can always rely on the hearty full English breakfast to fill you up. The pub has a good jukebox, and there's often a DJ or a band on summer weekends. ⊠ *121 Front St., Hamilton* ☎ *441/296–3333* ⊕ *www.dockies.com* ▭ *AE, MC, V.*

$ ✕ **Spring Garden Restaurant & Bar.** If you've never had Barbadian, or
CARIBBEAN   "Bajan" food, as Barbados natives like to call it, come sit under the indoor palm tree and try panfried flying fish—a delicacy in Barbados. Another good choice is the broiled mahimahi served in creole sauce, with peas and rice. During lobster season an additional menu appears, featuring steamed, broiled, or curried lobster ($38.50 for the complete dinner). For dessert, try coconut cream pie or raspberry-mango cheesecake. Or eat with the locals at the Friday lunchtime bargain buffet; help yourself to as many starters, mains, and desserts as you can eat for $21. ⊠ *19 Washington La., off Reid St., Hamilton* ☎ *441/295–7416* ▭ *AE, MC, V* ☉ *Closed Sun.*

BONAIRE (KRALENDIJK)

Vernon
O'Reilly
Ramesar

Starkly beautiful Bonaire is the consummate desert island. Surrounded by pristine waters, it is a haven for divers and snorkelers, who flock here from around the world to take advantage of the excellent visibility, easily accessed reefs, and bountiful marine life. Bonaire is the most rustic of the three ABC islands, and despite its dependence on tourism it manages to maintain its identity and simple way of life. There are many good restaurants, most of which are within walking distance of the port. Most of the island's 14,000-some inhabitants live in and around Kralendijk, which must certainly qualify as one of the cutest and most compact capitals in the Caribbean. The best shopping is to be found along the very short stretch of road that constitutes "downtown." Bonaire's beaches tend to be small and rocky, but there is a nice

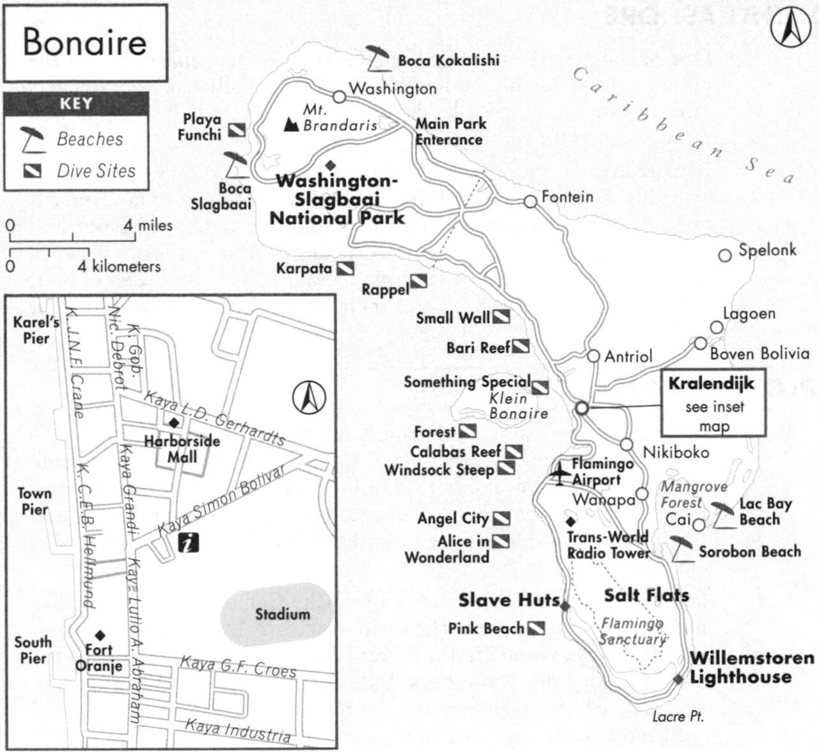
Bonaire
KEY
Beaches
Dive Sites
0 4 miles
0 4 kilometers
Boca Kokalishi
Washington
Caribbean Sea
Playa Funchi
Mt. Brandaris
Main Park Enterance
Boca Slagbaai
Washington-Slagbaai National Park
Fontein
Spelonk
Karpata
Rappel
Small Wall
Lagoen
Bari Reef
Antriol
Boven Bolivia
Something Special
Klein Bonaire
Kralendijk see inset map
Forest
Calabas Reef
Windsock Steep
Nikiboko
Flamingo Airport
Wanapa
Mangrove Forest
Cai
Lac Bay Beach
Angel City
Alice in Wonderland
Trans-World Radio Tower
Sorobon Beach
Slave Huts
Salt Flats
Pink Beach
Flamingo Sanctuary
Willemstoren Lighthouse
Lacre Pt.
Karel's Pier
K. J.N.E. Crane
Nic. Debrot
K. Gob.
Kaya L.D. Gerhardts
Harborside Mall
Town Pier
Kaya Grandi
Kaya Simon Bolivar
K. C.E.B. Hellmund
Kaya Lulio A. Abraham
Stadium
South Pier
Fort Oranje
Kaya G.F. Croes
Kaya Industria

stretch of sandy beach at Lac Bay. It is entirely possible to see almost all of the sights and sounds of the island in one day by taking one of the island tours on offer.

ESSENTIALS

CURRENCY The NAf guilder (NAF 1.79 to US$1); U.S. currency is accepted almost everywhere on the island, and the island has several ATMs, particularly in Kralendijk. At this writing, Bonaire is planning to transition to the US$ as the official currency by the beginning of 2011.

INTERNET **Bonaire Access** (✉ *Harbourside Mall, Kralendijk* ☎ *No phone*). **Cyber City** (✉ *City Café, Kaya Grandi 7, Kralendijk* ☎ *599/717–8286*).

TELEPHONE You can make international calls from from the Telbo central phone company office (next to the tourism office in Kralendijk), which is open 24 hours a day. The country code for Bonaire is 599; 717 is the exchange for every four-digit telephone number on the island. When making interisland calls, dial 717 plus the local four-digit number.

COMING ASHORE

One of the great benefits of Bonaire to cruise passengers is that the port is right in downtown Kralendijk. Ships usually tender passengers ashore. A four-minute walk takes you to most of the best shopping and restaurants on the island.

Bonaire lives for tourism, so upon the arrival of a cruise ship the locals are ready. Taxis wait right at the port and operate on fixed government rates. All the sights of Kralendijk are within easy walking distance, and a taxi ride to one of the larger resorts on the island will run between $9 and $12. A half-day island tour by taxi costs about $25 per hour for up to two passengers. Fares increase by 50% between midnight and 6 AM.

EXPLORING BONAIRE

Two routes, north and south from Kralendijk, the island's small capital, are possible on the 24-mi-long (39-km-long) island; either route will take from a few hours to a full day, depending on whether you stop to snorkel, swim, dive, or lounge. Those pressed for time will find that it's easy to explore the entire island in a day if stops are kept to a minimum.

Kralendijk. Bonaire's small, tidy capital city (population 3,000) is five minutes from the airport. The main drag, J. A. Abraham Boulevard, turns into **Kaya Grandi** in the center of town. Along it are most of the island's major stores, boutiques, and restaurants. Across Kaya Grandi, opposite the Littman jewelry store, is Kaya L. D. Gerharts, with several small supermarkets, a handful of snack shops, and some of the better restaurants. Walk down the narrow waterfront avenue called Kaya C.E.B. Hellmund, which leads straight to the **North and South piers.** In the center of town, the Harbourside Mall has chic boutiques. Along this route is **Ft. Oranje,** with its cannons. From December through April, cruise ships dock in the harbor once or twice a week. The diminutive ocher-and-white structure that looks like a tiny Greek temple is the **fish market;** local anglers no longer bring their catches here (they sell out of their homes these days), but you can find plenty of fresh produce brought over from Colombia and Venezuela. Pick up the brochure "*Walking and Shopping in Kralendijk*" from the tourist office to get a map and full listing of all the monuments and sights in the town.

♻ ★ **Rooi Lamoenchi Kunuku.** Owner Ellen Herrera restored her family's homestead north of Lac Bay, in the Bonairean *kadushi* (cactus) wilderness, to educate tourists and residents about the history and tradition of authentic *kunuku* living and show unspoiled terrain in two daily tours. You must make an appointment in advance and expect to spend a couple of hours. ⊠ *Kaya Suiza 23, Playa Baribe* ☎ *599/717–8489* ⊕ *www. webpagecur.com/rooilamoenchi* ☜ *$21* ۞ *By appointment only.*

Salt Flats. You can't miss the salt flats—voluptuous white drifts that look something like mountains of snow. Harvested once a year, the "ponds" are owned by Cargill, Inc., which has reactivated the 19th-century salt industry with great success (one reason for that success is that the ocean on this part of the island is higher than the land—which makes irrigation a snap). Keep a lookout for the three 30-foot obelisks—white, blue, and red—that were used to guide the trade boats coming to pick up the salt. Look also in the distance across the pans to the abandoned solar saltworks that's now a designated **flamingo sanctuary**. With the naked eye you might be able to make out a pink-orange haze just on the horizon; with binoculars you will see a sea of bobbing pink bodies. The sanctuary is completely protected, and no entrance is allowed (flamingos are extremely sensitive to disturbances of any kind).

○ **Slave Huts.** The salt industry's gritty history is revealed in Rode Pan, the site of two groups of tiny slave huts. The white grouping is on the right side of the road, opposite the salt flats; the second grouping, called the red slave huts (though they appear yellow), stretches across the road toward the island's southern tip. During the 19th century, slaves working the salt pans by day crawled into these huts to rest. Each Friday afternoon they walked seven hours to Rincon to weekend with their families, returning each Sunday. Only very small people will be able to enter, but walk around and poke your head in for a look.

○ **Washington–Slagbaai National Park.** Once a plantation producing dividi-divi trees (the pods were used for tanning animal skins), aloe (used for medicinal lotions), charcoal, and goats, the park is now a model of conservation. It's easy to tour the 13,500-acre tropical desert terrain on the dirt roads. As befits a wilderness sanctuary, the well-marked, rugged routes force you to drive slowly enough to appreciate the animal life and the terrain. There are two hiking routes: the long one (22 mi [35.5 km]) is marked by yellow arrows, the short one (15 mi [24 km]) by green arrows. Goats and donkeys may dart across the road, and if you keep your eyes peeled, you may catch sight of large iguanas camouflaged in the shrubbery. A useful guide to the park is available at the entrance for about $6. To get here, take the secondary road north from the town of Rincon. The Nature Fee for swimming and snorkeling also grants you free admission to this park—simply present proof of payment and some form of photo ID. ☎ 599/717–8444 ⊕ www.washingtonparkbonaire. org ✎ Free, but requires payment of Nature Fee ($10) ۞ Daily 8–5; you must enter before 3.

Willemstoren Lighthouse. Bonaire's first lighthouse was built in 1837 and is now automated (but closed to visitors). Take some time to explore the beach and notice how the waves, driven by the trade winds, play a crashing symphony against the rocks. Locals stop here to collect pieces

---

BONAIRE BEST BETS

■ **Diving.** Bonaire is one of the world's top diving destinations. Shore diving is especially good.

■ **Snorkeling.** With reefs close to shore, snorkeling is good right off the beach.

■ **Flamingo spotting.** These shy, graceful birds are one of Bonaire's scenic delights.

■ **Kralendijk.** The accessible town has a nice assortment of restaurants and stores.

■ **Washington–Slagbaai National Park.** Bonaire's best land-based sight is this well-preserved national park.

4

of driftwood in spectacular shapes and to build fanciful pyramids from objects that have washed ashore.

SHOPPING

Although it is a relatively small town, Kralendijk offers a good range of high-end items like watches and jewelry at attractive prices. There are a number of souvenir shops offering T-shirts and trinkets lining the main street of Kaya Grandi.

★ **Atlantis** (⊠ *Kaya Grandi 32B, Kralendijk* ☎ *599/717–7730*) carries a large range of precious and semiprecious gems. The tanzanite collection is especially beautiful. You will also find Sector, Raymond Weil, and Citizen watches, among others, all at great savings. Since gold jewelry is sold by weight here, it's an especially good buy.

Littman's (⊠ *Kaya Grandi 33, Kralendijk* ☎ *599/717–8160* ⊠ *Harbourside Mall, Kaya Grandi 31, Kralendijk* ☎ *599/717–2130*) is an upscale jewelry and gift shop where many items are handpicked by owner Steven Littman on his regular trips to Europe. Look for Rolex, Omega, Cartier, and Tag Heuer watches; fine gold jewelry; antique coins; nautical sculptures; resort clothing; and accessories.

ACTIVITIES

BICYCLING

Bonaire is generally flat, so bicycles are an easy way to get around. Because of the heat it's essential to carry water if you're planning to cycle for any distance, and especially if your plans involve exploring the deserted interior. There are more than 180 mi (290 km) of unpaved routes (as well as the many paved roads) on the island.

Cycle Bonaire (⊠ *Kaya Gobernador N. Debrot 77A, Kralendijk* ☎ *599/717–2229*) rents mountain bikes and gear (trail maps, water bottles, helmets, locks, repair and first-aid kits) for $20 a day or $100 for six days; half-day and full-day guided excursions start at $55, not including bike rental.

DIVING AND SNORKELING

Diving and snorkeling are almost a religion on Bonaire, and are by far the most popular activities for cruise passengers. Bonaire has some of the best reef diving this side of Australia's Great Barrier Reef. It takes only 5 to 25 minutes to reach many sites, the current is usually mild, and although some reefs have sudden, steep drops, most begin just offshore and slope gently downward at a 45-degree angle. General visibility runs 60 to 100 feet, except during surges in October and November. You can see several varieties of coral: knobby-brain, giant-brain, elkhorn, staghorn, mountainous star, gorgonian, and black.

☾ **Larry's Shore & Wild Side Diving** (☎ *599/790–9156* ⊕ *www.larry-*
★ *wildsidediving.com*) is run by a former army combat diver and offers a variety of appealing options ranging from the leisurely to downright scary. This company has become an extremely popular choice, so try to book as early as possible.

The **Mushi Mushi** (☎ 599/790–5399) is a catamaran offering a variety of two- and three-hour cruises starting at $45 per person. It departs from the Bonaire Nautico Marina in downtown Kralendijk (opposite the restaurant It Rains Fishes).

BEACHES

Don't expect long stretches of glorious powdery sand. Bonaire's beaches are small, and though the water is blue (several shades of it, in fact), the sand isn't always white. Bonaire's National Parks Foundation requires all nondivers to pay a $10 annual Nature Fee in order to enter the water anywhere around the island (divers pay $25). The fee can be paid at most dive shops.

Klein Bonaire. Just a water-taxi hop across from Kralendijk, this little island offers picture-perfect white-sand beaches. The area is protected, so absolutely no development has been allowed. Make sure to pack everything before heading to the island, including water and an umbrella to hide under, because there are no refreshment stands, no changing facilities, and almost no shade to be found. Boats leave from the Town Pier, across from the City Café, and the round-trip water-taxi ride costs roughly $18 per person.

Lac Bay Beach. It's a bumpy drive (10 to 15 minutes on a dirt road) to get here, but you'll be glad when you arrive. It's a good spot for diving, snorkeling, and kayaking (as long as you bring your own), and there are public restrooms and a restaurant for your convenience. ⊹ *Off Kaminda Sorobon, Lac Cai.*

Windsock Beach. Near the airport (just off E.E.G. Boulevard), this pretty little spot, also known as Mangrove Beach, looks out toward the north side of the island and has about 200 yards of white sand along a rocky shoreline. It's a popular dive site, and swimming conditions are also good. ⊹ *Off E.E.G. Blvd., near Flamingo Airport.*

WHERE TO EAT

$$–$$$ ⤫ **City Café/City Restaurant.** This busy waterfront eatery is also one of
ECLECTIC the most reliable nightspots on the island, so it's always hopping day or
Fodor's Choice night. Breakfast, lunch, and dinner are served daily at reasonable prices.
★ Seafood is always featured, as are a variety of sandwiches and salads. The pita sandwich platters are a good lunchtime choice for the budget challenged. Weekends, there's always live entertainment and dancing. This is the place to people-watch on Bonaire, as it seems everyone ends up at City Café eventually. ⊠ *Hotel Rochaline, Kaya Grandi 7, Kralendijk* ☎ *599/717–8286* ⊕ *www.citybonaire.com* ⊟ *AE, MC, V.*

$$–$$$ ⤫ **Le Flamboyant.** This intimate restaurant offers good food at afford-
CONTINENTAL able prices. The cozy historic house—conveniently downtown—also
★ has a small gourmet food shop, espresso bar, and lovely cocktail bar. The main attraction is the tree-covered courtyard in the back. Lunch offers a selection of ample sandwiches and salads; dinner is mostly seafood and pastas. There's also a comprehensive vegetarian menu. The restaurant is just a few steps away from the Tourism Corporation

Bonaire office. ✉ *Kaya Grandi 12, Kralendijk* ☎ *599/717–3919* ▤ *AE, MC, V* ☉ *Closed Sun.*

CALICA (PLAYA DEL CARMEN), MEXICO

Marlise Kast

Just minutes away from Calica, Playa del Carmen has become one of Latin America's fastest-growing communities, with a pace almost as hectic as Cancún's. Hotels, restaurants, and shops multiply here faster than you can say "Kukulcán." Some are branches of Cancún establishments whose owners have taken up permanent residence in Playa, while others are owned by American and European expats (predominately Italians) who came here years ago. It makes for a varied, international community. Avenida 5, the first street in town parallel to the beach, is a long, colorfully tiled pedestrian walkway with shops, cafés, and street performers; small hotels and stores stretch north from this avenue. Avenida Juárez, running east–west from the highway to the beach, is the main commercial zone for the Riviera Maya corridor. Here locals visit the food shops, pharmacies, hardware stores, and banks that line the curbs. People traveling the coast by car usually stop here to stock up on supplies—its banks, grocery stores, and gas stations are the last ones until Tulum.

ESSENTIALS

CURRENCY   The Mexican peso (MX$12.49 to US$1). U.S. dollars and credit cards are widely accepted in the area, from the port to Playa del Carmen, but it's best to have pesos—and small bills—when you visit ruins, where cashiers often run out of change. There is no advantage to paying in dollars, but there may be an advantage to paying in cash.

INTERNET   There are several Internet cafés on Avenida 5 in Playa del Carmen. **Atomic Internet Cafe** (✉ *Av. 8, between Calles 5 and 10, Playa del Carmen,* ☎ *984/873–0996*).

TELEPHONE   Most pay phones accept prepaid Ladatel cards, sold in 30-, 50-, or 100-peso denominations. To use the card, insert it in the pay phone's slot, dial 001 (for calls to the U.S.) or 01 (for calls within Mexico), followed by the area code and number. Credit is deleted from the card as you use it, and the balance is displayed on the small screen on the phone.

COMING ASHORE

The port at Calica, about 3 mi south of the town of Playa del Carmen (between Playa del Carmen and Xcarat), is small. Sometimes ships actually dock, and other times passengers are tendered to shore. There is a makeshift market at the port, where locals sell crafts. Beyond that, there is not much to do, and you'll need to head into Playa del Carmen proper to find restaurants and even tour operators. If you really want to shop, skip the vendors at the port and head to Playa del Carmen's Avenida 5, where you can easily spend an afternoon browsing shops and enjoying restaurants.

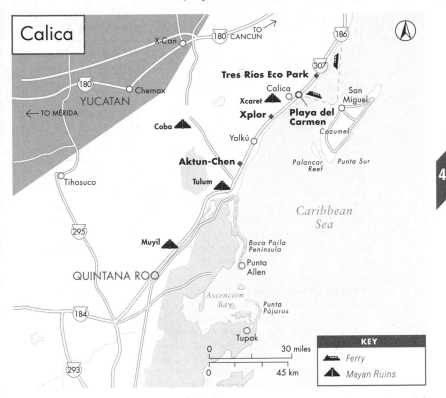

Calica

TO CANCUN

X-Can

Tres Ríos Eco Park

Calica
Xcaret
Xplor
Playa del
Carmen

San
Miguel

Chemax

YUCATAN

← TO MÉRIDA

Coba

Yalkú

Cozumel

Aktun-Chen

Palancar
Reef

Punta Sur

Tihosuco

Tulum

Caribbean
Sea

Muyil

Boca Paila
Peninsula

Punta
Allen

QUINTANA ROO

Ascencion
Bay

Punta
Pájaros

Tupak

| | 0 | 30 miles |
| | 0 | 45 km |

KEY

🚢 Ferry

▲ Mayan Ruins

4

Taxis and tour buses are available at the port to take you to Playa del
Carmen and other destinations, but lines often form as passengers wait
for taxis, so hurry to the front of the line if you really want to pack a
lot of activity into your day. Your taxi will have you in Playa del Carmen or in Xcaret in under 10 minutes, but you'll pay a whopping $10
for the short trip.

EXPLORING CALICA

Fodor's Choice **Aktun-Chen.** The name of these amazing underground caves is Mayan
★ for "the cave with cenote inside." Estimated to be about 5 million years
old, they are the area's largest. You walk through the underground pas-
sages, past stalactites and stalagmites, until you reach the cenote with
its various shades of deep green. There is also a canopy tour and one
cenote where you can swim. You don't want to miss this one. ⊠ *Carretera 307, Km 107* ☎ *984/109–2061* ⊕ *www.aktunchen.com* 🎫 *$25
cave tour, $36 canopy tour* ☉ *Daily 9–4.*

Muyil. This photogenic archaeological site at the northern end of the
Reserva de la Biosfera Sian Ka'an is underrated. Once known as Chu-
nyaxché, it's now called by its ancient name, Muyil (pronounced mool-
hill). It dates from the late preclassic era, when it was connected by
road to the sea and served as a port between Cobá and the Mayan

centers in Belize and Guatemala. The most notable site at Muyil today is the remains of the 56-foot Castillo—one of the tallest on the Quintana Roo coast—at the center of a large acropolis. During excavations of the Castillo, jade figurines representing the moon and fertility goddess Ixchel were found. Recent excavations at Muyil have uncovered some smaller structures. The ruins stand near the edge of a deep-blue lagoon and are surrounded by almost impenetrable jungle—so be sure to bring bug repellent. You can drive down a dirt road on the side of the ruins to swim or fish in the lagoon. The bird-watching is also exceptional here. ⊕ *muyil.smv.org* 🖾 *$3* ⊙ *Daily 8–5.*

> ### CALICA BEST BETS
>
> ■ **A Day at Xcaret.** Particularly for families, this ecological theme park is a great way to spend the day.
>
> ■ **Beaches.** The beaches in the Riviera Maya are stellar.
>
> ■ **Diving.** From Playa del Carmen it's only a short hop to some of the Yucatán's best dive sites.
>
> ■ **Shopping.** Playa del Carmen's Avenida 5 can easily keep you occupied for your day in port if you are a shopaholic.

Playa del Carmen. Once upon a time, Playa del Carmen was a fishing village with a ravishing deserted beach. The villagers fished and raised coconut palms to produce copra, and the only foreigners who ventured here were beach bums and travelers catching ferries to Cozumel. That was a long time ago, however. These days the beach is far from deserted, although it is still delightful, with its alabaster-white sand and turquoise-blue waters. In fact Playa has become one of Latin America's fastest-growing communities, with a population of more than 135,000 and a pace almost as hectic as Cancún's. The ferry pier, where the hourly boats arrive from and depart for Cozumel, is another busy part of town. The streets leading from the dock have shops, restaurants, cafés, a hotel, and food stands. If you take a stroll north from the pier along the beach, you'll find the serious sun worshippers. On the pier's south side is the sprawling Playacar complex. The development is a labyrinth of residences and all-inclusive resorts bordered by an 18-hole championship golf course. ✛ *3 mi (5 km) north of Calica.*

The excellent 32-acre **Xaman Ha Aviary** (⊠ *Paseo Xaman-Ha, Mza 13-A Lote 1, Playacar* 🖀 *984/873–0330* w*www.aviarioxamanha.com*), in the middle of the Playacar development, is home to more than 30 species of native birds. It's open daily 9 to 5, and admission is $20.

Tulum. Tulum (pronounced tool-*lum*) is a quickly growing town built near the spectacular ruins that draw most visitors here. But its charm extends past the famous ruins: pristine beaches, $10 cabanas, and open-air markets explain the town's increasing popularity with travelers.

The archaeological site itself is the Yucatán Peninsula's most-visited Mayan ruin, attracting more than 2 million people annually. Though most of the architecture is of unremarkable postclassic (1000–1521) style, the amount of attention that Tulum receives is not entirely undeserved. Its location—on a beach known for its sugar-white sand, by the blue-green Caribbean—is breathtaking. ✉ *Carretera 307, Km 133, Tulum* ☎ *983/837–2411* 🌐 *$5 entrance, $3 parking, $3 video fee, $1 shuttle from parking to ruins* ⊗ *Daily 8–5.*

↻ **Xcaret.** This popular outdoor theme park is packed with activities and

Fodor'sChoice shows. There are water sports and other water-based activities, a butter-

★ fly farm, a bird-feeding area, a replica Mayan village, a dolphinarium, a bee farm, a manatee lagoon, bat cave, orchid and bromeliad greenhouse, a 240-foot tower with a spectacular view, and even a small zoo. And this isn't even a complete list of attractions. The park also has almost a dozen restaurants as well as picnic areas. The entrance fee covers only access to the grounds and the exhibits; all other activities and equipment—from sea treks and dolphin tours to lockers and swim gear—are extra. The $99 Plus Pass includes park entrance, lockers, snorkel equipment, food, and drinks. You can buy tickets from any travel agency or major hotel along the coast. ☎ *984/871–5200; 998/883–0470 in Cancún* 🌐 *www.xcaret.com* 🌐 *$69 Basic Pass; $99 Plus Pass* ⊗ *Daily 8:30 AM–10 PM.*

Xplor. Designed for thrill-seekers, this 125-acre park features underground rafting in water caves and the cenotes of Riviera Maya. You can also swim in a stalactite river, ride in an amphibian-vehicle, or soar across the park on the longest zip line in Mexico. ✉ *Carretera 307, Km 282, Xcaret* ☎ *998/849–5275* 🌐 *www.xplor.travel* 🌐 *$99* ⊗ *Mon.–Sat. 9–5.*

SHOPPING

Playa del Carmen's Avenida 5 between calles 4 and 10 is the best place to shop along the coast. Boutiques sell folk art and textiles from around Mexico, and clothing stores carry lots of sarongs and beachwear made from Indonesian batiks. A shopping area called Calle Corazon, between calles 12 and 14, has a pedestrian street, art galleries, restaurants, and boutiques.

★ **Hacienda Tequila** (✉ *Av. 5 and Calle 14, Playa del Carmen* ☎ *984/873–1202*) sells traditional Mexican crafts and clothing as well as 480 different types of tequila. Free tastings are available, and there is a small museum displaying the various stages of tequila production.

ACTIVITIES

DIVING

The PADI and SSI-affiliated **Abyss** (✉ *Av. 1 between Calles 10 and 12* ☎ *984/873–2164* 🌐 *www.abyssdiveshop.com*) offers introductory courses and dive trips ($50 for one tank, $70 for two tanks). The oldest shop in town, **Tank-Ha Dive Center** (✉ *Calle 10 between Avs. 5 and 10, Playa del Carmen* ☎ *984/873–0302* 🌐 *www.tankha.com*), has PADI-certified teachers and runs diving and snorkeling trips to the reefs and caverns. A one-tank dive costs $45; for a two-tank trip it's $75. Dive packages are also available, as well as trips to Cozumel.

GOLF

Playa del Carmen's golf course is an 18-hole, par-72 championship course designed by Robert von Hagge. The greens fee is $180; there's also a special twilight fee of $120. Information is available from the **Casa Club de Golf** (☎ *984/873–0624 or 998/881–6088*).

WHERE TO EAT

$$ ✗**Babe's Noodles & Bar.** Photos and paintings of old Hollywood pinup
THAI   models decorate the walls and are even laminated onto the bar of this
★   Swedish-owned Thai restaurant known for its fresh and interesting fare. Everything is cooked to order—no prefab dishes here. Try the spring rolls with peanut sauce, or the sesame noodles, made with chicken or pork, veggies, lime, green curry, and ginger. In the Buddha Garden you can sip a mojito or sit at the bar and watch the crowds on nearby 5th Avenue. The lemonade, blended with ice and mint, is incredibly refreshing. If the place is crowded, head to their second location on Avenida 5 between calles 28 and 30. ⊠ *Calle 10 between Avs. 5 and 10* ☎ *984/120–2592* ⊕ *www.babesnoodlesandbar.com* ⊠ *Av. 5 between Calles 28 and 30* ☎ *984/803–0056* ▭ *No credit cards.*

¢–$ ✗**Hot.** This café is a great place to get an early start before a full day of
CAFÉ   sightseeing, shopping, or even sunbathing. It opens at 7 AM and whips up great egg dishes (the chili-and-cheese omelet is particularly good), baked goods, and hot coffee. Everything, including delicious bagels and bread, is made on the premises. Salads and sandwiches are available at lunch. ⊠ *Calle 14 Norte, between Avs. 5 and 10* ☎ *984/879–4520* ▭ *No credit cards.*

CARTAGENA, COLOMBIA

Jeffrey Van
Fleet

Ever wondered what the "Spanish Main" refers to? This is it. Colombia's Caribbean coast invokes ghosts of conquistadors, pirates, and missionaries journeying to the New World in search of wealth, whether material or spiritual. Anchoring this shore is Cartagena—poetically, officially *Cartagena de Indias* (Cartagena of the Indies)—founded in 1533 and one of Latin America's magnificent colonial cities. Gold and silver passed through here en route to Spain, making the city an obvious target for pirates, hence the construction of Cartagena's trademark walls and fortresses. Outside the *Ciudad Amurallada* (walled city) lie less historic (but no less interesting) beaches and water excursions. If Colombia conjures up images of drug lords and paramilitary guerillas, think again; security is quite visible (without being oppressive) here in the country's top tourist destination. Take the same precautions you'd follow visiting any city of one million people, and you should have a grand time.

ESSENTIALS

CURRENCY   The Colombian peso (COP 1,920 to US$1). In Colombia, peso prices are denoted with the "$" sign, too. If they carry a lot of zeros, they likely are not dollar prices, but always ask. ATMs are ubiquitous around town.

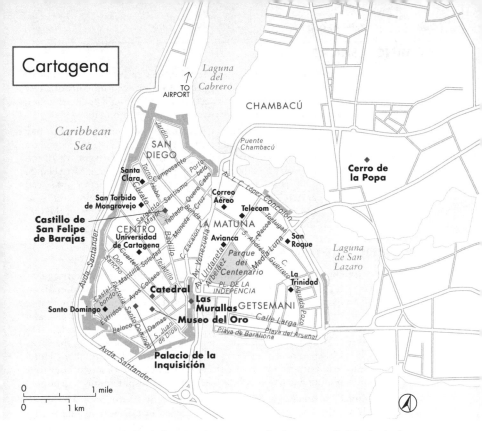

Cartagena

TO
AIRPORT

Laguna del Cabrero

CHAMBACÚ

Caribbean Sea

Puente Chambacú

SAN DIEGO

Cerro de la Popa

Santa Clara

San Torbido de Mongrovejo

Correo Aéreo

Telecom

Castillo de San Felipe de Barajas

CENTRO

LA MATUNA

Universidad de Cartagena

Avianca

San Roque

Laguna de San Lazaro

Avda. Santander

Parque del Centenario

La Trinidad

PL. DE LA INDEPENCIA

Catedral

Santo Domingo

Las Murallas

GETSEMANI

Museo del Oro

Calle Larga

Playa de Barañona

Playa del Arsenal

Avda. Santander

Palacio de la Inquisición

0   1 mile

0   1 km

INTERNET Upon arrival or before departure, you can check your e-mail at the bank of computers in the Terminal de Cruceros. In town, you can check your e-mail at **CaribeNet** (✉ *Calle Santo Domingo 3–19* ☎ *575/664–2326*).

SAFETY Security is tighter in Cartagena than elsewhere in Colombia, so you certainly can navigate the city on your own. (Knowing some Spanish helps.) However, the scarcity of English speakers or English signage at the city's tourist attractions and the persistence of vendors, street touts, and the periodic con artist—they *do* speak English—mean that many cruise passengers opt for the reassurance of an organized shore excursion. If you set out on your own, under no circumstances should you deal with anyone who approaches you on the street offering to change money; rip-offs are guaranteed.

TELEPHONE The Terminal de Cruceros has ample phones for your use. Local numbers in Cartagena have seven digits. For international calls, dial 009 followed by country and area codes and local number. The U.S. mobile carrier AT&T offers roaming options in this region of Colombia for calls back to the United States; if you have a tri-band GSM phone it should work.

COMING ASHORE

Cruise ships dock at the modern Terminal de Cruceros (cruise terminal) on Isla de Manga, an island connected by a bridge to the historic city center, about 2 mi (3 km) northwest of the docks. You'll find telephones, Internet computers, and a duty-free shop in the terminal.

A small army of taxis waits in front of the terminal. Expect to pay 14,000 pesos for the 10-minute drive to the walled city; the same fare will get you to the nearby beaches at Bocagrande. Drivers are all too happy to take you on your own do-it-yourself guided tour. Most charge around 18,000 pesos for an hour of waiting time. There's little need to rent a car here. Cartagena, at least the area of tourist interest, is so compact, and walking the labyrinth of cobblestone streets in the Old City is far more enjoyable than driving them.

EXPLORING CARTAGENA

Nothing says Cartagena quite like a ride in a horse-drawn carriage, or *coche,* as it known locally. Drivers are a wealth of information about Cartagena, and many do speak English. The downside for you is that the rides begin near dusk—it's a far cooler time of the day, after all—and your need to be back on ship may not coincide with that schedule. Do check. You can pick up carriages at many places, including the Plaza de los Coches, near the Puerta del Reloj in the walled city, or the Hotel Caribe in Bocagrande. Expect to pay around $200 for a two-hour tour (this kind of excursion is best when the cost is split among a group).

Castillo de San Felipe de Barajas. Designed by Antonio de Arévalo in 1639, the Fort of St. Philip's steep-angled brick and concrete battlements were arranged so that if part of the castle were conquered the rest could still be defended. A maze of tunnels, minimally lit today to allow for spooky exploration, still connects vital points of the fort. Acoustics were perfect in the tunnels, allowing occupants of the fort to hear the footsteps of the approaching enemy. You can walk here from the walled city in about 30 minutes; a 10,000-peso taxi ride is an easier option. ⊠ *Av. Pedro de Heredia at Carrera 17* ☎ *575/666–4790* ☎ *15,000 pesos* ☉ *Daily 8–6.*

Catedral. Any Latin American city centers on its cathedral and main square. Cartagena's Plaza de Bolívar is a shady place from which to admire the 16th-century cathedral, with its colorful bell tower and 20th-century dome. Inside is a massive gilded altar. A statue of South American liberator Simón Bolívar stands watch over his namesake plaza. ⊠ *Plaza de Bolívar.*

Fodor's Choice **Cerro de la Popa.** For spectacular views of Cartagena, ascend this hill,
★ the highest ground around. Because of its strategic location, the 17th-century hilltop convent did double duty as a fortress during the colonial era. It now houses a museum and a chapel dedicated to the Virgin de la Candelaria, Cartagena's patron saint. There is no public transport to get you here; taxis charge about 8,000 pesos. ⊠ *2 mi (3 km) southeast of Ciudad Amurallada* ☎ *575/666–2331* ☎ *7,000 pesos* ☉ *Daily 8:30–5:30.*

Las Murallas. Cartagena survived only because of its walls, and its *murallas* remain today the city's most distinctive feature. Repeated sacking by pirates and foreign invaders convinced the Spaniards of the need to enclose the region's most important port. Construction began about 1600 and was completed in 1796. Walking along the thick walls remains one of Cartagena's time-honored tourist pastimes. The Puerta del Reloj is the principal gate to the innermost sector of the Ciudad Amurallada. Its four-sided clock tower was a relatively late addition (1888), and has become the best-known symbol of the city. ⌧ *Area bounded by Bahía de las Ánimas, Caribbean Sea, and Laguna de San Lázaro* ☉ *24 hrs.*

Museo del Oro y Arqueología. The Gold and Archaeological Museum, a project of Colombia's Central Bank, displays an assortment of artifacts culled from the Sinús, an indigenous group that lived in the region 2,000 years ago. ⌧ *Carrera 4 No. 33–26* ☏ *575/660–0778* ⌧ *Free* ☉ *Tues.–Fri. 10–1 and 3–7, Sat. 10–1 and 2–5.*

Fodor's Choice **Palacio de la Inquisición.** Arguably Cartagena's most-visited tourist attrac-
★ tion documents the darkest period in the city's history. The 1770 Palace of the Inquisition served as the second headquarters of the repressive arbiters of political and spiritual orthodoxy who once exercised jurisdiction over northern South America. Although the museum also displays benign colonial and pre-Columbian artifacts, everyone heads to the ground floor to "Eeeewww" over the implements of torture—racks and thumbscrews, to name but two. ⌧ *Carrera 4 No. 33–26* ☏ *575/664–7381* ⌧ *4,000 pesos* ☉ *Daily 9–5.*

> ## CARTAGENA BEST BETS
>
> ■ **Cruise the Harbor.** A boat trip around the city's inner bay allows to you appreciate the city's formidable walls and fortresses.
>
> ■ **Islas del Rosario.** The beaches of nearby Islas del Rosario are an hour away by boat.
>
> ■ **Ride a Coche.** Take the quintessential horse-and-buggy ride through the streets.
>
> ■ **Walk Las Murallas.** Walking the city's massive stone walls is a favorite tourist pastime.
>
> ■ **Visit Palacio de la Inquisición.** Cartagena's most-visited sight is this historic—and creepy—center for the Spanish Inquisition.

SHOPPING

Think "Juan Valdez" if you're looking for something to take the folks back home. Small bags of fine Colombian coffee, the country's signature souvenir, are available in most tourist-oriented shops. Colombia also means emeralds, and you'll find plenty in the jewelry shops on or near Calle Pantaleón, beside the cathedral. Don't forget the duty-free shop in the Terminal de Cruceros for those last-minute purchases. The name of **Las Bóvedas** (⌧ *North of Plaza Fernández de Madrid*) translates as "the vaults," and the city's best crafts shops occupy this row of storerooms built in the 18th century to hold gunpowder and other military essentials. Your stockpile here will consist of hats, hammocks, and leather goods.

ACTIVITIES

DIVING

Coral reefs line the coast south of Cartagena, although warm-water currents have begun to erode them in recent years. There is still good diving to be had in the Islas del Rosario, an archipelago of 27 coral islands about 21 mi (35 km) southwest of the city. **Buzos de Barú** (✉ *Laguito Edificio Belmar L-103* ☎ *575/665–7675* ⊕ *www.buzosdebaru.com*) organizes snorkeling trips to the Islas del Rosario and scuba diving at underwater wrecks, as well as dive instruction.

BEACHES

For white sand and palm trees, your best bet is **Playa Blanca,** about 15 minutes away by boat. Many people opt for a visit to the **Islas del Rosario,** a verdant archipelago surrounded by aquamarine waters and coral reefs. Tour boats leave from the Muelle de los Pegasos, the pier flanked by statues of two flying horses that is just outside the city walls. Plenty of men with boats will also offer to take you on the one-hour journey. A final option is **Bocagrande,** the resort area on a 3-mi-long (5-km-long) peninsula south of the walled city. High-rise hotels and condos front the gray-sand beach. It gets quite crowded and is very lively, but Bocagrande is probably not the Caribbean beach of which you've always dreamed.

WHERE TO EAT

$–$$
CAFÉ

✕ **Café San Pedro.** Although it serves Colombian fare, this restaurant's eclectic menu includes dishes from Thailand, Italy, and Japan. You can also drop by to have a drink and to watch the activity on the plaza from one of the outdoor tables. ✉ *Plaza San Pedro* ☎ *575/664–5121* ▤ *MC, V* ☾ *Closed Sun.*

$–$$
LATIN AMERICAN

✕ **Paco's.** Heavy beams, rough terra-cotta walls, wooden benches, and tunes from an aging Cuban band are the hallmarks of this downtown eatery. Drop by for a drink and some tapas, or try the more substantial *langostinos a la sifú* (lobsters fried in batter). You can sit in the dining room or outside on the Plaza Santo Domingo. ✉ *Plaza Santo Domingo* ☎ *575/664–5057* ▤ *V.*

COLÓN, PANAMA

Jeffrey Van Fleet

When you consider the decades it took to build the canal, not to mention the lives lost and government failures and triumphs involved during its construction, it comes as no surprise that the Panama Canal is often called the Eighth Wonder of the Modern World. Best described as an aquatic bridge, the Panama Canal connects the Caribbean Sea with the Pacific Ocean by raising ships up and over Central America, through artificially created Gatún Lake, the highest point at 85 feet above sea level, and then lowering them back to sea level by using a series of locks, or water steps. A masterful engineering feat, three pairs of locks—Gatún, Pedro Miguel, and Miraflores—utilize gravity to fill

Panama Canal Zone

Caribbean Sea

○Portobelo

Colón

Futerte
San Lorenzo

Gatún Locks

Lago Gatún

◆Parque Nacional Chagres

◆Parque Nacional Soberanía

Panamá Railroad

Isla Barro Colorado

Gamboa

Pedro Miguel Locks

Miraflores Locks

Balboa

PANAMA CITY

Pacific Ocean

KEY

– – – Canal Transit Route

0   8 miles

0   10 km

and drain as ships pass through chambers 1,000 feet long by 110 feet wide that are "locked" by doors weighing 80 tons apiece, yet actually float into position. Most cruise ships pass through the canal seasonally, when repositioning from one coast to the other; however, partial transits have become an increasingly popular "destination" on regularly scheduled 10- and 11-night Caribbean itineraries. These loop cruises enter the canal from the Caribbean Sea and sail into Gatún Lake, where they remain for a few hours as passengers are tendered ashore for excursions. Ships then pass back through the locks, returning to the Caribbean and stopping at either Cristobal Pier or Colón 2000 Pier to retrieve passengers at the conclusion of their tours.

A day transiting the canal's Gatún Locks begins before dawn as your passenger ship passes through *Bahia Limon* and lines up with dozens of other vessels to await its turn to enter. Before your ship can proceed, two pilots and a narrator will board. The sight of a massive cruise ship being raised dozens of feet into the air by water is so mesmerizing that passengers eagerly crowd all forward decks at the first lock. If you don't find a good viewing spot, head for the rear decks, where there is usually more room and the view is just as intriguing. If you remain aboard, as many passengers do, you'll find plenty of room up front later in the day as your ship retraces its path down to the sea. Due to the tight scheduling of the day's activities—it takes at least 90 minutes for a ship to pass through Gatún Locks—passengers who wish to go ashore early in the day are advised to sign up for one of the many available shore excursions.

ESSENTIALS

CURRENCY   The U.S. dollar, called the balboa, is the currency in Panama; the country does mint its own coins.

INTERNET   There's an Internet café at the Colón 2000 Pier.

TELEPHONE   You'll find telephones inside Colón's cruise terminal, where you can purchase phone cards, which are a handy and inexpensive way to make calls.

COMING ASHORE

Colón, Panama's second-largest city, has little to offer of historic interest, and is simply a jumping-off point to the rain forest and a wide variety of organized tours. Infrequent cruise itineraries may include a day docked in Colón, rather than a partial canal transit. However, no matter how much time your ship spends in Colón, it is usually easier to take an organized shore excursion, and that's what we recommend. If you don't want to go on a ship-sponsored shore excursion, taxi drivers also await ship arrivals, and some can be acceptable private guides for $70 to $100 per day if you just want to explore Portabelo or San Lorenzo; however, as in any foreign port, before setting out with any unofficial car and driver, you should set a firm price and agree upon an itinerary as well as look over the vehicle carefully. It's also possible to rent a car from either Budget or Hertz, both of which have desks at the Colón 2000 terminal.

Although entry time into the canal is always approximate, passenger ships have priority, and most pass through Gatún Locks early in the morning. Passengers booked on shore excursions begin the tendering process soon after the ship sets anchor, which can be as early as 8:30 AM. Alternatives to excursions offered by your cruise ship are available from independent tour operators that can be arranged in advance through Web sites or, possibly, travel agents. You will likely be informed that Panamanian regulations restrict passengers going ashore in Gatún Lake to only those who have booked the cruise line's excursions; however, anyone who has a shore-excursion reservation with a local company should be able to leave the vessel. Before making independent tour arrangements, confirm with your cruise line that you will be allowed to go ashore after presenting your private tour confirmation to the shore-excursion staff on board the ship.

Upon completion of either full or partial canal transits, cruise ships generally dock at either Cristobal Pier or Colón 2000 Pier late in the afternoon, where they may remain for several hours. Passengers who remained on board throughout the canal passage have the opportunity to go ashore, and land tours end at the terminals, where passengers rejoin the ship. A second terminal opened in 2008 and became the home port for Royal Caribbean's *Enchantment of the Seas*, with the Panamanian government aggressively courting other cruise companies to set up shop here too. All of Colón is considered a high-crime area, and pickpockets have been known to strike even in the seemingly secure areas of the cruise-ship terminals. If you go ashore, you are well advised to leave jewelry and other valuables aboard your ship and carry only the cash you need.

EXPLORING THE PANAMA CANAL ZONE

Colón. The provincial capital of Colón, beside the canal's Atlantic entrance, has clearly seen better days, as the architecture of its older buildings attests. Its predominantly Afro-Caribbean population has long had a vibrant musical scene, and in the late 19th and early 20th centuries Colón was a relatively prosperous town. But it spent the second half of the 20th century in steady decay, and things have only gotten worse in the 21st century. For the most part, the city is a giant slum, with unemployment at 15% to 20% and crime on the rise.

⚠ Travelers who explore Colón on foot are simply asking to be mugged, and the route between the train station and the bus terminal is especially notorious; do all your traveling in a taxi or rental car. If you do the Panama Railway trip on your own without a tour company, take one of the shuttle vans or hire a taxi to the train station.

Twelve kilometers (7 mi) south of Colón are the **Esclusas de Gatún** *(Gatún Locks),* a triple-lock complex that is nearly a mile long and raises and lowers ships the 85 feet between sea level and Gatún Lake.

COLÓN BEST BETS

■ **Explore an Embera Village.** You'll travel through Chagres National Park by dugout canoe.

■ **Kayak on Gatún Lake.** You can paddle among the many islands and mangrove forests.

■ **Panama Railway.** Take a train trip to Panama City for a quick sightseeing tour (you can come back by taxi to save some time).

■ **Portobelo.** Visit historic Panamanian forts.

■ **Rain Forest Aerial Tram.** Travel to Gamboa Rainforest Resort and see the rain forest canopy from above.

There's a small viewing platform at the locks and a simple visitor center that's nothing compared to the center at Miraflores Locks. However, the sheer magnitude of the Gatún Locks—they are the canal's largest—is impressive, especially when packed with ships. You have to cross the locks on a swinging bridge to get to San Lorenzo and the **Represa Gatún** (Gatún Dam), which holds the water in Gatún Lake. At 1½ mi long, it was the largest dam in the world when it was built, a title it held for several decades. Get there by taking the first left after crossing the locks. ⊹ *12 km (7 mi) south of Colón* ⌘ *Free* ☉ *Daily 8–4.*

Fuerte San Lorenzo. Perched on a cliff overlooking the mouth of the Chagres River are the ruins of the ancient Spanish *fort* destroyed by pirate Henry Morgan in 1671. The Spaniards built Fort San Lorenzo in 1595, in an effort to protect the South American gold they were shipping down the Chagres River, which was first carried along the Camino de Cruces from Panamá Viejo. The fortress's commanding position and abundant cannons weren't enough of a deterrent for Morgan, whose men managed to shoot flaming arrows into the fort, causing a fire that set off stored gunpowder and forced the Spanish troops to surrender. In the 1980s UNESCO restored the fort to its current condition, which is pretty sparse—it hardly compares to the extensive colonial ruins of Portobelo. Nevertheless, the setting is gorgeous, and the view from that promontory of the blue-green Caribbean, the coast, and the vast jungle behind it is breathtaking. ⊠ *23 km (14 mi) northwest of Gatún Locks* ☎ *No phone* ⌘ *Free* ☉ *Daily 8–4.*

Lago Gatún (Gatún Lake). Covering about 163 square mi, an area about the size of the island nation Barbados, Gatún Lake extends northwest from Parque Nacional Soberanía to the locks of Gatún, just south of

Colón. The lake was created when the U.S. government dammed the Chagres River, between 1907 and 1910, so that boats could cross the isthmus at 85 feet above sea level. By creating the lake, the United States saved decades of digging that a sea-level canal would have required. It took several years for the rain to fill the convoluted valleys, turning hilltops into islands and killing much forest (some trunks still tower over the water nearly a century later). When it was completed, Gatún Lake was the largest man-made lake in the world. The canal route winds through its northern half, past several forest-covered islands (the largest is Barro Colorado, one of the world's first biological reserves). The lake itself is home to crocodiles, manatees, and peacock bass, a species introduced from South America and popular with fishermen. Fishing charters for bass, snook, and tarpon are out of Gamboa.

★ **Portobelo.** Portobelo is an odd mix of colonial fortresses, clear waters, lushly forested hills, and an ugly little town of cement-block houses crowded higgledy-piggledy amid the ancient walls. It holds some of Panama's most interesting colonial ruins, with rusty cannons still lying in wait for an enemy assault, and is a UNESCO World Heritage Site, together with San Lorenzo.

The forested hills that rise up behind the bay are part of **Parque Nacional Portobelo** *(Portobelo National Park)*, a vast marine and rain-forest reserve contiguous with Chagres National Park. Though several towns lie within the park, and much of its lowlands were deforested years ago, its inaccessible mountains are covered with dense forest that holds plenty of flora and fauna. Extending from offshore coral reefs up to the cloud forest atop 3,212-foot Cerro Brujo, the park comprises an array of ecosystems and is rich in biodiversity. While the coastal area is home to everything from ospreys to sea turtles, the mountains house spider monkeys, brocket deer, harpy eagles, and an array of other endangered wildlife. There is no proper park entrance, but you can explore patches of its forested coast and mangrove estuaries on boat trips from Portobelo, when you might see birds such as the ringed kingfisher and fasciated tiger heron.

Portobelo's largest and most impressive fort is **Fuerte San Jerónimo**, at the end of the bay, which is surrounded by the "modern" town. It was built in the 1600s but was destroyed by the pirate Edward Vernon and rebuilt to its current state in 1758. Its large interior courtyard was once a parade ground, but it is now the venue for all annual celebrations involving congo dancers, including New Year's, Carnival, the Festival de Diablos y Congos (shortly after Carnaval), and the town's patron saint's day (March 20).

Fuerte San Fernando, one of three Spanish forts you can visit at Portobelo, is surrounded by forest and is a good place to see birds. It lies directly across the bay from Batería Santiago, on the left as you drive toward town, a large structure with cannons pointed at the entrance to the bay. The youngest of Portobelo's forts, Batería Santiago was built in the 1860s, after Vernon's fateful attack. The thick walls are coral, which was cut from the platform reefs that line the coast. Coral was more abundant and easier to cut than the igneous rock found inland, so the Spanish used it for most construction in Portobelo. ■ **TIP**➔ **Local boatmen who are usually sitting near the dock next to Batería Santiago can take you across the bay to explore Fuerte San Fernando for $3.** They also offer transportation to several local beaches, as well as a trip into the estuary at the end of the bay. ✉ *Surrounding Portobelo* ☎ *448–2165 or 442–8348* 💲 *Free* ⊙ *24 hrs.*

One block east of the Real Aduana is the **Iglesia de San Felipe**, a large white church dating from 1814 that's home to the country's most venerated religious figure: the **Cristo Negro** (Black Christ). According to legend, the statue of a dark-skinned Jesus carrying a cross arrived in Portobelo in the 17th century on a Spanish ship bound for Cartagena, Colombia. Each time the ship tried to leave, it encountered storms and had to return to port, convincing the captain to leave the statue in Portobelo. Another legend has it that in the midst of a cholera epidemic in 1821 parishioners prayed to the Cristo Negro, and the community was spared. The statue spends most of the year to the left of the church's altar, but once a year it's paraded through town in the Festival del Cristo Negro. Each year the Cristo Negro is clothed in a new purple robe, donated by somebody who's earned the honor. Many of the robes that have been created for the statue over the past century are on display in the Museo del Cristo Negro (Black Christ Museum) in the Iglesia de San Juan, a smaller 17th-century church next to the Iglesia de San Felipe. ✉ *Calle Principal* ☎ *No phone* 💲 *$1* ⊙ *Weekdays 8–4, weekends 8:30–3.*

Near the entrance to Fuerte San Jerónimo is the **Real Aduana** *(Royal Customs House),* where servants of the Spanish crown made sure that the king and queen got their cut from every ingot that rolled through town. Built in 1630, the Real Aduana was damaged during pirate attacks and then destroyed by an earthquake in 1882, only to be rebuilt in 1998. It is an interesting example of colonial architecture—note the carved coral columns on the ground floor—and it houses a simple museum with some old coins, cannonballs, and displays on Panamanian folklore. ✉ *Calle de la Aduana* ☎ *No phone* 💲 *$1* ⊙ *Tues.–Sat. 9–4, weekends 8:30–3.*

SHOPPING

Both Cristobal Pier and Colón 2000 Pier have large shopping malls, where you will find Internet access, telephones, refreshments, and duty-free souvenir shopping in relatively secure environments. Stores in both locations feature local crafts such as baskets, wood carvings, and toys, as well as liquor, jewelry, and the ubiquitous souvenir T-shirts. In addition to shops and cafés, Cristobal Pier features an open-air arts and crafts market; Colón 2000 Pier has a well-stocked supermarket. Portobelo has a wide-ranging artisan market next to Iglesia de San Felipe.

The most unique locally made souvenirs are colorful appliquéd *molas,* the whimsical textile artwork created by native Kuna women, who come from the San Blas Islands; they are likely to be at hand stitching new designs while they sell the ones they just completed. The Kuna ladies drive a hard bargain, and considering the intricate nature of their handiwork, prices are quite fair. If you take an excursion to Portobelo, the prices may be better there; several Kuna women are usually there selling their molas in the artisan market next to the church.

COSTA MAYA, MEXICO

Marlise Kast

Puerto Costa Maya is an anomaly. Unlike other tourist attractions in the area (the island of Cozumel being the primary Yucatán cruise port), this port of call near Majahual has been created exclusively for cruise-ship passengers. The shops, restaurants, activities, and entertainment you'll find here aren't open to the general public. After major damage from Hurricane Dean in 2007, the port reopened ahead of schedule (and with an additional berth) in July 2008.

At first glance, the port complex itself may seem to be little more than an outdoor mall. The docking pier (which can accommodate three ships at once) leads to a 70,000-square-foot bazaar-type compound where shops selling local crafts—jewelry, pottery, woven straw hats and bags, and embroidered dresses—are interspersed with duty-free stores and souvenir shops. There are two alfresco restaurants, which serve seafood, American-friendly Mexican dishes like tacos and quesadillas, and cocktails at shaded tables. An outdoor amphitheater stages eight daily performances of traditional music and dance.

The strip of beach edging the complex has been outfitted with colorful lounge chairs and *hamacas* (hammocks), and may tempt you to linger and sunbathe. If you want to have a truly authentic Mexican experience, though, you'll take advantage of the day tours offered to outlying areas. These give you a chance to see some of the really spectacular sights in this part of Mexico, many of which are rarely visited. This is one port where the shore excursion is the point, and there are no options except to purchase what your ship offers. You can preview what excursions may be offered on the Puerto Costa Maya's own Web site.

Among the best tours are those that let you explore the gorgeous (and usually deserted) Mayan ruin sites of Kohunlich, Dzibanché, and Chacchoben. The ancient pyramids and temples at these sites, surrounded by jungle that's protected them for centuries, are still dazzling to behold. Since the sites are some distance from the port complex—and require some road travel in one of the port's air-conditioned vans—these tours are all-day affairs.

COSTA MAYA BEST BETS

■ **Chacchoben.** One of the major archaeological sites to undergo more recent excavation is near the Belize border. The ancient city was a contemporary of Kohunlich.

■ **Kohunlich.** This ruined city is best known for its great temples with sculpted masks.

■ **Majahual.** You might want to go into this small fishing village near the cruise pier; though heavily damaged by Hurricane Dean, it's being spruced up.

■ **Snorkeling at Banco Chinchorro.** Excellent catamaran snorkeling trips go to this nearby reef.

Prior to a devastating 2007 hurricane, there was no real reason to go into the small, nearby fishing village of Mahahual (pronounced ma-ha-*wal*). Though there are still about 200 residents, post-hurricane renovations have put the village on the map; it now has its own pier as well as a smattering of hotels, restaurants, and shops. The new cement boardwalk along the beach has made Mahahual an ideal spot for a sunset stroll. The crystal-clear waters and unspoiled beaches are delightful for snorkeling, diving, and fishing.

ESSENTIALS

CURRENCY The Mexican peso (MX$12.49 to US$1). U.S. dollars and credit cards are accepted by everyone at the port. There is no advantage to paying in dollars, but there may be an advantage to paying in cash.

INFORMATION **Puerto Costa Maya** (⊕ *www.puertocostamaya.com*).

TELEPHONE Most pay phones accept prepaid Ladatel cards, sold in 30-, 50-, or 100-peso denominations. To use the card, insert it in the pay phone's slot, dial 001 (for calls to the U.S.) or 01 (for calls within Mexico), followed by the area code and number. Credit is deleted from the card as you use it, and the balance is displayed on a small screen on the phone.

4

COZUMEL, MEXICO

Maribeth
Mellin

Cozumel, with its sun-drenched ivory beaches fringed with coral reefs, fulfills the tourist's vision of a tropical Caribbean island. It's a heady mix of the natural and the commercial. Despite a mini-construction boom in the island's sole city, San Miguel, there are still wild pockets scattered throughout the island where flora and fauna flourish. Smaller than Cancún, Cozumel surpasses its fancier neighbor in many ways. It has more history and ruins, superior diving and snorkeling, more authentic cuisine, and a greater diversity of handicrafts at better prices. The numerous coral reefs, particularly the world-renowned Palancar Reef, attract divers from around the world. On a busy cruise-ship day the island can seem completely overrun, but it's still possible to get away, and some good Mayan sights are within reach on long (and expensive) shore excursions.

ESSENTIALS

CURRENCY The Mexican peso (MX$12.49 to US$1). U.S. dollars and credit cards are widely accepted in the area, from the port to Playa del Carmen, but it's best to have pesos—and small bills—when you visit ruins, where cashiers often run out of change. There is no advantage to paying in dollars, but there may be an advantage to paying in cash.

INTERNET **CreWorld Internet** (✉ *Av. Rafael E. Melgar and Calle 11 Sur* ☎ *987/872–6509*). **Coffeenet** (✉ *Av. Rafael E. Melgar at Calle 11* ☎ *987/872–6394*).

TELEPHONE You may be able to find pay phones that accept prepaid Ladatel cards, sold in 30-, 50-, or 100-peso denominations at the cruise pier and at the plaza. To use the card, insert it in the pay phone's slot, dial 001 (for calls to the U.S.) or 01 (for calls within Mexico), followed by the area code and number. Credit is deleted

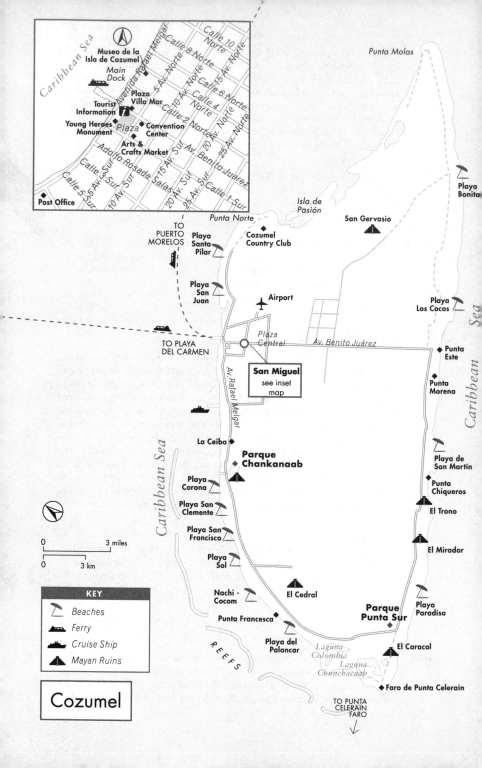

Cozumel

Inset map — San Miguel

Caribbean Sea

Museo de la Isla de Cozumel

Main Dock

Plaza Villa Mar

Tourist Information

Young Heroes Monument

Plaza

Convention Center

Arts & Crafts Market

Post Office

Calle 10 Norte
Calle 8 Norte
Calle 6 Norte
Calle 4 Norte
Calle 2 Norte
Avenida Rafael Melgar
5 Av. Norte
10 Av. Norte
15 Av. Norte
20 Av. Norte
25 Av. Norte
Av. Benito Juárez
Adolfo Rosada Salas
5 Av. Sur
10 Av. Sur
15 Av. Sur
20 Av. Sur
25 Av. Sur
Calle 1 Sur
Calle 3 Sur
Calle 5 Sur

Main map

Caribbean Sea

Punta Molas

Playa Bonita

Punta Norte

TO PUERTO MORELOS

Playa Santa Pilar

Playa San Juan

Airport

Isla de Pasión

San Gervasio

Cozumel Country Club

Playa Los Cocos

TO PLAYA DEL CARMEN

Plaza Central

Av. Benito Juárez

San Miguel see inset map

Punta Este

Punta Morena

Av. Rafael Melgar

La Ceiba

Parque Chankanaab

Playa Corona

Playa San Clemente

Playa San Francisco

Playa Sol

Nachi-Cocom

Punta Francesca

Playa del Palancar

Playa de San Martín

Punta Chiqueros

El Trono

El Mirador

El Cedral

Parque Punta Sur

Playa Paradíso

El Caracol

Laguna Colombia

Laguna Chunchacaab

Faro de Punta Celerain

Caribbean Sea

REEFS

TO PUNTA CELERAIN FARO

0   3 miles
0   3 km

KEY

- Beaches
- Ferry
- Cruise Ship
- Mayan Ruins

from the card as you use it, and the balance is displayed on a small screen on the phone. Most people use their own cell phones these days.

COMING ASHORE

As many as six ships call at Cozumel on a busy day, tendering passengers to the downtown pier in the center of San Miguel or docking at the two international piers 4 mi (6 km) away. From the downtown pier you can walk into town or catch the ferry to Playa del Carmen. Taxi tours are also available. An island tour, including the ruins and other sights, costs about $50 to $70, but negotiate the price before you get in the cab. The international pier is close to many beaches, but you'll need a taxi to get into town. There's rarely a wait for a taxi, but prices are high, and drivers are often aggressive, asking double or triple the reasonable fare. Expect to pay $10 for the ride into San Miguel from the pier. Tipping is not necessary.

Passenger ferries to Playa del Carmen leave Cozumel's main pier approximately every other hour from 5 AM to 10 PM. They also leave Playa del Carmen's dock about every other hour on the hour, from 6 AM to 11 PM (but note that service sometimes varies according to demand). The trip takes 45 minutes. Verify the times: bad weather and changing schedules can prompt cancellations.

EXPLORING COZUMEL

San Miguel is not tiny, but you can easily explore the waterfront and plaza area on foot. The main attractions are the small eateries and shops that line the streets and the main square, where the locals congregate in the evening.

El Cedral. Spanish explorers discovered this site, once the hub of Mayan life on Cozumel, in 1518. Later it became the island's first official city, founded in 1847. Today it's a farming community with small well-tended houses and gardens. Conquistadors tore down much of the Mayan temple, and during World War II the U.S. Army Corps of Engineers destroyed the rest to make way for the island's first airport. All that remains of the Mayan ruins is one small structure with an arch. Nearby is a green-and-white cinder-block church, decorated inside with crosses shrouded in embroidered lace; legend has it that Mexico's first Mass was held here. Vendors display embroidered blouses, hammocks, and other souvenirs at stands around the main plaza. ⊠ *Turn at Km 17.5 off Carretera Sur or Av. Rafael E. Melgar, then drive 3 km (2 mi) inland to site* ☎ *No phone* ☎ *Free* ☉ *Daily dawn–dusk.*

♻ **Faro Celarain Eco Park.** This 247-acre national preserve at Cozumel's southernmost tip is a protected habitat for numerous birds and animals, including crocodiles, flamingos, egrets, and herons. Cars aren't allowed, so you'll need to use park transportation (rented bicycles or park shuttles) to get around here. From observation towers you can spot crocodiles and birds in **Laguna Colombia** or **Laguna Chunchacaab.** Or visit the ancient Mayan lighthouse, **El Caracol,** designed to whistle when the wind blows in a certain direction. At the park's (and the island's) southernmost point is the Faro de Celarain, a lighthouse that is now a museum of navigation. Climb the 134 steps to the top; it's a steamy effort, but the views are incredible. Beaches here are wide and deserted, and there's great snorkeling offshore. Snorkeling equipment is available for rent, as are kayaks, and there are restrooms at the museum and by the beach. Without a rental car, expect to pay about $40 for a round-trip taxi ride from San Miguel. ⊠ *Southernmost point of Carretera Sur and coastal road* ☎ *987/872–2940 or 987/872–8462* 🖃 *$10* ☉ *Daily 9–4.*

⟳ ★ **Parque Chankanaab.** Chankanaab (which means "small sea") is a national park with a saltwater lagoon, an archaeological park, and a botanical garden. Scattered throughout are reproductions of a Mayan village, and of Olmec, Toltec, Aztec, and Mayan stone carvings. You can enjoy a cool walk along pathways leading to the sea, where parrotfish and sergeant majors swarm around snorkelers.

You can swim, scuba dive, or snorkel at the beach. There's plenty to see: underwater caverns, a sunken ship, crusty old cannons and anchors, and a sculpture of la Virgen del Mar (Virgin of the Sea). To preserve the ecosystem, park rules forbid touching the reef or feeding the fish.

Dive shops, restaurants, gift shops, a snack stand, and dressing rooms with lockers and showers are right on the sand. A small museum has exhibits on coral, shells, and the park's history, as well as some sculptures. ⊠ *Carretera Sur, Km 9* ☎ *987/872–2940* 🖃 *$16* ☉ *Daily 8–5.*

San Gervasio. Surrounded by a forest, these temples make up Cozumel's largest remaining Mayan and Toltec site. San Gervasio was the island's capital and ceremonial center, dedicated to the fertility goddess Ixchel. Its classic- and postclassic-style buildings and temples were continuously occupied from AD 300 to 1500. Typical architectural features include limestone plazas and arches atop stepped platforms, as well as stelae and bas-reliefs. Be sure to see the temple "Las Manitas," with red handprints all over its altar. Plaques clearly describe each structure in Mayan, Spanish, and English. ⊠ *From San Miguel, take cross-island road (follow signs to airport) east to San Gervasio access road; turn left and follow road 7 km (4½ mi)* 🖃 *$7* ☉ *Daily 8–4.*

San Miguel. Be sure to stroll along the *malecón* (boardwalk) and take in the ocean breeze. Cozumel's only town feels more traditional the farther you walk away from the water; the waterfront has been taken over by large shops selling jewelry, imported rugs, leather boots, and souvenirs to cruise-ship passengers. Head inland to the pedestrian streets around the plaza, where family-owned restaurants and shops cater to locals and savvy travelers.

☾ Cozumel's **Museo de la Isla de Cozu-**
★ **mel** is housed on two floors of a former hotel. It has displays on natural history—with exhibits on the island's origins, endangered species, topography, and coral-reef ecology—as well as the pre-Columbian and colonial periods. The photos of the island's transformation over the 20th and 21st centuries are especially fascinating, as is the exhibit of a typical Mayan home. Guided tours are available. ⌂ *Av. Rafael E. Melgar, between Calles 4 and 6 Norte* ☏ *987/872–1475* ⊠ *$3* ⊙ *Daily 9–5.*

SHOPPING

Cozumel's main souvenir-shopping area is downtown along Avenida Rafael E. Melgar and on some side streets around the plaza. There are also clusters of shops at **Plaza del Sol** (east side of the main plaza) and **Vista del Mar** (⌂ *Av. Rafael E. Melgar 45*). As a general rule, the newer, trendier shops line the waterfront, and the better crafts shops can be found around Avenida 5a. Malls at the cruise-ship piers aim to please passengers seeking jewelry, perfume, sportswear, and low-end souvenirs at high-end prices.

Most downtown shops accept U.S. dollars; many goods are priced in dollars. To get better prices, pay with cash or traveler's checks—some shops tack a hefty surcharge on credit-card purchases. Shops, restaurants, and streets are always crowded between 10 AM and 2 PM, but get calmer in the evening. Traditionally, stores are open from 9 to 1 (except Sunday) and 5 to 9, but those nearest the pier tend to stay open all day, particularly during high season. Most shops are closed Sunday morning.

ACTIVITIES

DIVING AND SNORKELING

Cozumel is famous for its reefs. In addition to Chankanaab Nature Park, a great dive site is La Ceiba Reef, in the waters off La Ceiba and Sol Caribe hotels. Here lies the wreckage of a sunken airplane blown up for a Mexican disaster movie. Cozumel has plenty of dive shops to choose from. **Aqua Safari** (⌂ *Av. Rafael E. Melgar 429, between Calles 5 and 7 Sur* ☏ *987/872–0101*) is among the island's oldest and most professional shops. Owner Bill Horn has long been involved in efforts to protect the reefs and stays on top of local environmental issues. The shop provides PADI certification, classes on night diving, deep diving and other interests, and individualized dives. **Blue Angel** (⌂ *Carretera Sur Km. 2.3* ☏ *987/872–1631 or 866/779–9986*) offers combo dive and snorkel trips so families who don't all scuba can still stick together. Along with dive trips to local reefs, they offer PADI courses. **Eagle Ray**

Divers (✉ *La Caleta Marina, near the Presidente InterContinental hotel* ☎ *987/872–5735 or 866/465–1616*) offers snorkeling trips (the three-reef trip lets nondivers explore beyond the shore) and dive instruction. As befits their name, the company keeps track of the eagle rays that appear off Cozumel from December to February and runs trips for advanced divers to walls where the rays congregate. Beginners can also see rays around some of the reefs.

FISHING

You can charter high-speed fishing boats for about $420 per half-day or $600 per day (with a maximum of six people). Your hotel can help arrange daily charters—some offer special deals, with boats leaving from their own docks.

Albatros Deep Sea Fishing (☎ *987/872–7904 or 888/333–4643* ⊕ *www.albatroscharters.com*) offers full-day trips that include boat and crew, tackle and bait, and lunch with beer and soda starting at $575 for up to six people.

3 Hermanos (☎ *987/872–6417; 651/755–4897 in the U.S.* ⊕ *www.cozumelfishing.com*) specializes in deep-sea and fly-fishing trips. Their rates for a half-day deep-sea fishing trip start at $350; a full day is $450. They also offer scuba-diving trips, and their boats are available for group charters (a great way to snorkel and cruise around at your own pace) for $400 for up to six passengers.

BEACHES

Cozumel's beaches vary from sandy treeless stretches to isolated coves to rocky shores. Most of the development is on the leeward (western) side. Beach clubs have sprung up on the southwest coast; admission, however, is usually free, as long as you buy food and drinks. Clubs offer typical tourist fare: souvenir shops, *palapa* (thatch-roofed) restaurants, kayaks, and cold beer. A cab ride from San Miguel to most clubs costs about $15 each way. Reaching beaches on the windward (eastern) side is more difficult, but the solitude is worth it.

★ South of the resorts lies the mostly ignored (and therefore serene) **Playa Palancar**. Offshore is the famous Palancar Reef, easily accessed by the on-site dive shop. There's also a water-sports center, a bar-café, and a long beach with hammocks hanging under coconut palms. The aroma of grilled fish with garlic butter is tantalizing. Playa del Palancar keeps prices low and rarely feels crowded. **Playa San Francisco** is an inviting 3-mi (5-km) stretch of sandy beach, which extends along Carretera Sur, south of Parque Chankanaab at about Km 10. Amenities include two outdoor restaurants, a bar, dressing rooms, gift shops, volleyball nets, beach chairs, and water-sports equipment rentals. Divers use this beach as a jumping-off point for the San Francisco reef and Santa Rosa wall. The abundance of turtle grass in the water, however, makes this a less-than-ideal spot for swimming. **Punta Chiqueros,** a half-moon-shaped cove sheltered by an offshore reef, is the first popular swimming area as you drive north on the coastal road (it's about 8 mi [12 km] north of Parque Faro Celarain Eco Park). Part of a longer beach that some locals call Playa Bonita, it has fine sand, clear water, and moderate waves. This is a great place to swim, watch the sunset, and eat fresh fish at the restaurant, also called Playa Bonita.

WHERE TO EAT

$$-$$$ ✗ **Guido's.** Chef Yvonne Villiger works wonders with fresh fish—if the
ITALIAN   wahoo with capers and black olives is on the menu, don't miss it.
★   But Guido's is best known for its pizzas baked in a wood-burning oven, which makes sections of the indoor dining room rather warm. Sit in the pleasant, recently expanded courtyard instead, and order a pitcher of sangria to go with the puffy garlic bread. ✉ *Av. Rafael E. Melgar 23, between Calles 6 and 8 Norte* ☎ *987/872–0946* 🖃 *MC, V* ☾ *Closed Sun.*

$$-$$$ ✗ **Pancho's Backyard.** Marimbas play beside the bubbling fountain in
MEXICAN   this gorgeous courtyard behind one of Cozumel's best folk-art shops.
★   Though Pancho's is always busy, the waitstaff is amazingly patient and helpful. Cruise-ship passengers seeking a taste of Mexico pack the place at lunch; dinner is a bit more serene. The menu is definitely geared toward tourists (written in English with detailed descriptions and prices in dollars), but regional ingredients make even the standard steak stand out when it's flavored with smoky chipotle chiles. Other stellar dishes include the cilantro cream soup and shrimp flambéed with tequila. ✉ *Av. Rafael Melgar between Calles 8 and 10 Norte* ☎ *987/872–2141* ⊕ *www. panchosbackyard.com* 🖃 *AE, MC, V* ☾ *Dinner only on Sun.*

CURAÇAO (WILLEMSTAD)

Vernon
O'Reilly-
Ramesar

Try to be on deck as your ship sails into Curaçao. The tiny Queen Emma floating bridge swings aside to allow ships to pass through the narrow channel. Pastel gingerbread buildings on shore look like dollhouses, especially from a large cruise ship. Although the gabled roofs and red tiles show a Dutch influence, the gleeful colors of the facades are peculiar to Curaçao. It's said that an early governor of the island suffered from migraines that were aggravated by the color white, so all the houses were painted in hues from magenta to mauve. Thirty-five mi (56 km) north of Venezuela and 42 mi (68 km) east of Aruba, Curaçao is, at 38 mi (61 km) long and 3 to 7.5 mi (5 to 12 km) wide, the largest of the Netherlands Antilles. Although always sunny, it's never stiflingly hot here because of the constant trade winds. Water sports attract enthusiasts from all over the world, and the reef diving is excellent.

ESSENTIALS

CURRENCY   The NAf guilder (NAf 1.79 to US$1); U.S. currency is accepted almost everywhere on the island, and ATMs are plentiful. At the time of this printing Curaçao is still considering making the U.S. dollar its official currency.

INTERNET   **Café Internet** (✉ *Handelskade 3B, Punda, Willemstad* ☎ *5999/465– 5088*). **Wireless Internet Café** (✉ *Hanchi Snoa 4, Punda, Willemstad* ☎ *5999/461–0590*).

4

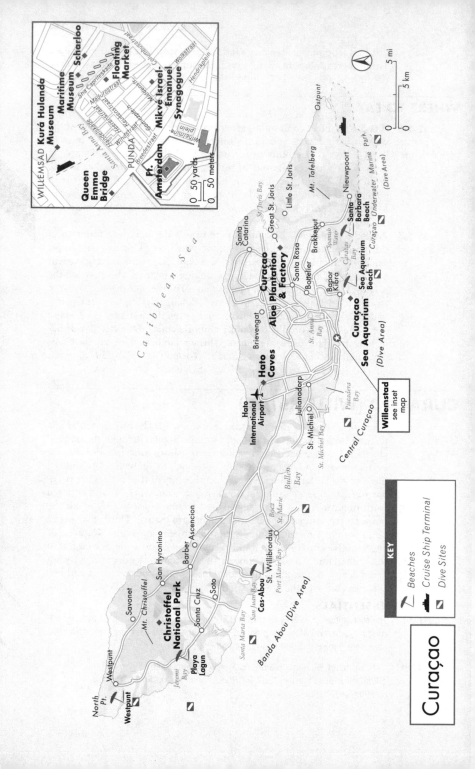

Curaçao

KEY

Beaches
Cruise Ship Terminal
Dive Sites

Inset map — WILLEMSTAD

Kurá Hulanda Museum
Maritime Museum
Scharloo
Floating Market
Mikvé Israel-Emanuel Synagogue
PUNDA
Queen Emma Bridge
Ft. Amsterdam

Columbusstraat
Pietermaaiweg
Workstraat
Hendrikplein
Breedestraat
Wilhelmina-plein
Windstraat
Gomezplein
Madurostraat
Hoogstraat
Heerenstraat
Keukenstraat
Sha Caprileskade
Santa Anna Bay

0   50 yards
0   50 meters

Main map labels

Caribbean Sea

North Pt.
Westpunt
Savonet
Mt. Christoffel
Christoffel National Park
Playa Lagun
Santa Cruz
San Hyronimo
Ascencion
Barber
Soto
St. Willibrordus
Cas-Abou (Dive Area)
San Juan Bay
Santa Marta Bay
Jeremi Bay
Port Marie Bay
Boca St. Marie
Bullen Bay
St. Michiel
St. Michiel Bay
Piscadera Bay
Central Curaçao
Willemstad
see inset map
Hato International Airport
Hato Caves
Brievengat
Julianadorp
St. Anna Bay
Santa Catarina
Curaçao Aloe Plantation & Factory
Santa Rosa
Bottelier
Bapor Kibra
Curaçao Sea Aquarium (Dive Area)
Sea Aquarium Beach
Spanish Water
Caracas Bay
Santa Barbara Beach
Curaçao Underwater Marine park (Dive Area)
Nieuwpoort
Mt. Tafelberg
Ostpunt
Brakkeput
Little St. Joris
Great St. Joris
St. Joris Bay
Banda Abou (Dive Area)

5 mi
5 km
0
0

TELEPHONE The telephone system is reliable. To place a local call, dial the seven-digit number. A local call costs NAf 0.50 from a pay phone. Direct-dial access is also available at the AT&T calling center at the cruise-ship terminal and at the mega-pier in Otrobanda. From other public phones, use phones marked LENSO; many more of these have been added around the island in recent years. You can also call direct from the air-conditioned Digicel center using a prepaid phone card (open 8 AM to 5:30 PM, Monday through Saturday; the center also offers Internet access).

COMING ASHORE

Ships dock at the terminal just beyond the Queen Emma Bridge, which leads to the floating market and the shopping district. The walk to downtown takes less than 10 minutes. Easy-to-read maps are posted dockside and in the shopping area. The terminal has a duty-free shop, telephones, and a taxi stand.

Taxis, which meet every ship, now have meters, although rates are still fixed from point to point of your journey. The government-approved rates, which do not include waiting time, can be found in a brochure called "Taxi Tariff Guide," available at the cruise-ship terminal and at the tourist board. Rates are for up to four passengers. There's a 25% surcharge after 11 PM. It's easy to see the sights on Curaçao without going on an organized shore excursion. Downtown can be done on foot, and a taxi for up to four people will cost about $35 an hour. Taxi fares to places in and around the city range from $8 to $20. Car rentals are available but are not cheap (about $40 per day, plus $10 compulsory insurance).

EXPLORING CURAÇAO

Willemstad. Willemstad is small and navigable on foot. You needn't spend more than two or three hours wandering around here, although the narrow alleys and various architectural styles are enchanting. English, Spanish, and Dutch are widely spoken. Narrow Santa Anna Bay divides the city into two sides: Punda, where you'll find the main shopping district, and Otrabanda (literally, the "other side"), where the cruise ships dock. Punda is crammed with shops, restaurants, monuments, and markets. Otrabanda has narrow, winding streets full of colonial homes notable for their gables and Dutch-influenced designs.

You can cross from Otrabanda to Punda in one of three ways: walk over the Queen Emma Bridge; ride the free ferry, which runs when the bridge swings open to let seagoing vessels pass; or take a cab across the Juliana Bridge (about $8). On the Punda side of the city, Handelskade is where you'll find Willemstad's most famous sights—the colorful colonial buildings that line the waterfront. The original red roof tiles came from Europe on trade ships as ballast.

★ Each morning dozens of Venezuelan schooners laden with tropical fruits and vegetables arrive at the bustling **Floating Market** on the Punda side of the city. Mangoes, papayas, and exotic vegetables vie for space with freshly caught fish and herbs and spices. The buying is best at

6:30 AM—too early for many people on vacation—but there's plenty of action through the afternoon. Any produce bought here should be thoroughly washed or peeled before being eaten. ⊠ *Sha Caprileskade, Punda, Willemstad.*

Step through the archway of **Ft. Amsterdam** and enter another century. The entire structure dates from the 1700s, when it was the center of the city and the island's most important fortification. Now it houses the governor's residence, a church (which has a small museum), and government offices. Outside the entrance, a series of majestic gnarled *wayaka* trees are fancifully carved with human forms—the work of local artist Mac Alberto. ⊠ *Foot of Queen Emma Bridge, Punda, Willemstad* ☎ *5999/461–1139* ⊡ *Fort free, church museum $2* ☉ *Weekdays 9:30–1, Sun. service at 10.*

Fodor's Choice   The fascinating **Kura Hulanda Museum** reveals the island's diverse roots.
★   Housed in a restored 18th-century village, the museum is built around a former mercantile square (Kura Hulanda means "Holland courtyard"), where the Dutch once sold slaves. An exhibit on the transatlantic slave trade includes a gut-wrenching replica of a slave-ship hold. Other sections feature relics from West African empires, examples of pre-Columbian gold, and Antillean art. The complex is the brainchild of Dutch philanthropist Jacob Gelt Dekker, and the museum grew from his personal collection of artifacts. ⊠ *Klipstraat 9, Otrobanda, Willemstad* ☎ *5999/462–1400* ⊕ *www.kurahulanda.com/museum* ⊡ *$9* ☉ *Thurs.–Sat. 10–5.*

The **Maritime Museum**—designed to resemble the interior of a ship—gives you a sense of Curaçao's maritime history, using model ships, historic maps, nautical charts, navigational equipment, and audiovisual displays. Topics explored in the exhibits include the development of Willemstad as a trading city, Curaçao's role as a contraband hub, the remains of *De Alphen* (a Dutch marine freighter that exploded and sank in St. Anna Bay in 1778 and was excavated in 1984), the slave trade, the development of steam navigation, and the role of the Dutch navy on the island. The museum also offers a two-hour guided tour (Wednesday and Saturday, 2 PM) on its "water bus" through Curaçao's harbor—a route familiar to traders, smugglers, and pirates. The museum is wheelchair accessible. ⊠ *Van der Brandhofstraat 7, Scharloo, Willemstad* ☎ *5999/465–2327* ⊕ *www.curacaomaritime.com* ⊡ *Museum $10, museum and harbor tour $15* ☉ *Tues.–Sat. 9–4.*

★   **Mikvé Israel-Emanuel Synagogue,** the oldest temple in continuous use in the Western Hemisphere, is one of Curaçao's most important sights, and draws thousands of visitors a year. The synagogue was dedicated in 1732 by the Jewish community, which had already grown from the original 12 families who came from Amsterdam in 1651. They were later joined by Jews from Portugal and Spain fleeing persecution from the Inquisition. White sand covers the synagogue floor for two symbolic reasons: a remembrance of the 40 years Jews spent wandering the desert, and a re-creation of the sand used by secret Jews, or *conversos,* to muffle sounds from their houses of worship during the Inquisition. The **Jewish Cultural Museum** in back of the synagogue displays antiques—including a set of circumcision instruments—and artifacts from around the world. Yarmulkes are provided to men for services and tours. ⊠ *Hanchi Snoa 29, Punda, Willemstad* ☎ *5999/461–1067* ⊕ *www.snoa. com* ✉ *$6; donations also accepted* ⊙ *Weekdays 9–4:30.*

Affectionately called the Swinging Old Lady by the locals, the **Queen Emma Bridge** connects the two sides of Willemstad—Punda and Otrobanda—across the Santa Anna Bay. The bridge swings open at least 30 times a day to allow passage of ships to and from the sea. The original bridge, built in 1888, was the brainchild of the American consul Leonard Burlington Smith, who made a mint off the tolls he charged for using it: 2¢ per person for those wearing shoes, free to those crossing barefoot. Today it's free to everyone. The bridge was dismantled and completely repaired and restored in 2005. ⊠ *Willemstad.*

The Wilhelmina Drawbridge connects Punda with the once-flourishing district of **Scharloo**, where the early Jewish merchants built stately homes. The architecture along Scharlooweg (much of it from the 17th century) is magnificent, and, happily, many of the colonial mansions that had become dilapidated have been meticulously renovated. The area closest to Kleine Werf is a red-light district and fairly run-down, but the rest is well worth a visit. ⊠ *Willemstad.*

★ **Christoffel National Park.** This 4,450-acre garden and wildlife preserve with Mt. Christoffel at its center consists of three former plantations. As you drive through the park, watch for deer, goats, and smaller wildlife that might suddenly dart in front of your car. If you skip everything else on the island, it's possible to drive to the park and climb 1,239-foot Mt. Christoffel, which takes two to three strenuous hours. On a clear day you can then see the mountain ranges of Venezuela, Bonaire, and Aruba. The park is an hour from Willemstad but worth a visit. ⊠ *Savonet* ☎ *5999/864–0363 for information and tour reservations, 5999/462–6262 for jeep tours, 5999/864–0535 for horseback tours* ✉ *$10* ⊙ *Mon.–Sat. 8–4, Sun. 6–3; last admission 90 min. before closing.*

Curaçao Aloe Plantation & Factory. Drop in for a fascinating tour that takes you through the various stages of production of aloe vera, renowned for its healing powers. You'll get a look at everything from the fields to the final products. At the gift shop you can buy CurAloe products, including homemade goodies like soap, pure aloe gel, and pure aloe

---

CURAÇAO BEST BETS

■ **Diving.** After Bonaire, Curaçao has probably the best diving in the region.

■ **Punda.** Willemstad's chic and beautiful shopping area is a joy to explore on foot.

■ **Curaçao Sea Aquarium.** Explore the wonders of the ocean without getting wet.

■ **Floating Market.** This unique market is a fun destination, even though it's mostly fruits and vegetables.

■ **Kurá Hulanda Museum.** This is the island's best historical museum.

4

juice, as well as sunscreen and other skin-care products. The plantation is on the way to the Ostrich Farm and run by the same owner. Tours begin throughout the day. ✉ *Weg Naar Groot St. Joris z/n, Groot St. Joris* ☎ *5999/767–5577* ⊕ *www. aloecuracao.com* ✉ *$6* ⊙ *Mon.– Sat. 9–4; last tour at 3.*

☕ ★ **Curaçao Sea Aquarium.** You don't have to get your feet wet to see the island's underwater treasures. The aquarium has about 40 saltwater tanks filled with more than 400

SUNGLASSES

When selecting sunglasses, the most important considerations are the amount of UV light that is blocked by the lenses and a proper fit. The lenses should shield your eyes from most angles. Darker lenses do not necessarily offer better UV protection. Look for sunglasses that block 99% of harmful UV rays.

---

varieties of marine life. For more up-close interaction, there are several mesmerizing options. You can hand-feed the sharks, stingrays, or sea turtles (or watch a diver do it) at the **Animal Encounters** section, which consists of a 12-foot-deep open-water enclosure. Snorkelers and divers of all skill levels swim freely with tarpon, stingrays, and such. If you prefer to stay dry, there's an underwater observatory in a stationary semi-submarine. It's also possible to swim with the aquarium's six lovable sea lions from Uruguay. Kids as young as 3 can have their photo taken kissing a sea lion. Reservations for Animal Encounters, including sea-lion programs, must be made 24 hours in advance. A restaurant, a snack bar, two photo centers, and souvenir shops are on-site. ✉ *Seaquarium Beach, Bapor Kibra z/n* ☎ *5999/461–6666* ⊕ *www. curacao-sea-aquarium.com* ✉ *Aquarium $19; animal encounters $54 for divers, $34 for snorkelers; sea lion programs $49–$169; Dolphin Academy $79–$169* ⊙ *Aquarium daily 8:30–5:30, Dolphin Academy daily 8:30–4:30.*

★ **Hato Caves.** Stalactites and stalagmites form striking shapes in these 200,000-year-old caves. Hidden lighting adds to the dramatic effect. Indians who used the caves for shelter left petroglyphs about 1,500 years ago. More recently, slaves who escaped from nearby plantations used the caves as a hideaway. Hour-long guided tours wind down to the pools in various chambers. Keep in mind that there are 49 steps to climb up to the entrance. To reach the caves, head northwest toward the airport, take a right onto Gosieweg, follow the loop right onto Schottegatweg, take another right onto Jan Norduynweg and a final right onto Rooseveltweg, and follow signs. ✉ *Rooseveltweg z/n, Hato* ☎ *5999/868–0379* ✉ *$7* ⊙ *Daily 10–4.*

SHOPPING

From Dutch classics like embroidered linens, delft earthenware, cheeses, and clogs to local artwork and handicrafts, shopping in Curaçao can turn up some fun finds. But don't expect major bargains on watches, jewelry, or electronics; Willemstad is not a duty-free port (the few establishments that claim to be "duty-free" are simply absorbing the cost of some or all of the tax rather than passing it on to consumers); however, if you come prepared with some comparison prices, you might still dig up some good deals. Hours are usually Monday through Saturday, from 8 to noon and 2 to 6. Most shops are within the six-block area of Willemstad described above. The main shopping streets are Heerenstraat, Breedestraat, and Madurostraat.

ACTIVITIES

BIKING

So you wanna bike Curaçao? **Wanna Bike Curaçao** (☎ *5999/527–3720* ⊕ *www.wannabike.com*) has the fix: kick into gear and head out for a guided mountain-bike tour through the Caracas Bay peninsula and the salt ponds at the Jan Thiel Lagoon. Although you should be fit to take on the challenge, mountain-bike experience is not required. Tour prices vary, depending on skill level and duration, and cover the bike, helmet, water, refreshments, park entrance fee, and guide—but don't forget to bring a camera.

DIVING AND SNORKELING

☾ **Ocean Encounters** (⊠ *Lions Dive & Beach Resort, Seaquarium Beach,*
★ *Bapor Kibra z/n* ☎ *5999/461–8131* ⊕ *www.oceanencounters.com*) is the largest dive operator on the island. Its operations cover the popular east-coast dive sites, including the *Superior Producer* wreck, where barracudas hang out,'and a tugboat wreck. West-end hot spots—including the renowned Mushroom Forest and Watamula dive sites—are accessible from the company's outlet at Westpunt. Ocean Encounters offers a vast menu of scheduled shore and boat dives and packages, as well as certified PADI instruction. In July, the dive center sponsors a kids' sea camp in conjunction with the Sea Aquarium.

BEACHES

Cas Abou has the brightest blue water in Curaçao, a treat for swimmers, snorkelers, and sunbathers alike. You can take respite beneath the hut-shaded snack bar. The restrooms and showers are immaculate. The entry fee is $3. Turn off Westpunt Highway at the junction onto Weg Naar Santa Cruz; follow until the turnoff for Cas Abou, and then drive along the winding country road for about 10 minutes to the beach. **Playa Knip** offers crystal clear turquoise waters. Big (Groot) Knip is an expanse of alluring white sand, perfect for swimming and snorkeling. You can rent beach chairs and hang out under the palapas or cool off with ice cream at the snack bar. There are restrooms here but no showers. Just up the road, also in a protected cove, Little (Kleine) Knip is a charmer, too, with picnic tables and palapas. There's no fee for these beaches. **Seaquarium Beach** is divided into separate sections, each uniquely defined by a seaside resort or restaurant as its central draw. By day, no matter where you choose to enter the palm-shaded beach, you can find lounge chairs in the sand, thatched shelters, and restrooms. The island's largest water-sports center (Ocean Encounters at Lion's Dive) caters to nearby hotel guests and walk-ins. Unless you're a guest of a resort on the beach, the entrance fee to any section is $3 until 5 PM, then free.

WHERE TO EAT

$-$$ ✕ **Mambo Beach.** Spread over the sand, this open-air bar and grill serves
CONTINENTAL hearty sandwiches and burgers for lunch; steaks, fresh seafood, and
☺ pasta fill the dinner menu. There's an excellent fish buffet on Friday,
and dinner with a movie on the beach on Tuesday. ⊠ *Seaquarium
Beach, Bapor Kibra z/n* ☎ *5999/461–8999* ⊕ *www.mambocuracao.
com* ⊟ *MC, V.*

¢-$ ✕ **Time Out Café.** In the shopping heartland of Punda, this outdoor spot
CAFÉ serves up light bites like tuna sandwiches and grilled cheese, as well as
heartier fare like chicken *shawarma* (a shaved-meat sandwich). From
Breedestraat facing Little Switzerland, take the alley to the left of the
store (Kaya A.M. Prince) and walk about 20 yards, or look for the
sign in Gomezplein Square and follow the arrow. This is more of a
place for lunch, but they are open until 7 PM if you're looking for a
cheap and cheerful early dinner. ⊠ *Keukenplein 8, Punda, Willemstad*
☎ *5999/524–5071* ⊟ *No credit cards* ☾ *Closed Sun.*

DOMINICA (ROSEAU)

Roberta
Sotonoff

In the center of the Caribbean archipelago, wedged between the two
French islands of Guadeloupe, to the north, and Martinique, to the
south, Dominica is a wild place. So unyielding is the terrain that colonists surrendered efforts at colonization, and the last survivors of the
Caribbean's original people, the Carib Indians, have made her rugged northeast their home. Dominica—just 29 mi (47 km) long and 16
mi (26 km) wide—is an English-speaking island, though family and
place names are a mélange of French, English, and Carib. The capital is
Roseau (pronounced rose-*oh*). If you've had enough of casinos, crowds,
and swim-up bars and want to take leave of everyday life—to hike, bike,
trek, spot birds and butterflies in the rain forest; explore waterfalls;
discover a boiling lake; kayak, dive, snorkel, or sail in marine reserves;
or go out in search of the many resident whale and dolphin species—
this is the place to do it.

ESSENTIALS

CURRENCY The Eastern Caribbean dollar (EC$2.61 to US$1). U.S. currency is readily
accepted, but you will get change in EC dollars. Most major credit cards are
accepted, as are traveler's checks.

INTERNET **Cyber Land Internet Café** (⊠ *George St., Roseau* ⊠ *Woodstone Shopping Mall,
Roseau* ⊠ *Grandby St., Portsmouth* ☎ *767/440–2605*). **Rituals Coffee** (⊠ *Bay-
front, next door to Cocrico, Roseau* ☎ *767/440–2233* ⊕ *www.tropicports.com/
rituals*).

COMING ASHORE

In Roseau most ships dock along the bay front. Across the street from
the pier, in the old post office, is a visitor information center. Taxis,
minibuses, and tour operators are available at the berths. If you do
decide to tour with one of them, choose one who is certified, and be
explicit when discussing where you will go and how much you will

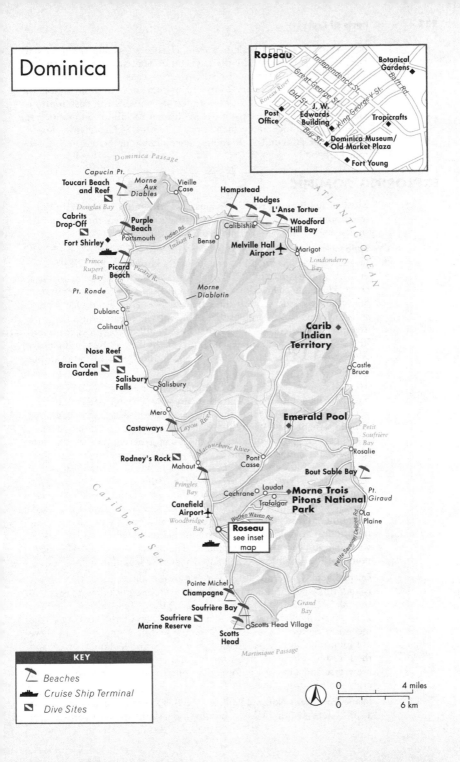

Dominica

Roseau

Independence St
Great George St
King George V St
Botanical Gardens
Bath Rd
Old St
Roseau River
Post Office
Bay St
J. W. Edwards Building
Tropicrafts
Dominica Museum/ Old Market Plaza
Fort Young

Dominica Passage

Capucin Pt.

Toucari Beach and Reef

Morne Aux Diables

Vieille Case

Hampstead

Hodges

L'Anse Tortue

Douglas Bay

Cabrits Drop-Off

Purple Beach

Portsmouth

Calibishie

Woodford Hill Bay

Fort Shirley

Prince Rupert Bay

Picard Beach

Bense

Melville Hall Airport

Marigot

Londonderry Bay

ATLANTIC OCEAN

Pt. Ronde

Dublanc

Colihaut

Morne Diablotin

Carib Indian Territory

Castle Bruce

Nose Reef

Brain Coral Garden

Salisbury Falls

Salisbury

Emerald Pool

Petit Soufrière Bay

Mero

Castaways

Layou River

Rosalie

Macoucherie River

Rodney's Rock

Mahaut

Pont Casse

Bout Sable Bay

Pringles Bay

Cochrane

Laudat

Morne Trois Pitons National Park

Pt. Giraud

Canefield Airport

Trafalgar

La Plaine

Caribbean Sea

Woodbridge Bay

Wotten Waven Rd.

Roseau see inset map

Pointe Michel

Champagne

Grand Bay

Soufrière Bay

Soufriere Marine Reserve

Scotts Head Village

Scotts Head

Martinique Passage

KEY

Beaches
Cruise Ship Terminal
Dive Sites

0 — 4 miles
0 — 6 km

pay—don't be afraid to ask questions. The drivers usually quote a fixed fare, which is regulated by the Division of Tourism and the National Taxi Association. Drivers also offer their services for tours anywhere on the island beginning at $25 to $30 an hour for up to four persons; a four- to five-hour island tour for up to four persons will cost approximately $150. You can rent a car in Roseau for about $45–$50, not including insurance and a mandatory EC$30 (US$12) driving permit, but it can be difficult to find things, so you might do better on a guided tour here.

EXPLORING DOMINICA

Most of Dominica's roads are narrow and winding, so you'll need a few hours to take in the sights. Be adventurous, whether you prefer sightseeing or hiking—you'll be amply rewarded.

Ⓒ **Carib Indian Territory.** In 1903, after centuries of conflict, the Caribbean's
★ first settlers, the Kalinago (more popularly known as the Caribs), were granted approximately 3,700 acres of land on the island's northeast coast. Here a hardened lava formation, L'Escalier Tête Chien (Snake's Staircase), runs down into the Atlantic. The name is derived from a snake whose head resembles that of a dog. The ocean alongside Carib Territory is particularly fierce. The shore is full of countless coves and inlets. According to Carib legend, every night the nearby Londonderry Islets transform into grand canoes to take the spirits of the dead out to sea.

The Kalinago resemble native South Americans and are mostly farmers and fishermen. Others are entrepreneurs who have opened restaurants, guesthouses, and little shops that offer exquisite baskets and handcrafted items. Craftspeople have retained their knowledge of basket weaving, wood carving, and canoe building through generations. They fashion long, elegant canoes from the trunk of a single *gommier* tree. You might catch canoe builders at work at **Kalinago Barana Autê** (✉ *Caryfish River, Carib Territory* ☎ *767/445–7979* ⊕ *www.kalinagobaranaaute. com* ✄ *Basic package is about $10* ☉ *Daily 9–5*), the Carib Territory's place to learn about Kalinago customs, history, and culture. A guided, 45-minute tour explores the village, stopping along the way to see some traditional dances and to learn about plants, dugout canoes, basket weaving, and cassava bread making. The path offers wonderful viewpoints of the Atlantic and a chance to glimpse Isukulati Falls.

Ⓒ **Emerald Pool.** Quite possibly the most-visited nature attraction on the island, this emerald-green pool fed by a 50-foot waterfall is an easy trip to make. To reach this spot in the vast Morne Trois Pitons National Park you follow a trail that starts at the side of the road near the reception center (it's an easy 20-minute walk). Along the way, there are lookout points with views of the windward (Atlantic) coast and the forested interior. If you don't want a crowd, check whether there are cruise ships in port before going out, as this spot is popular with cruise-ship tour groups.

Morne Trois Pitons National Park. A UNESCO World Heritage Site, this 17,000-acre swath of lush, mountainous land in the south-central interior (covering 9% of Dominica) is the island's crown jewel. Named after one of the highest (4,600 feet) mountains on the island, it contains the island's famous "boiling lake," majestic waterfalls, and cool mountain lakes. There are four types of vegetation zones here. Ferns grow 30 feet tall, wild orchids sprout from trees, sunlight leaks through green canopies, and a gentle mist rises over the jungle floor. A system of trails has been developed in the park, and the Division of Forestry and Wildlife works hard to maintain them—with no help from the excessive rainfall and the profusion of vegetation that seems to grow right before your eyes. Access to the park is possible from most points, though the easiest approaches are via the small mountaintop villages of Laudat (pronounced lau-*dah*) and Cochrane.

DOMINICA BEST BETS

■ **Kalinago Barana Autê.** This reserve is a great place to learn about the fierce Caribs.

■ **Rain-Forest Trips.** Hiking in Dominica's rain forest is the best way to experience its natural beauty.

■ **Snorkeling in Champagne.** A bubbling volcanic vent makes you feel as if you are snorkeling in champagne.

■ **Whale-Watching.** November through February offers the best whale-watching in the Caribbean.

■ **Indian River.** A rowboat ride on the river is relaxing and peaceful.

★ The undisputed highlight of the park is **Boiling Lake.** Reputedly the world's largest such lake, it's a cauldron of gurgling gray-blue water, 70 yards wide and of unknown depth, with water temperatures from 180°F to 197°F. Although generally believed to be a volcanic crater, the lake is actually a flooded fumarole—a crack through which gases escape from the molten lava below. As many visitors discovered in late 2004, the "lake" can sometimes dry up, though it fills again within a few months and, shortly after that, once more starts to boil. It has returned to its pre-2004 levels. The two- to four-hour (one way) hike up to the lake is challenging (on a very rainy day, be prepared to slip and slide the whole way up and back). You'll need attire appropriate for a strenuous hike, and a guide is a must. Most guided trips start early (no later than 8:30 AM) for this all-day, 7-mi (11-km) round-trip trek.

On your way to Boiling Lake you pass through the **Valley of Desolation,** a sight that definitely lives up to its name. Harsh sulfuric fumes have destroyed virtually all the vegetation in what must once have been a lush forested area. Small hot and cold streams with water of various colors—black, purple, red, orange—web the valley. Stay on the trail to avoid breaking through the crust that covers the hot lava. During this hike you'll pass rivers where you can refresh yourself with a dip (a particular treat is a soak in a hot-water stream on the way back). At the beginning of the Valley of Desolation trail is the **TiTou Gorge,** where you can swim in the pool or relax in the hot-water springs along one side. If you're a strong swimmer, you can head up the gorge to a cave (it's about a five-minute swim) that has a magnificent waterfall; a crack in the cave about 50 feet above permits a stream of sunlight to penetrate the cavern.

Also in the national park are some of the island's most spectacular waterfalls. The 45-minute hike to **Sari Sari Falls,** accessible through the east-coast village of La Plaine, can be hair-raising. But the sight of water cascading some 150 feet into a large pool is awesome. So large are these falls that you feel the spray from hundreds of yards away. Just beyond the village of Trafalgar and up a short hill is the reception facility, where you can purchase passes to the national park and find guides to take you on a rain-forest trek to the twin **Trafalgar Falls;** the 125-foot-high waterfall is called the Father, and the wider, 95-foot-high one, the Mother. If you like a little challenge, let your guide take you to the riverbed and the cool pools at the base of the falls (check whether there's a cruise ship in port before setting out; this sight is popular with the tour operators).

> **BIBS**
>
> With limited and expensive laundry facilities on ships, you may not want to spend your free time cleaning up after your child. It's convenient to bring along a pack of disposable bibs for mealtimes to keep baby's clothing cleaner and stain-free, avoiding messy garments after meals and a lot of laundry time on board the ship.

Roseau. Although it's one of the smallest capitals in the Caribbean, Roseau has the highest concentration of inhabitants of any town in the eastern Caribbean. Caribbean vernacular architecture and a bustling marketplace transport visitors back in time. Although you can walk the entire town in about an hour, you'll get a much better feel for the place on a leisurely stroll.

For some years now, the Society for Historical Architectural Preservation and Enhancement (SHAPE) has organized programs and projects to preserve the city's architectural heritage. Several interesting buildings have already been restored. **Lilac House,** on Kennedy Avenue, has three types of gingerbread fretwork, latticed veranda railings, and heavy hurricane shutters. The **J. W. Edwards Building,** at the corner of Old and King George V streets, has a stone base and a wooden second-floor gallery. The **Old Market Plaza** is the center of Roseau's historic district, which was laid out by the French on a radial plan rather than a grid, so streets such as Hanover, King George V, and Old radiate from this area. South of the marketplace is the Fort Young Hotel, built as a British fort in the 18th century; the nearby statehouse, public library, and Anglican cathedral are also worth a visit. New developments at the bay front on Dame M. E. Charles Boulevard have brightened up the waterfront.

The 40-acre **Botanical Gardens,** founded in 1891 as an annex of London's Kew Gardens, is a great place to relax, stroll, or watch a cricket match. In addition to the extensive collection of tropical plants and trees, there's also a parrot aviary. At the Forestry Division office, which is also on the garden grounds, you can find numerous publications on the island's flora, fauna, and national parks. The forestry officers are particularly knowledgeable on these subjects and can also recommend good hiking guides. ⊠ *Between Bath Rd. and Valley Rd.*

☎ *767/448–2401 Ext. 3417* ⊕ *www.da-academy.org/dagardens.html* ▦ *Free* ☉ *Daily 7–6.*

The old post office now houses the **Dominica Museum.** This labor of love by local writer and historian Dr. Lennox Honychurch contains furnishings, documents, prints, and maps that date back hundreds of years; you can also find an entire Carib hut as well as Carib canoes, baskets, and other artifacts. ✉ *Dame M. E. Charles Blvd., opposite cruise-ship berth* ☎ *767/448–2401* ▦ *$3* ☉ *Weekdays 9–4, Sat. 9–2; closed Sun. except when a cruise ship is in port.*

SHOPPING

Dominicans produce distinctive handicrafts, with various communities specializing in their specific products. The crafts of the Carib Indians include traditional baskets made of dyed *larouma* reeds and waterproofed with tightly woven *balizier* leaves. These are sold in the Carib Indian Territory and Kalinago Barana Autê as well as in Roseau's shops. Vertivert straw rugs, screw-pine tableware, *fwije* (the trunk of the forest tree fern), and wood carvings are just some examples. Also notable are local herbs, spices, condiments, and herb teas.

One of the easiest places to pick up a souvenir is the Old Market Plaza, just behind the Dominica Museum, in Roseau. Slaves were once sold here, but today handcrafted jewelry, T-shirts, spices, souvenirs, batik, and lacquered and woven bamboo boxes and trays are available from a group of vendors in open-air booths set up on the cobblestones. These are usually busiest when there's a cruise ship berthed across the street. On these days you can also find a vast number of vendors along the bay front.

ACTIVITIES

ADVENTURE PARKS

☉ The **Rainforest Aerial Tram** (✉ *Laudat* ☎ *767/448–8775, 767/440–3266, 866/759–8726 in U.S.* ⊕ *www.rfat.com*) gives you a bird's-eye view of a pristine forest aboard an open, eight-person gondola. For 90 minutes to two hours, you slowly skim the treetop canopy while a guide provides scientific information about the flora and fauna. At the top there is an optional walking tour that is worth the steps. The cost is $64. Transportation and lunch are extra. This is a popular attraction for cruise-ship passengers, so try to reserve ahead.

☉ **Wacky Rollers** (✉ *Front St., Roseau* ✉ *Box 900, Roseau* ☎ *767/440–4386* ⊕ *www.wackyrollers.com*) will make you feel as if you are training for the marines as you swing on a Tarzan-style rope and grab onto a vertical rope ladder, rappel across zip lines, and traverse suspended log bridges, a net bridge, and four monkey bridges (rope loops). It costs $65 for the adult course and should take from 1½ to 3½ hours to conquer the 28 "games." There is also an abbreviated kids' course for $35. Wacky Rollers also organizes adventure tours around the island. Although the office is in Roseau, the park itself is in Hillsborough Estate, about 20 to 25 minutes north of Roseau.

DIVING AND WHALE-WATCHING

Fodor's Choice
★
Dominica has been voted one of the top 10 dive destinations in the world by *Skin Diver* and *Rodale's Scuba Diving* magazines—and has won many other awards for its underwater sites. They are truly memorable. There are numerous highlights all along the west coast of the island, but the best are those in the southwest—within and around **Soufrière/Scotts Head Marine Reserve.** There is a $2 fee per person to dive, snorkel, or kayak in the reserve. The conditions for underwater photography, particularly macrophotography, are unparalleled. The rates are about $60 for a single tank dive and about $80–$100 for a two-tank dive or from about $95 for a resort course with one open-water dive. All scuba-diving operators also offer snorkeling. Equipment rents for $10 to $25 a day; trips with gear range from $15 to $35. A 10% tax is not included.

The **Anchorage Dive & Whale Watch Center** (⊠ *Anchorage Hotel, Castle Comfort* ☎ *767/448–2638* ⊕ *www.anchoragehotel.dm*) has two dive boats that can take you out day or night. It also offers PADI instruction (all skill levels), snorkeling and whale-watching trips, and shore diving. It has many of the same trips as Dive Dominica.

Dive Dominica (⊠ *Castle Comfort Lodge, Castle Comfort* ☎ *767/448–2188/2062, 646/502–6800 in U.S.* ⊕ *www.divedominica.com*), one of the island's dive pioneers, conducts NAUI, PADI, and SSI courses as well as Nitrox certification courses. With four boats, it offers diving, snorkeling, and whale-watching trips and packages including accommodation at the Castle Comfort Lodge. Its trips are similar to Anchorage's.

HIKING

★
Dominica's majestic mountains, clear rivers, and lush vegetation conspire to create adventurous hiking trails. The island is crisscrossed by ancient footpaths of the Arawak and Carib Indians and the Nègres Maroons, escaped slaves who established camps in the mountains. Existing trails range from easygoing to arduous. To make the most of your excursion, you'll need sturdy hiking boots, insect repellent, a change of clothes (kept dry), and a guide. Hikes and tours run $25 to $50 per person, depending on destinations and duration. Some of the natural attractions within the island's national parks require visitors to purchase a site pass. These are sold for varying numbers of visits. A single-entry site pass costs $5, and a week pass $12.

Local bird and forestry expert **Bertrand Jno Baptiste** (☎ 767/446–6358) leads hikes up Morne Diablotin and along the Syndicate Nature Trail; if he's not available, ask him to recommend another guide. Hiking guides can be arranged through the **Discover Dominica Authority** (⊠ *Valley Rd., Roseau* ☎ *767/448–2045* ⊕ *www.discoverdominica.com*).

BEACHES

On the west coast, just south of the village of Pointe Michel, **Champagne** is hailed as one of the best spots for swimming, snorkeling, and diving, but not for sunning. It gets its name from volcanic vents that constantly puff steam into the sea, which makes you feel as if you are swimming in warm champagne.

WHERE TO EAT

$–$$ ✕ **Cocorico.** It's hard to miss the umbrella-covered chairs and tables at
FRENCH   this Parisian-style café on a prominent bay-front corner in Roseau.
☺   Breakfast crepes, croissants, baguette sandwiches, and piping-hot café
au lait are available beginning at 8:30 AM. Throughout the day you
can relax indoors or out and enjoy any of the extensive menu's selections with the perfect glass of wine, and you can even surf the Internet
on their computers. In the cellar downstairs, the Cocorico wine store
has a reasonably priced selection from more than eight countries. You
can also choose from a wide assortment of pâtés and cheeses, crepes,
sausages, cigars, French bread, and chocolates. ✉ *Bay Front at Kennedy Ave., Roseau* ☎ *767/449–8686* ⊕ *www.natureisle.com/cocorico/*
⊙ *No dinner Sat. Closed Sun. unless ship is in port, then 10–4* ☐ *MC,
V* ⊙ *No dinner.*

¢–$$ ✕ **Pearl's Cuisine.** In a creole town house in central Roseau, chef Pearl,
CARIBBEAN   with her robust and infectious character, prepares some of the island's
best local cuisine, such as callaloo soup, fresh fish, and rabbit. Her menu
changes daily, but she offers such local delicacies as *sousse* (pickled pigs'
feet), blood pudding, and rotis. When sitting down, ask for a table on
the open-air gallery that overlooks Roseau and prepare for an abun-
dant portion, but make sure you leave space for dessert. If you're on
the go, enjoy a quick meal from the daily, varied menu in the ground-
floor snack bar. You're spoiled for choice when it comes to the fresh
fruit juices. ✉ *50 King George V St., Roseau* ☎ *767/448–8707* ☐ *AE,
D, MC, V* ⊙ *Closed Sun. No dinner.*

FREEPORT-LUCAYA, BAHAMAS

Chelle Koster   Grand Bahama Island, the fourth-largest island in the Bahamas, lies
Walton   only 52 mi (84 km) off Palm Beach, Florida. In 1492, when Columbus
first set foot in the Bahamas, Grand Bahama was already populated.
Skulls found in caves attest to the existence of the peaceable Lucayans,
who were constantly fleeing the more bellicose Caribs. But it was not
until the 1950s, when the harvesting of Caribbean yellow pine trees
(now protected by Bahamian environmental law) was the island's major
industry, that American financier Wallace Groves envisioned Grand
Bahama's grandiose future as a tax-free port for the shipment of goods
to the United States. It was in that era that the city of Freeport and
later Lucaya evolved. They are separated by a 4-mi (6-km) stretch of
East Sunrise Highway, although few can tell you where one commu-
nity ends and the other begins. Most of Grand Bahama's commercial
activity is concentrated in Freeport, the Bahamas' second-largest city.
Lucaya, with its sprawling shopping complex and water-sports reputa-
tion, stepped up to the role of island tourism capital. Resorts, beaches,
a casino, and golf courses make both cities popular with visitors.

ESSENTIALS

CURRENCY   The Bahamian dollar, which trades one-to-one with the U.S. dollar, which is uni-
versally accepted. There's no need to acquire any Bahamian currency.

INTERNET   Port Lucaya Marina has free Wi-Fi service if you have your own laptop.

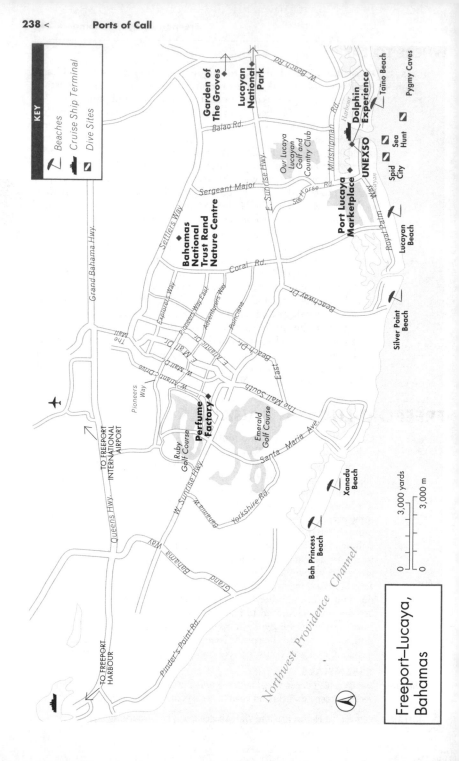

Freeport–Lucaya, Bahamas

TELEPHONE Calling locally or internationally is easy in the Bahamas. To place a local call, dial the seven-digit phone number. To call the United States, dial 1 plus the area code. Pay phones cost 25¢ per call; Bahamian and U.S. quarters are accepted, as are BATELCO phone cards. To place a call using a calling card, use your long-distance carrier's access code or dial 0 for the operator. But beware of using the dedicated long-distance public telephones, which are quite costly. Although most U.S. cell phones work in the Bahamas, the roaming coast can be very high, so check with your provider in advance.

COMING ASHORE

Cruise-ship passengers arrive at Lucayan Harbour, which has a clever Bahamian-style look, extensive cruise-passenger terminal facilities, and an entertainment-shopping village. The harbor lies about 10 minutes west of Freeport. Taxis and limos meet all cruise ships. Two passengers are charged $20 and $27 for trips to Freeport and Lucaya, respectively. Fare to Xanadu Beach is $21; it's $30 to Taïno Beach. The price per person drops $5 for larger groups. It's customary to tip taxi drivers 15%. A three-hour sightseeing tour of the Freeport-Lucaya area costs $25 to $35. Four-hour East or West End trips cost about $40. At this writing, an additional two-berth cruise-ship port in William's Town is undergoing the approval process, but no opening date is set yet.

Grand Bahama's flat terrain and straight, well-paved roads make for good scooter riding. Rentals run $35 a day (about $15 an hour). Helmets are required and provided. Look for small rental stands in parking lots and along the road in Freeport and Lucaya and at the larger resorts. It's usually cheaper to rent a car than to hire a taxi. Automobiles, jeeps, and vans can be rented at the Grand Bahama International Airport. Some agencies provide free pickup and delivery service to the cruise-ship port and Freeport and Lucaya, but prices are still not cheap; cars begin at $65 per day.

EXPLORING FREEPORT-LUCAYA

Grand Bahama is the only planned island in the Bahamas. Its towns, villages, and sights are well laid out but far apart. Downtown Freeport and Lucaya are both best appreciated on foot. Buses and taxis can transport you the 4-mi (6-km) distance between the two. In Freeport shopping is the main attraction. Bolstered by the Our Lucaya Resort complex, Lucaya has its beautiful beach and water-sports scene, plus more shopping and a big, beautiful new casino. Outside of town, isolated fishing villages, beaches, natural attractions, and the once-rowdy town of West End make it worthwhile to hire a tour or rent a car. The island stretches 96 mi (154 km) from one end to the other.

FREEPORT

★ **Bahamas National Trust Rand Nature Centre.** On 100 acres just minutes from downtown Freeport, a half-mile of self-guided botanical trails shows off 130 types of native plants, including many orchid species. The center is the island's birding hot spot, where you might spy a red-tailed hawk or a Cuban emerald hummingbird. Visit the caged one-eyed Bahama parrot the center has adopted, and a Bahama boa, a species that inhabits most Bahamian islands, but not Grand Bahama. On Tuesday and Thursday free (with admission) guided tours depart at 10:30 AM. The visitor center hosts changing local art exhibits. ⊠ *E. Settlers Way* ☎ *242/352–5438* ⚟ *$5* ⏱ *Weekdays 9–4; guided nature walk by advance reservation.*

> **HANGERS**
>
> Folding or inflatable travel hangers are useful if you need to dry out hand laundry or a bathing suit in your cabin. The ones in your cabin's closet may not be removable.

★ **Perfume Factory.** One good reason to visit the International Bazaar, the quiet and elegant Perfume Factory occupies a replica 19th-century Bahamian mansion—the kind built by Loyalists who settled in the Bahamas after the American Revolution. The interior resembles a tasteful drawing room. This is the home of Fragrance of the Bahamas, a company that produces perfumes, colognes, and lotions using the scents of jasmine, cinnamon, gardenia, spice, and ginger. Take a free five-minute tour of the mixology laboratory and get a free sample. For $30 an ounce, you can blend your own perfume using any of the 35 scents ($15 for 1½ ounces of blend-it-yourself body lotion). Sniff mixtures until they hit the right combination, then bottle, name, and take home the personalized potion. ⊠ *Behind International Bazaar, W. Sunrise Hwy. and Mall Dr., on access road* ☎ *242/352–9391* ⊕ *www. perfumefactory.com* ⚟ *Free* ⏱ *Weekdays 9:30–5, Sat. 11–3.*

LUCAYA

Lucaya, on Grand Bahama's southern coast and just east of Freeport, was developed as the island's resort center. These days it's booming with the megaresort complex called the Our Lucaya Resort, a fine sandy beach, championship golf courses, a casino, a first-class dive operation, and Port Lucaya's shopping and marina facilities. Most cruise ships offer excursions that include a day at Our Lucaya.

☺ **The Dolphin Experience.** Encounter Atlantic bottlenose dolphins in Sanctuary Bay at one of the world's first and largest dolphin facilities, about 2 mi east of Port Lucaya. A ferry takes you from Port Lucaya to the bay to observe and photograph the animals. If you don't mind getting wet, you can sit on a partially submerged dock or stand waist deep in the water and one of these friendly creatures will swim up to you. You can also engage in one of two swim-with-the-dolphins programs, but participants must be 55 inches or taller. The Dolphin Experience began in 1987, when it trained five dolphins to interact with people. Later, the animals learned to head out to sea and swim with scuba divers on the open reef. A two-hour dive program is available. You can buy tickets for the Dolphin Experience at UNEXSO in Port Lucaya, but be sure to make reservations as early as possible. ⊠ *Port Lucaya* ☎ *242/373–1244 or 800/992–3483* ⊕ *www.unexso.com* ⚟ *2-hr interaction program $75, 2-hr swim program $169, dolphin dive $219, open-ocean experience $199* ⏱ *Daily 8–5.*

❸ **Underwater Explorers Society (UNEXSO).**

Fodor's Choice One of the world's most respected

★ diving facilities, UNEXSO welcomes more than 50,000 individuals each year and trains hundreds of them in scuba diving. Facilities include a 17-foot-deep training pool with windows that look out on the harbor, changing rooms and showers, docks, equipment rental, an outdoor café, and an air-tank filling station. ⊠ *On wharf at Port Lucaya Marketplace* ☏ *242/373–1244 or 800/992–3483* ⊕ *www.unexso. com* ⊠ *Beginner reef dives $59, dives from $59, night dives $79, dolphin dives $219, shark dives $99* ☉ *Daily 8–5.*

BEYOND FREEPORT-LUCAYA

Grand Bahama Island narrows at picturesque West End, once Grand Bahama's capital and still home to

4

descendants of the island's first settlers. Seaside villages, with concrete-block houses painted in bright blue and pastel yellow, fill in the landscape between Freeport and West End. The East End is Grand Bahama's "back-to-nature" side. The road east from Lucaya is long, flat, and mostly straight. It cuts through a vast pine forest to reach McLean's Town, the end of the road.

Garden of the Groves. This vibrant 12-acre garden, featuring a trademark chapel and waterfalls, is filled with native Bahamian flora, butterflies, and birds. Interpretative signage identifies plant and animal species. First opened in 1973, the park was renovated and reopened in 2008; additions include a labyrinth modeled after the one at France's Cathedral of Chartres, colorful shops and galleries, a playground, and a multideck outdoor café. ⊠ *Midshipman Rd. and Churchill Dr., Eastern Grand Bahama* ☏ *242/374–7778* ⊠ *$15* ☉ *Daily 9–5; guided tours at 11 and 2.*

Fodor's Choice **Lucayan National Park.** In this extraordinary 40-acre seaside land pre-

★ serve, trails and elevated walkways wind through a natural forest of wild tamarind and gumbo-limbo trees, past an observation platform, a mangrove swamp, sheltered pools, and one of the largest explored underwater cave systems in the world (more than 6 mi long). You can enter the caves at two access points; one is closed in June and July, the bat-nursing season. Twenty miles east of Lucaya, the park contains examples of the island's five ecosystems: beach, hardwood forest, mangroves, rocky coppice, and pine forest. Across the road from the caves, two trails form a loop. Creek Trail's new boardwalk showcases impressive interpretive signage, and crosses a mangrove-clotted tidal creek to Gold Rock Beach, a narrow, lightly visited strand of white sand edged by some of the island's highest dunes and jewel-tone sea. ⊠ *Grand*

Bahama Hwy. ☎ *242/352–5438* ⊕ *www.bnt.bs/parks_lucayan.php* ✉ *$3* ⊙ *Daily 8:30–4:30.*

SHOPPING

In the stores, shops, and boutiques on Grand Bahama you can find duty-free goods costing up to 40% less than what you might pay back home. At the numerous perfume shops fragrances are often sold at a sweet-smelling 25% below U.S. prices. Be sure to limit your haggling to the straw markets.

★ **Port Lucaya Marketplace** (✉ *Sea Horse Rd.* ☎ *242/373–8446* ⊕ *www. portlucayamarketplace.com*) has more than 100 boutiques and restaurants in 13 pastel-color buildings in a harborside locale, plus an extensive straw market. Local musicians often perform at the bandstand in the afternoons and evenings.

ACTIVITIES

FISHING

Private boat charters for up to four people cost $300 and up for a half-day and $350 and up for a full day. Bahamian law limits the catching of game fish to six each of dolphinfish, kingfish, tuna, or wahoo per vessel.

Reef Tours Ltd. (✉ *Port Lucaya Marketplace* ☎ *242/373–5880* ⊕ *www. bahamasvacationguide.com/reeftours*) offers deep-sea fishing for four to six people on custom boats. Equipment and bait are provided free. All vessels are licensed, inspected, and insured. Trips run from 8:30 to 12:15 and from 1 to 4:45, weather permitting ($130 per angler, $60 per spectator). Full-day trips are also available, as are bottom-fishing excursions, glass-bottom-boat tours, snorkeling trips, and sailing–snorkeling cruises. Reservations are essential.

GOLF

Fodor's Choice ★ **Our Lucaya Beach and Golf Resort Lucayan Course**, designed by Dick Wilson, is a dramatic 6,824-yard, par-72, 18-hole course featuring a balanced six straight holes, six classic left-turning doglegs, and six right-turning holes. The 18th hole has a double lake, towering limestone structure, and a new clubhouse nearby. Its state-of-the-art instruction facilities include a practice putting green with bunker and chipping areas, covered teaching bays, and a teaching seminar area. A shared electric cart is included in greens fees. Ask about special "twilight" fees that are as low as $55 for 9 holes. ✉ *Our Lucaya Beach and Golf Resort, Lucaya* ☎ *242/373–2002* ✉ *Resort guests $120, nonguests $130.*

Ruby Golf Course reopened in 2008 with renovated landscaping but basically the same 18-hole, par-72 Jim Fazio design—a lot of sand traps and challenges on holes 7, 9, 10, and 18—especially playing from the blue tees. Hole 10 requires a tee shot onto a dogleg right fairway around a pond. There's a small restaurant-bar and pro shop at the 18th hole. ✉ *West Sunrise Hwy. and Wentworth Ave., Freeport* ☎ *242/352–1851* ⊕ *www.rubygolfclub.com* ✉ *$65–$90.*

BEACHES

Some 60 mi of magnificent, pristine stretches of sand extend between Freeport-Lucaya and the island's eastern end. Most are used only by people who live in adjacent settlements. The beaches have no public facilities, so beachgoers often headquarter at one of the local beach bars, which often provide

PLASTIC BAGS
Use Zip-loc bags for all toiletries and anything that might spill. Toss a few extras into your suitcase. You may need them later to pack dirty or damp clothes.

free transportation. **Lucayan Beach** is readily accessible from the town's main drag and is always lively and lovely. **Taïno Beach,** near Freeport, is fun for families, water-sports enthusiasts, and partyers. Near Freeport, **Xanadu Beach** provides a mile of white sand.

4

WHERE TO EAT

BAHAMIAN

$ ✕ **Becky's Bahamian Restaurant and Lounge.** Especially known for its wonderful breakfast, the restaurant's diner-style booths provide a comfortable backdrop for the inexpensive menu. It lists traditional Bahamian and American food, from conch salad and curried mutton to a BLT. Pancakes, eggs, and special Bahamian breakfasts—stew' fish, boil' fish, or chicken souse (the latter two are soups flavored with lime), with johnnycake or grits—are served all day. ⊠ *E. Beach Dr. and E. Sunrise Hwy.* ☎ *242/352–5247* ⊟ *D, MC, V.*

SEAFOOD

$$ ✕ **Pier One.** Blown down in the 2004 hurricanes, Pier One is back with a sturdier building decorated with the old trademark nautical paraphernalia. Diners have their choice of picnic tables around the balcony or inside the spacious dining and bar area. Popular with cruise-ship passengers because of its location at the port entrance, the restaurant also hosts shark feedings nightly at 7, 8, and 9. To go with this activity, order specialties such as smoked shark, blackened lemon shark fillet, or shark curry with bananas. The extensive menus also offer mussels, pan-fried mahi, grouper cordon bleu, lobster and mushrooms with cream, chicken curry, fettuccini with seafood, and steaks. ⊠ *Freeport Harbour,* ☎ *242/352–6674* ⊟ *AE, MC, V.*

GRAND CAYMAN, CAYMAN ISLANDS

Jordan Simon

The largest and most populous of the Cayman Islands, Grand Cayman is also one of the most popular cruise destinations in the Western Caribbean, largely because it doesn't suffer from the ailments afflicting many larger ports: panhandlers, hasslers, and crime. Instead, the Cayman economy is a study in stability, and the environment is healthy and prosperous. Though the island is rather featureless, Grand Cayman is a diver's paradise, with pristine waters and a colorful variety of marine life. Compared with other Caribbean ports, there are few things to see on land here; instead, the island's most impressive sights are underwater. Snorkeling, diving, and glass-bottom-boat and submarine rides top every ship's shore-excursion list, and can also be arranged at major aquatic shops if you don't go on a ship-sponsored excursion. Grand Cayman is also famous for the nearly 600 offshore banks in George Town; not surprisingly, the standard of living is high, and nothing is cheap.

ESSENTIALS

CURRENCY The Cayman Island dollar (CI$ to US$1.25). The U.S. dollar is accepted everywhere, and ATMs often dispense cash in both currencies, though you may receive change in Cayman dollars. Prices are often quoted in Cayman dollars, so make sure you know which currency you're dealing with so you don't end up paying 25% more than you expected.

INTERNET **Café del Sol Internet Cafe** (⊠ *Marquee Plaza, Seven Mile Beach, Grand Cayman* ☎ *345/946-2233* ⊕ *www.cafedelsol.ky*).

TELEPHONE To dial the United States, dial 1 followed by the area code and telephone number. To place a credit-card call, dial 800/744-7777; credit-card and calling-card calls can be made from any public phone.

COMING ASHORE

Ships anchor in George Town Harbour and tender passengers onto Harbour Drive, the center of the shopping district. If you just want to walk around town and shop or visit Seven Mile Beach, you're probably better off on your own, but the Stingray Sandbar snorkeling trip is a highlight of many Caribbean vacations and fills up quickly on cruise-ship days, so it's often better to order that excursion from your ship, even though it will be more crowded and expensive than if you took an independent trip.

A tourist information booth is on the pier, and taxis queue for disembarking passengers. Taxi fares are determined by an elaborate structure set by the government, and although rates may seem high, cabbies rarely try to rip off tourists. Ask to see the chart if you want to check a quoted fare. Taxi drivers won't usually do hourly rates for small-group tours; you must arrange a sightseeing tour with a company. Car rentals are not terribly expensive, beginning at about $40 a day (plus a $7.50 driving permit), so they are a good option if you want to do some independent exploring. You can easily see the entire island and have time to stop at a beach in a single day.

EXPLORING GRAND CAYMAN

ⓒ **Blowholes.** When the easterly trade winds blow hard, crashing waves force water into caverns and send impressive geysers shooting up as much as 20 feet through the ironshore. The blowholes were partially filled during Hurricane Ivan in 2004, so the water must be rough to recapture their former elemental drama. ⊠ *Frank Sound Rd., roughly 10 mi (16 km) east of Bodden Town, near East End.*

ⓒ **Boatswain's Beach.** Cayman's premier attraction, the Turtle Farm,
Fodor's Choice has been rebranded and transformed into a marine theme park. The
★ expanded complex now has several souvenir shops and restaurants. Still, the turtles remain a central attraction, and you can tour ponds in the original research/breeding facility with thousands in various stages

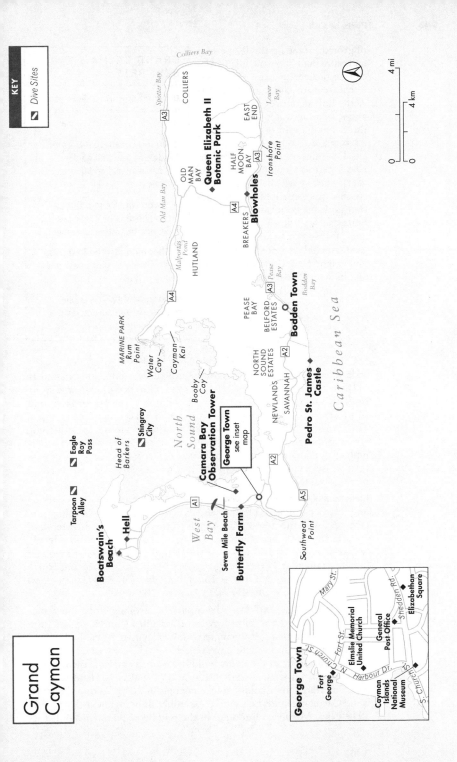

Grand
Cayman

KEY
◤ Dive Sites

Colliers Bay

Spotter Bay

COLLIERS

A3

Queen Elizabeth II
Botanic Park ◆

OLD
MAN
BAY

Lower
Bay

EAST
END

HALF
MOON
BAY

A3

Ironshore
Point

A4

Blowholes ◆

BREAKERS

Old Man Bay

Malportas
Pond

HUTLAND

A4

Pease
Bay

A3

Bodden
Bay

Bodden Town ◆

PEASE
BAY

BELFORD
ESTATES

MARINE PARK
Rum
Point

Water
Cay

Cayman
Kai

Booby
Cay

NORTH
SOUND
ESTATES

A2

North
Sound

Head of
Barkers

◤ Eagle
Ray
Pass

Stingray
City ◆

NEWLANDS

SAVANNAH

Pedro St. James
Castle ◆

Camara Bay
Observation Tower ◆

George Town
see inset
map

A2

◤ Tarpoon
Alley

West
Bay

A1

Seven Mile Beach

Butterfly Farm ◆

A5

Southwest
Point

Caribbean Sea

Boatswain's
Beach ◆ Hell

0 ————— 4 mi
0 ————— 4 km

George Town

Mary St.

Fort St.

Fort
George ◆

Elmslie Memorial
United Church

N. Church St.

Harbour Dr.

General
Post Office

Shedden Rd.

Elizabethan
Square

Cayman
Islands
National
Museum

S. Church St.

of growth, some up to 600 pounds and more than 70 years old. Turtles can be picked up from the tanks, a real treat for children and adults as the little creatures flap their fins and splash the water. Four areas— three aquatic and one dry—cover 23 acres; different-colored bracelets determine access (the steep full-pass admission includes snorkeling gear). The park helps promote conservation, encouraging interaction (a Tidal Pool houses invertebrates such as starfish and crabs) and observation. Animal Program Events include Keeper Talks, where you might feed birds or iguanas, and biologists speaking about conservation and their importance to the ecosystem. ✉ *825 Northwest Point Rd., Box 812, West Bay* ☎ *345/949–3894* ⊕ *www. boatswainsbeach.ky* 🎫 *Comprehensive ticket $45, Turtle Farm only $30* ☉ *Daily 8:30–4:30.*

> ## GRAND CAYMAN BEST BETS
>
> ■ **Diving.** If you're a diver, you'll find several good sites close to shore.
>
> ■ **Queen Elizabeth II Botanic Garden.** A beautiful garden has native plants and rare blue iguanas.
>
> ■ **Seven Mile Beach.** One of the Caribbean's best beaches is a short ride from the cruise pier.
>
> ■ **Shopping.** George Town has a wide range of shops near the cruise-ship pier.
>
> ■ **Stingray City.** This is one of the most fun adventures the Caribbean has to offer.

Bodden Town. In the island's original south-shore capital you can find an old cemetery on the shore side of the road. Graves with A-frame structures are said to contain the remains of pirates. There are also the ruins of a fort and a wall erected by slaves in the 19th century. The National Trust runs tours of the restored 1840s Mission House. A curio shop serves as the entrance to what's called the Pirate's Caves ($8), partially underground natural formations that are more hokey (decked out with fake treasure chests and mannequins in pirate garb, with an outdoor petting zoo) than spooky.

☉ ★ **Camana Bay Observation Tower.** This 75-foot structure provides striking 360-degree panoramas of otherwise flat Grand Cayman, sweeping from George Town and Seven Mile Beach to the North Sound. Afterward you can enjoy 500-acre Camana Bay's gardens, waterfront boardwalk, and pedestrian paths lined with shops and restaurants, or frequent live entertainment. ✉ *Extending between Seven Mile Beach and North Sound, 2 mi north of George Town, Camana Bay* ☎ *345/640–3500* ⊕ *www.camanabay.com* 🎫 *Free* ☉ *Sunrise–10* PM.

George Town. Begin exploring the capital by strolling along the waterfront Harbour Drive to **Elmslie Memorial United Church,** named after the first Presbyterian missionary to serve in Cayman. Its vaulted ceiling, wooden arches, and sedate nave reflect the religious nature of island residents. In front of the court building, in the center of town, names of influential Caymanians are inscribed on the **Wall of History,** which commemorates the islands' quincentennial in 2003. Across the street is the **Cayman Islands Legislative Assembly Building,** next door to the **1919 Peace Memorial Building.** In the middle of the financial district is the **General Post Office**, built in 1939. Let the kids pet the big blue iguana statues.

Fodor'sChoice ★ Built in 1833, the **Cayman Islands National Museum** has had several different incarnations over the years, including that of courthouse, jail (now the gift shop), post office, and dance hall. It features an ongoing archaeological excavation of the Old Gaol and excellent 3-D bathymetric displays, dioramas, and videos that illustrate local geology, flora and fauna, and island history. There are also temporary exhibits focusing on aspects of Caymanian culture, a local art collection, and interactive displays for kids. ✉ *Harbour Dr., Box 2189, George Town* ☎ *345/949–8368* ⊕ *www.museum.ky* 🎫 *$5* ☉ *Weekdays 9–5, Sat. 10–2.*

Fodor'sChoice ★ **Pedro St. James Castle.** Built in 1780, the greathouse is Cayman's oldest stone structure and the only remaining late-18th-century residence on the island. In its capacity as courthouse and jail, it was the birthplace of Caymanian democracy, where in December 1831 the first elected parliament was organized and in 1835 the Slavery Abolition Act signed. The structure still has original or historically accurate replicas of sweeping verandas, mahogany floors, rough-hewn wide-beam ceilings, outside louvers, stone and oxblood- or mustard-color lime-wash-painted walls, brass fixtures, and Georgian furnishings (from tea caddies to canopy beds to commodes). You can stroll through landscaping of native Caymanian flora and experience one of the most spectacular views on the island from atop the dramatic Great Pedro Bluff. First watch the impressive multimedia theater show, complete with smoking pots, misting rains, and two film screens where the story of Pedro's Castle is presented on the hour. The poignant Hurricane Ivan Memorial outside uses text, images, and symbols to represent important aspects of that horrific 2004 natural disaster. ✉ *Pedro Castle Rd., Box 305, Savannah* ☎ *345/947–3329* ⊕ *www.pedrostjames.ky* 🎫 *$10* ☉ *Daily 9–5.*

Fodor'sChoice ★ **Queen Elizabeth II Botanic Park.** This 65-acre wilderness preserve showcases a wide range of indigenous and nonindigenous tropical vegetation, approximately 2,000 species in total. Splendid sections include numerous water features, from limpid lily ponds to cascades; a Heritage Garden with a traditional cottage and "caboose" (outside kitchen) that includes crops that might have been planted on Cayman a century ago; and a Floral Colour Garden arranged by color, the walkway wandering through sections of pink, red, orange, yellow, white, blue, mauve, lavender, and purple. You'll encounter birds, lizards, turtles, agoutis, and more, but the park's star residents are the protected endemic blue iguanas, found only in Grand Cayman. The world's most endangered iguana, they're the focus of the National Trust's Blue Iguana Recovery Program, a captive breeding and reintroduction facility. The Trust conducts 90-minute behind-the-scenes safaris Monday–Saturday at 11 AM for $30. ✉ *367 Botanic Rd.* ✉ *Box 203, North Side, Grand Cayman* ☎ *345/947–9462* ⊕ *www.botanic-park.ky* 🎫 *$10* ☉ *Apr.–Sept., daily 9–6:30; Oct.–Mar., daily 9–5:30; last admission 1 hr before closing.*

4

SHOPPING

The **Anchorage Centre** across from the cruise-ship North Terminal has 10 of the most-affordable stores and boutiques selling duty-free goods from such great brand names as John Hardy, Movado, and Concord, as well as designer ammolite jewelry. Downtown is the **Kirk Freeport Plaza,** known for its boutiques selling fine watches, duty-free china, Gucci goods, perfumes, and cosmetics. Just keep walking—there's plenty of shopping in all directions. Stores in the **Landmark** in George Town sell perfumes, treasure coins, and upscale beachwear; Breezes by the Bay restaurant is upstairs.

★ **Cathy Church's Underwater Photo Centre and Gallery** (⊠ *S. Church St., George Town* ☎ *345/949–7415*) has a collection of the acclaimed underwater shutterbug's spectacular color and limited-edition black-and-white underwater photos.

★ **Pure Art** (⊠ *S. Church St., George Town* ☎ *345/949–9133* ⊕ *www. pureart.ky*), about 1½ mi (2½ km) south of George Town, purveys wit, warmth, and whimsy right from the wildly colored front steps. Its warren of rooms resembles a garage sale run amok or a quirky grandmother's attic spilling over with unexpected finds, from foodstuffs to functional art.

The **Tortuga Rum Company** (⊠ *N. Sound Rd., Industrial Park, George Town* ☎ *345/949–7701 or 345/949–7867*) bakes and then vacuum-seals more than 10,000 of its world-famous rum cakes daily, adhering to the original "secret" century-old recipe. Although available almost everywhere now, this is the source.

ACTIVITIES

DIVING AND SNORKELING

Pristine water (visibility often exceeding 100 feet [30 meters]), breath-taking coral formations, and plentiful and exotic marine life mark the **Great Wall**—a world-renowned dive site just off the north side of Grand Cayman. A must-see for adventurous souls is **Stingray City** in the North Sound, noted as the best 12-foot (3½-meter) dive in the world, where dozens of stingrays congregate, tame enough to suction squid from your outstretched palm. Nondivers gravitate to **Stingray Sandbar,** a shallower part of the North Sound, which has become a popular snorkeling spot; it is also a popular hangout for the stingrays.

Don Foster's Dive Cayman Islands (⊠ *218 S. Church St., George Town* ☎ *345/949–5679 or 345/945–5132* ⊕ *www.donfosters.com*) has a pool with a shower as well as snorkeling along the ironshore at Casuarina Point, easily accessed starting at 20 feet, extending to depths of 55 feet. There are Stingray City trips with divers and snorkelers in the same boat (perfect for families).

Eden Rock Diving Center (⊠ *124 S. Church St., George Town* ☎ *345/949–7243* ⊕ *www.edenrockdive.com*), south of George Town, provides easy access to Eden Rock and Devil's Grotto. It features full equipment rental, lockers, shower facilities, and a full range of PADI courses from a helpful, cheerful staff. Costs for guided shore dives and two-tank dives on its Pro 42 jet boat are cheaper than at most outfits, without sacrificing quality or comfort.

☺ **Red Sail Sports** (☎ *345/949–5965 or 877/733–7245* ⊕ *www.redsailcayman.com*) offers daily trips from most of the major hotels. Dives are often run as guided tours, a perfect option for beginners. If you're experienced and your air lasts a long time, consult the boat captain to see if he requires that you come up with the group as determined by the first person who runs low on air. There is a full range of kids' dive options for ages 5 to 15. The company also operates Stingray City tours, dinner and sunset sails, and just about every major water sport from Wave Runners to windsurfing.

> **STROLLERS**
>
> Parents should bring along an umbrella stroller for walks around the ship as well as the ports of call; people often underestimate how big ships are. It also comes in handy at the airport. Wheel baby right to the departure gate— the stroller is gate checked and will be waiting for you when you arrive at your port of embarkation.

FISHING

Cayman waters are abundant with blue and white marlin, yellowfin tuna, sailfish, dolphinfish, bonefish, and wahoo. Two-dozen boats are available for charter.

★ **Sea Star Charters** (☎ *345/949–1016, 345/916–5234 after 8* AM), aka Clinton's Watersports, is run by Clinton Ebanks, a fine and very friendly Caymanian who will do whatever it takes to make sure that you have a wonderful time on his two 25- and 31-foot cabin cruisers, enjoying light-tackle, bone-, and bottom-fishing. He's a good choice for beginners, and offers a nice cultural experience as well as sailing charters and snorkeling with complimentary transportation and equipment. Only cash and traveler's checks are accepted.

HIKING

★ The National Trust's internationally significant **Mastic Trail** (✉ *Frank Sound Rd., entrance by fire station at botanic park, Breakers, East End* ☎ *345/749–1121 for guide reservations* ⊕ *www.nationaltrust.org.ky*), used in the 1800s as the only direct path to and from the North Side, is a rugged 2-mi (3-km) slash through 776 dense acres of woodlands, black mangrove swamps, savannah, agricultural remnants, and ancient rock formations. Call the National Trust to determine suitability and to book a guide for $25; tours are run daily from 9 to 5 by appointment only, regularly on Wednesday at 9 AM. Or walk on the wild side with a $5 guidebook. The trip takes about three hours.

BEACHES

Fodor's Choice ★ **Seven Mile Beach.** Grand Cayman's west coast is dominated by the famous Seven Mile Beach—actually a 6½-mi-long (10-km-long) expanse of powdery white sand overseeing lapis water stippled with a rainbow of parasails and kayaks. The width of the beach varies with the season; toward the south end it narrows and disappears altogether south of the Marriott, leaving only rock and ironshore. It starts to broaden into its normal silky softness anywhere between Tarquyn Manor and the Reef Grill at Royal Palms. Free of litter and pesky peddlers, it's an unspoiled (though often crowded) environment. At the public beach toward the north end you can find chairs for rent ($10 for the day, including a beverage), a playground, water toys aplenty, two beach bars, restrooms, and showers. The best snorkeling is at either end, by the Marriott and Treasure Island or off the northern section called Cemetery Reef Beach. ⊠ *West Bay Rd., Seven Mile Beach.*

WHERE TO EAT

$$–$$$ ✕ **Breezes by the Bay.** There isn't a bad seat in the house at this nonstop
CARIBBEAN   feel-good fiesta. Wraparound balconies take in a dazzling panorama from South Sound to Seven Mile Beach. It's a joyous nonstop happy hour all day every day. Equally fresh food at bargain prices, including homemade baked goods and ice creams, isn't an afterthought. Chunky velvety conch chowder served in a bread bowl or near-definitive conch fritters are meals in themselves. Hefty sandwiches are slathered with yummy jerk mayo or garlicky aioli. Signature standouts include meltingly moist whole fish escoveitch, curry chicken, popcorn shrimp, and jerk-glazed pork chops. ⊠ *Harbor Dr., George Town* ☎ *345/943–8439* ⊕ *www.breezesbythebay.com* ▤ *AE, MC, V.*

$–$$ ✕ **MacDonald's.** One of the locals' favorite burger joints—not a fast-food
CARIBBEAN   outlet—MacDonald's does a brisk lunch business in stick-to-your-ribs basics such as rotisserie chicken and fish escoveitch. Yellows and pinks predominate, with appetizing posters of food, but decor is an afterthought to the politicos, housewives in curlers, and cops flirting shyly with the waitresses. ⊠ *99 Shedden Rd., George Town* ☎ *345/949–4640* ⩗ *Reservations not accepted* ▤ *MC, V.*

GRAND TURK, TURKS AND CAICOS ISLANDS

Ramona Settle   Just 7 mi (11 km) long and a little over 1 mi (1½ km) wide, Grand Turk, the political capital of the Turks and Caicos Islands, has been a longtime favorite destination for divers eager to explore the 7,000-foot-deep pristine coral walls that drop down only 300 yards out to sea. On shore, the tiny, quiet island is home to white-sand beaches, the National Museum, and a small population of wild horses and donkeys, which leisurely meander past the white-walled courtyards, pretty churches, and bougainvillea-covered colonial inns on their daily commute into town. The main settlement on the island is tranquil Cockburn Town, and that's where most of the small hotels, not to mention Pillory Beach, can be found. Although it has the second-largest number of inhabitants of all the Turks and Caicos Island, Grand Turk's permanent population has still not reached 4,000.

ESSENTIALS

CURRENCY   The U.S. dollar. You'll find branches of Scotiabank and FirstCaribbean on Grand Turk, with ATMs; all of these are in tiny Cockburn Town.

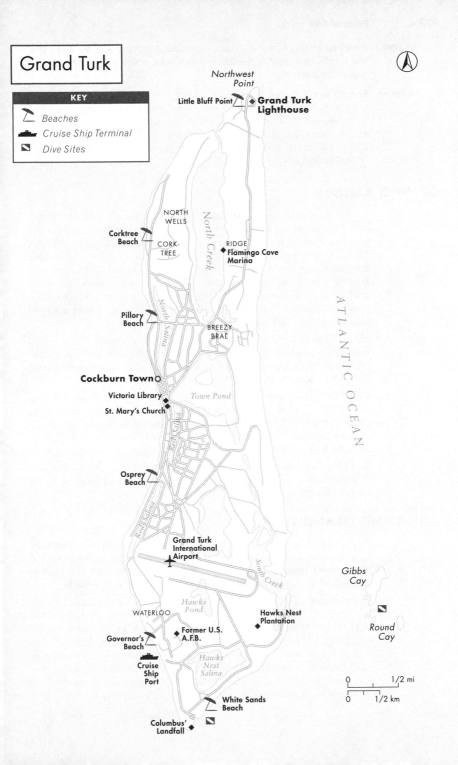

Grand Turk

KEY

⌐ Beaches

🚢 Cruise Ship Terminal

◣ Dive Sites

Northwest Point

Little Bluff Point

Grand Turk Lighthouse

NORTH WELLS

North Creek

Corktree Beach

CORK-TREE

RIDGE
♦ Flamingo Cove Marina

North Salina

Pillory Beach

BREEZY BRAE

Cockburn Town ○

Victoria Library

St. Mary's Church

Town Pond

Osprey Beach

Red Salina

Grand Turk International Airport

South Creek

Gibbs Cay

Hawks Pond

WATERLOO

Hawks Nest Plantation

Governor's Beach

Former U.S. A.F.B.

Round Cay

Cruise Ship Port

Hawks Nest Salina

White Sands Beach

Columbus' Landfall

ATLANTIC OCEAN

0   1/2 mi

0   1/2 km

INTERNET   There's no Internet café at the cruise center, but if you have a laptop, you might take it to the restaurant at the Osprey Beach Hotel, where you can take advantage of the hotel's free Wi-Fi.

TELEPHONE   To make local calls, dial the seven-digit number. To make calls from the Turks and Caicos, dial 0, then 1, the area code, and the number. All telephone service is provided by LIME (formerly Cable & Wireless), and your U.S. cell phone may work on Grand Turk. Calling cards are available, or you can make a call using AT&T's USADirect by dialing 800/872–2881 to charge the call to your credit card or an AT&T prepaid calling card.

COMING ASHORE

Cruise ships dock at the southern end of the island, near the former U.S. Air Force base south of the airport. The purpose-built, $40-million cruise center is about 3 mi (5 km) from tranquil Cockburn Town, Pillory Beach, and the Ridge, and far from most of the western shore dive sites. The center has many facilities, including shopping, a large, free-form pool, car-rental booths, and even a dock from which many sea-bound excursions depart. Governor's Beach is adjacent to the cruise-ship complex and one of the island's best beaches, but others are right in and around Cockburn Town.

If you want to come into Cockburn Town, it's reachable by taxi. Taxi rates are per person and by "zone"; you'll find a rate card outside the cruise terminal. You can also rent a car to explore the island on your own terms and schedule.

Grand Turk Cruise Terminal (✉ *South Base, Grand Turk Cruise Terminal* ☎ *649/946–1040* ⊕ *www.grandturkcc.com*) has a Web site that shows all the cruise schedules, lists all the shops at the terminal, and completely outlines options for excursions and transportation. A bonus is the live webcam so you can check the actual weather at any given moment.

Grace Bay Car Rentals (✉ *Providenciales* ☎ *649/941–8500* ⊕ *www.gracebaycarrentals.com*) has an office at the port, so you can see the sights on your own time. Remember, driving is on the left.

EXPLORING GRAND TURK

Pristine beaches with vistas of turquoise waters, small local settlements, historic ruins, and native flora and fauna are among the sights on Grand Turk. Fewer than 4,000 people live on this 7½-square-mi (19-square-km) island, and it's hard to get lost, as there aren't many roads.

Cockburn Town. The buildings in the colony's capital and seat of government reflect a 19th-century Bermudian style. Narrow streets are lined with low stone walls and old street lamps, which are now powered by electricity. The once-vital *salinas* (natural salt pans, where the sea leaves a film of salt) have been restored, and covered benches along the sluices offer shady spots for observing wading birds, including flamingos that frequent the shallows. Be sure to pick up a copy of the tourist board's *Heritage Walk* guide to discover Grand Turk's rich architecture.

Her Majesty's Prison (✉ *Pond St., Cockburn Town* ☎ *No phone*) was built in the 19th century to house runaway slaves and slaves who survived the wreck of the *Trouvadore* in 1841. After the slaves were granted freedom, the prison housed criminals and even modern-day drug runners until it closed in the 1990s. The last hanging here was in 1960. Now you can see the cells, solitary confinement area, and exercise patio. The prison is open only when there is a cruise ship at the port.

☾ ★ In one of the oldest stone buildings on the islands, the **Turks & Caicos National Museum** houses the Molasses Reef wreck, the earliest shipwreck—dating to the early 1500s—discovered in the Americas. The natural-history exhibits include artifacts left by Taíno, African, North American, Bermudian, French, and Latin American settlers. The museum has a 3-D coral reef exhibit, a walk-in Lucayan cave with wooden artifacts, and a gallery dedicated to Grand Turk's little-known involvement in the Space Race (John Glenn made landfall here after being the first American to orbit the Earth). An interactive children's gallery keeps knee-high visitors "edutained." The museum also claims that Grand Turk was where Columbus first landed in the New World. The most original display is a collection of messages in bottles that have washed ashore from all over the world. ✉ *Duke St., Cockburn Town* ☎ *649/946–2160* ⊕ *www.tcmuseum.org* ✍ *$5* ☉ *Mon., Tues., Thurs., and Fri. 9–4, Wed. 9–5, Sat. 9–1.*

Grand Turk Lighthouse. More than 150 years old, the lighthouse, built in the United Kingdom and transported piece by piece to the island, used to protect ships in danger of wrecking on the northern reefs. Use this panoramic landmark as a starting point for a breezy cliff-top walk by following the donkey trails to the deserted eastern beach. ✉ *Lighthouse Rd., North Ridge.*

GRAND TURK BEST BETS

■ **Beaches.** The sand is powdery soft, the water azure blue.

■ **Diving.** If you're certified, there are several world-class dive sights within each reach.

■ **Gibb's Cay.** To swim with stingrays, take a ship-sponsored trip here; it's an excellent beach.

■ **Front Street.** Colorful Front Street will give you the feeling you've stepped back in time.

■ **Turks and Caicos National Museum.** Small but worthy.

4

SHOPPING

There's not much to buy in Grand Turk, and shopping isn't a major activity here. However, there is a duty-free mall right at the cruise-ship center, where you'll find the usual array of upscale shops, including Ron Jon's Surf Shop, the largest Margaritaville in the world, and Piranha Joe's. There are also shops in Cockburn Town itself.

ACTIVITIES

Most of the activities offered to cruise-ship passengers can be booked only on your ship. These include a horseback ride and swim, dune-buggy safaris, and 4x4 safaris.

DIVING AND SNORKELING

★ In these waters you can find undersea cathedrals, coral gardens, and countless tunnels, but note that you must carry and present a valid certificate card before you'll be allowed to dive. As its name suggests, the **Black Forest** offers staggering black-coral formations as well as the occasional black-tip shark. In the **Library** you can study fish galore, including large numbers of yellowtail snapper. At the Columbus Passage separating South Caicos from Grand Turk, each side of a 22-mi-wide (35-km-wide) channel drops more than 7,000 feet. From January through March thousands of Atlantic humpback whales swim through en route to their winter breeding grounds. **Gibb's Cay,** a small cay a couple of miles off Grand Turk, where you can swim with stingrays, makes for a great excursion.

Blue Water Divers (⊠ *Duke St., Cockburn Town, Grand Turk* 🖭 *649/ 946–2432* ⊕ *www.grandturkscuba.com*) has been in operation on Grand Turk since 1983, and is the only PADI Gold Palm five-star dive center on the island. Owner Mitch will undoubtedly put some of your underwater adventures to music in the evening when he plays at the Osprey Beach Hotel or Salt Raker Inn. **Oasis Divers** (⊠ *Duke St., Cockburn Town* 🖭 *649/946–1128* ⊕ *www.oasisdivers.com*) specializes in complete gear handling and pampering treatment. It also supplies Nitrox and rebreathers. Besides daily dive trips to the wall, **Sea Eye Diving** (⊠ *Duke St., Cockburn Town* 🖭 *649/946–1407* ⊕ *www. seaeyediving.com*) offers encounters with friendly stingrays on a popular snorkeling trip to nearby Gibbs Cay.

BEACHES

Grand Turk is spoiled for choices when it comes to beach options: sunset strolls along miles of deserted beaches, picnics in secluded coves, beachcombing on the coralline sands, snorkeling around shallow coral heads close to shore, and admiring the impossibly turquoise-blue waters. **Governor's Beach,** a beautiful crescent of powder-soft sand and shallow, calm turquoise waters that fronts the official British Governor's residence, called Waterloo, is framed by tall casuarina trees that provide plenty of natural shade. On days when ships are in port, the beach is lined with lounge chairs. For more of a beachcombing experience, **Little Bluff Point Beach,** just west of the Grand Turk Lighthouse, is a low, limestone-cliff-edged, shell-covered beach that looks out onto shallow waters, mangroves, and often flamingos, especially in spring and summer. **Pillory Beach,** with sparkling neon turquoise water, is the prettiest beach on Grand Turk; it also has great off-the-beach snorkeling.

WHERE TO EAT

$ **✕ Jack's Shack.** For a more local
AMERICAN feel, walk 500 meters down the
beach from the cruise terminal and
you'll find Jack's Shack. This beach
bar gets lively with volleyball, and
offers chair rentals and tropical
drinks. Casual food such as burgers
and hot dogs satisfy your hunger.

WATER
Tap water on your ship is perfectly safe to drink; purchasing bottled water is only necessary if you prefer the taste.

Print a coupon from the Web site for a free shot of T&C's local rum,
Bamberra. ✉ *500 meters north of cruise terminal, Grand Turk Cruise
Port Terminal* ☎ *649/232–0099* ⌂ *Open when ship is at port* ▭ *AE,
MC, V* ☉ *Closed anytime a ship is not in port.*

$$ **✕ Jimmy Buffet's Margaritaville.** The only chain restaurant (so far) in all
AMERICAN of the Turks and Caicos is the place to partake in cruise activities even
when you're not on a cruise ship. One of the largest Margaritavilles in
the world is at the Grand Turk Cruise Terminal and open to all com-
ers (both cruisers and anyone else on the island) when a cruise ship is
parked at the dock. Tables are scattered around a large winding pool;
there's even a DJ and a FlowRider (a wave pool where you can surf
on land—for a fee). You can enjoy 52 flavors of margaritas or the res-
taurant's own beer, Landshark, while you eat casual bar food such as
wings, quesadillas, and burgers. The food is good, the people-watch-
ing is great. ✉ *Grand Turk Cruise Terminal* ☎ *649/946–1880* ⊕ *www.
margaritavillecaribbean.com* ▭ *AE, D, DC, MC, V* ☉ *Closed when no
cruise ship is at pier.*

GRENADA (ST. GEORGE'S)

Jane E. Zarem   Nutmeg, cinnamon, cloves, cocoa . . . those heady aromas fill the air in
Grenada (pronounced gruh-*nay*-da). Only 21 mi (33½ km) long and
12 mi (19½ km) wide, the Isle of Spice is a tropical gem of lush rain
forests, white-sand beaches, secluded coves, exotic flowers, and
locally grown spices to fill anyone's kitchen cabinet. St. George's is one
of the most picturesque capital cities in the Caribbean, St. George's
Harbour is one of the most picturesque harbors, and Grenada's Grand
Anse Beach is one of the region's finest beaches. The island has friendly,
hospitable people and enough good shopping, restaurants, historic sites,
and natural wonders to make it a popular port of call. About one-third
of Grenada's visitors arrive by cruise ship, and that number continues
to grow each year.

ESSENTIALS

CURRENCY   Eastern Caribbean (E.C.) dollar (EC$2.67 to US$1). U.S. dollars (but not coins) are
generally accepted, but change is given in E.C. currency.

INTERNET   **Java-Kool Internet Cafe** (✉ *The Carenage, St. George's* ☎ *473/435–3506*).

TELEPHONE   Prepaid phone cards, which can be used in special card phones throughout
the Caribbean for local or international calls, are sold in various denominations
at shops, attractions, transportation centers, and other convenient outlets. For

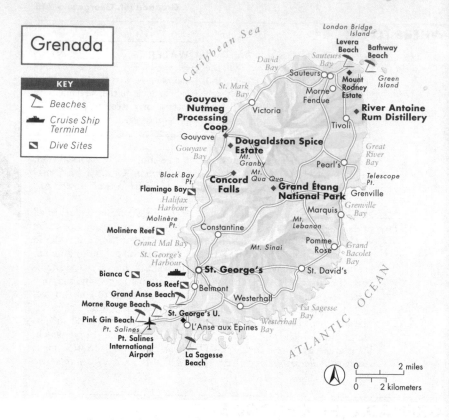

Grenada

KEY

Beaches

Cruise Ship Terminal

Dive Sites

international calls using a major credit card, dial 111; to place a collect call or use a calling card, dial 800/225–5872 from any telephone. Pay phones are available at the Cruise Ship Terminal welcome center, the LIME office on the Carenage in St. George's, shopping centers, and other convenient locations.

COMING ASHORE

The Cruise Ship Terminal near Market Square, on the north side of St. George's, allows larger ships to dock rather than anchor outside the harbor. A full range of passenger facilities is available at the terminal, which opens directly into the Esplanade Mall. You can easily tour the capital on foot, but be prepared to climb up and down steep hills. If you don't want to walk up and down through town, you can find a taxi ($3 or $4 each way) or a water taxi ($2 per person each way) right at the terminal to take you around to the Carenage. To explore areas outside St. George's, hiring a taxi or arranging a guided tour is more sensible than renting a car. Taxis are plentiful, and fixed rates to popular island destinations are posted at the terminal's welcome center.

A taxi ride from the terminal to the beach will cost $13, but water taxis are a less expensive and more picturesque way to get there; the one-way fare is about $6 per person to Grand Anse, depending on the number of passengers. Minibuses are the least expensive way to travel between St. George's and Grand Anse; pay EC$1.50 (55¢), but hold on to your hat. They're crowded with local people getting from here to there and often make quick stops and take turns at quite a clip! Still, it's an inexpensive, fun, and safe way to travel around the island. If you want to rent a car and explore on your own, be prepared to pay $12 for a temporary driving permit and about $55 to $75 for a day's car rental.

EXPLORING GRENADA

★ **Concord Falls.** About 8 mi (13 km) north of St. George's, a turnoff from the West Coast Road leads to Concord Falls—actually three separate waterfalls. The first is at the end of the road; when the currents aren't too strong, you can take a dip under the cascade. Reaching the two other waterfalls requires an hour's hike into the forest reserve. The third and most spectacular waterfall, at Fountainbleu, thunders 65 feet over huge boulders and creates a small pool. It's smart to hire a guide. The path is clear, but slippery boulders toward the end can be treacherous without assistance. ⊠ *Off West Coast Rd., St. John* ⌂ *Changing room $2* ⊙ *Daily 9–5.*

♻ **Dougaldston Spice Estate.** Just south of Gouyave, this historic plantation, now primarily a living museum, still grows and processes spices the old-fashioned way. You can see cocoa, nutmeg, mace, cloves, and other spices laid out on giant racks to dry in the sun. A worker will be glad to explain the process (and will appreciate a small donation). You can buy spices for about $2 a bag. ⊠ *Gouyave, St. John* ☎ *No phone* ⌂ *Free* ⊙ *Weekdays 9–4.*

♻ **Gouyave Nutmeg Processing Cooperative.** Touring the nutmeg-processing
★ co-op, in the center of the west-coast fishing village of Gouyave (pronounced *gwahv*), is a fragrant, fascinating way to spend half an hour. You can learn all about nutmeg and its uses, see the nutmegs laid out in bins, and watch the workers sort them by hand and pack them into burlap bags for shipping worldwide. The three-story plant turned out 3 million pounds of Grenada's most famous export each year before Hurricane Ivan's devastating effect on the crop in 2004, when most of the nutmeg trees were destroyed. Locals estimate it will be 2014 before the nutmeg industry returns to that level. It took about a year to source a large amount of new plants, and nutmeg trees take between 7 and 10 years to produce at economically viable levels. ⊠ *Gouyave, St. John* ☎ *473/444–8337* ⌂ *$1* ⊙ *Weekdays 10–1 and 2–4.*

♻ **Grand Étang National Park & Forest Reserve.** Deep in the mountainous
★ interior of Grenada is a bird sanctuary and forest reserve with miles of hiking trails, lookouts, and fishing streams. **Grand Étang Lake** is a 36-acre expanse of cobalt-blue water that fills the crater of an extinct volcano 1,740 feet above sea level. Although legend has it the lake is bottomless, maximum soundings are recorded at 18 feet. The informative **Grand Étang Forest Center** has displays on the local wildlife and vegetation. A forest manager is on hand to answer questions. A small snack bar and souvenir stands are nearby. ⊠ *Main interior road,*

between Grenville and St. George's, St. Andrew ☎ 473/440–6160 ☞ $1 ⊙ Daily 8:30–4.

River Antoine Rum Distillery. At this rustic operation, kept open primarily as a museum, a limited quantity of Rivers rum is produced by the same methods used since the distillery opened in 1785. The process begins with the crushing of sugarcane from adjacent fields. The result is a potent overproof rum, sold only in Grenada, that will knock your socks off. ✉ River Antoine Estate, St. Patrick ☎ 473/442–7109 ☞ $2 ⊙ Guided tours daily 9–4.

St. George's. Grenada's capital is a bustling West Indian city, most of which remains unchanged from colonial days. Narrow streets lined with shops wind up, down, and across steep hills. Brick warehouses and small shops cling to the waterfront, and pastel-painted homes rise from the waterfront and disappear into steep green hills.

GRENADA BEST BETS

■ **The Beach.** Grand Anse Beach is one of the Caribbean's most beautiful.

■ **Deep-Sea Fishing.** Fishing is excellent in the waters around Grenada.

■ **Market Square.** Market Square is a bustling produce and spice market.

■ **Nutmeg.** Don't miss a visit to a nutmeg cooperative (and get a pocketful to take home).

■ **Waterfalls.** Concord Falls, just south of Gouyave, and Annandale Falls are among the island's most spectacular.

Picturesque **St. George's Harbour,** a submerged volcanic crater, is arguably the prettiest harbor in the Caribbean and the center of town. Schooners, ferries, and tour boats tie up along the seawall or at the small dinghy dock. The **Carenage** (pronounced car-a-*nahzh*), which surrounds horseshoe-shaped St. George's Harbour, is the capital's main thoroughfare. Warehouses, shops, and restaurants line the waterfront. The *Christ of the Deep* statue that sits on the pedestrian plaza at the center of the Carenage was presented to Grenada by Costa Cruise Line in remembrance of its ship *Bianca C,* which burned and sank in the harbor in 1961 and is now a favorite dive site.

The **Grenada National Museum** (✉ Young and Monckton Sts. ☎ 473/440–3725 ☞ $1 ⊙ Weekdays 9–4:30, Sat. 10–1), a block from the Carenage, is built on the foundation of a French army barracks and prison that was originally built in 1704. The small museum has exhibitions of news items, photos, and proclamations relating to the 1983 intervention, along with the childhood bathtub of Empress Joséphine (who was born on Martinique), and other memorabilia.

Ft. George (✉ Church St.) is high on the hill at the entrance to St. George's Harbour. It's Grenada's oldest fort—built by the French in 1705 to protect the harbor. No shots were ever fired here until October 1983, when Prime Minister Maurice Bishop and some of his followers were assassinated in the courtyard. The fort now houses police headquarters but is open to the public daily; admission is free. The 360-degree view of the capital city, St. George's Harbour, and the open sea is spectacular.

An engineering feat for its time, the 340-foot-long **Sendall Tunnel** was built in 1895 and named for an early governor. It connects the harbor side of St. George's to the Esplanade on the bay side of town, where you can find the markets (produce, meat, and fish), the Cruise Ship Terminal, the Esplanade Mall, and the public bus station.

Don't miss St. George's **Market Square** (✉ *Granby St.*), a block from the Cruise Ship Terminal. It's open every weekday morning, but

> ## ID CASES
>
> You can keep track of your boarding pass, shipboard charge/key card, and picture ID when you go ashore by slipping them into a bi-fold business-card carrying case. Cases with a sueded finish are less likely to fall out of your pocket. With security as tight as it is these days, you don't want to lose your ID.

really comes alive on Saturday from 8 to noon. Vendors sell baskets, spices, brooms, clothing, knickknacks, coconut water, and heaps of fresh produce. A continuing renovation project is increasingly providing permanent cover for the vendors. Historically, Market Square is where parades begin and political rallies take place.

Overlooking the city of St. George's and the inland side of the harbor, historic **Ft. Frederick** (✉ *Richmond Hill*) provides a panoramic view of two-thirds of Grenada. The fort was started by the French and completed in 1791 by the British; it was also the headquarters of the People's Revolutionary Government during the 1983 coup. Today you can get a bird's-eye view of much of Grenada from here.

SHOPPING

Grenada's best souvenirs or gifts for friends back home are spice baskets filled with cinnamon, nutmeg, mace, bay leaves, cloves, turmeric, and ginger. You can buy them for as little as $3 and up to $10 in practically every shop, at the open-air produce market at **Market Square** in St. George's, at the vendor stalls near the pier, and at the **Vendor's Craft and Spice Market** on Grand Anse Beach. Vendors also sell handmade fabric dolls, coral jewelry, seashells, and hats and baskets handwoven from green palm fronds. Bargaining is not appropriate in the shops, and it isn't customary with vendors—although most will offer you "a good price."

ACTIVITIES

DIVING AND SNORKELING

You can see hundreds of varieties of fish and some 40 species of coral at more than a dozen sites off Grenada's southwest coast—only 15 to 20 minutes by boat—and another couple of dozen sites around Carriacou's reefs and neighboring islets. Depths vary from 20 to 120 feet, and visibility varies from 30 to 100 feet.

A spectacular dive is *Bianca C,* a 600-foot cruise ship that caught fire in 1961, sank to 100 feet, and is now encrusted with coral and serves as a habitat for giant turtles, spotted eagle rays, barracuda, and jacks. **Boss**

Reef extends 5 mi (8 km) from St. George's Harbour to Point Salines, with a depth ranging from 20 to 90 feet. **Flamingo Bay** has a wall that drops to 90 feet and is teeming with fish, sponges, sea horses, sea fans, and coral. **Molinère Reef** slopes from about 20 feet below the surface to a wall that drops to 65 feet. It's a good dive for beginners, and advanced divers can continue farther out to view the wreck of the *Buccaneer*, a 42-foot sloop.

Aquanauts Grenada (⊠ *Spice Island Beach Resort, Grand Anse Beach, Grand Anse, St. George* ☎ *473/444–1126, 888/446–9235 in U.S.*) has a multilingual staff, so instruction is available in English, German, Dutch, French, and Spanish. Two-tank dive trips, accommodating no more than eight divers, are offered each morning to both the Caribbean and Atlantic sides of Grenada. **EcoDive** (⊠ *Coyaba Beach Resort, Grand Anse, St. George* ☎ *473/444–7777* ⊕ *www.ecodiveandtrek.com*) offers two dive trips daily, both drift and wreck dives, as well as weekly trips to dive Isle de Rhonde. The company also runs Grenada's marine conservation and education center, which conducts coral-reef monitoring and turtle projects.

FISHING

Deep-sea fishing around Grenada is excellent, with marlin, sailfish, yellowfin tuna, and dolphin fish topping the list of good catches. You can arrange sportfishing trips that accommodate up to five people starting at $375 for a half day and $580 for a full day. **True Blue Sportfishing** (☎ *473/444–2048* ⊕ *www.yesaye.com*) offers big-game charters on its 31-foot *Yes Aye*. It has an enclosed cabin, a fighting chair, and professional tackle. British-born Captain Gary Clifford, who has been fishing since the age of 6, has run the company since 1998. Refreshments and courtesy transport are included.

BEACHES

Bathway Beach. A broad strip of sand with a natural reef that protects swimmers from the rough Atlantic surf on Grenada's far northern shore, this Levera National Park beach has changing rooms at the park headquarters. ⊠ *Levera, St. Patrick's.*

Fodor'sChoice ★ **Grand Anse Beach.** In the southwest, about 3 mi (5 km) south of St. George's, Grenada's loveliest and most popular beach is a gleaming 2-mi (3-km) semicircle of white sand lapped by clear, gentle surf. Sea grape trees and coconut palms provide shady escapes from the sun. Brilliant rainbows frequently spill into the sea from the high green mountains that frame St. George's Harbour to the north. The Grand Anse Craft and Spice Market is at the midpoint of the beach. ⊠ *Grand Anse, St. George's.*

WHERE TO EAT

Restaurants add an 8% government tax to your bill and usually add a 10% service charge; if not, tip 10% to 15% for a job well done.

$$ ✕**Belmont Estate.** Luncheon is served! If you're visiting the northern
CARIBBEAN reaches of Grenada island, plan to stop for lunch at Belmont Estate,
☺ a 400-year-old working nutmeg and cocoa plantation. Settle into the
★ breezy open-air dining room, which overlooks enormous trays of nut-
meg, cocoa, and mace drying in the sunshine. A waiter will offer some
refreshing local juice and a choice of callaloo or pumpkin soup. Then
head to the buffet and help yourself to salad, rice, stewed chicken, beef
curry, stewed fish, and vegetables. Dessert may be homemade ice cream,
ginger cake, or another delicious confection. Afterward, feel free to take
a tour of the museum, cocoa fermentary, sugarcane garden, and old
cemetery. Farm animals (and a couple of monkeys) roam the property,
and there's often folk music and dancing on the lawn. ⊠ *Belmont, St.
Patrick* ☎ *473/442–9524* ⊕ *www.belmontestate.net* ⊟ *MC, V* ⊗ *Closed
Sat. No dinner.*

$–$$$ ✕**Coconut Beach Restaurant.** Take local seafood, add butter, wine, and Gre-
CARIBBEAN nadian spices, and you have excellent French-creole cuisine. Throw in a
beautiful location on Grand Anse Beach, and this West Indian cottage
becomes a perfect alfresco spot. Lobster is a specialty, as lobster ther-
midor or perhaps wrapped in a crepe, dipped in garlic butter, or added
to pasta. Homemade coconut pie is a winner for dessert. Dine "wet
or fine," at a table on the beach or inside. On Wednesday and Sunday
nights in season, dinner is a beach barbecue with live music. ⊠ *Grand
Anse, St. George* ☎ *473/444–4644* ⊕ *www.coconutbeachgrenada.com*
⊟ *AE, D, MC, V* ⊗ *Closed Tues.*

GUADELOUPE (POINTE-À-PITRE)

Eileen Robin- On a map, Guadeloupe looks like a giant butterfly resting on the
son Smith sea between Antigua and Dominica. Its two wings—Basse-Terre
and Grande-Terre—are the two largest islands in the 659-square-mi
(1,054-square-km) Guadeloupe archipelago. The Rivière Salée, a 4-mi
(6-km) channel between the Caribbean and the Atlantic, forms the
"spine" of the butterfly. A drawbridge near Pointe-à-Pitre, the main city,
connects the two islands. Gorgeous scenery awaits, as Guadeloupe is
one of the most physically attractive islands in the Caribbean. If you're
seeking a resort atmosphere, casinos, and nearly white sandy beaches,
your target is Grande-Terre. On the other hand, Basse-Terre's Parc
National de la Guadeloupe, laced with trails and washed by waterfalls
and rivers, is a 74,100-acre haven for hikers, nature lovers, and anyone
brave enough to peer into the steaming crater of an active volcano. The
tropical beauty suggests the mythical Garden of Eden.

ESSENTIALS

CURRENCY The euro (€1 to US$1.31). Some of the larger liquor and jewelry stores may
accept dollars, but don't count on that. You cannot cash traveler's checks or dollars at the bank, only at a bureau de change, so ATMs are your best bet if you
need euros; facing the tourist office, there is one just to the right at the bank.

INTERNET Pointe-à-Pitre has several Internet cafés (there is one right at the new cruise
pier); the tourist office can point you in the direction of several more in the
immediate vicinity.

Guadeloupe

KEY

Beaches

Cruise Ship Terminal

Dive Sites

Guadeloupe Passage

La Pointe de la Grande Vigie

ATLANTIC OCEAN

Pte. Allègre

La Grande-Anse

Anse Bertrand

Port Louis

Campêche

Gros-Cap

Petit-Canal

Vieux-Bourg

G R A N D E

Deshaies

Ste-Rose

Morne-à-l'Eau

Le Moule

Anse de la Gourde

La Désirade Grande-Anse

Pointe-à-Pitre

Pointe-Noire

Lamentin

Abymes

T E R R E

Pointe Tarare

BASSE Destrelan

St-François

Ft. Fleur d'Épée

Ste-Anne

Mahaut

Cascade aux Ecrevisses

Gosier

Plage du Helleux

TO LA DÉSIRADE

Ilet de Pigeon

Les Mamelles

Plage Caravelle

Pigeon Island

Petit-Bourg

Ilet du Gosier

Iles de la Petite Terre

Malendure

Parc National

de Guadeloupe

Aquarium de la Guadeloupe

Bouillante

T E R R E

Ste-Marie

Vieux-Habitants

La Soufrière

Capesterre-Belle-Eau

Basse-Terre

Trois-Rivières

Saint Louis

Marie-Galante

Caribbean Sea

Vieux Fort

Grand-Bourg

Petite-Anse

Terre-de-Bas

Iles des Saintes (Les Saintes)

0   10 miles

0   10 kilometers

TELEPHONE To call the United States from Guadeloupe, dial 001, the area code, and the local number. For calls within Guadeloupe, you now have to put 0590 before the six-digit number. You'll need to purchase a *télécarte* at the post office or at tobacco and grocery shops in order to use the phone booths.

COMING ASHORE

Ships now dock at the new cruise terminal at Pier 5/6, which houses an Internet café, a duty-free shop, and the colorful Karuland Village, where cruisers can browse and buy spices, pareos, and souvenirs or just sit and listen to the local music while having coconut ice cream. In downtown Pointe-à-Pitre, it is about a five-minute walk from the shopping district. Passengers are greeted by local musicians and hostesses, usually dressed in the traditional madras costumes—and often dispensing samplings of local rum and creole specialties. These multilingual staffers operate the information booth and can pair you up with an English-speaking taxi driver for a customized island tour. To get to the main tourist office, walk along the quay to the Place de la Victoire; it is a large white Victorian building with wraparound veranda.

Taxi fares are regulated by the government (but expensive) and posted at taxi stands. Renting a car is a good way to see Guadeloupe, but it is expensive and best booked in advance. Be aware that traffic around Pointe-à-Pitre can be dreadful during rush hour, so allow plenty of time to drop off your car rental and get back to the ship. There are many rental agencies at the airport, but that is a €35 taxi ride from the city.

EXPLORING GUADELOUPE

☺ **Aquarium de la Guadeloupe.** Unique in the Antilles, this aquarium in the marina near Pointe-à-Pitre is a good place to spend an hour. The well-planned facility has an assortment of tropical fish, crabs, lobsters, moray eels, coffer fish, and some live coral. It's also a fascinating turtle rescue center and a spectacular shark tank. ⊠ *Pl. Créole off rte. N4, Pointe-à-Pitre* ☎ *0590/90–92–38* ☎ *€9* ☉ *Daily 9–7.*

Ft. Fleur d'Épée. The main attraction in Bas-du-Fort is this 18th-century fortress, which hunkers down on a hillside behind a deep moat. It was the scene of hard-fought battles between the French and the English in 1794. You can explore its well-preserved dungeons and battlements and take in a sweeping view of Iles des Saintes and Marie-Galante. ⊠ *Bas-du-Fort* ☎ *0590/90–94–61* ☎ *€6* ☉ *Mon. 10–5, Tues.–Sun. 9–5.*

★ **Parc National de la Guadeloupe.** This 74,100-acre park has been recognized by UNESCO as a Biosphere Reserve. Before going, pick up a *Guide to the National Park* from the tourist office; it rates the hiking trails according to difficulty, and most are quite difficult indeed. Most mountain trails are in the southern half. The park is bisected by the route de la Traversée, a 16-mi (26-km) paved road lined with masses of tree ferns, shrubs, flowers, tall trees, and green plantains. It's the ideal point of entry. Wear rubber-soled shoes and take along a swimsuit, a sweater, and perhaps food for a picnic. Try to get an early start to stay ahead of the hordes of cruise-ship passengers making a day of it. Check on the weather; if Basse-Terre has had a lot of rain, give it up. In the past, rockslides have closed the road for months after intense rainfall.

Within Parc National de la Guadeloupe, **Cascade aux Ecrevisses** is one of the island's loveliest (and most popular) spots. There's a marked trail (walk carefully—the rocks can be slippery) leading to this splendid waterfall, which dashes down into the Corossol River—a good place for a dip. Come early, though; otherwise you definitely won't have it to yourself. ⊠ *Administrative Headquarters, rte. de la Traversée, St-Claude* ☎ *0590/80–86–00* ⊛ *www.guadeloupe-parcnational. com* ☎ *Free* ☉ *Weekdays 8–5:30.*

Pointe-à-Pitre. Although not the capital, this is the island's largest city, a commercial and industrial hub in the southwest of Grande-Terre. The

GUADELOUPE BEST BETS

■ **Beaches.** The southern coast of Grand-Terre has stretches of soft, nearly white sand.

■ **Diving.** Jacques Cousteau called the reef off Pigeon Island one of the world's top dive sites.

■ **Hiking.** The Parc National de la Guadeloupe is one of the Caribbean's most spectacular scenic destinations.

■ **Shopping.** Though Point-à-Pitre itself can be frenetic, it does have a good choice of French goods.

Isles of Guadeloupe have 450,000 inhabitants, 99.6% of whom live in the cities. Pointe-à-Pitre is bustling, noisy, and hot—a place of honking horns and traffic jams and cars on sidewalks for want of a parking place. By day its pulse is fast, but at night, when its streets are almost deserted, you don't want to be there.

The city has suffered severe damage over the years from earthquakes, fires, and hurricanes. In recent years it took heavy hits by hurricanes Frederick (1979), David (1980), and Hugo (1989). On one side of rue Frébault you can see the remaining French colonial structures; on the other, the modern city. Some of the downtown area has been rejuvenated. An impressive terminal serves the ferries that depart for Iles des Saintes, Marie-Galante, Dominica, Martinique, and St. Lucia.

The heart of the old city is Place de la Victoire; surrounded by wooden buildings with balconies and shutters (including the tourism office) and by sidewalk cafés, it was named in honor of Victor Hugues's 1794 victory over the British. During the French Revolution, Hugues ordered the guillotine set up here so that the public could witness the bloody end of 300 recalcitrant royalists.

Even more colorful is the bustling marketplace, between rues St-John Perse, Frébault, Schoelcher, and Peynier. It's a cacophonous place, where housewives bargain for spices, herbs (and herbal remedies), and a bright assortment of papayas, breadfruits, christophenes, and tomatoes.

For fans of French ecclesiastical architecture, there's the imposing **Cathédrale de St-Pierre et St-Paul** (⊠ *Rue Alexandre Isaac at rue de l'Eglise*), built in 1807. Although battered by hurricanes, it has fine stained-glass windows and creole-style balconies and is reinforced with pillars and ribs that look like leftovers from the Eiffel Tower.

Anyone with an interest in French literature and culture (not your average sightseer) won't want to miss the **Musée St-John Perse,** which is dedicated to Guadeloupe's most famous son and one of the giants of world literature, Alexis Léger, better known as St-John Perse, winner of the Nobel Prize for literature in 1960. Some of his finest poems are inspired by the history and landscape—particularly the sea—of his beloved Guadeloupe. The museum contains a collection of his poetry and some of his personal belongings. Before you go, look for his birthplace at 54 rue Achille René-Boisneuf. ⊠ *At rues Noizières and Achille René-Boisneuf* ☎ *0590/90–01–92* 🖾 *€2.50* ☉ *Thurs.–Tues. 8:30–12:30 and 2:30–5:30.*

Musée Schoelcher celebrates Victor Schoelcher, a high-minded abolitionist from Alsace who fought against slavery in the French West Indies in the 19th century. The museum contains many of his personal effects, and exhibits trace his life and work. ⊠ *24 rue Peynier* ☎ *0590/82–08–04* 🖾 *€3* ☉ *Weekdays 9–5.*

SHOPPING

For serious shopping in Pointe-à-Pitre, browse the boutiques and stores along rue Schoelcher, rue Frébault, and rue Noizières. The multicolored market square and stalls of La Darse are filled mostly with vegetables, fruits, delicious homemade rum liqueurs, and housewares. The air is filled with the fragrance of spices, and they have lovely gift baskets of spices and vanilla lined with madras fabric.

ACTIVITIES

DIVING

The main diving area at the **Cousteau Underwater Park,** just off Basse-Terre near Pigeon Island, offers routine dives to 60 feet. The numerous glass-bottom boats and other crafts make the site feel like a marine parking lot; however, the underwater sights are spectacular. Guides and instructors are certified under the French CMAS (some also have PADI, but none have NAUI). Most operators offer two-hour dives three times per day for about €45 to €50 per dive; three-dive packages are €120 to €145. Hotels and dive operators usually rent snorkeling gear.

🌼 **Les Heures Saines** (✉ *Le Rocher de Malendure, Plage de Malendure, Bouillante, Basse-Terre* ☎ *0590/98–86–63* ⊕ *www.heures-saines.gp*) is the premier operator for dives in the Cousteau Underwater Park. Trips to Les Saintes offer one or two dives for average and advanced divers, with plenty of time for lunch and sightseeing. Wreck, night, and Nitrox diving are also available. The instructors, many of them English speakers, are excellent with children. The company also offers winter whale- and dolphin-watching trips with marine biologists as guides. These tours, aboard a 60-foot catamaran, cost €55, less for children.

HIKING

Fodor's Choice ★ With hundreds of trails and countless rivers and waterfalls, the **Parc National de la Guadeloupe** on Basse-Terre is the main draw for hikers. Some of the trails should be attempted only with an experienced guide. All tend to be muddy, so wear a good pair of boots. Know that even the young and fit can find these outings arduous; the unfit may find them painful. Start off slowly, with a shorter hike, and then go for the gusto. All water sports—even canoeing and kayaking—are forbidden in the center of the park. Scientists are studying the impact of these activities on the park's ecosystem. It will retain its prestigious award for ongoing sustainable tourism development, given by the EUROPARC Federation, until the year 2012.

Vert Intense (✉ *Route de la Soufrière, Mourne Houel, Basse-Terre* ☎ *0590/99–34–73 or 0690/55–40–47* ⊕ *www.vert-intense.com*) organizes fascinating hikes in the national park and to the volcano. You move from steaming hot springs to an icy waterfall in the same hike. Guides are patient and safety-conscious, and can bring you to heights that you never thought you could reach, including the top of Le Soufrière. The volcano hike costs only €30, but must be booked four days in advance. A mixed-adventure package spanning three days costs €225. The two-day bivouac and other adventures can be extreme sport, so before you decide to play Indiana Jones, know what is expected. The French-speaking guides, who also know some English and Spanish, can take you to other tropical forests and rivers, where the sport of canyoning can still be practiced. If you are just one or two people, the company can team you up with a group.

BEACHES

★ **Plage Caravelle.** Just southwest of Ste-Anne is one of Grande-Terre's longest and prettiest stretches of sand, the occasional dilapidated shack notwithstanding. Protected by reefs, it's also a fine snorkeling spot. Club Med occupies one end of this beach, and nonguests can enjoy its beach and water sports, as well as lunch and drinks, by buying a day pass. You can also have lunch at La Toubana, then descend the stairs to the beach below. ✉ *Rte. N4, southwest of Ste-Anne.*

La Grande-Anse. One of Guadeloupe's widest beaches has soft beige sand sheltered by palms. To the west it's a round verdant mountain. There's a large parking area and some food stands, but no other facilities. The beach can be overrun on Sunday, not to mention littered. Right after the parking lot, you can see signage for the creole restaurant Le Karacoli; if you have lunch there (it's not inexpensive), you can *sieste* on the chaise longues. ✉ *Rte. N6, north of Deshaies.*

Malendure. Across from Pigeon Island and Jacques Cousteau Underwater Park, this long, gray volcanic beach on the Caribbean's calm waters has restrooms, a few beach shacks offering cold drinks and snacks, and a huge parking lot. Don't come here for solitude, as the beach is the starting-off point for dive boats, sportfishing boats, glass-bottom boats, and whale-watching vessels. If you're scheduled to do any of the above, you can hang here afterward. Snorkeling from the beach is good. Le Rocher de Malendure, a fine seafood restaurant, is perched on a cliff over the bay. ✉ *Rte. N6, Bouillante.*

WHERE TO EAT

¢–$$ ✕ **Caraïbes Café.** This sidewalk café straight out of Paris is the "in" place
CAFÉ   for lunch and also a spot for a quick breakfast, a fresh juice cocktail—try *corossel* (a tropical fruit) and mango juices, a cappuccino, *un coupe* (a sundae), or a pastis while you people-watch and listen to French crooners. The *formule* (fixed-price menu) is always the best deal. Service is fast and friendly, and can even be in English. ✉ *Pl. de la Victoire, Pointe-à-Pitre* ☎ *0590/82–92–23* ▭ *MC, V* ⊘ *Closed Sun. No dinner.*

$$–$$$ ✕ **Le Rocher de Malendure.** Guests first climb the worn yellow stairs for
FRENCH   the panoramic sea views, but return again and again for the food. If
★   you arrive before noon, when the divers pull in, you might snag one of the primo tables in a gazebo that literally hangs over the Caribbean. Begin with a perfectly executed mojito. With fish just off the boat, don't hesitate to try the sushi *antillaise* or grilled crayfish and lobster from the pool. ✉ *Bord de Mer, Malendure de Pigeon, Bouillante* ☎ *0590/98–70–84* ▭ *AE, MC, V* ⊘ *Closed Wed. and Sept.–early Oct.*

KEY WEST, FLORIDA

Chelle Koster Walton

Along with the rest of Florida, Key West—the southernmost city in the continental United States—became part of American territory in 1821. In the late 19th century it was Florida's wealthiest city per capita. The locals made their fortunes from "wrecking"—rescuing people and

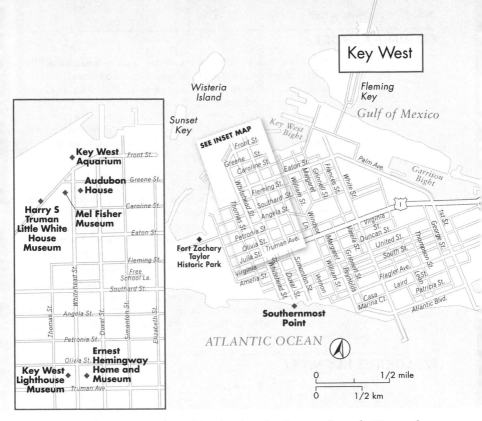

salvaging cargo from ships that foundered on nearby reefs. Cigar making, fishing, shrimping, and sponge gathering also became important industries. Capital of the self-proclaimed "Conch Republic," Key West today makes for a unique port of call. A genuinely American town, it nevertheless exudes the relaxed atmosphere and pace of a typical Caribbean island. Major attractions include the home of the Conch Republic's most famous residents, Ernest Hemingway and Harry Truman; the imposing Key West Museum of Art and History, a former U.S. Customs House and site of the military inquest of the USS *Maine*; and the island's renowned sunset celebrations.

ESSENTIALS

CURRENCY The U.S. dollar.

INTERNET Get your morning (or afternoon) buzz at **Coffee Plantation** (⊠ *713 Caroline St.* ☎ *305/295–9808* ⊕ *www.coffeeplantationkeywest.com*), where you can also hook up to the Internet in the comfort of a homelike setting in a circa-1890 Conch house. Poets, writers, and minstrels sometimes show up to perform while you munch pastries or luncheon sandwiches and wraps and sip your hot or cold espresso beverage.

TELEPHONE You'll be able to find plenty of public phones around Mallory Square. They're also along the major tourist thoroughfares.

COMING ASHORE

Cruise ships dock at three different locations. Mallory Square and Pier B are within walking distance of Duval and Whitehead streets, the two main tourist thoroughfares. Passengers on ships that dock at Outer Mole Pier (aka Navy Mole) are shuttled via Conch Train or Old Town Trolley to Duval and Front streets. At this writing, the tented passenger facilities at Outer Mole were being replaced by four permanent shelters to be completed by fall 2010. The adjacent Truman Waterfront project, with no estimated timeline at this point, will eventually add recreation facilities, including a marina.

Because Key West is so easily explored on foot, there is rarely a need to hire a taxi. If you plan to venture beyond the main tourist district, a fun way to get around is by bicycle or scooter (bike rentals begin at about $12 per day). Key West is a cycling town. In fact, there are so many bikes around that cyclists must watch out for one another as much as for cars. You can get tourist information from the Greater Key West Chamber of Commerce, which is just off Mallory Square.

The Conch Tour Train can be boarded at Mallory Square or Flagler Station every half-hour; it costs $29 per adult for the 90-minute tour. The Old Town Trolley operates trolley-style buses starting from Mallory Square every 30 minutes for the same price, but the smaller trolleys go places the train won't fit.

EXPLORING KEY WEST

Audubon House and Tropical Gardens. If you've ever seen an engraving by ornithologist John James Audubon, you'll understand why his name is synonymous with birds. See his works in this three-story house, which was built in the 1840s for Captain John Geiger and filled with period furniture. It now commemorates Audubon's 1832 stop in Key West while he was traveling through Florida to study birds. A children's room makes his work accessible to youngsters. Docents lead a guided tour that points out the rare indigenous plants and trees in the garden. An art gallery sells lithographs of the artist's famed portraits. ⊠ *205 White-head St.* ☎ *305/294–2116 or 877/294–2470* ⊕ *www.audubonhouse. com* 💲 *$11* ☉ *Daily 9:30–5, last tour starts at 4:30.*

★ **Ernest Hemingway Home and Museum.** Amusing anecdotes spice up the guided tours of Ernest Hemingway's home, built in 1801 by the town's most successful wrecker. While living here between 1931 and 1942, Hemingway wrote about 70% of his life's work, including classics like *For Whom the Bell Tolls.* Few of his belongings remain aside from some books, and there's little about his actual work, but photographs help you visualize his day-to-day life. The supposed six-toed descendants of Hemingway's cats—many named for actors, artists, authors, and even a hurricane—have free rein of the property. Tours begin every 10 minutes and take 25–30 minutes; then you're free to explore on your own. ⊠ *907 Whitehead St.* ☎ *305/294–1136* ⊕ *www.hemingwayhome. com* 💲 *$12* ☉ *Daily 9–5.*

★ **Fort Zachary Taylor Historic State Park.** Construction of the fort began in 1845, but was halted during the Civil War. Even though Florida seceded from the Union, Yankee forces used the fort as a base to block Confederate shipping. More than 1,500 Confederate vessels were detained in Key West's harbor. The fort, finally completed in 1866, was also used in the Spanish-American War. Take a 30-minute guided walking tour of the fort, a National Historic Landmark, at noon and 2. In February a celebration called Civil War Heritage Days includes costumed reenactments and demonstrations. From mid-January to mid-April the park serves as an open-air gallery for pieces created for Sculpture Key West. One of its most popular features is its man-made beach. ✉ *Box 6565; end of Southard St., through Truman Annex* ☎ *305/292–6713* ⊕ *www. floridastateparks.org/forttaylor* ✑ *$4.50 for 1 person, $7 for 2 people, 50¢ per additional person* ⊙ *Daily 8–sunset, tours noon and 2.*

> **KEY WEST BEST BETS**
>
> ■ **Boat Cruise.** Being out on the water is what Key West is all about.
>
> ■ **Conch Train.** Hop aboard for a narrated tour of the town's tawdry past and rare architectural treasures.
>
> ■ **Hemingway.** Visit Ernest Hemingway's historic home for a literary treat.
>
> ■ **Duval Crawl.** Shop, eat, drink, repeat.
>
> ■ **Sunset in Mallory Square.** The nightly street party is the quintessential Key West experience.

Harry S. Truman Little White House Museum. Recent renovations to this circa-1890 landmark have restored the home and gardens to the Truman era, down to the wallpaper pattern. A free photographic review of visiting dignitaries and presidents—John F. Kennedy, Jimmy Carter, and Bill Clinton are among the chief executives who passed through here—is on display in the back of the gift shop. Engaging 45-minute tours begin every 15 minutes until 4:30. They start with an excellent 10-minute video on the history of the property and Truman's visits. On the grounds of **Truman Annex,** a 103-acre former military parade grounds and barracks, the home served as a winter White House for presidents Truman, Eisenhower, and Kennedy. Note: the tour does require climbing steps. ✉ *111 Front St.* ☎ *305/294–9911* ⊕ *www.trumanlittlewhitehouse.com* ✑ *$12* ⊙ *Daily 9–5, grounds sunrise–6; last tour at 4:30.*

� **Key West Aquarium.** Pet a nurse shark and explore the fascinating underwater realm of the Keys without getting wet at this historic aquarium. Hundreds of tropical fish and enormous sea creatures live here. A touch tank enables you to handle starfish, sea cucumbers, horseshoe and hermit crabs, even horse and queen conchs—living totems of the Conch Republic. Built in 1934 by the Works Progress Administration as the world's first open-air aquarium, most of the building has been enclosed for all-weather viewing. Guided tours, included in the admission price, feature shark feedings. ✉ *1 Whitehead St.* ☎ *305/296–2051* ⊕ *www.keywestaquarium. com* ✑ *$12* ⊙ *Daily 10–6; tours at 11, 1, 3, and 4:30.*

4

Key West Lighthouse Museum & Keeper's Quarters Museum. For the best view in town, climb the 88 steps to the top of this 1847 lighthouse. The 92-foot structure has a Fresnel lens, which was installed in the 1860s at a cost of $1 million. The keeper lived in the adjacent 1887 clapboard house, which now exhibits vintage photographs, ship models, nautical charts, and lighthouse artifacts from all along the Key reefs. ⊠ *938 Whitehead St.* ☎ *305/295–6616* ⊕ *www. kwahs.com* ⊠ *$10* ⊙ *Daily 9:30–5; last admission at 4:30.*

> **USED BOOKS**
>
> Leave any paperback novels you have finished for the crew library. You will have more room in your suitcase, and crewmembers will have fresh reading material.

Fodor's Choice
★ **Key West Museum of Art & History in the Custom House.** When Key West was designated a U.S. port of entry in the early 1820s, a customs house was established. Salvaged cargoes from ships wrecked on the reefs were brought here, setting the stage for Key West to become for a time the richest city in Florida. The imposing redbrick-and–terra-cotta Richardsonian Romanesque–style building reopened as a museum and art gallery in 1999. Smaller galleries have long-term and changing exhibits about the history of Key West, including a Hemingway room and a fine collection of folk artist Mario Sanchez's wood paintings. ⊠ *281 Front St.* ☎ *305/295–6616* ⊕ *www.kwahs.com* ⊠ *$10* ⊙ *Daily 9:30–4:30.*

Mel Fisher Maritime Museum. In 1622 two Spanish galleons laden with riches from South America foundered in a hurricane 40 mi west of the Keys. In 1985 diver Mel Fisher recovered the treasures from the lost ships, the *Nuestra Señora de Atocha* and the *Santa Margarita.* Fisher's incredible adventure tracking these fabled hoards and battling the state of Florida for rights is as amazing as the loot you'll see, touch, and learn about in this museum. Artifacts include a gold bar (that you can lift to get an idea what $15,000 feels like) and a 77.76-carat natural emerald crystal worth almost $250,000. Exhibits on the second floor rotate, and might cover slave ships, including the excavated 17th-century *Henrietta Marie,* or Florida maritime history. ⊠ *200 Greene St.* ☎ *305/294–2633* ⊕ *www.melfisher.org* ⊠ *$12* ⊙ *Weekdays 8:30–5, weekends 9:30–5.*

The Southernmost Point. Possibly the most photographed site in Key West, this is a must-see for many visitors. Who wouldn't want his picture taken next to the big striped buoy that marks the southernmost point in the continental United States? A plaque next to it honors Cubans who lost their lives trying to escape to America, and other signs tell Key West history. ⊠ *Whitehead and South Sts.* ☎ *No phone.*

SHOPPING

On these streets you'll find colorful local art of widely varying quality, key limes made into everything imaginable, and the raunchiest T-shirts in the civilized world. Browsing the boutiques—with frequent pub stops along the way—makes for an entertaining stroll down Duval Street. Key West is filled with art galleries, and the variety is truly amazing. Much is locally produced by the town's large artist community, but many galleries carry international artists from as close as Haiti and as far away as France. Local artists do a great job of preserving the island's architecture and spirit.

Where to start? **Bahama Village** is an enclave of spruced-up shops, restaurants, and vendors responsible for the restoration of the colorful historic district where Bahamians settled in the 19th century. The village lies roughly between Whitehead and Fort streets and Angela and Catherine streets. Hemingway frequented the bars, restaurants, and boxing rings in this part of town.

ACTIVITIES

BOAT TOURS

Victoria Impallomeni, a 34-year wilderness guide and marine scientist, invites up to six nature lovers—especially children—aboard the *Imp II*, a 25-foot Aquasport, for four-hour ($500) and seven-hour ($700) **Dancing Dolphin Spirit Charters** (✉ *MM 5 OS at Murray's Marina, 5710 Overseas Hwy., Key West* ☎ *305/304–7562 or 888/822–7366* ⊕ *www.captainvictoria.com*) ecotours that frequently include encounters with wild dolphins. While island-hopping, you visit underwater gardens, natural shoreline, and mangrove habitats. For her Dolphin Day for Humans tour, Impallomeni pulls you through the water, equipped with mask and snorkel, on a specially designed "dolphin water massage board" that simulates dolphin swimming motions. Sometimes dolphins follow the boat and swim among participants. All equipment is supplied. Tours leave from Murray's Marina.

Lazy Dog Kayak Guides (✉ *5114 Overseas Hwy., Key West* ☎ *305/295–9898* ⊕ *www.lazydog.com*) runs four-hour guided sea kayak–snorkel tours around the mangrove islands just east of Key West. The $60 charge covers transportation, bottled water, a snack, and supplies, including snorkeling gear. A $35 two-hour guided kayak tour is also available.

DIVING AND SNORKELING

The Florida Keys National Marine Sanctuary extends along Key West and beyond to the Dry Tortugas. Key West National Wildlife Refuge further protects the pristine waters. Most divers don't make it this far out in the Keys, but if you're looking for a day of diving as a break from the nonstop party in Old Town, expect to pay about $45 and upward for a two-tank dive. Serious divers can book dive trips to the Dry Tortugas.

Captain's Corner (✉ *125 Ann St.* ☎ *305/296–8865* ⊕ *www.captainscorner.com*), a PADI–certified dive shop, has classes in several languages and twice-daily snorkel and dive trips ($40–$45) to reefs and wrecks aboard the 60-foot dive boat *Sea Eagle*. Equipment rental is extra. Safely dive the coral reefs without getting a scuba certification with **Snuba of Key West** (✉ *Garrison Bight Marina, Palm Ave. between Eaton St. and N. Roosevelt Blvd.* ☎ *305/292–4616* ⊕ *www.snubakeywest.com*). Ride out to the reef on a catamaran, then follow your guide underwater for a one-hour tour of the coral reefs. You wear a regulator with a breathing hose that is attached to a floating air tank on the surface. No prior diving or snorkeling experience is necessary, but you must know how to swim. The $99 price includes beverages.

FISHING

Any number of local fishing guides can take you to where the big ones are biting, either in the backcountry for snapper and snook or to the deep water for the marlins and shark that brought Hemingway here in the first place.

Key West Bait & Tackle (⊠ *241 Margaret St.* ☎ *305/292–1961* ⊕ *www. keywestbaitandtackle.com*) carries live bait, frozen bait, and fishing equipment. It also has the Live Bait Lounge, where you can sip ice-cold beer while telling fish tales. **Key West Pro Guides** (⊠ *G-31 Miriam St.* ☎ *866/259–4205* ⊕ *www.keywestproguides.com*) has several different trips, including flats and backcountry fishing ($400 for a half day) and reef and offshore fishing ($600 for half day).

BEACHES

★ **Fort Zachary Taylor Historic State Park.** The park's beach is the best and safest to swim in Key West. There's an adjoining picnic area with barbecue grills and shade trees, a snack bar, and rental equipment, including snorkeling gear. A café serves sandwiches and other munchies. ⊠ *Box 6565; end of Southard St., through Truman Annex* ☎ *305/292–6713* ⊕ *www. floridastateparks.org/forttaylor* ☜ *$4.50 for 1 person, $7 for 2 people, 50¢ per additional person* ☉ *Daily 8–sunset, tours noon and 2.*

WHERE TO EAT

$$

CARIBBEAN

✗ **El Meson de Pepe.** If you want to get a taste of the island's Cuban heritage, this is the place. Perfect for after Mallory Square sunset, you can dine alfresco or in the dining room on refined versions of Cuban classics. Begin with a megasize mojito while you enjoy the basket of bread and savory sauces. The expansive menu offers *tostones rellenos* (green plantains with different traditional fillings), ceviche (raw fish "cooked" in lemon juice), and more. Choose from Cuban specialties such as roasted pork in a cumin mojo sauce and *ropa vieja* (shredded beef stew). At lunch, the local Cuban population and cruise-ship passengers enjoy Cuban sandwiches and smaller versions of dinner's most popular entrées. A salsa band performs outside at the bar during sunset celebration. ⊠ *Mallory Sq., 410 Wall St.* ☎ *305/295–2620* ⊕ *www. elmesondepepe.com* ⊟ *AE, D, MC, V.*

¢

AMERICAN

✗ **Lobo's Mixed Grill.** White Castle attained national cult status with its burgers; the equivalent among Key West denizens is Lobo's belly buster. The 8-ounce, charcoal-grilled chunk of ground chuck is thick and juicy and served with lettuce, tomato, and pickle on a toasted bun. The 30 wraps (rib eye, oyster, grouper, and others) are equally popular. The menu includes salads and quesadillas, as well as a fried shrimp and oyster combo. Beer and wine are served. This courtyard food stand closes at 6, so eat early. Most of Lobo's business is takeout (it has a half-dozen outdoor picnic tables), and it offers free delivery within Old Town. ⊠ *5 Key Lime Sq., east of intersection of Southard and Duval*

Sts. ☎ *305/296–5303* ⊕ *www.loboskeywest.com* ▭ *No credit cards* ☽ *Closed Sun. Apr.–early Dec.*

NIGHTLIFE

Three spots stand out for first-timers among the saloons frequented by Key West denizens. All are within easy walking distance of the cruise-ship piers. **Capt. Tony's Saloon** (✉ *428 Greene St.* ☎ *305/294–1838* ⊕ *www.capttonyssaloon.com*) was the original Sloppy Joe's in the mid-1930s, when Hemingway was a regular. Later, a young Jimmy Buffett sang here and made this watering hole famous in his song "Last Mango in Paris." Bands play nightly. The **Schooner Wharf Bar** (✉ *202 William St.* ☎ *305/292–3302* ⊕ *www.schoonerwharf.com*), an open-air waterfront bar and grill in the historic seaport district, retains its funky Key West charm and hosts live entertainment daily. Its margarita ranks among Key West's best. There are history and good times at **Sloppy Joe's** (✉ *201 Duval St.* ☎ *305/294–5717* ⊕ *www.sloppyjoes.com*), the successor to a famous 1937 speakeasy named for its founder, Captain Joe Russell. Decorated with Hemingway memorabilia and marine flags, the bar is popular with travelers and is full and noisy all the time. A Sloppy Joe's T-shirt is a de rigueur Key West souvenir, and the gift shop sells them like crazy.

4

LA ROMANA, DOMINICAN REPUBLIC

Eileen Robinson Smith

The Dominican Republic is a beautiful island bathed by the Atlantic Ocean to the north and the Caribbean Sea to the south, and some of its most beautiful beaches are in the area surrounding La Romana, notably Bayahibe Bay. Ironically, the beach at the famed Casa de Campo resort, which will be the destination for most cruise passengers who land here at Casa de Campo Marina, is only middling, though it has a sense of Euro style. A port call here will allow you to explore the immediate region—even take a day-trip into Santo Domingo—or simply stay and enjoy some nice (but expensive) restaurants and shops. There is also a host of activities cruise passengers can take part in on organized shore excursions.

ESSENTIALS

CURRENCY The coin of the realm is the Dominican peso (RD$36.25 to US$1 at this writing). The exchange rate fluctuates continuously, but one thing is certain, the Dominican Republic, although still a good value, is not the cheap date it was up until a couple of years ago.

TELEPHONE Telephones are available at the dock, as soon as passengers disembark, and telephone cards can be purchased there as well. You'll also find phones at the Casa de Campo Marina, where a shuttle drops passengers off. Tele-cards can be bought at the supermarket. To call the U.S. or Canada from the D.R., just punch in 1 plus the area code and number. To make calls on the island, you must tap in the area code (809), plus the seven-digit number; if you are calling a Dominican cell phone, you must first punch in 1 then 809 or 829. Unfortunately, there is no Internet café where cruise-ship passengers can access their e-mail, either at the dock or at Casa de Campo.

COMING ASHORE

Ships enter the Casa de Campo International Tourist Port (Muelle Turïstico Internacional Casa de Campo). A group of folkloric dancers and local musicians, playing merengue, greets passengers as they come down the gangway. An information booth with English-speaking staffers is there to assist cruise-ship passengers; the desk is open the entire time the ship is in port.

It is a 15-minute walk into the town of La Romana, or you can jump into a waiting taxi. It's safe to stroll around town, but it's not particularly beautiful, quaint, or even historic; however, it is a real slice of Dominican life. Most people just board the complimentary shuttle and head for the Casa de Campo Marina and/or Altos de Chavón, both of which are at the Casa de Campo resort. Shuttles run all day long.

Taxis line up at the port's docks, and some, but not all, drivers speak English. Staff members from the information kiosk will help to make taxi arrangements. Most rates are fixed and spelled out on a board: $15 to Casa de Campo Marina, $20 to Altos de Chavón. You may be able to negotiate a somewhat lower rate if a group books a taxi for a tour. You can also rent a car at Casa de Campo from National Car Rental; rates are expensive, usually more than $70 a day. Driving into Santo Domingo can be a hair-raising experience, and isn't for the faint of heart, so we don't recommend it.

EXPLORING LA ROMANA

★ **Altos de Chavón.** This re-creation of a 16th-century Mediterranean village sits on a bluff overlooking the Río Chavón, about 3 mi (5 km) east of the main facilities of Casa de Campo. You feel transported to centuries past as you stroll the cobblestoned streets, stopping into the quaint shops, exclusive boutiques, and art galleries located near the archaeological museum, design school, and working artist studios, an amber museum, medieval-style cathedral, and a row of restaurants, along with a French bakery and coffee bar.

Isla Saona. Off the east coast of Hispaniola lies this island, now a national park inhabited by sea turtles, pigeons, and other wildlife. Caves here were once used by Indians. The beaches are beautiful, and legend has it that Columbus once strayed here. Getting here, on catamarans and other excursion boats, is half the fun, but know that it can be a crowd scene. Vendors are allowed to bother visitors, and there are a number of beach shacks serving lunch and drinks. If you go from a resort, like Viva, it will have its own designated area and the hotel will transport the catered lunch by boat. The largest island in the national park, it is no longer as pristine as a national park should be, but of all the excursions, it is one of the better ones.

LA ROMANA BEST BETS

■ **Altos de Chavón.** You'll find shopping and dining as well as great views.

■ **Golf.** The Teeth of the Dog is one of the Caribbean's best courses despite the cost.

■ **Horseback Riding.** Casa de Campo has an excellent equestrian center.

■ **Isla Saona.** The powder-soft beach and beautiful water are excellent.

■ **Kandela.** The tropical, Las Vegas-style review is a highlight if your ship stays late in port on a night it is performed.

Spanish civilization in the New World began in the 12-block Zona Colonial of **Santo Domingo.** Strolling its narrow streets, it's easy to imagine this old city as it was when the likes of Columbus, Cortés, and Ponce de León walked the cobblestones, pirates sailed in and out, and colonists were settling themselves. Tourist brochures tout that "history comes alive here"—a surprisingly truthful statement. A fun horse-and-carriage ride throughout the Zone costs $25 for an hour. The steeds are no thoroughbreds, but they clip right along, though any commentary will be in Spanish. The drivers usually hang out in front of the Hostal Nicolas de Ovando. History buffs will want to spend a day exploring the many "firsts" of our continent, which will be included in any cruise-ship excursion. Do wear comfortable shoes.

SHOPPING

Altos de Chavón is a re-creation of a 16th-century Mediterranean village on the grounds of the Casa de Campo resort, where you can find art galleries, boutiques, and souvenir shops grouped around a cobbled square. Casa Montecristo is a chic cigar lounge.

The **Casa de Campo Marina** is home to more than 60 shops and international boutiques, galleries, and jewelers scattered amid restaurants, an ice-cream parlor, Euro-style bars, and a yacht club. It is a great place to spend some hours shopping and sightseeing while you stare at the extravagant yachts. Although *upscale* is the operative word here, this does not mean that you cannot buy a postcard, a pair of shorts, or a logo T-shirt. Also, the *supermercado* Nacional at the marina has not only groceries but sundries, postcards, and snacks for much less than you would pay at a resort's shop.

ACTIVITIES

Most activities available at Casa de Campo are open to cruise-ship passengers. You'll need to make reservations on the ship, particularly for golf.

FISHING

Blue and white marlin, wahoo, sailfish, dorado, and mahimahi are among the most common catches in these waters. **Casa de Campo Marina** (⊠ *Casa de Campo, Calle Barlovento 3, La Romana* ☏ *809/523–8646*) is the best charter option in the La Romana area. Yachts are available for charters by day or night for a romantic sunset cruise. Boats for deep-sea and river fishing are available as well. Costs to charter a boat with a crew, refreshments, and bait and tackle generally range from $598 to $2,013 for a half-day, from $796 to $3,334 for a full day.

GOLF

Fodor's Choice

★

The famed 18-hole Teeth of the Dog course at **Casa de Campo** (⊠ *La Romana* ☏ *809/523–3333* ⊕ *www.casadecampo.com.do*), with seven holes on the sea, is often ranked as the number-one course in the Caribbean, and is among the top courses in the world. In 2009 it won the World Travel Award as the World's Leading Golf Resort! New also is the prestigious Golf Academy by David Leadbetter, offering high-quality instruction. Greens fees are $225 per round, per person (plus 16% tax for all courses; prices include a golf cart). A caddy is mandatory on this course, and costs $25 plus tip. Pete Dye has designed this and two other globally acclaimed courses here: Dye Fore, with 18 holes close to Altos de Chavón, hugs a cliff that looks over the sea, a river, and the stunning marina ($225); the Links is an 18-hole inland course ($150). Avid golfers should inquire about the resort's three-day and one-week supplements, or the new Simply Golf Packages. Tee times for all courses must be reserved at least one day in advance by resort guests (they enjoy a discount), earlier for nonguests.

HORSEBACK RIDING

The 250-acre **Equestrian Center at Casa de Campo** (⊠ *La Romana* ☏ *809/523–3333* ⊕ *www.casadecampo.com.do*) has something for both western and English riders—a dude ranch, a rodeo arena (where Casa's trademark Donkey Polo is played), guided trail rides, and jumping and riding lessons. Guided rides run about $35 an hour; lessons cost $56 an hour. There are early morning and sunset trail rides, too. Handsome, old-fashioned carriages are available for hire as well.

BEACHES

Cruise passengers can buy a day-pass to use the beach and facilities at Casa de Campo ($75 for adults, $45 for children 4–12 years); with that, you get a place in the sun at **Minitas Beach**, towels, non-motorized water sports, lunch in the Beach Club, and entrance to Altos de Chavón. Otherwise, excursions (sometimes cheaper) are available to several area beaches.

Catalina Island is a diminutive, picture-postcard Caribbean island off the coast of the mainland. Catalina is about a half-hour away by catamaran, and most excursions offer the use of snorkeling equipment as well as a beach barbecue. **Playa Bayahibe** is a beautiful stretch of beach. Shore excursions are organized by the cruise lines to the beach, which is about 30 minutes away from the cruise port by bus. You can also book your own taxi here, and the trip may be cheaper than the cost of a shore excursion if you come with a group. **Saona Island** was once a pristine, idyllic isle. Now, on a busy cruise-ship day there may be as many as 1,000 swimmers there. However, the beach is beautiful. Excursions here usually include a powerboat ride from Altos de Chavón; otherwise, you are bused to Bayahibe and board a boat there.

CABIN OUTLETS

Most ships' cabins have only one or two electrical outlets located near the desk/vanity table (not counting the shaver-only outlet in the bathroom). A short extension cord allows you to use more than one electrical appliance at once, and gives you a bit more flexibility to move around, particularly if you bring a laptop computer.

4

WHERE TO EAT

$$-$$$ ✗ **Peperoni.** Although the name sounds as Italian as *amore*, this restau-
ITALIAN   rant's menu is much more eclectic than Italian. It has a classy, contemporary, white-dominated decor; waiters are also dressed in white with long aprons. The marina setting is dreamy—you drink quietly, perhaps dreaming that you have just disembarked from one of the million-dollar yachts. Strolling musicians perpetuate the mood. An astounding appetizer is *pulpo* (octopus) with fava beans stewed in lemoncello vinaigrette; another is a crab cake with chipotle aioli and arugula in a warm vanilla vinaigrette. The classic pasta dishes, such as an inventive house-made pear and goat-cheese ravioli, as well as osso buco and risotto with rock shrimp or porcini mushrooms, are delectable. But you can also opt for stylishly simple charcoal-grilled steaks, burgers, gourmet pizzas, sandwiches, or even sushi and sashimi. Desserts are worthy here, including a tart key lime paired with mango sorbet. ⊠ *Casa de Campo, Plaza Portafino 16, Casa de Campo Marina, La Romana* ☎ *809/523–2228* ▭ *AE, MC, V.*

MARTINIQUE (FORT-DE-FRANCE)

Eileen Robin- The largest of the Windward Islands, Martinique is 4,261 mi (6,817 son Smith km) from Paris, but its spirit and language are decidedly French, with more than a soupçon of West Indian spice. Tangible, edible evidence of the fact is the island's cuisine, a superb blend of French and creole. Martinique is lushly landscaped with tropical flowers. Trees bend under the weight of fruits such as mangoes, papayas, lemons, limes, and bright-red West Indian cherries. Acres of banana plantations, pineapple fields, and waving sugarcane stretch to the horizon. The towering mountains and verdant rain forest in the north lure hikers, while underwater sights and sunken treasures attract snorkelers and scuba divers. Martinique is

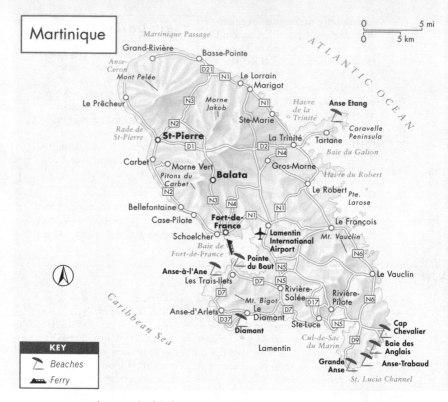

Martinique

ATLANTIC OCEAN

Caribbean Sea

KEY
☇ Beaches
⛴ Ferry

St. Lucia Channel

also wonderful if your idea of exercise is turning over every 10 minutes to get an even tan and your taste in adventure runs to duty-free shopping. A popular excursion goes to St-Pierre, which was buried by ash when Mount Pelée erupted in 1902.

ESSENTIALS

CURRENCY The euro (€1 to US$1.31). You will not be able to use dollars, so plan on getting some euros. You cannot cash traveler's checks or dollars at the bank, only at a bureau de change, so ATMs are your best bet if you need euros. There is a change office at the beginning of Ernest Deproge Street next to the Banque Francaise. Change Caraïbes—is at 14 rue Victor Hugo and Le Bord de Mer. They will still exchange both dollars and traveler's checks and usually offer fair rates.

INTERNET **Cyber Club Caraïbe** (✉ 16 rue François Arago, Fort-de-France ☎ 0596/70–31–62 ⊕ www.cyberclubcaraibe.com). **Internet Haut Depot** (✉ 61 rue Victor Hugo, Fort-de-France ☎ 0596/63–12–20).

TELEPHONE There are no coin-operated phone booths. Public phones now use a télécarte, which you can buy at post offices, café-tabacs, hotels, and bureaux de change. To call the United States from Martinique, dial 00 + 1, the area code, and the local seven-digit number. To call locally, you now have to dial 0596 before the six-digit number. You can make collect calls to Canada through the Bell operator; you can get the AT&T or MCI operators from blue, special-service phones at the cruise ports and in town (try Super Sumo snack bar, on rue de la Liberté, near the library).

COMING ASHORE

Most cruise ships call either at Tourelles (in the old port, about 1½ mi [2 km] from Fort-de-France) or at Pointe Simon, right in downtown Fort-de-France. (It is rare to have a ship anchor in the Baie des Flamands and tender passengers ashore.) Tourist information offices are at each cruise terminal. Uniformed dispatchers assist passengers in finding English-speaking taxi drivers. Passengers who do not wish to walk 20 minutes into Fort-de-France from Tourelles can take a taxi (set rate of €8 for up to four passengers in a van, or €2 for each additional passenger). Expect to pay about €40 per hour for touring; in larger vans the price is usually €10 per person per hour. Independent cruisers can explore the capital and the nearby open-air market on their own. Beaming and knowledge-able hostesses in creole dress greet cruise passengers. Civilian auxiliary police (in blue and orange uniforms) supplement the regular police.

Know that traffic in Fort-de-France can be nightmarish. If you want to go to the beach, a much cheaper option is to take a ferry from Fort-de-France. *Vedettes* (ferries) operate daily between the waterfront pier next to the public land transport terminal and the marina in Pointe du Bout, Anse-Mitan, and Anse-à-l'Ane. Any of the three trips takes about 15 minutes, and the ferries operate about every 30 minutes on weekdays. Renting a car in Fort-de-France is possible, but the heavy traffic can be forbidding. Rates are about €70 per day (high season) for a car with manual transmission; automatics are substantially more expensive and seldom available without reservations.

EXPLORING MARTINIQUE

If you want to see the lush island interior and St-Pierre on your own, take the N3, which snakes through dense rain forests, north through the mountains to Le Morne Rouge, then take the coastal N2 back to Fort-de-France via St-Pierre. You can do the 40-mi (64-km) round-trip in half a day—that is if you don't get lost, can comprehend the road signs, avoid collisions in the roundabouts, drive as fast as the flow of frenetic traffic, and can ask directions in French (probably of someone on the street who only speaks a creole patois). But your best option is to hire an English-speaking driver.

Balata. This quiet little town has two sights worth visiting. Built in 1923 to commemorate those who died in World War I, **Balata Church** is an exact model of Paris's Sacré-Coeur Basilica. The **Jardin de Balata** *(Balata Gardens)* has thousands of varieties of tropical flowers and plants. There are shaded benches from which to take in the mountain views and a plantation-style house furnished with period furniture. Just 15 minutes from Fort-de-France, direction St-Pierre, this worthy site explains why Martinique is called the Island of Flowers. ☒ *Rte. de Balata, Balata* ☎ *0596/64–48–73* ⊕ *www.jardindebalata.com* ☒ *€7* ☺ *Daily 9–5.*

Fort-de-France. With its historic fort and superb location beneath the towering Pitons du Carbet on the Baie des Flamands, Martinique's capital—home to about one-quarter of the island's 400,000 inhabitants—should be a grand place. It isn't, and hasn't been for decades. But an ambitious redevelopment project, under way, albeit progressing slowly, hopes to make it one of the most attractive cities in the Caribbean. The most pleasant districts, such as Didier, Bellevue, and Schoelcher, are on the hillside; there are some good shops with Parisian wares and lively street markets. Near the harbor is a marketplace where local crafts and souvenirs are sold.

> ## MARTINIQUE BEST BETS
>
> ■ **Beaches.** If you want to relax, the most beautiful beach is Les Salines.
>
> ■ **French culture.** Excellent French food and music make this a *paradis* for Francophiles.
>
> ■ **La Route des Rhums.** Visit a distillery and become a rum connoisseur.
>
> ■ **Shopping.** Browse Fort-de-France's many upscale boutiques and department stores for French wares.
>
> ■ **St-Pierre.** Wander the narrow, winding streets of this hill town.

The urban beach between the waterfront and the fort, La Française, has been cleaned up; white sand was brought in, and many cruise-ship passengers frequent it. Cruise-ship activity is strong because of all this revitalization, and Club Med, Holland America, Royal Caribbean, and Silver Sea are just a few of the cruise lines that pull into this port.

The wildly elaborate Romanesque **Bibliothèque Schoelcher** was named after Victor Schoelcher, who led the fight to free the slaves in the French West Indies in the 19th century. The eye-popping structure was built for the 1889 Paris Exposition, after which it was dismantled, shipped to Martinique, and reassembled piece by ornate piece. ⊠ *At rue de la Liberté, which runs along west side of La Savane* ☎ *0596/70–26–67* ✆ *Free* ☉ *Mon. 1–5:30, Tues.–Fri. 8:30–5:30, Sat. 8:30–noon.*

The heart of Fort-de-France, **La Savane** is a 12½-acre park filled with trees, fountains, and benches. It was a popular gathering place and the scene of promenades, parades, and impromptu soccer matches. Along the east side were numerous snack wagons. Alas, it was no longer a desirable oasis, what with a lot of litter and other negatives often found in urban parks. A statue of Pierre Belain d'Esnambuc, leader of the island's first settlers, is unintentionally upstaged by Vital Dubray's vandalized—now headless—white Carrara marble statue of the empress Joséphine, Napoléon's first wife. This park is cordoned off as it undergoes a massive revitalization, slated for completion in late 2010. It is to be a focal point of the city again, with entertainment and shopping and a pedestrian mall. Meanwhile, attractive wooden stands are being constructed along the edge of the park that will house a tourism information office, public restrooms, arts and crafts, a crepe stand, and an ice-cream parlor. Diagonally across from La Savane you can catch the ferries for the 20-minute run across the bay to Pointe du Bout and the beaches at Anse-Mitan and Anse-à-l'Ane. It's relatively cheap as well as stress-free—much safer, more pleasant, and faster than by car.

★ The **Musée Régional d'Histoire et d'Ethnographie** helps you understand the history, background, and people of the island. Housed in an elaborate former residence (circa 1888) with balconies and fretwork, it has everything from displays of

the garish gold jewelry that prostitutes wore after emancipation to reconstructed rooms of a home of proper, middle-class Martinicans. There's even a display of creole headdresses with details of how they were tied to indicate whether a woman was single, married, or otherwise occupied. ⊠ *10 bd. Général de Gaulle* ☎ *0596/72–81–87* ☒ *€3* ◷ *Mon. and Wed.–Fri. 8:30–5, Tues. 2–5, Sat. 8:30–noon.*

The Romanesque **St-Louis Cathedral** with its lovely stained-glass windows was built in 1878, the sixth church on this site (the others were destroyed by fires, hurricanes, and earthquakes). ⊠ *Rue Victor Schoelcher.*

St-Pierre. The rise and fall of St-Pierre is one of the most remarkable stories in the Caribbean. Martinique's modern history began here in 1635. By the turn of the 20th century St-Pierre was a flourishing city of 30,000, known as the Paris of the West Indies. As many as 30 ships stood at anchor at a time. By 1902 it was the most modern town in the Caribbean, with electricity, phones, and a tram. On May 8, 1902, two thunderous explosions rent the air. As the nearby volcano erupted, Mont Pelée split in half, belching forth a cloud of burning ash, poisonous gas, and lava that raced down the mountain at 250 MPH. At 3,600°F, it instantly vaporized everything in its path; 30,000 people were killed in two minutes.

The **Cyparis Express,** a small tourist train, will take you around to the main sights with running narrative (in French) for a half hour on Saturday, an hour on weekdays, for €10 (€5 for children).

An Office du Tourisme is on the *moderne* seafront promenade. Stroll the main streets and check the blackboards at the sidewalk cafés before deciding where to lunch. At night some places have live music. Like stage sets for a dramatic opera, there are the ruins of the island's first church (built in 1640), the imposing theater, and the toppled statues. This city, situated on its naturally beautiful harbor and with its narrow, winding streets, has the feel of a European seaside hill town. With every footstep you touch a page of history. Although many of the historic buildings need work, stark modernism has not invaded this burg. As much potential as it has, this is one town in Martinique where real estate is cheap—for obvious reasons.

◷ For those interested in the eruption of 1902, the **Musée Vulcanologique**
★ **Frank Perret** is a must. Established in 1932 by Frank Perret, a noted volcanologist, the museum houses photographs of the old town, documents, and a number of relics—some gruesome—excavated from the

ruins, including molten glass, melted iron, and contorted clocks stopped at 8 AM. ⊠ *Rue Victor Hugo* ☎ *0596/78–15–16* 🖃 *€5* ☉ *Daily 9–5.*

If you want to know more about volcanoes, earthquakes, and hurricanes, check out **Le Centre de Découverte des Sciences de la Terre.** Housed in a sleek building that looks like a dramatic white box, this earth-science museum has high-tech exhibits and interesting films. Watch the documentary on the volcanoes in the Antilles, highlighting the eruption of the nearby Mont Pelée. This site has fascinating summer programs on Wednesday on dance, cuisine, and ecotourism. ⊠ *Habitation Perinelle* ☎ *0596/52–82–42* ⊕ *www.cdst.cg972.fr* 🖃 *€5* ☉ *Tues.–Sun. 9–4:30, 9–5:30 in July and Aug.*

★ An excursion to **Depaz Distillery** is one of the island's nicest treats. For four centuries it has sat at the foot of the volcano. In 1902 the greathouse was destroyed in the eruption, but soon afterward it was courageously rebuilt and the fields were replanted. A self-guided tour includes the workers' gingerbread cottages, and sometimes there will be an exhibit of art and sculpture made from wooden casks and parts of distillery machinery. A video tells the Depaz story. The tasting room sells their rums, including golden and aged rum and distinctive liqueurs made from ginger and basil that can add creativity to your kitchen. Horse carriages take visitors through the cane fields, the garden, and to the greathouse, open for tours. The guided tour and movie tell the history of the Depaz family and their rum, and cost €10. A buffet restaurant has opened, and Le Moulina Canne serves creole specialties and . . . you guessed it, Depaz rum to wash it down with, for €20-plus. ■ **TIP→ Shutters are locked and the staff leaves exactly at 5 PM, so plan on being there by at least 4.** ⊠ *Mont Pelée Plantation* ☎ *0596/78–13–14* 🖃 *Free* ☉ *Weekdays 10–5, Sat. 9–4.*

SHOPPING

French fragrances, designer scarves and sunglasses, fine china and crystal, leather goods, wine (amazingly inexpensive at supermarkets), and liquor are all good buys in Fort-de-France. Purchases are further sweetened by the 20% discount on luxury items when paid for with certain credit cards. Among the items produced on the island, look for *bijoux creole* (local jewelry, such as hoop earrings and heavy bead necklaces), white and dark rum, and handcrafted straw goods, pottery, and tapestries.

The area around the cathedral in Fort-de-France has a number of small shops that carry luxury goods. Of particular note are the shops on rue Victor Hugo, rue Moreau de Jones, rue Antoine Siger, and rue Lamartine. The **Galleries Lafayette** department store on rue Schoelcher in downtown Fort-de-France sells everything from perfume to pâté.

ACTIVITIES

FISHING

Deep-sea fishing expeditions in these waters hunt down tuna, barracuda, dolphin fish, kingfish, and bonito, and the big ones—white and blue marlins. You can hire boats from the bigger marinas, particularly in Pointe du Bout, Le Marin, and Le François; most hotels arrange these Hemingway-esque trysts, but will often charge a premium. If you call several days in advance, companies can also put you together with other anglers to keep costs down. The **Centre de Peche** (⊠ *Port de Plaisance, bd. Allègre, Le Marin* ☎ *0596/76–24–20 or 0696/28–80–58*), a fully loaded Davis 47-foot fishing boat, is a sportfisherman's dream. It goes out with a minimum of five anglers for €195 per person for a half-day, or €390 per person for a full day, including lunch. Nonanglers can come for the ride for €95 and €190, respectively. Captain Yves speaks English fluently and is a fun guy.

GOLF

The 18-hole **Le Golf de l'Impératrice Josephine** (⊠ *Les Trois-Ilets* ☎ *0596/ 68–32–81*) has been renamed in honor of Empress Josephine Napoleon, whose birthplace, La Pagerie, adjoins this 150-acre track of rolling hills. However, the course is 100% American in design. It is a par-71 Robert Trent Jones course with an English-speaking pro, pro shop, bar, and restaurant. The club offers special greens fees to cruise-ship passengers. Normal greens fees are €23 for 9 holes (after 3 PM) and €43 for 18; a cart costs another €23 for 9, €39 for 18. For those who don't mind walking while admiring the Caribbean view between the palm trees, club trolleys are €6. There are no caddies.

HIKING

Two-thirds of Martinique is designated as protected land. Trails, all 31 of them, are well marked and maintained. At the beginning of each a notice indicates the level of difficulty and the duration of a hike, and relays any interesting facts. The **Parc Naturel Régional de la Martinique** (⊠ *9 bd. Général de Gaulle, Fort-de-France* ☎ *0596/73–19–30*) organizes inexpensive guided excursions year-round. If there have been heavy rains, though, give it up. The tangle of ferns, bamboo trees, and vines is dramatic, but during rainy season the wet, muddy trails will temper your enthusiasm.

HORSEBACK RIDING

Horseback-riding excursions can traverse scenic beaches, palm-shaded forests, sugarcane fields, and a variety of other tropical landscapes. Trained guides often include running commentaries on the history, flora, and fauna of the island.

At **Black Horse Ranch** (⊠ *Les Trois-Ilets* ☎ *0596/68–37–80*) one-hour trail rides (€35) go into the countryside and across waving cane fields; two hours on the trail (€40) bring riders near a river. Only western saddles are used for adults; children can ride English. Semiprivate lessons in French or English are €40 a person, less for kids if they can join a group.

Some guides are English-speaking at **Ranch de Caps** (⊠ *Cap Macré, Le Marin* ☎ *0596/74–70–65 or 0696/23–18–18*), where you can take a half-day ride (western) on the wild southern beaches and across the countryside for €48. Rides go out in the morning (8:30 to noon) and afternoon (1:30 to 5) every day but Monday. If you can manage a full day in the saddle, it costs €80. A real treat is the full-moon ride, but they need to assemble a group to orchestrate that. Most of the mounts are Anglo-Arabs. Riders are encouraged to help cool and wash their horses at day's end. Reserve in advance. Riders of all levels are welcomed.

Ranch Jack (⊠ *Anse-d'Arlets* ☎ *0596/68–37–69 or 0696/92–26–58* ✆ *ranch.jack@wanadoo.fr*) has trail rides (English-style) across some beautiful country for €36 for two hours; half-day excursions for €54 (€62 with transfers from nearby hotels) go through the fields and forests to the beach. Short rides can range from €16 to €25. The lessons for kids are recommendable.

BEACHES

Anse-Mitan (⊠ *Pointe du Bout, Les Trois-Ilets*) is not the French Riviera, though there are often yachts moored offshore. This long stretch of beach can be particularly fun on Sunday. Small, family-owned seaside restaurants are half hidden among palm trees and are footsteps from the lapping waves. Chaise longues are available for rent from hotels for about €6. **Pointe du Bout** (⊠ *Pointe du Bout, Les Trois-Ilets*) is small, man-made, and lined with resorts, including the Hotel Bakoua (formerly Sofitel Bakoua Martinique). Each little strip is associated with its resident hotel, and security guards and closed gates make access difficult. However, if you take a left across from the main pedestrian entrance to the marina—between the taxi stand and the former Kalenda Hotel—then go left again, you will reach Hotel Bakoua's beach, which has especially nice facilities and several options for lunch and drinks. If things are quiet—particularly during the week—one of the beach boys may rent you a chaise; otherwise, just plop your beach towel down, face forward, and enjoy the delightful view of the Fort-de-France skyline. **Les Salines** (⊠ *Ste-Anne*) is a mile-long cove lined with soft white sand and coconut palms. The beach is awash with families and children during holidays and on weekends but quiet during the week. The far end—away from the makeshift souvenir shops—is most appealing. The calm waters are safe for swimming, even for the kids. You can't rent chaise longues, but there are showers. Food vendors roam the sand. From Le Marin, take the coastal road toward Ste-Anne. You will see signs for Les Salines.

WHERE TO EAT

$$ ✕ **Mille & Une Brindilles.** At this trendy salon you can order anything from
CAFÉ a glass of wine to an aromatic pot of tea in flavors like vanilla or mango.
★ You'll find a litany of tapenades, olive cakes, and flans on the prix-fixe menu. Fred, the bubbly Parisian who is both chef and proprietress, is the queen of terrines, and she makes a delicious tart (like Roquefort and pear) or pâté out of any vegetable or fish. The Saturday brunch (€22) is

a very social occasion. The best-ever desserts, such as the Amadéus—as appealing as the classical music that plays—and *moelleux au chocolat*, are what you would want served at your last meal on earth. Look for the sign on the left side, for the place is easy to miss. ⊠ *27 rte. de Didier, Didier, Fort-de-France* ☎ *0596/71–75–61* ▭ *No credit cards* ۞ *Closed Sun. and Wed. No dinner.*

$ ✕ **Soup Bar du Centre Ville.** A sign reading NO OPIUM SMOKING is just
ECLECTIC   one of the details that make this artsy eatery so much fun. This is one place that the island's colorful characters will tell you about if they think you're hip. Wild-looking art decorates one wall; on the other is a surfboard, signed by its American owner, who added THANKS FOR THE SOUP. The list of soups is extensive, and includes local specialties such as *soupe z'habitant*, a flavorful puree of green vegetables with pigs' tails added for flavor. Because a German owns the place, you can also get goulash and cold cream-of-cucumber soup. No matter what you order, the price is right: a huge bowl with some rolls ranges from €7 to €10. This place is a venue for art exhibits and live music. And yes, there is German beer. Doors open at 4 PM. ⊠ *120 rue Martine, Fort-de-France* ☎ *0596/60–48–96* ▭ *MC, V* ۞ *Closed Sun. No lunch.*

MONTEGO BAY, JAMAICA

John Bigley
and Paris
Permenter

Today many explorations of MoBay are conducted from a reclining chair—frothy drink in hand—on Doctor's Cave Beach. As home of Jamaica's busiest cruise pier and the north-shore airport, Montego Bay—or MoBay—is the first taste most visitors have of the island. Travelers from around the world come and go in this bustling community, which ranks as Jamaica's second-largest city. The name Montego is derived from *manteca* (lard in Spanish). The Spanish first named this Bahía de Manteca, or Lard Bay. Why? The Spanish once shipped hogs from this port city. Jamaican tourism began here in 1924, when the first resort opened at Doctor's Cave Beach so that health-seekers could "take the waters." If you can pull yourself away from the water's edge and brush the sand off your toes, you can find some very interesting colonial sights in the surrounding area.

ESSENTIALS

CURRENCY   The Jamaican dollar (J$89 to US$1). Currency-exchange booths are set up on the docks at Montego Bay whenever a ship is in port, however, the U.S. dollar is accepted virtually everywhere, though change may be made in Jamaican dollars.

INTERNET   A growing number of Internet cafés have sprung up in recent years in Montego Bay hotels and cafés. A popular option for many cruise passengers is the Internet café at Doctor's Cave Beach Club (⊠ *Montego Bay* ☎ *876/952–2566*).

TELEPHONE   Public telephones (and faxes) are located at the communications center at the Montego Bay Cruise Terminal. Travelers also find public phones in major Montego Bay malls, such as the City Centre Shopping Mall. Some U.S. phone companies won't permit credit-card calls to be placed from Jamaica because they've been victims of fraud, so collect calls are often the top option. GSM cell phones equipped with tri-band or world-roaming service will find coverage throughout the Montego Bay region.

4

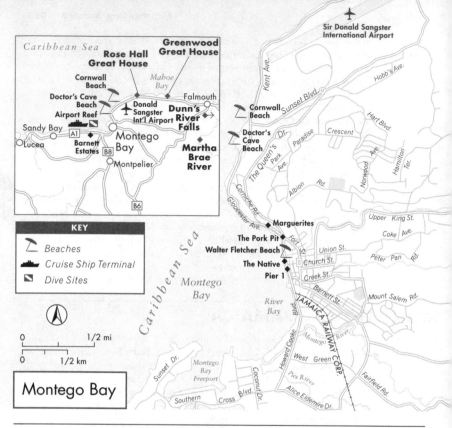

Montego Bay

KEY

- ⤴ Beaches
- 🚢 Cruise Ship Terminal
- ◪ Dive Sites

| 0 | | 1/2 mi |
| 0 | | 1/2 km |

COMING ASHORE

Ships dock at the Montego Cruise Terminal, operated by the Port Authority of Jamaica. West of Montego Bay, the cruise terminal has five berths and accommodates both cruise and cargo shipping. The terminal has shops, a communications center, a Jamaica Tourist Board visitor information booth, and a taxi stand supervised by the Jamaica Tourist Board. The cruise port in Montego Bay is not within walking distance of the heart of town; however, there's one shopping center within walking distance of the docks. If you just want to visit a beach, then Doctor's Cave, a public beach, is a very good nearby alternative, and it's right in town.

From the Montego Cruise Terminal both taxis and shuttle buses take passengers downtown. Taxi service is about US$10 each way to downtown. Expect to pay $2 per person each way by shuttle bus to the City Centre Shopping Mall or $3 each way to Doctor's Cave Beach. Jamaica is one place in the Caribbean where it's usually to your advantage to take an organized shore excursion offered by your ship unless you just want to do a bit of shopping in town. Taxis aren't particularly cheap, and a full-day tour for a small group will run $150 to $180 (because of road conditions and the distances in Jamaica, most tours take a full day).

If you take a private taxi, you should know that only some of Jamaica's taxis are metered; rates are per car, not per passenger. You can flag cabs on the street. All licensed and properly insured taxis display red Public Passenger (PP) license plates. Licensed minivans also bear the red PP plates. If you hire a taxi driver as a tour guide, be sure to agree on a price before the vehicle is put into gear. Because of the cost of insurance, which you must buy since most credit cards offering coverage exclude Jamaica, it's expensive to rent a car; you may also find it difficult to arrange a rental on-island. It's far easier to arrange a taxi.

EXPLORING MONTEGO BAY

Fodor's Choice
★
Dunn's River Falls. One of Jamaica's most popular attractions is an eye-catching sight: 600 feet of cold, clear mountain water splashing over a series of stone steps to the warm Caribbean. The best way to enjoy the falls is to climb the slippery steps: don a swimsuit, take the hand of the person ahead of you, and trust that the chain of hands and bodies leads to an experienced guide. The leaders of the climbs are personable fellows who reel off bits of local lore while telling you where to step; you can hire a guide's service for a tip of a few dollars. After the climb, you exit through a crowded market, another reminder that this is one of Jamaica's top tourist attractions. ⊠ *Off Rte. A1, between St. Ann's Bay and Ocho Rios, Ocho Rios* ☎ 876/974–4767 ⊕ *www.dunnsriverfallsja.com* ☜ *$15* ⊙ *Daily 8:30–5.*

★ **Greenwood Great House.** Unlike Rose Hall, Greenwood has no spooky legend to titillate, but it's much better than Rose Hall at evoking life on a sugar plantation. The Barrett family, from whom the English poet Elizabeth Barrett Browning descended, once owned all the land from Rose Hall to Falmouth; on their vast holdings they built this and several other greathouses. (The poet's father, Edward Moulton Barrett, "the Tyrant of Wimpole Street," was born at nearby Cinnamon Hill, later the estate of country singer Johnny Cash.) Highlights of Greenwood include oil paintings of the Barretts, china made for the family by Wedgwood, a library filled with rare books from as early as 1697, fine antique furniture, and a collection of exotic musical instruments. There's a pub on-site as well. It's 15 mi (24 km) east of Montego Bay. ⊠ *Greenwood* ☎ 876/953–1077 ⊕ *www.greenwoodgreathouse.com* ☜ *$14* ⊙ *Daily 9–6 (last tour at 5).*

Martha Brae River. This gentle waterway about 25 mi (40 km) southeast of Montego Bay takes its name from an Arawak woman who killed herself because she refused to reveal the whereabouts of a local gold mine. According to legend, she agreed to take her Spanish inquisitors there and, on reaching the river, used magic to change its course, drowning herself and the greedy Spaniards with her. Her *duppy* (ghost) is said to guard the mine's entrance. Rafting on this river is a very popular activity.

Fodor's Choice
★
Rose Hall. In the 1700s it may well have been the greatest of greathouses in the West Indies. Today it's popular less for its architecture than for the legend surrounding its second mistress, Annie Palmer. As the story goes, Annie was born in 1802 in England to an English mother and

Irish father. When she was 10, her family moved to Haiti, and soon her parents died of yellow fever. Annie was adopted by a Haitian voodoo priestess and soon became skilled in the practice of voodoo. Annie moved to Jamaica, married, and built Rose Hall, an enormous plantation spanning 6,600 acres with more than 2,000 slaves. There's a pub on-site. It's across the highway from the Rose Hall Resort & Country Club, A Hilton Resort.

> **BINOCULARS**
>
> Binoculars are as useful indoors as they are outside. You might think they are only for bringing far-off wildlife and sights within view, but take them into museums, churches, and other buildings to examine the details of artwork, sculptures, and architectural elements.

☒ *North Coast Hwy., St. James, 15 mi (24 km) east of Montego Bay* ☎ *876/953–2323* ✉ *$20* ☉ *Daily 9:15–5:15.*

SHOPPING

Jamaican artisans express themselves in silk-screening, wood carvings, resort wear, hand-loomed fabrics, and paintings. Jamaican rum makes a great gift, as do Tia Maria (the famous coffee liqueur) and Blue Mountain coffee. Wood carvings are one of the top purchases; the finest carvings are made from the Jamaican national tree, lignum vitae, or tree of life, a dense wood that talented carvers transform into dolphins, heads, or fish. Bargaining is expected with crafts vendors.

ACTIVITIES

DIVING AND SNORKELING

Jamaica isn't a major dive destination, but you can find a few rich underwater regions, especially off the north coast. MoBay, known for its wall dives, has **Airport Reef** at its southwestern edge. The site is known for its coral caves, tunnels, and canyons. The first marine park in Jamaica, the **Montego Bay Marine Park,** was established to protect the natural resources of the bay; a quick look at the area lets you see the treasures that lie beneath the surface. The north coast is on the edge of the Cayman Trench, so it boasts a wide array of marine life.

Scuba Jamaica (☒ *Half Moon Resort, North Coast Hwy., Montego Bay* ☎ *876/381–1113* ⊕ *www.scuba-jamaica.com*) offers serious scuba facilities for dedicated divers. This PADI and NAUI operation also offers Nitrox diving and instruction as well as instruction in underwater photography, night diving, and open-water diving. There's a pickup service for the Montego Bay, Runaway Bay, Discovery Bay, and Ocho Rios areas.

GOLF

Golfers appreciate both the beauty and the challenges offered by Jamaica's courses. Caddies are almost always mandatory throughout the island, and rates are $15 to $45 per round of golf. Cart rentals are available at most courses; costs are $20 to $40. Some of the best courses in the country are found near MoBay.

★ **Golf at Half Moon** (✉ *Half Moon Resort, North Coast Hwy., 7 mi [11 km] east of Montego Bay* ☎ *876/953–2560* ⊕ *www. halfmoongolf.com*), a Robert Trent Jones–designed 18-hole course, is the home of the Red Stripe Pro Am. Greens fees are $105 for guests, $150 for nonguests. In 2005 the course received an upgrade from Jones protégé Roger Rulewich and once again draws international attention. The course is also home of the Caribbean headquarters of the David Leadbetter Golf Academy, which offers one-day sessions, multiday retreats, and hour-long private sessions.

The newest course in Jamaica, which opened in January 2001, is the **White Witch** course at the **Ritz-Carlton Golf & Spa Resort, Rose Hall** (✉ *1 Ritz Carlton Dr., Rose Hall, St. James* ☎ *876/518–0174*). The greens fees at this 18-hole championship course are $175 for resort guests, $185 for nonguests, and $109 for a twilight round. Designed by Robert von Hagge and Rick Baril, it is literally on the grounds of historic Rose Hall greathouse.

Rose Hall Resort & Country Club, A Hilton Resort (*North Coast Hwy., St. James, 15 mi [24 km] east of Montego Bay* ☎ *876/953–2650*), 4 mi (6 km) east of the airport, hosts several invitational tournaments. Greens fees run $159 for guests, $169 for nonguests, and $99 for a twilight round of 9 holes at the 18-hole championship **Cinnamon Hill Ocean Course**. The course was designed by Robert von Hagge and Rick Baril (the designers of the White Witch course at the Ritz-Carlton) and is adjacent to historic Cinnamon Hill.

RIVER RAFTING

Jamaica's many rivers mean a multitude of freshwater experiences, from mild to wild. Relaxing rafting trips aboard bamboo rafts poled by local boatmen are almost a symbol of Jamaica, and the island's first tourist activity outside the beaches. Recently, soft-adventure enthusiasts have also been able to opt for white-water action as well with guided tours through several operators.

Fodor's Choice Bamboo rafting in Jamaica originated on the **Rio Grande,** a river in the
★ Port Antonio area. Jamaicans had long used the bamboo rafts to transport bananas downriver; decades ago actor and Port Antonio resident Errol Flynn saw the rafts and thought they'd make a good tourist attraction, and local entrepreneurs quickly rose to the occasion. Today the slow rides are a favorite with romantic travelers and anyone looking to get off the beach for a few hours. The popularity of the Rio Grande's

---

MONTEGO BAY BEST BETS

■ **Doctor's Cave Beach.** This public beach club is right in the heart of Montego Bay.

■ **Dunn's River Falls.** A visit to the falls is touristy but still exhilarating.

■ **Martha Brae Rafting.** A slow rafting trip down the river is relaxing and very enjoyable.

■ **Shopping.** MoBay has several good shopping centers, as well as bustling craft markets.

■ **Rose Hall Greathouse.** The island's most visited greathouse offers a peek back into the days of the plantations.

4

trips spawned similar trips down the **Martha Brae River**, about 25 mi (40 km) from MoBay. Near Ocho Rios, the **White River** has lazy river rafting in the daytime, followed by romantic river floats at night with the passage lighted by torches.

Jamaica Tours Limited (⊠ *Providence Dr., Montego Bay* ☏ *876/953–3700* ⊕ *www.jamaicatoursltd.com*) conducts trips down the River Lethe, approximately 12 mi (19 km) southwest of MoBay (a 50-minute trip); the four-hour excursion costs about $54 per person, includes lunch, and takes you through unspoiled hill country. Bookings can also be made through hotel tour desks. **River Raft Ltd.** (⊠ *66 Claude Clarke Ave., Montego Bay* ☏ *876/952–0889* ⊕ *www.jamaicarafting.com*) leads trips down the Martha Brae River, about 25 mi (40 km) from most hotels in MoBay. The cost is $45 per person for the 1½-hour river run, including transportation from the cruise pier.

If you're looking for a more rugged adventure, then consider a white-water rafting trip with **Caliche Rainforest** (☏ *876/940–1745* ⊕ *www. whitewaterraftingmontegobay.com*). Two tours, both offered in inflatable rafts, traverse the waters of the Great River. The Grade II Rainforest Rafting Tour glides along with stops for a swim; ages 4 and up can participate. The Canyon White Water Rafting tour traverses rapids up to Grade IV; travelers must be at least 14. The tour price includes the transfer cost from the cruise pier.

BEACHES

★ **Doctor's Cave Beach**. Montego Bay's tourist scene has its roots right on the Hip Strip, the bustling entertainment district along Gloucester Avenue. Here a sea cave's waters were said to be curative, and drew many travelers to bathe in them. Though the cave was destroyed by a hurricane generations ago, the beach is always busy and has a perpetual spring-break feel. It's the best beach in Jamaica outside one of the more-developed resorts, thanks to its plantation-style clubhouse with changing rooms, showers, gift shops, a bar, a grill, and even a cybercafé. There's a $5 fee for admission; beach chairs and umbrellas are also for rent. Its location within the Montego Bay Marine Park—where there are protected corals and marine life—makes it a good spot for snorkeling. More active travelers can opt for parasailing, glass-bottom boat rides, or jet-skiing. ⊠ *Gloucester Ave., Montego Bay.*

Walter Fletcher Beach. Though not as pretty as Doctor's Cave Beach, or as tidy, Walter Fletcher Beach is home to Aquasol Theme Park, which offers a large beach (with lifeguards and security), water trampolines, Jet Skis, Wave Runners, glass-bottom boats, snorkeling, tennis, go-kart racing, a disco at night, a bar, and a grill. The park is open daily from 9 to 6; admission is $5, with à la carte pricing for most activities. Near the center of town, the beach has protection from the surf on a windy day. This means you can find unusually fine swimming here; the calm waters make it a good bet for children. ⊠ *Gloucester Ave., Montego Bay.*

WHERE TO EAT

$–$$ ✗ **The Native.** Shaded by a large poinciana tree and overlooking Glouc-
CARIBBEAN   ester Avenue, this open-air stone terrace serves Jamaican and international dishes. To go native, start with smoked marlin, move on to the
boonoonoonoos platter (a sampler of local dishes), and round out with
coconut pie or *duckanoo* (a sweet dumpling of cornmeal, coconut,
and banana wrapped in a banana leaf and steamed). Live entertainment and candlelighted tables make this a romantic choice for dinner
on weekends. ✉ *29 Gloucester Ave., Montego Bay* ☎ *876/979–2769*
▭ *AE, D, MC, V.*

¢–$ ✗ **Pork Pit.** A favorite with many MoBay locals, this no-frills eatery
JAMAICAN   serves Jamaican specialties including some fiery jerk—note that it's
Fodor's Choice   spiced to local tastes, not watered down for tourist palates. Many get
★   their food to go, but you can also find picnic tables just outside. ✉ *27*
Gloucester Ave., Montego Bay ☎ *876/940–3008* ▭ D, MC, V.

NASSAU, BAHAMAS

Jessica
Robertson

Nassau, the capital of the Bahamas, has witnessed Spanish invasions
and hosted pirates, who made it their headquarters for raids along the
Spanish Main. The heritage of old Nassau blends the Southern charm of
British loyalists from the Carolinas, the African tribal traditions of freed
slaves, and a bawdy history of blockade-running during the Civil War
and rum-running in the Roaring 1920s. The sheltered harbor bustles
with crusie-ship hubbub, while a block away, broad, shop-lined Bay
Street is alive with commercial activity. Over it all is a subtle layer of
civility and sophistication, derived from three centuries of British rule.
Nassau's charm, however, is often lost in its commercialism. There's
excellent shopping, but if you look past the duty-free shops you'll also
find sights of historical significance that are worth seeing.

ESSENTIALS

CURRENCY   The Bahamian dollar, which trades one-to-one with the U.S. dollar, which is universally accepted. There's no need to acquire any Bahamian currency.

INTERNET   You'll find Internet kiosks at Prince George Wharf.

TELEPHONE   Calling locally or internationally is easy in the Bahamas. To place a local call,
dial the seven-digit phone number. To call the United States, dial 1 plus the area
code. Pay phones cost 25¢ per call; Bahamian and U.S. quarters are accepted,
as are BATELCO and Indigo phone cards. To place a call using a calling card, use
your long-distance carrier's access code or dial 0 for the operator. Be aware that
when placing a toll-free call from your hotel you are charged as if for a regular
long-distance call.

COMING ASHORE

Cruise ships dock at one of three piers on Prince George Wharf. Taxi
drivers who meet the ships may offer you a $2 "ride into town," but the
historic government buildings and duty-free shops lie just steps from the
dock area. As you leave the pier, look for a tall pink tower—diagonally

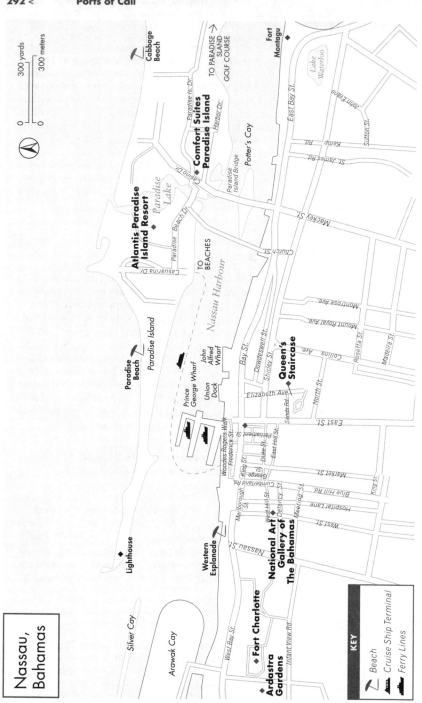

Nassau, Bahamas

300 yards
300 meters

Cabbage Beach

TO PARADISE ISLAND →
GOLF COURSE

Comfort Suites Paradise Island

Fort Montagu

Lake Waterloo

Paradise Is. Dr.

Harbour Dr.

Atlantis Paradise Island Resort

Paradise Lake

Castoo Dr.

Potter's Cay

Paradise Island Bridge

East Bay St.

John Evans

St. James Rd.

Kemp Rd.

Sutton St.

Paradise Beach Dr.

Casuarina Dr.

TO BEACHES

Church St.

Market St.

Montrose Ave.

Mount Royal Ave.

Paradise Island

Nassau Harbour

Bay St.

Dowdeswell St.

Shirley St.

Queen's Staircase

Collins Ave.

Rosetta St.

Madeira St.

Paradise Beach

Prince George Wharf

John Alfred Wharf

Union Dock

Elizabeth Ave.

Sands Rd.

North St.

East St.

Woodes Rogers Walk

Frederick St.

Parliament St.

Duke St.

East Hill St.

Market St.

Lighthouse

King St.

George St.

Cumberland Rd.

Blue Hill Rd.

Hospital Lane

Silver Cay

Marlborough St.

West Hill St.

Delancy St.

Meeting St.

West St.

Western Esplanade

Nassau St.

National Art Gallery of The Bahamas

Arawak Cay

West Bay St.

Fort Charlotte

Infant View Rd.

Ardastra Gardens

KEY

Beach
Cruise Ship Terminal
Ferry Lines

across from here is the tourist information office. Stop in for maps of the island and downtown Nassau. On most days you can join a one-hour walking tour ($10 per person) conducted by a well-trained guide. Tours generally start every hour on the hour from 10 AM to 4 PM; confirm the day's schedule in the office. Just outside, an ATM dispenses U.S. dollars.

As you disembark from your ship, you will find a row of taxis and air-conditioned limousines. Fares are fixed by the government by zones. The fare is $6 for trips within downtown Nassau and on Paradise Island, $9 (plus $1 toll) from downtown to Paradise Island, and $18 from downtown to Cable Beach. Fares are for two passengers; each additional passenger is $3, regardless of the destination. It's customary to tip taxi drivers 15%. You also can hire a car or small van for about $50 per hour. These are fixed costs for two passengers; each additional passenger is $3.

The cheapest way to get to Paradise Island on your own is to take the ferry from the dock area ($3 each way).

NASSAU BEST BETS

■ **Ardastra Gardens.** Flocks of flamingos, the country's national bird, "march" in three daily shows (you can mingle with the flamboyant pink stars afterward).

■ **Atlantis.** Though very costly, the water park here is a must for families.

■ **Shopping.** To many, shopping is one of Nassau's great delights.

■ **Junkanoo Beach.** Head to this beach (aka Long Wharf Beach) and sit in the shade of a coconut palm (it's a 10-minute walk from the duty-free shops on Bay Street).

EXPLORING NASSAU

Nassau's sheltered harbor bustles with cruise-ship hubbub, while a block away, broad, palm-lined Bay Street is alive with commercial activity. Shops angle for tourist dollars with fine imported goods at duty-free prices, yet you will find a handful of stores overflowing with authentic Bahamian crafts, foods, and other delights. Most of Nassau's historic sites are centered around downtown.

With its thoroughly revitalized downtown—the revamped British Colonial Hilton lead the way—Nassau is recapturing some of its glamour. Nevertheless, modern influence is apparent. Fancy restaurants, suave clubs, and trendy coffeehouses have popped up everywhere. This trend comes partly in response to the burgeoning upper-crust crowds that now supplement the spring-breakers and cruise passengers who have traditionally flocked to Nassau.

Today the seedy air of the town's not-so-distant past is almost unrecognizable. Petty crime is no greater than in other towns of this size, and the streets not only look cleaner but feel safer. You can still find a wild club or a rowdy bar, but you can also sip cappuccino while viewing contemporary Bahamian art or dine by candlelight beneath prints of old Nassau, serenaded by soft, island-inspired calypso music.

Saving on Atlantis

Frugal cruisers have long known about **Comfort Suites Paradise Island** (⊕ www.comfortsuites.com), which is right across the street from the Atlantis Resort. They use it to avoid paying for expensive and limited ship-sponsored day-passes to the resort, which cost well over $150 per person. Book a room here, and everyone in the room (up to four people, regardless of age) is entitled to a free day-pass to the Atlantis Resort's water park. In addition to the base rate (usually about $300 for two people depending on the season), you will also have to pay (at check-in) an additional energy surcharge of $12.95 per *adult* and a housekeeper gratuity of $5 per *adult* on top of the quoted rate, even if you prepay; the third and fourth person cost $40 each *plus* all the service charges. Frankly, this isn't as good a deal as it used to be, but families or groups of four can still save a little money by going this route, and then you will have a room in which to shower and change before returning to the ship. Of course, it's a better deal if you can get a discounted rate. (Be aware that you may not have more than four people on a single reservation regardless of their age, and you may not get access to the room in the morning, but it will be ready when you get back from your day of fun at the water park.) When it's time for lunch, you'll find cheaper restaurants within walking distance of Atlantis.

Arawak Cay. Known to Nassau residents as "The Fish Fry," Arawak Cay is one of the best places to knock back a Kalik beer, chat with locals, watch or join in a fast-paced game of dominoes, or sample traditional Bahamian fare. The two-story Twin Brothers and Goldie's Enterprises are two of the most popular places. Try their fried "cracked conch" and Goldie's famous Sky Juice (a sweet but potent gin, coconut-water, and sweet-milk concoction sprinkled with nutmeg). There's usually a live band on the outdoor stage Friday and Saturday nights. ⊠ *W. Bay St. and Chippingham Rd.*

⟳ **Ardastra Gardens, Zoo, and Conservation Centre.** Marching flamingos? These national birds give a parading performance at Ardastra daily at 10:30, 2:10, and 4:10. The brilliant pink birds are a delight—especially for children, who can walk among the flamingos after the show. The zoo, with more than 5 acres of tropical greenery and ponds, also has an aviary of rare tropical birds including the bright green Bahama parrot, native Bahamian creatures such as rock iguanas and the little (and harmless) Bahamian boa constrictors, and a global collection of small animals. ⊠ *Chippingham Rd. south of W. Bay St.* ☎ *242/323–5806* ⊕ *www.ardastra.com* ⊡ *$15* ⊘ *Daily 9–5.*

⟳ **Fort Charlotte.** Built in 1788, this imposing fort comes complete with a waterless moat, drawbridge, ramparts, and a dungeon, where children love to see the torture device where prisoners were "stretched." Young local guides bring the fort to life. (Tips are expected.) Lord Dunmore, who built it, named the massive structure in honor of George III's wife. At the time, some called it Dunmore's Folly because of the staggering expense of its construction. It cost eight times more than was originally planned. (Dunmore's superiors in London were less than ecstatic with the high costs, but he managed to survive unscathed.) Ironically, no shots were ever fired in battle from the fort. The fort and its surrounding 100 acres offer a wonderful view of the cricket grounds, the beach, and the ocean beyond. Inquire about Segway tours. ⊠ *W. Bay St. at Chippingham Rd.* ☎ *$5* ☉ *Tours daily 8–4.*

Fodor's Choice ★ **National Art Gallery of the Bahamas.** Opened in July 2003, the museum houses the works of esteemed Bahamian artists such as Max Taylor, Amos Ferguson, Brent Malone, John Cox, and Antonius Roberts. The glorious Italianate-colonial mansion, built in 1860 and restored in the 1990s, has double-tiered verandas with elegant columns. It was the residence of Sir William Doyle, the first chief justice of the Bahamas. Join locals on the lawn for movie night under the stars; call for schedule. Don't miss the museum's gift shop, where you'll find books about the Bahamas and Bahamian quilts, prints, and crafts. ⊠ *West and W. Hill Sts., across from St. Francis Xavier Cathedral* ☎ *242/328–5800* ⊕ *www. nagb.org.bs* ☎ *$5* ☉ *Tues.–Sat. 10–4.*

Parliament Square. Nassau is the seat of the national government. The Bahamian Parliament comprises two houses—a 16-member Senate (Upper House) and a 41-member House of Assembly (Lower House)—and a ministerial cabinet headed by a prime minister. If the House is in session, sit in to watch lawmakers debate. Parliament Square's pink, colonnaded government buildings were constructed in the late 1700s and early 1800s by Loyalists who came to the Bahamas from North Carolina. The square is dominated by a statue of a slim young Queen Victoria that was erected on her birthday, May 24, in 1905. In the immediate area are a handful of magistrates' courts. Behind the House of Assembly is the **Supreme Court.** Its four-times-a-year opening ceremonies (held the first weeks of January, April, July, and October) recall the wigs and mace-bearing pageantry of the Houses of Parliament in London. The Royal Bahamas Police Force Band is usually on hand for the event. ⊠ *Bay St.* ☎ *242/322–2041* ☎ *Free* ☉ *Weekdays 10–4.*

Queen's Staircase. A popular early-morning exercise regime for locals, the "66 Steps" (as Bahamians call them) are thought to have been carved out of a solid limestone cliff by slaves in the 1790s. The staircase was later named to honor Queen Victoria's reign. Pick up some souvenirs at the ad hoc straw market along the narrow road that leads to the site. ⊠ *Top of Elizabeth Ave. hill, south of Shirley St.*

SHOPPING

Most of Nassau's shops are on Bay Street between Rawson Square and the British Colonial Hotel, and on the side streets leading off Bay Street. Some stores are popping up on the main shopping thoroughfare's eastern end and just west of the Cable Beach strip. Bargains abound between Bay Street and the waterfront. Upscale stores can also be found in Marina Village and the Crystal Court at Atlantis and in the arcade joining the Sheraton Nassau Beach and the Wyndham on Cable Beach. You'll find duty-free prices—generally 25%–50% less than U.S.

prices—on imported items such as crystal, linens, watches, cameras, jewelry, leather goods, and perfumes.

ACTIVITIES

FISHING

The waters here are generally smooth and alive with many species of game fish, which is one of the reasons why the Bahamas has more than 20 fishing tournaments open to visitors every year. A favorite spot just west of Nassau is the Tongue of the Ocean, so called because it looks like that part of the body when viewed from the air. The channel stretches for 100 mi. For boat rental, parties of two to six will pay $600 or so for a half-day, $1,600 for a full day.

Born Free Charters (☎ 242/393–4144 ⊕ *www.bornfreefishing.com*) has three boats and guarantees a catch on full-day charters—if you don't get a fish, you don't pay. **Brown's Charters** (☎ 242/324–2061 ⊕ *www.brownscharters.shoreadventures.net*) specializes in 24-hour shark-fishing trips, as well as reef and deep-sea fishing. The **Charter Boat Association** (☎ 242/393–3739) has 15 boats available for fishing charters. **Chubasco Charters** (☎ 242/324–3474 ⊕ *www.chubascocharters.com*) has four boats for sportfishing and shark-fishing charters. **Nassau Yacht Haven** (☎ 242/393–8173 ⊕ *www.nassauyachthaven.com*) runs fishing charters out of its 150-slip marina.

GOLF

Cable Beach Golf Club (7,040 yards, par 72), the oldest golf course in the Bahamas, will be completely overhauled when Baha Mar gets on with its Cable Beach transformation. For now it remains a well-kept, competitive course that's a favorite with locals and visitors not staying on Paradise Island. *W. Bay St., SE end of Cable Beach strip* ☎ *242/327–6000 Ext. 6189* ⚑ *18 holes $95, 9 holes $70; carts included. Clubs $25* ⊗ *Daily 7–5:30; last tee off at 5:15.*

One & Only Ocean Club Golf Course (6,805 yards, par 72), designed by Tom Weiskopf, is a championship course surrounded by the ocean on three sides, which means that winds can get stiff. Call to check on current availability and up-to-date prices (those not staying at Atlantis or the One & Only Ocean Club may find themselves shut out completely). ⊠ *Paradise Island Dr. next to airport, Paradise Island* ☎ *242/363–3925, 800/321–3000 in U.S.* ⚑ *18 holes $260. Clubs $70* ⊗ *Daily 6 AM–sundown.*

BEACHES

New Providence is blessed with stretches of white sand studded with palm and sea grape trees. Some of the beaches are small and crescent-shaped; others stretch for miles. Paradise Island's real showpiece is 3-mi-long **Cabbage Beach,** which rims the north coast from the Atlantis lagoon to Snorkeler's Cove. At the west end you can rent Jet Skis and nonmotorized pedal boats, and go parasailing. **Cable Beach** is on New Providence's north shore, about 3 mi (5 km) west of downtown Nassau. Resorts line much of this beautiful, broad swath of white sand, but there is public access. Jet-skiers and beach vendors abound, so don't expect quiet isolation. Just west of Cable Beach is a rambling pink house on the Rock Point promontory, where much of the 1965 Bond film *Thunderball* was filmed. Right in downtown Nassau, **Junkanoo Beach** is spring-break central from

> **CAUTION**
>
> Mail overflowing your mailbox is a neon sign to thieves that you aren't home. Have someone pick it up, or better yet, have the post office hold all your mail for you.

late February through April. The man-made beach isn't the prettiest on the island, but it's conveniently located if you only have a few quick hours to catch a tan. Music is provided by bands and DJs to guys with boom boxes; a few bars keep the drinks flowing.

WHERE TO EAT

$ AMERICAN ✕ **Green Parrot.** Sip a green-color Parrot Crush while tackling the large Works Burger as you sit and enjoy the cool breeze and lovely Nassau Harbour scenery. This casual, all-outdoor restaurant and bar is popular with locals. The menu includes burgers, wraps, quesadillas, and other simple but tasty dishes. An extended all-night happy hour on Friday means the huge bar is lively and packed. There is live music on Thursday and Saturday nights and a DJ on Friday. ⊠ *E. Bay St. west of the bridges to Paradise Island* ☎ 242/322–9248 ⊕ *www.greenparrotbar. com* ⊟ MC, V.

$ BAHAMIAN ✕ **Double D's.** Don't let the dark-tinted windows and green lighting over the doorway put you off. Inside you'll find a simply decorated bar offering friendly service and good native food. This is a popular spot with locals for its Bahamian cuisine and 23-hour service in a town where most kitchens are closed at 10 PM. Try boil' fish—a peppery lime-based broth filled with chunks of boiled potatoes, onions, and grouper—or be adventurous and order a bowl of pigs' feet or sheep-tongue souse. Although souplike, these Bahamian delicacies are typically served only for breakfast. All come with a chunk of johnnycake or a bowl of steaming white grits. ⊠ *E. Bay St. at the foot of the bridges from Paradise Island* ☎ 242/393–2771 ⊟ MC, V.

NIGHTLIFE

Some ships stay late into the night or until the next day so that passengers can enjoy Nassau's nightlife. You'll find nonstop entertainment nightly along Cable Beach and on Paradise Island. All the larger hotels offer lounges with island combos for listening or dancing and restaurants with soft guitar or piano music. Large casinos can be found at Atlantis on Paradise Island and the Wyndham Nassau Resort & Crystal Palace Casino in Cable Beach.

NIGHTCLUBS

Club Waterloo. Claiming to be Nassau's largest indoor-outdoor nightclub, this club has five bars and nonstop dancing Monday through Saturday, and live bands on the weekend. Try the spring-break special Green

Lizard, a tropical mixture of rums and punches. ⊠ *E. Bay St., Nassau* 📞 *242/393–7324* ⊕ *www.clubwaterloo.com* ⏱ *Daily 8 PM–4 AM.*

NEVIS (CHARLESTOWN)

Jordan Simon

In 1493, when Columbus spied a cloud-crowned volcanic isle during his second voyage to the New World, he named it Nieves—the Spanish word for "snows"—because it reminded him of the peaks of the Pyrenees. Nevis rises from the water in an almost perfect cone, the tip of its 3,232-foot central mountain hidden by clouds. Even less developed than sister island St. Kitts—just 2 mi (3 km) away at their closest point, Nevis is known for its long beaches with white and black sand, its lush greenery, the charming if slightly dilapidated Georgian capital of Charlestown, mountain hikes, and its restored sugar plantations that now house charming inns. Even on a day trip Nevis feels relaxed and quietly upscale. You might run into celebrities at the Four Seasons (at this writing, reopening after extensive renovations in November 2010) or lunching at the beach bars on Pinney's, the showcase strand. Yet Nevisians (not to mention the significant expat American and British presence) never put on airs, offering warm hospitality to all visitors.

ESSENTIALS

CURRENCY   The Eastern Caribbean dollar (EC$2.67 to US$1). U.S. dollars, major credit cards, and traveler's checks are readily accepted, although large U.S. bills may be difficult to change in small shops—and you'll receive change in the local currency.

INTERNET   Charlestown usually has an operational Internet café, but they rarely last in one location. The tourist office will have the latest information.

TELEPHONE   Phone cards, which you can buy in denominations of $5, $10, and $20, are handy for making local phone calls, calling other islands, and accessing U.S. direct lines. To make a local call, dial the seven-digit number. To call Nevis from the United States, dial the area code 869, then access code 465, 466, 468, or 469 and the local four-digit number.

COMING ASHORE

Cruise ships dock in Charlestown harbor; all but the smallest ships bring passengers in by tender to the central downtown ferry dock. The pier leads smack onto Main Street, with shops and restaurants steps away. Taxi drivers often greet tenders, and there's also a stand a block away. Fares are fairly expensive, but a three-hour driving tour of Nevis costs about $80 for up to four people. Several restored greathouse plantation inns are known for their lunches; your driver can provide information and arrange drop-off and pickup. Before setting off in a taxi, be sure to clarify whether the rate quoted is in E.C. or U.S. dollars.

If your ship docks in St. Kitts, Nevis is a 30- to 45-minute ferry ride from Basseterre. You can tour Charlestown, the capital, in a half hour or so, but you'll need three to four hours to explore the entire island. Most cruise ships arrive in port at around 8 AM, and the ferry schedule (figure $18 round-trip) can be irregular, so many passengers sign up for

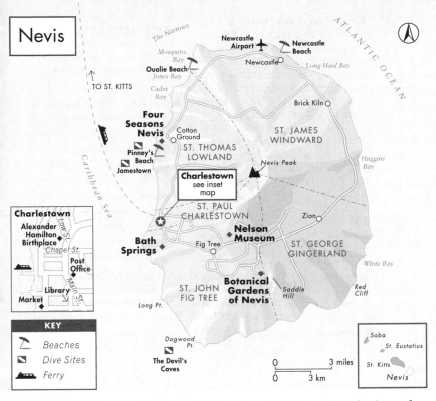

Nevis

Charlestown

Alexander Hamilton Birthplace

Chapel St.

Post Office

Library

Market

KEY

⌐ Beaches

◣ Dive Sites

⛴ Ferry

a cruise line–run shore excursion. If you travel independently, confirm departure times with the tourist office to be sure you'll make it back to your ship on time.

EXPLORING NEVIS

Bath Springs. The Caribbean's first hotel, the Bath Hotel, built by businessman John Huggins in 1778, was so popular in the 19th century that visitors, including such dignitaries as Samuel Taylor Coleridge and Prince William Henry, traveled two months by ship to "take the waters" in the property's hot thermal springs. It suffered extensive hurricane and probably earthquake damage over the years and languished in disrepair until recently. Local volunteers have cleaned up the spring and built a stone pool and steps to enter the waters; now residents and visitors enjoy the springs, which range from 104°F to 108°F, though signs still caution that you bathe at your own risk, especially if you have heart problems. Upon completion, this promising development will house the Nevis Island Administration offices, massage huts and changing rooms, a restaurant, and a cultural center and historic exhibit on the original hotel property. Follow Main Street south from Charlestown. ⊠ *Charlestown outskirts* ☎ *No phone.*

★ **Botanical Gardens of Nevis.** In addition to terraced gardens and arbors, this remarkable 7.8-acre site in the glowering shadow of Mt. Nevis has natural lagoons, streams, and waterfalls, superlative bronze mermaids, egrets and herons, and extravagant fountains. You can find a proper rose garden, sections devoted to orchids and bromeliads, cacti, and flowering trees and shrubs—even a bamboo garden. The entrance to the Rain Forest Conservatory— which attempts to include every conceivable Caribbean ecosystem and then some—duplicates an imposing Maya temple. A splendid re-creation of a plantation-style greathouse contains the Lemongrass restaurant with sweeping sea views, and the upscale Galleria shop selling art, textiles, jewelry, and Indonesian teak furnishings sourced during the owner's world travels. ⊠ *Montpelier Estate* ☎ *869/469–3509* ⊕ *www. botanicalgardennevis.com* ⊠ *$10, children 6–12 $7* ⊗ *Mon.–Sat. 9–5.*

NEVIS BEST BETS
■ **Charlestown.** The well-preserved little capital is worth a quick stroll.
■ **Golf.** The stunner at the Four Seasons provides challenge aplenty.
■ **Hiking.** Getting out in the countryside on foot is one of the best ways to experience Nevis.
■ **Pinney's Beach.** This long sensuous strand has several beach bars where you can "lime" with locals.

★ **Charlestown.** About 1,200 of Nevis's 10,000 inhabitants live in the capital. The town faces the Caribbean, about 12½ mi (20 km) south of Basseterre on St. Kitts. If you arrive by ferry, as most people do, you'll walk smack onto Main Street from the pier. It's easy to imagine how tiny Charlestown, founded in 1660, must have looked in its heyday. The weathered buildings still have their fanciful galleries, elaborate gingerbread fretwork, wooden shutters, and hanging plants. The stonework building with the clock tower (1825, but mostly rebuilt after a devastating 1873 fire) houses the courthouse and the second-floor **library** (a cool respite on sultry days). The little park next to the library is Memorial Square, dedicated to the fallen of World Wars I and II. Down the street from the square, archaeologists have discovered the remains of a Jewish cemetery and synagogue (Nevis reputedly had the Caribbean's second-oldest congregation), but there's little to see.

The **Alexander Hamilton Birthplace,** which contains the **Museum of Nevis History,** is on the waterfront, covered in bougainvillea and hibiscus. This Georgian-style house is a reconstruction of what is believed to have been the American patriot's original home, built in 1680 and thought to have been destroyed during an earthquake in the mid-19th century. Hamilton was born here in 1755 and moved to St. Croix when he was about 12. A few years later, at 17, he moved to the American colonies to continue his education; he became secretary of the treasury to George Washington and died in a duel with political rival Aaron Burr in 1804. The Nevis House of Assembly occupies the second floor of this building, and the museum downstairs contains Hamilton memorabilia, documents pertaining to the island's history, and displays on island geology, politics, architecture, culture, and cuisine. The gift shop is a wonderful source for historic maps, crafts, and books on Nevis. ⊠ *Low St., Charlestown* ☎ *869/469–5786* ⊕ *www.nevis-nhcs.org* ✑ *$5, with admission to Nelson Museum $7* ☉ *Weekdays 9–4, Sat. 9–noon.*

Nelson Museum. This collection merits a visit for its memorabilia of Lord Horatio Nelson, including letters, documents, paintings, and even furniture from his flagship; it is purportedly the Western Hemisphere's largest such compilation. Historical archives of the Nevis Historical and Conservation Society are housed here and are available for public viewing. Nelson was based in Antigua but came on military patrol to Nevis, where he met and eventually married Frances Nisbet, who lived on a 64-acre plantation here. Half the space is devoted to often-provocative displays on island life, from leading families to vernacular architecture to the adaptation of traditional African customs, from cuisine to Carnival. ⊠ *Bath Rd. outside Charlestown* ☎ *869/469–0408* ⊕ *www. nevis-nhcs.org* ✑ *$5, with Museum of Nevis History $7* ☉ *Weekdays 9–4, Sat. 9–noon.*

SHOPPING

Nevis is certainly not the place for a shopping spree, but there are some wonderful surprises, notably the island's stamps, fragrant honey, ceramics, and batik and hand-embroidered clothing. Other than a few hotel boutiques and isolated galleries, virtually all shopping is concentrated on or just off Main Street in Charlestown. The lovely old stonework and wood floors of the waterfront Cotton Ginnery Complex make an appropriate setting for shops of local artisans.

★ The **Philatelic Bureau** (⊠ *Off Main St., Charlestown* ☎ *869/469–0617*), opposite the tourist office, is the place to go for stamp collectors. St. Kitts and Nevis are famous for their decorative, and sometimes valuable, stamps. Real beauties include the butterfly, hummingbird, and marine-life series.

ACTIVITIES

GOLF

Fodor's Choice Duffers doff their hats to the beautiful, impeccably maintained Robert
★ Trent Jones Jr.–designed **Four Seasons Golf Course** (⚐ *18 holes, par 72, 6,766 yd* ⊠ *Four Seasons Resort Nevis, Pinney's Beach* ☎ *869/469–1111*): the virtual botanical gardens surrounding the fairways almost qualify as a hazard in themselves. The front 9 holes are fairly flat until Hole 8, which climbs uphill after your tee shot. Most of the truly stunning views are along the back 9. The signature hole is the 15th, a 660-yard monster that encompasses a deep ravine; other holes include bridges, steep drops, rolling pitches, extremely tight and unforgiving fairways, sugar-mill ruins, and fierce doglegs. Attentive attendants canvas the course with beverage buggies, handing out chilled, peppermint-scented towels and preordered Cubanos that help test the wind. Greens fees per 18 holes had been $190 for hotel guests, $290 for nonguests, but as of this writing have been discounted to $100 for everyone until the hotel reopens, which may not happen until late 2010.

HIKING

The center of the island is Nevis Peak—also known as Mt. Nevis—which soars 3,232 feet and is flanked by Hurricane Hill on the north and Saddle Hill on the south. If you plan to scale Nevis Peak, a daylong affair, it's highly recommended that you go with a guide. The **Upper Round Road Trail** is a 9-mi (14.5-km) road constructed in the late 1600s that was cleared and restored by the Nevis Historical and Conservation Society. It connects the Golden Rock Plantation Inn, on the east side of the island, with Nisbet Plantation Beach Club, on the northern tip. The trail encompasses numerous vegetation zones, including pristine rain forest, and impressive plantation ruins. The original cobblestones, walls, and ruins are still evident in many places.

★ **Herbert Heights Village Experience** (☎ *869/469–2856 or 869/665–6926* ⊕ *www.herbertheights.com*) is run by the Herbert family, who lead four-hour nature hikes up to panoramic Herbert Heights, where you drink in fresh local juices and the views of Montserrat; the powerful telescope, donated by Greenpeace, makes you feel as if you're staring right into that island's simmering volcano (or staring down whales during their migratory season). The trail formed part of an escape route for runaway slaves. Numerous hummingbirds, doves, and butterflies flit and flutter through the rain forest. The Herberts painstakingly reconstructed thatched cottages that offer a glimpse of village life a century ago, dubbed Peak Haven, at Nelson's Lookout, where Coal Pot restaurant offers affordable island fare. Hike prices start at $25. **Sunrise Tours** (☎ *869/469–2758* ⊕ *www.nevisnaturetours.com*), run by Lynell and Earla Liburd, offers a range of hiking tours, but their most popular is Devil's Copper, a rock configuration that figures in ghostly legends. Local people gave it its name because at one time the water was hot—a volcanic thermal stream. The area features pristine waterfalls and splendid bird-watching. They also do a Nevis village walk, a Hamilton Estate Walk, an Amerindian walk along the wild southeast Atlantic coast, and trips to the rain forest and Nevis Peak. They love highlighting Nevisian heritage, explaining time-honored cooking techniques, the many uses of dried grasses, and medicinal plants. Hikes range from $20 to $40 per person, and you receive a certificate of achievement.

WINDSURFING

★ Waters are generally calm and northeasterly winds steady yet gentle, making Nevis an excellent spot for beginners and intermediates. **Windsurfing Nevis** (✉ *Oualie Beach* ☎ *869/469–9682*) offers top-notch instructors (Winston Crooke is one of the best in the islands) and equipment for $30 per hour; beginners for two hours ($55). Groups are kept small (eight maximum), and the equipment is state-of-the-art from Mistral, North, and Tushingham. They also offer kayak rentals and tours along the coast, stopping at otherwise inaccessible beaches.

BEACHES

All beaches are free to the public (the plantation inns cordon off "private" areas on Pinney's Beach for guests), but there are no changing facilities, so wear a swimsuit under your clothes.

★ **Oualie Beach,** south of Mosquito Bay and north of Cades and Jones bays, is lined with palms and sea grapes, and the folks at Oualie Beach Hotel can mix you a drink and fix you up with water-sports equipment. **Pinney's Beach,** the island's showpiece, has almost 4 mi (6.5 km) of soft, golden sand on the calm Caribbean, lined with a magnificent grove of palm trees, punctuated by beach bars such as Sunshine's, Chevy's and the Double Deuce.

WHERE TO EAT

$$$
SEAFOOD
★
✗ **Double Deuce.** Mark Roberts, the former chef at Montpelier, decided to chuck the "five-star lifestyle" and now co-owns this jammed, jamming beach bar, which lures locals with fine, fairly priced fare, creative cocktails, and a Hemingway-esque feel (the shack is plastered with sailing and fishing pictures, as well as Balinese masks, Sabrett hot dog umbrellas, and wind chimes). Peer behind the ramshackle bar and you'll find a gleaming modern kitchen where Mark (and fun-loving firebrand partner Lyndeta) prepare sublime seafood he often catches himself, as well as organic beef burgers, velvety pumpkin soup, creative pastas, and lip-smacking ribs. The "DD" is as cool and mellow as it gets. Stop by for free Wi-Fi and proper espresso, a game of pool, riotous Thursday-night karaoke, or just to hang out with a Double Deuce Stinger (Lyndy's answer to Sunshine's Killer Bee punch). You'll find more than 5,000 songs on the "jukebox"—Akon to ZZ Top, Sarah Vaughan to Van Morrison; if you can't find your favorite, the "DJ" will download it for you while you take a quick dip. ⊠ *Pinney's Beach* ☎ *869/469–2222* ⊕ *www.doubledeucenevis.com* ⚞ *Reservations essential* ▭ No *credit cards* ☾ *Closed Mon.*

$–$$$
CARIBBEAN
✗ **Sunshine's.** Everything about this shack overlooking (and spilling onto) the beach is larger than life, including the Rasta man Llewelyn "Sunshine" Caines himself. Flags and license plates from around the world complement the international patrons (including an occasional movie or sports star). Picnic tables are splashed with bright sunrise-to-sunset colors; even the palm trees are painted, though "it gone upscaled," as locals say, with VIP cabanas. Fishermen cruise up with their catch—you might savor lobster rolls or snapper creole. Don't miss the lethal house specialty, Killer Bee rum punch. As Sunshine boasts, "One and you're stung, two, you're stunned, three, it's a knockout." ⊠ *Pinney's Beach* ☎ *869/469–5817* ⊕ *www.sunshinenevis.com* ▭ *MC, V.*

OCHO RIOS, JAMAICA

John Bigley and Paris Permenter

About two hours east of Montego Bay lies Ocho Rios (often just "Ochi"), a lush destination that's favored by honeymooners for its tropical beauty. Often called the garden center of Jamaica, this community is perfumed by flowering hibiscus, bird of paradise, bougainvillea, and other tropical blooms year-round. Ocho Rios is a popular cruise port, and the destination where you'll find one of the island's most recognizable attractions: the stairstep Dunn's River Falls, which invites travelers to climb in daisy-chain fashion, hand-in-hand behind a sure-footed guide. This spectacular waterfall is actually a series of falls that cascades from the mountains to the sea. That combination of hills, rivers, and sea also means many activities in the area, from seaside horseback rides to mountain biking and lazy river rafting.

> ## OCHO RIOS BEST BETS
>
> ■ **Chukka Caribbean.** Any of the great adventure tours here is sure to please.
>
> ■ **Dunn's River Falls.** A visit to the falls is touristy, yet it's still exhilarating.
>
> ■ **Mystic Mountain.** Live out your *Cool Runnings* fantasies on the bobsled ride.
>
> ■ **Dolphin Cove at Treasure Reef.** Swim with a dolphin, stingray, or shark at this popular stop.
>
> ■ **Firefly.** The former home of playwright Noël Coward can be seen on a guided tour.

ESSENTIALS

CURRENCY The Jamaican dollar (J$89 to US$1). Currency-exchange booths are set up on the docks at Ocho Rios whenever a ship is in port. The U.S. dollar is accepted virtually everywhere; at some places change is made in Jamaican dollars. Prices given are in U.S. dollars unless otherwise indicated.

INTERNET A growing number of facilities offer Internet service; expect to pay about US$2 for 20 minutes. At the Taj Mahal Centre, **Jerkin @ Taj Internet Bar and Grill** (✉ *Ocho Rios* ☎ *876/974–7438*) offers numerous terminals for staying in touch by e-mail while traveling.

TELEPHONE Public telephones are found at the communications center at the Ocho Rios Cruise Pier. Travelers also find public phones in major Ocho Rios malls. Some U.S. phone companies won't permit credit-card calls to be placed from Jamaica because they've been victims of fraud, so collect calls are often the top option. GSM cell phones equipped with tri-band or world-roaming service will find coverage throughout the Ocho Rios region.

COMING ASHORE

Most cruise ships are able to dock at this port on Jamaica's north coast, near Dunn's River Falls. Less than 1 mi (2 km) from the Ocho Rios pier are Island Village (within walking distance), Taj Mahal Duty-Free Shopping Center, and the Ocean Village Shopping Center. Getting anywhere else in Ocho Rios will require a taxi; expect to pay $10 for a taxi ride downtown. The pier, which includes a cruise terminal with the

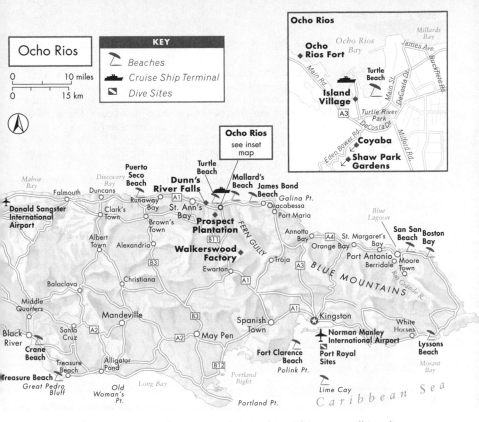

Ocho Rios

KEY

⊿ Beaches
⛴ Cruise Ship Terminal
◻ Dive Sites

0 — 10 miles
0 — 15 km

Ocho Rios
see inset
map

Ocho Rios

Millards
Bay

**Ocho
Rios Fort**

Ocho Rios
Bay

James Ave.

**Turtle
Beach**

**Island
Village**

Turtle River
Park

A3

DeCosta Dr.

Coyaba

**Shaw Park
Gardens**

Main Rd.

Eden Bower Rd.

Main St.

Milford Rd.

Mahoe
Bay

Falmouth

Discovery
Bay

Duncans

**Puerto
Seco
Beach**

Runaway
Bay

Clark's
Town

Brown's
Town

**Turtle
Beach**

**Dunn's
River Falls**

A1

St. Ann's
Bay

**Mallard's
Beach**

**James Bond
Beach**

Galina Pt.

Oracabessa

Port Maria

**Prospect
Plantation**

B11

**Walkerswood
Factory**

Ewarton

Annotto
Bay

A4

St. Margaret's
Bay

Orange Bay

Port Antonio

Berridale

Moore
Town

Blue
Lagoon

**San San
Beach**

**Boston
Bay**

Rio Grande R.

Albert
Town

Alexandria

B3

Christiana

Troja

A3

BLUE MOUNTAINS

**Donald Sangster
International
Airport**

Balaclava

Middle
Quarters

Mandeville

A2

B3

Spanish
Town

A1

May Pen

A2

Santa
Cruz

Alligator
Pond

B12

Portland
Bight

Kingston

**Norman Manley
International Airport**

White
Horses

**Lyssons
Beach**

Morant
Bay

**Fort Clarence
Beach**

**Port Royal
Sites**

Polink Pt.

Lime Cay

**Black
River**

**Crane
Beach**

Treasure
Beach

Treasure Beach

Great Pedro
Bluff

Old
Woman's
Pt.

Long Bay

Portland Pt.

Caribbean Sea

basic services and transportation, is also within easy walking distance
of Turtle Beach.

Licensed taxis are available at the pier; expect to pay about $35 per
hour for a guided taxi tour. Jamaica is one place in the Caribbean where
it's usually to your advantage to take an organized shore excursion
offered by your ship unless you just want to go to the beach or do a bit
of shopping in town. Car rental isn't recommended in Jamaica due to
high prices, bad roads, and aggressive drivers.

EXPLORING OCHO RIOS

Fodor'sChoice ★ **Dunn's River Falls.** One of Jamaica's most popular attractions is an eye-
catching sight: 600 feet of cold, clear mountain water splashing over
a series of stone steps to the warm Caribbean. The best way to enjoy
the falls is to climb the slippery steps: don a swimsuit, take the hand of
the person ahead of you, and trust that the chain of hands and bodies
leads to an experienced guide. The leaders of the climbs are personable
fellows who reel off bits of local lore while telling you where to step;
you can hire a guide's service for a tip of a few dollars. After the climb,
you exit through a crowded market, another reminder that this is one of
Jamaica's top tourist attractions. ⊠ Off Rte. A1, between St. Ann's Bay

and Ocho Rios, Ocho Rios ☎ *876/974–4767* ⊕ *www.dunnsriverfallsja. com* ✉ *$15* ⊙ *Daily 8:30–5.*

Prospect Plantation. To learn about Jamaica's agricultural heritage, a trip to this working plantation, just east of town, is a must. It's not just a place for history lovers, however. Everyone enjoys the views over the White River Gorge and the tour in a tractor-pulled cart. The grounds are full of exotic flowers and tropical trees, some planted over the years by such celebrities as Winston Churchill and Charlie Chaplin. The estate includes a small aviary with free-flying butterflies. You can also saddle up for horseback rides and camel safaris on the plantation's 900 acres, but the actual tour times are usually geared toward the cruise-ship schedule, so call ahead. ✉ *Rte. A1, 4 mi (3.2 km) east of Ocho Rios* ☎ *876/994–1058* ⊕ *www.prospectplantationtours.com* ✉ *$32* ⊙ *Daily 8–5; tour times vary.*

Walkerswood Factory. To learn more about Jamaican cuisine (as well as the island's bountiful supply of herbs, fruits, and spices), visit the source of many sauces and seasonings. Walkerswood Factory produces everything from jerk sauces to jams and pepper sauces. A one-hour guided tour provides a look at herb gardens, a visit to a re-created hut to learn more about historic countryside life, a jerk marinade demonstration, and a sampling of Walkerswood products. The site includes a gift shop and snack bar with local dishes. Tours are based on cruise-ship schedules, so call ahead. ✉ *About 6 mi (10 km) south of Ocho Rios on A3 in Walkerswood, St. Ann's Bay* ☎ *876/917–2318* ✉ *$15* ⊙ *Tour times vary.*

SHOPPING

Ocho Rios has several malls, and they are less hectic than the one in MoBay. Shopping centers include **Pineapple Place, Ocean Village, Taj Mahal,** and **Coconut Grove.** A fun mall that also serves as an entertainment center is **Island Village,** the place nearest to the cruise port. The open-air mall includes shops selling Jamaican handicrafts, duty-free goods and clothing, a Margaritaville restaurant, and a small beach area with a water trampoline and water sports.

ACTIVITIES

DOLPHIN-SWIM PROGRAMS

☾ **Dolphin Cove at Treasure Reef** (✉ *North Coast Hwy., adjacent to Dunn's River Falls, Box 21, Ocho Rios* ☎ *876/974–5335* ⊕ *www. dolphincovejamaica.com*) offers dolphin swims as well as lower-price dolphin encounters for ages 8 and up; dolphin touch programs for ages 6 and over; or simple admission to the grounds, which also includes a short nature walk. Programs cost between $45 and $195, depending on your depth of involvement with the dolphins. Advance reservations are required for dolphin and shark programs.

GOLF

Ocho Rios courses don't have the prestige of those around Montego Bay, but duffers will find challenges at a few lesser-known courses. The golf course at **Sandals Golf and Country Club** (*5 mi [8 km] southeast of Ocho Rios, turn south at White River and continue 4 mi [6 km], Ocho Rios* ☎ *876/975–0119*) is 700 feet above sea level (greens fees are $100 for 18 holes or $70 for 9 holes for nonguests; free for guests).

HORSEBACK RIDING

With its combination of hills and beaches, Ocho Rios is a natural for horseback excursions. Most are guided tours taken at a slow pace and perfect for those with no previous equestrian experience. Many travelers opt to pack long pants for horseback rides, especially those away from the beach.

Fodor's Choice Ocho Rios has excellent horseback riding, but the best of the operations ★ is **Chukka Caribbean Adventures** (✉ *Llandovery, St. Ann's Bay* ☎ *876/972–2506* ⊕ *www.chukkacaribbean.com*). Horse trainers at Chukka Cove originally exercised polo ponies by taking them for therapeutic rides in the sea; soon there were requests from visitors to ride the horses in the water. The company now offers a 2½-hour beach ride that ends with a bareback swim on the horses in the sea from a private beach ($76). It's a highlight of many trips to Jamaica. **Prospect Plantation** (✉ *Rte. A1, about 3 mi [5 km] east of Ocho Rios* ☎ *876/994–1058* ⊕ *www. prospectplantationtours.com*) offers a 3½-hour ride for ages 8 and older. The price ($70) includes use of helmets; advance reservations are required. For the adventurous, Prospect Plantation also offers guided camel rides.

WHITE-WATER RAFTING

White-water rafting is increasingly popular in the Ocho Rios area. **Chukka Caribbean Adventures** (✉ *Llandovery, St. Ann's Bay* ☎ *876/972–2506* ⊕ *www.chukkacaribbean.com*) offers white-water fun on the White River—an easy trip that doesn't require any previous experience. Rafters travel in a convoy along the river and through some gentle rapids. The 3½-hour tour costs $63 for adults.

BEACHES

Beach World. Especially popular with cruise passengers thanks to its proximity to the pier, Beach World offers a small beach and a full array of water toys at Island Village. Admission to the beach is $5; for an extra fee you can rent umbrellas, towels, and beach chairs. Activities include kayaking, snorkeling, scuba diving, and glass-bottom-boat rides. Changing rooms and lockers are also available. ✉ *Island Village Shopping Complex, Main St., Ocho Rios* ☎ *876/842–9406.*

★ **Dunn's River Falls Beach.** You'll find a crowd (especially if there's a cruise ship in town) at the small beach at the foot of the falls. Although tiny—especially considering the masses of people—its got a great view, as well as a beach bar and grill. Look up from the sands for a spectacular view of the cascading water, whose roar drowns out the sea as you approach. ✉ *Rte. A1, between St. Ann's Bay and Ocho Rios.*

WHERE TO EAT

¢–$ ✕ **Ocho Rios Village Jerk Centre.** This blue-canopied, open-air eatery is
JAMAICAN a good place to park yourself for frosty Red Stripe beer and fiery jerk
pork, chicken, or seafood. Milder barbecued meats, also sold by weight
(typically, a quarter or half pound makes a good serving), turn up on
the fresh-daily chalkboard menu posted on the wall. It's lively at lunch,
especially when passengers from cruise ships swamp the place. ⊠ *Da
Costa Dr., Ocho Rios* ☎ *876/974–2549* ▭ *D, MC, V.*

¢–$ ✕ **Scotchies Too.** The Ocho Rios branch of the longtime Montego Bay
CARIBBEAN favorite has already been lauded by international chefs for its excel-
Fodor'sChoice lent jerk. The open-air eatery offers plates of jerk chicken, sausage,
★ fish, pork, and ribs, all accompanied by *festival, bammy,* and some
fire-breathing hot sauce. Be sure to step over to the kitchen to watch
the preparation of the jerk over the pits. ⊠ *N. Coast Hwy., Drax Hall,
Ocho Rios* ☎ *876/794–9457* ▭ *MC, V.*

PROGRESO, MEXICO

Michele Joyce The waterfront town closest to Mérida, Progreso is not particularly
historic. It's also not terribly picturesque; still, it provokes a certain
sentimental fondness for those who know it well. On weekdays during
most of the year the beaches are deserted, but when school is out (Easter
week, July, and August) and on summer weekends it's bustling with families from Mérida. Progreso's charm—or lack of charm—seems to hinge
on the weather. When the sun is shining, the water looks translucent
green and feels bathtub-warm, and the fine sand makes for lovely long
walks. When the wind blows during one of Yucatán's winter *nortes,* the
water churns with whitecaps and looks gray and unappealing. Whether
the weather is good or bad, however, everyone ends up eventually at one
of the restaurants lining the main street, Calle 19. Across the street from
the oceanfront malecón, these all serve up cold beer, seafood cocktails,
and freshly grilled fish. Most cruise passengers head immediately for
Mérida or one of the nearby archaeological sites.

ESSENTIALS

CURRENCY The Mexican peso (MX$12.22 to US$1). U.S. dollars and credit cards are accepted
by everyone at the port. There is no advantage to paying in dollars, but there
may be an advantage to paying in cash.

INTERNET The cruise terminal isn't terribly close to Progreso's downtown area, but if you
take a bus or taxi into town, you'll easily find an Internet café with pretty cheap
service. If you take an excursion to Mérida, you'll find that Internet cafés there
are ubiquitous, particularly on the main square and calles 61 and 63; most
charge $1 to $3 per hour.

TELEPHONE Most pay phones accept prepaid Ladatel cards, sold in 30-, 50-, or 100-peso
denominations. To use the card, insert it in the pay phone's slot, dial 001 (for
calls to the U.S.) or 01 (for calls within Mexico), followed by the area code and
number. Credit is deleted from the card as you use it, and the balance is displayed on the small screen on the phone.

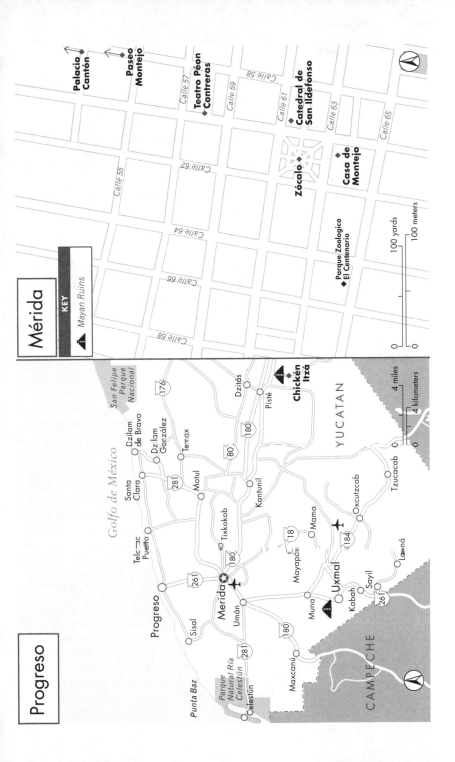

Progreso

Mérida

KEY

◄ Mayan Ruins

Palacio Cantón
Paseo Montejo
Teatro Péon Contreras
Catedral de San Ildefonso
Zócalo
Casa de Montejo
Parque Zoologico El Centenario

Calle 57
Calle 58
Calle 59
Calle 61
Calle 63
Calle 65
Calle 55
Calle 62
Calle 64
Calle 66
Calle 68

100 yards
100 meters

Golfo de México

San Felipe Parque Nacional

Punta Baz
Celestún
Parque Natural Ria Celestún
Sisal
Telchac Puerto
Santa Clara
Dzilam de Bravo
Dzilam González
Temax
Motul
Tixkokob
Progreso
Umán
Maxcanú
Muna
Mayapán
Mama
Kantunil
Dzitás
Pisté
Chichén Itzá
Uxmal
Kabah
Sayil
Labná
Oxcutzcab
Tzucacab

Mérida

YUCATAN
CAMPECHE

176
281
281
180
180
180
80
18
184
261
261

4 miles
4 kilometers

COMING ASHORE

The pier in Progreso is long, and cruise ships dock at its end, so passengers are shuttled to the foot of the pier, where the Progreso Cruise Terminal offers visitors their first stop. The terminal houses small restaurants and shops selling locally produced crafts. These are some of the best shops in sleepy Progreso (a much wider selection is available in nearby Mérida). The beach lies just east of the pier and can easily be reached on foot. If you want to enjoy the sun and a peaceful afternoon, a drink at one of the small palapa-roof restaurants that line the beach is a good option.

If you are looking to explore, there are plenty of taxis around the pier. A trip around town should not cost more than $5, but ask the taxi driver to quote you a price. If you want to see more of Progresso, a cab can also take you to the local sightseeing tour bus (which departs about every 10 minutes from the Casa de Cultura), a bright blue, open-air, double-decker bus that travels through town and only costs $2. A taxi ride from Progreso to Mérida runs about $25, and most drivers charge around $12 per hour to show you around. If you plan on renting the cab for a good part of the day, talk about the number of hours and the cost with the driver before you take off. It's difficult to rent a car, so most people just band together in a taxi.

EXPLORING MÉRIDA

Just south of Progreso (about 20 or 30 minutes by taxi), Mérida, the cultural and intellectual hub of the Yucatán, offers a great deal to explore. Mérida is rich in art, history, and tradition. Most streets are numbered, not named, and most run one-way. North–south streets have even numbers, which descend from west to east; east–west streets have odd numbers, which ascend from north to south. One of the best ways to see the city is to hire a *calesa*, a horse-drawn carriage. They congregate on the main square or at the Palacio Cantón, near the anthropology museum. Choose your horse and driver carefully, as some of the horses look dispirited, but others are fairly well cared for. Drivers charge about $13 for an hour-long circuit around downtown and up Paseo de Montejo, and $22 for an extended tour.

Casa de Montejo. Francisco de Montejo—father and son—conquered the peninsula and founded Mérida in 1542; they built their stately "casa" 10 years later. In the late 1970s it was restored by banker Agustín Legorreta, converted to a branch of Banamex bank, and now sits on the south side of the plaza. It is the city's finest—and oldest—example of colonial plateresque architecture, a Spanish architectural style popular in the 16th century and typified by the kind of elaborate ornamentation you'll see here. A bas-relief on the doorway—the facade is all that remains of the original house—depicts Francisco de Montejo the younger, his wife, and daughter, as well as Spanish soldiers standing on the heads of the vanquished Maya. Even if you have no banking to do, step into the building to glimpse the leafy inner patio. ⊠ *Calle 63, Centro* ⊗ *Weekdays 9–5 and Sat. 9–1.*

Catedral de San Ildefonso. Begun in 1561, St. Ildefonso is believed to be the oldest cathedral in the Americas. It took several hundred Mayan laborers, working with stones from the pyramids of the ravaged Mayan city, 36 years to complete it. Designed in the somber Renaissance style by an architect who had worked on the Escorial in Madrid, its facade is stark and unadorned, with gunnery slits instead of windows, and faintly Moorish spires. Inside, the black Cristo de las Ampollas (Christ of the Blisters)—at 7 meters (23 feet) tall, perhaps the tallest Christ in Mexico—occupies a side chapel to the left of the main altar. The statue is a replica of the original, which was destroyed during the revolution in 1910; this is also when the gold that typically decorated Mexican cathedrals was carried off. According to one of many legends, the Christ figure burned all night yet appeared the next morning unscathed—except that it was covered with the blisters for which it is named. You can hear the pipe organ play at the 11 AM Sunday mass. ⊠ *Calles 60 and 61, Centro* ☎ *No phone* ⊘ *Daily 7–11:30 and 4:30–8.*

> **PROGRESO BEST BETS**
>
> ■ **Chichén Itzá.** Difficult to reach from Cancún and most other Yucatan ports, the famous Maya city is an easy day trip from Progreso.
>
> ■ **Mérida.** This delightful, though busy, town is where you should head immediately upon landing if you aren't interested in the region's archaeological sites.
>
> ■ **Uxmal.** One of the most beautiful Mayan cities is reachable on a day trip from Progreso. If you've seen Chichén Itzá, go here.

Palacio Cantón. The most compelling of the mansions on **Paseo Montejo**, this stately palacio was built as the residence for a general between 1909 and 1911. Designed by Enrique Deserti, who also did the blueprints for the Teatro Peón Contreras, the building has a grandiose air that seems more characteristic of a mausoleum than a home: there's marble everywhere, as well as Doric and Ionic columns and other Italianate Beaux-Arts flourishes. The building also houses the air-conditioned **Museo de Antropología e Historia,** which introduces visitors to ancient Mayan culture. Temporary exhibits sometimes brighten the standard collection. ⊠ *Paseo Montejo 485, at Calle 43, Paseo Montejo* ☎ *999/923–0469* ⊠ *$5* ⊘ *Tues.–Sat. 9 AM–8 PM, Sun. 9–2.*

Paseo Montejo. North of downtown, this 10-block-long street was *the* place to reside in the late 19th century, when wealthy plantation owners sought to outdo each other with the opulence of their elegant mansions. Mansion owners typically opted for the decorative styles popular in New Orleans, Cuba, and Paris—imported Carrara marble, European antiques—rather than any style from Mexico. The broad boulevard, lined with tamarind and laurel trees, has lost much of its former panache; some of the mansions have fallen into disrepair. Many are now used as office buildings; others have been or are being restored as part of a citywide, privately funded beautification program. The street is a lovely place to explore on foot or in a horse-drawn carriage.

Teatro Peón Contreras. This 1908 Italianate theater was built along the same lines as grand turn-of-the-20th-century European theaters and opera houses. In the early 1980s the marble staircase, dome, and frescoes were restored. Today, in addition to performing arts, the theater houses the **Centro de Información Turística** (Tourist Information Center), which provides maps, brochures, and details about attractions in the city and state. The theater's most popular attraction, however, is the café-bar spilling out into the street facing Parque de la Madre. It's crowded every night with people enjoying the balladeers singing romantic and politically inspired songs. ⊠ *Calle 60 between Calles 57 and 59, Centro* 🕾 *999/924–9290 Tourist Information Center, 999/923–7344 theater, 999/924–9290* ☉ *Tourist Information Center daily 8–9.*

Zócalo. Méridians traditionally refer to this main square as the Plaza de la Independencia, or the Plaza Principal. Whichever name you prefer, it's a good spot from which to begin a tour of the city, in which to watch music or dance performances, or to chill in the shade of a laurel tree when the day gets too hot. The plaza was laid out in 1542 on the ruins of T'hó, the Mayan city demolished to make way for Mérida, and is still the focal point around which the most important public buildings cluster. *Confidenciales* (S-shaped benches) invite intimate tête-à-têtes; lampposts keep the park beautifully illuminated at night. ⊠ *Bordered by Calles 60, 62, 61, and 63, Centro.*

FARTHER AFIELD

Fodor's Choice
★

Chichén Itzá. One of the most dramatically beautiful of the ancient Mayan cities, Chichén Itzá was discovered by Europeans in the mid-1800s, and much here remains a mystery. Experts have little information about who the Itzás might have been, and the reason why they abandoned the city around 1224 is also unknown. ⊠ *Approximately 75 mi (120 km) east of Mérida on Carretera 180* 🖼 *Site, museum, and sound-and-light show $MX 111; parking $2; use of video camera $3 (keep this receipt if visiting other archaeological sites on same day)* ☉ *Daily 8–5; sound-and-light show just after 5* PM *(at 8* PM *in Spanish with translations for $2.50)* ⊕ *www.inah.gob.mx.*

Fodor's Choice
★

Uxmal. If Chichén Itzá is the most expansive Mayan ruin in Yucatán, Uxmal is arguably the most elegant. The architecture here reflects the late classical renaissance of the 7th to the 9th century and is contemporary with that of Palenque and Tikal. ⊠ *48 mi (78 km) south of Mérida on Carretera 261* 🖼 *Site, museum, and sound-and-light show $MX 111; parking $1; use of video camera $2 (keep this receipt if visiting other archaeological sites along Ruta Puuc on same day)* ☉ *Daily 8–5; sound-and-light show just after dusk (at 7* PM *in winter or 8* PM *in summer, tickets to only show $3); official English language tour guide $55.*

SHOPPING

In Progreso there is also a small downtown area that is a better place to walk than to shop, between Calle 80 and Calle 31, with small restaurants that serve simple Mexican fare (like *tortas* and *tacos*), small shops with everyday goods for locals, banks, and supermarkets.

Mérida offers more places to shop, including colorful Mexican markets selling local goods. Sunday brings an array of wares into Mérida;

starting at 9 AM, the Handicrafts Bazaar, or **Bazar de Artesanías** (⊠ *At main square, Centro*), sells lots of *huipiles* (traditional, white embroidered dresses) as well as hats and costume jewelry. As its name implies, popular art, or handicrafts, are sold at the **Bazar de Artes Populares** (⊠ *Parque Santa Lucía, at Calles 60 and 55, Centro*) beginning at 9 AM on Sunday. If you're interested in handicrafts, **Bazar García Rejón** (⊠ *Calles 65 and 62, Centro*) has rows of indoor stalls that sell items like leather goods, palm hats, and handmade guitars.

The **Mercado Municipal** (⊠ *Calles 56 and 67, Centro*) has lots of things you won't need, but which are fascinating to look at: songbirds in cane cages, mountains of mysterious fruits and vegetables, dippers made of hollow gourds (the same way they've been made here for a thousand years). There are also lots of crafts for sale, including hammocks, sturdy leather *huaraches,* and piñatas in every imaginable shape and color. ■ TIP➔ Guides often approach tourists near this market. They expect a tip and won't necessarily bring you to the best deals. You're better off visiting some specialty stores first to learn about the quality and types of hammocks, hats, and other crafts; then you'll have an idea of what you're buying—and what it's worth—if you want to bargain in the market. Also be wary of pickpockets within the markets.

WHERE TO EAT

$ ✕ **Café La Habana.** A gleaming wood bar, white-jacketed waiters, and the scent of cigarettes contribute to the Old European feel at this overwhelmingly popular spot, a branch of a Mexico City café that has been around since the 1950s. Overhead, brass-studded ceiling fans swirl the air-conditioned air. Sixteen specialty coffees are offered (some spiked with spirits like Kahlúa or cognac), and the menu has light snacks as well as some entrées, including tamales, fajitas, and enchiladas. The waiters are friendly, and there are plenty of them, although service is not always brisk. Both the café and upstairs Internet joint are open 24 hours a day; free Wi-Fi is available downstairs for laptop-toting customers. ⊠ *Calle 59 No. 511A, at Calle 62, Centro* ☎ *999/928–6502* ▤ *MC, V.*

MEXICAN

$ ✕ **La Casa de Frida.** Chef-owner Gabriela Praget puts a healthful, cosmopolitan spin on Mexican fare at her restaurant. This is a great place to sample foods from around Mexico. Praget prepares all the dishes herself and is usually on hand to greet guests. Traditional dishes like duck in a dark, rich mole sauce (made with chocolate and chiles) share the menu with gourmet vegetarian cuisine: potato and cheese tacos, ratatouille in puff pastry, and crepes made with *huitlacoche* (a delicious trufflelike corn fungus). The flavors here are so divine that diners have been known to hug Praget after a meal. The dining room—a casual covered patio decorated with plants, copies of Frida Kahlo self-portraits, several Frida dolls, and other art—is a comfortable place to enjoy a leisurely meal. ⊠ *Calle 61 No. 526, at Calle 66, Centro* ☎ *999/928–2311* ▤ *No credit cards* ⊙ *Closed Sun. No lunch.*

MEXICAN
Fodor'sChoice
★

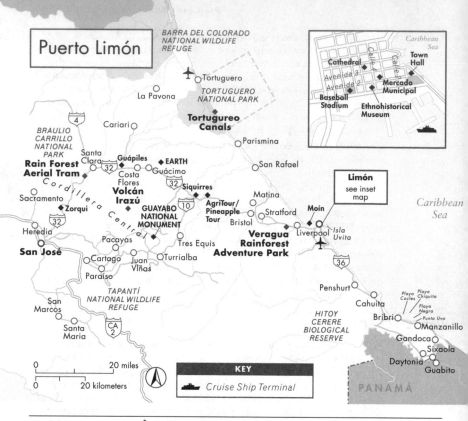

PUERTO LIMÓN, COSTA RICA

Jeffrey Van Fleet

Christopher Columbus became Costa Rica's first tourist when he landed on this stretch of coast in 1502 during his fourth and final voyage to the New World. Expecting to find vast mineral wealth, he named the region "Costa Rica" (rich coast). Imagine the Spaniards' surprise eventually to find there was none. Save for a brief skirmish some six decades ago, the country *did* prove itself rich in a long tradition of peace and democracy. No other country in Latin America can make that claim. Costa Rica is also abundantly rich in natural beauty, managing to pack beaches, volcanoes, rain forests, and diverse animal life into an area the size of Vermont and New Hampshire combined. It has successfully parlayed those qualities into its role as one the world's great ecotourism destinations. A day visit is short, but time enough for a quick sample.

ESSENTIALS

CURRENCY The colón (¢569 to US$1). Most businesses in port gladly accept U.S. dollars.

INTERNET A bank of Internet computers is yours to use at the cruise terminal. **Internet Cinco Estrellas** (⊠ *50 meters north of Terminal de Cruceros* ☎ *2758–5752*).

TELEPHONE Telephone numbers have eight digits. Merely dial the number. There are no area codes. You'll find ample phones for use in the cruise terminal. Public phones accept locally purchased calling cards.

COMING ASHORE

Ships dock at Limón's spacious, spiffy Terminal de Cruceros (cruise terminal), one block south of the city's downtown. You'll find telephones, Internet computers, a crafts market, and tourist information and tour operators' desks inside the terminal, as well as a small army of manicurists who do a brisk business. Step outside and walk straight ahead one block to reach Limón's downtown.

A fleet of red taxis waits on the street in front of the terminal. Drivers are happy to help you put together a do-it-yourself tour. Most charge $100 to $150 per carload for a day of touring. There is no place to rent a car here, but you're better off leaving the driving to someone else. Cruise lines offer dozens of shore excursions in Costa Rica, and if you want to go any farther afield than Limón or the coast south, we suggest you take an organized tour. The country looks disarmingly small on a map—it is—but hills give rise to mountains the farther inland you go, and road conditions range from "okay" to "abysmal." Distances are short as the toucan flies, but travel times are longer than you'd expect.

EXPLORING PUERTO LIMÓN

Limón. "Sultry and sweltering" describes this port community of 60,000. The country's most ethnically diverse city mixes the Latino flavor of the rest of Costa Rica with Afro-Caribbean and Asian populations, descendants of laborers brought to do construction and farming in the 19th century. As in most of the rest of Costa Rica, you'll see no street signs here. Locals use a charmingly archaic system of designating addresses: The place you're looking for may be "100 meters south and 75 meters west of some landmark," where "100 meters" equals one city block, regardless of actual distance. Just north and east of the cruise terminal lies the city's palm-lined central park, **Parque Vargas,** with a promenade facing the ocean. Nine or so Hoffman's two-toed sloths live in its trees; ask a passerby to point them out, as spotting them requires a trained eye.

Rain Forest Aerial Tram. This 2½-square-mi (4-square-km) preserve houses a privately owned and

PUERTO LIMÓN BEST BETS

■ **The Rain Forest Tram.** This attraction takes you up into the canopy of the rain forest to see it from a unique angle.

■ **Tortuguero Canals.** Whether you go on a ship-sponsored tour or arrange it on your own, you see a wild part of Costa Rica that isn't reachable by anything but boat.

■ **Zip-Line Tours.** If you have never done one of these thrilling tours, flying from tree to tree, Costa Rica is the original place to do it.

operated engineering marvel: a series of gondolas strung together in a modified ski-lift pulley system. (To lessen the impact on the jungle, the support pylons were lowered into place by helicopter.) The tram gives you a way of seeing the rain-forest canopy and its spectacular array of epiphyte plant life and birds from just above, a feat you could otherwise accomplish only by climbing the trees yourself. Though purists might complain that it treats the rain forest like an amusement park, it's an entertaining way to learn the value and beauty of rain-forest ecology. ☒ *Braulio Carrillo National Park, 76 mi (120 km) west of Limón* ☎ *2257–5961, 866/759–8726 in North America* ⊕ *www.rainforestrams.com* ⌨ *$55, children under 12, $27.50* ⊗ *Mon. 9–4, Tues.–Sun. 6:30–4.*

San José. Costa Rica's sprawling, congested capital sits in the middle of the country about three hours inland from the coast. Despite the distance, San José figures as a shore excursion—a long one to be sure—on most ships' itineraries. (The vertical distance is substantial, too; the capital sits on a plateau just under a mile above sea level. You'll appreciate a jacket here after so many days at sea level.) Although the city dates from the mid-18th century, little from the colonial era remains. The northeastern San José suburb of **Moravia** is chock-full of souvenir stores lining a couple of blocks behind the city's church. The **Teatro Nacional** (*National Theater;* ☒ *Plaza de la Cultura, Barrio La Soledad* ☎ *221–1329* ⊕ *www.teatronacional.go.cr* ⌨ *$7* ⊗ *Mon.–Sat. 9–4.*) is easily the most enchanting building in Costa Rica, and San José's must-see sight. Coffee barons constructed the Italianate sandstone building, modeling it on a composite of European opera houses, and inaugurating it in 1897. ✦ *100 mi (160 km) west of Limón.*

The **Museo Nacional** (*National Museum;* ☒ *C. 17, between Avs. Central and 2, Barrio La Soledad* ☎ *257–1433* ⊕ *www.museocostarica.go.cr* ⌨ *$7* ⊗ *Tues.–Sat. 8:30–4:30, Sun. 9–4:30*) is housed in a white-washed fortress dating from 1870. Notice the bullet holes: this former army headquarters saw fierce fighting during a brief 1948 civil war. But it was also here that the government abolished the country's military in 1949. ✦ *100 mi (160 km) west of Limón.*

Tortuguero Canals. The largely forested region north of Limón is one of those Costa Rican anomalies: roadless and remote, it's nevertheless one of the country's most-visited places. A system of inland canals runs parallel to the shoreline, providing safer access to the region than a dangerous journey for smaller vessels up the seacoast. Some compare the densely layered greenery highlighted by brilliantly colored flowers, whose impact is doubled by the jungle's reflection in the mirror-smooth canal surfaces, to the Amazon. That might be stretching it, but there's still an Indiana Jones mystique to the journey up here, especially when you get off the main canals and into the narrower lagoons. Your guide will point out the abundant wildlife: sloths hang in the trees; howler monkeys let out their plaintive calls; egrets soar above the river surface; and crocodiles laze on the banks. ☒ *North of Limón.*

☾ **Veragua Rainforest Adventure Park.** The region's newest attraction is a 4,000-acre nature theme park, about 30 minutes west of Limón. It's popular with cruise-ship passengers in port for the day, but if you're in the area, it's well worth a stop. Veragua's great strength is its small army of enthusiastic, super-informed guides who take you through a network of nature trails and exhibits of hummingbirds, snakes, frogs, and butterflies and other insects. A gondola ride overlooks the complex and transports you through the rain-forest canopy. A branch of the **Original Canopy Tour** is here, too, and offers you the chance to zip from platform to platform—10 in all—through the rain-forest canopy. The $50 tour lasts 1½ hours, and can be done separately from the other attractions. The canopy tour is not included in the admission price for the park. ⊠ *Veragua de Liverpool* ✛ *9 mi (15 km) west of Limón* 🕾 *2296–5056 in San José* ⊕ *www.veraguarainforest.com* ⊠ *Half-day tour $65, children under 12, $45; full-day tour $99, children under 12, $70* ⊙ *Tues.–Sun. 8–4.*

Volcán Irazú. Five active volcanoes loom over Costa Rica's territory (as well as many inactive ones). Irazú clocks in at the highest at about 11,000 feet (3,700 meters) and the farthest east and most accessible from Limón, though still a three-hour drive. The volcano last erupted in 1965, but gases and steam have billowed from fumaroles on its northwestern slope ever since. You can go right up to the top, although cloudy days—there are many—can obscure the view. ⊠ *84 mi (140 km) southwest of Limón* 🕾 *2551–9398, 8200–5025 for ranger station* ⊠ *$7* ⊙ *Daily 8–3:30.*

SHOPPING

The cruise-ship terminal contains an orderly maze of souvenir stands. Vendors are friendly; there's no pressure to buy. Many shops populate the restored port building across the street as well. Spelling is not its forte, but the **Caribbean Banana** (⊠ *50 meters north Terminal de Cruceros, west side of Parque Vargas*) stands out from the other shops in the cruise-terminal area with a terrific selection of wood carvings.

ACTIVITIES

WHITE-WATER RAFTING

You can experience some of the world's premier white-water rafting in Costa Rica. Old standby **Ríos Tropicales** (⊠ *On highway in Siquirres* 🕾 *2233–6455, 866/722–8273 in North America* ⊕ *www.riostropicales. com*) has tours on a Class III–IV section of the Pascua sector of the Río Reventación for experienced rafters only. Not quite so wild, but still with Class II–III rapids, is the nearby Florida section of the Reventazón. You can kick off your excursion in this part of the country at the company's operations center in Siquirres, 45 mi (75 km) west of Limón.

ZIP-LINE TOURS

Costa Rica gave birth to the so-called canopy tour, a system of zip lines that transports you from platform to platform in the rain-forest treetops courtesy of a very secure harness. Though billed as a way to get up close with nature, your Tarzan-like yells will probably scare any wildlife away. Think of it more as an outdoor amusement-park ride.

The nearest zip-line tour is at **Veragua Rainforest Adventure Park** (*see the listing, above*).

BEACHES

The dark-sand beaches on this sector of the coast are pleasant enough, but won't dazzle you if you've made previous stops at Caribbean islands with their white-sand strands. Nicer beaches than Limón's Playa Bonita lie farther south along the coast and can be reached by taxi or organized shore excursion. Strong undertows make for ideal surfing conditions on these shores, but risky swimming. Exercise caution.

Playa Bonita (⌧ *1 mi [2 km] north of Limón*), the name of Limón's own strand, translates as "pretty beach," but it's your typical urban beach, a bit on the cluttered side. **Playa Blanca** (⌧ *26 mi [44 km] southeast of Limón, Cahuita*), one of the coast's only white-sand beaches, lies within the boundaries of Cahuita National Park, right at the southern entrance of the pleasant little town of Cahuita. The park's rain forest extends right to the edge of the beach, and the waters here offer good snorkeling. **Playa Cocles** (⌧ *38 m [63 km] southeast of Limón, Puerto Viejo de Talamanca*), the region's most popular strand of sand, lies just outside Puerto Viejo de Talamanca, one of Costa Rica's archetypal beach towns, with its attendant cafés and bars and all-around good times to be had.

WHERE TO EAT

$ ✕ **Brisas del Caribe.** Here's a case study in what happens when cruise
SEAFOOD ships come to town. This old downtown standby, once as charmingly off-kilter as the crooked umbrellas on its front tables, got rid of its video poker machines (and the locals who always hoped to get lucky playing them), tiled the floors, and remodeled. The food is still good—seafood and surprisingly decent hamburgers, a real rarity in Costa Rica, are the fare here—but a bit of the local color has faded. This place does it up big with a lunch buffet on cruise days. ⌧ *North side of Parque Vargas* ☎ 2758–0138 ▭ AE, D, DC, MC, V.

$ ✕ **Park Hotel.** Take refuge from the sweltering midday heat in the air-
SEAFOOD conditioned restaurant of Limón's pastel-and-pink, mid-range business-class hotel. Decent pastas, seafood, and desserts are on the menu, and the pleasant ocean view is tossed in for free. ⌧ *Av. 3, Calles 2–3* ☎ 2798–0555 ▭ AE, D, DC, MC, V

ROATÁN, HONDURAS

Melanie
Wetzel

You'll swear you hear Jimmy Buffett singing as you step off the ship onto Roatán. The flavor is decidedly Margaritaville, but with all there is to do on this island off the north coast of Honduras you'll never waste away here. Roatán is the largest and most important of the Bay Islands, though at a mere 40 mi (65 km) from tip to tip, and no more than 3 mi (5 km) at its widest; "large" is relative here. As happened elsewhere on Central America's Caribbean coast, the British got here first—the Bay

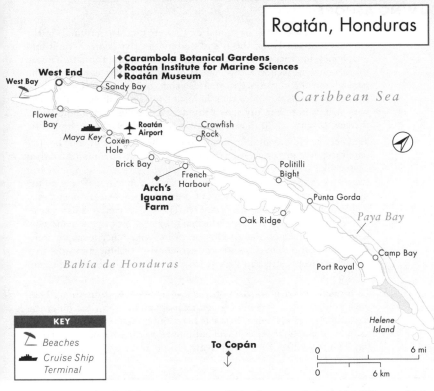

Roatán, Honduras

◆ Carambola Botanical Gardens
◆ Roatán Institute for Marine Sciences
◆ Roatán Museum

West End
West Bay
West End
Sandy Bay

Caribbean Sea

Flower Bay
Maya Key
Coxen Hole
Roatán Airport
Crawfish Rock
Brick Bay
French Harbour
Arch's Iguana Farm
Politilli Bight
Punta Gorda
Oak Ridge
Paya Bay

Bahía de Honduras

Camp Bay
Port Royal

Helene Island

KEY

⊿ *Beaches*
🚢 *Cruise Ship Terminal*

To Copán

0 _____ 6 mi
0 _____ 6 km

Islands didn't become part of Honduras until the mid-1800s—and left an indelible imprint in the form of place names such as Coxen Hole, French Harbour, and West End, and of course their language, albeit a Caribbean-accented English. The eyes of underwater enthusiasts mist over at the mention of Roatán, one of the world's premier diving destinations, but plenty of topside activity will keep you busy, too.

ESSENTIALS

CURRENCY The Honduran leimpira (L18.9 to US$1). You'll find an ATM at Banco BAC in the town of Coxen Hole, where cruise ships arrive. There are also ATMs in West End at the Dolphin Resort and in West Bay at the Mayan Princess Resort. Credit cards are widely accepted, although merchants frequently add a surcharge to offset the high processing fees they are charged by card companies

INTERNET Check your e-mail and make international phone calls at **Paradise Computers** (✉ *Megaplaza Mall French Harbour*), in their main location inside the new Megaplaza Mall, or at their satellite location on the main drag in West End Village.

TELEPHONE Land lines in Honduras have seven digits, while cell phones have eight. There are no area codes, so just dial the number. Public phones are hard to find, but some hotels and businesses will offer phone services to walk-up users for a small fee.

COMING ASHORE

Some ships dock at the Terminal de Cruceros (cruise terminal) in the village of Coxen Hole, the island's administrative center. You'll find telephones, Internet computers, and stands with tour information inside the terminal, as well as a flea market of crafts vendors just outside the gate. Carnival completed a new cruise-ship dock in 2010, and its ships now dock at this new $80 million installation in Mahogany Bay. The new dock is not near any major towns, but it is just a few miles from the new Megaplaza Mall and the town of French Harbour.

Taxis are readily available outside the cruise-ship docks, but be prepared to pay a premium for services there. Trips to the major tourism centers like West End and West Bay beach will cost around $20. If you would like to save money on your taxi fares, you can walk out to the main highway (or into the town of Coxen Hole if you dock near there) and look for taxis marked COLECTIVO. These taxis charge a flat rate of L25–L30, depending on the distance. They also pick up as many passengers as they can hold, so plan on riding with other locals or tourists. The local public-transport system consists of blue minivans that leave from Main Street in Coxen Hole to various points on the island until 6 PM.

Look for the cadre of tourist police if you need help with anything. They wear yellow shirts and dark-green trousers and are evident on cruise days. You certainly can rent a car here, but the island's compact size makes it unnecessary. Taxis will happily take you anywhere; expect to pay $60 to $120 for a day's private tour, depending on how far you wish to travel.

EXPLORING ROATÁN

Arch's Iguana Farm. West of French Harbour you'll find this farm where you can get a close look at hundreds of indigenous reptiles. There are tropical birds as well, and a marine viewing area where you can see many species of fish and live lobsters from the dock. ⊠ *French Harbour* ☏ *445–1498* ✉ *L75.*

Carambola Botanical Gardens. With one of the country's most extensive orchid collections, this is home to many different varieties of tropical plants. It is also a breeding area for iguanas. There are several trails to follow, and many of the trees and plants are identified by small signs. The longest trail leads up to the top of the hill, where you find an amazing view of the West End and Anthony's Key Resort. ⊠ *Sandy Bay, across from Anthony's Key Resort* ☏ *445–3117* ⊕ *www. carambolagardens.com* ✉ *$5* ☉ *Daily 7–5.*

Maya Key. One of the premier day excursions for cruisers visiting Roatán is this small, private island near Coxen Hole. The park offers a wide variety of amenities and activities, including sandy beaches, tropical gardens, a museum with cultural displays, and an animal rescue center, where you can meet the animals. Carnival and Norwegian cruise lines offer this option as a shore excursion, or you can book independently on the park's Web site. You can also buy snacks and beverages. This is a great place for families with children. Maya Key is operated by Anthony's Key Resort, which is one of the oldest and most famous resorts in Honduras. ⊹ *3-minute water shuttle ride from the shuttle pier 50 yeards east of the Terminal de Cruceros near Coxen Hole* ☎ *9995–9589* ⊕ *www.mayakeyroatan.com* ✉ *$30 (includes boat shuttle, advance reservations required)* ☉ *Mon.–Sat. 7 AM–4 PM.*

☾ **Roatán Institute for Marine Sciences.** One of the attractions at Anthony's Key Resort, the Institute is an educational center that researches bottlenose dolphins and other marine animals. There are dolphin shows twice a day, which are free to the public. For an additional fee you can participate in a "dolphin encounter," which allows you to interact with the dolphins either swimming or snorkeling. There are also programs for children ages 5 to 14, including snorkeling experiences, and the "Dolphin Trainer for a Day" program. ✉ *Anthony's Key Resort* ☎ *445–1327* ⊕ *www.anthonyskey.com* ✉ *L64* ☉ *Daily 8:30–5.*

Roatán Museum. Well worth a visit is the tiny museum, which has been called one of the best small museums in Central America. The facility, at Anthony's Key Resort, displays archaeological discoveries from Roatán and the rest of the Bay Islands. ✉ *Anthony's Key Resort* ☎ *445–1327* ⊕ *www.anthonyskey.com* ✉ *L64* ☉ *Daily 8:30–5.*

West End. One of the most popular destinations for budget travelers, West End offers idyllic beaches stretching as far as the eye can see. One of the loveliest spots is Half Moon Bay, a crescent of brilliant white sand. A huge number of dive shops offer incredibly low-price diving courses. ✉ *West End.*

SHOPPING

At the cruise ship dock in Coxen Hole you can find craft vendors, who set up shop outside the cruise-terminal gates; a small number of souvenir shops are scattered around the center of Coxen Hole, a short walk from the docks. Few of the souvenirs for sale here—or anywhere else on the island for that matter—were actually made in Roatán; most come from mainland Honduras. The new cruise-ship dock in Mahogany Bay has a shopping area as well. If you get as far as West End, there are a variety of souvenir and craft sellers in small shops lining the main sand road that runs parallel to the beach.

ACTIVITIES

DIVING AND SNORKELING

Most of the activity on Roatán centers on scuba diving and snorkeling, as well as the newest sensation, snuba, a cross between the two, whereby your mask is connected to an air tube above. Warm water, great visibility, and thousands of colorful fish make the island a popular destination. Add to this a good chance of seeing a whale shark, and you'll realize why so many people head here each year. Dive sites cluster off the island's western and southern coasts. Competition among the dive shops is fierce in West End, so check out a few. When shopping around, ask about class size (eight is the maximum), the condition of the diving equipment, and the safety equipment on the dive boat.

In West Bay, **Bananarama Dive Center** (✉ West Bay ☎ 445–5005 ⊕ www.bananaramadive.com) is a top-notch dive operation. The staff are particularly good with kids and families, and they offer a variety of services for cruisers, such as snorkel rental, snacks and drinks right on the beach. Just at the entrance to West End, **Coconut Tree Divers** (✉ West End ☎ 445–4081 ⊕ www.coconuttreedivers.com) is a PADI Gold Palm resort, offering a wide range of dives and dive courses. They also have cabins with air-conditioning and fridges, with a discount for their divers. **Native Sons** (✉ West End ☎ 445–4003 ⊕ www.nativesonsroatan.com) is one of the most popular dive shops in town. It's run by a native of Roatán who really knows the area.

FISHING

Early Bird Fishing Charters (✉ Sandy Bay ☎ 9955–0001 ⊕ www.earlybirdfishingcharters.com) is a great charter fishing company operated by a Roatán native. In addition to deep-sea and flats fishing, you'll have a great opportunity to see the island. Roatán has traditionally had a sea-based economy, and many of the small towns and villages look better from the vantage point of a boat.

FLIGHTSEEING

Bay Island Airways (⊕ www.bayislandairways.com) offer sightseeing tours in a multi-engine, three-seat seaplane. The experience is thrilling, since the cockpit is open and the plane takes off from the water; it is a fantastic photo opportunity. The company also offers packages that include landing near inaccessible beaches for a private picnic far from the crowds of other cruisers.

BEACHES

You almost can't go wrong with any of Roatán's white-sand beaches. Even those adjacent to populated areas manage to stay clean and uncluttered, thanks to efforts of residents. Water is rougher for swimming on the less-protected north side of the island.

Half Moon Bay, Roatán's most popular beach, is also one of its prettiest. Coconut palms and foliage come up to the crescent shoreline. The beach lies just outside the tourist-friendly West End. Crystal-clear waters offer abundant visibility for snorkeling.

Roatán is famous for the picturesque **West Bay Beach.** It's a de rigueur listing on every shore-excursions list. Once there, you can lounge on the beach or snorkel; on cruise days, most ships offer an excursion to nearby **Gumba Limba Park** (⊕ *www.gumbalimbapark.com*), which offeres close encounters with monkeys and birds, as well as canopy zip-line tours and other activities; to visit on a cruise-ship day, passengers must purchase an excursion from their ship that includes the park.

WHERE TO EAT

$$ ✕ **Cool Beans Coffee Shop.** Cool Beans has a wide variety of coffees,
CAFÉ teas, and frozen drinks (iced coffee, milkshakes, and fruit shakes). You can also get great pastries as well as sandwiches for lunch. During the evening there is often live music here, as well as Spanish classes or other events. ⊠ *West Bay Mall, West Bay* ☎ *445–5048* ⊕ *www. coolbeansroatan.com* ⊟ *No credit cards.*

$$$ ✕ **Foster's West End Pier.** This bar and grill sits over the water in West End,
AMERICAN just before Crystal Beach Cabins and across from Barefoot Charlie's Internet café. Foster's was the original West End bar and restaurant, and has had many different operators over the years. It is a spectacular location for relaxing and dining on the water, and viewing the boat traffic around West End. The menu is currently heavy on Southern-style food; there's a full bar. On Friday and Saturday nights this becomes the West End party spot, with a DJ and full crowd of locals and tourists. ⊠ *West End* ☎ *9481–2595* ⊟ *AE, MC, V.*

SAMANÁ (CAYO LEVANTADO), DOMINICAN REPUBLIC

Eileen Robin-son Smith

Samaná, the name of both a peninsula in the Dominican Republic as well as the largest town on Samaná Bay, is one of the least-known regions of the country, but the new international airport that opened in nearby El Catey in 2006, and the new highway from Santo Domingo that has cut drive-time to two hours, are changing that perception quickly. (Still, only charters fly into El Catey.) Much development is planned, so a visit now will be to a place that is not yet geared to a great deal of mainstream, mass tourism. But with the use of the port by some mega-ships, that, too, is changing rapidly. Samaná is one of the Dominican Republic's newest cruise-ship destinations, with one of the island's greatest varieties of shore excursions. You can explore caves and see an amazing waterfall. And since many humpback whales come here each year to mate and give birth, it's a top whale-watching destination from January through March. While some cruise lines still use Cayo Levantado as a private-island type of experience, for other lines it is just one of several options.

ESSENTIALS

CURRENCY The Dominican peso (RD$36.25 to US$1). Get local currency if you are touring on your own, but most places accept U.S. dollars, though any change will be in pesos. Banks and *cambios* (currency exchange offices) are plentiful.

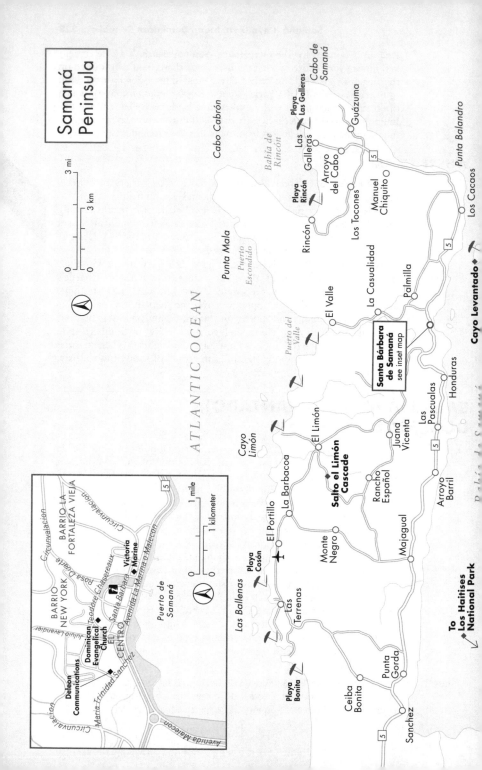

Samaná Peninsula

ATLANTIC OCEAN

3 mi

3 km

Cabo Cabrón

Punta Mala

Bahía de Rincón

Cabo de Samaná

Playa Las Galleras

Las Galleras

Guázuma

Playa Rincón

Arroyo del Cabo

Puerto Escondido

Rincón

Los Tocones

Manuel Chiquito

Punta Balandro

5

Los Cacaos

El Valle

La Casualidad

Palmilla

Cayo Levantado

Puerto del Valle

Santa Bárbara de Samaná
see inset map

Honduras

5

Cayo Limón

El Limón

Salto el Limón Cascade

Las Pascualas

Juana Vicenta

Rancho Español

Arroyo Barril

Bahía de Samaná

La Barbacoa

Monte Negro

Majagual

To Los Haitises National Park

El Portillo

Playa Cosón

Las Terrenas

Las Ballenas

Playa Bonita

Ceiba Bonita

Punta Gorda

Sanchez

5

BARRIO LA FORTALEZA VIEJA

BARRIO NEW YORK

Circunvalación

Rosa Duarte

Julio Lavandier

Teodoro Chassereaux

Dominican Evangelical Church

Deleon Communications

María Trinidad Sánchez

CENTRO

EL

Santa Bárbara

Victoria Marine

Avenida La Marina o Malecón

Puerto de Samaná

Avenida Malecón

Circunvalación

5

1 mile

1 kilometer

INTERNET You'll find several convenient Internet cafés in town. The price of going online ranges between RD$30 and RD$80 per hour, inexpensive to be sure. However, don't be surprised if you go and are told that the computers: *"No sirve, porque no hay electricidad."* Translation: This is still a developing destination, and sometimes half the day is spent without electricity. Although most hotels and restaurants have generators, usually these shops do not. **Centro Llamada Edwards** (✉ *4 Francisco Rosario Sanchez, Samaná* ☎ *809/538–2476*) has five computers and charges only RD$30 an hour to connect. **Deleon Communications** (✉ *13 Maria Trinidad Sanchez, Samaná, across from landmark Palacio Justicia* ☎ *809/538–3538*) has just two computers but four phone booths.

TELEPHONE You can call U.S. or Canadian numbers easily; just dial 1 plus the area code and number. **Centro de Communicationes Verizon** (✉ *8 Francisco Rosario Sanchez (near the market), Samaná* ☎ *809/538–2901* ✉ *Maria Trinidad Sanchez, Samaná, next door to Pharmacia Gisella)*is a good place to make phone calls. Only cash is taken, preferably pesos. At the first location, there are public computers for checking your e-mails; at the second, you won't be able to go online.

COMING ASHORE

Cruise ships anchor at a point equidistant between the town of Samaná and Cayo Levantado, an island at the mouth of Samaná Bay with a great beach and facilities to receive 1,500 cruise-ship passengers. Tenders will take you to one of three docks, located on the malecón, referred to as the Samaná Bay Piers. The farthest is a five-minute walk from the town center.

Renting a car, although possible, isn't a good option. Driving in the D.R. can be a hectic and even harrowing experience; if you are only in port one day, don't risk it. You'll do better if you combine your resources with friends from the ship and share a taxi to do some independent exploring. Negotiate prices, and settle before getting in the taxi. To give you an idea of what to expect, a minivan that can take eight people will normally charge $90 for the round-trip to Las Terranas, including a two-hour wait while you explore or enjoy the beach. Similarly, you'll pay $80 to travel to Las Galleras or Playa Rincón. Many of the drivers speak some English. Within Samaná, rickshaws are far less costly and are also fun. Called *motoconchos de carretas*, they are not unlike larger versions of the Thai tuk-tuk, but can hold up to six people. The least you will pay is RD$10. They're fine

SAMANÁ BEST BETS

■ **Cayo Levantado.** This resort island puts on an excellent show for day-trippers.

■ **El Limón Waterfall.** A horseback ride into the forest culminates in dazzling falls cascading into a natural pool.

■ **Los Haitises National Park.** The caves are filled with Taíno drawings; the mangroves are magnificent.

■ **Playa Rincón.** This rarely accessed beach offers a river, unspoiled mountainside, perfect beach, and privacy.

■ **Whale-watching.** In season, this is the top activity on the Samaná Peninsula.

for getting around town, but don't even think about going the distance with them.

EXPLORING SAMANÁ

Samaná. The official name of the city is Santa Barbara de Samaná; alas, that saint's name is falling into disuse, and you'll more often hear simply "Samaná" these days. An authentic port town, not just a touristic zone, it has a typical *malecón* (seaside promenade) with gazebos and park benches, ideal for strolling and watching the boats in the harbor. The main avenue that borders this zone is lined with restaurants, shops, and small businesses. A small but bustling town, Samaná is filled with friendly residents, skilled local craftesmen selling their wares, and many outdoor cafés.

The **Whale Museum and Nature Center** is dedicated to the mighty mammals of the sea, and you will learn everything you have ever wanted to know about whales here. Samaná has one of the largest marine-mammal sanctuaries in the world, and is a center for whale-watching in the migration season. The C.E.B.S.E (Center for Conservation and Ecodevelopment of Samaná Bay and its Environment) manages this facility. ⊠ *Av. La Marina, Tiro Blanco* ☎ *809/538–2042* ⊕ *samana.org. do* ☒ *RD$50* ⊙ *Daily 8–noon and 2–5.*

The historic **Dominican Evangelical Church** is the oldest original building left in Samaná. It actually came across the ocean from England in 1881 in a hundred pieces, and was reassembled here, serving the spiritual needs of African-American freedmen who emigrated here from Philadelphia, Pennsylvania, in 1824. ⊠ *Calle Chaseurox, in front of Catholic church* ☎ *809/538–2579* ☒ *Donations appreciated* ⊙ *Daily dawn–dusk.*

Cayo Levantado. Residents of Samaná call Cayo Levantado their *pasa dia en la playa* (the place to pass the day on the beach). Today the small island in Samaná Bay has been improved to receive up to 1,500 cruise-ship passengers per day, with dining facilities, bars, restrooms, and lounge chairs on the beautiful beach. The company that runs cruise-ship services on the island has even applied for the coveted "Blue Flag" that designates a beach as clean and unpolluted. Independent restaurants and vendors also ply their wares. This isn't the most tranquil island, but you can quite happily spend the day here if you don't want to go into the town of Samaná. The new Grand Bahía Principe Cayo Levantado, an upscale, all-inclusive resort, claims the eastern two-thirds of the island for its private use. Day-use of the island will either be included in your cruise fare or will be treated as a regular shore excursion, for which the lines usually charge $40 to $60. ⊠ *Samaná Bay* ☎ *No phone* ☒ *Public beach free* ⊙ *Daily dawn–dusk.*

Los Haitises National Park. A guided tour is the only way to explore Los Haitises (pronounced Hi-*tee*-sis), which is across Samaná Bay from the peninsula. The park is famous for its karst limestone formations, caves, and grottoes filled with pictographs and petroglyphs left by the indigenous Taíno before the discovery of the Americas. Mangrove forests shelter many coastal bird species, including black-crowned night herons and the magnificent American frigate birds, making this a bird-watchers delight as well. Typical trips cruise the coastline dotted with small islands and spectacular cliff faces, finally docking to allow passengers to walk quietly around a mangrove swamp and visit the various caves.

Salto el Limón Cascade. Provided that you are fit, an adventurous guided trip to this spectacular waterfall is a delight. The journey is usually done mostly on horseback, but includes walking down rocky, sometimes muddy trails. The well-mannered horses take you across rivers and up mountains to El Limón, where you'll find the waterfall amidst luxuriant vegetation. Some snacks and drinks are usually included in the guided trip. ⊠ *Santi Rancho, El Limón.*

SHOPPING

Rum, coffee, and cigars are popular local products. You may also find good coconut handicrafts, including coconut-shell candles. Whale-oriented gift items are particularly popular. Most of the souvenir shops are on Samaná's malecón or in the market plaza; you will find more on the major downtown streets in town, all within easy walking distance of the tender piers. A shopping mall called **Pueblo Principe** (⊠ *20 Francisco Rosario Sanchez, Santa Barbara de Samaná*) is near the piers; it has a bevy of shops and food outlets (including American fast food).

ACTIVITIES

DIVING AND SNORKELING

In 1979 three atolls disappeared following a seaquake off Las Terrenas, providing an opportunity for truly memorable dives. Also just offshore from Las Terrenas are the Islas Las Ballenas ("The Whale Islands"), a cluster of four little islands with good snorkeling. A coral reef is off Playa Jackson, a beach accessible only by boat. **Las Terrenas Divers** (⊠ *Playa Bonita, Las Terrenas* ☎ *809/889–2422* ⊕ *www.lt-divers. com*) offers diving lessons and trips; diving equipment rentals start at $50, snorkeling equipment at $10 per day, $25 with an excursion. It is closed Sunday.

WHALE-WATCHING

Humpback whales come to Samaná Bay to mate and give birth each year, from approximately January 15 through March 30. Samaná Bay is considered one of the top 10 destinations in the world for watching whales. If you're here in season, this can be the experience of a lifetime. You can listen to the male humpback's solitary courting song and witness incredible displays as the whales flip their tails and breach (humpbacks are the most active species of whales in the Atlantic). **Whale Samaná** (⊠ *Av. Malecón 3, across street from cement town dock, beside park, Santa Barbara de Samaná* ☎ *809/538–2494* ⊕ *www.whalesamana. com*) is owned by Kim Beddall, a Canadian who is incredibly knowledgeable about whales and Samaná in general, having lived here for 20-some years. Now a certified marine mammal specialist, Kim leads the regions' best trips on board the *Victoria II,* a 50-foot motor vessel. Trips are $58, which includes the Marine Mammal Sanctuary entrance fee. Kim welcomes cruise passengers but requires advance reservations; in most cases the trip times have been modified to accommodate cruise schedules, but be sure to ask about timing in advance to make sure it will work with your port call.

BEACHES

There are no recommendable beaches in Samaná de Santa Barbara itself. You will have to travel to one of the beautiful ones elsewhere on the peninsula, another reason why the Cayo Levantado excursion is very popular on most ships.

On **Playa Bonita** (⊠ *Las Terrenas*) you can bounce between the golden beach (BYO towel—no chaises) and one of the hotels and restaurants directly across the rough road, where you can have lunch. The beach can disappear in flooding and high tides. It's a quiet stretch of gold sand with leaning coconut trees.

Fodor's Choice   **Playa Cosón** (⊠ *Las Terrenas*) is a long, wonderful stretch of white sand
★   and best beach close to the town of Las Terrenas. At the time of this writing, it was completely undeveloped, but there are a dozen condo developments under construction, so that sense of solitude is not going to last. One restaurant, the Beach, serves the entire 15-mi shore.

Playa Las Galeras (⊠ *Las Galeras*) is within this tiny coastal town, a 30-minute drive northeast from Samaná town. It's a lovely, long, and uncluttered beach. The sand is white, the Atlantic waters generally calm. It has been designated a "Blue Flag" beach, which means that it's crystal-clean, with no pollution, though there are several small hotels here. This is a good snorkeling spot, too. That said, this is really just a departure point to the nearby virgin beaches closer to the cape to west. Hire a boat and get to them!

Fodor's Choice   **Playa Rincón** (⊠ *5 km [3 mi] by boat, 15 km [9 mi] by road from Las*
★   *Galeras*), a beautiful, white-sand beach, is considered one of the top beaches in the Caribbean. It's relatively undeveloped, and at the far-right end is a sheltered area, where you can snorkel. There are no facilities per se, but local ladies will sell you the freshest lobster and fish in coconut sauce with rice, and other creole dishes as well as cold drinks. You can reach Playa Rincón by boat or bus or car from Las Galeras. A boat is preferable; expect to pay about $15.

WHERE TO EAT

$ ✕ **La Mata Rosada.** Next door to El Sabor Sabanés, La Mata represents
SEAFOOD   more than a step up in comfort and gastronomic complexity. The French owner-chef Yvonne Bastian has been luring local expats and foodies since the late 1990s. She sets tables up with white linens in an all-white interior including an army of ceiling fans to keep you cool; breezes sneak in from the bay across the street. There's a plentiful array of choices, starting with a sea and country salad of conch, potatoes, greens, and bacon; or the "gourmet" plate, a mix of grilled lobster and other shellfish. Ceviche, a specialty of this port town, is made with dorado (mahimahi) and conch. Whether you go local or international, order

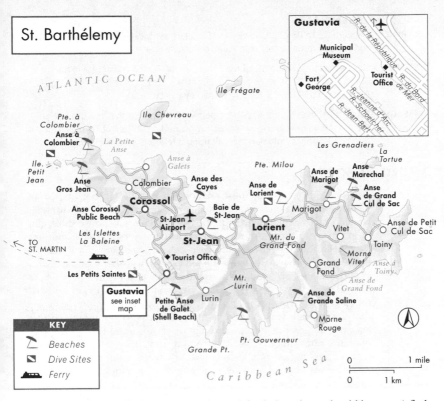

St. Barthélemy

ATLANTIC OCEAN

Ile Frégate

Pte. à Colombier
Anse à Colombier
La Petite Anse
Ile Chevreau

Anse à Galets

Pte. Milou

Les Grenadiers
La Tortue

Ile Petit Jean
Anse Gros Jean
Colombier
Anse des Cayes
Anse de Lorient
Anse de Marigot
Anse Marechal
Anse de Grand Cul de Sac

Anse Corossol Public Beach
Corossol
Baie de St-Jean
Marigot

TO ST. MARTIN
Les Islettes
La Baleine
St-Jean Airport
Lorient
Mt. du Grand Fond
Vitet
Anse de Petit Cul de Sac
Toiny

Les Petits Saintes
St-Jean
♦ Tourist Office
Grand Fond
Morne Vitet
Anse à Toiny

Gustavia
see inset map
Petite Anse de Galet (Shell Beach)
Lurin
Mt. Lurin
Anse de Grande Saline
Anse de Grand Fond

KEY
⟋ Beaches
◣ Dive Sites
▅ Ferry

Grande Pt.
Pt. Gouverneur
Morne Rouge

C a r i b b e a n   S e a

0 ——— 1 mile
0 ——— 1 km

Gustavia
Municipal Museum
Fort George
Tourist Office
R. de la République
R. du Bord de Mer
R. Jeanne d'Arc
R. Schoelcher
R. Jean Bart

---

the creole shrimp or a substantial salad, and you should leave satisfied. But save room: desserts are presented with pride. ⊠ *5B Av. Malecón* ☎ *809/538–2388* ▭ *AE, MC, V* ☺ *June–Nov., closed Tues.*

ST. BARTHÉLEMY (GUSTAVIA)

Elise Meyer

Hilly St. Barthélemy, popularly known as St. Barth (or St. Barts) is just 8 square mi (21 square km), but the island has at least 20 good beaches. What draws visitors is its sophisticated but unstudied approach to relaxation: the finest food, excellent wine, high-end shopping, and lack of large-scale commercial development. A favorite among upscale cruise-ship passengers, who also appreciate the shopping opportunities and fine dining, St. Barth isn't really equipped for mega-ship visits, which is why most ships calling here are from smaller premium lines. This is one place where you don't need to take the ship's shore excursions to have a good time. Just hail a cab or rent a car and go to one of the many wonderful beaches, where you will find some of the best lunch-time restaurants, or wander around Gustavia, shopping and eating. It's the best way to relax on this most relaxing of islands.

ESSENTIALS

CURRENCY   The euro (€1 to US$1.30); however, U.S. dollars are accepted in almost all shops and in many restaurants. Credit cards are widely accepted.

INTERNET   Most restaurants on the island now offer free Wi-Fi for customers, and there is also a free hotspot at the port area.**Centre Alizes** (⊠ *Rue de la République, Gustavia* ☎ *0590/29–89–89*) offers Internet service.

TELEPHONE   Public telephones accept *télécartes*, prepaid calling cards that you can buy at the gas station next to the airport and at post offices in Lorient, St-Jean, and Gustavia. Making an international call using a télécarte is the best way to go.

COMING ASHORE

Even medium-size ships must anchor in Gustavia Harbor and bring passengers ashore on tenders. The tiny harbor area is right in Gustavia, which is easily explored on foot. Taxis, which meet all cruise ships, can be expensive. Technically, there's a flat rate for rides up to five minutes long. Each additional three minutes is an additional amount. In reality, however, cabbies usually name a fixed rate—and will not budge. Fares are 50% higher on Sunday and holidays. St. Barth is one port where it's really worth it to arrange a car rental for a full-day exploration of the island, including the island's out-of-the-way beaches. But be aware that during high season there is often a three-day minimum, so this may not be possible except through your ship (and then you'll pay premium rates indeed). Most car-rental firms operate at the airport; however, renting on your own is usually cheaper than what you'll get if you go with one of the ship's car rentals (you may be able to find a car for €50 per day).

EXPLORING ST. BARTH

With a little practice, negotiating St. Barth's narrow, steep roads soon becomes fun. Free maps are everywhere, roads are well marked, and painted signs will point you where you want to be. Take along a towel, sandals, and a bottle of water, and you will surely find a beach upon which to linger.

☺   **Corossol.** The island's French-provincial origins are most evident in this two-street fishing village with a little rocky beach.

Ingenu Magras's **Inter Oceans Museum** has more than 9,000 seashells and an intriguing collection of sand samples from around the world. You can buy souvenir shells. ⊠ *Corossol* ☎ *0590/27–62–97* ▢ *€3* ☉ *Tues.–Sun. 9–12:30 and 2–5.*

Gustavia. You can easily explore all of Gustavia during a two-hour stroll. Most shops close from noon to 2 or 3, so plan lunch accordingly, but stores stay open past 7 in the evening.

A good spot to park your car is rue de la République, alongside the catamarans, yachts, and sailboats. The **tourist office** on the pier can provide maps and a wealth of information. It's open Monday from 8:30 to 12:30, Tuesday through Friday from 8 to noon and 2 to 5, and Saturday from 9 to noon. During busier holiday periods, the office may be open all day. ⊠ *Rue de la République, Gustavia* ☎ *0590/27–87–27* ⊕ *www.saintbarth-tourisme.com/*.

On the far side of the harbor known as La Pointe is the charming **Municipal Museum**, where you can find watercolors, portraits, photographs, and historic documents detailing the island's history as well as displays of the island's flowers, plants, and marine life. ⊠ *La Pointe, Gustavia* ☎ *0590/29–71–55* ⊠ €2 ☉ *Mon., Tues., Thurs., and Fri. 8:30–12:30 and 2:30–6, Sat. 9–12:30.*

Lorient. Site of the first French settlement, Lorient is one of the island's two parishes; a restored church, a school, and a post office mark the spot. Note the gaily decorated graves in the cemetery.

St-Jean. There is a monument at the crest of the hill that divides St-Jean from Gustavia. Called *The Arawak*, it symbolizes the soul of St. Barth. A warrior, one of the earliest inhabitants of the area (AD 800–2,500), holds a lance in his right hand and stands on a rock shaped like the island; in his left hand he holds a conch shell, which sounds the cry of nature; perched beside him are a pelican (which symbolizes the air and survival by fishing) and an iguana (which represents the earth). The half-mile-long crescent of sand at St-Jean is the island's most favored beach. A popular activity is watching and photographing the hair-raising airplane landings, but be sure not to stand in the area at the beach end of the runway, where someone was seriously injured. You'll also find some of the best shopping on the island here, as well as several restaurants.

ST. BARTHÉLEMY BEST BETS

■ **Soaking up the Atmosphere.** It's the French Riviera transported to the Caribbean.

■ **Beautiful Beaches.** Pick any of the lovely, uncrowded beaches.

■ **French Food.** St. Barth has some of the best restaurants in the Caribbean.

■ **Shopping.** There is no better fashion shopping in the Caribbean, especially if you are young and slim.

SHOPPING

St. Barth is a duty-free port, and with its sophisticated crowd of visitors, shopping in the island's 200-plus boutiques is a definite delight. In Gustavia boutiques line the three major shopping streets: Quai de la République, which is right on the harbor, rivals New York's Madison Avenue or Paris's avenue Montaigne for high-end designer retail, including shops for **Louis Vuitton, Bulgari, Cartier, Chopard,** and **Hermès**. These shops often carry items that are not available in the United States. The Carré d'Or plaza is great fun to explore. Shops are also clustered in **La Savane Commercial Center** (across from the airport), **La Villa Créole** (in St-Jean), and **Espace Neptune** (on the road to Lorient). It's worth working your way from one end to the other at these shopping complexes—just to see or, perhaps, be seen. Boutiques in all three areas carry the latest in French and Italian sportswear and some haute couture. Bargains may be tough to come by, but you might be able to snag that *pochette* that is sold out stateside, and in any case, you'll have a lot of fun hunting around.

ACTIVITIES

BOATING AND SAILING

St. Barth is a popular yachting and sailing center, thanks to its location midway between Antigua and St. Thomas. Gustavia's harbor, 13 to 16 feet deep, has mooring and docking facilities for 40 yachts. There are also good anchorages available at Public, Corossol, and Colombier. You can charter sailing and motorboats in Gustavia Harbor for as little as a half day. Stop at the tourist office in Gustavia for an up-to-the-minute list of recommended charter companies.

Marine Service (⊠ *Gustavia* ☎ *0590/27–70–34* ⊕ *www.st-barths.com/ marine.service*) offers full-day outings, either on a 42- or 46-foot catamaran, to the uninhabited Île Fourchue for swimming, snorkeling, cocktails, and lunch. The cost is $100 per person; an unskippered motor rental runs about $260 a day.

DIVING AND SNORKELING

Several dive shops arrange scuba excursions to local sites. Depending on weather conditions, you may dive at **Pain de Sucre, Coco Island,** or toward nearby **Saba.** There's also an underwater shipwreck to explore, plus sharks, rays, sea tortoises, coral, and the usual varieties of colorful fish. The waters on the island's leeward side are the calmest. For the uncertified who still want to see what the island's waters hold, there's an accessible shallow reef right off the beach at Anse de Cayes that you can explore if you have your own mask and fins.

Plongée Caraïbe (☎ *0590/27–55–94* ⊕ *www.plongee-caraibes.com*) is recommended for its up-to-the-minute equipment and dive boat. Marine Service operates the only five-star, PADI-certified diving center on the island, called **West Indies Dive** (☎ *0590/27–70–34* ⊕ *www. westindiesdive.com*). Scuba trips, packages, resort dives, night dives, and certifications start at $90, including gear.

BEACHES

There are many *anses* (coves) and nearly 20 *plages* (beaches) scattered around the island, each with a distinctive personality and each open to the general public. Even in season you can find a nearly empty beach. Topless sunbathing is common, but nudism is forbidden—although both Grande Saline and Gouverneur are de facto nude beaches.

Anse de Grand Cul de Sac. The shallow, reef-protected beach is nice for small children, fly-fishermen, kayakers, and windsurfers—and lots of the amusing pelicanlike frigate birds that dive-bomb the water fishing for their lunch.

Fodor's Choice ★ **Anse de Grande Saline.** Secluded, with its sandy ocean bottom, this is just about everyone's favorite beach and is great for swimmers, too. However, there can be a bit of wind here, so you can enjoy yourself more if you go on a calm day. In spite of the prohibition, young and old alike go nude. The beach is a 10-minute walk up a rocky dune trail, so be sure to wear sneakers or water shoes. Although there are several good restaurants for lunch near the parking area, once you get there, the beach is just sand, sea, and sky.

★ **Anse du Gouverneur.** Because it's so secluded, this beach is a popular place for nude sunbathing. It is truly beautiful, with blissful swimming and views of St. Kitts, Saba, and St. Eustatius. Venture here at the end of the day and watch the sun set behind the hills. The road here from Gustavia also offers spectacular vistas. Legend has it that pirates' treasure is buried in the vicinity. There are no restaurants or other services here, so plan accordingly.

Baie de St-Jean. Like a mini–Côte d'Azur—beachside bistros, terrific shopping, bungalow hotels, bronzed bodies, windsurfing, and day-trippers who tend to arrive on BIG yachts—the reef-protected strip is divided by Eden Rock promontory. You can rent chaises and umbrellas at La Plage restaurant or at Eden Rock, where you can lounge for hours over lunch.

WHERE TO EAT

A service charge is always added by law, but you should leave the server 5% to 10% extra in cash. It is generally advisable to charge restaurant meals on a credit card, as the issuer will offer a better exchange rate than the restaurant.

$$–$$$ ✕ **Le Tamarin.** A leisurely lunch here en route to Grand Saline beach is a
FRENCH St. Barth *must*. But new management makes it tops for dinner, too. Sit
★ on one of the licorice-colored Javanese couches in the lounge area and nibble excellent sushi, or settle at a table under the wondrous tamarind tree for which the restaurant is named. There is a unique cocktail each day. Ultrafresh fish is provided by the restaurant's designated fisherman, and gentle prices accommodate local residents as well as the holiday crowd. The restaurant is also open year-round. ⌧ *Grande Saline* ☎ *0590/27–72–12* ☐ *AE, MC, V* ☉ *Closed Tues.*

$$–$$$ ✕ **Wall House.** The food is excellent—and the service is always friendly—
ECLECTIC at this restaurant on the far side of Gustavia Harbor. The pesto gnocchi are out of this world, and the rare fresh-caught tuna with sea salt and lime-ginger mousse is a universal favorite. Local businesspeople crowd the restaurant for the bargain €10 prix-fixe lunch menu. The daily €29 dinner menu is a pretty good deal, too. An old-fashioned dessert trolley showcases some really yummy sweets. ⌧ *La Pointe, Gustavia* ☎ *0590/27–71–83* ⚐ *Reservations essential* ☐ *AE, MC, V* ☉ *Closed Sept. and Oct.*

ST. CROIX (FREDERIKSTED)

Lynda Lohr | St. Croix is the largest of the three U.S. Virgin Islands (USVI) that form the northern hook of the Lesser Antilles; it's 40 mi (64 km) south of its sister islands, St. Thomas and St. John. Christopher Columbus landed here in 1493, skirmishing briefly with the native Carib Indians. Since then, the USVI have played a colorful, if painful, role as pawns in the game of European colonialism. Theirs is a history of pirates and privateers, sugar plantations, slave trading, and slave revolt and liberation. Through it all, Denmark had staying power. From the 17th to the 19th century, Danes oversaw a plantation slave economy that produced molasses, rum, cotton, and tobacco. Many of the stones you tread on in the streets were once used as ballast on sailing ships, and the yellow fort of Christiansted is a reminder of the value once placed on this island treasure. Never a major cruise destination, it is still a stop for several ships each year.

ESSENTIALS

CURRENCY   The U.S. dollar is the official currency of St. Croix.

INTERNET   There's a convenient Internet café in Christiansted if you make it there during your day ashore. **A Better Copy** (✉ *52A Company St., Christiansted, St. Croix* ☎ *340/692–5303*).

TELEPHONE   Calling the United States from St. Croix works the same way as calling within the U.S. Local calls from a public phone cost up to 35¢ for every five minutes. You can use your regular toll-free connections for long-distance services. Most U.S. cell phone plans include the Virgin Islands for no additional cost.

COMING ASHORE

Cruise ships dock in Frederiksted, on the island's west end. You'll find an information center at the pier, and the town is easy to explore on foot. Beaches are nearby. The only difficulty is that you are far from the island's main town, Christiansted. Some cruise lines offer bus transportation there; otherwise, you are probably better off renting a car to explore the island, since both car-rental rates and gasoline prices are reasonable; just remember to drive on the left. **Midwest** (☎ *340/772–0438 or 877/772–0438* ⊕ *www.midwestautorental.com*) is outside Frederiksted, but will pick you up at the pier.

Taxis of all shapes and sizes are available at the cruise-ship pier and at various shopping and resort areas. Remember, too, that you can hail a taxi that's already occupied. Drivers take multiple fares and sometimes even trade passengers at midpoints. Taxis don't have meters, so you should check the list of official rates (available at the visitor centers or from drivers) and agree on a fare before you start, but there are standard rates for most trips. A taxi to Christiansted will cost about $24 for two people for transportation only; an island tour including Christiansted will cost $110 for two people.

EXPLORING ST. CROIX

Frederiksted speaks to history buffs with its quaint Victorian architecture and historic fort. There's very little traffic, so this is the perfect place for strolling and shopping. Christiansted is a historic Danish-style town that served as St. Croix's commercial center. Your best bet is to see the historic sights in the morning, when it's still cool. This two-hour endeavor won't tax your walking shoes and will leave you with energy to poke around the town's eclectic shops.

Christiansted. In the 1700s and 1800s Christiansted was a trading center for sugar, rum, and molasses. Today there are law offices, tourist shops, and restaurants, but many of the buildings, which start at the harbor and go up the gently sloped hillsides, still date from the 18th century.

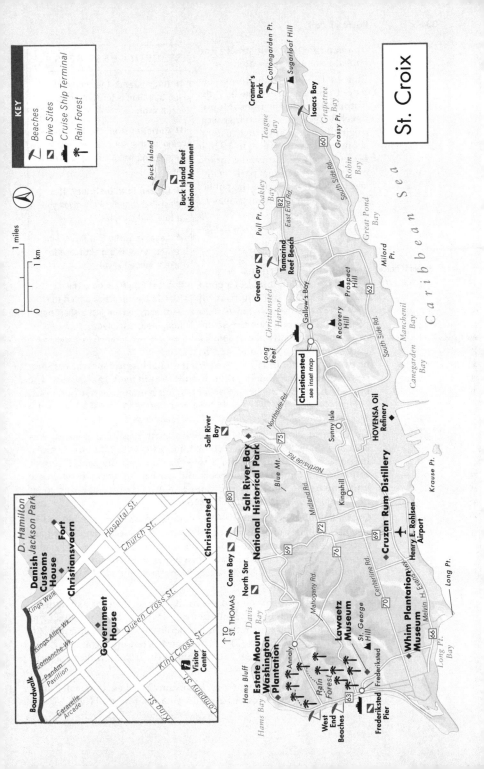

St. Croix

KEY
⚓ Beaches
▣ Dive Sites
⚓ Cruise Ship Terminal
✳ Rain Forest

0   1 miles
0   1 km

Buck Island
Buck Island Reef National Monument

Caribbean Sea

Cramer's Park
Cotongarden Pt.
Sugarloaf Hill
Isaacs Bay
Grapetree
Grassy Pt. Bay
60
Teague Bay
South Side Rd.
Robin Bay
Pull Pt. Coakley Bay
82
East End Rd.
Great Pond Bay
Milord Pt.
62
Prospect Hill
Manchenil Bay
Canegarden Bay
Krause Pt.

Green Cay
Tamarind Reef Beach
Christiansted Harbor
Gallow's Bay
Christiansted
see inset map
Long Reef
Recovery Hill
South Side Rd.

HOVENSA Oil Refinery
Sunny Isle
75
Northside Rd.
Blue Mt.
Kingshill
Midland Rd.
Cruzan Rum Distillery
72
69
Henry E. Rohlsen Airport
Centerline Rd.
70
Melvin H. Evans Hwy
66
Long Pt. Bay
Long Pt.

Salt River Bay
Salt River Bay National Historical Park
80
↑ TO ST. THOMAS
Davis Bay
North Star
Cane Bay
Mahogany Rd.
69
St. George Hill
76
Lawaetz Museum
63
Annaly
Rain Forest
St. George
Frederiksted
Frederiksted Pier
West End Beaches
Hams Bluff
Hams Bay
Estate Mount Washington Plantation
Whim Plantation Museum

Inset map (Christiansted):

D. Hamilton
Hospital St.
Church St.
Queen Cross St.
Boardwalk
Kings Walk
Kings Alley Wk.
Comanche Wk.
PanAm Pavilion
Caravelle Arcade
Danish Jackson Park
Danish Customs House
Fort Christiansvaern
Government House
ℹ **Visitor Center**
King Cross St.
Queen Cross St.
Company St.
King St.
Christiansted

You can't get lost. All streets lead back downhill to the water.

Built in 1830 on foundations that date from a century earlier, the historic **Danish Customs House,** which is near Ft. Christiansvaern, originally served as both a customs-house and a post office. In 1926 it became the Christiansted Library, and it's been a national park facility since 1972. It's closed to the public, but the sweeping front steps make a nice place to take a break. ⊠ *King St.* ☎ *340/773–1460* ⊕ *www.nps. gov/chri.*

☾ Fodor's Choice ★ The large yellow **Ft. Christiansvaern** dominates the waterfront. Because it's so easy to spot, it makes a good place to begin a walking tour. In 1749 the Danish built the fort to protect the harbor, but the structure was repeatedly damaged by hurricane-force winds and had to be partially rebuilt in 1771. It's now a national historic site, the best preserved of the few remaining Danish-built forts in the Virgin Islands. The park's visitor center is here. Rangers are on hand to answer questions. ⊠ *Hospital St.* ☎ *340/773–1460* ⊕ *www.nps.gov/chri* ⊠ *$3 (includes Steeple Building)* ☾ *Weekdays 8–4:30, weekends 9–4:30.*

Government House, one of the town's most elegant structures, was built as a home for a Danish merchant in 1747. Today it houses offices. If you're here weekdays from 8 to 4:30, slip into the peaceful inner courtyard to admire the still pools and gardens. A sweeping staircase leads you to a second-story ballroom, still used for official government functions. ⊠ *King St.* ☎ *340/773–1404.*

Cruzan Rum Distillery. A tour of the company's factory, established in 1760, culminates in a tasting of its products, all sold here at bargain prices. It's worth a stop to look at the distillery's charming old buildings even if you're not a rum connoisseur. ⊠ *West Airport Rd., Estate Diamond* ☎ *340/692–2280* ⊕ *www.cruzanrum.com* ⊠ *$4* ☾ *Weekdays 9–11:30 and 1–4:15.*

Frederiksted. This town is noted less for its Danish than for its Victorian architecture, which dates from after the slave rebellion and great fire of July 1848. Across from the pier, Federiksted's **visitor center** (⊠ *200 Strand St.* ☎ *340/772–0357*) has brochures from numerous St. Croix businesses, as well as a few exhibits about the island. You can stop in weekdays from 8 to 5.

Sitting across from the waterfront in a historic building, the small **Caribbean Museum Center for the Arts** (⊠ *10 Strand St.* ☎ *340/772–2622*

ST. CROIX BEST BETS

■ **Buck Island.** The snorkeling trail here is fun, but go by catamaran.

■ **Christiansted.** The best shopping on the island as well as interesting historical sights are here.

■ **Cruzan Rum Distillery.** This West End rum distillery gives you a tour and samples.

■ **Kayaking.** The Salt River, with few currents, is a great place to take a guided kayak trip.

■ **West End Beaches.** The island's best beaches are on the west end, and are just a short hop from the cruise pier.

⊕ *www.cmcarts.org*) hosts an always-changing roster of exhibits. Many are cutting-edge multimedia efforts that you might be surprised to find in such an out-of-the way location. The openings are popular events. It's open Wednesday, Thursday, and Saturday from 10 to 6 and Friday noon to 6; admission is free.

Ft. Frederik (⊠ *Waterfront* ☎ *340/772–2021*), completed in 1760, houses an art gallery and a number of interesting historical exhibits, including some focusing on the 1848 Emancipation and the 1917 transfer of the Virgin Islands from Denmark to the United States. It's within earshot of the Frederiksted Visitor Center. The fort is open weekdays from 8:30 to 4; admission is $3.

Lawaetz Museum. For a trip back in time, tour this circa-1750 farm. Owned by the prominent Lawaetz family since 1896, just after Carl Lawaetz arrived from Denmark, the lovely two-story house is in a valley at La Grange. A Lawaetz family member shows you the four-poster mahogany bed Carl and Marie shared, the china Marie painted, the family portraits, and the fruit trees that fed the family for several generations. Initially a sugar plantation, it was subsequently used to raise cattle and grow produce. ⊠ *Rte. 76, Mahogany Rd., Estate Little La Grange* ☎ *340/772–1539* ⊕ *www.stcroixlandmarks.com* ⬛ *$10* ⊗ *Tues., Thurs., and Sat. 10–4.*

Salt River Bay National Historical Park & Ecological Preserve. This joint national and local park commemorates the area where Christopher Columbus's men skirmished with the Carib Indians in 1493 on his second visit to the New World. The peninsula on the bay's east side is named for the event: Cabo de las Flechas (Cape of the Arrows). Although the park is just in the developing stages, it has several sights with cultural significance. A ball court, used by the Caribs in religious ceremonies, was discovered at the spot where the taxis park. Take a short hike up the dirt road to the ruins of an old earthen fort for great views of Salt River Bay. The area also encompasses a coastal estuary with the region's largest remaining mangrove forest, a submarine canyon, and several endangered species, including the hawksbill turtle and the roseate tern. A visitor center, open winter only, sits just uphill to the west. The water at the beach can be on the rough side, but it's a nice place for sunning. ⊠ *Rte. 75 to Rte. 80, Salt River* ☎ *340/773–1460* ⊕ *www.nps.gov/sari* ⊗ *Tues.–Thurs. 9–4.*

☺ **Whim Plantation Museum.** The lovingly restored estate, with a windmill,
★ cook house, and other buildings, will give you a sense of what life was like on St. Croix's sugar plantations in the 1800s. The oval-shaped greathouse has high ceilings and antique furniture and utensils. Notice its fresh, airy atmosphere—the waterless stone moat around the greathouse was used not for defense but for gathering cooling air. If you have kids, the grounds are the perfect place for them to run around, perhaps while you browse in the museum gift shop. It's just outside of Frederiksted. ⊠ *Rte. 70, Estate Whim* ☎ *340/772–0598* ⊕ *www.stcroixlandmarks.com* ⬛ *$10* ⊗ *Mon.–Sat. 10–4.*

SHOPPING

The selection of duty-free goods on St. Croix is fairly good. The best shopping is in Christiansted, where most stores are in the historic district near the harbor. King Street, Strand Street, and the arcades that lead off them compose the main shopping district and where you'll find **Sonya's**, the jewelry store that first sold the locally popular hook bracelet. The longest arcade is **Caravelle Arcade,** adjacent to the hotel of the same name. In Frederiksted a handful of shops face the cruise-ship pier.

ACTIVITIES

BOAT TOURS

Many people take a day trip to Buck Island aboard a charter boat. Most leave from the Christiansted waterfront or from Green Cay Marina and stop for a snorkel at the island's eastern end before dropping anchor off a gorgeous sandy beach for a swim, a hike, and lunch. Sailboats can often stop right at the beach; a larger boat might have to anchor a bit farther offshore. A full-day sail runs about $100, with lunch included on most trips. A half-day sail costs about $68.

Big Beard's Adventure Tours (⊠ *Christiansted* ☎ *340/773–4482* ⊕ *www. bigbeards.com*) takes you on catamarans, either the *Renegade* or the *Adventure,* from the Christiansted waterfront to Buck Island for snorkeling before dropping anchor at a private beach for a barbecue lunch.

DIVING AND SNORKELING

In Frederiksted, **N2 the Blue** (⊠ *Frederiksted Beach, Rte. 631, Frederiksted* ☎ *340/772–3483 or 888/789–3483* ⊕ *www.n2blue.com*) takes divers right off the beach near Coconuts restaurant, on night dives off the Frederiksted Pier, or on boat trips to wrecks and reefs.

GOLF

The spectacular 18-hole course at **Carambola Golf Club** (⊠ *Rte. 80, Davis Bay* ☎ *340/778–5638* ⊕ *www.golfcarambola.com*), in the northwest valley, was designed by Robert Trent Jones Sr. It sits near Carambola Beach Resort. Greens fees are $90 for 18 holes, which includes the use of a golf cart.

HORSEBACK RIDING

Well-kept roads and expert guides make horseback riding on St. Croix pleasurable. At Sprat Hall, just north of Frederiksted, Jill Hurd runs **Paul & Jill's Equestrian Stables** (⊠ *Rte. 58, Frederiksted* ☎ *340/772–2880 or 340/332–0417* ⊕ *www.paulandjills.com*). She will take you through the rain forest, across the pastures, along the beaches, and through valleys—explaining the flora, fauna, and ruins on the way. A 1½-hour ride costs $90.

KAYAKING

Caribbean Adventure Tours (⊠ *Salt River Marina, Rte. 80, Salt River* ☎ *340/778–1522* ⊕ *www.stcroixkayak.com*) takes you on trips through Salt River Bay National Historical Park and Ecological Preserve, one of the island's most pristine areas. All tours run $45.

BEACHES

The waters aren't always gentle at **Cane Bay,** a breezy north-shore beach, but there are seldom many people around, and the scuba diving and snorkeling are wondrous. You can see elkhorn and brain corals, and less than 200 yards out is the drop-off called Cane Bay Wall. There are several unnamed **West End Beaches** along the coast road north of Frederiksted, but it's best if you don't stray too far from civilization. For safety's sake, it's best to visit with a group. The beach at the Rainbow Beach Club, a five-minute drive outside Frederiksted, has a bar, a casual restaurant, water sports, and volleyball.

WHERE TO EAT

$$$ ✕ **Blue Moon.** This terrific little bistro, which has a loyal local follow-
ECLECTIC ing, offers a changing menu that draws on Cajun and Caribbean fla-
Fodor'sChoice vors. Try the spicy gumbo with andouille sausage or crab cakes with
★ a spicy aioli for your appetizer. A grilled chicken breast served with spinach and artichoke hearts and topped with Parmesan and cheddar cheeses makes a good entrée. The Almond Joy sundae should be your choice for dessert. There's live jazz on Wednesday and Friday. ⊠ *7 Strand St.* ☎ *340/772–2222* ⊕ *www.bluemoonstcroix.com* ⊟ *AE, MC, V* ⊘ *Closed Mon.*

$$$ ✕ **Rum Runners.** The view is as stellar as the food at this highly popular
CONTINENTAL local standby. Sitting right on Christiansted boardwalk, Rum Runners
ⓒ serves everything, including a to-die-for salad of crispy romaine lettuce
★ and tender grilled lobster drizzled with lemongrass vinaigrette. More hearty fare includes baby back ribs cooked with the restaurant's special spice blend and Guinness stout. ⊠ *Hotel Caravelle, 44A Queen Cross St.* ☎ *340/773–6585* ⊕ *www.rumrunnersstcroix.com* ⊟ *AE, MC, V.*

ST. JOHN (CRUZ BAY)

Lynda Lohr St. John's heart is Virgin Islands National Park, a treasure that takes up a full two-thirds of St. John's 20 square mi (53 square km). The park helps keep the island's interior in its pristine and undisturbed state, but if you go at midday you'll probably have to share your stretch of beach with others, particularly at Trunk Bay. The island is booming, and while it can get a tad crowded at the ever-popular Trunk Bay Beach during the busy winter season, you won't find traffic jams or pollution. It's easy to escape from the fray, however: just head off on a hike. St. John doesn't have a grand agrarian past like her sister island, St. Croix, but if you're hiking in the dry season, you can probably stumble upon the stone ruins of old plantations. The less adventuresome can visit the repaired ruins at the park's Annaberg Plantation and Caneel Bay resort. Of the

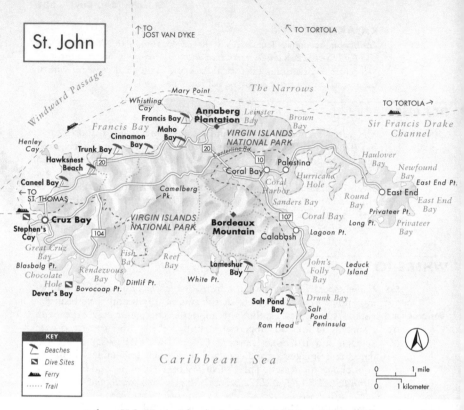

St. John

TO
JOST VAN DYKE

TO TORTOLA

Windward Passage

The Narrows

Mary Point

Whistling Cay

Francis Bay

Annaberg Plantation

Leinster Bay

Brown Bay

Sir Francis Drake Channel

TO TORTOLA →

Francis Bay

Cinnamon Bay

Maho Bay

VIRGIN ISLANDS NATIONAL PARK

Henley Cay

Trunk Bay

Hawksnest Beach

Centerline Rd.

Palestina

Haulover Bay

Newfound Bay

East End Pt.

Caneel Bay

← TO ST. THOMAS

Camelberg Pk.

Coral Bay

Coral Harbor

Hurricane Hole

Sanders Bay

Round Bay

East End

East End Bay

Cruz Bay

VIRGIN ISLANDS NATIONAL PARK

Bordeaux Mountain

Calabash

Long Pt.

Privateer Pt.

Privateer Bay

Stephen's Cay

Great Cruz Bay

Fish Bay

Reef Bay

Lameshur Bay

John's Folly Bay

Lagoon Pt.

Coral Bay

Leduck Island

Blasbalg Pt.

Chocolate Hole

Rendezvous Bay

Dittlif Pt.

White Pt.

Dever's Bay

Bovocoap Pt.

Salt Pond Bay

Drunk Bay

Salt Pond Peninsula

Ram Head

Caribbean Sea

KEY

⤢ Beaches
◩ Dive Sites
⛴ Ferry
⋯⋯ Trail

0   1 mile
0   1 kilometer

three U.S. Virgin Islands, St. John, which has 5,000 residents, has the strongest sense of community, which is primarily rooted in a desire to protect the island's natural beauty.

ESSENTIALS

CURRENCY   The U.S. dollar is the official currency of U.S. Virgin Islands; you'll find a few ATMs in Cruz Bay.

INTERNET   **Quiet Mon Pub** (✉ *1 block up from ferry dock, across from First Bank and Julius E. Sprauve School, Cruz Bay* ☎ *340/779–4799* ⊕ *www.quietmon.com*).

TELEPHONE   Both Sprint and AT&T phones work in most of St. John (take care that you're not roaming on the Tortola cell network on the island's north coast, though). It's as easy to call home from St. John as from any city in the United States. On St. John public phones are near telephone poles mid-way along the Cruz Bay waterfront.

COMING ASHORE

While smaller ships drop anchor at St. John, most people taking a cruise aboard a larger ship visit St. Thomas's sister island on a shore excursion or on an independent day trip from St. Thomas. If you prefer to not take a tour, ferries leave St. Thomas from the Charlotte Amalie waterfront and Red Hook. You'll have to take a taxi to reach the ferry dock.

If you're aboard a smaller ship that calls in St. John, your ship may simply pause outside Cruz Bay Harbor to drop you off or drop anchor if it's spending the day. You'll be tendered to shore at the main town of Cruz Bay. The shopping district starts just across the street from the tender landing. You'll find an eclectic collection of shops, cozy restaurants, and places where you can just sit and take it all in. The island has few sights to see. Your best bet is to take a tour of the Virgin Islands National Park. (If your ship doesn't offer such a tour, arrange one with one of the taxi drivers who will meet your tender.) The drive takes you past luscious beaches to a restored sugar plantation. With only a single day in port, you're better off just using the island's shared taxi vans rather than renting a car, but if you want to do some independent exploring, you can rent a car in Cruz Bay.

ST. JOHN BEST BETS

■ **Hiking in the National Park.** Hiking trails that crisscross the terrain are easy enough for beginners and offer breathtaking scenery.

■ **Snorkeling Cruises.** The best snorkeling sites are reachable only by boat.

■ **Trunk Bay Beach.** St. John's national park beach is beautiful and has an underwater snorkeling trail.

EXPLORING ST. JOHN

★ **Annaberg Plantation.** In the 18th century, sugar plantations dotted the steep hills of this island. Slaves and free Danes and Dutchmen toiled to harvest the cane that was used to create sugar, molasses, and rum for export. Built in the 1780s, the partially restored plantation at Leinster Bay was once an important sugar mill. Although there are no official visiting hours, the National Park Service has regular tours, and some well-informed taxi drivers will show you around. Occasionally you may see a living-history demonstration—someone making johnnycake or weaving baskets. For information on tours and cultural events, contact the V.I. National Park Visitors Center. ⊠ *Leinster Bay Rd., Annaberg* ☎ *340/776–6201* ⊕ *www.nps.gov/viis* ⊠ *Free* ☉ *Daily dawn–dusk.*

★ **Bordeaux Mountain.** St. John's highest peak rises to 1,277 feet. Route 10 passes near enough to the top to offer breathtaking vistas. Don't stray into the road here—cars whiz by at a good clip along this section. Instead, drive nearly to the end of the dirt road that heads off next to the restaurant and gift shop for spectacular views at Picture Point and the trailhead of the hike downhill to Lameshur. Get a trail map from the park service before you start. ⊠ *Rte. 10, Bordeaux.*

Cruz Bay. St. John's main town may be compact (it consists of only several blocks), but it's definitely a hub: the ferries from St. Thomas and the British Virgin Islands pull in here, and it's where you can get a taxi or rent a car to travel around the island. There are plenty of shops in which to browse, a number of watering holes where you can stop for a breather, many restaurants, and a grassy square with benches where you can sit back and take everything in. Look for the current edition of the handy, amusing *"Road Map: St. Thomas–St. John"* featuring Max the Mongoose.

To pick up a useful guide to St. John's hiking trails, see various large maps of the island, and find out about current park service programs, including guided walks and cultural demonstrations, stop by the **V.I. National Park Visitors Center** (⊠ *Near baseball field, Cruz Bay* ☎ *340/776–6201* ⊕ *www.nps.gov/viis*). It's open daily from 8 to 4:30.

SHOPPING

Luxury goods and handicrafts can be found on St. John. Most shops carry a little of this and a bit of that, so it pays to poke around. The Cruz Bay shopping district runs from **Wharfside Village**, just around the corner from the ferry dock, to **Mongoose Junction**, an inviting shopping center on North Shore Road. (The name of this upscale shopping mall, by the way, is a holdover from a time when those furry island creatures gathered at a nearby garbage bin.) Out on Route 104 stop in at the **Marketplace** to explore its gift and crafts shops. At the island's other end, there are a few stores—selling clothes, jewelry, and artwork—here and there from the village of **Coral Bay** to the small complex at **Shipwreck Landing**.

On St. John, store hours run from 9 or 10 to 5 or 6. Wharfside Village and Mongoose Junction shops in Cruz Bay are often open into the evening.

ACTIVITIES

DIVING AND SNORKELING

Cruz Bay Watersports (⊠ *Lumberyard Shopping Complex, Cruz Bay* ☎ *340/776–6234* ⊠ *Westin St. John, Great Cruz Bay* ☎ *340/776–6234* ⊕ *www.divestjohn.com*) actually has two locations: in Cruz Bay at the Lumberyard Shopping Complex and at the Westin St. John Resort. Owners Marcus and Patty Johnston offer regular reef, wreck, and night dives and USVI and BVI snorkel tours. The company holds both PADI five-star-facility and NAUI-Dream-Resort status.

Low Key Watersports (⊠ *Wharfside Village, Strand St., Cruz Bay* ☎ *340/693–8999 or 800/835–7718* ⊕ *www.divelowkey.com*) offers two-tank dives and specialty courses. It's certified as a PADI five-star training facility.

FISHING

Well-kept charter boats—approved by the U.S. Coast Guard—head out to the north and south drops or troll along the inshore reefs, depending on the season and what's biting. The captains usually provide bait, drinks, and lunch, but you need to bring your own hat and sunscreen. Half-day fishing charters run between about $700 for the boat. **Captain Byron Oliver** (☎ *340/693–8339*) takes you out to the north and south drops.

HIKING

Although it's fun to go hiking with a Virgin Islands National Park guide, don't be afraid to head out on your own. To find a hike that suits your ability, stop by the park's visitor center in Cruz Bay and pick up the free trail guide; it details points of interest, trail lengths, and estimated hiking times, as well as any dangers you might encounter. Although the park staff recommends long pants to protect against thorns and insects, most people hike in shorts because it can get very hot. Wear sturdy shoes or hiking boots even if you're hiking to the beach. Don't forget to bring water and insect repellent.

Fodor'sChoice
★ The **Virgin Islands National Park** (⊠ *1300 Cruz Bay Creek, St. John* ☎ *340/776–6201* ⊕ *www.nps.gov/viis*) maintains more than 20 trails on the north and south shores and offers guided hikes along popular routes. A full-day trip to Reef Bay is a must; it's an easy hike through lush and dry forest, past the ruins of an old plantation, and to a sugar factory adjacent to the beach. It can be a bit arduous for young kids, however. Take the $6 safari bus from the park's visitor center to the trailhead, where you can meet a ranger who'll serve as your guide. The park provides a boat ride back to Cruz Bay for $15 to save you the walk back up the mountain. The schedule changes from season to season; call for times and reservations, which are essential.

BEACHES

Cinnamon Bay Beach. This long, sandy beach faces beautiful cays and abuts the national park campground. The facilities are open to the public and include cool showers, toilets, a commissary, and a restaurant. You can rent water-sports equipment here—a good thing, because there's excellent snorkeling off the point to the right; look for the big angelfish and large schools of purple triggerfish. ⊠ *North Shore Rd., Rte. 20, Cinnamon Bay, about 4 mi (6 km) east of Cruz Bay.*

Hawksnest Beach. Sea grape and waving palm trees line this narrow beach, and there are restrooms, cooking grills, and a covered shed for picnicking. A patchy reef just offshore means snorkeling is an easy swim away, but the best underwater views are reserved for ambitious snorkelers who head farther to the east along the bay's fringes. ⊠ *North Shore Rd., Rte. 20, Hawksnest Bay, about 2 mi (3 km) east of Cruz Bay.*

Fodor'sChoice
★ **Trunk Bay Beach.** St. John's most photographed beach is also the preferred spot for beginning snorkelers because of its underwater trail. Crowded or not, this stunning beach is one of the island's most beautiful. There are changing rooms with showers, bathrooms, a snack bar, picnic tables, a gift shop, phones, lockers, and snorkeling-equipment rentals. ⊠ *North Shore Rd., Rte. 20, Trunk Bay, about 2½ mi (4 km) east of Cruz Bay.*

WHERE TO EAT

$ ╳ **Deli Grotto.** At this air-conditioned but no-frills sandwich shop you
ECLECTIC place your order at the counter and wait for it to be delivered to your table or for takeout. The portobello panini with savory sautéed onions

are favorites, but the other sandwiches, such as the smoked turkey and artichoke, get rave reviews. Order a delicious brownie or cookie for dessert. ✉ *Mongoose Junction Shopping Center, North Shore Rd., Cruz Bay* ☎ *340/777–3061* 🍴 *No credit cards* ⊗ *No dinner.*

$ ✕ **Sun Dog Cafe.** There's an unusual assortment of dishes at this charm-
ECLECTIC   ing alfresco restaurant, which you'll find tucked into a courtyard in the upper reaches of the Mongoose Junction shopping center. Kudos to the white pizza with artichoke hearts, roasted garlic, mozzarella cheese, and capers. The Jamaican jerk chicken salad and the black-bean quesadilla are also good choices. ✉ *Mongoose Junction, North Shore Rd., Cruz Bay* ☎ *340/693–8340* 🍴 *AE, MC, V* ⊗ *No dinner.*

ST. KITTS (BASSETERRE)

Jordan Simon   Mountainous St. Kitts, the first English settlement in the Leeward Islands, crams some stunning scenery into its 65 square mi (168 square km). Vast, brilliant green fields of sugarcane (the former cash crop, now slowly being replanted) run to the shore. The fertile, lush island has some fascinating natural and historical attractions: a rain forest replete with waterfalls, thick vines, and secret trails; a central mountain range dominated by the 3,792-foot Mt. Liamuiga, whose crater has long been dormant; and Brimstone Hill, known in the 18th century as the Gibral-tar of the West Indies. St. Kitts and Nevis, along with Anguilla, achieved self-government as an associated state of Great Britain in 1967. In 1983 St. Kitts and Nevis became an independent nation. English with a strong West Indian lilt is spoken here. People are friendly but shy; always ask before you take photographs. Also, be sure to wear wraps or shorts over beach attire when you're in public places.

ESSENTIALS

CURRENCY   Eastern Caribbean (E.C.) dollar (EC$2.67 to US$1). U.S. dollars are accepted prac-tically everywhere, but you'll usually get change in E.C. currency.

INTERNET   Basseterre usually has an operational Internet café, but it rarely lasts in one location. The tourist office in Pelican Mall will have the latest information.

TELEPHONE   Phone cards, which you can buy in denominations of $5, $10, and $20, are handy for making local phone calls, calling other islands, and accessing U.S. direct lines. To make a local call, dial the seven-digit number. To call St. Kitts from the United States, dial the area code 869, then access code 465, 466, 468, or 469 and the local four-digit number.

COMING ASHORE

Cruise ships calling at St. Kitts dock at Port Zante, which is a deep-water port directly in Basseterre, the capital of St. Kitts. The cruise-ship terminal is right in the downtown area, two minutes' walk from sights and shops. Taxi rates on St. Kitts are fixed, and should be posted right at the dock. If you'd like to go to Nevis, several daily ferries (30 to 45 minutes, $8–$10 one-way) can take you to Charlestown in Nevis; the byzantine schedule is subject to change, so double-check times.

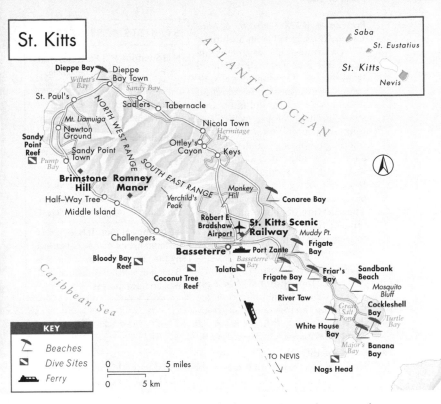

St. Kitts

Saba
St. Eustatius
St. Kitts
Nevis

ATLANTIC OCEAN

Caribbean Sea

Dieppe Bay
Dieppe Bay Town
Willett's Bay
Sandy Bay
St. Paul's
Sadlers
Tabernacle
NORTH WEST RANGE
Mt. Liamuiga
Newton Ground
Nicola Town
Hermitage Bay
Sandy Point Reef
Pump Bay
Sandy Point Town
Ottley's
Cayon
Keys
SOUTH EAST RANGE
Brimstone Hill
Romney Manor
Verchild's Peak
Monkey Hill
Conaree Bay
Half-Way Tree
Middle Island
Challengers
Robert E. Bradshaw Airport
St. Kitts Scenic Railway
Muddy Pt.
Basseterre
Port Zante
Frigate Bay
Bloody Bay Reef
Basseterre Bay
Talata
Frigate Bay
Friar's Bay
Sandbank Beach
Coconut Tree Reef
River Taw
Mosquito Bluff
Great Salt Pond
Cockleshell Bay
Turtle Bay
White House Bay
Major's Bay
Banana Bay
TO NEVIS
Nags Head

KEY

⅄ Beaches
◥ Dive Sites
🚢 Ferry

0   5 miles
0   5 km

Taxi rates on St. Kitts are fairly expensive, and you may have to pay
$32 for a ride to Brimstone Hill (for one to four passengers). A four-
hour tour of St. Kitts runs about $80. It's often cheaper to arrange an
island tour with one of the local companies than to hire a taxi driver
to take your group around. Several restored plantation greathouses
are known for their lunches; your driver can provide information and
arrange drop-off and pickup. Before setting off in a cab, be sure to
clarify whether the rate quoted is in E.C. or U.S. dollars.

EXPLORING ST. KITTS

Basseterre. On the south coast, St. Kitts's walkable capital is graced with
tall palms and flagstone sidewalks; although many of the buildings
appear run-down, there are interesting shops, excellent art galleries, and
some beautifully maintained houses. Duty-free shops and boutiques line
the streets and courtyards radiating from the octagonal **Circus,** built in
the style of London's famous Piccadilly Circus.

There are lovely gardens on the site of a former slave market at **Independence Square** (⊠ *Off Bank St., Basseterre*). The square is surrounded
on three sides by 18th-century Georgian buildings.

Port Zante (⊠ *Waterfront, behind Circus, Basseterre*) is an ambitious 27-acre cruise-ship pier and marina in an area that has been reclaimed from the sea. The domed welcome center is an imposing neoclassical hodgepodge, with columns and stone arches, shops, walkways, fountains, and West Indian–style buildings housing luxury shops, galleries, restaurants, and a small new casino. A second pier, 1,434 feet long, has a draft that accommodates even leviathan cruise ships. The selection of shops and restaurants (Tiffany Bar and Deli is a find for fantastic local fare) is gradually expanding as well.

In the restored former Treasury Building, the **National Museum** presents an eclectic collection reflecting the history and culture of

---

ST. KITTS BEST BETS

■ **Brimstone Hill Fortress.** Stop here for some of the best views on St. Kitts and historic ambience.

■ **Nevis.** A trip to Nevis is a worthwhile way to spend the day.

■ **Plantation Greathouses.** Stop for a lunch at Ottley's or Rawlins Plantation.

■ **Rain-forest Hikes.** Several operators on the island lead day-long hikes through the rain forest.

■ **Romney Manor.** This partially restored manor house is enhanced by the chance to shop at Caribelle Batik and watch the elaborate wax-and-dye process.

---

the island. ⊠ *Bay Rd., Basseterre* ☎ *869/465–5584* 🖾 *EC$1 residents, US$1 nonresidents* ⊘ *Weekdays 9–5, Sat. 9–1.*

★ **Brimstone Hill.** The well-restored 38-acre fortress, a UNESCO World Heritage Site, is part of a national park dedicated by Queen Elizabeth in 1985. The steep walk up the hill from the parking lot is well worth it if military history and/or spectacular views interest you. After routing the French in 1690, the English erected a battery here, and by 1736 the fortress held 49 guns, earning it the moniker Gibraltar of the West Indies. In 1782, 8,000 French troops laid siege to the stronghold, which was defended by 350 militia and 600 regular troops of the Royal Scots and East Yorkshires. When the English finally surrendered, the French allowed them to march from the fort in full formation out of respect for their bravery (the English afforded the French the same honor when they surrendered the fort a mere year later). A hurricane severely damaged the fortress in 1834, and in 1852 it was evacuated and dismantled. The beautiful stones were carted away to build houses. The citadel has been partially reconstructed and its guns remounted. A seven-minute orientation film recounts the fort's history and restoration. You can see what remains of the officers' quarters, the redoubts, the barracks, the ordnance store, and the cemetery. Its museum collections were depleted by hurricanes, but some pre-Columbian artifacts, objects pertaining to the African heritage of the island's slaves (such as masks and ceremonial tools), weaponry, uniforms, photographs, and old newspapers remain. The view from here includes Montserrat and Nevis to the southeast; Saba and St. Eustatius to the northwest; and St. Barth and St. Maarten to the north. Nature trails snake through the tangle of surrounding hardwood forest and savanna (a fine spot to catch the green vervet monkeys—inexplicably brought by the French and now outnumbering the residents— skittering about). ✉ *Main Rd., Brimstone Hill* ☎ *869/465–2609* ⊕ *www.brimstonehillfortress.org* 💳 *$8* ⊙ *Daily 9:30–5:30.*

★ **Romney Manor.** The ruins of this somewhat restored house (reputedly once the property of Thomas Jefferson) and surrounding cottages that duplicate the old chattel-house style are set in 6 acres of glorious gardens, with exotic flowers, an old bell tower, and an enormous,

> **STORAGE**
>
> Take along a hanging shoe organizer for the closet to extend storage space for small items and to keep shoes off the floor. An over-the-door, pocket-style shoe organizer can be hung on the bathroom door. Slip bathroom necessities in the pockets so they are handy and out of the way.

gnarled 350-year-old saman tree (sometimes called a rain tree). Inside, at **Caribelle Batik,** you can watch artisans hand-printing fabrics by the 2,500-year-old Indonesian wax-and-dye process known as batik. Look for signs indicating a turnoff for Romney Manor near Old Road. ✉ *Old Road* ☎ *869/465–6253* ⊕ *www.caribellebatikstkitts.com* 💳 *Free* ⊙ *Daily 9–5.*

St. Kitts Scenic Railway. The old narrow-gauge train that had transported sugarcane to the central sugar factory since 1912 is all that remains of the island's once-thriving sugar industry. Two-story cars bedecked in bright Kittitian colors circle the island in just under four hours. Each passenger gets a comfortable, downstairs air-conditioned seat fronting vaulted picture windows and an upstairs open-air observation spot. The conductor's running discourse embraces not only the history of sugar cultivation but also the railway's construction, local folklore, island geography, even other agricultural mainstays from papayas to pigs. You can drink in complimentary tropical beverages (including luscious guava daiquiris) along with the sweeping rain-forest and ocean vistas, accompanied by an a cappella choir's renditions of hymns, spirituals, and predictable standards like "I've Been Workin' on the Railroad." ✉ *Needsmust* ☎ *869/465–7263* ⊕ *www.stkittsscenicrailway.com* 💳 *$89, children 4–12 $44.50* ⊙ *Departures vary according to cruise-ship schedules (call ahead, but at least once daily Dec.–Apr.).*

SHOPPING

St. Kitts has limited shopping, but there are a few small duty-free shops with good deals on jewelry, perfume, china, and crystal. Several galleries sell excellent paintings and sculptures. The batik fabrics, scarves, caftans, and wall hangings of Caribelle Batik are well known. British expat Kate Spencer is an artist who has lived on the island for years, reproducing its vibrant colors on everything from silk pareus (beach wraps) to note cards to place mats. Other good island buys include crafts, jams, and herbal teas. Don't forget to pick up some CSR (Cane Spirit Rothschild), which is distilled from fresh wild sugarcane right on St. Kitts. The Brinley Gold company has made a splash among spirits connoisseurs for its coffee, mango, coconut, lime, and vanilla rums (there is a tasting room at Port Zante). Most shopping plazas are in downtown Basseterre, on the streets radiating from the Circus. **All Kind of Tings**, a peppermint-pink edifice on Liverpool Row at College Street Ghaut, functions as a de facto vendors' market, where several booths sell local crafts and cheap T-shirts. Its courtyard frequently hosts folk-

> **CAUTION**
>
> Pack a small flashlight just in case there's an emergency. You don't want to be stumbling around in the dark.

loric dances, fashion shows, poetry readings, and steel-pan concerts. The **Pelican Mall**—a shopping arcade designed to look like a traditional Caribbean street—has 26 stores, a restaurant, tourism offices, and a bandstand near the cruise-ship pier. **Shoreline Plaza** is next to the Treasury Building, right on Basseterre's waterfront. **TDC Mall** is just off the Circus in downtown.

ACTIVITIES

DIVING AND SNORKELING

Though unheralded as a dive destination, St. Kitts has more than a dozen excellent sites, protected by several new marine parks. The surrounding waters feature shoals, hot vents, shallows, canyons, steep walls, and caverns at depths from 40 to nearly 200 feet. **Dive St. Kitts** (⊠ *2 mi [3 km] east of Basseterre, Frigate Bay* ☎ *869/465–1189* ⊕ *www.divestkitts. com*), a PADI–NAUI facility, offers competitive prices and friendly, laid-back dive masters. The Bird Rock location features superb shore diving: common sightings 20 to 30 feet out include octopuses, nurse sharks, manta and spotted eagle rays, and sea horses. Shore dives are unlimited when you book packages. Kenneth Samuel of **Kenneth's Dive Center** (⊠ *Bay Rd., Newtown* ☎ *869/465–2670* ⊕ *www.kennethsdivecenter. com*), a PADI company, takes small groups of divers with C cards to nearby reefs. Rates average $70 for single-tank dives, $95 for double-tank dives; add $10 for equipment. Night dives, including lights, are $80–$90, and snorkeling trips (four-person minimum) are $40, drinks included. After 25 years' experience, former fisherman Samuel is considered an old pro (Jean-Michel Cousteau requested his guidance upon his first visit in the 1990s) and strives to keep groups small and prices reasonable. **Pro-Divers** (⊠ *Ocean Terrace Inn, Basseterre* ☎ *869/466–3483* ⊕ *www.prodiversstkitts.com*) is owned by Austin Macleod, a PADI-certified dive master–instructor, and offers resort and certification courses running $115–$420. Dive computers are included gratis. He offers free introductory scuba courses twice weekly at Ocean Terrace Inn. He also takes groups to snorkeling sites accessible only by boat via his custom-built 38-foot cat.

GOLF

The **Royal St. Kitts Golf Club** (⊠ *St. Kitts Marriott Resort, Frigate Bay* ☎ *869/466–2700 or 866/785–4653* ⊕ *www.royalstkittsgolfclub.com*) is an 18-hole, par-71 links-style championship course that underwent a complete redesign by Thomas McBroom to maximize Caribbean and Atlantic views and increase the challenge (there are now 12 lakes and

83 bunkers). Holes 15 through 17 (the latter patterned after Pebble Beach #18) actually skirt the Atlantic in their entirety, lending new meaning to the term sand trap. The sudden gusts, wide but twisting fairways, and extremely hilly terrain demand pinpoint accuracy and finesse, yet holes such as 18 require pure power. Greens fees are $150 for Marriott guests in high season, $180 for nonguests, with twilight and super-twilight discounts. The development includes practice bunkers, a putting green, a short-game chipping area, and the fairly high-tech Royal Golf Academy.

HIKING

Trails in the central mountains vary from easy to don't-try-it-by-yourself. Monkey Hill and Verchild's Peak aren't difficult, although the Verchild's climb will take the better part of a day. Don't attempt Mt. Liamuiga without a guide. You'll start at Belmont Estate—at the west end of the island—on horseback, then proceed on foot to the lip of the crater, at 2,600 feet. You can go down into the crater—1,000 feet deep and 1 mi (1.5 km) wide, with a small freshwater lake—clinging to vines and roots and scaling rocks, even trees. Expect to get muddy. There are several fine operators (each hotel recommends its favorite); tour rates range from $50 for a rain-forest walk to $95 for a volcano expedition, and usually include round-trip transportation from your hotel and picnic lunch.

★ Earl of **Duke of Earl's Adventures** (☎ 869/465–1899 or 869/663–0994) is as entertaining as his nickname suggests—and his prices are slightly cheaper ($45 for a rain-forest tour includes refreshments, $70 volcano expeditions add lunch; hotel pickup/drop-off is complimentary). He genuinely loves his island and conveys that enthusiasm, encouraging hikers to swing on vines or sample unusual-looking fruits during his rain-forest trip. He also conducts a thorough volcano tour to the crater's rim and a drive-through ecosafari tour ($50 with lunch). Greg Pereira of **Greg's Safaris** (☎ 869/465–4121 ⊕ www.gregsafaris.com), whose family has lived on St. Kitts since the early 19th century, takes groups on half-day trips into the rain forest and on full-day hikes up the volcano and through the grounds of a private 18th-century greathouse. The rain-forest trips include visits to sacred Carib sites, abandoned sugar mills, and an excursion down a 100-foot coastal canyon containing a wealth of Amerindian petroglyphs. The Off the Beaten Track 4x4 Plantation Tour provides a thorough explanation of the role sugar and rum played in the Caribbean economy and colonial wars. He and his staff relate fascinating historical, folkloric, and botanical information.

HORSEBACK RIDING

Wild North Frigate Bay and desolate Conaree Beach are great for riding, as is the rain forest. Guides from **Trinity Stables** (☎ 869/465–3226) offer beach rides ($50) and trips into the rain forest ($60), both including hotel pickup. The latter is intriguing, as guides discuss plants' medicinal properties along the way (such as sugarcane to stanch bleeding) and pick oranges right off a tree to squeeze fresh juice. Otherwise, the staffers are cordial but shy; this isn't a place for beginners' instruction.

ZIP-LINING

☺ **Sky Safari Tours** (✉ *Wingfield Estate* ☎ *869/466–4259 or 869/465–4347* ⊕ *www.skysafaristkitts.com*) whisks would-be Tarzans and Janes through the "Valley of the Giants" (so dubbed for the towering trees) at speeds up to 50 MPH (80 KPH) along five cable lines; the longest (nicknamed "The Boss") stretches 1,350 feet and is suspended 250 feet above the ground. Following the Canadian-based company's mantra of "faster, higher, safer," it uses a specially designed trolley with secure harnesses attached. Many of the routes afford unobstructed views of Brimstone Hill and the sea beyond. Admission is usually $65–$75, depending on the tour chosen. It's open daily 9–6, with the first and last tours departing at 10 and 3.

BEACHES

The powdery white-sand beaches of St. Kitts, free and open to the public (even those occupied by hotels), are in the Frigate Bay area or on the lower peninsula. Chair rentals cost around $3, though if you order lunch you can negotiate a freebie. Caution: The Atlantic waters are rougher.

Friar's Bay. Locals consider Friar's Bay, on the Caribbean (southern) side, the island's finest beach. It's a long, tawny scimitar where the water always seems warmer and clearer. Chair rentals cost around $3, though if you order lunch at one of the beach bars, you can negotiate a freebie. Friar's is the first major beach along Southeast Peninsula Drive (aka Simmonds Highway), approximately a mile (1½ km) southeast of Frigate Bay. ✉ *Friar's Bay.*

Frigate Bay. The Caribbean side offers talcum-powder-fine beige sand framed by coconut palms and sea grapes, and the Atlantic side (a 15-minute stroll)—sometimes called North Frigate Bay—is a favorite with horseback riders. Most of the beach bars charge $3 to $5 to rent a chair, though they'll often waive the fee if you ask politely and buy lunch. Waters are generally calm for swimming; the rockier eastern end offers fine snorkeling. The incomparably scenic Atlantic side attracts occasional pesky vendors. The surf is choppier and the undertow stronger here. Frigate Bay is easy to find, just less than 3 mi (5 km) from downtown Basseterre. ✉ *Frigate Bay.*

WHERE TO EAT

$$–$$$ ✗ **Reggae Beach Bar & Grill.** Treats at this popular daytime watering hole
ECLECTIC   include honey-mustard ribs, coconut shrimp, grilled lobster, decadent bread pudding with rum sauce, and an array of tempting tropical libations. Business cards and pennants from around the world plaster the bar, and the open-air space is decorated with a variety of nautical accoutrements, from fishnets and turtle shells to painted wooden crustaceans. You can snorkel here, spot hawksbill turtles and the occasional monkey, laze in a palm-shaded hammock, or rent a kayak or snorkeling gear. Beach chairs are free. Locals come Sunday afternoons for dancing to live bands and for fun but fiercely contested volleyball. ✉ *S.E. Peninsula*

Rd., Cockleshell Beach ☎ *869/762–5050* ⊕ *www.reggaebeachbar.com*
▭ *AE, D, MC, V* ⊗ *No dinner.*

ST. LUCIA (CASTRIES)

Jane E. Zarem

Magnificent St. Lucia—with its towering mountains, dense rain forest, fertile green valleys, and acres of banana plantations—lies in the middle of the Windward Islands. Nicknamed "the Helen of the West Indies" because of its natural beauty, St. Lucia is distinguished from its neighbors by its unusual geological landmarks, the Pitons—the twin peaks on the southwest coast that soar nearly ½ mi (1 km) above the ocean floor. Named a World Heritage Site by UNESCO in 2004, the Pitons are the symbol of this island. Nearby, in the former French colonial capital of Soufrière, are a "drive-in" volcano, its neighboring sulfur springs that have rejuvenated bathers for nearly three centuries, and one of the most beautiful botanical gardens in the Caribbean. A century and a half of battles between the French and English resulted in St. Lucia's changing hands 14 times before 1814, when England established possession. In 1979 the island became an independent state within the British Commonwealth of Nations. The official language is English, although most people also speak a French-creole patois.

4

ESSENTIALS

CURRENCY Eastern Caribbean (E.C.) dollar (EC$2.67 to US$1). U.S. dollars (but not coins) are generally accepted, but change is given in E.C. currency.

INTERNET Internet cafés can be found in Castries and at the Rodney Bay Marina. **CIBS Café** (⊠ *Castries* ☎ *758/458–2195*). **Cyber Connections** (⊠ *Rodney Bay Marina, Gros Islet* ☎ *758/450–9309*).

TELEPHONE You can make direct-dial overseas and interisland calls from St. Lucia, and the connections are excellent. You can charge an overseas call to a major credit card with no surcharge by dialing 811. Phone cards can be purchased at many retail outlets.

COMING ASHORE

Most cruise ships dock at the capital city of Castries, on the island's northwest coast. Either of two docking areas is used: Pointe Seraphine, a port of entry and duty-free shopping complex, or Port Castries, a commercial wharf across the harbor. Ferry service connects the two piers. Smaller vessels occasionally call at Soufrière, on the island's southwest coast. Ships calling at Soufrière must anchor offshore and bring passengers ashore via tender. Tourist information booths are located at Pointe Seraphine and across from the commercial wharf in Castries and along the waterfront on Bay Street in Soufrière. Downtown Castries is within walking distance of the pier, and the produce market and adjacent crafts and vendors' markets are the main attractions. Soufrière is a sleepy West Indian town, but it's worth a short walk around the central square to view the French colonial architecture; many of the island's interesting natural sights are in or near Soufrière.

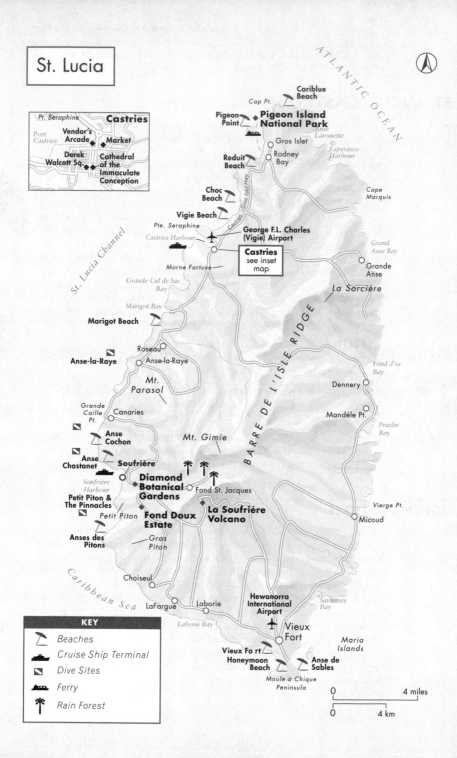

St. Lucia

Castries

Pt. Seraphine
Port Castries
Vendor's Arcade ◆ ◆ Market
Derek Walcott Sq. ◆ ◆ Cathedral of the Immaculate Conception

ATLANTIC OCEAN

Cap Pt.
Cariblue Beach
Pigeon Point
Pigeon Island National Park
Anse Lavouette
Gros Islet
Esperance Harbour
Rodney Bay
Reduit Beach
Cape Marquis
Choc Beach
Castries Gros Islet Hwy.
Vigie Beach
Pte. Seraphine
Grand Anse Bay
George F.L. Charles (Vigie) Airport
Castries Harbour
Grande Anse
Castries see inset map
Morne Fortune
La Sorcière
Grande Cul de Sac Bay
Marigot Bay
Marigot Beach
Fond d'or Bay
Roseau
Anse-la-Raye
Anse-la-Raye
Mt. Parasol
Dennery
Grande Caille Pt.
Canaries
Mandéle Pt.
Praslin Bay
Anse Cochon
Mt. Gimie
Anse Chastanet
Soufrière
Soufrière Harbour
Diamond Botanical Gardens
Fond St. Jacques
Vierge Pt.
Petit Piton & The Pinnacles
Fond Doux Estate
La Soufrière Volcano
Micoud
Petit Piton
Anses des Pitons
Gros Piton
BARRE DE L'ISLE RIDGE
Caribbean Sea
Choiseul
Hewanorra International Airport
Savannes Bay
LaFargue
Laborie
Maria Islands
Laborie Bay
Vieux Fort
Vieux Fort Honeymoon Beach
Anse de Sables
Moule à Chique Peninsula

St. Lucia Channel

KEY
- ⚐ Beaches
- 🚢 Cruise Ship Terminal
- ◻ Dive Sites
- 🚤 Ferry
- 🌴 Rain Forest

0   4 miles
0   4 km

Taxis are available at the docks in Castries. Although they are unmetered, the standard fares are posted at the entrance to Pointe Seraphine. Taxi drivers are well informed, and can give you a full tour—often an excellent one—thanks to government-sponsored training programs. From the Castries area, full-day island tours cost about $160 for up to four people; sightseeing trips to Soufrière, around $150. If you plan your own day, expect to pay the driver at least $25 per hour plus a 10% tip. Whatever your destination, negotiate the price with the driver before you depart—and be sure that you both understand whether the rate is quoted in E.C. or U.S. dollars.

ST. LUCIA BEST BETS

■ **The Pitons.** You must see the Pitons, St. Lucia's unique twin peaks.

■ **The Rain Forest.** St. Lucia's lush rain forest is striking.

■ **Diamond Botanical Garden.** Stroll through this tropical paradise to Diamond Waterfall.

■ **Reduit Beach.** St. Lucia's nicest white-sand beach is north of Castries.

■ **Pigeon Island.** This national park is both a historic site and a natural playground.

4

EXPLORING ST. LUCIA

CASTRIES AND THE NORTH

Castries. The capital, a busy commercial city of about 65,000 people, wraps around a sheltered bay. Morne Fortune rises sharply to the south of town, creating a dramatic green backdrop. The charm of Castries lies almost entirely in its liveliness, since most of the colonial buildings were destroyed by four fires that occurred between 1796 and 1948. Freighters (exporting bananas, coconut, cocoa, mace, nutmeg, and citrus fruits) and cruise ships come and go daily, making Castries Harbour one of the Caribbean's busiest ports. Pointe Seraphine is a duty-free shopping complex on the north side of the harbor; a launch ferries passengers across the harbor when ships are in port. Pointe Seraphine's attractive Spanish-style architecture houses more than 20 upscale duty-free shops, a tourist information kiosk, a taxi stand, and car-rental agencies.

At the corner of Jeremie and Peynier streets, spreading beyond its brilliant orange roof, is the **Castries Market.** Full of excitement and bustle, the market is open every day except Sunday. It's liveliest on Saturday morning, when farmers bring their fresh produce and spices to town, as they have for more than a century. Next door to the produce market is the **Craft Market,** where you can buy pottery, wood carvings, and handwoven straw articles. Across Peynier Street from the Craft Market, at the **Vendor's Arcade,** there are still more handicrafts and souvenirs.

Directly across Laborie Street from Derek Walcott Square is the Roman Catholic **Cathedral of the Immaculate Conception,** which was built in 1897. Though it's rather somber on the outside, its interior walls are decorated with colorful murals reworked by St. Lucian artist Dunstan St. Omer in 1985, just prior to Pope John Paul II's visit. This church has an active parish and is open daily for both public viewing and religious services.

Derek Walcott Square is a green oasis bordered by Brazil, Laborie, Micoud, and Bourbon streets. Formerly Columbus Square, it was renamed to honor the hometown poet who won the 1992 Nobel Prize for Literature—one of two Nobel laureates from St. Lucia (the late Sir W. Arthur Lewis won the 1979 Nobel Prize in economics). Some of the 19th-century buildings that have survived fire, wind, and rain can be seen on Brazil Street, the square's southern border. On the Laborie Street side there's a huge, 400-year-old *samaan* tree with leafy branches that shade a good portion of the square.

☺
★ **Pigeon Island National Park.** Jutting out from the northwest coast, Pigeon Island is connected to the mainland by a causeway. Tales are told of the pirate Jambe de Bois (Wooden Leg), who once hid out on this 44-acre hilltop islet—a strategic point during the French and British struggles for control of St. Lucia. Now it's a national park and a venue for concerts, festivals, and family gatherings. There are two small beaches with calm waters for swimming and snorkeling, a restaurant, and picnic areas. Scattered around the grounds are ruins of barracks, batteries, and garrisons that date from 18th-century French and English battles. In the Museum and Interpretative Centre, housed in the restored British officers' mess, a multimedia display explains the island's ecological and historical significance. ⊠ *Pigeon Island, St. Lucia National Trust, Rodney Bay* ☎ *758/452–5005* ⊕ *www.slunatrust.org* ⊠ *$5* ☺ *Daily 9–5.*

Rodney Bay. About 15 minutes north of Castries, the natural bay and an 80-acre man-made lagoon—surrounded by hotels and many popular restaurants—are named for Admiral George Rodney, who sailed the British Navy out of Gros Islet Bay in 1780 to attack and ultimately decimate the French fleet. With 250 slips, Rodney Bay Marina is one of the Caribbean's premier yachting centers and the destination of the Atlantic Rally for Cruisers (transatlantic yacht crossing) each December. Yacht charters and sightseeing day trips can be arranged at the marina. The Rodney Bay Ferry makes hourly crossings between the marina and the shopping complex, as well as daily excursions to Pigeon Island.

SOUFRIERE AND THE SOUTH

☺
Fodor's Choice
★ **Diamond Botanical Gardens and Waterfall.** These splendid gardens are part of Soufrière Estate, a 2,000-acre land grant presented by King Louis XIV in 1713 to three Devaux brothers from Normandy in recognition of their services to France. The estate is still owned by their descendants; Joan Du Bouley Devaux maintains the gardens. Water bubbling to the surface from underground sulfur springs streams downhill in rivulets to become Diamond Waterfall, deep within the botanical gardens. For a small fee you can slip into your swimsuit and soak for 30 minutes in one of the outside pools; a private bath costs slightly more. ⊠ *Soufrière Estate, Diamond Rd., Soufrière* ☎ *758/452–4759 or 758/454–7565* ⊕ *www.diamondstlucia.com* ⊠ *$5, outside bath $4, private bath $6* ☺ *Mon.–Sat. 10–5, Sun. 10–3.*

☺
★ **Fond Doux Estate.** One of the earliest French estates established by land grant (1745 and 1763), this plantation still produces cocoa, citrus,

bananas, coconut, and vegetables on 135 hilly acres; the restored 1864 plantation house is still in use as well. Cool drinks and a creole buffet lunch are served at the restaurant. Souvenirs, including just-made chocolate balls, are sold at the boutique. ⊠ *Chateaubelair, Soufrière* ☎ *758/459–7545* ⊕ *www.fonddouxestate.com* ⊑ *Estate $30, includes buffet lunch* ⊘ *Daily 9–4.*

Ⅽ **La Soufrière Drive-In Volcano.** As you approach, your nose will pick up
Fodor's Choice the strong scent of the sulfur springs—more than 20 belching pools of
★ muddy water, multicolor sulfur deposits, and other assorted minerals baking and steaming on the surface. Actually, you don't drive in. You drive up within a few hundred feet of the gurgling, steaming mass and then walk behind your guide—whose service is included in the admission price—around a fault in the substratum rock. It's a fascinating, educational half hour, though it can also be pretty stinky on a hot day. ⊠ *Bay St., Soufrière* ☎ *758/459–5500* ⊑ *$2* ⊘ *Daily 9–5.*

Fodor's Choice **The Pitons.** These two unusual mountains, which are, in fact, a symbol
★ of St. Lucia and were named a UNESCO World Heritage Site in 2004, rise precipitously from the cobalt-blue Caribbean Sea just south of Soufrière. Covered with thick tropical vegetation, the massive outcroppings were formed by lava from a volcanic eruption 30 to 40 million years ago. They are not identical twins since—confusingly—2,619-foot Petit Piton is taller than 2,461-foot Gros Piton, though Gros Piton is, as the word translates, broader. It's possible to climb the pitons as long as you have permission and use a guide, but it's a strenuous trip. Gros Piton is the easier climb, though the trail up even this shorter Piton is one very tough trek and requires the permission of the Forest & Lands Department and a knowledgeable guide. ☎ *758/450–2231, 758/450–2078 for St. Lucia Forest & Lands Department, 758/459–9748 for Pitons Tour Guide Association* ⊑ *Guide services $45* ⊘ *Daily by appointment only.*

Soufrière. The oldest town in St. Lucia and the former French-colonial capital, Soufrière was founded by the French in 1746 and named for its proximity to the volcano of the same name. The wharf is the center of activity in this sleepy town (which currently has a population of about 9,000), particularly when a cruise ship is moored in pretty Soufrière Bay. French-colonial influences can be noticed in the architecture of the wooden buildings, with second-story verandas and gingerbread trim that surround the market square. The market building itself is decorated with colorful murals. The **Soufrière Tourist Information Centre** (⊠ *Bay St., Soufrière* ☎ *758/459–7200*) provides information about area attractions. Outside some of the popular attractions in and around Soufrière, souvenir vendors can be persistent. Be polite but firm if you're not interested in their wares.

SHOPPING

The island's best-known products are artwork and wood carvings; clothing and household articles made from batik and silk-screen fabrics, designed and printed in island workshops; and clay pottery. You can also take home straw hats and baskets and locally grown cocoa, coffee, and spices. The only duty-free shopping is at **Pointe Seraphine** or **La Place Carenage**, on opposite sides of the harbor. You must show your passport and cabin key card to get duty-free prices. You'll want to experience the **Castries Market** and scour the adjacent **Vendor's Arcade** and **Craft Market** for handicrafts and souvenirs at bargain prices.

ACTIVITIES

DIVING AND SNORKELING

Fodor's Choice

★

The coral reefs at Anse Cochon and Anse Chastanet, on the southwest coast, are popular beach-entry dive sites. In the north, Pigeon Island is the most convenient site. **Dive Fair Helen** (✉ *Vigie Marina, Castries* ☎ *758/451–7716, 888/855–2206 in U.S. and Canada* ⊕ *www.divefairhelen.com*) is a PADI center that offers half- and full-day excursions to wreck, wall, and marine reserve areas, as well as night dives.

Scuba St. Lucia (✉ *Anse Chastanet Resort, Anse Chastanet Rd., Soufrière* ☎ *758/459–7755* ⊕ *www.scubastlucia.com*) is a PADI five-star training facility. Daily beach and boat dives and resort and certification courses are offered; underwater photography and snorkeling equipment are available. Day trips from the north of the island include round-trip speedboat transportation.

FISHING

Among the deep-sea creatures you can find in St. Lucia's waters are dolphin (the fish, not the mammal—also called dorado or mahimahi), barracuda, mackerel, wahoo, kingfish, sailfish, and white and blue marlin. Sportfishing is generally done on a catch-and-release basis, but the captain may permit you to take a fish back to your hotel to be prepared for your dinner. Neither spearfishing nor collecting live fish in coastal waters is permitted. Half- and full-day deep-sea fishing excursions can be arranged at either Vigie Marina or Rodney Bay Marina. A half-day of fishing on a scheduled trip runs about $75 to $80 per person. Beginners are welcome. **Captain Mike's** (✉ *Vigie Marina, Castries* ☎ *758/452–1216 or 758/452–7044* ⊕ *www.captmikes.com*) has a fleet of Bertram powerboats (31 to 38 feet) that accommodate as many as eight passengers; tackle and cold drinks are supplied. **Mako Watersports** (✉ *Rodney Bay Marina, Rodney Bay* ☎ *758/452–0412*) takes fishing enthusiasts out on the well-equipped six-passenger *Annie Baby*.

HORSEBACK RIDING

Creole horses, a breed indigenous to South America and popular on the island, are fairly small, fast, sturdy, and even-tempered animals suitable for beginners. Established stables can accommodate all skill levels and offer countryside trail rides, beach rides with picnic lunches, plantation tours, carriage rides, and lengthy treks. Prices run about $45 for one hour, $60 for

---

BAG IT

A mesh laundry bag or a "pop-up" mesh clothes hamper are two fairly light items that pack flat in your suitcase. The bag can hang from the closet, but either will keep your closet neat, allow damp clothing to dry out, and help you tote dirty clothes to the self-service laundry room so you can avoid high cleaning charges.

two hours, and $75 for a three-hour beach ride and barbecue. Transportation is usually provided between the stables and nearby hotels. Local people sometimes appear on beaches with their steeds and offer 30-minute rides for $10 to $15; ride at your own risk. **International Riding Stables** (⊠ *Beauséjour Estate, Gros Islet* ☎ *758/452–8139 or 758/450–8665*) offers English- and western-style riding. The beach-picnic ride includes time for a swim—with or without your horse. **Trim's National Riding Stable** (⊠ *Cas-en-Bas, Gros Islet* ☎ *758/452–8273* ⊕ *www.trimsnationalridingacademy.com*), the island's oldest riding stable, offers four sessions per day, plus beach tours, trail rides, and carriage tours to Pigeon Island.

BEACHES

All of St. Lucia's beaches are open to the public, but beaches in the north are particularly accessible to cruise-ship passengers.

Pigeon Point. At this small beach within Pigeon Island National Park, on the northwestern tip of St. Lucia, a restaurant serves snacks and drinks, but this is also a perfect spot for picnicking. ⊠ *Pigeon Island.*

Fodor's Choice ★ **Reduit Beach.** This long stretch of golden sand frames Rodney Bay, and is within walking distance of many hotels and restaurants in Rodney Bay Village. The Rex St. Lucian hotel, which faces the beach, has a water-sports center, where you can rent sports equipment and beach chairs and take windsurfing or waterskiing lessons. Many feel that Reduit (pronounced red-*wee*) is the island's finest beach. ⊠ *Rodney Bay.*

Vigie Beach. This 2-mi (3-km) strand runs parallel to the George F.L. Charles Airport runway in Castries and continues on to become Malabar Beach, the beachfront in front of the Rendezvous resort. ⊠ *Castries, next to airport.*

WHERE TO EAT

$$$–$$$$
ECLECTIC
Fodor's Choice ★
✕ **Jacques Waterfront Dining.** Chef–owner Jacky Rioux creates magical dishes in his open-air garden restaurant (known for years as Froggie Jack's) overlooking Vigie Cove. The cooking style is decidedly French, as is Rioux, but fresh produce and local spices create a fusion cuisine that's memorable at either lunch or dinner. You might start with a bowl of creamy tomato-basil or pumpkin soup, a grilled portobello mushroom, or octopus and conch in curried coconut sauce. Main courses include fresh seafood, such as oven-baked kingfish with a white wine and sweet pepper sauce, or breast of chicken stuffed with smoked salmon in a citrus butter sauce. The wine list is also impressive. ⊠ *Vigie Marina, Castries* ☎ *758/458–1900* ⊕ *www.jacquesrestaurant.com* ⚐ *Reservations essential* ⊟ *AE, MC, V* ⊘ *Closed Sun.*

$$
CARIBBEAN
★
✕ **The Still.** When you're visiting Diamond Waterfall, this is a great lunch spot. The two dining rooms seat up to 400 people, so it's a popular stop for tour groups and cruise passengers. The emphasis is on local cuisine, using vegetables such as christophene, breadfruit, yam, and callaloo along with grilled fish or chicken, but there are also pork and beef dishes. All fruits and vegetables used in the restaurant are organically

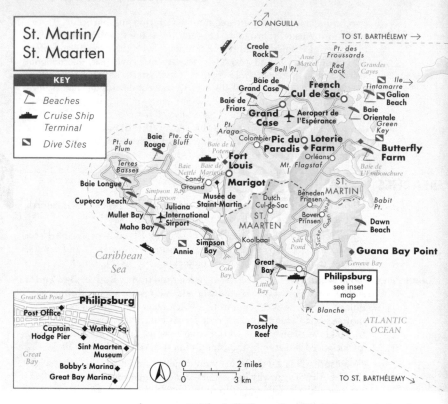

St. Martin/ St. Maarten

KEY

⅂ *Beaches*

⚓ *Cruise Ship Terminal*

◣ *Dive Sites*

TO ANGUILLA

TO ST. BARTHÉLEMY →

Creole Rock ◣

Anse Marcel

Pt. des Froussards

Bell Pt.

Red Rock

Grandes Cayes

Baie de Grand Case ⅂

French Cul de Sac

Ile → Tintamarre ◣

Galion Beach

Baie de Friars ⅂

Grand Case

Aeroport de l'Espérance

Baie Orientale

Green Key

Pt. Arago

Colombier **Pic du Paradis**

Loterie Farm ◆

Butterfly Farm ⅂

Orléans

Baie de L'Embouchure

Fort Louis

Mt. Flagstaf

Baie Rouge ⅂

Pt. du Plum

Baie Pte. du Bluff

Baie de la Potenie

ST. MARTIN

Terres Basses

Baie Nettlé

Baie de Marigot

Sandy Ground

Marigot

Béneden Prinsen

Babit Pt.

Baie Longue ⅂

Simpson Bay Lagoon

Dutch Cul-de-Sac

Cupecoy Beach ◣

Musée de Staint-Martin

ST. MAARTEN

Boven Prinsen

Dawn Beach ⅂

Mullet Bay ⅂

Juliana International Airport ⚓

Maho Bay ⅂

Koolbaai

Salt Pond

Caribbean Sea

◣ Annie

Simpson Bay ◣

Guana Bay Point ◆

Cole Bay

Great Bay ⅂

Geneve Bay

Little Bay

Philipsburg see inset map

Pt. Blanche

ATLANTIC OCEAN

Proselyte Reef ◣

0 — 2 miles
0 — 3 km

TO ST. BARTHÉLEMY ↘

Great Salt Pond

Philipsburg

Post Office ◆

Captain Hodge Pier ⚓

◆ Wathey Sq.

Sint Maarten Museum ◆

Great Bay

Bobby's Marina ◆

Great Bay Marina ◆

grown on the estate. ✉ *The Still Plantation, Sir Arthur Lewis St., Soufrière* ☎ *758/459–7261* ▭ *MC, V.*

ST. MAARTEN (PHILLIPSBURG)

Elise Meyer and Roberta Sotonoff

St. Martin/St. Maarten: one tiny island, just 37 square mi (59 square km), with two different accents and ruled by two sovereign nations. Here French and Dutch have lived side by side for hundreds of years, and when you cross from one country to the next there are no border patrols, no customs agents. In fact, the only indication that you have crossed a border at all is a small sign and a change in road surface. St. Martin/St. Maarten epitomizes tourist islands in the sun, where services are well developed but there's still some Caribbean flavor. The Dutch side is ideal for people who like plenty to do. The French side has a more genteel ambience, more fashionable shopping, and a Continental flair. The combination makes an almost ideal port. On the negative side, the island has been completely developed. It can be fun to shop, and you'll find an occasional bargain, but many goods are cheaper in the United States.

ESSENTIALS

CURRENCY   Legal tender on the Dutch side is the Netherlands Antilles florin (guilder), written NAf or ANG. At this writing, ANG 1.79 equals $1. On the French side, the currency is the euro (€1 to US$1.22 at this writing). There's little need to exchange money. Prices are usually quoted in both florins and dollars on the Dutch side and euros on the French side, but dollars are accepted all over the island.

INTERNET   There is Wi-Fi service on the boardwalk behind Front Street if you have your own laptop. **Cyber Link** (✉ *53 Front St., Philipsburg*).

TELEPHONE   To phone from the Dutch side to the French, you first must dial (00–590–590) for local numbers, or (00–590–690) for cell phones, then the six-digit local number. To call from the French side to the Dutch, dial "00–599" then the seven-digit local number. Remember that a call from one side to the other is an international call.

At the Landsradio in Philipsburg there are facilities for overseas calls and a USA-Direct phone, where you're directly in touch with an operator who will accept collect or credit-card calls. To call direct with an AT&T credit card or operator, dial 001–800/872-2881. On the French side, AT&T can be accessed by calling 080-099-00-11. If you need to use public phones, go to the special desk at Marigot's post office and buy a *télécarte*. There's a public phone at the tourist office in Marigot where you can make credit-card calls: the operator takes your card number (any major card) and assigns you a PIN, which you then use to charge calls to your card.

COMING ASHORE

Most cruise ships drop anchor off the Dutch capital of Philipsburg or dock in the marina at the southern tip of the Philipsburg harbor; a very few small or medium-size ships drop anchor in Marigot Bay and tender passengers ashore in the French capital. If your ship anchors, tenders will ferry you to the town pier in the middle of town, where taxis await passengers. If your ship docks at the marina, downtown is a 15-minute taxi ride away. The walk is not recommended. The island is small, and most spots aren't more than a 30-minute drive from Marigot or Phillipsburg.

Doing your own thing will be much less expensive here than a ship-sponsored tour, and since rental cars are cheap (starting at $30 per day for a local car rental), you can easily strike out as soon as your ship docks. This is the best thing to do if you just want to see the island and spend a little time at a beach. Taxis are government-regulated and fairly costly, so they aren't really an option if you want to do much exploring. Authorized taxis display stickers of the St. Maarten Taxi Association. Taxis are also available at Marigot. You may be able to negotiate a favorable deal with a taxi driver for a two- to three-hour island tour for as little as $50 plus $15 for each additional person.

EXPLORING ST. MAARTEN/ST-MARTIN

& **Butterfly Farm.** If you arrive early in the morning, when the butterflies
Fodor's Choice first break out of their chrysalis, you'll be able to marvel at the abso-
★ lute wonder of dozens of butterflies and moths from around the world
and the particular host plants with which each evolved. At any given
time, some 40 species of butterflies—numbering as many as 600 individual insects—flutter inside the lush screened garden and hatch on the
plants housed there. Butterfly art and knickknacks are for sale in the
gift shop. In case you want to come back, your ticket, which includes
a guided tour, is good for your entire stay. ⊠ *Le Galion Beach Rd.,*
Quartier d'Orléans ☎ *590/87–31–21* ⊕ *www.thebutterflyfarm.com*
⊠ *$12* ⊙ *Daily 9–3:30.*

Fort Louis. Though not much remains of the structure itself, this fort,
which was completed by the French in 1789, is great fun if you want to
climb the 92 steps to the top for the wonderful views of the island and
neighboring Anguilla. On Wednesday and Saturday there is a market
in the square at the bottom. ⊠ *Marigot.*

French Cul de Sac. North of Orient Bay Beach, the French-colonial mansion of St. Martin's mayor is nestled in the hills. Little red-roof houses
look like open umbrellas tumbling down the green hillside. The area is
peaceful and good for hiking. From the beach here, shuttle boats make
the five-minute trip to **Ilêt Pinel,** an uninhabited island that's fine for
picnicking, sunning, and swimming. There are full-service beach clubs
there, so just pack the sunscreen and head over.

Grand Case. The Caribbean's own Restaurant Row is the heart of this
French-side town, a 10-minute drive from either Orient Bay or Marigot,
stretching along a narrow beach overlooking Anguilla. You'll find a
first-rate restaurant for every palate, mood, and wallet. At lunchtime,
or with kids, head to the casual *lolos* (open-air barbecue stands) and
feet-in-the-sand beach bars. Twilight drinks and tapas are fun. At night,
stroll the strip and preview the sophisticated offerings on the menus
posted outside before you settle in for a long and sumptuous meal. If
you still have the energy, there are lounges with music (usually a DJ)
that get going after 11 PM.

Marigot. This town's southern European flavor is most in evidence at
its beautiful harborfront, with its shopping stalls, open-air cafés, and
fresh-food vendors. From here, you can catch the ferry for Anguilla
or St. Barth.

Philipsburg. The capital of Dutch St. Maarten stretches about a mile (1½
km) along an isthmus between Great Bay and the Salt Pond, and has five
parallel streets. Most of the village's dozens of shops and restaurants
are on Front Street, narrow and cobblestone, closest to Great Bay. It's
generally congested when cruise ships are in port, because of its many
duty-free shops and several casinos. Little lanes called *steegjes* connect
Front Street with Back Street, which has fewer shops and considerably
less congestion. Along the beach is a ½-mi-long (1-km-long) boardwalk
with restaurants and several Wi-Fi hot spots.

Wathey Square (pronounced watty) is in the heart of the village. Directly across from the square are the town hall and the courthouse, in the striking white building with the cupola. The structure was built in 1793, and has served as the commander's home, a fire station, a jail, and a post office. The streets sur-

rounding the square are lined with hotels, duty-free shops, fine restaurants, and cafés. **Captain Hodge Pier,** just off the square, is a good spot to view Great Bay and the beach that stretches alongside.

The **Sint Maarten Museum** hosts rotating cultural exhibits and a permanent historical display called Forts of St. Maarten–St. Martin. Artifacts range from Arawak pottery shards to objects salvaged from the wreck of the HMS *Proselyte.* ⊠ *7 Front St., Philipsburg* ☎ *599/542–4917* 🖰 *Free* ☉ *Weekdays 10–4.*

Fodor's Choice ★ **Pic du Paradis.** Between Marigot and Grand Case, "Paradise Peak," at 1,492 feet, is the island's highest point. There are two observation areas. From them the tropical forest unfolds below, and the vistas are breathtaking. The road is quite isolated and steep, best suited to a four-wheel-drive vehicle, so don't head up here unless you are prepared for the climb. There have also been some problems with crime in this area, so it might be best to go with an experienced local guide.

Halfway up the road to Pic du Paradis is **Loterie Farm,** a peaceful 150-acre private nature preserve opened to the public in 1999 by American expat B. J. Welch. There are hiking trails and maps, so you can go on your own (🖰 €5) or arrange a guide for a group (🖰 €25 for six people). Along the marked trails you will see native forest with tamarind, gum, mango, and mahogany trees, and wildlife including greenback monkeys if you are lucky. Don't miss a treetop lunch or dinner at **Hidden Forest Café,** Loterie Farm's restaurant, where Julie, B. J.'s wife, cooks. If you are brave—and over 4 feet 5 inches—try soaring over trees on one of the longest zip lines in the Western Hemisphere. ⊠ *Rte. de Pic du Paradis* ☎ *590/87–86–16 or 590/57–28–55* 🖰 *€35–€55* ☉ *Daily sunrise–sunset.*

SHOPPING

It's true that the island sparkles with its myriad outdoor activities—diving, snorkeling, sailing, swimming, and sunning—but shopaholics are drawn to the sparkle within the jewelry stores. The huge array of such stores is almost unrivaled in the Caribbean. In addition, duty-free shops offer substantial savings—about 15% to 30% below U.S. and Canadian prices—on cameras, watches, liquor, cigars, and designer clothing. It's no wonder that each year 500 cruise ships make Philipsburg a port of call. On both sides of the island, be alert for idlers. They can snatch unwatched purses. Prices are in dollars on the Dutch side, in euros on the French side. As for bargains, there are more to be had on the Dutch side.

Philipsburg's **Front Street** has reinvented itself. Now it's mall-like, with a redbrick walk and streets, palm trees lining the sleek boutiques, jewelry stores, souvenir shops, outdoor restaurants, and the old reliables, like McDonald's and Burger King. Here and there a school or a church appears to remind visitors there's more to the island than shopping. Back Street is where you'll find the **Philipsburg Market Place,** a daily open-air market where you can haggle for bargains on such goods as handicrafts, souvenirs, and beachwear. **Old Street,** near the end of Front Street, has stores, boutiques, and open-air cafés offering French crepes, rich chocolates, and island mementos.

On the French side, wrought-iron balconies, colorful awnings, and gingerbread trim decorate Marigot's smart shops, tiny boutiques, and bistros in the **Marina Royale** complex and on the main streets, **Rue de la Liberté** and **Rue de la République.** Also in Marigot are the pricey **West Indies Mall** and the **Plaza Caraïbes,** which house designer shops, although some shops are closing in the economic downturn.

ACTIVITIES

For a wide range of water sports, including parasailing and waterskiing, head to Orient Beach, where a variety of operators have their headquarters.

DIVING AND SNORKELING

Although St. Maarten is not generally known as a dive destination, the water temperature here is rarely below 70°F (21°C). Visibility is often excellent, averaging about 100 feet to 120 feet. The island has more than 40 good dive sites, from wrecks to rocky labyrinths. For snorkelers, the area around Orient Bay, Caye Verte (Green Key), Ilêt Pinel, and Flat Island is especially lovely, and is officially classified, and protected, as a regional underwater nature reserve. The average cost of an afternoon snorkeling trip is about $45 to $55 per person.

Dive Safaris (⊠ *La Palapa Marina, Simpson Bay* ☎ *599/545–3213* ⊕ *www.divestmaarten.com*) has a shark-awareness dive where participants can watch professional feeders give reef sharks a little nosh. **Ocean Explorers Dive Shop** (⊠ *113 Welfare Rd., Simpson Bay* ☎ *599/544–5252* ⊕ *www.stmaartendiving.com*) is St. Maarten's oldest dive shop, and offers different types of certification courses.

FISHING

You can angle for yellowtail snapper, grouper, marlin, tuna, and wahoo on deep-sea excursions. Costs range from $150 per person for a half-day to $250 for a full day. Prices usually include bait and tackle, instruction for novices, and refreshments. Ask about licensing and insurance.

Big Sailfish Too (⊠ *Anse Marcel* ☎ *690/27–40–90*) is your best bet on the French side of the island. **Lee's Deepsea Fishing** (⊠ *Welfare Rd. 82, Simpson Bay* ☎ *599/544–4233* ⊕ *www.leesfish.com*) organizes excursions, and when you return, Lee's Roadside Grill will cook your tuna, wahoo, or whatever else you catch and keep. **Rudy's Deep Sea Fishing** (⊠ *14 Airport Rd., Simpson Bay* ☎ *599/545–2177 or 599/522–7120*

⊕ *www.rudysdeepseafishing.com*) has been around for years, and is one of the more experienced sport-angling outfits.

BEACHES

The island's 10 mi (16 km) of beaches are all open to cruise-ship passengers. You can rent chairs and umbrellas at most of the beaches, primarily from beachside restaurants. The best beaches are on the French side. Topless bathing is common on the French side. If you take a cab to a remote beach, be sure to arrange a specific time for the driver to return for you. Don't leave valuables unattended on the beach or in a rental car, even in the trunk.

Baie des Péres (*Friars Bay*). This quiet cove close to Marigot has beach grills and bars, with chaises and umbrellas, calm waters, and a lovely view of Anguilla. To get to the beach, take National Road 7 from Marigot, go toward Grand Case to the Morne Valois hill, and turn left on the dead-end road at the sign. ⊠ *Friar's Bay.*

★ **Dawn Beach.** True to its name, Dawn Beach is the place to be at sunrise. On the Atlantic side of Oyster Pond, just south of the French border, this is a first-class beach for sunning and snorkeling. It's not usually crowded, and there are several good restaurants nearby. To find it, follow the signs to Mr. Busby's restaurant. ⊠ *South of Oyster Pond, Dawn Beach.*

Fodor'sChoice **Baie Orientale** (*Orient Bay*). Many consider this the island's most beautiful beach, but its 2 mi (3 km) of satiny white sand, underwater marine reserve, variety of water sports, beach clubs, and hotels also make it one of the most crowded. Lots of "naturists" take advantage of the clothing-optional policy, so don't be shocked. To get to Baie Orientale from Marigot, take National Road 7 past Grand Case, past the Aéroport de L'Espérance, and watch for the left turn. ⊠ *Baie Orientale.*

Ilêt Pinel. A protected nature reserve, this kid-friendly island is a five-minute ferry ride from French Cul de Sac ($7 per person round-trip). The ferry runs every half-hour from midmorning until dusk. The water is clear and shallow, and the shore is sheltered. If you like snorkeling, don your gear and paddle along both coasts of this pencil-shaped speck in the ocean. You can rent equipment on the island or in the parking lot before you board the ferry for about $10. You can buy lunch on-island except in September, when the beach bar there is closed. ⊠ *Ilêt Pinel.*

WHERE TO EAT

$ ✕**Enoch's Place.** The blue-and-white-stripe awning on a corner of the
CARIBBEAN Marigot Market makes this place hard to miss. But Enoch's cooking is what draws the crowds. Specialties include garlic shrimp, fresh lobster, and rice and beans (like your St. Martin mother used to make). Try the saltfish and fried johnnycake—a great breakfast option. The food more than makes up for the lack of decor, and chances are you'll be counting the days until you can return. ⊠ *Marigot Market, Front de Mer, Marigot* ☎ *590/29–29–88* ▭ *No credit cards* ☉ *Closed Sun. No dinner.*

$$ ✕ **Taloula Mango's.** Ribs are the specialty at this casual beachfront res-
ECLECTIC   taurant, but the jerk chicken and thin-crust pizza, not to mention a
ℭ   few vegetarian options like the tasty falafel, are not to be ignored. On
weekdays lunch is accompanied by live music; every Friday during
happy hour a DJ spins tunes. In case you're wondering, the restaurant
got its name from the owner's golden retriever. ⊠ *Sint Rose Shopping
Mall, off Front St. on beach boardwalk, Philipsburg* ☎ *599/542–1645*
⊕ *www.taloulamango.com* ☰ *AE, D, MC, V.*

ST. THOMAS (CHARLOTTE AMALIE)

Carol
Bareuther

St. Thomas is the busiest cruise port of call in the world. Up to eight
mega ships may visit in a single day. Don't expect an exotic island expe-
rience: one of the three U.S. Virgin Islands (with St. Croix and St. John),
St. Thomas is as American as any place on the mainland, complete
with McDonald's and HBO. The positive side of all this development
is that there are more tours here than anywhere else in the Caribbean,
and every year the excursions get better. Of course, shopping is the big
draw in Charlotte Amalie, but experienced travelers remember the days
of "real" bargains. Today so many passengers fill the stores that it's a
seller's market. On some days there are so many cruise passengers on
St. Thomas that you must book a ship-sponsored shore excursion if
you want to do more than just take a taxi to the beach or stroll around
Charlotte Amalie.

ESSENTIALS

CURRENCY   The U.S. dollar is the official currency of U.S. Virgin Islands, and ATMs are
plentiful.

INTERNET   **Beans, Bytes and Websites** (⊠ *Royal Dane Mall, behind Tavern on Water-
front, Charlotte Amalie* ☎ *340/775–5262* ⊕ *www.beansbytesandwebsites.com*).
Havensight Cafe (⊠ *Havensight Mall, Charlotte Amalie* ☎ *340/774–5818*).

TELEPHONE   Both GSM and Sprint phones work in St. Thomas (and the USVI are normally
included in most U.S. cell phone plans). It's as easy to call home from St.
Thomas and St. John as from any city in the United States. On St. Thomas, public
phones are easily found, and AT&T has a telecommunications center across from
the Havensight Mall.

COMING ASHORE

Depending on how many ships are in port, cruise ships drop anchor in
the harbor at Charlotte Amalie and tender passengers directly to the
waterfront duty-free shops, dock at the Havensight Mall at the eastern
end of the crescent bay, or dock at Crown Bay Marina a few miles west
of town (Holland America almost always docks at Crown Bay).

The distance from Havensight to the duty-free shops is 1½ mi (3 km),
which can be walked in less than half an hour; a taxi ride there costs
$6 per person ($5 for each additional person). Tourist information
offices are at the Havensight Mall (across from Building No. 1) for
docking passengers and downtown near Fort Christian (at the eastern

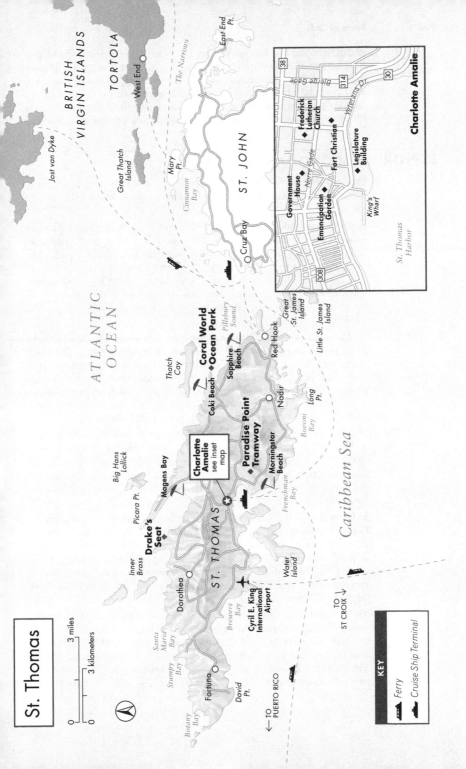

end of the waterfront shopping area) for those coming ashore by tender. Both offices distribute free maps. From Crown Bay it's also a half-hour walk or a $5 per person cab ride ($4 for each additional person). V.I. Taxi Association drivers offer a basic 2-hour island tour for $29 per person. You can rent a car in St. Thomas, but with all the tour options it's often easier and cheaper to take an organized excursion or just hop in a cab.

EXPLORING ST. THOMAS

Charlotte Amalie. St. Thomas's major burg is a hilly shopping town. There are also plenty of interesting historic sights—so take the time to see at least a few.

Built to commemorate the freeing of slaves in 1848, the **Emancipation Garden** was the site of a 150th anniversary celebration of emancipation. A bronze bust of a freed slave blowing a symbolic conch shell commemorates this anniversary. The gazebo here is used for official ceremonies. Two other monuments show the island's Danish-American connection—a bust of Denmark's King Christian and a scaled-down model of the U.S. Liberty Bell. ☒ *Between Tolbod Gade and Ft. Christian.*

St. Thomas's oldest standing structure, **Ft. Christian** was built between 1672 and 1680 and now has U.S. National Landmark status. The clock tower was added in the 19th century. This remarkable building has, over time, been used as a jail, governor's residence, town hall, courthouse, and church. A multimillion-dollar renovation project is under way and will stabilize the structure and halt centuries of deterioration. ☒ *Waterfront Hwy. east of shopping district* ☎ *340/776–8605.*

Historic **Frederick Lutheran Church** has a massive mahogany altar, and its pews—each with its own door—were once rented to families of the congregation. Lutheranism is the state religion of Denmark, and when the territory was without a minister, the governor—who had his own elevated pew—filled in. ☒ *Norre Gade* ☎ *340/776–1315* ☉ *Mon.–Sat. 9–4.*

Built in 1867, the neoclassical white brick-and-wood **Government House** houses the offices of the governor of the Virgin Islands. Inside, the staircases are of native mahogany, as are the plaques hand-lettered in gold with the names of the governors appointed and, since 1970, elected. Brochures detailing the history of the building are available, but you may have to ask for them. ☒ *Government Hill* ☎ *340/774–0294* 🖅 *Free* ☉ *Weekdays 8–5.*

The pastoral-looking lime-green exterior of the **Legislature Building** conceals the vociferous political wrangling of the Virgin Islands Senate. Constructed originally by the Danes as a police barracks, the building was later used to billet U.S. Marines, and much later it housed a public school. You're welcome to sit in on sessions in the upstairs chambers. ☒ *Waterfront Hwy. across from Ft. Christian* ☎ *340/774–0880* ☉ *Daily 8–5.*

☺ **Coral World Ocean Park.** This inter-
Fodor's Choice active aquarium and water-sports
★ center lets you experience a vari-
ety of sea life and other animals.
The park has several outdoor pools
where you can pet baby sharks, feed
stingrays, touch starfish, and view
endangered sea turtles. Other activities include the Sea Trek Helmet
Dive that allows you to walk along
an underwater trail with a high-tech
helmet that provides a continuous
supply of air. A Shark Encounter
program lets you observe and pet
juvenile sharks as they swim around
you. Get a big, wet, whiskered kiss
while taking a swim in the sea-lion
pool. A Sea Lion Painting program
started in 2009—you hold a 12- by
16-inch canvas as one of the South
American Sea Lion artists creates a
unique masterpiece using two col-
ors of your choice. Buy a cup of nectar for $2 and let the parrot-look-
alike lorikeets perch on your hand and drink. Coral World also has an
offshore underwater observatory, an 80,000-gallon coral reef exhibit
(one of the largest in the world), and a nature trail full of lush tropical
flowers, ducks, and tortoises. Daily feedings take place at most exhibits. ⊠ *Coki Point north of Rte. 38, Estate Frydendal* ☎ *340/775–1555*
⊕ *www.coralworldvi.com* ⛱ *$21, Sea Lion Splash $106, Sea Lion
Painting $96, Sea Trek $79, Shark Encounter $53* ☉ *Daily 9–5.*

☺ **Drake's Seat.** Sir Francis Drake is supposed to have kept watch over his
fleet and looked for enemy ships from this vantage point. The panorama
is especially breathtaking (and romantic) at dusk, and if you arrive late
in the day you can miss the hordes of day-trippers on taxi tours who
stop here to take a picture and buy a T-shirt from one of the many
vendors. ⊠ *Rte. 40, Estate Zufriedenheit.*

☺ **Paradise Point Tramway.** Fly skyward in a gondola to Paradise Point, an
★ overlook with breathtaking views of Charlotte Amalie and the harbor.
For an extra thrill, try the Sky Jump, a high-tech trampoline that lets
you jump up to 20 feet—it's almost like touching the sky from this
elevation. There are several shops, a bar, a restaurant, and a wedding
gazebo; kids enjoy the tropical bird show held daily at 10:30 AM and
1:30 PM. A ¼-mi (½-km) hiking trail leads to spectacular views of St.
Croix. Wear sturdy shoes, as the trail is steep and rocky. ⊠ *Rte. 30
across from Havensight Mall, Havensight* ☎ *340/774–9809* ⊕ *www.
paradisepointtramway.com* ⛱ *$21, Sky Jump $30* ☉ *Thurs.–Tues. 9–5,
Wed. 9–9.*

ST. THOMAS BEST BETS

■ **Coral World Ocean Park.** This
aquarium attraction is a great bet
for families, and it's on one of
best snorkeling beaches.

■ **Magen's Bay Beach.** St.
Thomas has one of the most
picture-postcard perfect beaches
you'll ever see. It's great for
swimming.

■ **St. John.** It's easy to hop on
the ferry to St. John for a day of
hiking, then relax for an hour or
two on the beach afterward.

■ **Shopping.** Charlotte Amalie
is one of the best places in the
Caribbean to shop.

4

SHOPPING

The prime shopping area in **Charlotte Amalie** is between Post Office and Market squares; it consists of two parallel streets that run east–west (Waterfront Highway and Main Street) and the alleyways that connect them. Particularly attractive are the historic **A. H. Riise Alley, Royal Dane Mall, Palm Passage,** and pastel-painted **International Plaza. Vendors Plaza,** on the waterfront side of the Emancipation Garden in Charlotte Amalie, is a central location for vendors selling handmade earrings, necklaces, and bracelets; straw baskets and handbags; T-shirts; fabrics; African artifacts; and local fruits. Look for the many brightly colored umbrellas.

Havensight Mall, next to the cruise-ship dock, may not be as charming as downtown Charlotte Amalie, but it does have more than 60 shops. It also has an excellent bookstore, a bank, a pharmacy, a gourmet grocery, and smaller branches of many downtown stores.The shops at **Port of $ale,** adjoining Havensight Mall (its buildings are pink instead of brown), sell discount goods. Next door to Port of $ale is the **Yacht Haven Grande** complex, with many upscale shops. At the Crown Bay cruise-ship pier, the **Crown Bay Center,** off the Harwood Highway in Sub Base about ½ mi (¾ km), has quite a few shops.

ACTIVITIES

DIVING AND SNORKELING

☾ **Coki Beach Dive Club** (✉ *Rte. 388, at Coki Point, Estate Frydendal* ☎ *340/775–4220* ⊕ *www.cokidive.com*) is a PADI Gold Palm outfit run by avid diver Peter Jackson. Snorkeling and dive tours in the fish-filled reefs off Coki Beach are available, as are classes from beginner to underwater photography.

Snuba of St. Thomas (✉ *Rte. 388, at Coki Point, Estate Smith Bay* ☎ *340/693–8063* ⊕ *www.visnuba.com*) offers something for nondivers, a cross between snorkeling and scuba diving: a 20-foot air hose connects you to the surface. The cost is $68. Children must be 8 or older to participate.

FISHING

Big Wave (✉ *Crown Bay Marina, Rte 304, Estate Conant* ☎ *340/642–7423*), owned by a long-time islander, offers fishing trips on its 28-foot World cat multihull.

The **Charter Boat Center** (✉ *6300 Red Hook Plaza, Red Hook* ☎ *340/775–7990* ⊕ *www.charterboat.vi*) is a major source for sportfishing charters, both marlin and inshore.

GOLF

★ The **Mahogany Run Golf Course** (✉ *Rte. 42, Estate Lovenlund* ☎ *340/777–6006 or 800/253–7103* ⊕ *www.mahoganyrungolf.com*) attracts golfers for its spectacular view of the British Virgin Islands and the challenging three-hole Devil's Triangle. At this Tom and George Fazio–designed, par-70, 18-hole course, there's a fully stocked pro shop, snack bar, and open-air clubhouse. Greens fees and half-cart fees for 18 holes are $150.

The course is open daily, and there are frequently informal weekend tournaments. It's the only course on St. Thomas.

BEACHES

☺ **Coki Beach.** Funky beach huts selling local foods such as meat pâté (fried turnovers with a spicy ground-beef filling), picnic tables topped with umbrellas sporting beverage logos, and a brigade of hair braiders and taxi men give this beach overlooking picturesque Thatch Cay a Coney Island feel. But this is the best place on the island to snorkel and scuba dive. ⊠ *Rte. 388, next to Coral World Ocean Park.*

Fodor's Choice
★

☺ **Magens Bay.** Deeded to the island as a public park, this heart-shaped stretch of white sand is considered one of the most beautiful in the world. The bottom of the bay is flat and sandy, so this is a place for sunning and swimming rather than snorkeling. There's a bar, snack shack, and beachwear boutique; bathhouses with restrooms, changing rooms, and saltwater showers are close by. If you arrive between 8 AM and 5 PM, you pay an entrance fee of $4 per person, $2 per vehicle; it's free for children under 12. ⊠ *Rte. 35, at end of road on north side of island.*

Fodor's Choice
★

4

Morningstar Beach. Nature and nurture combine at this ¼-mi-long (½-km-long) beach between Marriott Frenchman's Reef and Morning Star Beach Resorts, where amenities range from water-sports rentals to beachside bar service. A concession rents floating mats, snorkeling equipment, sailboards, and Jet Skis. Swimming is excellent; there are good-size rolling waves year-round, but do watch the undertow. ⊠ *Rte. 315, 2 mi (3 km) southeast of Charlotte Amalie, past Havensight Mall and cruise-ship dock.*

Sapphire Beach. A steady breeze makes this beach a boardsailor's paradise. The swimming is great, as is the snorkeling, especially at the reef near Pettyklip Point. Beach volleyball is big on the weekends. Sapphire Beach Resort & Marina has a restaurant, bar, and water-sports rentals. ⊠ *Rte. 38, Sapphire Bay.*

WHERE TO EAT

$$
CARIBBEAN

✕ **Cuzzin's Caribbean Restaurant & Bar.** This is the place to sample bona-fide Virgin Islands cuisine. For lunch, order tender slivers of conch stewed in a rich onion-and-butter sauce, savory braised oxtail, or curried chicken. At dinner the island-style mutton, served in thick gravy and seasoned with locally grown herbs, offers a tasty treat that's deliciously different. Side dishes include peas and rice, boiled green bananas, fried plantains, and potato stuffing. In a 19th-century livery stable on Back Street, this restaurant is hard to find but well worth it if you like sampling local foods. ⊠ *7 Wimmelskafts Gade, also called Back St.* ☎ *340/777–4711* ⊟ *AE, MC, V.*

$$
CARIBBEAN
Fodor's Choice
★

✕ **Gladys' Cafe.** Even if the local specialties—conch in butter sauce, salt fish and dumplings, hearty red bean soup—didn't make this a recommended café, it would be worth coming for Gladys's smile. Her cozy alleyway restaurant is rich in atmosphere, with its mahogany bar and native stone walls, making dining a double delight. While you're here, pick up a $5 or $10 bottle of her special hot sauce. There are mustard-, oil and vinegar-, and tomato-based versions; the tomato-based sauce is the hottest. ✉ *Waterfront at Royal Dane Mall* ☎ *340/774–6604* ✉ *AE* ⊙ *No dinner.*

ST. VINCENT (KINGSTOWN)

Jane E. Zarem   You won't find glitzy resorts or flashy discos in St. Vincent. Rather, you'll be fascinated by its busy capital, mountainous beauty, and fine sailing waters. St. Vincent is the largest and northernmost island in the Grenadines archipelago; Kingstown, the capital city of St. Vincent and the Grenadines, is the government and business center and major port. Except for one barren area on the island's northeast coast—remnants of the 1979 eruption of La Soufrière, one of the last active volcanoes in the Caribbean—the countryside is mountainous, lush, and green. St. Vincent's topography thwarted European settlement for many years. As colonization advanced elsewhere in the Caribbean, in fact, the island became a refuge for Carib Indians—descendants of whom still live in northeastern St. Vincent. After years of fighting and back-and-forth territorial claims, British troops prevailed by overpowering the French and banishing Carib warriors to Central America. Independent since 1979, St. Vincent and the Grenadines remains a member of the British Commonwealth.

ESSENTIALS

CURRENCY   Eastern Caribbean (E.C.) dollar (EC$2.67 to US$1). U.S. dollars (but not coins) are generally accepted, but change is given in E.C. currency.

INTERNET   **E@gles Internet Cafe** (✉ *Halifax St., opposite the General Post Office, Kingstown, St. Vincent*).

TELEPHONE   Your cell phone should operate in St. Vincent, but roaming charges can be hefty. Pay phones are readily available and best operated with the prepaid phone cards that are sold at many stores. Telephone services are available at the Cruise Ship Complex in Kingstown. For an international operator, dial 115; to charge your call to a credit card, call 117.

COMING ASHORE

The Cruise Ship Complex at Kingstown, St. Vincent's capital city, accommodates two cruise ships; additional vessels anchor outside the harbor and bring passengers to the jetty by launch. The facility has about two-dozen shops that sell duty-free items and handicrafts. There's a communications center, post office, tourist information desk, restaurant, and food court.

Buses and taxis are available at the wharf. Taxi drivers are well equipped to take you on an island tour; expect to pay $25 per hour for up to four passengers. The ferry to Bequia (one hour each way) is at the adjacent pier. Renting a car for just one day isn't advisable, since car rentals are expensive (at least $55 per day) and require a $20 temporary driving permit on top of that. It's almost always more financially favorable to

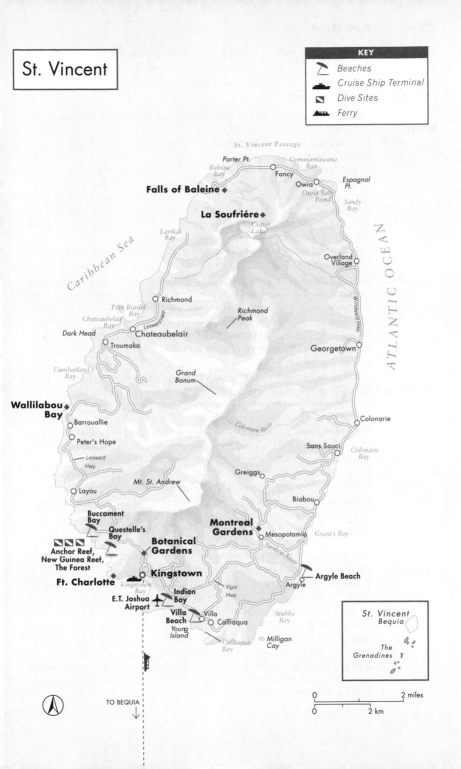

St. Vincent

KEY

Beaches

Cruise Ship Terminal

Dive Sites

Ferry

St. Vincent Passage

Porter Pt.

Baleine Bay

Fancy

Commantawana Bay

Owia

Espagnol Pt.

Falls of Baleine ◆

Owia Salt Pond

Sandy Bay

La Soufriére ◆

Crater Lake

Larikai Bay

Overland Village

Caribbean Sea

Richmond

Richmond Peak

ATLANTIC OCEAN

Petit Bordel Bay

Chateaubelair Bay

Leeward Hwy.

Chateaubelair

Georgetown

Windward Hwy.

Dark Head

Troumaka

Cumberland Bay

Grand Bonum

Wallilabou Bay ◆

Colonarie River

Colonarie

Barrouallie

Sans Souci

Colonarie Bay

Peter's Hope

Greiggs

Leeward Hwy.

Layou

Mt. St. Andrew

Biabou

Buccament Bay

Montreal Gardens ◆

Questelle's Bay

Mesopotamia

Grant's Bay

Anchor Reef, New Guinea Reet, The Forest

Botanical Gardens

Yambou River

Ft. Charlotte ◆

Kingstown

Kingstown Bay

Argyle Beach

Argyle

Vigie Hwy.

E.T. Joshua Airport

Indian Bay

Villa Beach

Villa

Calliaqua

Stubbs Bay

Young Island

Calliaqua Bay

Milligan Cay

St. Vincent

Bequia

The Grenadines

TO BEQUIA ↓

| 0 | | 2 miles |
| 0 | | 2 km |

take a tour, though you don't have to limit yourself to those offered by your ship.

EXPLORING ST. VINCENT

Botanical Gardens. A few minutes north of downtown by taxi is St. Vincent's famous Botanical Gardens. Founded in 1765, it's the oldest botanical garden in the Western Hemisphere. Captain Bligh—of *Bounty* fame—brought the first breadfruit tree to this island for landowners to propagate. The prolific bounty of the breadfruit trees was used to feed the slaves. You can see a direct descendant of this original tree among the specimen mahogany, rubber, teak, and other tropical trees and shrubs in the 20 acres of gardens. Two-dozen rare St. Vincent parrots, confiscated from illegal collectors, live in the small aviary. Guides explain all the medicinal and ornamental trees and shrubs; they also appreciate a tip at the end of the tour. ⊠ *Off Leeward Hwy., Montrose* ☎ *784/457–1003* 🖅 *Free* ☉ *Daily 7–6.*

Falls of Baleine. The falls are impossible to reach by car, so book an escorted, all-day boat trip from Villa Beach or the Lagoon Marina. The boat ride along the coast offers scenic island views. When you arrive, you have to wade through shallow water to get to the beach. Then local guides help you make the easy five-minute trek to the 60-foot falls and the rock-enclosed freshwater pool the falls create—wear a bathing suit so you can take a dip.

Ft. Charlotte. Started by the French in 1786 and completed by the British in 1806, the fort was named for King George III's wife. It sits on Berkshire Hill, a dramatic promontory 2 mi (3 km) north of Kingstown and 636 feet above sea level, with a stunning view of the capital city and the Grenadines. Interestingly, cannons face inward—the fear of attack by the French and their native allies was far greater than any threat approaching from the sea, though, truth be told, the fort saw no action. Nowadays the fort serves as a signal station for ships; its ancient cells house historical paintings of the island by Lindsay Prescott.

Kingstown. The capital city of St. Vincent and the Grenadines is on the island's southwestern coast. The town of 13,500 residents wraps around Kingstown Bay; a ring of green hills and ridges, studded with homes, forms a backdrop for the city. This is very much a working city, with a busy harbor and few concessions to tourists. Kingstown Harbour is the only deepwater port on the island.

A few gift shops can be found on and around **Bay Street,** near the harbor. Upper Bay Street, which stretches along the bay front, bustles with daytime activity—workers going about their business and housewives doing their shopping. Many of Kingstown's downtown buildings are built of stone or brick brought to the island in the holds of 18th-century ships as ballast (and replaced with sugar and spices for the return trip to Europe). The Georgian-style stone arches and second-floor overhangs on former warehouses create shelter from midday sun and the brief, cooling showers common to the tropics.

An almost infinite selection of produce fills the **Kingstown Produce Market,** a three-story building that takes up a whole city block on Upper Bay, Hillsboro, and Bedford streets in the center of town. It's noisy, colorful, and open Monday through Saturday—but the busiest times (and the best times to go) are Friday and Saturday mornings. In the courtyard, vendors sell local arts and crafts. On the upper floors, merchants sell clothing, household items, gifts, and other products.

St. George's Cathedral, on Grenville Street, is a pristine, creamy yellow Anglican church built in 1820. The dignified Georgian architecture includes simple wooden pews, an ornate chandelier, and beautiful stained-glass windows; one window was a gift from Queen Victoria, who actually commissioned it for London's St. Paul's Cathedral in honor of her first grandson. When the artist created an angel with a red robe, she was horrified by the color and sent it abroad. The markers in the cathedral's graveyard recount the history of the island. Across the street is **St. Mary's Roman Catholic Cathedral of the Assumption,** built in stages beginning in 1823. The strangely appealing design is a blend of Moorish, Georgian, and Romanesque styles applied to black brick. Nearby, freed slaves built the **Kingstown Methodist Church** in 1841. The exterior is brick, simply decorated with quoins (solid blocks that form the corners), and the roof is held together by metal straps, bolts, and wooden pins. **Scots Kirk** was built from 1839 to 1880 by and for Scottish settlers but became a Seventh-Day Adventist church in 1952.

La Soufrière. This towering volcano, which last erupted in 1979, is 4,000 feet high and so huge in area that its surrounding mountainside covers virtually the entire northern third of the island. The eastern trail to the rim of the crater, a two-hour ascent, begins at Rabacca Dry River.

Fodor's Choice ★ **Montreal Gardens.** Welsh-born landscape designer Timothy Vaughn renovated 7½ acres of neglected commercial flower beds and a falling-down plantation house into a stunning yet informal garden spot. Anthurium, ginger lilies, birds of paradise, and other tropical flowers are planted in raised beds; tree ferns create a canopy of shade along the walkways. The gardens are in the shadow of majestic Grand Bonhomme Mountain, deep in the Mesopotamia Valley, about 12 mi (19 km) from Kingstown. ⊠ *Montreal St., Mesopotamia* ☎ *784/458–1198* ⌑ *$2* ⊙ *Dec.–Aug., weekdays 9–4.*

☼ ★ **Wallilabou Bay.** The *Pirates of the Caribbean* left its mark at Wallilabou (pronounced wally-la-*boo*), a location used for filming the recent movies. Many of the buildings and docks built as stage sets remain, giving the pretty bay an intriguingly historic appearance. You can sunbathe, swim, picnic, or buy your lunch at Wallilabou Anchorage. This is a favorite stop for day-trippers returning from the Falls of Baleine and boaters anchoring for the evening. Nearby there's a river with a small waterfall where you can take a freshwater plunge.

SHOPPING

The 12 small blocks that hug the waterfront in **downtown Kingstown** compose St. Vincent's main shopping district. Among the shops that sell goods to fulfill household needs are a few that sell local crafts, gifts, and souvenirs. Bargaining is neither expected nor appreciated. The **cruise-ship complex,** on the waterfront in Kingstown, has a collection of a dozen or so boutiques, shops, and restaurants that cater primarily to cruise-ship passengers but welcome all shoppers. **St. Vincent Craftsmen's Centre** (⊠ *Frenches St., Kingstown* ☎ *784/457–2516*), three blocks from the wharf, sells locally made grass floor mats, place mats, and other straw articles, as well as batik cloth, handmade West Indian dolls, hand-painted calabashes, and framed artwork. No credit cards are accepted. On the leeward coast about a half-hour's drive north of Kingstown, **Wallilabou Craft Centre** (⊠ *Leeward Hwy., Wallilabou* ☎ *784/456–0078*) was established in 1986 as a local cooperative where villagers can learn various techniques for weaving straw and other natural fibers. Workers create baskets, handbags, hats, toys, and other items that are sold in the Kingstown market and make good souvenirs of a visit to St. Vincent.

ACTIVITIES

DIVING AND SNORKELING

Novices and advanced divers alike will be impressed by the marine life in the waters surrounding St. Vincent and the Grenadines—brilliant sponges, huge deepwater coral trees, and shallow reefs teeming with colorful fish. The best dive spots on St. Vincent are in the small bays along the coast between Kingstown and Layou; many are within 20 yards of shore and only 20 feet to 30 feet down.

Anchor Reef has excellent visibility for viewing a deep-black coral garden, schools of squid, seahorses, and maybe a small octopus. The **Forest,** a shallow dive, is still dramatic, with soft corals in pastel colors and schools of small fish. **New Guinea Reef** slopes to 90 feet (28 meters) and can't be matched for its quantity of corals and sponges. The pristine waters surrounding the **Tobago Cays,** in the Southern Grenadines, will give you a world-class diving experience.

Dive Fantasea (⊠ *Villa Beach* ☎ *784/457–5560 or 784/457–5577*) offers dive and snorkeling trips to the St. Vincent coast and the Tobago Cays. **Dive St. Vincent** (⊠ *Young Island Dock, Villa Beach* ☎ *784/457–4714 or 784/457–4928* ⊕ *www.divestvincent.com*) is where NAUI- and PADI-certified instructor Bill Tewes and his two certified dive masters offer beginner and certification courses for ages 8 and up, advanced water excursions along the St. Vincent coast and to the southern Grenadines for diving connoisseurs, and an introductory scuba lesson for novices.

FISHING

From Villa Beach or Indian Bay on St. Vincent, you can go on a full-day fishing trip or boat ride around the Grenadines for about $120–$140 per person, including all equipment and lunch. **Crystal Blue Sportfishing Charters** (⊠ *Indian Bay* ☎ *784/457–4532*) offers sportfishing charters on a 34-foot pirogue for both amateur and serious fishermen.

BEACHES

St. Vincent's origin is volcanic, so its beaches range in color from golden-brown to black. Swimming is recommended only in the lagoons and bays along the leeward coast. By contrast, beaches on Bequia and the rest of the Grenadines have pure white sand, palm trees, and crystal-clear aquamarine water; some are even within walking distance of the jetty.

Indian Bay. South of Kingstown and just north of Villa Beach, this beach has golden sand but is slightly rocky; it's good for snorkeling.

Questelle's Bay. This beach (pronounced keet-*ells*), north of Kingstown and next to Campden Park, has a black-sand beach.

Villa Beach. The long stretch of sand in front of the row of hotels and restaurants along the Young Island Channel varies from 20–25 feet wide to practically nonexistent. The broadest, sandiest part is in front of Beachcombers Hotel, which is also the perfect spot for sunbathers to get lunch and liquid refreshments.

WHERE TO EAT

$-$$ ✗ **Basil's Bar and Restaurant.** It's not just the air-conditioning that makes
CARIBBEAN   this restaurant cool. Downstairs at the Cobblestone Inn, Basil's is owned by Basil Charles, whose Basil's Beach Bar on Mustique is a hangout for the vacationing rich and famous. This is the Kingstown power-lunch venue. Local businesspeople gather for the daily buffet (weekdays) or full menu of salads, sandwiches, barbecued chicken, or fresh seafood platters. Dinner entrées of pasta, local seafood, and chicken are served at candlelit tables. There's a Chinese buffet on Friday, and takeout is available that night only. ⊠ *Cobblestone Inn, Upper Bay St., Kingstown* ☎ *784/457–2713* ➌ *AE, MC, V* ⊗ *Closed Sun.*

$-$$ ✗ **Cobblestone Roof-Top Bar & Restaurant.** To reach what is perhaps the
CARIBBEAN   most pleasant, the breeziest, and the most satisfying breakfast and lun-
★   cheon spot in downtown Kingstown, diners must climb the equivalent of three flights of interior stone steps within the historic Cobblestone Inn. But getting to the open-air rooftop restaurant is half the fun, as en route diners get an up-close view of the 19th-century sugar (and later arrowroot) Georgian warehouse that is now a very appealing boutique inn. A full breakfast menu is available to hotel guests and the public alike. The luncheon menu ranges from homemade soups, salads (tuna, chicken, fruit, or tossed), sandwiches, or burgers and fries to full meals of roast beef, stewed chicken, or grilled fish served with rice, plantains, macaroni pie, and fresh local vegetables. Dee-licious! ⊠ *Upper Bay St., Kingstown* ☎ *784/456–1937* ➌ *AE, D, MC, V* ⊗ *No dinner.*

SAN JUAN, PUERTO RICO

Heather Rodino

Although Puerto Rico is a commonwealth of the United States, few cities in the Caribbean are as steeped in Spanish tradition as San Juan. Within a seven-square-block area in Old San Juan are restored 16th-century buildings, museums, art galleries, bookstores, and 200-year-old

houses with balustraded balconies overlooking narrow, cobblestone streets. In contrast, San Juan's sophisticated Condado and Isla Verde areas have glittering hotels, fancy boutiques, casinos, and discos. Out in the countryside is 28,000-acre El Yunque National Forest, a rain forest with more than 240 species of trees growing at least 100 feet high. You can stretch your sea legs on dramatic mountain ranges, numerous trails, in vast caves, at coffee plantations, old sugar mills, and hundreds of beaches. No wonder San Juan is one of the busiest ports of call in the Caribbean. Like any other big city, San Juan has its share of petty crime, so guard your wallet or purse, especially in crowded markets and squares.

ESSENTIALS

CURRENCY   The U.S. dollar is the official currency of Puerto Rico.

INTERNET   You can check your e-mail at **CyberNet Café** (✉ 1128 Av. Ashford, Condado ☎ 787/724–4033 ✉ 5980 Av. Isla Verde, Isla Verde ☎ 787/728–4195).

TELEPHONE   Calling the United States from Puerto Rico is the same as calling within the United States, and all U.S. cell phone plans work here just as they do at home. You can use the long-distance telephone service office in the cruise-ship terminal, or you can use your calling card by dialing the toll-free access number of your long-distance provider from any pay phone. You'll find a phone center by the Paseo de la Princesa.

COMING ASHORE

Most cruise ships dock within a couple of blocks of Old San Juan; however, there is a second cruise pier across the bay, and if your ship docks there you'll need to take a taxi to get anywhere on the island. The Paseo de la Princesa, a tree-lined promenade beneath the city wall, is a nice place for a stroll—you can admire the local crafts and stop at the refreshment kiosks. Major sights in the Old San Juan area are mere blocks from the piers, but be aware that the streets are narrow and steeply inclined in places.

It's particularly easy to get to Cataño and the Bacardí Rum Plant on your own; take the ferry (50¢) that leaves from the cruise piers every half hour and then a taxi from the other side. Taxis, which line up to meet ships, are the best option if you want to explore the city itself. White taxis labeled TAXI TURISTICO charge set fares of $10 to $19. Metered cabs authorized by the Public Service Commission charge an initial $1; after that, it's about 10¢ for each additional 1/13 mi. If you take a metered taxi, insist that the meter be turned on, and pay only what is shown, plus a tip of 15% to 20%. You can negotiate with taxi drivers for specific trips, and you can hire a taxi for as little as $30 per hour for sightseeing tours. If you want to see more of the island but don't want to drive, you may want to consider a shore excursion, though almost all trips can be booked more cheaply with local tour operators.

EXPLORING SAN JUAN

Old San Juan, the original city founded in 1521, contains carefully preserved examples of 16th- and 17th-century Spanish-colonial architecture. More than 400 buildings have been beautifully restored. Graceful wrought-iron balconies with lush hanging plants extend over narrow streets paved with *adoquines* (blue-gray stones originally used as ballast on Spanish ships). The Old City is partially enclosed by walls that date from 1633 and once completely surrounded it. Designated a U.S. National Historic Zone in 1950, Old San Juan is chockablock with shops, open-air cafés, homes, tree-shaded squares, monuments, and people. You can get an overview on a morning's stroll (bear in mind that this "stroll" includes some steep climbs). However, if you plan to immerse yourself in history or to shop, you'll need a couple of days.

> ### SAN JUAN BEST BETS
>
> ■ **El Morro.** Explore the giant labyrinthine fort.
>
> ■ **El Yunque National Forest.** This rain forest east of San Juan is a great half-day excursion.
>
> ■ **Casa Bacardí.** Rum lovers can jump on the public ferry and then taxi over to the factory.
>
> ■ **Old San Juan.** Walk the cobblestone streets of Old San Juan.
>
> ■ **Shopping.** Within a few blocks of the port there are plenty of factory outlets and boutiques.

4

OLD SAN JUAN

Alcaldía. San Juan's city hall was built between 1604 and 1789. In 1841 extensive alterations were made so that it would resemble the city hall in Madrid, with arcades, towers, balconies, and an inner courtyard. Renovations have refreshed the facade of the building and some interior rooms, but the architecture remains true to its colonial style. Only the patios are open to public viewings. A municipal tourist information center and an art gallery with rotating exhibits are in the lobby. ⊠ *153 Calle San Francisco, Plaza de Armas, Old San Juan* ☎ *787/724–7171* ☜ *Free* ☉ *Weekdays 8–4.*

Casa Blanca. The original structure on this site was a wooden house built in 1521 as a home for Ponce de León; he died in Cuba without ever having lived here. His descendants occupied the house's sturdier replacement, a lovely colonial mansion with tile floors and beamed ceilings, for the next 250 years. It was the home of the U.S. Army commander in Puerto Rico from the end of the Spanish-American War in 1898 to 1966. Several rooms decorated with colonial-era furnishings are open to the public. A guide will show you around, and then you can explore on your own. Don't miss the stairway descending from one of the bedrooms—which, despite local lore, leads to a small room and not to a tunnel to nearby El Morro. The lush garden, complete with watchtower, is a quiet place to unwind. As of this writing, Casa Blanca was closed for a lengthy restoration to last well into 2010. ⊠ *1 Calle San Sebastián, Old San Juan* ☎ *787/725–1454* ⊕ *www.icp.gobierno.pr* ☜ *$3* ☉ *Wed.–Sun. 9–noon and 1–4.*

☾ **Castillo San Cristóbal.** This huge stone fortress, built between 1634 and 1785, guarded the city from land attacks from the east. Even larger than El Morro, San Cristóbal was known in the 17th and 18th centuries as the Gibraltar of the West Indies. Five freestanding structures divided by dry moats are connected by tunnels. You're free to explore the gun turrets (with cannon in situ), officers' quarters, re-created 18th-century barracks, and gloomy passageways. Along with El Morro, San Cristóbal is a National Historic Site administered by the U.S. Park Service; it's a World Heritage Site as well. Rangers conduct tours in Spanish and English. ⊠ *Calle Norzagaray at Calle Muñoz Rivera, Old San Juan* ☎ *787/729–6777* ⊕ *www.nps.gov/saju* ☜ *$3, $5 includes admission to El Morro* ☉ *Daily 9–6.*

☾ **Castillo San Felipe del Morro** *(El Morro).* On a rocky promontory at the
Fodor's Choice northwestern tip of the Old City is El Morro ("the promontory"), a
★ massive, six-level fortress built by the Spaniards between 1540 and 1783. Rising 140 feet above the sea, it is a labyrinth of cannon batteries, ramps, barracks, turrets, towers, and tunnels. Built to protect the port, El Morro has a commanding view of the harbor. The fort's small but enlightening museum displays ancient Spanish guns and other armaments, military uniforms, and blueprints for Spanish forts in the Americas, although Castillo San Cristóbal has more extensive and impressive exhibits. ⊠ *Calle del Morro, Old San Juan* ☎ *787/729–6960* ⊕ *www. nps.gov/saju* ☜ *$3, $5 includes admission to Castillo San Cristóbal* ☉ *Daily 9–6.*

Catedral de San Juan Bautista. The Catholic shrine of Puerto Rico had humble beginnings in the early 1520s as a thatch-roof, wooden structure. After a hurricane destroyed the church, it was rebuilt in 1540, when it was given a graceful circular staircase and vaulted Gothic ceilings. Most of the work on the present cathedral, however, was done in the 19th century. The remains of Ponce de León are behind a marble tomb in the wall near the transept, on the north side. The trompe-l'oeil work on the inside of the dome is breathtaking. Unfortunately, many of the other frescoes suffer from water damage. ⊠ *151 Calle Cristo, Old San Juan* ☎ *787/722–0861* ⊕ *www.catedralsanjuan.com* ⊠ *$1 donation suggested* ☉ *Mon.–Sat. 8–5, Sun. 8–4:30.*

❼ La Fortaleza. Sitting atop the fortified city walls overlooking the harbor, ★ the Fortaleza was built in 1533 as a fortress—and not a very good one. It was attacked numerous times and was occupied twice, by the British in 1598 and the Dutch in 1625. When El Morro and the city's other fortifications were finished, the Fortaleza was transformed into the governor's palace. It is still the official residence of the island's governor and is the Western Hemisphere's oldest executive mansion in continual use. Guided tours are conducted several times a day in English and Spanish; both include a short video presentation. Call ahead, as tours are often canceled because of official functions. ⊠ *Western end of Calle Fortaleza, Old San Juan* ☎ *787/721–7000* ⊕ *www.fortaleza.gobierno. pr* ⊠ *Free* ☉ *Weekdays 8–4.*

Museo de las Américas. On the second floor of the imposing former military barracks, Cuartel de Ballajá, the museum's permanent exhibit, Las Artes Populares en las Américas, focuses on the popular art and folk art of Latin America, including religious figures, musical instruments, basketwork, costumes, and farming and other implements. It's a small exhibit, worth a look if you're visiting other nearby attractions. ⊠ *Calle Norzagaray and Calle del Morro, Old San Juan* ☎ *787/724–5052* ⊕ *www.museolasamericas.org* ⊠ *$3* ☉ *Tues. and Wed. and weekends 10–4, Thurs. and Fri. 9–4.*

ELSEWHERE IN SAN JUAN

Casa Bacardí Visitor Center. Exiled from Cuba, the Bacardí family built a small rum distillery here in the 1950s. Today it's the world's largest, with the capacity to produce 100,000 gallons of spirits a day and 21 million cases a year. You can hop on a little tram to take an approximately 45-minute tour of the visitor center, though you can no longer visit the distillery itself. Yes, you'll be offered a sample. If you don't want to drive, you can reach the factory by taking the ferry from Pier 2 for 50¢ each way and then a *público* (public van service) from the ferry pier to the factory for about $2 or $3 per person. ⊠ *Road 165, Rte. 888, Km 2.6, Cataño* ☎ *787/788–1500 or 787/788–8400* ⊕ *www. casabacardi.org* ⊠ *Free* ☉ *Mon.–Sat. 9–6, last tour at 4:30; Sun. 10–5, last tour at 3:45.*

❷ Museo de Arte de Puerto Rico. One of the biggest museums in the Caribbean, this 130,000-square-foot building was once known as San Juan ☺ Municipal Hospital. The beautiful neoclassical building, dating from the **Fodor's Choice** 1920s, has been supplemented by a modern east wing. The collection ★

starts with works from the colonial era. There's much more to the museum, including a beautiful garden filled with a variety of native flora and a 400-seat theater that's worth seeing for its remarkable hand-crocheted lace curtain. ⊠ *299 Av. José De Diego, Santurce* ☎ *787/977–6277* ⊕ *www.mapr.org* ⊠ *$6* ⊙ *Tues.–Sat. 10–4, Sun. noon–4.*

SHOPPING

San Juan is not a duty-free port, so you won't find bargains on electronics and perfumes. However, shopping for native crafts can be fun. Popular souvenirs and gifts include *santos* (small, hand-carved figures of saints or religious scenes), hand-rolled cigars, local coffee, handmade lace, and carnival masks.

In Old San Juan—especially on Calles Fortaleza and Cristo—you can find everything from T-shirt emporiums to selective crafts stores, bookshops, art galleries, jewelry boutiques, and even shops that specialize in made-to-order Panama hats. Calle Cristo is lined with factory-outlet stores, including Coach and Ralph Lauren.

ACTIVITIES

GOLF

★ The spectacular **Río Mar Country Club** (⊠ *Rio Mar Beach Resort & Spa, a Wyndham Grand Resort, 6000 Río Mar Blvd., Río Grande* ☎ *787/888–7060* ⊕ *www.wyndhamriomar.com*) has a clubhouse with a pro shop, two restaurants between two 18-hole courses, and a recently added fire pit that doubles as a place to grab a quick beverage and bite. The River Course, designed by Greg Norman, has challenging fairways that skirt the Mameyes River. The Ocean Course, designed by Tom and George Fazio, has slightly wider fairways than its sister; iguanas can usually be spotted sunning themselves near its fourth hole. If you're not a resort guest, be sure to reserve tee times at least 24 hours in advance. Greens fees for hotel guests range from $70 to $199, depending on tee time. Fees for walk-ins start at $150.

BEACHES

San Juan does not have the island's best beaches, but anyone can rent a chair for the day at one of the public entry points.

Balneario de Carolina. When people talk of a "beautiful Isla Verde beach," this is the one they're talking about. A government-maintained beach, this *balneario* east of Isla Verde is so close to the airport that the leaves rustle when planes take off. There's plenty of room to spread out and lots of amenities: lifeguards, restrooms, changing facilities, picnic tables, and barbecue grills. ⊠ *Carolina* ⊠ *Parking $3* ⊙ *Daily 8–5.*

Playa del Condado. East of Old San Juan and west of Ocean Park, this long, wide beach is overshadowed by an unbroken string of hotels and apartment buildings. Beach bars, water-sports outfitters, and chair-rental places abound. You can access the beach from several roads off Avenida Ashford, including Calle Cervantes and Calle Candina. The protected water at the small stretch of beach west of the Conrad San Juan Condado Plaza hotel is particularly calm and popular with families; surf elsewhere in Condado can be a bit strong. The stretch of sand near Calle Vendig (behind the Atlantic Beach Hotel) is especially popular with the gay community. ⊠ *Condado* ☉ *Daily dawn–dusk.*

NIGHTLIFE

Almost every ship stays in San Juan late or even overnight to give passengers an opportunity to revel in the nightlife—the most sophisticated in the Caribbean.

CASINOS

By law, all casinos are in hotels. The atmosphere is refined, and many patrons dress to the nines, but informal attire (no shorts or tank tops) is usually fine. Casinos set their own hours, which change seasonally, but generally operate from noon to 4 AM, although the casino in the Conrad Condado Plaza Hotel and Casino is open 24 hours. Other hotels with casinos include the InterContinental San Juan Resort and Casino, the Ritz-Carlton San Juan Hotel, Spa and Casino, and the Sheraton Old San Juan Hotel and Casino.

BARS AND DANCE CLUBS

Atlantic Beach. The oceanfront-deck bar of this hotel is famed in the gay community for its early-evening happy hours. But the pulsating tropical music, the wide selection of exotic drinks, and the ever-pleasant ocean breeze make it a hit regardless of sexual orientation. Good food is also served on deck. ⊠ *1 Calle Vendig, Condado* ☎ *787/721–6100.*

Blend. This hip SoFo nightspot draws fashionistas enamored of the black walls, neon-blue lighting, and eye-candy female waitstaff. You can settle in at the marble-top bar, nestle cozily in a banquet sofa, or dance to salsa, techno, and world beat music in the dance hall to the rear. It serves late-night nouvelle native cuisine. ⊠ *309 Calle Fortaleza, Old San Juan* ☎ *787/977–7777.*

The wildly popular **El Batey** (⊠ *101 Calle Cristo, Old San Juan, San Juan* ☎ *787/725–1787*) won't win any prizes for its decor. Grab a marker to add your own message to the graffiti-covered walls, or add your business card to the hundreds that cover the lighting fixtures. The jukebox, packed with vintage 45s, has one of the best music selections on the island.

Wet. On the roof of the San Juan Water & Beach Club Hotel, this sexy spot offers some of the best ocean views anywhere in Isla Verde. On weekends there's a DJ, and locals pack in to relax at the bar or on the leather beds reserved for bottle service. ⊠ *San Juan Water & Beach Club, 2 Calle Tartak, Isla Verde* ☎ *787/725–4664.*

WHERE TO EAT

$$–$$$ ✕ **El Picoteo.** You could make a meal of the small dishes that dominate
SPANISH   the menu at this tapas restaurant, on a mezzanine balcony at the Hotel El Convento. You won't go wrong ordering the sweet sausage in brandy or the turnovers stuffed with lobster and passing them around the table.

If you're not into sharing, there are five different kinds of paella that arrive on huge plates. There's a long, lively bar inside; one dining area overlooks a pleasant courtyard, whereas the other looks out onto Calle Cristo. Even if you have dinner plans elsewhere, consider stopping here for a nightcap or a midday pick-me-up. ✉ *Hotel El Convento, 100 Calle Cristo, Old San Juan* ☎ *787/723–9202* ⊕ *www.elconvento.com* ▭ *AE, DC, MC, V.*

$–$$

CARIBBEAN

Fodor'sChoice

★

✕ **La Fonda del Jíbarito.** The menus are handwritten and the tables wobble, but *sanjuaneros* have favored this casual, no-frills, family-run restaurant—tucked away on a quiet cobbled street—for years. The conch ceviche, goat fricassee, and shredded beef stew are among the specialties on the menu of typical Puerto Rican comida criollo dishes. The tiny back porch is filled with plants, and the dining room is filled with fanciful depictions of life on the street outside. The ever-present owner, Pedro J. Ruíz, is filled with the desire to ensure that everyone is happy. Troubadors serenade patrons, among them plenty of cruise-ship passengers when ships are in port. ✉ *280 Calle Sol, Old San Juan* ☎ *787/725–8375* ⊕ *www.eljibaritopr.com* ⟁ *Reservations not accepted* ▭ *AE, MC, V.*

SANTO DOMINGO, DOMINICAN REPUBLIC

Eileen Robin-
son Smith

Spanish civilization in the New World began in Santo Domingo's 12-block Zona Colonial (Colonial Zone). As you stroll its narrow streets, it's easy to imagine this old city as it was when the likes of Columbus, Cortés, and Ponce de León walked the cobblestones, when pirates sailed in and out of the harbor, and when colonists first started building the New World's largest city. Tourist brochures tout that "history comes alive here"—a surprisingly truthful statement. However, many tourists bypass the large, sprawling, and noisy city; it's their loss. The Dominican Republic's seaside capital—despite such detractions as poverty and sprawl, not to mention a population of some 2 million people—has some of the country's best hotels, restaurants, and nightlife (not to mention great casinos). Many of these are right on or near the Malecón and within the historic Zona Colonial area, which is separated from the rest of the city by Parque Independencia. If your ship calls or even embarks here, you'll be treated to a vibrant Latin cultural center unlike any other in the Caribbean.

ESSENTIALS

CURRENCY   The Dominican peso (RD$36.2 to US$1). Independent merchants willingly accept U.S. dollars, but you may need to change some money. Cambios (money exchange offices) are abundant, but you'll get the best rates at either a bank or a casino. Banco Popular has ATMS in the Zona Colonial, but you will be able to get only pesos.

INTERNET   Look up, and you will see many Internet shops on the Conde, usually with second-floor locations. Also, in the Colonial Zone, a convenient place to check your e-mail is **Verizon Comunicaciones** (✉ *256 Calle Conde, Zona Colonial* ☎ *809/221–4249*), where you can also make phone calls. You will have to pay cash—pesos or dollars.

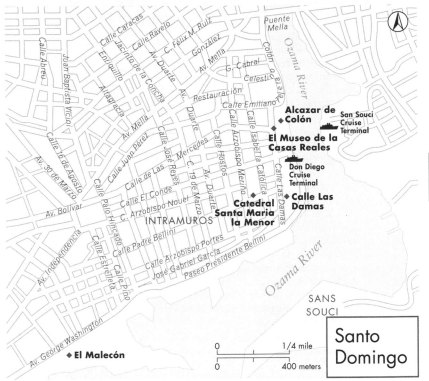

Santo Domingo

♦ El Malecón   0 — 1/4 mile
                0 — 400 meters

TELEPHONE   From the D.R. you need only dial 1 plus the area code and number to call the U.S. To make a local call, you must now dial 809 plus the seven-digit number. Phone cards, which are sold at gift shops and grocery stores, can give you considerable savings on your calls home. If you have a tri-band GSM phone, it should work on the island.

COMING ASHORE

Santo Domingo has two cruise-ship terminals. The Port of Don Diego is on the Ozuma River, facing the Avenida del Puerto, and across the street are steps that lead up to the main pedestrian shopping street of the Zona Colonial, Calle Conde. Don Diego has a lovely yellow-and-white building, with stained-glass windows and faux gas lights. It now has a small cafeteria, and potted palms soften the cordoned-off lines of passengers waiting to have their tickets checked and go through immigration. Just down the dock is an ATM machine; in front of that is a counter where you can get cold drinks and snacks. Across from it is a booth offering new self-guided audio tours. Should you want to go to the Malecón or shop in the modern city, $20 an hour is the going taxi rate. Don't rent a car; it's expensive, and traffic and parking are stressful.

The newer Sans Souci Terminal is still a work in progress, and some shops and other infrastructure are not yet finished. It is diagonally across the river from Don Diego, on Avenida Francisco Alberto Caaman. If you dock there, you will need transportation to get to the Colonial Zone.

Just a few paces in front of the Don Diego cruise terminal is the office of **Audio Guide Dominicana** (⊕ *www.jccolonialservice.com*). Tours come in three languages, and include information on more than 29 historic sites in the Colonial City and seven museums, plus a map and informative booklet. All museum entrances are included, as well as a nonalcoholic beverage at Hard Rock Café. The total cost is US$29, and credit cards are accepted. The company will also store luggage and provide airport transfers.

> ## SANTO DOMINGO BEST BETS
>
> ■ **Zona Colonial.** Santo Domingo's Colonial Zone is a World Heritage Site and a great place to stroll. It is a trip to the Old World; it is Spain in the 16th century.
>
> ■ **Dining.** Some of the D.R.'s best restaurants can be found in the capital. Take advantage of them if you have any extra time to spend here.
>
> ■ **Shopping.** The country's best shopping can be found in Santo Domingo. You can go souvenir shopping right on Calle Conde, a pedestrian street that is the main drag of the Zona Colonial.

AIRPORT TRANSFERS

If you are embarking in Santo Domingo, you should fly into **Las Américas International Airport** (*SDQ* ⊠ *Santo Domingo* ☎ *809/549–0450*), about 15 mi (24 km) east of downtown. Upon arrival you will have to pay $10 for a tourist tax. Transportation into the city is usually by taxi; figure on $40 to or from hotels on the Malecón or in the Zona Colonial. You'll be greeted by a melee of hawking taxi drivers and sometimes their English-speaking solicitors (who expect to be tipped, as do the freelance porters who will undoubtedly scoop up your luggage). If you are spending a night or two in Santo Domingo before a cruise, you can probably arrange a driver through your hotel, so you'll be met with someone holding a sign with your name (it's worth the extra $10 or so to avoid the hassle). If you're going straight to your cruise ship, consider taking the cruise line's prearranged transfer. When you disembark from your ship, expect long lines at check-in, and be sure to give yourself a full two hours for check-in and security. The government departure tax should be included in your airline ticket.

EXPLORING SANTO DOMINGO

History buffs will want to spend a day exploring the many "firsts" of our continent. A horse-and-carriage ride throughout the Colonial Zone costs $25 an hour. The steeds are no thoroughbreds, but they clip right along, though any commentary will be in Spanish. You can also negotiate to use them as a taxi, say down to the Malecón. The drivers hang out in front of the Hostal Nicolas de Ovando hotel.

Alcazar de Colón. The castle of Don Diego Colón, built in 1517, has 40-inch-thick coral-limestone walls. The Renaissance-style structure, with its balustrade and double row of arches, has strong Moorish, Gothic, and Isabelline influences. The 22 rooms are furnished in a style to which the viceroy of the island would have been accustomed—right down to the dishes and the viceregal shaving mug. Multi-lingual audio guides can be rented for RD$50. Do it. Costumed docents appear on Saturday morning, and on Saturday night history comes alive. The Colón family walks again throughout the castle, as actors in period costume play the roles of Diego and his family. ⌧ *Plaza de España off Calle Emiliano Tejera at foot of Calle Las Damas, Zona Colonial* ☎ *809/682–4750* ⌧ *RD$60* ⊗ *Mon.–Sat. 9–5 and 8 PM–midnight, Sun. 9–4. Closed if no cruise ship in port.*

★ **Calle Las Damas.** The Ladies Street was named after the elegant ladies of the court who, in the Spanish tradition, promenaded in the evening. Here you can see a sundial dating from 1753 and the Casa de los Jesuitas, which houses a fine research library for colonial history as well as the **Institute for Hispanic Culture**; admission is free, and it's open weekdays from 8 to 4:30. If you follow the street going toward the Malecón, you will pass a picturesque alley fronted by a wrought-iron gate that has perfectly maintained colonial structures owned by the Catholic Church.

Catedral Santa María la Menor. The coral-limestone facade of the first cathedral in the New World towers over the south side of the Parque Colón. Spanish workmen began building the cathedral in 1514, but left to search for gold in Mexico. The church was finally finished in 1540. Its facade is composed of architectural elements from the late Gothic to the lavish plateresque style. Inside, the high altar is made of hammered silver. At this writing, a museum is being built for the cathedral's treasures. ⌧ *Calle Arzobispo Meriño, Zona Colonial* ☎ *809/689–1920* ⌧ *Free* ⊗ *Mon.–Sat. 9–4; Sun. Masses begin at 6 AM.*

El Malecón. Avenida George Washington, better known as the Malecón, runs along the Caribbean and has tall palms, cafés, high-rise hotels, and sea breezes.

★ **El Museo de las Casas Reales.** This is a remarkable museum that helps you understand the New World that was discovered by Columbus and the ensuing history of exploration and colonization in the 16th century. Built in the Renaissance style, it was the seat of Spanish government and housed the governor's office as well as the Royal Court. ⌧ *Calle Las Damas, right before Plaza de Espana, Zona Colonial* ☎ *809/682–4202* ⌧ *RD$50* ⊗ *Tues.–Sun. 9–5.*

SHOPPING

Exquisitely hand-wrapped cigars continue to be the hottest commodity coming out of the D.R. Only reputable cigar shops sell the real thing. Dominican rum and coffee are also good buys. *Mamajuana*, an herbal liqueur, is said to be the Dominican answer to Viagra. Look also for the delicate, faceless ceramic figurines that symbolize Dominican culture. Though locally crafted products are often very affordable, expect to pay for designer jewelry made of amber and larimar, an indigenous semiprecious stone the color of the Caribbean. Amber, a fossilization of resin from a prehistoric pine tree, often encasing ancient animal and plant life, from leaves to spiders to tiny lizards, is mined extensively. (Beware of fakes, which are especially prevalent in street stalls.)

One of the main shopping streets in the Zone is **Calle El Conde,** a pedestrian thoroughfare. With the advent of so many restorations, the dull and dusty stores with dated merchandise are giving way to some hip, new shops. However, many of the offerings, including local designer shops, are still of a caliber and cost that the Dominicans can afford. Some of the best shops are on **Calle Duarte,** north of the Colonial Zone, between Calle Mella and Avenida de Las Américas. **El Mercado Modelo,** a covered market, borders Calle Mella in the Colonial Zone; vendors here sell a dizzying selection of Dominican crafts. The **Malecón Center,** the latest complex, adjacent to the classy Hilton Santo Domingo, will eventually house 170 shops, boutiques, and services plus several movie theaters. In the tower above are luxury apartments and Sammy Sosa, in one of the penthouses. **Plaza Central** (✉ *Avs. Winston Churchill and 27 de Febrero, Piantini* ☎ *809/541–5929*) is a major shopping center with high-end shops, including a Jenny Polanco shop (an upscale Dominican designer who has incredible white linen outfits, artistic jewelry, purses, and more).

NIGHTLIFE

Santo Domingo's nightlife is vast and ever changing. Check with the concierges and hip capitaleños. Get a copy of the free newspapers *Touring, Flow,* and *Aqui o Guía de Bares Restaurantes*—available at the tourist office and at hotels—to find out what's happening. At this writing, there is still a curfew for clubs and bars; they must close at midnight during the week, and 2 AM on Friday and Saturday nights. There are some exceptions to the latter, primarily those clubs and casinos located in hotels. Sadly, the curfew has put some clubs out of business, but it has cut down on crime and late-night noise, particularly in the Zone.

WHERE TO EAT

$–$$$ ✕ **Café Bellini.** This café has always had a panache far and above its
ITALIAN   counterparts, for the Italian owners also have the adjacent furniture
★   design center. The modern, wicker-weave barrel chairs and the contemporary art and light fixtures are all achingly hip. It has recently had a renovation and looks refreshed. The menu is the same at lunch and dinner. The democratic pricing usually offers pasta dishes, such as the trio of raviolis (spinach, beet, and pumpkin), for about $10, which works for those on a slim budget. Also, know that an amuse-bouche, perhaps a tomato bruschetta, can usually suffice as an appetizer. The addition of grilled portobellos to a classic arugula-and-shaved-Parmesan salad is brilliant. Main courses of meat or seafood are accompanied by pasta or grilled vegetables and potato. You can enjoy French and Italian liquors here (like pastis and grappa); dessert might be dark-chocolate mousse and fresh mango sorbet. Service is laudable, as is the

music. ⊠ *Arzobispo Merino, corner of Padre Bellini, Zona Colonial* ☏ *809/686–3387* ⊜ *Reservations essential* ▭ *AE, MC, V* ☉ *Closed Sun. No lunch Mon.*

$–$$$ ✕ **La Residence.** This fine-dining enclave has always had the setting—
FRENCH Spanish colonial architecture, with pillars and archways overlooking a
★ courtyard—and an esoteric lunch-dinner menu with high prices that did not always deliver. Now it has a French Certified Master Chef, Denis Schetrit (there are only 300 such designated chefs in the world), who is serving classic yet innovative cuisine. He bows to more recent culinary trends while cleverly using local produce and offering many moderately priced choices. The three-course, daily Menu del Chef is less than $28 and includes tax. It could be brochettes of spit-roasted duck, chicken au poivre, or vegetable risotto. You could start with a salad of pan-fried young squid and segue to a luscious French pastry. Veer from the daily specials menu and prices can certainly go higher, but they are still fair; even the grilled fillet and braised oxtail with foie-gras sauce and wild mushrooms is reasonable. Anything that Chef Denis prepares is heaven on a plate. Diners are often serenaded by musicians; sometimes the service is not right on. ⊠ *Hostal Nicolas de Ovando, Calle Las Damas, Zona Colonial* ☏ *809/685–9955* ▭ *AE, MC, V.*

WHERE TO STAY

Since Santo Domingo is a port of embarkation for some ships, we list these hotel recommendations for those who want or need to stay overnight.

$ ⌂ **Coco Boutique Hotel.** Behind the soft, Caribbean turquoise facade,
BED AND you'll find a most un-typical B&B, with earth tones and white almost
BREAKFAST everywhere—the reception and lounge, the stark wooden staircase, the
★ grillwork on the French doors. **Pros:** amazingly quiet for the Zona Colonial; opposite the Plaza Pellerano Castro; rooftop terrace with Balinese sun beds. **Cons:** not steeped in creature comforts, bathrooms are small, as is one upstairs room. ⊠ *Arzobispo Porte 7, corner of Las Damas, Zona Colonial, Santo Domingo* ☏ *809/685–8467* ⊕ *www. cocoboutique-hotel.com* ⌁ *5 rooms* ⌂ *In-room: no phone, no TV. In-hotel: bar, laundry service, Wi-Fi, parking (free), no-smoking rooms* ▭ *AE, MC, V* ⓧ *BP.*

₵ ₵₵ ⌂ **Hilton Santo Domingo.** This has become *the* address on the Malecón
HOTEL for businesspeople, convention attendees, and leisure travelers. **Pros:**
★ Sunday brunch is one of the city's top tickets; great music in the lobby lounge; best service in Santo Domingo. **Cons:** little about the property is authentically Dominican; hotel can feel large and impersonal. ⊠ *Av. George Washington 500, Gazcue* ☏ *809/685–0000* ⊕ *hiltoncaribbean. com/santodomingo* ⌁ *228 rooms, 32 suites* ⌂ *In-room: safe, refrigerator, Internet. In-hotel: 2 restaurants, bars, pool, gym, spa, Internet terminal, Wi-Fi* ▭ *AE, D, MC, V* ⓧ *EP.*

$$$–$$$$ ⌂ **Hostal Nicolas de Ovando.** This luxury hotel, sculpted from the resi-
HOTEL dence of the first governor of the Americas, is the best thing to happen in
Fodor's Choice the Zone since Diego Columbus's palace was finished in 1517. **Pros:** lav-
★ ish breakfast buffet; beautifully restored historic section. **Cons:** pricey.

✉ *Calle Las Damas, Zona Colonial* ☎ *809/685–9955 or 800/763–4835*
🌐 *www.sofitel.com* ⇆ *100 rooms, 4 suites* ♿ *In-room: safe, refrigerator. In-hotel: restaurant, room service, bars, pool, gym, laundry service, Internet terminal, Wi-Fi, parking (free), some pets allowed* 🞕 *AE, MC, V* ¶🞘¶ *BP.*

SANTO TOMÁS DE CASTILLA, GUATEMALA

Jeffrey Van Fleet

Guatemala's short Caribbean shoreline doesn't generate the buzz of those of neighboring Belize and Mexico. The coast weighs in at a scant 74 mi (123 km), and this mostly highland country, which wears its indigenous culture on its sleeve and has historically looked inland rather than to the sea. You'll be drawn inland, too, with a variety of shore excursions. This is the land of the Maya, after all. But there's plenty to keep you occupied here in the lowlands. Tourist brochures tout the Caribbean coast as "The Other Guatemala." The predominantly indigenous and Spanish cultures of the highlands give way to an Afro-Caribbean tradition that listens more closely to the rhythms of far-off Jamaica rather than taking its cue from Guatemala City. Think of it as mixing a little reggae with your salsa.

ESSENTIALS

CURRENCY The Guatemalan quetzal, named for the brightly plumed bird that is the symbol of the country (Q8 to US$1). Take care of any banking matters in the cruise terminal in Santo Tomás de Castilla. You'll find ATMs in Puerto Barrios and Livingston but nowhere else in this region.

INTERNET The Terminal de Cruceros in Santo Tomás de Castilla has Internet computers for your use, the easiest option if you're a day visitor.

TELEPHONE Guatemalan phone numbers have eight digits. There are no city or area codes. Simply dial the number for any in-country call. Most towns have offices of Telgua, the national telephone company, where you can place both national and international calls. Avoid the ubiquitous public phones with signs promising FREE CALLS TO THE USA. The number back home being called gets socked with a hefty bill.

COMING ASHORE

Cruise ships dock at the modern, spacious Terminal de Cruceros, where you'll find a bank, post office, money exchange, telephones, Internet access, a lively craft market, and an office of INGUAT, Guatemala's national tourist office. A marimba band serenades you with its clinking xylophone-like music; a Caribbean ensemble dances for you (and may even pull you in to take part).

Taxis, both vehicular and water, take you to various destinations in the area. Plan on paying $2 to Santo Tomás de Castilla proper, and $5 to Puerto Barrios. Boats transport cruise visitors to Livingston, charging about $6 for the 20-minute trip. The Amatique Bay Resort provides water taxis from port to resort of $9 per person. Vehicular taxis charge $20 per head to travel by land to the resort.

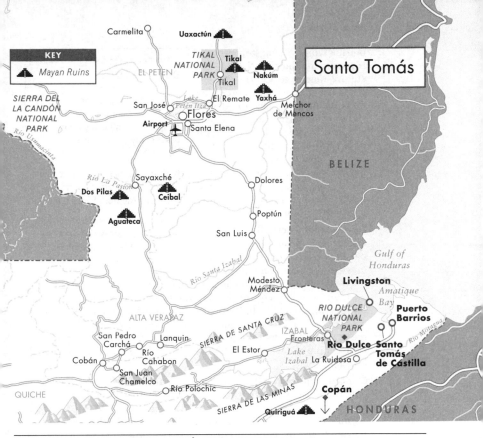

EXPLORING SANTO TOMÁS DE CASTILLA

Amatique Bay. "Bahía de Amatique" denotes the large bay that washes the Caribbean coast of Guatemala and southern Belize, but for most travelers the name is inexorably linked with the **Amatique Bay Resort and Marina**, part of the Clarion chain, and the region's only five-star hotel. The 61-room resort opens itself up for day visitors, and many cruise passengers stop by for a drink, a meal, or an entire day of swimming, watersliding, kayaking, horseback riding, or bicycling. ⊠ *6 mi (10 km) north of Santo Tomás* ☎ *7948–1800, 2421–3333 in Guatemala City* ⊕ *www.amatiquebay.com.*

Copán. The famous Mayan ruins of Copán lie just across the border from this region in neighboring Honduras, but are accessible enough from Santo Tomás to be an excursion on many itineraries. Bring your passport, since this entails an international border crossing. ⊠ *½ mi (1 km) east of Copán Ruinas, Honduras; 122 mi (203 km) southeast of Santo Tomás* ☎ *No phone* ☑ *$15* ☉ *Daily 8–4.*

Livingston. Visitors compare Livingston with Puerto Barrios across the bay, and the former wins hands down, for its sultry, seductive Caribbean flavor. Wood houses, some on stilts, congregate in this old fishing town, once an important railroad hub, but today inaccessible by land from the outside world. Livingston proudly trumpets its Garífuna heritage, a culture unique to Central America's eastern coast and descended from the intermarriage of African slaves with Caribbean indigenous peoples. Music and dance traditions and a Caribbean-accented English remain, even if old-timers lament the creeping outside influences, namely Spanish, rap, and reggae. ⊠ *15 mi (25 km) by water northwest of Santo Tomás.*

Puerto Barrios. Puerto Barrios maintains the atmosphere of an old banana town, humid and a tad down at the heels, perhaps longing

> ### SANTO TOMÁS BEST BETS
>
> ■ **Quiriguá.** If you want to see Mayan ruins but don't want to spend an entire day on the bus, nearby Quiriguá can be impressive.
>
> ■ **Copán.** In neighboring Honduras, this Mayan site is a worthwhile day trip from Santo Tomás.
>
> ■ **Riding on the Río Dulce.** The ride on this river is one of Guatemala's most beautiful boat trips.

for better days. Santo Tomás has replaced it as the country's largest port, and you'll likely zip through the Caribbean coast's biggest city on your way to somewhere else, but the cathedral and municipal market are worth a look if you find yourself here. Water taxis depart from the municipal docks for Livingston, across the bay, where you start your trip up the Río Dulce. ⊠ *3 mi (5 km) north of Santo Tomás de Castilla.*

Quiriguá. Construction began on the Guatemalan lowlands' most important Mayan ruins about AD 500. Its hieroglyphics tell its story: Quiriguá served at the time as a satellite state under the control of Copán, about 30 mi (50 km) away in present-day Honduras. By the height of its power in the 7th century, Quiriguá had overpowered Copán, but just as quickly fell back into submissive status. Quiriguá's ruins still today live in the shadow of their better-known neighbor across the border, and of the Tikal ruins in the northern part of Guatemala, but a visit here is rewarding for the carvings of *stelae,* the ornate sculptures depicting the city's rulers, and the largest such works in Central America. (Quiriguá's stelae stand 33 feet [10 meters] tall, dwarfing those of Copán.) Ease of access from the Caribbean coast makes Quiriguá well worth a visit, too. ⊠ *54 mi (90 km) southwest of Santo Tomás* ▱ Q60 ⊙ *Daily 7:30–4.*

Río Dulce. The natural crown jewel of this region is the 13,000-hectare (32,000-acre) national park that protects the river leading inland from Livingston to Lago de Izabal, Guatemala's largest lake. Pelicans, herons, egrets, and terns nest and fly along the Río Dulce, which cuts through a heavily forested limestone canyon. Excursions often approach the park by land, but we recommend making the trip upriver from Livingston to immerse yourself in the entire Indiana Jones experience. ⊠ *Southwest of Livingston.*

Once an important Mayan trade route, the Río Dulce later became the route over which the conquistadors sent the gold and silver they plundered back to Spain. All this wealth attracted Dutch and English pirates, who attacked both the ships and the warehouses on shore.

In hopes of curtailing these buccaneers, colonists built a series of fortresses on the river's northern banks. In 1955 the Guatemalan government reconstructed the ruined fortress of **Castillo de San Felipe de Lara** (⊠ *Southwest of Fronteras* 🕾 *No phone* ⌑ *Q25*). Spanish colonists constructed the fortress in 1595 to guard the inland waterway from pirate incursions. It was used as a prison between 1655 and 1660. You can reach it by the road leading west from Río Dulce or by a short boat ride. A 1999 earthquake in this region destroyed the river pier as well as damaging portions of the fort. If you wish to visit, rather than simply see the structure from the water, you'll need to approach the park overland rather than upriver.

A short launch from Fronteras takes you to **Hacienda Tijax** (⊠ *Northeast of Fronteras* 🕾 *7930–5505*), an old rubber plantation, now a reforestation project, which offers hiking and kayaking and a chance to view the cultivation of orchids and spices.

Santo Tomás de Castilla. Belgian immigrants settled Santo Tomás in the 19th century, but little remains of their heritage today, save for the preponderance of French and Flemish names in the local cemetery. Most visitors move on. Santo Tomás has experienced a small renaissance as the country's most important port, receiving growing numbers of cruise and cargo ships, and serving as the headquarters of the Guatemalan navy.

FodorśChoice
★
Tikal. The high point of any trip to Guatemala is a visit to Central America's most impressive ruins. There's nothing quite like the sight of the towering temples, ringed on all sides by miles of virgin forest, but you need a lot of quetzales to get here, since you'll travel by plane from the airstrip outside Santo Tomás to the small airport in Santa Elena, near the ruins. Although this region was home to Mayan communities as early as 600 BC, Tikal wasn't established until around 200 BC. By AD 500 it's estimated that the city covered more than 18 square mi (47 square km) and had a population of close to 100,000. For almost 1,000 years Tikal remained engulfed by the jungle. Excavation began in earnest in the mid-1800s. Today, after more than 150 years of digging, researchers say that Tikal includes some 3,000 buildings. Countless more are still covered by the jungle. Temple IV, the tallest-known structure built by the Maya, offers an unforgettable view from the top. ⊠ *Parque Nacional Tikal* 🕾 *No phone* ⌑ *Q150* ☉ *Daily 6–6.*

SHOPPING

The rest of Guatemala overflows with indigenous crafts and art, but the famous market towns of the highlands are nowhere to be found in Caribbean region. Quite honestly, your best bet for shopping is the Terminal de Cruceros at Santo Tomás de Castilla, and you'll have plenty of opportunity to buy before you board your ship. What you'll find here comes from Guatemala's highlands—the Caribbean has never developed a strong artisan tradition—with a good selection of fabrics, weavings, woodwork, and basketry to choose from. Markets in Puerto Barrios and Livingston, the only real urban areas you'll encounter in this region, are more geared to the workaday needs of residents rather than visitors.

ACTIVITIES

BEACHES AND WATER SPORTS

A beach culture has just never developed in this region of Guatemala the way it has in neighboring Belize and Mexico. The only real beach in the region is found within the confines of the **Amatique Bay Resort and Marina** (⊠ *6 mi [10 km] north of Santo Tomás* ☎ *7948–1800, 2421–3333 in Guatemala City* ⊕ *www.amatiquebay.com*), which is the only place here that has a resort feel to it. Day visitors partake of swimming, water-slides, and kayaking. The resort's launch will bring you over from the cruise-ship terminal in Santo Tomás.

HIKING AND KAYAKING

Hacienda Tijax (⊠ *Northeast of Fronteras* ☎ *7930–5505* ⊕ *www. tijax. com*), which is pronounced tee-*hahsh*, is inland, near the point where the Río Dulce meets Lake Izabal, and provides kayaking and hiking for day visitors.

TOBAGO (SCARBOROUGH)

Vernon
O'Reilly
Ramesar

The smaller and quieter of the sister islands that make up Trinidad and Tobago offers pristine beaches and friendly people. Tobago has long been a favorite of European visitors, who enjoy the rustic feel of the island and the laid-back pace. There are numerous fine restaurants, though many are not located in Scarborough, where cruise ships dock. The culinary thrill here is exploring the local cuisine that can be found at food stalls across the island, and you could easily make eating the focus of your shore excursion and be all the happier for it. No trip here is complete without trying the quintessential Tobago dish, curry crab and dumplings. This can be a slow (and messy) experience, but it fits in perfectly with the pace of life on the island.

ESSENTIALS

CURRENCY The Trinidad and Tobago dollar (TT$6.30 to US$1). Most places catering to tourists will accept U.S. currency, but the exchange rate may vary wildly from place to place.

INTERNET Internet cafés spring up and disappear quickly. A quick look around the port area should reveal the latest incarnations.

TELEPHONE Pay phones are located in the cruise terminal. To make an international call from a pay phone, you must first purchase a prepaid "companion" card, which is readily available from most convenience shops at or near the port, then simply follow the instructions on the card. Cards are available in various denominations.

COMING ASHORE

Scarborough, Tobago's lazy and hilly capital, is where all cruise ships dock. The cruise terminal is at the base of the city, near the market, many colorful shops, and fast-food restaurants. There are shops selling

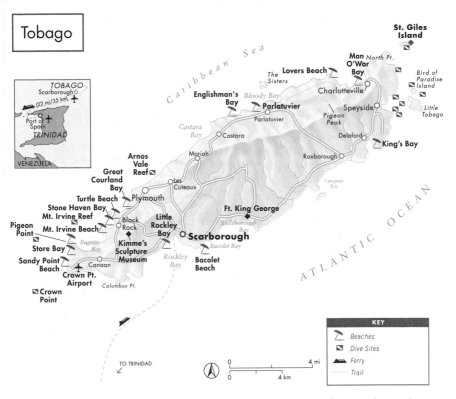

Tobago

KEY
↘ Beaches
◪ Dive Sites
⛴ Ferry
⋯ Trail

goods specifically marketed to tourists right at the port, but a short stroll around the streets of downtown can yield considerably more interesting treasures.

While you can easily walk into town, the island's best beaches and restaurants are in Crown Point. Because of the narrow roads and hilly terrain—not to mention aggressive drivers who like to drive very fast—it is not advisable to rent a car. But if you choose to drive yourself, remember that driving is on the left, British style. Taxis flock to the port whenever a cruise ship arrives. Authorized taxis always have a license plate starting with the letter "H" (for "hire"). Although rates are technically fixed, it is never a bad idea to negotiate with the driver.

EXPLORING TOBAGO

Ft. King George. On Mt. St. George, a short drive up the hill from Scarborough, Tobago's best-preserved historic monument clings to a cliff high above the ocean. Ft. King George was built in the 1770s and operated until 1854. It's hard to imagine that this lovely, tranquil spot commanding sweeping views of the bay and landscaped with lush tropical foliage was ever the site of any military action, but the prison, officers' mess, and several stabilized cannons attest otherwise. Just to the left of the tall wooden figures dancing a traditional Tobagonian jig is the former barrack guardhouse, now housing the small **Tobago Museum.** Exhibits include weapons and other pre-Columbian artifacts found in the area; the fertility figures are especially interesting. Upstairs are maps and photographs of Tobago's past. Be sure to check out the gift display cases for the perversely fascinating jewelry made from embalmed and painted lizards and sea creatures; you might find it hard to resist a pair of bright-yellow shrimp earrings. The **Fine Arts Centre** at the foot of the Ft. King George complex shows the work of local artists. ⊠ *84 Fort St., Scarborough* ☎ *868/639–3970* ⊠ *Fort free, museum TT$5* ☉ *Weekdays 9–5.*

TOBAGOS BEST BETS

■ **Bird-Watching.** For such a small island, the diversity of bird life is fascinating.

■ **Buccoo Reef.** The reef at the southwestern tip of the island is teeming with life.

■ **Beaches.** If you're craving an excellent Caribbean beach, this is one place where you can take your pick of beaches, each lovelier than the last.

■ **Golf.** The island has one excellent and one very good golf course.

★ **Kimme Sculpture Museum.** The diminutive and eccentric German-born sculptress Luise Kimme fell in love with the form of Tobagonians and has devoted her life to capturing them in her sculptures. Her pieces can exceed 12 feet in height and are often wonderfully whimsical. Much of her work is done in wood (none of it local), but there are many bronze pieces as well. The museum itself is a turreted structure with a commanding view of the countryside. Most locals refer to it as "The Castle." There are numerous signs in Mt. Irvine directing visitors to the museum. ⊠ *Mt. Irvine* ☎ *868/639–0257* ⊕ *www.luisekimme.com* ⊠ *TT$20* ☉ *Sun. 10–2 or by appointment.*

Scarborough. Around Rockley Bay on the island's leeward hilly side, this town is both the capital of Tobago and a popular cruise-ship port, but it conveys the feeling that not much has changed since the area was settled two centuries ago. It may not be one of the delightful pastel-color cities of the Caribbean, but Scarborough does have its charms, including several interesting little shops. Whatever you do, be sure to check out the busy Scarborough Market, an indoor and outdoor affair featuring everything from fresh vegetables to live chickens and clothing. Note the red-and-yellow Methodist church on the hill, one of Tobago's oldest churches.

SHOPPING

Determined shoppers should manage to find a few things to take home. Scarborough has the largest collection of shops on the island, and Burnett Street, which climbs sharply from the port to St. James Park, is a good place to browse.

ACTIVITIES

BIRD-WATCHING

★ Some 200 varieties of birds have been documented on Tobago: look for the yellow oriole, scarlet ibis, and the comical motmot—the male of the species clears sticks and stones from an area and then does a dance complete with snapping sounds to attract a mate. The flora is as vivid as the birds. Purple-and-yellow *poui* trees and spectacular orange immortelles splash color over the countryside, and something is blooming virtually every season. Pat Turpin and Renson Jack at **Pioneer Journeys** (☎ *868/660–4327 or 868/660–5175* ✉ *pturpin@tstt.net.tt*) can give you information about their bird-watching tours of Bloody Bay rain forest and Louis d'Or River valley wetlands. Naturalist and ornithologist David Rooks operates **Rooks Nature Tours** (✉ *462 Moses Hill, Lambeau* ☎ *868/756–8594* ⊕ *www.rookstobago.com*), offering bird-watching walks inland and trips to offshore bird colonies. He's generally considered the best guide on the island.

BOAT TOURS

Tobago offers many wonderful spots for snorkeling. Although the reefs around Speyside in the northeast are becoming better known, **Buccoo Reef**, off the island's southwest coast, is still the most popular—perhaps too popular. Over the years the reef has been badly damaged by the ceaseless boat traffic and by the thoughtless visiting divers who take pieces of coral as souvenirs. Still, it's worth experiencing, particularly if you have children. Daily 2½-hour tours by glass-bottom boats let you snorkel at the reef, swim in a lagoon, and gaze at Coral Gardens—where fish and coral are as yet untouched. Most dive companies in the Black Rock area also arrange snorkeling tours. There's also good snorkeling near the **Arnos Vale Hotel** and the **Mt. Irvine Bay Hotel.**

Hew's Glass Bottom Boat Tours (✉ *Pigeon Point* ☎ *868/639–9058*) are perfect excursions for those who neither snorkel nor dive. Boats leave daily at 11:30 AM.

GOLF

★ The 18-hole, PGA-designed championship par-72 course at **Tobago Plantations Golf & Country Club** (✉ *Lowlands* ☎ *868/631–0875*) is set amid rolling greens and mangroves. It offers some amazing views of the ocean as a bonus. Greens fees are $85 for one 18-hole round, $150 for two rounds (these rates include a golf cart and taxes). This is the newer of the two main courses on the island and is by far the most popular. The course is well maintained, and contains areas of mangrove and forest that are home to many bird species.

BEACHES

You won't find manicured country-club sand here. But those who enjoy feeling as though they've landed on a desert island will relish the untouched quality of these shores.

Bacolet Beach. This dark-sand beach was the setting for the films *Swiss Family Robinson* and *Heaven Knows, Mr. Allison*. Though used by the Blue Haven Hotel, like all local beaches it's open to the public. If you are not a guest at the hotel, access to the beach is down a track next door to the hotel. The bathroom and changing facilities on the beach are for hotel guests only. ⊠ *Windward Rd. east of Scarborough.*

Great Courland Bay. Near Ft. Bennett, the bay has clear, tranquil waters. Along the sandy beach—one of Tobago's longest—you can find several glitzy hotels. A marina attracts the yachting crowd. ⊠ *Leeward Rd. northeast of Black Rock, Courland.*

King's Bay. Surrounded by steep green hills, this is the most visually satisfying of the swimming sites off the road from Scarborough to Speyside—the bay hooks around so severely, you can feel like you're in a lake. The crescent beach is easy to find because it's marked by a sign about halfway between the two towns. Just before you reach the bay, there's a bridge with an unmarked turnoff that leads to a gravel parking lot; beyond that, a landscaped path leads to a waterfall with a rocky pool. You'll likely meet locals who can offer to guide you to the top of the falls; however, you may find the climb not worth the effort. ⊠ *Delaford.*

Pigeon Point Beach. This stunning locale is often displayed on Tobago travel brochures. The white-sand beach is lined with swaying coconut trees, and there are changing facilities and food stalls nearby. Although the beach is public, it abuts part of what was once a large coconut estate, and you must pay a token admission (about TT$18) to enter the grounds and use the facilities. ⊠ *Pigeon Point.*

Store Bay. The beach, where boats depart for Buccoo Reef, is little more than a small sandy cove between two rocky breakwaters, but the food stands here are divine: several huts licensed by the tourist board to local ladies who sell roti, *pelau* (meat stewed in coconut milk with peas and rice), and the world's messiest dish—crab and dumplings. Near the airport, just walk around the Crown Point Hotel to the beach entrance. ⊠ *Crown Point.*

WHERE TO EAT

$–$$
CARIBBEAN
Fodor's Choice
★
✕ **Blue Crab Restaurant.** The Sardinha family has been serving the best local lunches at their home since the 1980s. The ebullient Alison entertains and hugs diners while her husband Ken does the cooking. The food is hearty and usually well seasoned in the creole style. The only bad news here is that the restaurant is rarely open for dinner; the good news is that you may not have room for dinner after lunch. ⊠ *Robinson and Main Sts., Scarborough* ☎ *868/639-2737* ⊕ *www.tobagobluecrab. com* ⊟ *AE, MC, V* ☉ *Closed weekends. No dinner.*

¢
CAFÉ
Fodor's Choice
★
✕ **Shore Things Café & Craft.** With a dramatic setting over the ocean on the Milford Road between Crown Point and Scarborough, this is a good spot to stop for a lunch or coffee break. Survey the view from the deck tables while enjoying a variety of freshly prepared juices (the tamarind is particularly refreshing) and nibbling on excellent sandwiches. The whole-wheat pizza here may well be the best on the island. While waiting for your meal, you can shop for local crafts in the lovely and comprehensive gift shop. ⊠ *25 Old Milford Rd., Lambeau* ☎ *868/635-1072* ⊟ *MC, V* ☉ *Closed Sun. No dinner.*

TORTOLA (ROAD TOWN)

Lynda Lohr

Once a sleepy backwater, Tortola is definitely busy these days, particularly when several cruise ships tie up at the Road Town dock. Passengers crowd the streets and shops, and open-air jitneys filled with cruise-ship passengers create bottlenecks on the island's byways. That said, most folks visit Tortola to relax on its deserted sands or linger over lunch at one of its many delightful restaurants. Beaches are never more than a few miles away, and the steep green hills that form Tortola's spine are fanned by gentle trade winds. The neighboring islands glimmer like emeralds in a sea of sapphire. Tortola doesn't have many historic sights, but it does have abundant natural beauty. Beware of the roads, which are extraordinarily steep and twisting, making driving demanding. The best beaches are on the north shore.

4

ESSENTIALS

CURRENCY The U.S. dollar is the official currency. Some places accept cash only, but major credit cards are widely accepted. You'll find ATMs in Road Town.

TELEPHONE To call anywhere in the BVI once you've arrived, dial all seven digits. A local call from a pay phone costs 25¢, but such phones are sometimes on the blink. An alternative is a Caribbean phone card, available in $5, $10, and $20 denominations. They're sold at most major hotels and many stores, and can be used to call within the BVI as well as all over the Caribbean, and to access USADirect from special phone-card phones. If you're coming ashore at the cruise-ship dock, you'll find pay phones right on the dock. If a tender drops you right in Road Town at the ferry dock, phones are located in the terminal.

AT&T has service in nearby St. John, USVI, so it's possible to get service from there in some spots in Road Town and along the waterfront highway that leads to the West End. You may not have to pay international roaming charges on some U.S. cell-phone plans if you can connect with this network.

COMING ASHORE

Large cruise ships usually anchor in Road Town Harbor and bring passengers ashore by tender. Small ships can sometimes tie up at Wickham's Cay dock. Either way, it's a short stroll to Road Town. If your ship isn't going to Virgin Gorda, you can make the 12-mi (19-km) trip by ferry from the dock in Road Town in about 30 minutes for about $30 round-trip, but you'll still have to take a taxi to get to the Baths for swimming and snorkeling, so it's not necessarily a bad deal to go on your ship's shore excursion.

There are taxi stands at Wickham's Cay and in Road Town. Taxis are unmetered, and there are minimums for travel throughout the island, so it's usually cheaper to travel in groups. Negotiate to get the best fares, as there is no set fee schedule. If you are in the islands for just a day, it's usually more cost-effective to share a taxi with a small group than to rent a car, since you'd have to pay an agency at Wickham's Cay or in Road Town car-rental charges of at least $50 a day. You must be at least age 25 to rent a car.

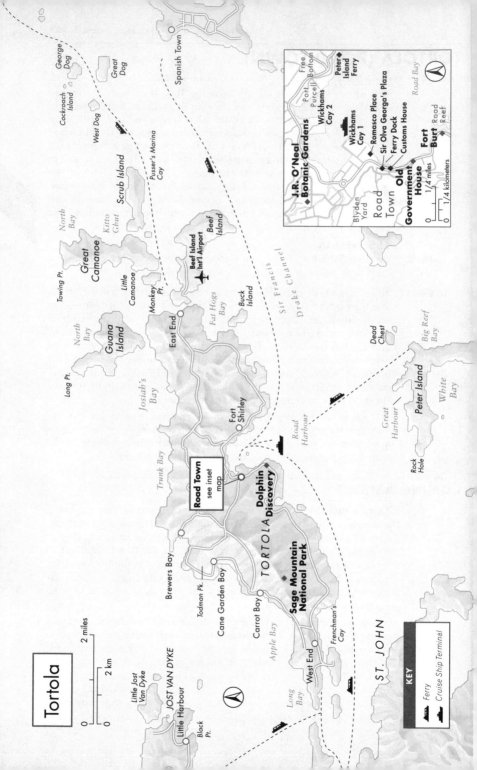

Tortola

0   2 km
0   2 miles

JOST VAN DYKE
Little Jost Van Dyke

Little Harbour
Black Pt.

George Dog
Great Dog
Cockroach Island
West Dog
Spanish Town

Pusser's Marina Cay
Scrub Island
Kitto Ghut
North Bay

Great Camanoe
Little Camanoe
Towing Pt.
North Bay
Long Pt.
Guana Island

Monkey Pt.
East End
Beef Island Int'l Airport
Beef Island
Fat Hogs Bay
Buck Island

Sir Francis Drake Channel

Dead Chest
Big Reef Bay

Josiah's Bay
Fort Shirley

Trunk Bay
Road Harbour

Road Town
see inset map

Dolphin Discovery

TORTOLA

Peter Island
Great Harbour
White Bay
Rock Hole

Brewers Bay
Todman Pk.
Cane Garden Bay
Carrot Bay

Sage Mountain National Park

Apple Bay
Long Bay
West End
Frenchman's Cay

ST. JOHN

KEY

Ferry
Cruise Ship Terminal

Peter Island Ferry
Road Bay
Free Purcell Bottom
Pott Purcell

Wickhams Cay 2
Wickhams Cay 1
Romasco Place
Sir Olva George's Plaza
Ferry Dock
Customs House
J.R. O'Neal Botanic Gardens
Blyden Yard
Road Town
Old Government House
Fort Burt
Road Reef

1/4 miles
1/4 kilometers
0
0

EXPLORING TORTOLA

The bustling capital of the BVI looks out over Road Harbour. It takes only an hour or so to stroll down Main Street and along the waterfront, checking out the traditional West Indian buildings painted in pastel colors and with corrugated-tin roofs, bright shutters, and delicate fretwork trim. For sightseeing brochures and the latest information on everything from taxi rates to ferry schedules, stop in at the BVI Tourist Board office. Or just choose a seat on one of the benches in Sir Olva Georges Square, on Waterfront Drive, and watch the people come and go from the ferry dock and customs office across the street.

4

☺ ★ **Dolphin Discovery.** Get up close and personal with dolphins as they swim in a spacious seaside pen. There are three different programs that provide a range of experiences. In the Royal Swim, dolphins tow participants around the pen. The less expensive Adventure and Discovery programs allow you to touch the dolphins. ✉ *Prospect Reef Resort, Road Town* ☎ *284/494–7675* ⊕ *www.dolphindiscovery.com* ✉ *Royal Swim $139, Adventure $99, Discovery $79* ☉ *Royal Swim daily at 10 and noon, Adventure and Discovery daily at 11 and 1.*

Ft. Burt. The most intact historic ruin on Tortola was built by the Dutch in the early 17th century to safeguard Road Harbour. It sits on a hill at the western edge of Road Town and is now the site of a small hotel and restaurant. The foundations and magazine remain, and the structure offers a commanding view of the harbor. ✉ *Waterfront Dr., Road Town* ☎ *No phone* ✉ *Free* ☉ *Daily dawn–dusk.*

★ **J.R. O'Neal Botanic Gardens.** Take a walk through this 4-acre showcase of lush plant life. There are sections devoted to prickly cacti and succulents, hothouses for ferns and orchids, gardens of medicinal herbs, and plants and trees indigenous to the seashore. From the tourist office in Road Town, cross Waterfront Drive and walk one block over to Main Street and turn right. Keep walking until you see the high school. The gardens are on your left. ✉ *Botanic Station, Road Town* ☎ *284/494–3904* ✉ *$3* ☉ *Mon.–Sat. 8:30–4:30.*

★ **Old Government House Museum.** The official government residence until 1997, this gracious building now displays a nice collection of artifacts from Tortola's past. The rooms are filled with period furniture, hand-painted china, books signed by Queen Elizabeth II on her 1966 and 1977 visits, and numerous items reflecting Tortola's seafaring legacy.

✉ *Waterfront Dr., Road Town* ☎ *284/494–4091* ✉ *$3* ⊙ *Weekdays 9–3, Sat. 9–1.*

★ **Sage Mountain National Park.** At 1,716 feet, Sage Mountain is the highest peak in the BVI. From the parking area, a trail leads you in a loop not only to the peak itself (and extraordinary views) but also to a

small rain forest that is sometimes shrouded in mist. Most of the forest was cut down over the centuries to clear land for sugarcane, cotton, and other crops; to create pastureland; or simply to use the stands of timber. In 1964 this park was established to preserve what remained. Up here you can see mahogany trees, white cedars, mountain guavas, elephant-ear vines, mamey trees, and giant bullet woods, to say nothing of such birds as mountain doves and thrushes. Take a taxi from Road Town or drive up Joe's Hill Road and make a left onto Ridge Road toward Chalwell and Doty villages. The road dead-ends at the park. ✉ *Ridge Rd., Sage Mountain* ☎ *284/494–3904* ⊕ *www.bvinationalparkstrust. org* ✉ *$3* ⊙ *Daily dawn–dusk.*

SHOPPING

Many shops and boutiques are clustered along and just off Road Town's **Main Street.** You can shop in Road Town's **Wickham's Cay I** adjacent to the marina. The **Crafts Alive Market** on the Road Town waterfront is a collection of colorful West Indian–style buildings with shops that carry items made in the BVI. You might find pretty baskets or interesting pottery or perhaps a bottle of home-brewed hot sauce. An ever-growing number of art and clothing stores are opening at **Soper's Hole** in West End.

ACTIVITIES

DIVING AND SNORKELING

The *Chikuzen,* sunk northwest of Brewers Bay in 1981, is a 246-foot vessel in 75 feet of water; it's home to thousands of fish, colorful corals, and big rays. In 1867 the **RMS Rhone,** a 310-foot royal mail steamer, split in two when it sank in a devastating hurricane. It's so well preserved that it was used as an underwater prop in the movie *The Deep.* You can see the crow's nest and bowsprit, the cargo hold in the bow, and the engine and enormous propeller shaft in the stern. Its four parts are at various depths from 30 to 80 feet. Get yourself some snorkeling gear and hop aboard a dive boat to this wreck near Salt Island (across the channel from Road Town). Every dive outfit in the BVI runs scuba and snorkel tours to this part of the BVI National Parks Trust; if you have time for only one trip, make it this one. Rates start at around $75 for a one-tank dive and $100 for a two-tank dive.

Blue Waters Divers (✉ *Nanny Cay* ☎ *284/494–2847* ✉ *Soper's Hole, West End* ☎ *284/495–1200* ⊕ *www.bluewaterdiversbvi.com*) teaches resort, open-water, rescue, and advanced diving courses, and also makes daily dive trips. If you're chartering a sailboat, the company's boat will meet your boat at Peter, Salt, Norman, or Cooper Island for a rendezvous dive. Rates include all equipment as well as instruction. Reserve two days in advance. **Dive Tortola** (⊠ *Prospect Reef Resort, Road Town* ☎ *284/494–9200* ⊕ *www.divetortola.com*) offers beginner and advanced diving courses and daily dive trips. Trainers teach open-water, rescue, advanced diving, and resort courses. Dive Tortola also offers a rendezvous diving option for folks on charter sailboats.

FISHING

Most of the boats that take you deep-sea fishing for bluefish, wahoo, swordfish, and shark leave from nearby St. Thomas, but local anglers like to fish the shallower water for bonefish. A half day runs about $480, a full day around $850. Call **Caribbean Fly Fishing** (⊠ *Nanny Cay* ☎ *284/494–4797* ⊕ *www.caribflyfishing.com*).

SAILING

The BVI are among the world's most popular sailing destinations. They're close together and surrounded by calm waters, so it's fairly easy to sail from one anchorage to the next. **Aristocat Charters** (⊠ *West End* ☎ *284/499–1249* ⊕ *www.aristocatcharters.com*) sets sail daily to Jost Van Dyke, the Indians, and Peter Island aboard a 48-foot catamaran. **White Squall II** (⊠ *Village Cay Marina, Road Town* ☎ *284/494–2564* ⊕ *www.whitesquall2.com*) takes you on regularly scheduled day sails to the Baths at Virgin Gorda, Cooper, the Indians, or the Caves at Norman Island on an 80-foot schooner.

⟲ **Fodor's Choice** ★

BEACHES

Tortola's north side has several perfect palm-fringed white-sand beaches that curl around turquoise bays and coves. Nearly all are accessible by car (preferably one with four-wheel-drive), albeit down bumpy roads that corkscrew precipitously. Facilities run the gamut from absolutely none to a number of beachside bars and restaurants as well as places to rent water-sports equipment.

Brewers Bay (⊠ *Brewers Bay Rd. E off Cane Garden Bay Rd., or Brewers Bay Rd. W off Ridge Rd.*) is good for snorkeling, and you can find a campground with showers and bathrooms and beach bar tucked in the foliage right behind the beach. An old sugar mill and ruins of a rum distillery are off the beach along the road. The beach is easy to find, but the steep, twisting paved roads leading down the hill to it can be a bit daunting. You can get there from either Brewers Bay Road East or Brewers Bay Road West.

Cane Garden Bay (⊠ *Cane Garden Bay Rd. off Ridge Rd.*), a silky stretch of sand, has exceptionally calm, crystalline waters—except when storms at sea turn the water murky. Snorkeling is good along the edges. Casual guesthouses, restaurants, bars, and even shops are steps from the beach in the growing village of the same name. The beach is a laid-back, even somewhat funky place to put down your towel. It's the closest beach to Road Town—one steep uphill and downhill drive—and one of the BVI's best-known anchorages (unfortunately, it can be very crowded). Water-sports shops rent equipment.

WHERE TO EAT

$ ✕**Capriccio di Mare.** The owners of the well-known Brandywine Bay
ITALIAN restaurant also run this casual, authentic Italian outdoor café. Stop by
★ for an espresso, a fresh pastry, a bowl of perfectly cooked penne, or a
crispy tomato-and-mozzarella pizza. Drink specialties include a mango
Bellini, an adaptation of the famous cocktail served at Harry's Bar in
Venice. ✉ *Waterfront Dr., Road Town* ☎ *284/494–5369* ⚲ *Reservations not accepted* ▤ *MC, V* ⊗ *Closed Sun.*

$$$ ✕**Village Cay Restaurant.** Docked sailboats stretch nearly as far as the
CARIBBEAN eye can see at this busy Road Town restaurant. For lunch, try the grouper club sandwich with an ancho chili mayonnaise. Dinner offerings
run to fish served a variety of ways, including West Indian–style with
okra, onions, and peppers, as well as a seafood jambalaya with lobster,
crayfish, shrimp, mussels, crab, and fish in a mango-passion-fruit sauce.
✉ *Wickhams Cay I, Road Town* ☎ *284/494–2771* ▤ *AE, MC, V.*

VIRGIN GORDA (THE VALLEY)

Lynda Lohr Virgin Gorda, or "Fat Virgin," received its name from Christopher
Columbus. The explorer envisioned the island as a pregnant woman in
a languid recline with Gorda Peak being her big belly and the boulders
of the Baths her toes. Different in topography from Tortola, with its
arid landscape covered with scrub brush and cactus, Virgin Gorda has
a slower pace of life, too. Goats and cattle own the right-of-way, and
the unpretentious friendliness of the people is winning. The top sight
(and beach for that matter) is the Baths, which draws scores of cruise-ship passengers and day-trippers to its giant boulders and grottoes that
form a perfect snorkeling environment. While ships used to stop only
in Tortola, saving Virgin Gorda for shore excursions, smaller ships are
coming increasingly to Virgin Gorda directly.

ESSENTIALS

CURRENCY The U.S. dollar is the official currency here. Some places accept cash only, but
major credit cards are widely accepted. First Caribbean International, which has
an ATM, isn't far from the ferry dock in Spanish Town.

TELEPHONE To call anywhere in the BVI once you've arrived, dial all seven digits. A local call
from a pay phone costs 25¢, but such phones are sometimes on the blink. An
alternative is a Caribbean phone card, available in $5, $10, and $20 denominations. They're sold at most major hotels and many stores, and can be used to
call within the BVI, as well as all over the Caribbean, and to access USADirect
from special phone-card phones. If you're coming ashore at the cruise-ship dock,
you'll find pay phones right on the dock. You'll find pay phones in Spanish Town
at the public dock, Virgin Gorda Yacht Harbor, and the Post Office, all located
near spots where cruise-ship tenders land. If Leverick Bay is your destination,
you'll find pay phones in the marina. Passengers coming ashore in North Sound
will find pay phones at the Gun Creek public dock.

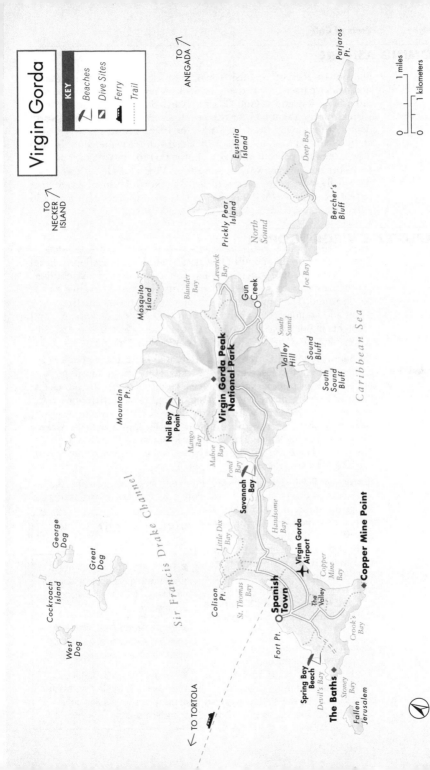

Virgin Gorda

KEY

◿ *Beaches*
▨ *Dive Sites*
⛴ *Ferry*
·········· *Trail*

TO
NECKER
ISLAND ↗

TO
ANEGADA ↗

← TO TORTOLA

West Dog

Cockroach Island

George Dog

Great Dog

Sir Francis Drake Channel

Mountain Pt.

Mosquito Island

Blunder Bay

Leverick Bay

Prickly Pear Island

Eustatia Island

North Sound

Gun
Creek ○

Virgin Gorda Peak National Park ◆

Nail Bay Point ◿

Mango Bay

Mahoe Bay

Pond Bay

Savannah Bay ◿

Valley Hill

South Sound

Sound Bluff

South Sound Bluff

Joe Bay

Deep Bay

Bercher's Bluff

Pajaros Pt.

Caribbean Sea

Handsome Bay

Little Dix Bay

Colison Pt.

St. Thomas Bay

Fort Pt.

Spanish Town ○

✈ Virgin Gorda Airport

The Valley

Copper Mine Bay

Copper Mine Point ◆

Crook's Bay

Spring Bay Beach ◿

Devil's Bay

The Baths ◆

Stoney Bay

Fallen Jerusalem

0 ───── 1 miles

0 ───── 1 kilometers

COMING ASHORE

Ships often dock off Spanish Town, Leverick Bay, or in North Sound and tender passengers to the ferry dock. A few taxis will be available at Leverick Bay and at Gun Creek in North Sound—you can set up an island tour for about $45 for two people—but Leverick Bay and North Sound are far away from the Baths, the island's must-see beach, so a shore excursion is often the best choice. If you are tendered to Spanish Town, then it's possible to take a shuttle taxi to the Baths for as little as $4 per person each way. If you are on Virgin Gorda for just a day, it's usually more cost-effective to share a taxi with a small group than to rent a car, since you'd have to pay car-rental charges of at least $50 a day. You must be at least age 25 to rent a car.

EXPLORING VIRGIN GORDA

There are few roads, and most byways don't follow the scalloped shoreline. The main route sticks resolutely to the center of the island, linking the Baths on the southern tip with Gun Creek and Leverick Bay at North Sound. The craggy coast, scissored with grottoes and fringed by palms and boulders, has a primitive beauty. If you drive, you can hit all the sights in one day. Stop to climb Gorda Peak, which is in the island's center. Signage is erratic, so come prepared with a map.

Ở

Fodor's Choice

★

The Baths. At Virgin Gorda's most celebrated sight, giant boulders are scattered about the beach and in the water. Some are almost as large as houses and form remarkable grottoes. Climb between these rocks to swim in the many placid pools. Early morning and late afternoon are the best times to visit if you want to avoid crowds. If it's privacy you crave, follow the shore northward to quieter bays—Spring Bay, the Crawl, Little Trunk, and Valley Trunk—or head south to Devil's Bay. ⊠ *Off Tower Rd., The Baths* ☏ *284/494–3904* ⊕ *www.bvinationalparkstrust. org* ⊑ *$3* ☉ *Daily dawn–dusk.*

Copper Mine Point. Here stand a tall stone shaft silhouetted against the sky and a small stone structure that overlooks the sea. These are the ruins of a copper mine established 400 years ago and worked first by the Spanish, then by the English, until the early 20th century. The route is not well marked, so turn inland near LSL Restaurant and look for the hard-to-see sign pointing the way. ⊠ *Copper Mine Rd.* ☏ *No phone* ⊕ *www.bvinationalparkstrust.org* ⊑ *Free.*

Spanish Town. Virgin Gorda's peaceful main settlement, on the island's southern wing, is so tiny that it barely qualifies as a town at all. Also known as the Valley, Spanish Town has a marina, some shops,

VIRGIN GORDA BEST BETS

■ **The Baths.** This unique beach strewn with giant boulders and grottos is a favorite snorkeling destination.

■ **Virgin Gorda Peak.** This lofty peak has excellent views and is a great hiking destination.

■ **Sailing Trips.** Like Tortola, Virgin Gorda is within easy reach of many small islets and good snorkeling sights.

and a couple of car-rental agencies. Just north of town is the ferry slip. At the Virgin Gorda Yacht Harbour you can stroll along the dock and do a little shopping.

★ **Virgin Gorda Peak National Park.** There are two trails at this 265-acre park, which contains the island's highest point, at 1,359 feet. Small

> **CAUTION**
>
> If you pick an outside cabin, check to make sure your view of the sea is not obstructed by a lifeboat. The ship's deck plan will help you figure it out.

signs on North Sound Road mark both entrances; sometimes, however, the signs are missing, so keep your eyes open for a set of stairs that disappears into the trees. It's about a 15-minute hike from either entrance up to a small clearing, where you can climb a ladder to the platform of a wooden observation tower and a spectacular 360-degree view. ⌧ *North Sound Rd., Gorda Peak* ☎ *No phone* ⊕ *www.bvinationalparkstrust. org* ⌫ *Free.*

SHOPPING

Most boutiques are within hotel complexes or at Virgin Gorda Yacht Harbour. Two of the best are at Biras Creek and Little Dix Bay. Other properties—the Bitter End and Leverick Bay—have small but equally select boutiques.

ACTIVITIES

DIVING AND SNORKELING

The dive companies on Virgin Gorda are all certified by PADI. Costs vary, but count on paying about $75 for a one-tank dive and $110 for a two-tank dive. All dive operators offer introductory courses as well as certification and advanced courses. Should you get an attack of the bends, which can happen when you ascend too rapidly, the nearest decompression chamber is at Roy L. Schneider Regional Medical Center in St. Thomas.

Dive BVI (⌧ *Virgin Gorda Yacht Harbour, Spanish Town* ☎ *284/495–5513 or 800/848–7078* ⌧ *Leverick Bay Resort and Marina, Leverick Bay* ☎ *284/495–7328* ⊕ *www.divebvi.com*) offers expert instruction, certification, and day trips. **Sunchaser Scuba** (⌧ *Bitter End Yacht Club, North Sound* ☎ *284/495–9638 or 800/932–4286* ⊕ *www.sunchaserscuba. com*) offers resort, advanced, and rescue courses.

SAILING AND BOATING

The BVI waters are calm, and terrific places to learn to sail. You can also rent sea kayaks, waterskiing equipment, dinghies, and powerboats, or take a parasailing trip.

If you just want to sit back, relax, and let the captain take the helm, choose a sailing or power yacht from **Double "D" Charters** (⌧ *Virgin Gorda Yacht Harbour, Spanish Town* ☎ *284/499–2479* ⊕ *www. doubledbvi.com*). Rates are $60 for a half-day trip and $110 for a full-day island-hopping excursion. Private full-day cruises or sails for up to 12 people run $1,299. If you'd rather rent a Sunfish or Hobie

Wave, check out **Leverick Bay Watersports** (⊠ *Leverick Bay, North Sound* ☎ *284/495–7376* ⊕ *www.watersportsbvi.com*).

BEACHES

The best beaches are easily reached by water, although they're also accessible on foot, usually after a moderately strenuous 10- to 15-minute hike. Anybody going to Virgin Gorda should experience swimming or snorkeling among its unique boulder formations, which can be visited at several beaches along Lee Road. The most popular of these spots is the Baths, but there are several others nearby that are easily reached. **The Baths** is usually crowded midday with day-trippers. Public bathrooms and a handful of bars and shops are close to the water and at the start of the path that leads to the beach. Beach lockers are available to keep belongings safe. Admission is $3. **Savannah Bay** is a wonderfully private beach close to Spanish Town. It may not always be completely deserted, but it's a long stretch of soft, white sand. There are no facilities. **Spring Bay Beach,** just off Tower Road, gets much less traffic than the nearby Baths and has the similarly large, imposing boulders that create interesting grottos for swimming. The snorkeling is excellent, and the grounds include swings and picnic tables.

WHERE TO EAT

$$

AMERICAN

✕ **Bath & Turtle.** You can sit back and relax at this informal tavern with a friendly staff—although the noise from the television can sometimes be a bit much. Well-stuffed sandwiches, homemade pizzas, pasta dishes, and daily specials such as conch soup round out the casual menu. Local musicians perform Wednesday and Friday nights. ⊠ *Virgin Gorda Yacht Harbour, Spanish Town* ☎ *284/495–5239* ▤ *AE, MC, V.*

$$$

AMERICAN

✕ **Top of the Baths.** At the entrance to the Baths, this popular restaurant starts serving at 8 AM. Tables are on an outdoor terrace or in an open-air pavilion; all have stunning views of the Sir Francis Drake Channel. Hamburgers, coconut chicken sandwiches, and fish-and-chips are among the offerings at lunch. For dessert, the key lime pie is excellent. The Sunday barbecue, served from noon until 3 PM, is an island event. ⊠ *The Valley* ☎ *284/495–5497* ▤ *AE, MC, V* ◷ *No dinner.*

INDEX

NOTES